A COMPANION TO GREEK DEMOCRACY AND THE ROMAN REPUBLIC

BLACKWELL COMPANIONS TO THE ANCIENT WORLD

This series provides sophisticated and authoritative overviews of periods of ancient history, genres of classical literature, and the most important themes in ancient culture. Each volume comprises approximately twenty-five and forty concise essays written by individual scholars within their area of specialization. The essays are written in a clear, provocative, and lively manner, designed for an international audience of scholars, students, and general readers.

Ancient History

A Companion to the Roman Army
Edited by Paul Erdkamp

A Companion to the Roman Republic
Edited by Nathan Rosenstein and Robert Morstein-Marx

A Companion to the Roman Empire
Edited by David S. Potter

A Companion to the Classical Greek World
Edited by Konrad H. Kinzl

A Companion to the Ancient Near East
Edited by Daniel C. Snell

A Companion to the Hellenistic World
Edited by Andrew Erskine

A Companion to Late Antiquity
Edited by Philip Rousseau

A Companion to Ancient History
Edited by Andrew Erskine

A Companion to Archaic Greece
Edited by Kurt A. Raaflaub and Hans van Wees

A Companion to Julius Caesar
Edited by Miriam Griffin

A Companion to Byzantium
Edited by Liz James

A Companion to Ancient Egypt
Edited by Alan B. Lloyd

A Companion to Ancient Macedonia
Edited by Joseph Roisman and Ian Worthington

A Companion to the Punic Wars
Edited by Dexter Hoyos

A Companion to Augustine
Edited by Mark Vessey

A Companion to Marcus Aurelius
Edited by Marcel van Ackeren

A Companion to Ancient Greek Government
Edited by Hans Beck

A Companion to the Neronian Age
Edited by Emma Buckley and Martin T. Dinter

A Companion to Greek Democracy and the Roman Republic
Edited by Dean Hammer

A Companion to Livy
Edited by Bernard Mineo

Literature and Culture

A Companion to Classical Receptions
Edited by Lorna Hardwick and Christopher Stray

A Companion to Greek and Roman Historiography
Edited by John Marincola

A Companion to Catullus
Edited by Marilyn B. Skinner

A Companion to Roman Religion
Edited by Jörg Rüpke

A Companion to Greek Religion
Edited by Daniel Ogden

A Companion to the Classical Tradition
Edited by Craig W. Kallendorf

A Companion to Roman Rhetoric
Edited by William Dominik and Jon Hall

A Companion to Greek Rhetoric
Edited by Ian Worthington

A Companion to Ancient Epic
Edited by John Miles Foley

A Companion to Greek Tragedy
Edited by Justina Gregory

A Companion to Latin Literature
Edited by Stephen Harrison

A Companion to Greek and Roman Political Thought
Edited by Ryan K. Balot

A Companion to Ovid
Edited by Peter E. Knox

A Companion to the Ancient Greek Language
Edited by Egbert Bakker

A Companion to Hellenistic Literature
Edited by Martine Cuypers and James J. Clauss

A Companion to Vergil's Aeneid and its Tradition
Edited by Joseph Farrell and Michael C. J. Putnam

A Companion to Horace
Edited by Gregson Davis

A Companion to Families in the Greek and Roman Worlds
Edited by Beryl Rawson

A Companion to Greek Mythology
Edited by Ken Dowden and Niall Livingstone

A Companion to the Latin Language
Edited by James Clackson

A Companion to Tacitus
Edited by Victoria Emma Pagán

A Companion to Women in the Ancient World
Edited by Sharon L. James and Sheila Dillon

A Companion to Sophocles
Edited by Kirk Ormand

A Companion to the Archaeology of the Ancient Near East
Edited by Daniel Potts

A Companion to Roman Love Elegy
Edited by Barbara K. Gold

A Companion to Greek Art
Edited by Tyler Jo Smith and Dimitris Plantzos

A Companion to Persius and Juvenal
Edited by Susanna Braund and Josiah Osgood

A Companion to the Archaeology of the Roman Republic
Edited by Jane DeRose Evans

A Companion to Terence
Edited by Antony Augoustakis and Ariana Traill

A Companion to Roman Architecture
Edited by Roger B. Ulrich and Caroline K. Quenemoen

A Companion to Sport and Spectacle in Greek and Roman Antiquity
Edited by Paul Christesen and Donald G. Kyle

A Companion to Plutarch
Edited by Mark Beck

A Companion to Greek and Roman Sexualities
Edited by Thomas K. Hubbard

A Companion to the Ancient Novel
Edited by Edmund P. Cueva and Shannon N. Byrne

A Companion to Ethnicity in the Ancient Mediterranean
Edited by Jeremy McInerney

A Companion to Ancient Egyptian Art
Edited by Melinda Hartwig

A Companion to the Archaeology of Religion in the Ancient World
Edited by Rubina Raja and Jörg Rüpke

A COMPANION TO GREEK DEMOCRACY AND THE ROMAN REPUBLIC

Edited by

Dean Hammer

WILEY Blackwell

This edition first published 2015

Registered Office
John Wiley & Sons Ltd, The Atrium, Southern Gate, Chichester, West Sussex, PO19 8SQ, UK

Editorial Offices
350 Main Street, Malden, MA 02148-5020, USA
9600 Garsington Road, Oxford, OX4 2DQ, UK
The Atrium, Southern Gate, Chichester, West Sussex, PO19 8SQ, UK

For details of our global editorial offices, for customer services, and for information about how to apply for permission to reuse the copyright material in this book please see our website at www.wiley.com/wiley-blackwell.

Library of Congress Cataloging-in-Publication Data

A companion to Greek democracy and the Roman republic / edited by Dean Hammer.
pages cm
Includes bibliographical references and index.
ISBN 978-1-4443-3601-6 (cloth)
1. Greece—Politics and government—To 146 B.C. 2. Rome—Politics and government—265-30 B.C. 3. Greece—Economic conditions—To 146 B.C. 4. Rome—Economic conditions—510-30 B.C. I. Hammer, Dean, 1959–
JC73.C673 2015
320.938— dc23

2014012679

A catalogue record for this book is available from the British Library.

Cover image: Cesare Maccari, Cicero Denounces Catiline (detail of fresco), 1880. Palazzo Madama, Rome. © akg-images / Album / Oronoz

Typeset in 10/12.5pt GalliardStd by Laserwords Private Limited, Chennai, India

1 2015

Contents

Notes on Contributors

Valentina Arena is Lecturer in Roman History at University College London. Her work focuses mainly on the history of ideas and political thought, its relationship with the practice of politics and the study of Roman oratory and rhetorical techniques. She is the author of *Libertas and the Practice of Politics in the late Roman Republic* (2012). Her essays have appeared in a wide range of scholarly journals and edited volumes.

Larissa M. Atkison is a PhD candidate at the University of Toronto and is currently finishing work on her dissertation, entitled "Tragic Rhetoric: Sophocles and the Politics of Good Sense." During the 2013–2014 academic year, she will hold the Classics and Contemporary Perspectives Post-Doctoral Fellowship at the University of South Carolina. Atkison has contributed an entry on Sophocles to the forthcoming *Blackwell Encyclopedia of Political Thought*. She specializes in classical political thought, rhetoric, and contemporary democratic theory.

Ryan K. Balot is Professor of Political Science and Classics at the University of Toronto. The author of *Greed and Injustice in Classical Athens* (2001), *Greek Political Thought* (2006), and *Courage in the Democratic Polis: Ideology and Critique in Classical Athens* (2014), and editor of *A Companion to Greek and Roman Political Thought* (2009), Balot specializes in American, early modern, and classical political thought.

Sarah Bolmarcich, after a year spent in Greece studying on a Fulbright, received her PhD in Classics from the University of Virginia with a dissertation on Greek interstate diplomacy in the archaic and classical periods. She has taught at the universities of Michigan, Minnesota, and Texas (Austin), and currently teaches at the Arizona State University.

Craige B. Champion teaches ancient history at Syracuse University. He is the author of *Cultural Politics in Polybius's Histories* (2004), editor of *Roman Imperialism: Readings and Sources* (2004), one of the general editors of the Wiley Blackwell *Encyclopedia of Ancient History* (2013), and co-editor of the forthcoming *Landmark Edition of the Histories of Polybius*. He is currently completing a book tentatively titled *Pax Deorum: Elite Religious Practices in the Middle Roman Republic*.

David Cohen is Emeritus Professor of Rhetoric and Classics at University of California, Berkeley and currently the director of the WSD HANDA Center for Human Rights and International Justice at Stanford and Professor of Law at the University of Hawaii, Manoa. He has authored *Indifference and Accountability: The United Nations and the Politics of International Justice in East Timor* (2006), *The Legacy of the Serious Crimes Trials in East Timor* (2006), *Law, Violence, and Community in Classical Athens* (1995), *Law, Society, and Sexuality: The Enforcement of Morals at Classical Athens* (1991), and *The Athenian Law of Theft* (1983).

Luuk de Ligt is Professor of Ancient History at Leiden University. He is the author of *Fairs and Markets in the Roman Empire* (1993) and of *Peasants, Citizens and Soldiers: Studies in the Demographic History of Roman Italy 225 BC–AD 100* (2012), and co-editor (with Simon Northwood) of *People, Land, and Politics. Demographic Developments and the Transformation of Roman Italy, 300 BC–AD 14* (2008). He has published extensively on Roman economic history, the history of Roman associations, and Roman demography.

Vincent Farenga is Professor of Classics and Comparative Literature at the University of Southern California. He is the author of *Citizen and Self in Ancient Greece: Individuals Performing Justice and the Law* (2006). He has published a number of articles on expressions of individualism in Greek literature and political history (especially on Greek tyranny), and he is currently completing a study of literature and justice within a global context in contemporary authors and political philosophers.

Nick Fisher is Professor Emeritus of Ancient History at Cardiff University. He has published widely on the political, social, and cultural history of ancient Greece. He has published *Aeschines, Against Timarchos* (2001), *Slavery in Classical Greece* (1993), *HYBRIS. A Study in the Values of Honour and Shame in Ancient Greece* (1992), a sourcebook on *Social Values in Classical Athens* (1976), and many articles and co-edited volumes.

Michael P. Fronda is Associate Professor in the Department of History and Classical Studies at McGill University. His research focuses on domestic and interstate politics in Roman and pre-Roman Italy. He is author of *Between Rome and Carthage: Southern Italy in the Second Punic War* (2010) as well as articles on the Hannibalic War, Roman political culture, foreign policy and imperialism, Roman–Italian relations, and the Italiote League.

Dean Hammer is the John W. Wetzel Professor of Classics and Professor of Government at Franklin and Marshall College (USA). He has authored *The Puritan Tradition in Revolutionary, Federalist, and Whig Political Theory* (1998), *The* Iliad *as Politics: The Performance of Political Thought* (2002), *Roman Political Thought and the Modern Theoretical Imagination* (2008), and *Roman Political Thought: From Cicero to Augustine* (2015), as well as numerous articles on Greek, Roman, and modern political thought.

Tonio Hölscher, born in 1940, is Professor Emeritus of Classical Archaeology at the University of Heidelberg, Germany. He was Meyer Shapiro Visiting Professor at Columbia University in New York, Fellow of the Institute for Advanced Study at Berlin, Jerome Lecturer at the University of Michigan and the American Academy in Rome, Research Professor at the German Archaeological Institute in Rome, Sather Guest Professor at the University of Berkeley and Visiting Professor at the University of California Berkeley, and Princeton. His main interests are art, policy, and society in ancient Greece and Rome, Greek and Roman urbanism, and theories of art.

Mary Jaeger is Professor of Classics at the University of Oregon, where she has taught since 1990. She is the author of *Livy's Written Rome* (1997), *Archimedes and the Roman Imagination* (2008), and *A Livy Reader* (2011).

David Konstan is Professor of Classics at New York University and Professor Emeritus of Classics and Comparative Literature at Brown University. Among his books are *Sexual Symmetry: Love in the Ancient Novel and Related Genres* (1994), *Greek Comedy and Ideology* (1995), *Friendship in the Classical World* (1997), *Pity Transformed* (2001), *The Emotions of the Ancient Greeks: Studies in Aristotle and Classical Literature* (2006), *"A Life Worthy of the Gods": The Materialist Psychology of Epicurus* (2008), *Terms for Eternity: Aiônios and aïdios in Classical and Christian Texts* (with Ilaria Ramelli, 2007), *Before Forgiveness: The Origins of a Moral Idea* (2010), and *Beauty: The Fortunes of an Ancient Greek Idea.*

Kathryn A. Morgan is Professor of Classics at UCLA, where she has taught since 1996. She is the author of *Myth and Philosophy from the Presocratics to Plato* (2000), and editor of *Popular Tyranny: Sovereignty and its Discontents in Ancient Greece* (Austin, 2003). Her most recent book is *Pindar and the Construction of Syracusan Monarchy in the Fifth Century BC* (forthcoming).

Robert Morstein-Marx is Professor of Classics at the University of California, Santa Barbara. He is the author of two books, *Hegemony to Empire: The Development of the Roman Imperium in the East from 148 to 62* B.C. (1995), and *Mass Oratory and Political Power in the Late Roman Republic* (2004). He is also co-editor (with N. Rosenstein) of *A Companion to the Roman Republic* (2006). His current research focuses on political culture and communication in the late Roman Republic.

Henrik Mouritsen is Professor of Roman History at King's College London. He has published widely on Roman political and social history, Roman Italy and Latin epigraphy. His books include *Elections, Magistrates and Municipal Elite* (1988), *Italian Unification* (1998), *Plebs and Politics* (2001), and *The Freedman in the Roman World* (2011).

Shawn O'Bryhim is Professor of Classics at Franklin & Marshall College. He edited and contributed to *Greek and Roman Comedy* (2001) and has written several articles on Plautus, Catullus, Ovid, and ancient Mediterranean religions.

Ellen Perry is Associate Professor in the Department of Classics at the College of the Holy in Worcester, Massachusetts. She has published articles on Roman sarcophagi, the aesthetics of ancient painting, the history of plaster cast collections, and the Roman imitation of Greek art. Her book *The Aesthetics of Emulation in the Visual Arts of Ancient Rome* appeared in 2005, and she is currently writing a book about the Capitoline Temple.

Kurt A. Raaflaub is Professor Emeritus of Classics and History at Brown University. His research has focused on the social, political, and intellectual history of archaic and classical Greece and of the Roman Republic, and the comparative history of the ancient world. His recent books include *The Discovery of Freedom in Ancient Greece* (2004), *War and Peace in the Ancient World* (edited, 2007), and *Origins of Democracy in Ancient Greece* (co-authored, 2007).

P.J. Rhodes was Professor of Ancient History and is now Honorary Professor at the

University of Durham (UK), and is particularly interested in Greek politics and political institutions. His books include *The Athenian Boule* (1972), *A Commentary on the Aristotelian Athenaion Politeia* (1981), and *The Decrees of the Greek States* (with D.M. Lewis, 1997).

Joseph Roisman is a Professor of Classics at Colby College, USA. Among his rhetoric-related publications are *The Rhetoric of Manhood: Masculinity According to the Attic Orators* (2005), *The Rhetoric of Conspiracy in Ancient Athens* (2006), and *Pseudo-Plutarch and Photius on the Lives of the Ten Orators* (with I. Worthington, forthcoming).

Malcolm Schofield is Emeritus Professor of Ancient Philosophy, University of Cambridge, and a Fellow of St. John's College. He was co-editor with Christopher Rowe of *The Cambridge History of Greek and Roman Political Thought* (2000). *The Stoic Idea of the City* (1991) and *Plato: Political Philosophy* (2006) are among his major solo publications. Current projects include a book on Cicero's political thought and a new translation (with Tom Griffith) of Plato's *Laws*.

Keith Sidwell is Emeritus Professor of Latin and Greek at University College Cork and Adjunct Professor of Classics at the University of Calgary. He has published widely on Greek comedy and tragedy, including a recent study of politics in Old Comedy, *Aristophanes the Democrat: The Politics of Satirical Comedy during the Peloponnesian War* (2009).

Roberta Stewart is Professor of Classics at Dartmouth College. She has authored two books, *Public Office in Early Rome: Ritual Procedure and Political Practice* (1998) and *Plautus and Roman Slavery* (2012). She has published articles on Roman religion, Roman numismatics, Latin literature, and Latin lexicography (for the Thesaurus Linguae Latinae in Munich).

David W. Tandy, Research Fellow in Classics at the University of Leeds and Professor Emeritus of Classics at the University of Tennessee, concentrates on Near Eastern and Greek economic history, on Homer, Hesiod, lyric poets, on Athenian taxation and aspects of fourth-century Greece.

W. Jeffrey Tatum is Professor of Classics at the Victoria University of Wellington. He is the author of *The Patrician Tribune: Publius Clodius Pulcher* (1999), *Always I Am Caesar* (2008), *A Caesar Reader* (2012), and *Plutarch: The Rise of Rome* (with Chris Pelling, 2013), in addition to numerous papers and chapters on Roman history and Latin literature.

Robert W. Wallace is Professor of Classics at Northwestern University. He is the author of books on Athens' Areopagus Council and the music theorist (and Pericles' adviser) Damon, co-author of a book on the origins of Greek democracy, and co-editor of four other books. He has published some eighty-five articles in different areas of archaic and classical Greek history, literature, law, numismatics, and music theory.

Callie Williamson is an independent scholar and attorney. Her first book, *The Laws of the Roman People*, won the 2005 American Historical Association Breasted Prize for best book in the English language on any period before 1000 CE. She has also written on the significance of Roman laws engraved on bronze tablets, and contributed to the definitive edition of early Roman laws published as *Roman Statutes* (1996), edited by Michael Crawford.

Abbreviations

AUTHORS AND WORKS

AE	*l'Année épigraphique*
Aeschin.	Aeschines
In Ctes.	*Against Ctesiphon*
Andoc.	Andocides
Antiph.	Antiphon
App.	Appian
B. civ.	*Bella civile*
Arist.	Aristotle
[*Ath. Pol.*	*Constitution of the Athenians*]
Cat.	*Categories*
EE	*Eudemian Ethics*
NE	*Nicomachean Ethics*
Poet.	*Poetics*
Pol.	*Politics*
Rhet.	*Rhetoric*
Aristoph.	Aristophanes
Ach.	*Acharnians*
Thesm.	*Thesmophoriazusae*
Ascon.	Asconius
Aug.	Augustine
Civ. Dei	*De civitate Dei*
Conf.	*Confessions*
De fid. inv.	*De fide rerum invisibilium*
De lib. arb.	*De libero arbitrio*
De ord.	*De ordine*
Caesar	
B. civ.	*Bellum civile*
Cato	
DA	*De agricultura*

Cic.	Cicero
Arch.	*Pro Archia*
Att.	*Epistulae ad Atticum*
Balb.	*Pro Balbo*
Brut.	*Brutus*
Caec.	*Pro Caecina*
Cat.	*In Catilinam*
Cest.	*Pro Cestio*
Clu.	*Pro Cluentio*
Corn.	*Pro Cornelio*
De fin.	*De finibus*
De leg.	*De legibus*
De off.	*De officiis*
De orat.	*De oratore*
De rep.	*De republica*
Dom	*De domo sua*
Fam.	*Epistulae ad familiares*
Flac.	*Pro Flacco*
Font.	*Pro Fonteio*
Inv.	*De inventione rhetorica*
Leg. agr.	*De lege agraria*
Leg. Man.	*Pro lege Manilia*
Mur.	*Pro Murena*
Parad.	*Paradoxa Stoicorum*
Part. or.	*Partitiones oratoriae*
Phil.	*Philippics*
Planc.	*Pro Plancio*
Prov. cons.	*De provinciis consularibus*
Q. fr.	*Epistolae ad Quintum fratrem*
Q. Rosc.	*Pro Roscio comoedo*
Quinct.	*Pro Quinctio*
Red. pop.	*Post reditum ad populum*
Red. sen.	*Post reditum in senatu*
Sen.	*De senectute*
Sest.	*Pro Sestio*
Tusc.	*Tusculanae disputationes*
CIL	*Corpus Inscriptionum Latinarum*
Colum.	Columella
Dem.	Demosthenes
DFA[2]	A. Pickard-Cambridge, *The Dramatic Festivals of Athens.* 2nd edn., rev. J. Gould and D.M. Lewis, reissued with a new supplement (Oxford, 1988)
Dio Cass.	Dio Cassius
Diod. Sic.	Diodorus Siculus
Diog. Laert.	Diogenes Laertius
Dionys.	Dionysius of Halicarnassus
Ant. Rom.	*Roman Antiquities*
Donat.	Aelius Donatus
Eur.	Euripides
Supp.	*Suppliants*
FGH	F. Jacoby, *Fragmente der grieschischen Historiker*
Fornara	C.W. Fornara, ed. and trans., *Archaic Times to the End of the Peloponnesian War.* Translated Documents of Greece and Rome, 1. 2nd edn. (Cambridge, 1983)
Gaius	
Inst.	*Institutiones*

Gell.	Aulus Gellius
NA	*Noctes Atticae*
Hdt.	Herodotus
Hell. Oxy.	*Hellenica Oxyrhynchia*
Hes.	Hesiod
Theog.	*Theogony*
WD	*Works and Days*
Hyp.	Hyperides
Homer	
Il.	*Iliad*
Od.	*Odyssey*
IC	*Inscriptiones Creticae*
IG	*Inscriptiones Graecae*
ILLRP	*Inscriptiones Latinae Liberae Rei Republicae*
ILS	*Inscriptiones Latinae Selectae*
Isae.	Isaeus
Isid.	Isidorus
Etym.	*Etymologiae*
Isoc.	Isocrates
Panath.	*Panathenaicus*
Josephus	
AJ	*Antiquitates Josephae*
Livy	
Per.	*Periochae*
LSCG	F. Sokolowski, *Lois sacrées des cités grecques*
LTUR	*Lexicon Topographicum Urbis Romae*
Lycurg.	Lycurgus
Leoc.	*Against Leocrates*
Lys.	Lysias
Macr.	Macrobius
Sat.	*Saturnalia*
Malcovati	
ORF	*Oratorum romanorum fragmenta*
Mar.	Martial
ML	R. Meiggs and D. Lewis, *A Selection of Greek Historical Inscriptions to the End of the Fifth Century BC* (Oxford, 1988)
Nep.	Nepos
De excel. duc.	*De excellentibus ducibus*
ORF	H. Malcovati, *Oratorum Romanorum Fragmenta*
Oros.	Orosius
Paus.	Pausanias
PCG	R. Kassel and C. Austin, eds., *Poetae Comici Graeci*
Ph.	Phaedrus
Plato	
Ap.	*Apology*
Crit.	*Critias*
Gor.	*Gorgias*
Menex.	*Menexenus*
Phdr.	*Phaedrus*
Prot.	*Protagoras*
Rep..	*Republic*
Them.	*Themistocles*
Tht.	*Thaetetus*
Tim.	*Timaeus*

Plaut. Plautus
- *Amph.* *Amphitruo*
- *Asin.* *Asinaria*
- *Bacch.* *Bacchides*
- *Capt.* *Captivi*
- *Cas.* *Casina*
- *Cist.* *Cistellaria*
- *Curc.* *Curculio*
- *Men.* *Menaechmi*
- *Merc.* *Mercator*
- *Most.* *Mostellaria*
- *Poen.* *Poenulus*
- *Pseud.* *Pseudolus*
- *Rud.* *Rudens*
- *Stich.* *Stichus*
- *Trin.* *Trinummus*

Pliny
- *NH* *Natural History*

Plut. Plutarch
- *Aem.* *Aemilius Paulus*
- *Ages.* *Agesilaus*
- *Alc.* *Alcibiades*
- *Arist.* *Aristeides*
- *C. Gracch.* *Gaius Gracchus*
- *Caes.* *Caesar*
- *Cat.* *Cato*
- *Cic.* *Cicero*
- *Cim.* *Cimon*
- *Luc.* *Lucullus*
- *Lyc.* *Lycurgus*
- *Lys.* *Lysander*
- *Nic.* *Nicias*
- *Per.* *Pericles*
- *Pomp.* *Pompeius*
- *Quaest. Rom.* *Quaestiones Romanae*
- *Rom.* *Romulus*
- *Sol.* *Solon*
- *Them.* *Themistocles*
- *Ti. Gracch.* *Tiberius Gracchus*
- *X orat.* *Vitae decem oratorum*

Polyb. Polybius

Prop. Propertius

Ps.-Asc. Pseudo-Asconius

Ps.-Xenophon
- *Ath. Pol.* *Athenaiōn politeia*

Q. Cic. Q. Tullius Cicero
- *Comm. pet.* *Commentariolum petitionis*

Quint. Quintilian
- *Inst. or.* *Institutio oratoria*

Rhet. Her. *Rhetorica ad Herennium*

RO P.J. Rhodes and R. Osborne, *Greek Historical Inscriptions 404–323 BC* (Oxford, 2003)

Sal. Sallust
- *Cat.* *De bellum Catilinae*
- *Hist.* *Historiae*
- *Iug.* *Bellum Iugurthinum*

SEG *Supplementum epigraphicum Graecum*

Sen.	Seneca the Younger
De ben.	*De beneficiis*
SIG	W. Dittenberger, *Sylloge Inscriptionum Graecarum*
Soph.	Sophocles
Ant.	*Antigone*
Suet.	Suetonius
Aug.	*Divus Augustus*
De rhet.	*De rhetoribus*
Iul.	*Divus Iulius*
Poet.	*De poetis*
Tib.	*Tiberius*
Tac.	Tacitus
Ann.	*Annales*
Ter.	Terence
Adel.	*Adelphoe*
Phor.	*Phormio*
Tert.	Tertullian
Apol.	*Apologeticus*
De. spect.	*De spectaculis*
Thuc.	Thucydides
Val. Max.	Valerius Maximus
Var.	Varro
Ling.	*De lingua Latina*
Log	*Logistoricon libri LXXVI*
RR	*De re rustica*
Vell. Pat.	Velleius Paterculus
Xen.	Xenophon
Lac. Pol.	*Lacedaimonion politeia*
Hell.	*Hellenika*
Mem.	*Memorabilia*
Oec.	*Oeconomicus*
Zon.	Zonaras

JOURNALS

AHB	*Ancient History Bulletin*
AJA	*American Journal of Archaeology*
AJP	*American Journal of Philology*
ANRW	*Aufstieg und Niedergang der römischen Welt*
Ath	*Athenaeum*
AW	*Antike Welt*
BCEH	*Bulletin de Correspondence Hellénique*
CA	*Classical Antiquity*
CÉFR	*Collection de l'École française de Rome*
CJ	*The Classical Journal*
ClAnt	*Classical Antiquity*
C&M	*Classica et Medievalia*
CPh	*Classical Philology*
CQ	*Classical Quarterly*
CR	*Classical Review*
CW	*Classical World*
DArch	*Dialoghi di Archeologia*
EMC	*Echos du Monde Classique*

G&R	*Greece & Rome*
GRBS	*Greek, Roman and Byzantine Studies*
HSPh	*Harvard Studies in Classical Philology*
HZ	*Historische Zeitschrift*
ICS	*Illinois Classical Studies*
JBL	*Journal of Biblical Literature*
JDI	*Jahrbuch des Deutschen Archäologischen Instituts*
JHS	*Journal of Hellenic Studies*
JITE	*Journal of Institutional and Theoretical Economics*
JRA	*Journal of Roman Archaeology*
JRS	*Journal of Roman Studies*
LCM	*Liverpool Classical Monthly*
MBAH	*Münstersche Beiträge zur Antiken Handelgeschichte*
MDAI	*Mitteilungen de deutschen archäologischen Instituts*
MH	*Museum Helveticum*
PdP	*La Parola del Passato*
P&P	*Past & Present*
RD	*Revue internationale des droits d'antiquité*
RE	Pauly-Wissowa, *Real-Encyclopädie der klassischen Altertumswissenschaft* (1893–)
REG	*Revue des études grecques*
REL	*Revue des études latines*
RFIC	*Rivista di filologia e di istruzione classica*
RhM	*Rheinisches Museum für Philologie*
SCI	*Scripta Classica Israelica*
SE	*Studi Etruschi*
SMEA	*Studi Micenei ed Egeo-Anatolici*
SO	*Symbolae Osloenses*
TAPA	*Transactions of the American Philological Association*
YCS	*Yale Classical Studies*
ZPE	*Zeitschrift für Papyrologie und Epgraphik*

Introduction

Dean Hammer

Scholarship on Greek democracy and the Roman Republic has proceeded largely on two separate paths, rarely noticing each other, let alone intersecting. There are many reasons for this. One is specialization, which has led scholars to pursue questions unique to Greek or Roman life without necessarily recognizing or exploring how similar questions resonate in a comparative perspective. A second reason is that there does not seem to be much to compare. Ancient Greece, with the emphasis by scholars on Athens, appears as an open, vibrant, creative democracy while ancient Rome, in contrast, looks like a closed, plodding oligarchy.

But much has changed in our evaluations of both Greece and Rome. Greece's democratic picture has become as complex as Rome's oligarchic one, particularly as new methodologies and approaches have analyzed the formal and informal ways in which political, economic, social, and cultural meanings are enacted and enforced, as well as resisted (see Hammer 2009 for a review of methodological approaches to the ancient world). These approaches view literary texts, institutional forms, community spaces, human bodies, and economic transactions as ideological enactments. By that I do not mean that there is a univocal ideology expressed, but that we can read in these artifacts the expressions, tensions, contradictions, and even transformations in the thoughts and practices of these communities (on conceptualizations of ideologies, see Geertz 1973; Douglas 1966, 1978, 1982; Turner 1974, 1988; Bourdieu 1977; Ricoeur 1986; Hammer 2006). Moreover, an understanding of the politics of these communities requires more than an analysis of formal political institutions, not because institutions are unimportant but because they are types of formalized practices that are embedded in and comprehensible by way of other practices.

This volume builds on these approaches by providing a comprehensive and comparative exploration of the origins, concepts, and practices that emerge in the *enactment* of what we can understand as *participatory communities* in ancient Greece and Rome.

A Companion to Greek Democracy and the Roman Republic, First Edition. Edited by Dean Hammer.

The term *participatory community* draws attention to the range of different types of communities and different forms of participation one encounters in the ancient world, not only between Greece and Rome but within Greece, as well. A participatory community is one in which politics is no longer seen as the exclusive preserve of one small group but premises the legitimacy of important political outcomes on some aspect of broad participation. The term provides a common language by which we can think about and compare Greek participatory communities with the Roman Republic (understanding the term as designating a participatory community dating from roughly 509–31 BCE) rather than categorizing these communities beforehand (and not particularly helpfully) as democracies, aristocracies, or oligarchies. Furthermore, the term allows us to distinguish these communities from ancient kingdoms and dynasties.

The term *enactment* draws attention to how institutional forms, informal norms, myths and legends, community spaces, philosophic and literary texts, rhetoric, political vocabulary, public displays, entertainment, economic transactions, and global relations are interconnected practices by which communities negotiate their identities, identify and respond to crises, and reflect on their own cultures. As practices, they may arise in response to specific situations or conditions, coming into conflict or existing in tension with other practices. As they bear the imprint of the past, these practices may serve as an impediment to change as well as provide the language and experiences by which change can be articulated and imagined. Drawing on some of the challenging questions raised in contemporary scholarship, each chapter explores how different enactments give us insight into the origins, concepts, and practices of these participatory communities. Together these chapters provide a complex portrait of the interaction of different practices in forming, ordering, sustaining, developing, and imperiling participatory communities.

The Companion is distinct in viewing ancient Greek and Roman participatory communities through a comparative lens. Unlike other books that either analyze Greece and Rome separately or organize them chronologically, focusing on texts, authors, and subjects unique to either Greece or Rome, this volume is organized by topic (or types of enactments, using the language above) with parallel chapters that examine the Greek and Roman participatory contexts. The volume brings into conversation with each other an international array of Greek and Roman scholars with diverse methodological orientations. The authors of each of the parallel chapters worked with each other throughout the project, organizing each chapter with an eye toward the other, reading each other's chapters, and ultimately highlighting comparisons that emerge from each of the cases. The result is a distinct resource for students and scholars. One can use material specific to Greece or Rome (for courses, for example). But one can also look at how these same enactments play out in the comparison community (for courses, but also as a starting point for comparative inquiry for students and scholars). What emerges from this comparative context is an enriched understanding of the types of relationships that sustained these participatory communities, the challenges these communities faced, and how they responded.

In the opening chapter, David Konstan asks in what way we can profitably compare Greek and Roman participatory communities, given the different types of institutions, the little we know about many of these communities (not the least of which early Rome), and the historical interrelationship between Greek and Roman politics and ideas. What emerges, as Konstan writes, are "two stories of the evolution of participatory government, in which relative exclusiveness in respect to citizenship, both vertical along class divisions or horizontal among adjacent communities, was the most salient factor" (14). In the chapters that follow, one sees played out these different trajectories of inclusiveness: one in which the equality and autonomy associated with citizenship in Greek *poleis* extended no further than their borders and the other in which the hierarchical gradations of rights and responsibilities associated with Rome provided greater opportunities for incorporation. The importance of comparison is not to decide which of these choices is best, or even to pronounce general laws of politics, but to note the stress points, limits, and tradeoffs of different participatory paths.

Kurt Raaflaub and Michael Fronda trace the origins and different trajectories of Greek and Roman participatory communities, noting, for example, the similar early city-state structures and social roots for such important political ideas as freedom and liberty. But Greek and Roman developments get mediated through different international pressures (the Greek city-states developing without such international pressures until Persian expansion versus Rome emerging in a continuously hostile environment), class structures (an elite never able to separate itself from the non-elite versus a highly cohesive elite in Rome forged by continual outside pressure), and different available solutions to such crises as debt-bondage (limits on the aristocracy versus conquest). In Greece, the weakness of the elite combined with the indispensable role of non-elite citizens moved these communities toward increased equality of citizenship with strong boundaries limiting new membership. In Rome, expanding claims for protection and participation by non-elites did not result in equality, but occurred within a hierarchic culture with gradations of opportunities and obligations, dominated by strong aristocratic clans. Unlike the more egalitarian Greek *poleis*, Rome had both the structures and the need to expand and integrate outside groups.

Kathryn Morgan and Mary Jaeger examine how these participatory communities constructed their pasts, looking at how the respective conceptions of land informed their imagination. The myths of these pasts are themselves creations of the present, evolving to suit supra-regional affiliations, reinforce claims of military supremacy (as in the case of Sparta), maintain exclusive identities (with myths of autochthony in Thebes and Athens), justify notions of incorporation and inclusion (Rome), and instill habits of discipline, moderation, and vigor (with the idealization of agrarian origins shared by Athens and Rome). What Morgan and Jaeger identify is how these myths are not just propagandistic, but also the basis for critical reflection, differing interpretations, and debate within the community.

Vincent Farenga and Malcolm Schofield analyze the different expressions of liberty, equality, and authority. There are some fundamental similarities in how freedom comes to be defined against the experience of domination and associated with demands for equality (though an equality that is understood in fundamentally different ways in Greece and Rome). But there are striking differences, particularly in conceptions of authority. Although the Greeks, as Farenga argues, had a notion of authority as a recognition of legitimate claims to be obeyed, a claim that is in tension with an egalitarian *dēmos* ideology, the Roman concept of *auctoritas* is distinctive in joining together a "mutually reinforcing union of social and political standing and of impressiveness in character and judgment, with a consequential power to exert influence" (Schofield: 125). Liberty, equality, and authority took on very different resonances in the practices of these communities: one tied to contending ideologies, the other as a broader corporate framework in which that competition occurred.

P.J. Rhodes and Henrik Mouritsen identify how the institutional structures of these participatory communities reflected different political ideologies. Across Greece one sees a correspondence of government with citizenship in the sense that citizens, as an undifferentiated group, shared in ruling and being ruled, extending into legislative, legal, and religious matters. In contrast, Roman institutions rested on a differentiated citizen-body that defined gradations of rights and duties. But underlying these institutions is a paradox: it was the Roman Republic that collapsed from the failure of its institutions to curb individual ambition. The Roman elite found itself without the means to enforce its authority and secure political order. Roman institutions could prevent the revolt of the masses; they just could not, in ways that Greek institutions could, stem the excesses of the elite.

David Cohen and Callie Williamson continue this discussion of institutions, looking specifically at law. Cohen points to the participatory nature of law in Athenian democracy, identifying the fiction of the "rule of law" since neither laws nor a body with authority to interpret the laws had priority over the people (even as attempts were made to provide some consistency to the law). In Rome, though, the law code of the Twelve Tables occupied a much more prominent role in the evolution of law and legal procedure, an evolution shaped by citizen participation, Rome's hierarchic social structure, and the inclusion of new groups.

Nick Fisher and Valentina Arena tap into the less visible ways in which participatory cultures operate, examining the mechanisms by which citizens learned to be citizens, whether by instilling awareness of these norms through civic instruction or through participation in particular rituals and celebrations. In Greece, even in communities as different as Sparta and Athens, there was an emphasis on the similarity of all citizens, united in their civic devotion, reinforcing ideals of discipline and athleticism (in the more regimented forms of education in Sparta) and freedom and democracy (in the more open, panhellenic festivals and performances of Athens). In Rome, civic values were bound closely to appeals to the *mos maiorum*, the ancestral customs. Although traditional and aristocratic, the *mos* were also fluid and adaptable, their meanings reinforced through elite orations, public displays, social spaces, and tightly controlled forms of education.

Robert Wallace and Jeffrey Tatum reveal the complexities and some of the paradoxes of the operation of power in these participatory communities. Although the *dēmos* held sway in the Greek participatory communities, it was a sway that could still be strongly influenced by strong leaders, notably Pericles, who, Wallace argues, may have wielded quite undemocratic power. In Rome, by contrast, power lay with reputation that operated within a competitive, hierarchical political order that was organized by traditions of popular sovereignty and the ways of one's ancestors. But, as Tatum notes, "What obtrudes is the uncertainty ... of the outcome whenever these elements [of prestige and popular sovereignty] combined or came into conflict ... It is not the constituents of clout, then, that elude modern historians so much as their effective application in specific circumstances" (270).

Joseph Roisman and Robert Morstein-Marx develop how rhetoric and persuasion operated in these participatory contexts in which oral communication was central. Roisman shows how epideictic, forensic, and deliberative forms of rhetoric served to reinforce a *dēmos* ideology that was central to Athens' identity, exclusivity, and sense of superiority. The chapter, like Morstein-Marx's, also points to the often unpredictable and tumultuous aspects of this rhetorical climate in which others in the audience could and did respond.

This clamor functions in a Greek participatory context to align the views of the speaker with that of the *dēmos*, even if such actions served to silence some views or preclude good advice. As in Greece, Roman oratory functioned to promote the norms and values of the Republic, though in contrast emphasizing norms of *dignitas*, *honor*, *virtus*, and *auctoritas*. A combination of the lack of transparency in Roman politics (in dramatic contrast to Greece) and the norms of respect for *dignitas* and *auctoritas* "ensured that in open, public deliberation, those who spoke were senators while ordinary citizens were reduced strictly to listening and reacting to what they heard." The result was that "the balance of 'communicative power' was tilted heavily toward senators and toward the collective perspective of the Senate" (Morstein-Marx: 300). If Roman oratory worked to assert the supremacy of the nobility (rather than as a response to *dēmos* authority), it did so only incompletely, subject to the pull of the crowd.

Sarah Bolmarcich and Craige Champion look at the global contexts in which these participatory communities operated, examining how the social values of these communities informed their relations with other states. Bolmarcich traces how Greek federations, although trading on the language of equality and reciprocity, tended to be transformed into forms of power and domination. Ultimately, the ideology of these participatory communities existed in tension with broader relations: democratic claims based on sovereignty inhibited attempts at broader interstate participation or were, in fact, undermined as this sovereignty was ceded. In contrast, Champion demonstrates how Roman hierarchical social relations formed the thread by which Rome constituted its relations with other states. Unlike the egalitarian Greek communities, Rome had a variety of mechanisms by which it could form agreements and expand while incorporating new citizens.

David Tandy and Luuk de Ligt situate economic life in these participatory communities, noting their similar origins as small, agrarian societies with views of economic activity as necessary but not admirable. Greece and Rome diverged most notably in the relative integration of their domestic economies to a world economy. Where the Greek city-states remained closed, protective of their identities, Rome underwent dramatic changes in agrarian and non-agrarian production, commerce, and consumption that were set in motion by imperialism. The expanding economy increased the flow of wealth into Rome, both undermining the traditional austerity associated with elite virtue and providing resources by which particular social tensions could be postponed.

Ryan Balot, Larissa Atkison, and Roberta Stewart explore the rhetoric of exclusion in these participatory communities. One important aspect of the status of these marginal groups lies in their lack of any public voice, leaving us to piece together this world largely through the concerns of male citizens. What emerges in these chapters is an understanding of the status and roles of women and slaves as more negotiated, and the subject of more cultural anxiety, than often assumed. Balot and Atkison analyze how civic identities were shaped and affirmed in rhetorical encounters with and exclusions of the "other" as well as challenged by way of tragedy and philosophy. Stewart explores the interactions of slave and master as well as the gender dynamics of social relations, noting the complex ways in which non-Roman outsiders could be made insiders or could be incorporated in a status of subordination as non-Roman within the Roman system. We see in both the Greek and Roman cases how categories of "insider" and "outsider" emerge as narratives of power that affirm (and may provide the basis for critical reflection on) the identity and status of citizens.

Keith Sidwell and Shawn O'Bryhim place entertainment in its participatory context. Sidwell challenges the conception of Greek theater as simply mirroring the values of the *dēmos*, arguing that the actual relationship between performance and democracy operated more as a "private–public partnership" in which the plays reflected both broader, public concerns and personal agendas. As Sidwell writes, "the politics of the plays themselves were dictated by private agendas, within a system that was entirely controlled otherwise (in terms of buildings, occasion, choice of participants, and judging) by the *dēmos*." The aim was "to influence the members of the audience in some way towards acceptance of one view of things rather than another" (442). In this influence there is some relationship to Roman entertainment, though some marked divergences. Rome was much more suspicious of theater than the Greeks, placing restrictions on the permanence of any theater, concerned in part with the license it might give to the people. More than in Athens, though, theater became a form of elite competition for honor and support, meant as lavish spectacle and visual demonstration of hierarchy. The plays themselves were less critical of political leaders, though particular lines may have been employed by elites to test audience reaction or support.

Tonio Hölscher and Ellen Perry complete our picture, looking at the complexities of generalizing about the interaction between art and participatory communities. Temples and cult places provided a new concept of religious topography, conceived and reshaped in the spirit of a participatory community. As in the *agora*, the decisive feature of this sacred topography is that it is not only a static "image," but also a semantic space to be used by the population, in which large parts of the Athenian citizen-body made a concrete experience of their city and territory. There is no "democratic architecture and art," but there is massive use of architecture and art by and for democracy (Hölscher: 478). One also sees in Roman visual culture a semantic space in which art and architecture reinforced differences in status rather than equality, but nonetheless forged a common identity, reflecting the incorporation of different groups and traditions as well as extending to other conquered territories. Like the *agora* in Greek *poleis*, the Roman Forum constituted the center of participatory life, the civic presence of citizens acting, speaking, and appearing before each other.

Each chapter can be read on its own. But each companion chapter also brings into relief both what is similar and what is distinctive in how these communities constructed, imagined, and responded to participatory claims. Each reader will find his or her own salient comparisons, perhaps stimulated to pursue some of the questions that arise from these chapters. The final chapter is one such exercise, drawing on the complex portrait painted in this volume to reflect on fundamental questions of power that underlie the practices of contemporary participatory communities in both a domestic and an international context. A study of the past cannot tell us what to do or what will happen. But it can broaden our sense of the choices and deepen our appreciation of the struggles that all participatory communities must face.

REFERENCES

Bourdieu, P. 1977. *Outline of a Theory of Practice*. Trans. R. Nice. Cambridge.
Douglas, M. 1966. *Purity and Danger: An Analysis of Concepts of Pollution and Taboo.* London.
Douglas, M. 1978. *Cultural Bias* (occasional paper No. 34). London.

Douglas, M. 1982. *Natural Symbols: Exploration in Cosmology*. New York.
Geertz, C. 1973. *The Interpretation of Cultures*. New York.
Hammer, D. 2006. "Bourdieu, Ideology, and the Ancient World." *American Journal of Semiotics* 22: 87–108.
Hammer, D. 2009. "What Is Politics in the Ancient World?" In R.K. Balot, ed., *A Companion to Greek and Roman Political Thought*. Oxford and Malden, MA, 20–36.
Ricoeur, P. 1986. *Lectures on Ideology and Utopia*. Ed. G. Taylor. New York.
Turner, V. 1974. *Dramas, Fields and Metaphors: Symbolic Action in Human Society*. Ithaca, NY.
Turner, V. 1988. *The Anthropology of Performance*. New York.

CHAPTER 1

Reading the Past (On Comparison)

David Konstan

This volume is a study in comparisons—but what does it mean to compare? Does comparing presuppose an underlying similarity, so that one cannot draw useful comparisons between things that are fundamentally different? The conventional expression, "comparing apples and oranges" (in fact, this expression is itself a comparison, usually introduced by "like"), suggests that only items that belong to a single class, such as apples, can fruitfully be compared. Yet apples and oranges do not seem so very different: both are round, sweetly acidic fruits, of about the same size; if one said, "comparing apples and skyscrapers," the contrast would be much sharper. But even so, is it useful to accept such restrictions on what can profitably be compared? Marcel Detienne has published a book with the provocative title, *Comparing the Incomparable* (Detienne 2008), in which he argues that the comparative approach should move beyond the focus on contiguous or closely related political forms and widen its scope to take in remote and diverse societies, as far removed as China and Africa. To this end, he proposes an active dialogue between historians and anthropologists (cf. Lloyd 2004, 2007; Morris 2010; Morris and Scheidel 2009; Scheidel 2009). But it may also be that societies that have traditionally been seen as similar in fact diverge more than they seem, and that despite close contact are fundamentally distinct in character. Indeed, classical Greece and Rome may differ more radically than, say, Rome and ancient Persia, or Athens and Carthage. One purpose of this book is to raise just such doubts and questions.

But the problem of comparing ancient Greek and Roman communities is still deeper. For it is inevitable to see these communities through the lens of modern social forms, all the more so because it is often assumed that modern democracies and republics—the participatory communities of today—are descended from their ancient prototypes. Although *dēmokratia* and *res publica* are, respectively, Greek and Latin words, the notions conveyed by the English terms "democracy" and "republic," and the idea that they represent in

A Companion to Greek Democracy and the Roman Republic, First Edition. Edited by Dean Hammer.

some sense contrasting political systems, are modern, and reflect developments in social and intellectual history that have only a tangential relation to classical antiquity. When James Madison observed in the tenth of the *Federalist Papers*, "The two great points of difference between a democracy and a republic are: first, the delegation of the government, in the latter, to a small number of citizens elected by the rest; secondly, the greater number of citizens, and greater sphere of country, over which the latter may be extended," he was speaking a language, and engaged in a debate, that were foreign to the ways in which thinkers in the classical world imagined their polities: the Roman Senate, for example, was scarcely conceived of as a representative body, its powers delegated to it by an electorate. Thomas Jefferson, indeed, categorically dismissed the relevance of ancient models to modern republicanism: "The introduction of this principle of representative democracy has rendered useless almost everything written before on the structure of government; and in great measure, relieves our regret, if the political writings of Aristotle, or of any other ancient, have been lost, or are unfaithfully rendered or explained" (quoted in Saxonhouse 2006: 13; cf. Finley 1973). A comparison between ancient Greek and Roman communities always implicitly involves a comparison between classical and modern societies as well.

If the contrast between democracy and republic is complicated by modern conceptions, it is a further wrinkle that the distinction between Greek city-states and Rome was not typically imagined in these terms in antiquity. Some Greek cities were democracies, some were not: they might also be characterized as aristocracies, oligarchies, or tyrannies, among other things (see Rhodes, Chapter 8). Some Greek observers of Rome, beginning at least with the historian Polybius (second century BCE), described it as a mixed regime, with elements of democracy, aristocracy, and monarchy—government by the many, by the few or best, and by a single ruler or at most two (the two consuls at Rome, with their plenipotentiary powers, were analogized to the double kingship in Sparta). But nothing prevented Greek cities from adopting this model, and it was equally possible to characterize the Roman state as fundamentally oligarchic (a view that is prevalent today among classical scholars, although some have recently maintained that it was in fact more of a democracy; see especially Millar 1998, 2002). Beneath these distinctions in the form of regime, Greek and Roman political thinkers might describe both the Greek communities and their Italian counterparts, including Rome, simply as cities (in Greek, *poleis*, plural of *polis*; in Latin, *civitates*), which set them off from kingdoms such as Egypt or Babylon, and from looser groups that they called *ethnē* (plural of *ethnos*), which shared a common heritage or identity but lacked the civic structures of the *polis*. Modern historians typically refer to classical *poleis* as city-states, and include under this category Italian Renaissance cities (whether monarchies, democracies, or republics, as they are sometimes styled) and also, at times, cities in Phoenicia (as well as Carthage) and the Hittite region (Raaflaub, Emlen, and Molho 1991; Raaflaub and Hansen 1995; Raaflaub and Hansen 1996). Are city-states an elementary type of polity, so that it is reasonable to compare variations among different instances, whether in the Greek-speaking world or Italy (comparing one variety of apple with another, so to speak), or are the differences between Greek *poleis* and Rome too great to be assimilated in this manner?

It may be that early Rome was a *polis* on the model of the Greek or Etruscan city-states, but that it ceased to be one as it grew to include all of Italy under its sway and finally the entire Mediterranean world and beyond, as far north as Britain. Here, there arises another distinction in terminology that can prove treacherous for comparisons. The appellation Roman Republic (in this sense conventionally written with a capital R) is often applied to the period in Roman history following the expulsion of the kings (traditionally dated to 509 BCE) and ending with the defeat of Antony and Cleopatra at Actium in 31 BCE and the concentration of power in the hands of Octavian, whose reign (sometimes characterized as a principate) inaugurated the Roman Empire. The Empire in this context refers to the succession of authoritarian rulers from Augustus onward, as opposed to the predominance of the senatorial class and its allies among the *equites* or knights. The Empire (majuscule) is thus not synonymous with empire in the sense of rule over subject populations, which was as true of Rome in the republican period as under the Empire proper. Clearly, there was some kind of rupture in the shift from Republic to Empire (Sir Ronald Syme [1939] described it as "The Roman Revolution"), even if Augustus, as the Senate dubbed Octavian, boasted precisely of having restored the Republic to the Senate and People of Rome (*Res gestae* 6). However we date the shift from Republic to Empire (Cicero foresaw the menace in his own lifetime, but others date it to Tiberius' reign), if the Republic is understood as the opposite of authoritarian control under an emperor—and this view of it was to some extent shared by the founding fathers of the United States—then it is not necessarily incompatible with democracy; indeed, it summons up the founding ideals of the American republic, even if it fails to correspond to Madison's and Jefferson's conception of a republic as representative government (some offices were elective, but these were magistracies; membership in the Senate was mainly hereditary).

If we take the Roman Republic, at least in the early centuries, to be a *polis*, like Athens—and these are the two polities that have loomed largest in the historical imagination of the modern world, with Athens in the fifth and fourth centuries BCE seen as the democracy par excellence and Rome as the model of a republic—then what are the fundamental features of this formation that the two societies have in common? Athens and Rome were, at least early on, small, independent agricultural communities—small by the standards of a modern state, of course, but also in comparison with monarchies such as ancient Egypt or Lydia or Persia. Nevertheless, they were larger than mere villages or groups comprising just a few families, and had developed political institutions. It is plausible that the emergence of polities of this form was facilitated to some extent by the geographical terrains of Greece and Italy, where mountains and rivers provided protection from neighbors as well as well-watered plains suitable for agriculture. The use of iron, which became widespread in the region in the early part of the first millennium BCE, would also seem to have been a factor in the development of such cities: iron plowshares were tough enough to permit deep cultivation, so that a limited amount of land could now support a sizeable population (Heichelheim 1968 is still worth consulting in this regard). What is more, farmers might produce enough on a plot of land worked by a single extended family (including dependent labor) to achieve a certain degree of self-sufficiency; this relative autarky in turn may have helped to engender a sense of autonomy in the individual farmer, and of the community as a collection of households that are conceptually prior to the state (cf. Arist. *Pol.* 1252b10–12, where he cites with approval Hesiod's verse: "first of all the household and wife and ox and plow," *Works and Days* 405). In the absence of adequate information about Mediterranean and near-eastern cities during the Bronze Age, however, it is hazardous to tie the emergence of government based on communal participation too closely to a particular stage of technological development.

If the above—or comparable—preconditions for the city-state form of social organization made possible the emergence of a democracy or republic, something more was needed for these to become self-conscious political regimes. In the case of both Athens and Rome, the governments that they identified as *dēmokratia* and *res publica* were founded, or imagined as having been founded, in the wake of revolutionary action, by which a previous regime was modified or overthrown and a new political formation was inaugurated (see Raaflaub, Chapter 2, and Fronda, Chapter 3). In both cases, revolution was conceived of as liberation from tyranny (in this respect, they resembled the inauguration of the French and American republics), by means of which a broad stratum of the population obtained the right to engage in political activity. This right, or set of rights, was associated in turn with a new status, that of citizen (*politēs* in Greek, *civis* in Latin): for Athens and Rome alike were premised on the idea of citizenship. To be sure, citizen status was inherited (as it is today), and this might give rise to a myth of kinship as the original basis of community, but this does not compromise the novelty of citizenship as a basis of social organization. It is perhaps fair to say that the concept of citizenship, and the attendant notion of the individual (or, more specifically, the adult male head of household) as the elementary constituent of the political community, are the most salient contribution of classical Greece and Rome to modern political thought and practice. It is the basis of every social contract theory, from Democritus and Plato down to Hobbes, Rousseau, and Rawls.

Citizenship is compatible with a variety of regimes, including monarchy, and both Athens and Rome underwent changes that put their notions of *dēmokratia* and *res publica* to the test (see Raaflaub, Chapter 2, Fronda, Chapter 3, Rhodes, Chapter 8, and Mouritsen, Chapter 9). The transformation of Rome is of course the more evident one, since it expanded from a community roughly comparable in size to Greek or Etruscan city-states to a metropolis of more than a million inhabitants by the first century BCE, and commanded a territory that reached from Britain to Tunisia, from Spain to Egypt and the borders of Iran. What is more, by the early third century Roman citizenship had been extended to most free inhabitants of the Empire (by the so-called Decree of Caracalla), thus turning Rome into what may be imagined as a vast polity, as opposed to an imperial center governing tributary states or satrapies. Athens and the other Greek *poleis* no longer functioned as independent city-states, but were now local municipalities in one or another Roman province—in the case of Athens, the province of Achaea, which is as close as ancient Greece ever came to acquiring a political unity over a territory more or less corresponding to the imagined boundaries of Hellas. The provinces were under the jurisdiction of a Roman governor, to whom the local administration was responsible; the governor himself was answerable to the regime in Rome, which under the Empire was subject to the supreme authority of the emperor. And yet, by virtue of the geographical range over which Rome now extended, citizenship had become divorced from effective participation in the central government. No mechanism for voting at a distance for offices at Rome, such as obtained in the American republic, was even imagined. Roman citizenship carried with it many legal entitlements, but these had nothing to do with ideas such as democracy or republicanism.

The loss of independence among the Greek *poleis*, however, did not mean a cessation of political institutions or activity on the level of the city. On the contrary, cities continued to be arenas of a vital political life well into the later Empire (for the Hellenistic period, see Carlsson 2010; for the Roman period, Dmitriev 2005). What is more, although the radical democracy that prevailed in fifth- and fourth-century BCE Athens, which eliminated property qualifications for participation in the assembly and council and as a qualification for all but a few offices, was curtailed after the suzerainty of Macedon and later Rome, not only Athens but pretty much all the Greek city-states continued to style themselves as democracies, and many modeled their institutions closely on Athens' own. Thus, Greek city-state democracies of one sort or another continued to flourish under Roman rule, albeit with certain restrictions on their decision-making and liberty (they could not act openly against the interests of Rome). Participatory government was not over, though it took new forms.

The persistence of local loyalties among the Greek cities differs in another respect from the expansive conception of citizenship that developed at Rome. In the heyday of the democracy, Athens was especially tight-fisted with the bestowal of citizenship and jealous of the purity of its lineage, whereas Rome was far more ready to absorb others into the citizen body, thereby increasing its numbers and its territory. The foundation myths of Athens and Rome (created, needless to say, after the fact) reflect their distinct paths. Thus, Athens, boasted of the autochthony of its population, understanding by this term the original birth of its population from the native soil and thus, by way of descent, its uninterrupted connection with the land (the term autochthony seems to have acquired this sense precisely in the fifth century; cf. Rosivach 1987). Rome, on the contrary, traced its lineage to a mixture of native Latins and Trojan immigrants, and imagined that the city itself, which was originally the site of a kingdom deriving from Greek Arcadia, was subsequently populated by granting asylum to refugees from all over Italy (see Morgan, Chapter 4, and Jaeger, Chapter 5). This all-male community proceeded, according to tradition, to acquire wives by seizing them from the Sabines, which led to the political integration of the two communities; further wars each time ended up widening Rome's boundaries (cf. Konstan 1986; Wiseman 2004). The practice of granting citizenship to manumitted slaves further augmented the enfranchised population and contributed to its mixed character.

This is not to say that all sense of local participation was lost at Rome: Rome continued to have its own identity and institutions, as did other cities in Italy and the west. But there developed a rupture between local ties that involved the entire community (at one or another level, and always with exclusions based on status, class, gender, and the like) and more extended forms of association, such as obtained among the elites of different cities and regions in the empire. Just why Athens failed to develop in this direction is difficult to say. It has been suggested that the very deepening of the Athenian democracy may have inhibited the extension of citizenship beyond its territory, despite Athenian hegemony over as many as 300 *poleis* at the height of its empire (Andrew Monson, personal communication). For the chief privilege of the citizenry under the democracy, that is, participation in the ruling organs of the city, would have been compromised by such inclusiveness. At Rome, the absence, from the beginning, of a comparably broad democracy, combined with the overwhelming weight of the aristocracy, represented by the

Senate, meant that increments to the citizen population might be welcomed as providing a greater power base for the ruling caste rather than a dilution of its privileges.

Control by the aristocracy at Rome was by no means unchallenged, and the system was not entirely stable. Threats to the dominant stratum took various forms. In the earliest period (according to tradition), senators were drawn from a hereditary caste known as patricians, and intermarriage with other strata was prohibited; breaking down this barrier and permitting the admission of plebeians to the ruling group was an initial step toward creating a democratic structure. Although the lower classes could vote for magistrates, conflicts between the orders broke out with some frequency, leading even to such extreme ruptures as secession on the part of the plebs. To what extent such tensions reflected genuine class warfare, or were rather maneuvers resulting from dissension within the ruling echelon, is hard to determine: the conflicts under the Gracchi in the second century BCE, and the rebellion of Catiline in the first, are typically ambiguous cases (see Raaflaub, Chapter 2, Mouritsen, Chapter 9, Arena, Chapter 13, Tatum, Chapter 15). Even the civil wars that led to the establishment of the Empire can be read as manifestations of class struggle, and were sometimes imagined or promoted as such by the participants. The Roman Republic retained elements of popular government, even as the Greek city-state democracies accommodated rule by elite segments of the population, which often received support from Rome itself. The relationship between the two models—if they can be usefully distinguished as such—was as much symbiotic or complementary as it was contrastive or discordant.

The upshot is that the difference between *dēmokratia* and *res publica*, in the original sense of the words, is perhaps not best expressed as obtaining between forms of political regime, but as two stories of the evolution of participatory government, in which relative exclusiveness in respect to citizenship, both vertical along class divisions or horizontal among adjacent communities, was the most salient factor. The differences between Athens and Rome are of course numerous and manifest in domains such as law, patronage, military organization, economy, the structure of the family, and so forth, and are discussed in detail in the chapters that follow. Without anticipating these studies here, it may be useful to consider briefly how political freedom and participation were conceived in Athens and in Rome—the two exemplary societies under investigation—insofar as these ideological commitments are what have borne most importantly on modern conceptions of democracy and republicanism.

The most striking feature of the Athenian democratic ideology is the emphasis on equality, whether before the law (*isonomia*) or in respect to freedom of speech (*isēgoria*, *parrhēsia*) (see Raaflaub, Chapter 2, Rhodes, Chapter 8, Fisher, Chapter 12, and Wallace, Chapter 14). The revolution at the end of the sixth century associated with the name of Cleisthenes, together with subsequent reforms that extended the democracy still further, resulted in a radical conception of popular sovereignty that is virtually without parallel in history. The idea rested on two basic principles. First, the governing body is the people as a whole, that is, the *dēmos*; its decisions are final and supreme. Although the word *dēmos* can refer to the entire citizen population, it was often employed to designate the poorer strata, as opposed to the elite; thus, democracy in Athens always smacked of the rule of ordinary folk, a reminder that the lower classes had achieved—or usurped—the power that had formerly been monopolized by noble or wealthy families. Democracy could thus be construed by its enemies as the unfair domination of the aristocracy by the common man. Insofar as the *dēmos* signified the entire citizenry, however, it was not a particular constituency but coincided with the population as a whole (that is, the free adult native males who made up the citizen body). Seen this way, one could not distinguish the interests of the rulers from those of the ruled, since rulers and ruled were the same. At the heart of American democracy, by contrast, is the idea that, in James Madison's words, "the great object in view is to limit and qualify the powers of Government" (the idea goes back ultimately to Milton's famous tract, *Areopagitica: A Speech for the Liberty of Unlicenc'd Printing*); the view is understandable in a system of representative government, where elected individuals have great power over their fellow countrymen and may be thought to put their own interests, or those of some special constituency, ahead of those of the society at large. If, in classical Athens, the people conceived of themselves as the government, then there was no separate regime whose powers needed to be checked or curtailed. President Barack Obama has affirmed: "When our government is spoken of as some menacing, threatening foreign entity, it ignores the fact that, in our democracy, government is us" (Obama 2010). He is of course right to insist that government is not necessarily an adversary of the people it represents, but it is misleading to suggest that the modern state can be straightforwardly assimilated to the people as a whole, as was the case—or was believed to be the case—in classical Athens.

The second foundational principle of classical Athenian democracy is the autonomy and equality of all citizens. Each and every one had the right to speak in the assembly, to cast his vote, to take turns in participating in the executive council and even to be president for a day, as virtually all offices were assigned by lot. Indeed, any other method of selection was viewed with the deepest suspicion, as potentially undoing the democratic system and opening the door to the domination or tyranny of a privileged class. If the idea of the *dēmos* represented the collective identity of the Athenian citizenry, it was counterbalanced by a strong sense of individualism that was idealized in the notion of personal autarky or self-sufficiency, freedom from subservience, yes—and wage labor was regarded as a kind of servility not far removed from slavery—but even from economic interdependency with others. Athenian society was fraught with rivalry. The reverse side of political equality was the need to maintain one's station and dignity before one's peers, and Athenians seem to have been exceptionally sensitive to any kind of slight that might diminish their reputation or standing. Aristotle, indeed, in his analysis of anger, defines it as a desire for revenge in response to an insult or snub: an unanswered put-down was tantamount to acknowledging one's own social inferiority (*Rhet.* 2.2, 1378a31–33; discussion in Konstan 2006). This quality of assertiveness, so much admired in the classical democracy, is evident in Aristophanic comedy, with its feisty protagonists who take matters into their own hands and promote the wildest schemes to realize their goals: an example is Dicaeopolis in the *Acharnians*, who, in protest against the war with Sparta, makes a separate truce with the enemy and thus enjoys all the benefits of peace, while his fellow citizens suffer the deprivations caused by embargos on trade (see Fisher, Chapter 12, and Sidwell, Chapter 24). "Dicaeopolis" means something like "Just City," and it is easy to see the contradiction here, by which a man who isolates his household from the rest of the community and strikes his own bargain with the foe is nevertheless styled as though he were the *polis* in its entirety.

The power of the people might also run up against the force of tradition, enshrined in a combination of customs and laws which in Greek were both called ***nomoi*** (singular, ***nomos***). Where the community is the dominant force, whether in legislation or in the judiciary (there was no system of precedents in Athenian law, and the jury, embodying the will of the *dēmos*, was paramount), it can set limits to the free speech exercised by individuals in the name of the society as a whole. This is how Socrates, for example, met his death: he was accused of introducing new gods and corrupting the youth, both matters of persuasion; nor were there any pre-existing laws that precisely addressed these offenses, so far as one can tell. It was up to the discretion of the jurors to decide whether Socrates' unorthodox habit of publicly cross-examining the conventional beliefs of his peers constituted a threat to the city. It has been argued that, over the course of the fifth and fourth centuries, popular sovereignty was gradually rejected in favor of the sovereignty of law (see Ostwald 1989), but the question remains a murky one, since laws were also enacted with a view to protecting the authority of the *dēmos*, and not for the purpose of abrogating or controlling it. For all the emphasis on *parrhēsia* in classical Athens, it is difficult to imagine a popular sentiment such as that expressed by Thomas Jefferson in regard to freedom of the press (that is, of expression in its most public form): "were it left to me to decide whether we should have a government without newspapers or newspapers without a government, I should not hesitate a moment to prefer the latter" (Thomas Jefferson to Edward Carrington, 1787).

A civic democracy does not grant unrestricted rights to all, but only to those who are acknowledged citizens. These rights can be bestowed by the governing body and also taken away in part or in whole, as happened, for example, to many partisans of the short-lived oligarchic revolution after its defeat in 411 BCE (another example is the Athenian practice of ostracism). I suggested above that Athenians may have been niggardly in their extension of citizen rights to outsiders as a way of maintaining their privileged status, but restrictions on intermarriage with outsiders (a law promulgated by Pericles in 451 BCE restricted legitimate unions to citizens on both sides, that is, the husband's family and the wife's) may also have been aimed at the elite, who had more occasion to form marital connections with foreigners and fewer inhibitions about ties with aristocratic communities abroad. A likely consequence of this rule is that Athenians were encouraged to think of themselves as a race apart, defined by their relation to the land—the notion of autochthony mentioned earlier (for the most extreme expression of this attitude, see the Platonic dialogue *Menexenus*). Although there is no reason to suppose that a majority of Athenians agreed with Aristotle's view (*Pol.* 1, 1252a31–b1) that non-Greeks were by nature mentally inferior to Greeks and therefore fit to be enslaved, in part for their own good (since they would be ruled by people capable of reason), the tendency in a democracy toward ever greater inclusiveness might be checked by a doctrine of racial superiority that classified outgroups as naturally unworthy of civic participation (see Balot and Atkison, Chapter 22).

To what extent early Rome was beset by similar problems is impossible to say, given the absence of documentary evidence (see Stewart, Chapter 23). During the period of the high Republic, one of the principal concerns of political thinkers and historians was harmony among the several orders or classes, rather than the sovereignty of the people as a whole (cf. Connolly 2007: 42, who remarks that the distribution of power in Rome "cannot be understood as a matter of two identities and ideologies, one ruling, one ruled"; Connolly suggests that the senatorial class, with its privileged access to rhetorical training, sought to include the populace by producing the image of a common identity). The formula, *senatus populusque romanus*, "the Roman people and senate," is revealing (see Mouritsen, Chapter 9). On the one hand, it marks a distinction between the senatorial class and the rest of the population; on the other hand, the singular adjective *romanus* suggests that the preceding pair of nouns is thought of as a single unit (the plural *romani*, at all events, would have emphasized the distinction between them). Sovereignty is shared, and danger to the republic arises when orders—not individuals—fail to observe their proper limits and encroach on the rights of others. This hierarchical structure was underpinned by the institution of patronage, which was a relationship between unequal parties, as opposed to friendship, which ideally obtained among equals. As a sentimental bond, friendship could cross class lines, and patrons and clients could come to regard themselves as friends. But the tension between the two paradigms made such relations exceptional (cf. Konstan 2010). Patronage between classes was mirrored within the family by the custom of *patria potestas*, by which the father retained absolute authority over his sons until his death, unless he formally granted them independence.

Class barriers were not airtight. Very occasionally, men of lower station were elected to the consulship, and thereby entered the senatorial order (Cato the Censor and Cicero are the two most prominent examples). Movement downward was also possible: an aristocrat might renounce his status to join the plebeians, with a view to obtaining the office of tribune of the people and thus developing an alternative basis of political power. Such a move was naturally regarded with misgivings by the upper classes, and members of the nobility who were thought to be currying the favor of the people were invariably branded by their opponents as corrupt and motivated by their own personal interests and depravities. Undoubtedly, a highly ambitious senator who had thoughts of monopolizing power within his class might exploit popular institutions as a fulcrum, and the populace at large might conceivably benefit from such internal divisions among the ruling caste. There were of course organs for the popular election of candidates, however skewed their function was in practice, and leading figures cultivated the favor of the people by gestures of amity and direct handouts (cf. the *Commentariolum ambitionis*; these institutions are the basis of descriptions of Rome as a popular democracy). But the dominant rhetoric at Rome was never egalitarian, as it was in Athens at the height of the democracy, and the tension between individualism and service to the community was acted out primarily among senatorial families and factions, where the goal was not autarky but autocracy.

The modern republican ideal of representative government can be seen as an attempt to square the circle: the best will rule, as in an aristocracy, but as an expression of the popular will. Let us return to the passage from the Federalist Paper quoted above; Madison continues: "The effect of the first difference [that is, the delegation of government] is, on the one hand, to refine and enlarge the public views, by passing them through the medium of a chosen body of citizens, whose wisdom may best discern the true interest of their country, and whose patriotism and love of justice will be least likely to sacrifice it to temporary or partial considerations. Under such a regulation, it may well happen that the public voice, pronounced by the representatives of the people, will be more consonant to the public good than if pronounced by the people themselves, convened for the purpose." Delegates are not mouthpieces for their constituencies; they are independent-minded legislators, who ideally exercise a judgment superior to the collective view of the electorate. Madison was of course aware that individual representatives might seek to promote their private interests: "On the other hand, the effect may be inverted. Men of factious tempers, of local prejudices, or of sinister designs, may, by intrigue, by corruption, or by other means, first obtain the suffrages, and then betray the interests, of the people." One might suppose that the best safeguard against such a breach between elected representatives and the people is the rapid rotation of office: in a democratic republic, there is no ruling caste, as there was in Rome, but a succession of office-holders who return, after their terms, to the status of ordinary voters. Madison in fact looks in this essay to a different remedy, namely, the size of the republic, on the grounds that there is likely to be a larger number of suitable candidates in a larger population, whereas the size of the representative organs does not increase proportionally (or else they would become too cumbersome). But the central incongruity in the passage is in the notion that the public voice is not that of the people, but is rather ventriloquized through their representatives; this counts as the public voice because it is "more consonant to the public good than if pronounced by the people themselves." The question of who decides what is in the public's interest is not addressed.

No ideology is free from inconsistencies, insofar as it constitutes an attempt to reconcile individual freedoms with structures of power. But the stress points differ according to the kind of state in question, and where it locates responsibility for determining the general good. Matching up ancient Greek and Roman participatory communities—and, inevitably, modern democracies and republics as well—may be an exercise in comparing incomparables, but just for this reason it may reveal the limits of these systems of government, not excluding our own.

REFERENCES

Carlsson, S. 2010. *Hellenistic Democracies: Freedom, Independence and Political Procedure in Some East Greek City-States*. Stuttgart (= *Historia* Einzelschriften 206).

Connolly, J. 2007. *The State of Speech: Rhetoric and Political Thought in Ancient Rome*. Princeton.

Detienne, M. 2008. *Comparing the Incomparable*. Trans. J. Lloyd. Stanford. Original French edn., *Comparer l'incomparable*. Paris 2000.

Dmitriev, S. 2005. *City Government in Hellenistic and Roman Asia Minor*. Oxford.

Finley, M.I. 1973. *Democracy Ancient and Modern*. New Brunswick.

Heichelheim, F.M. 1968. *An Ancient Economic History: From the Paleolithic Age to the Migrations of the Germanic, Slavic, and Arabic Nations*. Trans. J. Stevens. Revised edn. Leiden.

Jefferson, T. 1787. *Papers*. Vol. 11: 48–49. Available at http://press-pubs.uchicago.edu/founders/documents/amendI_speechs8.html. Accessed Mar. 28, 2014.

Konstan, D. 1986. "Ideology and Narrative in Livy, Book I." *ClAnt* 5: 197–215.

Konstan, D. 2006. *The Emotions of the Ancient Greeks: Studies in Aristotle and Classical Literature*. Toronto.

Konstan, D. 2010. "Are Fellow Citizens Friends? Aristotle versus Cicero on *Philia*, *Amicitia*, and Social Solidarity." In R. Rosen and I. Sluiter, eds., *Valuing Others: Papers from the Penn-Leiden Colloquium V*. Leiden, 233–248.

Lloyd, G.E.R. 2004. *Ancient Worlds, Modern Reflections: Philosophical Perspectives on Greek and Chinese Science and Culture*. Oxford.

Lloyd, G.E.R. 2007. *Cognitive Variations: Reflections on the Unity and Diversity of the Human Mind*. Oxford.

Madison, J. 1787. *Federalist Paper #10*. Originally published in *The New York Packet*. Collected with other papers in *The Federalist; or, The New Constitution*, 2 vols. (New York, 1788). Available at Library of Congress website ("Thomas") http://thomas.loc.gov/home/histdox/fedpapers.html#skip_menu. Accessed Mar. 28, 2014.

Millar, F. 1998. *The Crowd in Rome in the Late Republic*. Ann Arbor.

Millar, F. 2002. *The Roman Republic in Political Thought*. Hanover.

Morris, I. 2010. *Why the West Rules—For Now: The Patterns of History, and What They Reveal about the Future*. New York.

Morris, I. and W. Scheidel, eds. 2009. *The Dynamics of Ancient Empires: State Power from Assyria to Byzantium*. Oxford.

Obama, B. 2010. "Remarks by the President at University of Michigan Spring Commencement" (Big House, University of Michigan, Ann Arbor, Michigan, May 01, 2010). Available at http://www.whitehouse.gov/the-press-office/remarks-president-university-michigan-spring-commencement. Accessed Mar. 28, 2014.

Ostwald, M. 1989. *From Popular Sovereignty to the Sovereignty of Law: Law, Society, and Politics in Fifth-Century Athens*. Berkeley.

Raaflaub, K., J. Emlen, and A. Molho, eds. 1991. *Athens and Rome, Florence and Venice: City-States in Classical Antiquity and Medieval Italy*. Stuttgart.

Raaflaub, K. and M.H. Hansen, eds. 1995. *Studies in the Ancient Greek Polis*. Stuttgart (= *Historia* suppl. vol. 95).

Raaflaub, K. and M.H. Hansen, eds. 1996. *More Studies in the Ancient Greek Polis*. Stuttgart (= *Historia* suppl. vol. 108).

Rosivach, V.J. 1987. "Autochthony and the Athenians." *CQ* 37: 294–306.

Saxonhouse, A. 2006. *Free Speech and Democracy in Ancient Athens*. Cambridge.

Scheidel, W. ed. 2009. *Rome and China: Comparative Perspectives on Ancient World Empires*. New York.

Syme, R. 1939. *The Roman Revolution*. Oxford.

Wiseman, T.P. 2004. *The Myths of Rome*. Exeter.

FURTHER READING

Comparative studies of ancient cultures are still comparatively rare, and scholars have tended to shy away from exploring analogies with the modern world. Moses Finley's *Democracy Ancient and Modern* (1973) is an early and still exciting contribution. Fergus Millar has argued forcefully (albeit controversially) for a far more democratic interpretation of Roman republican politics than has usually been admitted; see his *The Crowd in Rome in the Late Republic* (1998). Geoffrey Lloyd has done a great deal to stimulate comparison between ancient Greece and China; see his *Ancient Worlds, Modern Reflections: Philosophical Perspectives on Greek and Chinese Science and Culture* (2004), and *Cognitive Variations: Reflections on the Unity and Diversity of the Human Mind* (2007). Ian Morris and Walter Scheidel have taken a long view of the evolution of ancient societies, using modern demographic and other analytic methods; see Morris' controversial *Why the West Rules—For Now: The Patterns of History, and What They Reveal about the Future* (2010), Scheidel's edited collection, *Rome and China: Comparative Perspectives on Ancient World Empires* (2009), and their jointly edited *The Dynamics of Ancient Empires: State Power from Assyria to*

Byzantium (2009). Finally, Kurt Raaflaub, together with various scholars, has edited a series of volumes covering a wide range of ancient civilizations, from classical Greece and Rome to China and India, Africa, and the Americas, and more; see in particular Raaflaub, Emlen, and Molho, eds., *Athens and Rome, Florence and Venice: City-States in Classical Antiquity and Medieval Italy* (1991); Raaflaub and Ian Morris, eds., *Democracy 2500? Questions and Challenges* (1997); Raaflaub and Nathan Rosenstein, eds., *War and Society in the Ancient and Medieval Worlds* (1999); Raaflaub, ed., *War and Peace in the Ancient World* (2006); Raaflaub and David Konstan, eds., *Epic and History* (2009); and Raaflaub and Richard Talbert, eds., *Geography and Ethnography: Perceptions of the World in Pre-Modern Societies* (2010).

PART I

The Emergence of Participatory Communities

CHAPTER 2

Why Greek Democracy? Its Emergence and Nature in Context

Kurt A. Raaflaub

1 Introduction, Questions, Sources

Ancient Greek democracy emerged in its most fully developed form in Athens in the mid-fifth century BCE. Naturally, under the conditions prevailing in the ancient world, women, noncitizens, and slaves were excluded from political rights (Cartledge 2002a: chs. 4–5; Raaflaub 1998: 26–36); in world history, the political enfranchisement of women and the full integration of the descendants of slaves are very recent phenomena, and noncitizens generally remain excluded. Despite these limitations, Athenian democracy was most radical in realizing the idea of an egalitarian and participatory citizen community; it was unparalleled in the ancient world, and after its demise at the end of the fourth century it was not matched again for more than two millennia. Emerging in an extraordinary constellation after the Persian Wars and, remarkably, in an imperial city, this democracy remained exceptional. But more moderate democracies sprang up in other Greek communities as well.

Earlier, by the end of the sixth century, "proto-democratic" or "isonomic" constitutions, based on the equal participation of at least the landowning citizens who qualified for service in the army, became quite common in the Greek world. They resulted from a long process of development that the extant evidence permits us to follow from the mid-seventh to the late sixth century. Even earlier, reflecting conditions in the eighth to early seventh century, the epics of Homer and Hesiod offer insights into the interaction of leaders, councils, and assemblies, and the role of these as yet informal institutions in communal life. Other evidence too suggests a widespread political culture that, lacking centralized power and authoritarian structures, was to some extent based on civic equality and elements of "people's power." This was the foundation upon which the Greek *polis* (pl. *poleis*, see below) developed in the ninth and eighth centuries.

A Companion to Greek Democracy and the Roman Republic, First Edition. Edited by Dean Hammer.

This chapter will discuss the development of participatory *polis* constitutions from their earliest informal traces to fully developed democracy. Unlike historians of early Rome, those of archaic (c.750–480 BCE) and classical Greece (480–c.320) are able to rely on contemporaneous written sources, whether literary or epigraphical. Initially, with the exception of written laws, such evidence is limited to poetry. Prose emerged only in the late sixth century (Grethlein 2011), and literature with specifically political content was not produced before the fifth. But in the small face-to-face societies of Greek *poleis*, the poets not only entertained but also educated their audiences and voiced public concerns (Maehler 1963; Nagy 1989). Hence political thinking is pervasive in early Greek poetry (Raaflaub 2000). The dramatic poets and historians of the fifth century inherited this public function and often reflected on issues that agitated their contemporaries (Meier 1993; Boedeker and Raaflaub 2005; Raaflaub 2010). From the late fifth century, political pamphlets, inscriptions, political and court speeches, the *Constitution of the Athenians* (*Ath. Pol.*) produced in Aristotle's school, and Xenophon's, Plato's, and especially Aristotle's works of political theory and philosophy illuminate political decisions, procedures, structures, and constitutions on an ever broader scale. Later writers, such as Plutarch and Pausanias, add valuable material that, however, requires critical assessment.

Those readers who wish to learn more about the historical background to the developments discussed in this chapter will find rich information in the titles listed in "Further Reading" at the end of this chapter.

2 Foundations and Early Stages: The Eighth and Early Seventh Centuries

The magnificent "Mycenaean" Bronze Age civilization ended around 1200 BCE in a wave of destruction that affected the entire eastern Mediterranean (Ward and Joukowsky 1992; Dickinson 1994) initiated a long period of decline. The subsequent centuries (c.1200–800), often called the "Dark Age" (Osborne 1996; Snodgrass 2000; Dickinson 2006), were characterized by regional and local focuses. People lived in villages under the leadership of "chiefs," who counted their wealth in herds and excelled in raids of neighboring villages or coasts (*Od.* 9.39–61; 14.211–275; see also Farenga, Chapter 6, on early notions of authority).

Gradual recovery began around 1000 BCE. Populations increased, farming became more prominent, international contacts intensified, and new types of communities, the *poleis*, emerged. The *polis* was a citizen community rather than a city-state (Hansen 1993a). It had a main settlement, but cities developed much later, if at all. "The men are the polis," says Thucydides (7.77.7; cf. Hdt. 8.61), preceded centuries earlier by the poet Alcaeus (frs. 112.10; 426 in Campbell 1982); hence Homer's Greek soldiers in their fortified camp near Troy or Xenophon's 10,000 mercenaries form *poleis*, though temporary ones (Raaflaub 1993: 47–48; Hornblower 2004). This explains the *polis*' egalitarian foundations. Despite their ambitions and pretensions, members of an emerging elite were large farmers and did not stand far above the other free farmers. The landowning citizens fought in the army and sat in the assembly; members of the elite formed a council and provided leadership. As *polis* territories filled up, land became scarce and was contested both within and among *poleis*. Wars between neighboring communities for booty or land became more frequent, well attested in the *Iliad* (11.670–761; 18.509–540) and in traditions about early Greek warfare (Raaflaub 1997b).

By the eighth century, in many parts of Greece the *polis* was the normal type of community (Thomas and Conant 1999). A more rapid pace of development began. This is also the "age of Homer." The historicity of "epic society" has elicited much controversy but, in contrast to the foregrounded events and heroic actions, their social background is depicted with sufficient consistency to reflect a historical society that can be dated to the eighth or early seventh century (Finkelberg 2011: 359–361, 682, 810–813). In this society, and in the epics' narrative, collective decision-making plays a prominent role.

In the story of his adventures, Odysseus mentions the outrageous and lawless Cyclopes.

> These people have no institutions, no meetings for counsels;
> rather they make their habitations in caverns hollowed
> among the peaks of the high mountains, and each one is the law
> for his own wives and children, and cares nothing about the others.
> (*Od.* 9.112–115, trans. Lattimore 1967)

The poet conceptualizes here an atomized "non-community," consisting of unconnected, autonomous family units: the extreme opposite of civilized society. By contrast, normal human society is organized by the structures of a *polis*. The idealized epic Phaeacians too live in a *polis* with all its essential features (6.262–268: walls, harbor, sanctuary, and a permanent assembly place); they have shared norms and meetings for communal decision making, and are governed by a council of elders and a recognized leader (bks. 6–8, 13; Scully 1990).

A strong focus on the community pervades the epics, signaled already in the proem of the *Iliad* (1.1–7) that emphasizes not great deeds of mighty heroes but the misery caused by the quarrel of two leaders. The epic's story line highlights good and bad leadership, exemplified by Hector and Agamemnon (Raaflaub 2000: 29–31), and the leaders' interaction with peers and community in council and assembly. The leader, a *primus inter pares*, owes his privileges (materially and ideally) to the community and must justify them through good leadership (*Il.* 12.310–321). His duty is to make sure that his "people be safe, not perish" (1.117; 2.233–334).

In the epic *polis* all citizens, except for the poor and landless, have important communal functions in army and assembly (Raaflaub 1997a, 2008). There is a sense of a public realm, separated from the private, and an awareness of a communal will and action, attributed collectively to the people, both domestically and in dealing with other *poleis*. Leader and community depend on each other. The *agorē* represents the middle of the community where important communal acts take place. Descriptions of meetings and scattered references illustrate procedures (Finkelberg 2011: 104, 143). Though not regulated, the assembly plays an indispensable communal role: every decision is made in assembly (*agorē*), and even the gods meet in assembly (*Il.* 4.1–72; *Od.* 1.22–95; Flaig 1994). Although they do not vote, the men express their opinion unmistakably by voice or feet, and it is difficult to act against their firmly expressed opinion (*Od.* 13.239; cf. *Il.* 15.721–723). If the leader ignores their will and fails he is in trouble. A good leader listens to his peers' advice and follows the best proposal. Consensus and conflict resolution are important; hence the ideal leader is best in fighting *and speaking* (*Il.* 1.274; 3.216–224; 9.440–443; *Od.* 8.169–173).

Normally the elite leaders speak; despite a hierarchy of power and age (*Il.* 9.31–36, 50–62; 14.109–227), they are roughly equal. Yet any man who has something useful to contribute will be heard. Lowly Thersites (2.211–277) gets disciplined not for venting the anger of the masses and berating Agamemnon for his neglect of duty (222–223, 233–242) but because he speaks "not according to order" (*kosmos,* 213–214) and thus violates traditional norms.

An especially informative assembly takes place at the beginning of the *Odyssey* (2.6–257; Raaflaub 2000: 32–33). Clearly, the assembly is expected to deal only with public (*dēmion*: 30–32), not with private business, not even that of the leader. The people therefore remain silent and passive, when Telemachus appeals to them for support in his quarrel with his mother's suitors. But in a crucial episode (229–241) a speaker directs attention precisely to the question of when the community should get involved. What appears to be a private conflict, he says, is in fact of utmost importance to the community because it determines the relationship between leader and *polis* and thereby the well-being of all (230–234; cf. 4.687–695; 16.424–432). For the first time in extant Greek thinking a cause-and-effect relationship is here observed on a primarily political level and then applied to a political issue.

Although this effort to stir the people into action remains unsuccessful, the suitors are alarmed by Telemachus' initiative and the potential danger he poses to them (4.630–672). Their attempt to assassinate him fails. And now they have reason to fear the people:

> So act! before he can gather his people in assembly.
> ... He'll rise and rage away, shouting out to them all how we,
> we schemed his sudden death but never caught him.
> Hearing of our foul play ... they might do us damage, run us off our lands,
> drive us abroad ...
>
> (16.361ff., esp. 374–383; trans. Fagles 1996)

The people thus represent a potential force, and if provoked sufficiently, their collective will might translate into uncontrolled action (cf. 16.424–432). In the *Iliad*, Paris and the war he has provoked are not popular among the Trojans (3.454; 7.390). Chastising him for his poor performance, Hector says:

> What cowards, the men of Troy—or years ago
> they'd have decked you out in a suit of rocky armor,
> stoned you to death for all the wrongs you've done!
>
> (*Il.* 3.56–57; trans. Fagles 1990)

On the Greek side, Agamemnon experiences humiliation when the masses, instead of rising to his challenge, rush to the ships, thus voting with their feet to abandon the war (*Il.* 2.84–154).

To sum up, the epics show us early citizen communities in which council and assembly are firmly established forums for the performance of politics (Hammer 2002) and the centers of communal and political life. The poet takes them for granted and usually thinks *with* these institutions, occasionally even *about* them. Although not formally regulated, these institutions are crucial for sounding out popular opinion and forming as well as expressing a communal will that a leader disregards at his peril. The masses of citizens are seen as capable of taking common action and perceived as a potential power factor. Hence the leader's and the elite's ability to control this factor by persuasion, and a positive relationship between leaders and masses are decisive for the communal well-being.

The poet who dramatizes these issues from a communal perspective that can be critical of the leaders is not an elite person but an itinerant specialist, a *dēmiourgos* ("worker among the people"; *Od.* 17.382–386; Qviller 1980), and thus, even if he settles down, an outsider (*metanastēs*, "resident alien"; Gschnitzer 1981: 29, 33–34), competing with others for acclaim and remuneration (Hes. *WD* 17–26, 654–659). Hesiod, Homer's younger contemporary and author of didactic epics, presents himself as an average farmer who keeps away from the town with its legal or political fights, relies primarily on his neighbors, and chastises the elite judges as corrupt and prone to render "crooked judgments" (220–224, 248–251, 260–264; Millett 1984; Raaflaub 2000: 34–37). Conversely, in characterizing Zeus as an ideal leader, Hesiod links him with the personifications of justice, good order, peace, memory (important for upholding communal norms), and the Muses who bless a leader with a "honeyed tongue" (persuasive speech) to lead his people with expert knowledge and "straight judgments" (*Theog.* 901–903, 81–93). Again, the poet's choice of words and images makes clear that leadership rests on persuasion, not sheer power. This requires as a corollary a citizen body and assembly that play a communally significant role.

3 From Civil Strife to Civic Integration: The Formalization of Institutions in the Late Seventh and Sixth Centuries

The eighth century was a period of rapid change and "structural revolution" (Snodgrass 1980; Morris 1998). From the late eighth to the sixth century (Osborne 1996; Fisher and van Wees 1998; Hall 2007; Raaflaub and van Wees 2009) Greeks founded new *poleis* along the coasts from the western Mediterranean to the Black Sea. Social and economic tensions caused civil strife, facilitated the rise of temporary monarchies ("tyrannies"; Murray 1993: ch. 9; Lewis 2009), and necessitated new ways of resolving conflicts through communal legislation and the appointment of lawgivers (below). In this period the Greeks formed their unique culture (Meier 2011) and developed political thought (Meier 1990; Raaflaub 2000), philosophy (Barnes 1979; Kirk et al. 1983), and a variety of literary genres (Raaflaub 2009b). They stabilized the *polis* by regulating officials and institutions and aspired to realize a "good order" (*eunomia*) based on justice, responsible and accountable leadership, and the political involvement of large numbers of citizens. Prompted by opposition to tyranny and based on the political involvement of at least the landowning citizens capable of fighting on equal terms in the heavily armed infantry (hoplite) army (van Wees 2004), new "isonomic" *polis* constitutions emerged (Robinson 1997), reflecting the value of political equality (*isonomia*; Raaflaub 1996). Three cases of broad reform in Sparta and Athens, based on the newly discovered potential of communally enacted laws, best represent these developments.

Legal texts had been inscribed in the ancient Near East for millennia. Influenced by this habit but using it differently (Raaflaub 2009a: 41–48), Greek *poleis* began in the mid-seventh century to enact and inscribe laws. Prompted by negative experiences, many of these laws dealt with political issues and government, attesting to the process of formalizing institutions and "institutionalizing" the *polis* (Gagarin 1986, 2008; Thomas 2005; Farenga 2006; Hawke 2011).

The earliest extant law begins with "This was decided by the polis" (Meiggs and Lewis 1988: 2; Effenterre and Ruzé 1994: 81; trans. Fornara 11); similar formulae occur in other laws: it was thus the collectivity of citizens that enacted laws. This particular law shows that by 650 BCE the small *polis* of Dreros on Crete had several officials and regulated rotation in the chief office. From other laws we learn about a variety of officials, a council of elders, and a "popular council" with specific powers (ML 8; Effenterre and Ruzé 1994: 62; Fornara 19). Tradition remembered lawgivers (below) who enacted clusters of laws (Hölkeskamp 1999). An inscribed collection of laws has survived in Gortyn on Crete (Willetts 1967), while much of Solon's comprehensive legislation is cited by later authors (below).

Early laws suggest that *poleis* acted with a collective will and voice, had a differentiated government apparatus they tried to regulate, and defined their membership and relations with others. Laws were tools to realize the community's will and to change its order and institutions. They were inscribed, mostly on stone monuments, and thus intended to be visible and to last; that they were often placed in sacred places under divine protection demonstrated respect for the law and the gods (Thomas 1996; Whitley 1998). Laws were thus fixed and made accessible, which improved the security of law (Eder 2005), but they also became changeable. Realizing that they had control over their law, and recognizing its significance for communal stability, communities expanded, refined, and adapted it to changing needs. Greek law thus was dynamic. Like Greek culture in general (Meier 2011), Greek legal culture was developed from a position in the middle of citizen communities. This facilitated constitutional creativity and reform.

4 Sparta's "Great Rhetra," the Sovereignty of the *Dēmos*, and the Restoration of *Eunomia*

In several wars the Spartans subdued Laconia and Messenia. Their *polis* subsequently comprised an exceptionally large slave population (helots) and numerous dependent communities (*perioikoi*). According to tradition, the Messenians rose in revolt around the mid-seventh century and were subjected again in a long and difficult war that caused civil strife (*stasis*) and disorder (*kakonomia*), until a lawgiver, Lycurgus, restored internal stability and a "good order" (*eunomia*; Hdt. 1.65–66; Thuc. 1.18). Lycurgus' historicity is disputed, and many of the reforms attributed to him (Plut. *Lyc.*) date to a later period. As archaeological evidence and poetry show, Sparta long shared the culture of other Greek *poleis*. Its rigidly militaristic system evolved gradually from the late seventh to the fifth century, probably in response to the need to control the large dependent population. Although much of this continues to be debated, recent research has profoundly improved our understanding of early Spartan history (Finley 1981; Hodkinson 2000; Cartledge 2002b; Welwei 2004; Luraghi 2008).

Perhaps also as a consequence of the Messenian crisis, the precarious minority status of the citizens (Spartiates) in their large *polis*, and the crucial importance the Spartiate army assumed in defending the citizens' privileges, Sparta enacted the earliest known *polis* constitution, the "Great Rhetra" ("Pronouncement"; Effenterre and Ruzé 1994: 61,

Fornara 12). Scholars agree on its essential authenticity, though not on details (van Wees 1999; Cartledge 2002b: 113–117; Welwei 2004: 59–69). Plutarch (*Lyc.* 6) mentions a new sanctuary, new civic subdivisions, and a *gerousia* (council of elders), including the two leaders (*archagetai,* also called *basileis,* kings); assembly meetings were to be held regularly on the festival day of Apollo at a specified place, "so as to propose and stand aside. But to the people shall belong the authority to respond[?] and power [*kratos*]." "Making proposals" is unproblematic, while "to stand aside" seems corrupted; perhaps the *dēmos* responded to proposals made by others. Undoubtedly, the *dēmos* was intended to hold power. In an elegy entitled "Eunomia" (fr. 4.3–10 in West 1992), the poet Tyrtaeus defines a hierarchy of speaking: first the "kings," second the other members of the *gerousia*, last the commoners. The *dēmos* has the final decision (*nikē*) and in this sense power (*kratos*).

The two documents complement each other, suggesting both a civic/military and a political reform. New civic subdivisions elsewhere (in Athens and early Rome) reflect organizational adjustments necessitated by hoplite fighting. The reform's communal importance was emphasized by placing it under the protection of Zeus and Athena. The institutions and process of decision-making were regulated. The *gerousia* (Schulz 2011) now consisted specifically of thirty men, distinguished by age and experience. The fixed number implies an election; the method was collective shouting (Plut. *Lyc.* 26). Attested in early Rome as well (*suffragium*, vote, from *fragor*, noise), this method is valuable because it takes into account both numbers and the strength of voters' feelings (Flaig 1993). Although the *dēmos* ultimately decided, the councilors introduced proposals, spoke first, and apparently retained some kind of veto power (Plut. *Lyc.* 6.7–8). Whether there was open discussion remains unclear. Five ephors were later added to the system. Elected for one-year terms by the assembly, they somehow represented the *dēmos* and balanced the power of leaders and *gerousia* (Richer 1998).

Overall, the Rhetra formalized the assembly's decision-making power by placing the final decision firmly in the hands of the citizen-soldiers, the *homoioi*, "peers" (Cartledge 2001: 68–75). Despite all restrictions, it sealed the *dēmos*' sovereignty in a system that was characterized by "good order" (*eunomia*).

5 Solon's Reforms in Athens, the Restoration of *Eunomia*, and the Institutionalization of Civic Responsibility

Widespread social and economic crisis, intense rivalries among elite families, and their ruthless exploitation of dependent labor, debt, and debt bondage (Finley 1981: ch. 9) resulted in social unrest (*stasis*) that prompted the Athenians in 594 BCE to appoint Solon chief magistrate (*archōn*) and mediator with full power to enact necessary reforms (Welwei 1992: 150–206; Blok and Lardinois 2006; Wallace 2007; Meier 2011: ch. 21).

Offering a peaceful resolution, such mediators or "straighteners" (*katartistēres*) were a uniquely Greek response to *stasis* and the threat of tyranny. They were connected with the Delphic oracle (that advocated moderation) and, standing above the conflicting parties, represented a "third position" (Meier 1990: 40–52). As "sages," they enjoyed far-reaching authority (Wallace 2009). Their power was similar to that of a tyrant—Aristotle calls Pittacus of Mytilene an "elected tyrant" (*Pol.* 1285a35ff.), and

Solon apparently could easily have assumed the same position (fr. 33, cf. 32 in West 1992)—but the crucial difference was that these "straighteners" were appointed by the community and acted on its behalf. Solon explicitly addresses the Athenians as a fellow citizen (fr. 4.1–8, 30, 36.1–2 in West 1992), standing between the conflicting parties and preventing either from hurting the other or profiting unjustly (fr. 5; 36.20–27; 37 in West 1992).

Solon formulated his ideas and justified his actions in extant poems (collected in West 1992: pp. 139–165; trans. in West 1994: 74–83); many of his laws survive (Ruschenbusch 1966, 2010). Aristotle's (*Ath. Pol.* 5–13) and Plutarch's (*Solon*) description of his activities draw mostly on this evidence. A programmatic elegy (also entitled "Eunomia") offers insight into the theoretical foundations of his reforms (fr. 4 in West 1992). Emphasizing that not the gods but the citizens themselves are responsible for their fate (ibid., lines 1–4) and that it is greed and abuses especially of the leaders (5–6) that cause *stasis* with disastrous consequences for all (ibid., lines 18–25), Solon constructs an inescapable chain of cause and effect that is based on empirical observation, comparable to laws of nature (such as thunder following upon lightning: fr. 9 in West 1992), and links socio-political wrongdoing by citizens with socio-political harm suffered by the community (fr. 4.5–25 in West 1992: such as civil strife or enslavement by a tyrant). In Hesiod Dikē (goddess of justice) exacts her punishment through the power of her father, Zeus (Hes. *WD* 256–262); Solon conceives of Dikē as an independent demon of revenge, almost an abstract principle: justice will prevail—with certainty (fr. 4.14–17 in West 1992), and it will affect the entire city; nobody can escape (ibid., lines 26–29).

A political process is here analyzed entirely on the political level—a breakthrough in political thought. Using empirical knowledge and theoretical insight, Solon understands the political causes of communal problems. This enables him to devise specific measures to eliminate these problems and thus prevent their aggravation or recurrence. Afflicted by "bad order" (*dysnomia*), the community, "taught" by the mediator (4.30), can re-establish "good order" (*eunomia*, 4.30–39). Equally affected, the aristocracy has a strong interest in collaborating (Eder 2005). As in Hesiod (*Theog.* 901–903) and Tyrtaeus' Sparta (Tyrt. fr. 4 in West 1992), *eunomia* appears here as a central communal value (Sol. fr. 4.31–39 in West 1992) that lawgiver and community, suffering from crisis and conflict, aim to restore.

Solon's legislation affected most spheres of communal life (Andrewes 1982a). He abolished debt bondage and guaranteed the citizens' personal freedom (Raaflaub 2004: 45–53). He improved certainty of law by giving citizens access to justice and involve them in jurisdiction: for example, any person who wished (*ho boulomenos*) was empowered to take legal action on behalf of an injured third party (Rhodes 2006b). Solon's statement, "I wrote down ordinances for low and high alike, providing straight justice fitted for each man (or case)" (fr. 36.18–20 in West 1992), approximates the principle of equality before the law (later expressed fully by *isonomia*; below). In the political sphere (Hansen 1999: 29–32), Solon divided the citizens into "classes" (based on military and economic capacity) that determined political participation and access to political office. This made it more difficult for the aristocracy to monopolize power and introduced more openness into politics. An annually elected council with 400 members, if authentic (Rhodes 1981: 153–154), was intended to balance the aristocratic Areopagus Council's power and enhance the assembly's role. Hence Solon probably also regulated the assembly's meetings and procedures (as the Rhetra did in Sparta). Protecting the Athenian institutions from subversion, he outlawed tyranny and made it mandatory for citizens to take sides in the event of *stasis* ([Arist.] *Ath. Pol.* 8.5, 16.10; Plut. *Sol.* 20.1; Rhodes 2006b: 156, 220–222).

All these measures served three purposes: to stabilize the community by eliminating abuses and establishing a firm system of justice, to balance elite power by creating avenues for political participation by non-elite citizens, and to prevent civil discord with the potential result of tyranny. They reflect Solon's understanding of civic responsibility: if every citizen suffered from political abuses, every citizen had to assume responsibility for the common good. Even so, Solon's thinking was far from democratic (below) but some of his measures were crucial in setting Athens on a path that eventually led to democracy. The community itself had become the object of the citizens' political action: legislation enabled them to change and improve their communal order.

6 *Isonomia* and the Integration of the Athenian *Polis* in the Late Sixth Century

Solon's reforms had not cut deep enough to prevent the recurrence of factional strife and the establishment of a tyranny. Peisistratus and his sons ruled for almost forty years (until 510 BCE). In suppressing elite rivalries, weakening aristocratic power structures, enhancing the central role of Athens through cults, festivals, temples, and other public buildings, and introducing measures that fostered peace and prosperity and especially benefited non-elite citizens, the Peisistratids' rule deeply influenced the community and was a crucial condition for future changes (Andrewes 1982b; Stahl 1987; Lewis 1988; Shapiro 1989; Welwei 1992: 229–265).

After the fall of tyranny, aristocratic factions renewed their fierce rivalry. In 508/7, Cleisthenes secured the people's support by announcing reform plans that proved popular. When his rival Isagoras summoned outside support to consolidate his own faction's control, he prompted a popular uprising that crushed his party (Hdt. 5.66–73.1; [Arist.] *Ath. Pol.* 20–22.1). Cleisthenes now realized his reforms. Although he left no personal statements or laws, we are able to reconstruct the details of his reform and subsequent measures that profoundly transformed the Athenian *polis* (Ostwald 1988; Ober 1996: ch. 4; Ober 2007; Welwei 1999: 1–27; Anderson 2003).

A comprehensive territorial reorganization combined local districts (demes) into thirty "thirds" (*trittyes*, ten each in Attica's central plain, coastal areas, and interior hill-country) and one of these from each region into ten tribes (*phylai*). Each tribe, comprising a similar number of citizens from all regions of Attica (Traill 1975, 1986; Whitehead 1986), provided teams for competitive performances at *polis* festivals, one regiment of the reorganized hoplite army (Siewert 1982), and fifty members of the "Council of 500" that replaced Solon's popular council. Elected by the demes in proportion to their citizen numbers, serving for one year, and eventually restricted to two non-consecutive terms, the councilors thus evenly represented the citizen population in the first representative council known in world history (Larsen 1955: ch. 1; Rhodes 1972). This council had important functions in the *polis*' government and prepared motions for the assembly. Moreover, the fifty councilors of one tribe served for one-tenth of the year as the council's executive committee, and for a third of this time the members of a *trittys* of that tribe were constantly present in a specific building in the *agora* (Camp 1986: 76–77). The quota of representation (about 1:60) was dense: the councilors, connecting their demes with the *polis* center and serving as information carriers, thus virtually made the citizens present in Athens (Meier 1990: ch. 4). Eventually, therefore, an extraordinary proportion of citizens (below) gained intensive experience of politics and the way government worked (Hansen 1999: 249). The demes in turn had their own officials, assemblies, cults, and cultural events: their "grassroots democracies" provided another arena for learning participatory politics.

The challenge had been to eliminate the scourge of destructive factional and regional rivalry. Cleisthenes' intention thus probably was to make the citizens present and active in the community, and to "mix" them, enhancing familiarity, solidarity, collaboration, and shared knowledge (Ober 2008). Virtually on a drawing board, in a complex and sophisticated reform embedded in a host of other changes (Anderson 2003), the entire structure of the civic community and relations among citizens were radically redesigned. The result was an integrated community encompassing all of Attica. This made spectacular successes in outside relations possible, culminating in the decision to fight the invading Persians at Marathon (490 BCE).

Another sophisticated innovation was "ostracism," a vote without announced "candidates," in which citizens wrote on potsherds (*ostraka*) the name of the person they wanted exiled. If the prescribed high quorum was met the "winner" was banished for ten years, without loss of citizenship or property. Ostracism thus was a "negative election" that made it possible to choose between alternatives offered by two political rivals, especially when their competition ended in a stalemate (Hansen 1999: 35–36; Forsdyke 2005).

Herodotus explained Athens' success with its liberation from tyranny: when the Athenians gained their liberty and achieved equality (*isēgoria*, equality of speech), they were enabled to pursue their own interest in their common cause (Hdt. 5.78). *Isēgoria* is closely related to *isonomia* (equality before the law, political equality; Ostwald 1969: esp. pt. 2). Both terms are attested in the late sixth century (Raaflaub 1996: 143–148). "Equality" was thus probably crucial in propagating Cleisthenes' system. His reform illustrates the extent to which the citizens had assumed control over their communal order. Everything could be changed, even profoundly, if the citizens wanted it and voted for it.

7 *Eunomia*, *Isonomia*, and Democracy

Sparta's "Rhetra" gave power (*kratos*) to the *dēmos*, making us think of *dēmokratia*. In Solonian Athens too the assembly passed final decisions. Some scholars thus date the beginning of democracy to this early period (Hansen 1994: 33; Ruschenbusch 1995). For Sparta this seems more than doubtful (Raaflaub, Ober, and Wallace 2007: 39–40): Sparta was later perceived as an ideal of oligarchy (Rawson 1969), and the council's prerogatives severely constrained the assembly (above). The *dēmos* was sovereign but certainly did not rule the *polis*. This corresponds to a widespread pattern in the Graeco-Roman world: despite the assemblies' decision-making monopoly, republican Rome was no democracy either (Jehne 2006: 14–22).

Although Solon adjusted the institutions to make broader citizen participation possible, his ideal was not democratic (Stahl 1992; Wallace 2007) but rather conservative

(Raaflaub, Ober, and Wallace. 2007: 142–144): the aristocracy was to lead, the *dēmos*, clearly not considered capable of leading, was to follow (Sol. fr. 5–6 in West 1992). Access to political office was restricted by law to the propertied classes who were eligible for service in the hoplite army; the same restriction perhaps applied *de facto* to *active* political participation in the assembly (Rhodes 1981: 140–141; Raaflaub 2006: 404–423). Even if the latter was not the case democracy in any meaningful sense was far beyond Solon's horizon.

Herodotus claims that Cleisthenes gave the Athenians their democracy (6.131), although he fails to explain how the new *phylai* achieved this. Through the activities of the demes, the Council of 500, and probably more frequent assembly meetings, his system certainly formalized and intensified citizen participation. Whether *all* citizens were fully included, and whether this really instituted democracy remains debated (Ober 2007; Raaflaub 2007a: esp. 144–150). Decades after Cleisthenes, the third form of constitution (besides monarchy and aristocracy), often simply called *dēmos*, was still identified with *stratos*, the army (e.g., Pindar, *Pythian* 2.86–88; Raaflaub 2007a: 107–108). Cleisthenes' system, although probably more sophisticated than others, fits well into the broad range of "isonomic" (egalitarian) constitutions that were quite frequent by that time (Robinson 1997). Democracy in the strict sense of the word was yet to emerge.

8 The Emergence of Fully Participatory Democracy in Mid-Fifth-Century Athens

Militarily, the reformed hoplite army proved Athens' decisive weapon, achieving victories in 506 BCE and over a Persian army at Marathon in 490. In the 480s, debates about whether or not to resist a second Persian invasion prompted a series of ostracisms, while the discovery of a new silver mine in Attica permitted the construction of a large fleet. When the Persians returned in 480–479, the Athenians decided in assembly to bank their survival on this fleet (Hdt. 7.142–144); sacrificing their city, they contributed decisively to the Greek victories (Green 1996). After 479, the Greeks continued the war, to liberate Greeks still under Persian control, secure the gains, and prevent another Persian attempt at conquest. When Sparta lost interest in this war, Athens and the liberated Greeks founded a new alliance, centered on Delos (the "Delian League"). Within two decades, the Athenians turned leadership in this alliance into rule over a naval empire (*archē*) that eventually comprised close to 200 *poleis* around the Aegean and beyond. They treated attempts to leave the league as treason and suppressed them ruthlessly. In the late 450s hostilities with the Persians ended, and in a time of crisis the Athenians moved the league's seat to Athens and henceforth used their own assembly to make decisions concerning its policies and the allies. By then Athens had long been involved in wars with Sparta and her allies, but in 446, under Pericles' leadership, concluded a thirty-year peace (Meiggs 1972; Fornara and Samons 1991: chs. 3–4; Rhodes 1992b).

In the emergency of 480–479, citizens of all classes, resident aliens, and slaves had manned the fleet. Had the war ended in 479 and most of the fleet become unnecessary, constitutional development probably would not have moved much beyond Cleisthenes' system. But the continuation of the Persian War and the creation of the *archē* transformed the dynamics of Athenian social, economic, and political life (Raaflaub 1998). The improvisation of 480–479 became permanent. Although the hoplites remained important, success in war and control over the *archē*—and with it Athenian security, power, and prosperity—increasingly and constantly depended on the fleet that was rowed by lower-class citizens, together with resident aliens (metics), slaves, and mercenaries. The shipyards in the Piraeus, where hundreds of triremes were built and maintained, required a huge labor force; large numbers of citizens moved from rural Attica to the Piraeus, which became a large, planned city, connected with Athens by the Long Walls in the 450s (Garland 1987; Gabrielsen 1994; but see Bissa 2009). Thousands of lower-class citizens, employed on the fleet and in the shipyards, now lived close enough to the political center in Athens to make their voices and wishes heard there. They had previously counted little politically because they did not qualify as hoplites. In their new military role, they assumed vital importance for the community. This changed the distribution of military responsibility among the citizens and called for political adjustments. Moreover, because of Athens' *archē* and active foreign policy (an exception among Greek *poleis*), political activities on every level and the range of administrative offices in the *polis* and empire multiplied. The intensity of political life and the individual citizen's involvement in it increased enormously.

In 462/1 reforms were enacted under the leadership of Ephialtes (Meier 1987; Fornara and Samons 1991: ch. 2; Rhodes 1992a; Raaflaub 2007a). Details are debated, but overall powers and responsibilities were shifted from the Areopagus Council to the Council of 500, assembly, and law courts. The institutions that directly represented the citizen body became responsible for the entire political process (below). The *dēmos* now really ruled (Eur. *Supp.* 352, 406). Subsequent measures, realized until 450, partly under Pericles' leadership, were intended not least to facilitate the involvement of all citizens. Although democracies emerged in other *poleis* as well (Robinson 2011; see also Rhodes, Chapter 8), most of these lacked the specific conditions prevailing in Athens and were thus probably more moderate.

The reformers of 462–450 apparently had a clear concept of what democracy ideally should be—while of course taking slave labor and the political exclusion of women for granted (above). Through pay for time-consuming offices, the extensive and sophisticated use of the lot, "term limits" for councilors (Rhodes 1972: 3), and the distribution of executive and administrative responsibility among many sizable committees (Bleicken 1994: 530–538; Hansen 1999: 230–242), they intended to achieve the broadest possible citizen involvement in government, according to the principle of "ruling and being ruled in turn" (Eur. *Supp.* 406–407), and to exclude manipulation, group interests, and bribery. Many thousand citizens were needed every year to run this system (Hansen 1999: 313) that was based on belief in civic equality and every citizen's ability to serve in communally useful functions (Thuc. 2.37.1). Discussions of democracy that pervade fifth-century literature illuminate these ideas (Raaflaub 1989).

Probably in the mid-460s, the Athenians coined for this system the word *dēmokratia* (Hansen 1987: 69–71). Resistance to Ephialtes' reforms was strong and violent; they were seen as the victory of a faction that served the interests of only part of the citizen body; *stasis* seemed a real threat. Intense debates ensued (visible in Aeschylus' tragedies: Meier 1990: ch. 5; 1993: ch. 5), resulting in terminological differentiation, ideological contrasts (especially between democracy and oligarchy), constitutional conflicts, and constitutional theory (Farrar 1988; Winton 2000: 89–101; Raaflaub 2004: 21). The need to close ranks against foreign threats, constant involvement in war, the success, despite setbacks, of imperial policies and the profits of empire, and Pericles' strong and charismatic leadership helped restore and maintain internal stability. Only under the pressures of the long and bitter Peloponnesian War and especially the crisis after the Sicilian disaster *stasis* surfaced again and prompted two short-lived and violent oligarchic coups (Munn 2000; Osborne 2011; Shear 2011). Constitutional measures introduced in the late fifth and early fourth century were intended to prevent hasty and arbitrary decisions by the assembly (Ostwald 1989), and a comprehensive revision of laws between 410 and 399 produced a system of somewhat clearly defined institutions that approached a "constitution" (Hansen 1999: 162–165). In this more moderate version, democracy survived without further interruptions to the late fourth century, when it was abolished by outside interference (Rhodes 1979/80, 2010; Ober 1989; Eder 1995).

9 Participatory Democracy at Its Height

Despite these and other changes, in all essential respects democracy was fully developed by the middle of the fifth century. This democracy was "unparalleled in world history" (Hansen 1999: 313). It mobilized a multidimensional and intense commitment to communal affairs of extraordinary numbers of citizens of all classes, generated enormous enthusiasm, and prompted the citizens to develop a "political identity" that was supposed to take priority over their social identity (Meier 1990: ch. 6); it was also both uniquely productive, stimulating an amazing cultural upswing (Sakellariou 1996; Boedeker and Raaflaub 1998), and sadly destructive, tied to aggressive imperialism, shocking brutality in war, and the systematic exploitation of others. Defeated by Sparta in 404, Athens barely escaped wholesale destruction.

What does unparalleled citizen participation mean concretely? The systematic part of Aristotle's *Ath. Pol.* (42–69) offers valuable details. Most time-consuming was the year-long membership in the Council of 500 (above). Due to term-limits, at least every third citizen over 30, and about two-thirds of those over 40, held this office (Hansen 1999: 249). The council dealt with foreign policy issues, reports of officials, issues and motions to be decided by the assembly, and the supervision of the entire administrative apparatus ([Arist.] *Ath. Pol.* 45–49; Rhodes 1972). The assembly (***ekklēsia***) met numerous times during the year (forty in the fourth century); meetings lasting from several hours to whole days, often with a prescribed agenda ([Arist.] *Ath. Pol.* 44–46), were attended by several thousand citizens—the assembly place on the Pnyx hill provided space for 6,000, and this was the quorum prescribed for ostracisms and a few other issues. Assembly and council were presided over by citizens selected by lot for only one day ([Arist.] *Ath. Pol.* 44). Assisted by the council and law courts (***dikastēria***), the ***ekklēsia*** controlled the entire political process from planning policies to making decisions on a vast number of small and large issues, to supervising their execution in every phase, controlling the officials, and holding them accountable (Hansen 1987).

Professional personnel was limited to a few hundred state-owned slaves who served officials in various functions and provided a rudimentary police force (Hunter 1994: 3). Numerous committees of various sizes were in charge of a wide range of administrative duties, some of them every day year-round; they assisted the council and various officials and were in turn supervised by them. Their membership totaled about 700 (Hansen 1999: ch. 9), and in the fifth century hundreds of other officials served in various functions throughout the empire ([Arist.] *Ath. Pol.* 24.3 with Rhodes 1981: 305;

Balcer 1976). Except for very few offices with major financial or military responsibilities that were filled by election (*Ath. Pol.* 43.1, 44.4), all officials were selected by lot (*Ath. Pol.* 8.1, 43.1, 47–48, 50–55.1). About 2,000 citizens, also selected by lot and assigned to various courts by a sophisticated allotment machine that made abuses virtually impossible (*Ath. Pol.* 63–66; Boegehold 1995: 58, 230–234; Demont 2003), served in several large boards as collective judges (rather than jurors) who on court days (about 200 per year) tried cases simultaneously in various locations. In democracy, the law courts had an important function as, so to speak, a continuation of politics by different means (Christ 1998; Hansen 1999: ch. 8 and 313; Herman 2006).

In the mid-fifth century the Athenian citizen numbers rose to perhaps more than 60,000; after the losses of the Peloponnesian War they shrank to about 30,000 and hardly rose above that level throughout the fourth century (Patterson 1981; Hansen 1986; Akrigg forthcoming). Of these, every year many thousands were politically active, and many were so year after year. Many thousands of these same citizens also regularly served in the cavalry, hoplite army, or as rowers on the fleet. Hence Athenian democracy was not only direct in that decisions were made in open assembly, but the most direct imaginable because a fantastically large proportion of citizens was involved constantly in the business of governing their community and controlling all aspects of government and administration. Moreover, the principle of rotation of offices (Arist. *Pol.* 1317b2–7) guaranteed that those not involved in one year would be in another. Finally, through all these activities, the citizens acquired an exceptional level of knowledge about politics and administration (Thuc. 2.40.2).

Such involvement was voluntary, but lack of involvement was despised. "We do not say that a man who takes no interest in politics is a man who minds his own business; we say that he has no business here at all" (Thuc. 2.40.2; trans. Warner 1954). Literally, the passive (*apragmōn*) citizen was useless (*achreios*) to the community (Carter 1986; Christ 2006; Demont 1990). The Athenians' ideal was the active, involved citizen (*polypragmōn*, doing a lot; Thuc. 1.70). This ideal shaped their private and public lives, their "political identity" (above), and their communal policies (Raaflaub 1994, 2001). It led them to extreme heights of power and achievement and, eventually, over the top into the abyss of defeat and near-destruction.

In the fifth century, this democracy was closely and in multiple ways connected with the empire. No other *polis* at the time was so active in so many directions and required such an intense citizen involvement. Hence democracy in its Athenian version was extreme and unique, an exciting experiment we might not want to imitate but from which we can still learn a lot (Ober 2005).

10 Greek Democracy and Roman Republicanism: Elements of a Comparison

In many ways, Greek and Roman state formation followed similar paths, and in their early phases Greek *poleis* and Rome were very similar, just as "city-state systems" on both sides of the Adriatic shared some important characteristics (Raaflaub 1990). For example, the Greek and Roman concepts of liberty developed from the same linguistic and social roots (Raaflaub 1984; 2004: 265–77). Yet a few hundred years later the differences were enormous, in both the value and political systems (see Eder 1996; Meier 1996). Why did developments lead into such different directions? This is a big question that requires careful and detailed discussion, but it might be useful as a start to emphasize a few aspects that emerge from the two chapters in this section.

First, the Greek *polis* emerged as a citizen-state with strong egalitarian foundations. This expressed itself early on in the indispensable role the non-elite citizens played in army and assembly. In Rome citizenship was initially mediated through powerful aristocratic clans and their followers and dependants (clients). Hence when voting was introduced, this happened on an individual basis in Greece, collectively by voting groups in Rome. Rome had citizens but never became a citizen-state.

Second, for reasons that are probably connected with the influence of the strongly hierarchical Etruscan city-states, Rome's aristocratic clans were strong and powerful and retained their predominance throughout the regal into the republican period. Despite high aspirations, the Greek aristocracies never succeeded in dominating their communities or controlling power and politics in the way the Roman senatorial class did. Greek oligarchies were not confined to a political elite but always comprised elite and non-elite landowners.

Third, in both Greece and Rome problems caused by elite abuse of debt and exploitation of debt bondage prompted serious conflicts. The Roman aristocracy was able to resolve these and other problems at the expense of defeated enemies, while in Greece solutions could only be achieved by imposing limits on the aristocracy and setting the community on a broader base of citizen responsibility and participation. In Rome such internal conflicts were resolved without violent civil war by compromises within the existing power structures; in Greece they prompted frequent civil strife and war and often necessitated the intervention of lawgivers and reformers.

Fourth, in its formative period in the early republic, Rome was confronted for a very long time with serious outside pressure (to which many other Italian communities succumbed); this strengthened aristocratic leadership, a commitment to communal survival, and an ability to find compromise solutions for communal problems. Before Persian expansion reached the Aegean in the mid-sixth century, Greek *poleis* never faced such outside pressure. Strong and cohesive aristocratic leadership was thus not needed; the aristocracies could afford to exhaust themselves in rivalries and factional strife and lost much of their collective predominance when "tyrants" exploited such rivalries to establish sole rule, and the people were no longer willing to tolerate elite abuses.

Fifth, bolstered by elite solidarity and strong vertical ties between elite and non-elite, Rome opened itself to the integration of ever new groups (immigrants, allies, defeated enemies, former slaves) and thus constantly strengthened its manpower base. Greek *poleis* remained closed societies that jealously protected their citizen privileges. Within these narrowly defined citizen bodies, though, broader political integration and in exceptional cases an unprecedented maximum of power-sharing became possible. Hence Greece was able to develop democracy, and the tension between democracy and oligarchy became the motor that drove political and constitutional thought and development. In the framework of Roman republicanism, despite the decision-making power of the assemblies, democracy was never an option.

REFERENCES

CAH = *The Cambridge Ancient History*. 2nd edn. Cambridge, 1989.

Akrigg, B. Forthcoming. *Population and Economy in Classical Athens*. Cambridge.

Anderson, G. 2003. *The Athenian Experiment: Building an Imagined Political Community in Ancient Attica, 508–490 B.C.* Ann Arbor.

Andrewes, A. 1982a. "The Growth of the Athenian State," *CAH* 3(3): 360–391.

Andrewes, A. 1982b. "The Tyranny of Pisistratus." *CAH* 3(3): 392–416.

Balcer, J.M. 1976. "Imperial Magistrates in the Athenian Empire." *Historia* 25: 257–287.

Barnes, J. 1979. *The Presocratic Philosophers, I*. London.

Bissa, E. 2009. *Governmental Intervention in Foreign Trade in Archaic and Classical Greece*. Leiden.

Bleicken, J. 1994. *Die athenische Demokratie*. 2nd rev. and exp. edn. Paderborn.

Blok, J. and A. Lardinois, eds. 2006. *Solon of Athens: New Historical and Philological Approaches*. Leiden.

Boedeker, D. and K. Raaflaub, eds. 1998. *Democracy, Empire, and the Arts in Fifth-Century Athens*. Cambridge, MA.

Boedeker, D. and K. Raaflaub. 2005. "Tragedy and the City." In R. Bushnell, ed., *A Companion to Tragedy*. Oxford and Malden, MA, 109–127.

Boegehold, A.L. 1995. *The Lawcourts at Athens: Sites, Buildings, Equipment, Procedure, and Testimonia*. Princeton.

Camp, J.M. 1986. *The Athenian Agora*. London.

Campbell, D.A. 1982. *Greek Lyric, I*. Cambridge, MA.

Carter, L.B. 1986. *The Quiet Athenian*. Oxford.

Cartledge, P. 1998. *The Cambridge Illustrated History of Ancient Greece*. Cambridge.

Cartledge, P. 2001. *Spartan Reflections*. London and Berkeley.

Cartledge, P. 2002a. *The Greeks: A Portrait of Self and Others*. 2nd edn. Oxford.

Cartledge, P. 2002b. *Sparta and Laconia: A Regional History, 1300–362 B.C.* 2nd edn. London.

Christ, M. 1990. "Liturgy Avoidance and Antidosis in Classical Athens." *TAPA* 120:147–169.

Christ, M. 1998. *The Litigious Athenian*. Baltimore.

Christ, M. 2006. *The Bad Citizen in Classical Athens*. Cambridge.

Demont, P. 2003. "Le *klērotērion* ('machine à tirer au sort') et la démocratie athénienne." *Bull. Ass. G. Budé* 2003(1): 26–52.

Demont, P. 2009. *La cité grecque archaïque et classique et l'idéal de tranquillité*. Paris.

Dickinson, O. 1994. *The Aegean Bronze Age*. Cambridge.

Dickinson, O. 2006. *The Aegean from Bronze Age to Iron Age*. London.

Eder, W., ed. 1995. *Die athenische Demokratie im 4. Jahrhundert v. Chr. Vollendung oder Verfall einer Verfassungsform?* Stuttgart.

Eder, W. 1996. "Rechtsentwicklung und Verfassungskrise in Athen und Rom." In E.G. Schmidt, Hg., *Griechenland und Rom. Vergleichende Untersuchungen zu Entwicklungstendenzen und -höhepunkten der antiken Geschichte, Kunst und Literatur*. Tbilissi, Erlangen, and Jena, 131–151.

Eder, W. 2005. "The Political Significance of the Codification of Law in Archaic Societies." In K. Raaflaub, ed., *Social Struggles in Archaic Rome*. Oxford and Malden, MA, 239–67.

Effenterre, H. van and F. Ruzé, eds. 1994. *Nomima: Recueil d'inscriptions politiques et juridiques de l'archaïsme grec*, I. Paris.

Fagles, R., trans. 1990. *Homer: The Iliad*. New York.

Fagles, R., trans. 1996. *Homer: The Odyssey*. New York.

Farenga, Vincent. 2006. *Citizen and Self in Ancient Greece: Individuals Performing Justice and the Law*. Cambridge.

Farrar, C. 1988. *The Origins of Democratic Thinking: The Invention of Politics in Classical Athens*. Cambridge.

Finkelberg, M., ed. 2011. *Homer Encyclopedia*. 3 vols. Oxford and Malden, MA.

Finley, M.I. 1981. *Economy and Society in Ancient Greece*. Ed. B.D. Shaw and R.P. Saller. London.

Fisher, N. and H. van Wees, eds. 1998. *Archaic Greece: New Approaches and New Evidence*. London.

Flaig, E. 1993. "Die spartanische Abstimmung nach Lautstärke." *Historia* 42: 139–160.

Flaig, E. 1994. "Das Konsensprinzip im homerischen Olymp. Überlegungen zum göttlichen Entscheidungsprozess Ilias 4.1–72." *Hermes* 122: 13–31.

Fornara, C.W., ed. and trans. 1983. *Archaic Times to the End of the Peloponnesian War*. Translated Documents of Greece and Rome, 1. 2nd edn. Cambridge.

Fornara, C.W. and L.J. Samons II. 1991. *Athens from Cleisthenes to Pericles*. Berkeley.

Forsdyke, S. 2005. *Exile, Ostracism, and Democracy: The Politics of Expulsion in Ancient Greece*. Princeton.

Gabrielsen, V. 1994. *Financing the Athenian Fleet: Public Taxation and Social Relations*. Baltimore.

Gagarin, M. 1986. *Early Greek Law*. Berkeley.

Gagarin, M. 2008. *Writing Greek Law*. Cambridge.

Garland, R. 1987. *The Piraeus*. Ithaca, NY.

Green, P. 1996. *The Greco-Persian Wars*. New edn. Berkeley.

Grethlein, J. 2011. "The Rise of Greek Historiography and the Invention of Prose." In A. Feldherr and G. Hardy, eds., *The Oxford History of Historical Writing*. Oxford, 148–170.

Gschnitzer, F. 1981. *Griechische Sozialgeschichte. Von der mykenischen bis zum Ausgang der klassischen Zeit*. Wiesbaden.

Hall, J. 2007. *A History of the Archaic Greek World*. Oxford and Malden, MA.

Hammer, D. 2002. *The* Iliad *as Politics: The Performance of Political Thought*. Norman, OK.

Hansen, M.H. 1986. *Demography and Democracy: The Number of Athenian Citizens in the Fourth Century* B.C. Herning.

Hansen, M.H. 1987. *The Athenian Assembly in the Age of Demosthenes*. Oxford.

Hansen, M.H. 1991. *The Athenian Democracy in the Time of Demosthenes*. Oxford.

Hansen, M.H. 1993a. "The *Polis* as a Citizen-State." In Hansen 1993b: 7–29.

Hansen, M.H., ed. 1993b. *The Ancient Greek City-State*. Copenhagen.

Hansen, M.H. 1994. "The 2500th Anniversary of Cleisthenes' Reforms and the Tradition of Athenian Democracy." In R. Osborne and S. Hornblower, eds., *Ritual, Finance, Politics: Athenian Democratic Accounts Presented to David Lewis*. Oxford, 25–37.

Hansen, M.H. 1999. *The Athenian Democracy in the Age of Demosthenes: Structure, Principles, and Ideology*. Exp. edn. Norman, OK.

Hawke, J. 2011. *Writing Authority: Elite Competition and Written Law in Early Greece*. DeKalb, IL.

Herman, G. 2006. *Morality and Behaviour in Democratic Athens: A Social History*. Cambridge.

Hodkinson, S. 2000. *Property and Wealth in Classical Sparta*. London.

Hölkeskamp, K.-J. 1999. *Schiedsrichter, Gesetzgeber und Gesetzgebung im archaischen Griechenland*. Stuttgart.

Hornblower, S. 1983. *The Greek World 479–323* BC. London.

Hornblower, S. 2004. "'This was Decided' (*edoxe tauta*): The Army as *Polis* in Xenophon's *Anabasis*—and Elsewhere." In R.L. Fox, ed., *The Long March: Xenophon and the Ten Thousand*. New Haven, 243–263.

Hunter, V. 1994. *Policing Athens*. Princeton.

Jehne, M. 2006. "Methods, Models, and Historiography." In N. Rosenstein and R. Morstein-Marx, eds., *A Companion to the Roman Republic*. Oxford and Malden, MA, 3–28.

Kirk, G.S., J.E. Raven, and M. Schofield. 1983. *The Presocratic Philosophers: A Critical History with a Selection of Texts*. 2nd edn. Cambridge.
Kinzl, K. 2006. *A Companion to Classical Greece*. Oxford and Malden, MA.
Larsen J.A.O. 1955. *Representative Government in Greek and Roman History*. Berkeley.
Lattimore, R. 1967. *The Odyssey of Homer.* Trans. with an Introduction. New York.
Lewis, D.M. 1988. "The Tyranny of the Pisistratidae." *CAH* 4: 287–302.
Lewis, S. 2009. *Greek Tyranny*. Exeter.
Luraghi, N. 2008. *The Ancient Messenians: Constructions of Ethnicity and Memory*. Cambridge.
Maehler, H. 1963. *Die Auffassung des Dichterberufes im frühen Griechentum bis zur Zeit Pindars*. Göttingen.
Meier, C. 1987. "Der Umbruch zur Demokratie in Athen 462/61 v. Chr." In R. Herzog and R. Koselleck, eds., *Epochenschwelle und Epochenbewusstsein*. Munich, 353–380.
Meier, C. 1990. *The Greek Discovery of Politics*. Cambridge, MA.
Meier, C. 1993. *The Political Art of Greek Tragedy*. Baltimore.
Meier, C. 1996. "Der griechische und der römische Bürger. Gemeinsamkeiten und Unterschiede im Ensemble gesellschaftlicher Bedingungen." In E.G. Schmidt, Hg., *Griechenland und Rom. Vergleichende Untersuchungen zu Entwicklungstendenzen und -höhepunkten der antiken Geschichte, Kunst und Literatur*. Tbilissi, Erlangen, and Jena, 41–66.
Meier, C. 1999. *Athens: A Portrait of the City in Its Golden Age*. London.
Meier, C. 2011. *A Culture of Freedom: Ancient Greece and the Origins of Europe*. Oxford.
Meiggs, R. 1972. *The Athenian Empire*. Oxford.
Meiggs, R. and D. Lewis, eds. 1988. *A Selection of Greek Historical Inscriptions to the End of the Fifth Century* B.C. Rev. edn. Oxford.
Millett, P. 1984. "Hesiod and His World." *Proceedings of the Cambridge Philological Society* 30: 84–115.
Morris, I. 1998. "Archaeology and Archaic History." In Fisher and van Wees 1998: 1–91.
Munn, M. 2000. *The School of History: Athens in the Age of Socrates*. Berkeley.
Murray, O. 1993. *Early Greece*. 2nd edn. Cambridge, MA.
Nagy, G. 1989. "Early Greek Views of Poets and Poetry." In G.A. Kennedy, ed., *The Cambridge History of Literary Criticism*. Cambridge, 1: 1–77.
Ober, J. 1989. *Mass and Elite in Democratic Athens*. Princeton.
Ober, J. 1996. *The Athenian Revolution: Essays on Ancient Greek Democracy and Political Theory*. Princeton.
Ober, J. 1998. *Political Dissent in Democratic Athens: Intellectual Critics of Popular Rule*. Princeton.
Ober, J. 2005. *Athenian Legacies: Essays on the Politics of Going On Together*. Princeton.
Ober, J. 2007. "'I Besieged that Man': Democracy's Revolutionary Start." In Raaflaub, Ober, and Wallace 2007: 83–104.
Ober, J. 2008. *Democracy and Knowledge: Innovation and Learning in Classical Athens*. Princeton.
Osborne, R. 1996. *Greece in the Making, 1200–479* BC. London.
Osborne, R., ed. 2011. *Debating the Athenian Cultural Revolution: Art, Literature, Philosophy and Politics 430–380* BC. Cambridge.
Ostwald, M. 1969. *Nomos and the Beginnings of the Athenian Democracy*. Oxford.
Ostwald, M. 1988. "The Reform of the Athenian State by Cleisthenes." *CAH* 4: 303–346.
Ostwald, M. 1989. *From Popular Sovereignty to the Sovereignty of Law: Law, Society, and Politics in Fifth-Century Athens*. Berkeley.
Patterson, C. 1981. *Pericles' Citizenship Law of 451–50* B.C. New York.
Qviller, B. 1980. "Prolegomena to a Study of the Homeric Demiurgoi (Murakawa's Theory Reexamined)." *SO* 55: 5–22.
Raaflaub, K.A. 1984. "Freiheit in Athen und Rom: Ein Beispiel divergierender politischer Begriffsentwiclung in der Antike." *HZ* 238: 529–567.

Raaflaub, K.A. 1989. "Contemporary Perceptions of Democracy in Fifth-Century Athens." *Classica et Mediaevalia* 40: 33–70.

Raaflaub, K.A. 1990. "Expansion und Machtbildung in frühen Polis-Systemen." In W. Eder, ed., *Staat und Staatlichkeit in der frühen römischen Republik*. Stuttgart, 511–545.

Raaflaub, K.A. 1991. "Homer und die Geschichte des 8. Jh. s v. Chr." In J. Latacz, ed., *Zweihundert Jahre Homer-Forschung*. Stuttgart, 205–256.

Raaflaub, K.A. 1993. "Homer to Solon: The Rise of the Polis." In Hansen 1993b: 41–105.

Raaflaub, K.A. 1994. "Democracy, Power, and Imperialism in Fifth-Century Athens." In J.P. Euben, J.R. Wallach, and J. Ober, eds., *Athenian Political Thought and the Reconstruction of American Democracy*. Ithaca, NY, 103–146.

Raaflaub, K.A. 1996. "Equalities and Inequalities in Athenian Democracy." In J. Ober and C. Hedrick, eds., *Dēmokratia: A Conversation on Democracies, Ancient and Modern*. Princeton, 139–174.

Raaflaub, K.A. 1997a. "Politics and Interstate Relations in the World of Greek Poleis: Homer and Beyond." *Antichthon* 31: 1–27.

Raaflaub, K.A. 1997b. "Soldiers, Citizens and the Evolution of the Early Greek *Polis*." In L.G. Mitchell and P.J. Rhodes, eds., *The Development of the* Polis *in Archaic Greece*. London, 49–59.

Raaflaub, K.A. 1998. "The Transformation of Athens in the Fifth Century." In Boedeker and Raaflaub 1998: 15–41, 348–357.

Raaflaub, K.A. 2000. "Poets, Lawgivers, and the Beginnings of Greek Political Reflection." In C. Rowe and M. Schofield, eds., *The Cambridge History of Greek and Roman Political Thought*. Cambridge, 23–59.

Raaflaub, K.A. 2001. "Father of All, Destroyer of All: War in Late Fifth-Century Athenian Discourse and Ideology." In D. McCann and B.S. Strauss, eds., *War and Democracy: A Comparative Study of the Korean War and the Peloponnesian War*. Armonk NY, 307–56.

Raaflaub, K.A. 2004. *The Discovery of Freedom in Ancient Greece*. 1st English edn. rev. and updated from the German. Trans. Renate Franciscono (and revised by the author). Chicago.

Raaflaub, K.A. 2006. "Athenian and Spartan *eunomia*, or: What to Do with Solon's Timocracy?" In Blok and Lardinois 2006: 390–428.

Raaflaub, K.A. 2007a. "The Breakthrough of *Dēmokratia* in Mid-Fifth-Century Athens." In Raaflaub, Ober, and Wallace 2007: 105–54.

Raaflaub, K.A., ed. 2007b. *War and Peace in the Ancient World*. Oxford.

Raaflaub, K.A. 2008. "Homeric Warriors and Battles: Trying to Resolve Old Problems." *CW* 101: 469–483.

Raaflaub, K.A. 2009a. "Early Greek Political Thought in Its Mediterranean Context." In R. Balot, ed., *A Companion to Greek and Roman Political Thought*. Oxford and Malden, MA, 37–56.

Raaflaub, K.A. 2009b. "Intellectual Achievements." In Raaflaub and van Wees 2009: 564–584.

Raaflaub, K.A. 2010. "Ulterior Motives in Ancient Historiography: What Exactly, and Why?" In L. Foxhall, H.-J. Gehrke, and N. Luraghi, eds., *Intentional History: Spinning Time in Ancient Greece*. Stuttgart, 189–210.

Raaflaub, K.A. and H. van Wees, eds.. 2009. *A Companion to Archaic Greece*. Oxford and Malden, MA.

Raaflaub, K.A., J. Ober, and R.W. Wallace. 2007. *Origins of Democracy in Ancient Greece*. Berkeley.

Rawson, E. 1969. *The Spartan Tradition in European Thought*. Oxford.

Rhodes, P.J. 1972. *The Athenian Boule*. Oxford.

Rhodes, P.J. 1979/80. "Athenian Democracy after 403 B.C." *CJ* 75: 305–323.

Rhodes, P.J. 1981. *A Commentary on the Aristotelian Athenaion Politeia*. Oxford.

Rhodes, P.J., trans. 1984. *Aristotle, The Athenian Constitution*. Harmondsworth.

Rhodes, P.J. 1986. "Political Activity in Classical Athens," *JHS* 106: 132–144; repr. in Rhodes, ed., *Athenian Democracy* (Edinburgh, 2004), 185–206.

Rhodes, P.J. 1992a. "The Athenian Revolution." *CAH* 5: 62–95.

Rhodes, P.J. 1992b. "The Delian League to 449 B.C." *CAH* 5: 34–61.
Rhodes, P.J. 2006a. *A History of the Classical Greek World, 478–323 BC*. Oxford and Malden, MA.
Rhodes, P.J. 2006b. "The Reforms and Laws of Solon: An Optimistic View." In Blok and Lardinois 2006: 248–260.
Rhodes, P.J. 2010. "Stability in the Athenian Democracy after 403 B.C." In B. Linke, M. Meier, and M. Strothmann, eds. *Zwischen Monarchie und Republik. Gesellschaftliche Stabilisierungsleistungen und politische Transformationspotentiale in den antiken Stadtstaaten*. Stuttgart, 67–75.
Richer, N. 1998. *Les éphores*. Paris.
Robinson, E.W. 1997. *The First Democracies: Early Popular Government Outside Athens*. Stuttgart.
Robinson, E.W. 2011. *Democracy beyond Athens: Popular Government in the Greek Classical Age*. Cambridge.
Ruschenbusch, E. 1966. *SOLŌNOS NOMOI. Die Fragmente des solonischen Gesetzeswerkes mit einer Text- und Überlieferungsgeschichte*. Wiesbaden.
Ruschenbusch, E. 1995. "Zur Verfassungsgeschichte Griechenlands." In K. Kinzl, ed., *Demokratia. Der Weg zur Demokratie bei den Griechen*. Darmstadt, 432–445.
Ruschenbusch, E. 2010. *Solon: Das Gesetzeswerk—Fragmente. Übersetzung und Kommentar*. Ed. K. Bringmann. Stuttgart.
Sakellariou, M., ed. 1996. *Démocratie athénienne et culture*. Athens.
Schulz, F. 2011. *Die homerischen Räte und die spartanische Gerusie*. Düsseldorf.
Scully, S. 1990. *Homer and the Sacred City*. Ithaca, NY.
Shapiro, H.A. 1989. *Art and Cult under the Tyrants in Athens*. Mainz. With supp., Mainz 1995.
Shear, J.L. 2011. *Polis and Revolution: Responding to Oligarchy in Classical Athens*. Cambridge.
Siewert, Peter. 1982. *Die Trittyen Attikas und die Heeresreform des Kleisthenes*. Munich.
Snodgrass, A. 1980. *Archaic Greece: The Age of Experiment*. Berkeley.
Snodgrass, A. 2000. *The Dark Age of Greece*. 2nd edn. Edinburgh.
Stahl, M. 1987. *Aristokraten und Tyrannen im archaischen Athen*. Stuttgart.
Stahl, M. 1992. "Solon F 3D. Die Geburtsstunde des demokratischen Gedankens." *Gymnasium* 99: 385–408.
Thomas, C. and C. Conant. 1999. *Citadel to City-State: Transformation of Greece, 1200–700 BCE*. Bloomington.
Thomas, R. 1996. "Written in Stone? Liberty, Equality, Orality, and the Codification of Law." In L. Foxhall and A.D.E. Lewis, eds., *Greek Law in Its Political Setting: Justifications not Justice*. Oxford, 9–31.
Thomas, R. 2005. "Writing, Law, and Written Law." In M. Gagarin and D. Cohen, eds., *The Cambridge Companion to Greek Law*, 41–60. Cambridge.
Traill, J.S. 1975. *The Political Organization of Attica: A Study of the Demes, Trittyes, and Phylai, and Their Representation in the Athenian Council*. Princeton.
Traill, J.S. 1986. *Demos and Trittys: Epigraphical and Topographical Studies in the Organization of Attica*. Toronto.
van Wees, H. 1999. "Tyrtaeus' Eunomia: Nothing To Do with the Great Rhetra." In S. Hodkinson and A. Powell, eds., *Sparta: New Perspectives*. London, 1–41.
van Wees, H. 2004. *Greek Warfare: Myths and Realities*. London.
Wallace, R.W. 2007. "Revolutions and a New Order in Solonian Athens and Archaic Greece." In Raaflaub, Ober, and Wallace 2007: 49–82.
Wallace, R.W. 2009. "Charismatic Leaders." In Raaflaub and van Wees 2009: 411–426.
Ward, W.A. and M.S. Joukowsky, eds. 1992. *The Crisis Years: The 12th Century B.C. from beyond the Danube to the Tigris*. Dubuque, IA.
Warner, R., trans. 1954. *Thucydides, History of the Peloponnesian War*. Harmondsworth.
Welwei, K.-W. 1992. *Athen. Vom neolithischen Siedlungsplatz zur archaischen Grosspolis*. Darmstadt.
Welwei, K.-W. 1999. *Das klassische Athen. Demokratie und Machtpolitik im 5. und 4. Jahrhundert*. Darmstadt.

Welwei, K.-W. 2004. *Sparta*. Stuttgart.

West, M.L., ed. 1992. *Iambi et Elegi Graeci ante Alexandrum Cantati*, II. 2nd edn. Oxford.

West, M.L., trans. 1994. *Greek Lyric Poetry*. Oxford.

Whitehead, D. 1986. *The Demes of Attica, 508/7–ca.250* B.C. Princeton.

Whitley, J. 1998. "Literacy and Law-Making: The Case of Archaic Crete." In Fisher and van Wees 1998: 311–331.

Willetts, R.F., ed. 1967. *The Law Code of Gortyn*. Berlin.

Winton, R. 2000. "Herodotus, Thucydides and the Sophists." In C. Rowe and M. Schofield, eds., *The Cambridge History of Greek and Roman Political Thought*. Cambridge, 89–121.

FURTHER READING

On Greek history in general, see *The Cambridge Ancient History*, 2nd edn., vols. 4–6; Cartledge 1998, 2002a; on early and archaic Greece, Osborne 1996; Fisher and van Wees 1998; Hall 2007; Raaflaub and van Wees 2009; Meier 2011; on classical Greece, Hornblower 1983; Kinzl 2006; Rhodes 2006a; on Sparta, Cartledge 2001, 2002b; on Athens, Meier 1999; on democracy and its evolution, Hansen 1999; Raaflaub, Ober, and Wallace 2007; on democracy and political thought or theory, Farrar 1988; Raaflaub 1989; Meier 1990; Ober 1998.

CHAPTER 3

Why Roman Republicanism? Its Emergence and Nature in Context

Michael P. Fronda

1 Introduction and Sources

The participatory government in ancient Rome, which is commonly referred to as the Roman Republic, was strongly republican in nature. My intention is not to begin with a tautology or to be funny. Rather, I wish to point out and clarify terminology. "Republic" comes from the Latin phrase *res publica* (the public business, the commonwealth), and refers to the system of government established in Rome in c.509 BCE that continued to function into the late first century, when, although never officially abolished, it was *de facto* replaced by a semi-hereditary military dictatorship (the Roman imperial system of government). The Republic featured an executive branch comprising several annually elected magistrates, a number of people's assemblies where Roman citizens from all social-economic strata voted on legislation and elected officials, and an aristocratic advisory body, the Senate, which was the main locus for political deliberation and policy formation. It was republican in the contemporary sense of the term: in both its formal constitutional structures and informal practices and traditions the system greatly blunted majoritarian democratic tendencies. The Republic featured a separation of powers, elected magistrates who wielded much power, a strong Senate, and, perhaps most importantly, weak popular assemblies where the political influence of each individual citizen was lessened through an elaborate system of group-voting schemes.

Polybius' (c.200–c.118 BCE) lengthy excursus on the Roman *Politea* (the "Roman constitution"), in the sixth book of his *Histories*, is the most systematic source for the Roman republican system of government. It is the only extended theoretical-legal description of the Roman constitution of the republican period to come to us from antiquity, and it is the starting point for any discussion of Roman republicanism. However, by the time Polybius composed his work, the Roman Republic had existed for more than three centuries: Roman republicanism was fully developed and republican traditions were firmly

A Companion to Greek Democracy and the Roman Republic, First Edition. Edited by Dean Hammer.

established. This chapter will consider why Roman republicanism, whose roots trace back to the archaic period, developed in the first place.

The sources for Rome's archaic period are highly problematic. There survive practically no contemporary written documents detailing social and political developments during the regal period (traditionally 753–509 BCE) and the early Republic (509–287 BCE). A handful of inscriptions written in archaic Latin and Etruscan have been discovered, such as the famous Lapis Niger inscription. These are difficult to interpret and provide at best only glimpses into the world of Latium and southern Etruria. For specific political or institutional developments we must rely on the literary tradition.

Two major narrative accounts of Rome from the time of the kings through the early Republic survive: *Roman Antiquities* by the Greek scholar Dionysius of Halicarnassus, and *From the Founding of the City* by the Roman historian Titus Livius (Livy). Both were published in the late first century BCE, hundreds of years after the formative period of the Roman republican system. The genre of antiquarian texts, for example Aulus Gellius' *Attic Nights*, is an important corpus for additional information about archaic Roman history and institution, often preserved as passing references, or included in dubious etiological passages. Nearly all of these sources, too, were composed in the first century BCE or later. In other words, by the time the authors of surviving texts wrote, archaic Rome was already ancient history. Yet the problems are even more profound: Roman historiography only began c.200, already three centuries after the traditional date of the foundation of the Roman Republic. Thus, the authors of our main sources for the archaic period not only wrote long after the events, but also relied on sources that were themselves far removed from the events.

Some archival material may have been available for Roman and Greek historians to consult, such as archaic treaties (e.g. see Polyb. 3.22–26), and at some point events such as temple dedications, eclipses, famines, floods, and religious prodigies were recorded by the *pontifex maximus* in the so-called *Annales Maximi* or *Annales Pontificum Maximorum*. It is uncertain, however, when these records were begun, and one doubts that much archival material from the early Republic would have survived for later historians to use. One "archival" source, the *fasti Capitolini*, warrants further comment. This fragmentary inscription records two lists: the names of all Roman consuls and other high magistrates from the earliest times down to the death of Augustus (14 CE), and the names of *triumphators* down to 19 BCE. The lists are critical to the reconstruction of early republican history, though their authenticity is widely debated, especially with respect to the fifth and fourth centuries. This is because the lists were not inscribed until the late first century BCE, and so the compilers were probably forced to reconstruct the early lists from the same faulty sources that Roman historians had at their disposal. Lastly, Roman historians may have used the private records maintained by prominent noble families, which recorded the alleged deeds of their ancestors. Unfortunately, we do not know when the great clans began to produce family histories, how the stories were transmitted, or whether families kept documentary or archival evidence to back up their claims (Ridley 1983). Already in antiquity family histories were assumed to be full exaggerations, omissions, and falsehoods (Cic. *Brut.* 62; Livy 8.40.2).

Archaeology offers only partial remedy (Scott 2005). To be sure, ongoing archaeological research has shed light on the development of Rome and other communities in Latium and Etruria, c.800–300 BCE. "The problem," as Timothy Cornell (1995: 29) puts it, "is that archaeological evidence and textual evidence provide answers to very different types of questions, and combining them is extremely hard." Archaeology typically says very little about specific political events or constitutional reforms of the regal and early republican periods, though archaeological evidence may provide some clues as to the general social-economic conditions in which Roman republicanism developed.

Livy (6.1.2–3) famously compared the study of the ancient past to looking at a faraway object whose details are obscured by the distance. While we are not completely blind in our search for the origins of Roman republicanism, given the apparent "wealth of textual material," including "inscriptions, historical narratives, religious and antiquarian texts, [and] legal codes" (Terrenato 2011: 232) and the growing body of archaeological evidence, nevertheless we are squinting at a very distant target through a very cloudy lens (see e.g. Wiseman 1979, 1983, 1989; Cornell 1995: 1–30; 2005; Oakley 1997: 13–110; Forsythe 2005: 59–77; Bispham 2007; Raaflaub 2006: 126–135; Fronda 2010: 5–13; Smith 2011).

2 Urbanization, State Formation and Aristocratic Clans, c.900–500 BCE

By the end of the Bronze Age hilltop settlements appear on the tops of volcanic plateaus in Etruria, and in the ninth century some grew into large sites comprising distinct habitation clusters ("villages"). By the end of the seventh and beginning of the sixth centuries, these villages began to coalesce into larger, contiguous settlements. A similar process played out in Latium, as "proto-urban" centers appear in the eighth century, for example at Rome, Gabii, and perhaps Ardea and Antium (Holloway 1994; Cornell 1995: 92–97; Terrenato 2011: 237–240). Rome was highly urbanized by the late sixth–early fifth centuries (Forsythe 2005: 86–88). This is indicated by monumental architectural projects such as the draining and paving of the Forum, the construction of a series of large buildings where the Regia now stands, and the building of several large temples. The most spectacular was Temple of Jupiter Optimus Maximus on the Capitoline Hill, whose earliest construction phase have been dated to the sixth century, corresponding roughly to the literary tradition that the temple was dedicated in the first year of the Republic (Coarelli 1983; Holloway 1994: 68–90; Cornell 1995: 93–97; Torelli 2006: 81–84).

Urbanization ran parallel to increased social stratification and the rise of a wealthy elite class, whose emergence is documented through the excavation of opulent tombs containing splendid burial goods. Aristocratic tombs containing jewelry, weapons, bronze tripods, silver and gold vessels, and fine imported pottery, dated from the end of the eighth century, have been excavated at sites in Latium and Etruria, such as Castel di Decima and Caere. Moreover, some tombs appear to be intentionally grouped together, with individual burials within the group separated chronologically by several years. Even more striking are the massive chamber tombs, family vaults where successive burials, sometimes stretching over multiple generations, were made. The earliest chamber tombs are found in southern Etruria: these were underground tombs cut into the soft volcanic tufa typical of the local geology. In other places chamber tombs were constructed above ground out of cut blocks. From the second half of the seventh century aristocratic chamber tombs were common throughout Etruria and appear in numerous sites in Latium, including Rome. Ostentatious tombs containing expensive grave goods, as well as the intentional grouping of tombs, presumably from the same family, over multiple generations, suggest a highly stratified society with a permanent aristocracy that consolidated wealth and perpetuated family memory, solidarity, and identity (Holloway 1994: 56–64; Cornell 1995: 81–86; Raaflaub 2006: 135–137; Terrenato 2011).

Their appearance is bound up with the emergence of extended patriarchal kin groups, or clans (called *gentes* in Latin; singular: *gens*), and indeed the development and endurance of powerful aristocratic clans is critical to our understanding of early Roman social and political structures. Roman *gentes* were extended groups who claimed a common ancestry—whether the ancestral connection was real or fictitious is not important. Common ancestry was demonstrated through a peculiar naming system: each member of a *gens* had a first name or personal name (*praenomen*) and a clan name or gentilic name (*nomen gentilicium*), which all clan members shared. This system is the forerunner of the famous Roman trinomial system. Clans and the associated double-naming system were not limited to Rome, but rather the phenomenon was widespread throughout Italy. Thus, two-name inscriptions appear as early as the early seventh century in Etruria and in Latium a little later, and we can assume that *gentes* were an established social institution in Rome no later than about 600 (Cornell 1995: 84–85; Smith 2006; Terrenato 2011). Roman *gentes* were hierarchal, centering on the dominant male line headed by a clan leader but also incorporating various dependants such as slaves, former slaves, and retainers. The clans were also territorially based, with each clan possessing considerable property, perhaps partly or mostly as communal property, which would be assigned to members for usage and otherwise regulated by the clan leader. Occasionally clans moved en masse, presumably at the direction of the clan leader perhaps in consultation with other prominent members. The literary tradition preserves a famous example: Attus Clausus (Latin: Appius Claudius) allegedly moved from the Sabine Hills to Rome with a large number of armed supporters in 504, thus establishing the *gens claudia* (Livy 2.16.2–6; Dionys. *Ant. Rom.* 5.40; Suet. *Tib.* 1.1; see Cornell 1995: 144; Terrenato 2011: 233–237). This relates to another peculiar feature of central Italic society in the sixth and early fifth centuries: aristocratic warlords supported by armed personal dependants known variously as clients (*clientes*) and companions (*sodales*). These warlords and their retainers operated more or less as private armies independent of the state, often moving from city to city, and vying with each other or local authorities. In archaic Rome, the phenomenon of aristocratic warlords and their companions merged with the rise of prominent clans. For example, members of the *gens fabia* and their companions fought a private war against the city of Veii in 479, and a famous fragmentary inscription, the Lapis Satricanus, dated to c.500, mentions the "companions of Poplios Valesios (=Publius Valerius)—this may refer to Publius Valerius Publicola, a prominent aristocrat of the early republic (Cornell 1995: 143–145).

What is striking about these three examples is that they come from the early republican period: that is, after the foundation of the Republic, and certainly well after the processes of urbanization and state formation was underway. To say that Rome was a state by the end of the sixth century is not particularly controversial. Monumental projects such as the draining and paving of the Forum indicate the capacity to marshal communal resources on a large scale and the desire to create a public space, presumably for political and other communal functions. The building of temples implies the institution of civic cults. Permanent political institutions were also founded during the regal period. For example, the Romans' most ancient assembly, the *comitia curiata* (curiate assembly), is alleged to have been founded by Rome's mythical founder-king, Romulus (Dionys. *Ant. Rom.* 2.12.14). Few doubt the great antiquity of the curiate assembly, even if the fabulous accounts of its Romulan foundation are to be rejected. In historical times the curiate assembly was reduced to a largely symbolic body whose meetings were attended by only thirty representatives, one from each of the ancient *curiae*. Little can be said about its organizations and function in the archaic period (Botsford 1909: 152–200; Richard 1978: 197–222; Cornell 1995: 114–118; Forsythe 2005: 108–110). Scanty literary evidence suggests that membership in the *curiae* was determined by *gens*. Since the *gentes* were originally territorially based, the thirty *curiae* may have been administrative wards into which the archaic city was divided, with each ward dominated by one or a few *gentes*. If so, then perhaps the curiate assembly was initially a sort of clan council, where powerful Roman aristocratic clan leaders and their companions could meet to deliberate and resolve conflicts. In later times voting in the curiate assembly was determined by a majority of *curiae*, regardless of how many people voted in each *curia*. This surely had its roots in the archaic period, as each clan (or perhaps small groups of clans) possessed a single "vote" in the curiate assembly.

The *curiae* also served a military function. The thirty *curiae* were subdivisions of the three tribes into which Romulus allegedly placed all Roman citizens, ten *curiae* to each tribe, and the tribes were each responsible for supplying 1,000 men and 100 cavalry for the Roman army. Thus, each *curia* presumably supplied 100 infantry and 10 cavalry, making an army of 3,000 men and 300 cavalry (Cornell 1995: 114; Forsythe 2007: 25–26). The great clans probably contributed warriors on occasion to joint military ventures, but this neat division of three tribes and thirty *curiae* is surely a later development, an artificial administrative arrangement designed to regularize military recruitment and service. It may even reflect an early effort by the Roman state to control the military resources wielded by the great clan leaders.

This system was allegedly overhauled by Rome's sixth king, Servius Tullius, who replaced the three Romulan tribes with a new system of four urban tribes and some unknown number of rural tribes. He also allegedly instituted the census to count citizens, enroll them in tribes, and place them in property classes. Lastly he instituted the centuriate assembly, where citizens voted in blocs according to property class (Livy 1.42.5–1.44.2; Dionys. *Ant. Rom.* 4.14–19). Archaeological evidence suggests that Greek-style hoplite armor was used in Latium by the middle of the sixth century, which in turn implies the adoption of hoplite tactics (Snodgrass 1965; Torelli 1974–75: 13–17; Stary 1981; Cornell 1995: 183–186; Keppie 1998: 14–17; Raaflaub 2006: 137; Rich 2007: 16–18; Forsythe 2007: 26–28). Meanwhile, literary sources indicate that the Servian property classes were related to military service, as each class was defined by the sorts of armor and weapons an individual of that class could provide (Livy 1.43; Dionys. *Ant. Rom.* 4.16–18; cf. Polyb. 6.22–23; Cic. *De rep.* 2.39–40). According to Livy and Dionysius, there were seven property classes responsible for providing recruits for the Roman army, each armed differently depending on the property class he was in—and so presumably what arms he could afford. Several property classes were also divided into two groups, the younger men (*iuniores*) and the older men (*seniores*). The scheme as presented by Livy and Dionysius, with some modifications, is summarized in Table 3.1.

This complicated scheme reflects the political organization of the *comitia centuriata* in the middle Republic, and there is general consensus that it does not accurately reflect the

Table 3.1 The centuriate organization of Servius Tullius, according to Livy and Dionysius of Halicarnassus

Class	Property according to Livy (asses)	Armament according to Livy	Property according to Dionysius (asses)*	Armament according to Dionysius	Centuries (*iuniores*)	Centuries (*seniores*)	Centuries (total)
Knights (equites)**	"leading men of state"	Cavalry	Listed with First Class	Cavalry			18
First Class	more than 100,000	Bronze helmet, round shield, breastplate, greaves, long spear, sword	more than 100,000	Bronze helmet, Argolic shield, corselet, greaves, spear, sword	40	40	80
Second Class	75,000 to 100,000	Bronze helmet, oblong shield, greaves, long spear, sword	75,000 to 100,000	Bronze helmet, oblong shield, greaves, spear, sword	10	10	20
Third Class	50,000 to 75,000	Bronze helmet, oblong shield, long spear, sword	50,000 to 75,000	Bronze helmet, oblong shield, spear, sword	10	10	20
Fourth Class	25,000 to 50,000	Long spear and short spear	25,000 to 50,000	Oblong shield, spear, sword	10	10	20
Fifth Class	11,000 to 25,000	Slings	12,500 to 25,000	Javelins and slings	15	15	30
Proletarii	below 11,000	exempt from military service	below 12,500	Exempt from military service			1
Carpenters and Metalworkers	Listed with First Class	none	Listed with Second Class	none			2
Buglers and trumpeters	Listed with Fifth Class	none	Listed with Fourth Class	none			2
Total							193

*Dionysius gives his figures in minae, drachmae, and denarii, and he assumes that 1 drachma = 1 denarius = 10 asses. Dionysius' figures here have been converted to asses for easier comparison to Livy's version.

**Livy lists the knights in two groups, 12 centuries of knights formed by Servius Tullius, and 6 centuries of knights formed by Romulus and later augmented by Tarquinius Priscus. Both authors agree that the knights totaled 18 centuries.

military organization of the late regal and early republican periods. The original centuriate system was probably much simpler, differentiating only between those of the military class, who could afford to bear arms, and those who fell below this class. The former was probably known as the *classis* and comprised the cavalry and hoplite classes, while everyone was deemed *infra classem* (below the class) and fought as light-armed troops or not at all. It is also likely the division of Classes I–V into *iuniores* and *seniores* was a later development—originally there would have been only 40 centuries in Class I, 10 in Class II, and so forth. The only question is how many of the later property classes comprised the original *classis*. Raaflaub (2006: 135–137) suggests that the first class alone represented Rome's hoplite class, and was required to contribute 40 centuries of infantry to the Roman army. Since term "century" (*centuria*) means "a group of one hundred," that makes a hoplite army of 4,000 strong. Cornell (1995: 179–186) follows Fraccaro's (1931) reconstruction that the first three classes, each described as heavy infantry, originally formed a single hoplite class that contributed 60 centuries, or 6,000 hoplites. Either reconstruction suggests that the Roman state had a robust hoplite army by the end of the sixth century. To this poorer landholders (Classes IV–V) may have contributed another 25 centuries (2,500 men) of light-armed troops, and, in addition, there would have been 6 or 12 or 18 centuries of cavalry (600, 1,200 or 1,800 cavalry). This is consistent with the general view that Rome was by far the most powerful city-state in Latium in the late sixth and early fifth century (Cornell 1995: 198–214; Raaflaub 2006: 135–137; cf. Polyb. 3.22; Livy 2.33; Dionys. *Ant. Rom.* 6.95.2).

The centuriate system was also related to political participation (see Mouritsen, Chapter 9, and Tatum, Chapter 15). In the middle Republic the 193 centuries represented the relative political representation of the different property classes in the *comitia centuriata*. Each property class was divided into a fixed number of centuries, which served as voting units. The main five property classes were further divided into older men (*seniores*) and younger men (*iunores*), with the total number of centuries for the class divided equally between each group. Voting was conducted by century, starting with those of the *equites*, then the *seniores* of the first class, the *iuniores* of the first class, and so on. Elections were determined by a group-voting system: the majority of votes in a century carried that century, and the majority of centuries carried the election or decision. A quick glance at the organization of centuries, summarized in Table 3.1, reveals that that the wealthiest tier of Roman society had disproportionate electoral power, since the higher property classes, with presumably a much smaller population, were assigned the lion's share of centuries. In fact, since the *equites* and first class comprised 98 total centuries, these two classes could potentially control all legislative and electoral outcomes.

This highly complex voting scheme was probably not devised in the sixth century, but rather evolved over time as the centuriate system decoupled from military recruitment and the centuries transformed into strictly political units. Yet, this does not deny the existence of the centuriate assembly in the sixth century. Indeed, Livy (1.60.4) records the centuriate assembly functioning already in the first year of the Republic. It is plausible that the *comitia centuriata* was initially closely related to the military obligation of the *classis*: that those who performed military service were granted specific political representation. Wealth, measured primarily in terms of property, military obligation, and political participation were intrinsically linked in Greek *poleis* of the archaic and classical periods, and the relationship was personified in the citizen-hoplite who voted in the *ekklēsia*. The appearance of a hoplite-style political structures in Rome makes perfect sense in light of the apparent adoption of hoplite armor and tactics. In later times the *comitia centuriata* met outside the *pomerium* on the Campus Martius and was tasked with the election of consuls and praetors and declarations of war. These were vestiges of its original function as an assembly of Roman citizens under arms (Dionys. *Ant. Rom.* 37.28.3). Presumably the organization of the archaic centuriate assembly reflected the military function of the centuries, with voting restricted to citizens who constituted the *classis* and presumably weighted in relation to the number of centuries each property class contributed.

The development of political institutions, the reorganization of Roman citizens into territorially based administrative units, the rationalization of military recruitment and the adoption of hoplite warfare, the consolidation of power in the hands of the political office-holders (the kings) and their enhanced ability to marshal resources, reflected in Rome's territorial gains and large-scale monumental architecture and other urban improvements—taken together these suggest that the process of state formation was well advanced by the time of the foundation of the Republic. It is usually assumed that state formation corresponds to a weakening of clans and other "pre-political" structures. Yet, as we have seen, this was not the case in Rome, though the kings surely tried to curtail the power of the clan leaders. Instead, the Roman *gentes* remained robust, even semi-autonomous entities, and individual aristocratic clan leaders were able to operate as warlords largely independent of state authority into the fifth century, even as Rome emerged as a hegemonic, territorially expansionist state. Thus, the Roman state remained relatively weak, and its archaic political institutions continued to be dominated by powerful aristocratic families.

3 Kingship in Rome

This inability of the Roman state to tame powerful clan leaders can only be understood in light of the nature of the Roman kingship. The Roman kingship was an elected rather than a hereditary position, though kin relationship to the previous ruler was presumably an important consideration in the selection of a new king. When a king died, the heads of the powerful clans (*patres*) took turns holding the office of *interrex*, and after a period of time the *patres* would advance a candidate for king, for whom the people would give their assent. Thus, the selection of the king involved the people's assembly but was heavily influenced by the powerful clan leaders.

A second important characteristic is that several of Rome's kings were foreign. Most notably, two of the last three legendary kings (Tarquinius Priscus and Tarquinius Superbus) were Etruscan. The origins of Servius Tullius, the sixth king of Rome, are nebulous, but he too may have been Etruscan, or possibly his family came from Corniculum. This acceptance of foreign rulers is consistent with our previous discussion of aristocrat warlords and powerful clan leaders who occasionally migrated from one city to another, and also fits a more general phenomenon throughout archaic Italy of such warlords (sometimes called *condottieri*) occasionally seizing political power in a community, whether though legitimate means or by force as usurpers or strongmen. These *condottieri* roughly parallel the tyrants (*tyrannoi*) of the archaic Greek world. Like the tyrants, they pursued ambitious foreign and domestic policies to enhance their own prestige, and they often introduced reforms meant to weaken pre-existing political structures (Cornell 1995: 141–143). The massive urban building program and significant military and political reforms of Servius Tullius can be seen in this context, as can his appeals to divine sanction to bolster his political legitimacy (Cornell 1995: 132–133; cf. Livy 1.39, 1.45). According to Roman tradition he was a beneficent reformer, but his policies can be interpreted as an effort to strengthen his own position vis-à-vis the Roman aristocracy. Indeed, the reform of the Roman tribal system and the creation of the centuriate military organization—whether introduced by Servius Tullius or another king, or whether introduced piecemeal over time—may have been aimed at undermining the influence of the clans who must have dominated the curial system, while at the same time providing the king with a more formidable army.

Nevertheless, the Roman kingship remained relatively weak, while the leaders of great clans retained considerable political influence. This is reflected in the archaic Roman political institutions themselves. If the centuriate system was linked to adoption of hoplite tactics, then the creation of centuriate assembly probably represented the ceding of some political power to the relatively broad strata of society who bore military responsibility. In theory, granting voting power to the hoplite class might have threatened the power of the aristocracy, yet it certainly indicates that monarchs such as Servius Tullius had to give up some political power in exchange for the military service necessary to maintain aggressive foreign policies. In addition, the aristocracy could influence the centuriate assembly in informal ways, and indeed they later came to dominate it through the formal organization of weighted, bloc voting by property class, just as the curiate assembly was also dominated by aristocratic clan leaders.

We should also briefly consider the archaic Senate in light of the present discussion. By the middle Republic the Roman Senate was a permanent and extremely influential aristocratic advisory body, and according to the later literary tradition it had functioned as such since the time of Romulus, yet the truth is surely more complicated. The *lex Ovinia*, passed c.320, gave the censors the right to select membership in the Senate, rather than the consuls (Festus, *Glossaria Latina*, 290L; Cornell 1995: 248, 369), which indicates that before the end of the fourth century, the Senate was an ad hoc advisory council (*consilium*) for the consuls. This arrangement probably descended from the regal period when the Senate was the king's *consilium* (Cornell 1995: 245–251), its membership undoubtedly drawn from the aristocracy, including the great clan leaders. Thus in practice the kings ruled in consultation with leading aristocrats, who exercised influence through both the archaic Senate and the assemblies. Unlike what happened in some archaic Greek *poleis* (for example, in Corinth, where the Cypselid dynasty destroyed the old aristocratic families known as the Bacchiadai), the Roman aristocracy survived the tyrant-like monarchs of the late regal period with its status and influence largely intact. In fact, it is very likely that the great clan leaders were behind the abolition of the kingship and the introduction of a new political system at the end of sixth century (Terrenato 2011).

4 Foundation of the Republic, c.509 BCE

According to Roman tradition, the last king Tarquinius Superbus ruled tyrannically. When his son Sextus Tarquinius raped a noblewoman, it sparked a rebellion: aggrieved Roman aristocrats seized the city, deposed the king, and established a new system of government that featured annually elected magistrates as the highest political officers (Livy 1.49, 1.57–60; Dionys. *Ant. Rom.* 4.41–44, 4.64–85). The birth of the republic, then, allegedly involved a rapid sequence of events, a political revolution rather than a gradual evolution. The sources agree that the abolition of the monarchy was relatively bloodless, and the political retributions were selective and limited. Only the king, his wife, his sons and their offspring were permanently banished from the city (Livy 1.59–60; Dionys. *Ant. Rom.* 5.1.2–3). Otherwise, there was no bloodshed, at least until Tarquinius Superbus tried to recapture the city. In fact, according to the tradition, the leaders of the republican revolution and Rome's first consuls, Lucius Iunius Brutus and Lucius Tarquinius Collatinus, were both related to the royal family. Collatinus was later pressured to abdicate because the people were apprehensive about anyone named Tarquinius; he retired to Lanuvium (Livy 2.2; Dionys. *Ant. Rom.* 5.12), but there were no further reprisals, no massacre of the king's family or former court officials, no widespread purge of Etruscan aristocrats or their Roman supporters. It is true that archaeological evidence suggests widespread destruction at this time—the Regia, the archaic sanctuary of Sant'Omobono, and the Comitium were all burned around 500—and this may indicate that the transition from monarchy to republic was more disruptive than the literary tradition claims (Coarelli 1983: 137–138; Cornell 1995: 236–241). Nevertheless, the appearance of Etruscan names in the early consular *fasti* implies a high degree of political continuity (Pallottino 1963; Scullard 1967: 263; Ampolo 1975). The great clans, including Etruscan families, survived the political revolution and retained their dominant position. The republican revolution resulted in a new system of government, but not a radically transformed ruling class.

According to Livy (2.1), annually elected magistrates were a hallmark of the Roman Republic, a safeguarded against tyranny. The practice of having two supreme magistrates of equal authority, the consuls, was undoubtedly designed to limit the potential for an individual to wield too much power. There is some debate, however, when the Romans settled on electing two consuls. The literary tradition and the consular *fasti* record that the consulship was instituted at the same time as the Republic, in 509. This remained the norm until the middle of the fifth century, when the Romans began to experiment with other offices, including boards of three to six magistrates known as consular tribunes. In 367, however, the double consulship was restored as part of a major reorganization of the government that included the creation of a third high magistracy, the office of praetor, which ranked just below the consuls. Some scholars doubt the veracity of this tradition and suggest that the consuls were instituted only in 367. One theory posits that the chief magistrates of the early Republic were initially called praetors (*praetor* simply means "the leader"), though whether there were initially one or two annually elected praetors is also debated (varying views: Beloch 1926: 231–236; De Sanctis 1956: 392–393; De Martino 1972; Cornell 1995: 226–230; Forsythe 2005: 150–155). I tend to accept the traditional account that two annually elected chief magistrates holding equal power were part of the initial republican set-up, but the precise details are not important. Rather, what is significant is that the government of the early Republic comprised only a handful of high political offices. Although the system was designed to guarantee power-sharing, power was shared among only a very few. Political leadership was presumably dominated by a small number of important clan leaders who rotated among themselves a few powerful magistracies. In other words, the basic pattern of Roman republicanism—relatively weak citizen assemblies with a tradition of group voting and dominated by a handful of aristocratic clans, an influential aristocratic advisory body, and strong magistrates—was present already from the very foundation of the Republic.

5 Developments in Roman Republicanism, c.500–300 BCE: A Response to Internal and External Pressures

As discussed, Roman aristocratic *gentes* were successful in perpetuating their status, wealth, and power over many generations. On the one hand, the Roman aristocracy of the late regal and early republican periods appears to have been relatively open to horizontal mobility, allowing for new elite families occasionally to be incorporated into the ruling class. On the other hand, a number of highly successful clans began to close ranks by the middle of the fifth century, forming what would become known as the patrician order. The nature of the patriciate has been greatly debated, but it is probable that these families claimed special religious competence. If so, we may imagine the patricians as a sort of priestly class. Since even "secular" high offices had some religious functions, over time the patricians laid claim to a virtual monopoly on all priestly and political offices. Patrician privilege was further justified by historical-mythical appeals, as each patrician *gens* claimed descent from Rome's founding fathers or, in some cases, divinities. Eventually everyone else in Roman society who was not patrician was called a *pleb* (the plebeians), though it is not clear when the term developed or what it would have meant in an early republican context (see Mitchell 1992, 2005; Cornell 1995: 242–258; Forsythe 2005: 157–170; Linderski 2005; Richard 2005; Raaflaub 2006: 139–141).

The so-called Struggle of the Orders, a two-century conflict between patricians and plebeians, is a dominant theme in narrative sources for the early Republic. It is beyond the scope of this chapter to discuss fully the nature of the conflict(s), though there appear to have been major several points of contention (see also Mouritsen, Chapter 9). The most important was political, as wealthy non-patricians (the plebeian aristocracy) sought access to the political and religious offices increasingly monopolized by the patrician clans. Plebeians also wanted greater political representation and protection from abuses on the part of patrician aristocrats. A third, related, grievance was economic: poorer plebeians complained of food shortages, unfair land distribution, and the condition of debt bondage into which impoverished plebeians had allegedly fallen. Archaeological evidence hints at a widespread economic downturn between c.475 and 400, so there may be some veracity to reports that political agitation was related to economic distress (Colonna 1990; Cornell 1995: 266–267; though see Scott 2005: 104–105). The Struggle of the Orders probably encompassed several separate but related conflicts, with different issues pressing more at different times (Raaflaub 2005b; 2006: 139–141). The plebeians were ultimately successful in their bid to obtain greater representation and access to high offices, but this was achieved only slowly.

The political side of the Struggle of the Orders was resolved mostly through compromises and concessions by the patrician aristocracy, who periodically created new offices and political institutions for the plebeians, and gradually opened magistracies and priesthoods to plebeian aristocrats. The office of plebeian tribune, which could only be held by plebeians, was created in 494. Initially there were probably only two plebeian tribunes elected each year. The number was increased from two to five in 471, and from five to ten in 457 (Livy 2.33.1–3, 2.58.1 (citing the second-century historian L. Calpurnius Piso Frugi = HRF Piso F 23 = FRH 7 F25); Dionys. *Ant. Rom.* 6.89; cf. Diod. 11.68.8). The office of aedile was also created in 494: the two aediles were charged with assisting the tribunes (Dionys. *Ant. Rom.* 6.90.3). Meanwhile the plebeian assembly (*concilium plebis*), which was attended only by plebeians, was reportedly formed in 471 (Livy 2.56.1–3). The literary tradition implies that the tribal assembly (*comitia tributa*) was created soon thereafter, since its first recorded action was the election of quaestors in 447 (Tac. *Ann.* 11.22). Both of these assemblies were organized around the Servian tribes: all members of the same tribe voted together in a group voting system, and the outcome was determined by a majority of tribes. We do not know how many Servian tribes were created initially, but by 495 there were twenty-one, four urban tribes and seventeen rural tribes (Livy 2.21.7; Cornell 1995: 173–175). Thus, legislation in the tribal or plebeian assembly would have passed if eleven tribes voted for it. This bloc-voting scheme probably derived from a similar protocol used in the *comitia curiata*. There is some question as to whether there were two separate assemblies organized along the Servian tribes, or if there was only one citizen assembly organized according to the reformed tribal units (Forsythe 2005: 177–183). There is also reason to reject the traditional narrative that the plebeian assembly was only formed in 471, more than twenty years after the number of tribes was expanded to twenty-one, and even longer after Servius Tullius allegedly reformed the tribes. The details of the debate are not a serious concern here, however. What matters is that one or more citizen assemblies organized according to the Servian tribes were functioning at a very early point in republican history. These assemblies (or this assembly) theoretically gave the plebeians more legislative and electoral influence, because the votes within the tribes were equal rather than weighted in favor of the wealthy, as in the centuriate assembly. Between 451 and 449, Roman law was codified and published for the first time: inscribed on twelve bronze tablets and put up in public (Livy 3.9, 32–34, 57; Dionys. *Ant. Rom.* 10.3.34; Diod. 12.26.1; see Cornell 1995: 272–292; Eder 2005; Forsythe 2005: 201–233; also Williamson, Chapter 11). The laws included a notorious prohibition on marriage between patricians and plebeians (Dion. 10.60.5; Cic. *De rep.* 2.61–63), which proved unpopular and was lifted in 445 (Livy 4.1.2; though see Forsythe 2005: 225–230). Between 444 and 367 the Romans experimented with a new office call the consular tribunate: in certain years a board of three to six consular tribunes was chosen instead of the usual two annual consuls, and the consular tribunate was open to plebeians (Boddington 1959; Sealey 1959; Pinsent 1975; Drummond 1989; Ridley 1986; Cornell 1995: 334–337; Forsythe 2005: 234–239). The Sexto-Licinian laws of 367 doubled the number of aediles to four (two curule, two plebeian) and allowed plebeians to hold the consulship (Livy 6.42, 7.1). The *lex Genucia* of 342 mandated that at least one consul each year be plebeian (Livy 7.42; Cornell 1995: 337–338). The *lex Ogulnia* (300) both increased the number of priesthoods and opened most major priesthoods to plebeians (Livy 10.6.2–6, 10.9.1–2). Finally, in 287, the *lex Hortensia* made any law passed by the plebeian assembly binding on all Romans (Livy *Per.* 11; Pliny *NH* 16.37; Gell. 15.274; Gaius 1.3), a re-enactment and/or modification of similar measures passed already in 449 and 339 (see Cornell 1995: 276–278; Oakley 2004). This rather brisk survey of some of the key junctures in the Struggle of the Orders indicates a general pattern in the development of the republican political system. On the one hand, the gradual increase in the number of more specialized magistracies, coupled with the push to codify law, reflect the emergence of a more sophisticated state structure, while on the other hand the opening of offices to plebeians allowed the Roman ruling class slowly to incorporate new members from the plebeian aristocracy

Patrician concessions were granted, we are told, in response to local heightening of tension between the two orders. Yet rarely did these more acute confrontations result in significant bloodshed, if the literary tradition can be trusted. Indeed, a striking feature of the Struggle of the Orders is the degree to which it was characterized by non-violent compromise, revealing the Roman aristocracy's knack for finding political solutions to social and political problems. This tradition of compromise, as we have seen, stretches back to the birth of the Republic, when the aristocracy came through the political revolution with its power still largely unaffected. During the Struggle of the Orders, the Roman ruling class accepted a limited horizontal widening of political power-sharing, as the opening up of certain offices, the creation of new offices, and the formal legalization of intermarriage between the orders allowed new elite families to participate in high-level politics and slowly integrate into the aristocracy. Meanwhile, the slow transformation of the patrician ruling class into the patrician-plebeian *nobilitas* guaranteed that the old powerful clans continued to exert influence and dominate the political scene (on the *nobilitas*: Cornell 1989: 334–347; 1995: 340–344; Forsythe 2005: 268–281). In a way, the outcome of the Struggle of the Orders was as much a victory for the most powerful patrician clans as it was for aspiring plebeian aristocratic families.

Similarly the ruling class made concessions to the people—vertical power-sharing—that quelled any popular discontent and satisfied the people's political demands without seriously jeopardizing aristocratic privilege (see also Tatum, Chapter 15). This can be seen in the way the various popular assemblies functioned. Assemblies had to be called by a magistrate; assemblies were called only for the purpose of voting rather than for open debate or deliberation; legislative proposals were introduced only by the assembly's overseeing magistrate, while the people's role was strictly reactive, voting yes or no. The system was geared to limit but not completely eliminate the people's participation and democratic power. The group-voting schemes employed in the assemblies, a practice that appears to have pre-dated the birth of the Republic, were another mechanism for limiting democratic expression.

This is seen most clearly in the *comitia centuriata*. As we have discussed, the centuriate assembly was probably from its inception a group-voting institution, with votes weighted proportionally to the military obligation of each class. Roman military organization evolved over the course of the fifth and fourth centuries, with the result that already before the end of the fifth century the *centuriae* ceased to have a meaningful link to military recruitment (Cornell 1995: 186–190; Forsythe 2007: 35–36). With the *centuriae* decoupled from military service, the property class structure became more important for political purposes. What developed by the middle Republic was the complicated centuriate system described by Livy and others, with the Roman people placed into one of several precise property classes and further divided into groups of older and younger voters. In this system, even the poorest of class of Roman society, the *proletarii*, had nominal political influence, but in reality the system was slanted heavily toward the wealthy. As mentioned, group voting meant that the wealthiest two classes (the *equites* and first class) were sufficient to determine the outcome in any election. The voting in assemblies arranged by tribe theoretically should have been more democratic, since the votes of rich and poor counted the same, yet these assemblies, too, were highly republican in function. A relatively small number of wealthier voters distributed throughout the rural tribes, whose poorer members would have had difficulty coming to Rome for a meeting of the assembly, could guarantee a majority of tribal votes even if a large number of poorer urban citizens turned out to vote.

The willingness of the ruling class to make any sort of political concessions to the people, albeit largely symbolic concessions, must be understood in the context of the highly competitive interstate environment of archaic Italy (Raaflaub 1996; Eckstein 2006: 120–147). The Romans were profoundly affected by intense external military pressure—by threats both real and perceived—and they were successful in dealing with external threats in large part because they adopted policies to expand the pool for military recruitment. This meant not relying only the hoplite and equestrian classes, but instead recruiting from poorer levels of society. By the middle Republic the Romans had already greatly lowered the property qualification to serve in the legions (Livy 1.43; Polyb. 6.19; Cic. *De rep.* 2.40), and as early as the end of the fifth century the Roman state paid each citizen-soldier a small *stipendium* to support his military service (Livy 4.59.11; Diod. 14.16.5). Moreover, a significant proportion of the legions was made up of lightly armed skirmishers drawn from the lower property classes (see Keppie 1998: 14–23; Forsythe 2007; Rawlings 2007). Put simply, the Roman ruling class needed people to fight, and this in turn gave the lower classes political leverage. The various "secessions of the plebs" make this dynamic very clear, regardless of the historicity of the accounts. Thus, the ruling class found it advantageous to give the people some political voice. Indeed, even the very poorest were allowed to vote, as the Romans enforced no minimum property qualification to participate in any assembly. I would argue the occasional concessions to the plebeians and the theoretical inclusion of the people in political decision-making, even if their role was greatly circumscribed and controlled by the ruling elite, were critical in promoting social cohesion, and were thus key to the Roman aristocracy's maintenance of power and status (on vertical bonds and social cohesion see Gelzer 1969; Hölkeskamp 2010: 98–106). Through such gestures the aristocracy avoided the danger of a truly democratic revolution, such as occurred in the late sixth and early fifth century in Athens. Careful negotiation, compromise, and willingness to allow some power-sharing benefited the ruling class over the long run

Lastly, the Roman aristocracy applied the practice of careful compromise, limited political concessions, and the successful political integration of outsiders on a larger scale, making Rome a relatively open society by ancient standards. Let us return briefly to the tribal system allegedly introduced by Servius Tullius. In 495 there were twenty-one tribes, four urban and seventeen rural, and between 387 and 241 another fourteen tribes were added in stages, corresponding roughly to the expansion of the Roman territorial state throughout the Italian peninsula. Roman citizenship was determined by enrolment into one of these tribes, which were organized more or less geographically. In other words, Roman citizenship, which originally had been based on birth into one of the old curial tribes, was now determined by residence. The office of censor was reportedly created in 443, suggesting that this new conception of citizenship was already developed by the middle of the fifth century (Livy 4.8.2–7). This was one aspect of a larger process in which the Romans re-imagined citizenship as a cluster of legal rights and privileges, rather than a birthright. This is expressed very clearly in the recognition of the *Ius Latinum* ("Latin right") and *civitas sine suffragio* ("citizenship without the vote"), two categories of "partial" citizenship that shared specific rights and privileges with "full" Roman citizenship and could be granted to outsiders as the Romans deemed desirable. The expandable tribal system and partible citizenship allowed for the periodic incorporation of conquered peoples into the Roman state. This organization of citizenship into different "levels" or categories was part of the so-called Settlement of 338, which Rome imposed upon the defeated Latins and other allies after the Latin War, 341–338 (Cornell 1995: 347–352; Forsythe 2005: 289–292; Champion, Chapter 19). This contrasts with the ancient Greek *poleis*, who tended to closely guard citizenship as an exclusive birthright. The Roman political system could handle this sort of expansion with little threat to stability because of its strongly republican traditions and structures: the core *nobilitas* endured while slowly absorbing new members, while the inclusion of new citizens provided Rome with enormous military resource. Meanwhile, the new citizens were essentially satisfied by the nominal political voice they were granted in exchange for military service. Thus the Romans found a way to break free from the structural constraints that limited all but a handful of ancient city-states from creating an extensive territorial empire.

6 *Nobilitas*, Republicanism, and the Conquest of Italy and Sicily, c.300–241 BCE

By the close of the fourth century BCE, the community emerged as the most important locus of military and political legitimacy, while the autonomy of the great clans was increasingly circumscribed. Nevertheless, the political system continued to emphasize elite political privilege, and it allowed for successful aristocratic clans to maintain and perpetuate their status. Thus, such clans as the *gentes Cornelia*, *Aemilia*, *Claudia*, and *Valeria* appear repeatedly in the consular *fasti* for the first half of the third century BCE, indicating that they successfully preserved their position into the middle Republic. Yet membership in the *nobilitas* was also not a birthright: although members of the great clans had clear political advantages, they still needed to work to preserve their political capital from generation to generation. They needed to compete to win elections to high office and, more importantly, obtain military glory.

This is well exemplified by a very important document, the *Elogium of Scipio Barbatus* (*CIL* I² 7). The text was inscribed on the sarcophagus of Lucius Cornelius Scipio Barbatus (consul, 298 BCE), which was buried in the tomb of the Cornelii Scipiones. Recent scholarship has argued that the text was composed and inscribed at the time of Scipio Barbatus' death (c.280 BCE) rather than a later copy or composition added to an older sarcophagus (see Flower 1996: 173–177). If so, the inscription is perhaps the earliest Roman historical narrative. It reads:

> Cornelius Lucius Scipio Barbatus Gnaivod patre prognatus / fortis vir sapiensque / quoius forma virtutei parisuma fuit / consol censor aidilis quei fuit apud vos / Taurasia Cisauna Samnio cepit / subigit omne Loucana opsidesque abdoucit.
>
> Lucius Cornelius Scipio Barbatus, descended from his father Gnaeus, a strong and wise man whose beauty was most equal to his manly excellence, who was consul, censor and aedile among you, he took Taurasia, Cisauna, and Samnium and he subjugated all Lucania and he led away hostages.

Attention to family lineage is clear, and the family's corporate identity and self-representation would have been reinforced by the burial context, as the tomb of the

Scipios comprised several joined rock-cut chambers holding approximately thirty burials. Members of the Cornelii Scipiones were buried in the tomb for six generations, until the middle of the second century BCE, by which time the tomb was adorned with a monumental facade and statues of most prominent members in the history of the family, Publius Cornelius Scipio Africanus and his brother Lucius Cornelius Scipio Asiaticus (Cic. *Pro Arch.* 22, *Tusc.* 1.13, *De leg.* 2.57; Livy 38.56; cf. Pliny *NH* 7.114; Suet. *De poet.* 8; Coarelli 1988; Claridge 2010: 365–368). The inscription also calls attention to Barbatus' political rank and offices obtained, but the greatest stress is martial in nature, both in the list of foreign peoples conquered and the highlighting of martial values such as *fortis* (strong, courageous) and *virtus* (manliness, courage, military talent).

Barbatus' achievements are placed in relation to the broader community: the *elogium* advertises that he was aedile, consul, and censor *apud vos* (among you), referring to the Roman people. Through the second person pronoun the inscription addresses the reader directly, and it may mimic in abbreviated form the performances at a Roman aristocrat's public funeral, where his great deeds and those of his ancestors were recounted before the entire populace (Polyb. 6.53). In this way the family's achievements were advertised and memorialized, and its social standing justified. Meanwhile, the people too played an important role in, giving sanction to and legitimating the aristocratic family's position. Scipio Barbatus and his relatives merited their rank and status because of their achievements in the eyes of the Roman people. The *elogium* nicely encapsulates the two-way street of Roman republicanism, which largely secured elite privilege while various social rituals and symbolic yet important political concession to the people promoted social harmony (on the *elogium*, see Hölkeskamp 2010: 91–92).

Scipio Barbatus' consulship coincides with the outbreak of the Third Samnite War (298–290), which saw the Romans fighting on multiple fronts against a diverse and formidable coalition of Samnites, Etruscans, Umbrians, and Gauls. The war brought nearly the entire peninsula under Rome's hegemony, and it underscores how Roman warfare was now conducted on a much larger scale. Between 350 and 264 there were only six years when the Romans were not at war. Already by the late fourth century the normal annual levy was four legions of citizen-soldiers, and from c.312 the Romans regularly conducted campaigns in two or more theaters of Italy. After the difficult campaigns against the Samnites, the Romans weathered a major challenge from Pyrrhus of Epirus, whose highly skilled mercenary army inflicted severe defeats on the Romans at Heraclea (280) and Asculum (279). Nevertheless, Rome refused to yield and ultimately Pyrrhus was driven from Italy after the battle of Beneventum (275). The Romans then completed their subjugation of Italy, with victories over communities in both the southern and northern reaches of the peninsula. The total area of the *ager Romanus* grew from an estimated 1,900 km^2 in 340 to nearly 27,000 km^2 in 264, or approximately one-sixth of the Italian peninsula (Cornell 1995: 380; Rawlings 2007: 47–49), as the Romans confiscated land from various conquered communities and incorporated it into the Roman state. However, creating this enormous territorial state required an enormous and sustained military effort, which put a significant burden on the Roman people. They in turn must have pressured the ruling class for further political concessions. The last Secession of the Plebs, which allegedly resulted in the passing of the *lex Hortensia* (287), makes sense in light of Rome's emergence in the early third century as major territorial state and pan-Italian power.

The reform of the *comitia centuriata* in the middle of the third century BCE, if historical, can be understood in the same context. The Senate's decision to invade Sicily in 264, Rome's first significant trans-peninsular military venture, brought the Romans into conflict with the Carthaginians. The First Punic War (264–241) was an epic struggle of unprecedented scale in terms of men and materiel. Rome emerged victorious, but victory was costly, as perhaps 50,000 Roman citizens perished in more than two decades of fighting (Goldsworthy 2001: 122; Rankov 2011). Literary sources suggest that the *comitia centuriata* was reorganized in the same year the First Punic War concluded. This is also when the last two Roman citizen tribes were created, bringing the total to thirty-five tribes. The exact details of the reform are much debated, but it may have involved trying to link the centuriate organization with the number of tribes. More importantly, the number of centuries assigned to the first class was reduced from 80 to 70 (Cic. *De rep.* 2.22.39; Livy 1.43.12–13, *Per.* 19; Dionys. *Ant. Rom.* 4.21.3). Thus, the combined weight of the *equites* and first class (88 centuries) no longer formed a majority of the total number of centuries (193), and so they could not, strictly speaking, determine the outcome of all votes and elections. Although the highest classes still exercised disproportionate electoral power, nevertheless the reform may have been understood as an important concession to the people. To this another reform was added, possibly also in 241, but no later than 215: the centuries of *equites* no longer voted first, but instead a century from another class—probably always the first class—was chosen by lot to vote first (Livy 24.7.12, 26.22.2, 27.6.3). Again, this would not have lessened the actual electoral power of the wealthiest citizens, but removing from the *equites* the privilege of voting first surely had a significant symbolic value (for various views on the reforms see Staveley 1952; Nicholls 1956; Taylor 1957; Sumner 1962; Develin 1978; Grieve 1985).

Both the rhetoric of the *Elogium of Scipio Barbatus* and the reforms of the *comitia centuriata* highlight the need to emphasize the people's function in sanctioning aristocratic power. Indeed, the very practice of holding elections in which the people could vote, even if their actual political power was negligible, was a critical in the creation and sustaining of Rome's republican ideology. As Hölkeskamp (2010: 93) notes, eventually "there were more than seventy official positions of one kind or another that had to be filled every year" by elections in Rome's various citizen assemblies. Each election reaffirmed the people's legitimizing role and reinforced the vertical bonds between the elite and *populus Romanus.*

7 Conclusion

Three main factors were discussed to explain the origins and emergence of Roman republicanism. The first were deep-rooted social-political structures and traditions that go back to the archaic period. These include the emergence of very powerful aristocratic clan leaders whose position was not seriously undermined by urbanization and the beginnings of state formation, and the longstanding practice of group voting (itself perhaps tied to the creation of early Roman assemblies as councils of clans). One could say that Roman republicanism developed because republican tendencies had always been part of the Rome's political machinery. Second, Rome's ruling class was deft at political compromise, allowing the Romans to resolve internal political pressures without violence or the radical reordering of the political hierarchy. Third, Roman political thought and practice developed in the context of profound external pressure, which compelled the ruling class to find ways to integrate outsiders and power-share both horizontally and vertically. To this I will add a fourth: Roman conservatism, the tendency of the Romans to keep older practices and institutions rather than discard them, and to prefer gradual evolution over punctuated political change.

The Roman Republic shared several important characteristics with the citizen-states of ancient Greece. In both Greece and Rome, final decision-making power was placed—theoretically—in the hands of a citizen assembly. Political power was exercised primarily by the landed citizenry, who also served as heavily armed infantry in the citizen militia, though some political voice was sometimes extended to poorer members of the society. Practically speaking, the assembly's power was usually circumscribed by an executive council (*boulē*) and magistrates. At the same time, magistrates tended to be elected or selected annually, to minimize the chance that one or a few men would accumulate too much power.

However, the functioning of the Roman Republic differed significantly from the citizen governments of the Greek world, especially the most "extreme" example of participatory government, democratic Athens. Primarily, the citizens' political voice, expressed through the various assemblies, was far weaker in Rome than in Athens, in large part because of the peculiar and uniquely Roman practice of bloc voting. It is hard to pinpoint precisely why the Romans adopted this practice, though, as argued above, it was probably related to another key feature of archaic and early republican Rome, the endurance of powerful clans as social-political entities.

Also, specific historical and geopolitical circumstances encouraged Rome and Athens to develop along different trajectories. As Kurt Raaflaub discussed (see Chapter 2), Athens' wars with Persia and the development of her thalassocratic empire compelled the Athenians to maintain a permanent fleet, giving greater political leverage to the poorest citizens who made up the rower class. The empire also needed large numbers of magistrates and other officials. Combined with a large *boulē* with rotating membership, the Athenian imperial-political system required a high level of active citizen participation. By contrast, Rome was an extensive territorial state, and Rome's response to external threat was to increase the size of its infantry. This was done mostly by increasing the citizen population through the incorporation of conquered peoples into pre-existing or newly created citizen tribes. The Roman Senate was a relative small body that remained the domain of the ruling class, and the Romans used relatively few magistrates to govern their territory. Thus, the Roman Republic functioned without needing lots of political participation from a significant percentage of the citizenry. In this context, the token political concessions to the poor, for example the single vote in the *comitia centuriata*, combined with economic advantages and certain measures of social care, were sufficient to maintain social cohesion.

REFERENCES

CAH = *The Cambridge Ancient History*. 2nd edn. Cambridge, 1989.

FRH = H. Beck and U. Walter, eds., *Die frühen römischen Historiker*. 2 vols. Darmstadt, 2001–2004.

HRF = H. Peter, ed., *Historicorum Romanorum Fragmenta*. 2nd edn. Leipzig, 1914.

Ampolo, C. 1975. "Gli Aquilii del V secolo a.C. e il problema dei Fasti consolari più antichi." *PdP* 30: 410–416.

Beloch, J. 1926. *Römische Geschichte bis zum Beginn der punischen Kriege*. Berlin.

Bispham, E. 2007. "Literary Sources." In Rosenstein and Morstein-Marx 2006: 29–50.

Boddington, A. 1959. "The Original Nature of the Consular Tribunate." *Historia* 8: 356–364.

Botsford, G. 1909. *The Roman Assemblies from their Origin to the End of the Republic*. New York.

Coarelli, F. 1983. *Il foro romano I: Periodo arcaico*. Rome.

Coarelli, F. 1988. *Il Sepolcro degli Scipioni a Roma*. Rome.

Claridge, A. 2010. *Rome: An Oxford Archaeological Guide*. 2nd edn. Oxford.

Colonna, G. 1990. "Città e territorio nell'Etruria meridionale del V secolo." In T. Colonna, ed., *Crise et transformation des sociétés archaïques de l'Italie antique au Ve siècle*. Rome, 7–21.

Cornell, T. 1989. "The Recovery of Rome." *CAH* 7(2): 309–350.

Cornell, T. 1995. *The Beginnings of Rome: Italy and Rome from the Bronze Age to the Punic Wars (c.1000–264 BC)*. London.

Cornell, T. 2005. "The Value of the Literary Tradition Concerning Archaic Rome." In Raaflaub 2005a, 47–74.

De Martino, F. 1972. "Intorno all'origine della repubblica romana e delle magistrature." *ANRW* 2(1): 217–249.

De Sanctis, G. 1956. *Storia Dei Romani*. 2nd edn., vol. 2. Florence.

Develin, R. 1978. "The Third Century Reform of the *Comitia Centuriata*." *Ath* 56: 346–377.

Drummond, A. 1989. "Rome in the Fifth Century II: The Citizen Community." *CAH* 7(2): 172–242.

Eckstein, A. 2006. *Mediterranean Anarchy, Interstate War, and the Rise of Rome*. Berkeley.

Eder, W. 2005. "The Political Significance of the Codification of Law in Archaic Societies." In Raaflaub 2005a: 239–267.

Erdkamp, P., ed. 2007. *A Companion to the Roman Army*. Oxford.

Flower, H. 1996. *Ancestor Masks and Aristocratic Power in Roman Culture*. Oxford.

Forsythe, G. 2005. *A Critical History of Early Rome*. Berkeley.

Forsythe, G. 2007. "The Army and the Centuriate Organization in Early Rome." In Erdkamp 2007: 24–41.

Fraccaro, P. 1931. "La storia dell'antichissimo esercito romano e l'eta dell'ordinamento centuriato." *Atti II Congresso nazionale di studi romani* 3: 91–97.

Fronda, M. 2010. *Between Rome and Carthage*. Cambridge.

Gelzer, M. 1969. *The Roman Nobility*. Oxford.

Goldsworthy, A. 2001. *The Punic Wars*. London.

Grieve, L. 1985. "The Reform of the *Comitia Centuriata*." *Historia* 34: 278–309.

Hölkeskamp, K.-J. 2010. *Reconstructing the Roman Republic: An Ancient Political Culture and Modern Research*. Princeton.

Holloway, R. 1994. *The Archaeology of Early Rome and Latium*. London.

Keppie, L. 1998. *The Making of the Roman Army*. 2nd edn. Norman, OK.

Linderski, J. 2005. "Religious Aspects of the Conflict of the Orders: the Case of *confarreatio*." In Raaflaub 2005a: 223–238.

Marincola, J., ed. 2007. *A Companion to Greek and Roman Historiography*. 2 vols. Oxford and Malden, MA.

Mehl, A. 2011. *Roman Historiography: An Introduction to its Basic Aspects and Development*. Trans. Hans-Friedrich Müller; 1st published 2001. Chichester and Malden, MA.

Mitchell, R. 1992. *Patricians and Plebeians*. Ithaca, NY.

Mitchell, R. 2005. "The Definition of *Patres* and *Plebs*: An End to the Struggle of the Orders," in Raaflaub 2005a: 128–167.

Nicholls, J. 1956. "The Reform of the Comitia Centuriata." *AJP* 77: 225–254.

Oakley, S. 1997. *A Commentary on Livy Books VI–X*, vol. 1. Oxford.

Oakley, S. 1998. *A Commentary on Livy Books VI–X*, vol. 2. Oxford.

Oakley, S. 2004. "The Early Republic." In H. Flower, ed., *The Cambridge Companion to the Roman Republic*. Cambridge, 15–30.

Oakley, S. 2005a. *A Commentary on Livy Books VI–X*, vol. 3. Oxford.

Oakley, S. 2005b. *A Commentary on Livy Books VI–X*, vol. 4. Oxford.

Ogilvie, R.M. 1965. *A Commentary on Livy Books 1–5*. Oxford.

Ogilvie, R.M. 1989. "The Sources for Early Roman History." *CAH* 7(2): 1–29.

Pallottino, M. 1963. "Fatti e leggende (moderne) sulla più antica storia di Roma." *SE* 31: 3–37.

Pinsent, J. 1975. *Military Tribunes and Plebeian Consuls: The Fasti from 444 V. To 342 V*. Wiesbaden.

Raaflaub, K. 1996. "Born to be Wolves? Origins of Roman Imperialism." In R. Wallace and E. Harris, eds., *Transitions to Empire: Essays in Greco-Roman History, 360–146 BC, in Honor of E. Badian*. Norman, OK, 273–314.

Raaflaub, K., ed. 2005a. *Social Struggles in Archaic Rome*. 2nd edn. London.

Raaflaub, K. 2005b. "From Protection and Defense to Offense and Participation: Stages in the Conflict of the Orders." In Raaflaub 2005a: 168–184.

Raaflaub, K. 2006. "Between Myth and History: Rome's Rise from Village to Empire (the Eighth Century to 264)." In Rosenstein and Morstein-Marx 2006: 125–146.

Rankov, B. 2011. "A War of Phases: Strategies and Stalemates 264–241 BC." In D. Hoyos, ed., *A Companion to the Punic Wars*. Oxford, 159–166.

Rawlings, L. 2007. "Army and Battle during the Conquest of Italy (350–264 BC)." In Erdkamp 2007: 45–62.

Rich, J. 2007. "Warfare and the Army in Early Rome." In Erdkamp 2007: 7–23.

Richard, J.-C. 1978. *Les origines de la plèbe romaine*. Paris.

Richard, J.-C. 2005. "Patricians and Plebeians: The Origins of a Social Dichotomy." In Raaflaub 2005a: 107–127.

Ridley, R. 1983. "Falsi triumphi, plures sonsulatus." *Hermes* 42: 372–382.

Ridley, R. 1986. "The Consular Tribunate: the Testimony of Livy." *Klio* 62: 337–354.

Rosenstein, N. and R. Morstein-Marx, eds. 2006. *A Companion to the Roman Republic*. Oxford and Malden, MA.

Scott, R. 2005. "The Contribution of Archaeology to Early Roman History." In Raaflaub 2005a: 98–106.

Scullard, H.H. 1967. *The Etruscan Cities and Rome*. London.

Sealey, R. 1959. "The Consular Tribunate Once More." *Latomus* 18: 521–530.

Smith, C. 1996. *Early Rome and Latium: Economy and Society c.1000 to 500 BC*. Oxford.

Smith, C. 2006. *The Roman Clan: The* Gens *from Ancient Ideology to Modern Anthropology*. Cambridge.

Smith, C. 2011. "Citizenship and Community: Inventing the Roman Republic." In Terrenato and Haggis 2011: 217–230.

Snodgrass, A. 1965. "The Hoplite Reform and History." *JHS* 85: 110–122.

Stary, P. 1981. *Zur eisenzeitliche Bewaffnung und Kampfesweise in Mittelitalien*. Mainz.

Staveley, E. 1952. "The Reform of the Comitia Centuriata." *AJP* 74: 1–33.

Sumner, G. 1962. "Aspects of the History of the Comitia Centuriata in the Middle and Late Republic." *Ath* 50: 37–84.

Taylor, L.R. 1957. "The Centuriate Assembly Before and After the Reform." *AJP* 78: 337–354.

Terrenato, N. 2011. "The Versatile Clans: Archaic Rome and the Nature of Early City-States in Central Italy." In Terrenato and Haggis 2011: 231–244.

Terrenato, N. and D. Haggis, eds. 2011. *State Formation in Italy and Greece*. Oxford.

Torelli, M. 1974–75. "Trè studi di storia etrusca." *DArch* 8: 3–78.

Torelli, M. 2006. "The Topography and Archaeology of Republican Rome." In Rosenstein and Morstein-Marx 2006: 81–101.

Wiseman, T.P. 1979. *Clio's Cosmetics: Three Studies in Greco-Roman Literature*. Leicester.
Wiseman, T.P. 1983. "The Credibility of the Early Annalists." *LCM* 8: 20–22.
Wiseman, T.P. 1989. "Roman Legend and the Oral Tradition." *JRS* 79: 129–137.

FURTHER READING

On the history Roman in the archaic and early republican periods, Cornell 1995 and Forsythe 2005 are essential; see also *The Cambridge Ancient History* 2nd edn., 7(2), and Smith 1996. On the Struggle of the Orders, see Raaflaub 2005. On the evolution of the Roman army and its relationship to state formation and political developments, see the relevant chapters in Rosenstein and Morstein-Marx 2006; Erdkamp 2007. On Roman historiography in general, see Marincola 2007; Mehl 2011. Commentaries on the first ten books of Livy, see Ogilvie 1965; Oakley 1997–2005.

PART II

Constructing a Past

CHAPTER 4

Autochthony and Identity in Greek Myth

Kathryn A. Morgan

1 Introduction

Creating a vision of the past is tied inescapably to the needs of the present. Mythical aetiology, as Barbara Kowalzig (2007: 27) has remarked, "while pretending to connect cause with effect, really related [the] present with a mythical past. It seems to establish a timeless continuity from the moment of origins to the present day." Getting a grip on the construction of the past thus involves unpicking the threads that constitute what seems to be a coherent mythico-historical picture. I say "mythico-historical" because the Greek construction of history wove together categories that we are inclined to separate. Even though historians such as Herodotus and Thucydides attempted to carve out a space for their work that separated off the time of myth, the majority of Greeks would still have encountered their past in forms like oratory and choral poetry that used myth and mythologized history to underpin the present. The multitude of cities that constituted the ancient Greek world imagined their past in a complex network of interlocking and conflicting traditions, traditions that changed as the needs of the present changed in accordance with shifting identities (ethnic and otherwise), new priorities, and new allegiances. When we talk of constructing a past we must, then, always ask "Whose past?" and "Whose past when?" The Greek cities and intellectuals of the Roman empire constituted their identity and thus their past differently from the Athenians or Spartans of the classical period (Konstan 2001; Saïd 2001).

For present purposes I shall be focusing (for the most part) on the construction of the past in the classical period in Athens, and in particular on the late fifth and first half of the fourth century BCE. This is due partly to the richness of the sources for Athens, but also to the opportunity provided by the works of Plato, that refracting prism who simultaneously presents and deconstructs the ideologies of his day. The following chapter in this volume will examine the idealization of agriculture in creating a vision of the Roman Republic.

A Companion to Greek Democracy and the Roman Republic, First Edition. Edited by Dean Hammer.

This chapter will pursue a closely related issue: the connection of agrarian ideology with the Athenian idea of autochthony, whereby the citizens of Athens imagined themselves in a unique relationship to the land in which they lived. Plato's canny manipulation of pastoral and agrarian ideologies in the context of his several fantasies about the development of utopian and historical societies is the goal towards which this chapter will move, but in order to appreciate the extent of his subtlety it will be necessary first to sketch a more general picture of the Greeks and their pasts.

2 The Land

There were two broad possibilities for imagining the relationship of a community to the land in which it dwelt. Either the inhabitants were native to the land or they had migrated there (or perhaps a combination of both). The histories of Herodotus and Thucydides transmit shadowy stories of population movement both before and after the Trojan War (Hdt. 1.56; Thuc. 1.2, 1.12). The most famous of these migrations was the Return of the Heracleidae, when the descendants of Heracles, accompanied by the Dorians, were thought to have invaded and taken control of the Peloponnese in the period after the fall of Troy. The historicity of the "Dorian invasion" has long been a disputed issue; what is important in the present context is, as Jonathan Hall has pointed out, that the Greeks conceived of early history as characterized by migration and instability and used stories of population movement to explore supra-regional affiliations (Hall 2002: 34–35; cf. 73–89 for a measured consideration of the "Dorian invasion"). The Return of the Heracleidae and the concomitant arrival of the Dorians formed the foundational charter myth for Sparta with its dual Heraclid kings (Malkin 1994: 15–19). The myth carried with it strong implications of military supremacy. The Spartan poet Tyrtaeus exhorted his countrymen to courage in battle by telling them that their race came from "unconquered Heracles" (fr. 11.1–2 W^2). In his elegy on good government, he declared that "Zeus himself gave this city to the Heracleidae, with whom we left windy Erineus and arrived at the broad island of Pelops" (fr. 1.12–15 W^2). The paradigm of Dorian/Heraclid conquest followed by constitutional continuity was foregrounded by Pindar in 470 BCE, when he praised Hieron, tyrant of Syracuse, for the foundation of his Dorian city of Aetna by telling him that "the descendants of Pamphylus and the Heraclids who live on the slopes of Taygetus wish always to remain Dorians in the institutes of Aegimius. The blessed ones set out from Pindus and took Amyclae." (*Pythian* 1.62–66). The same paradigm of conquest and subsequent continuity recurs in Plato's *Laws*, where the foundation of Sparta by the Dorians marks the point at which the interlocutors in the dialogue pass from the time of myth to a more historical time: "our fourth city or if you wish, race, has arrived, founded in the past and still now founded" (683a7–8). The sequence of arrival (and conquest), foundation, and continuity is a flexible construction that accommodates movement and rupture as well as unbroken tradition.

A people might also imagine that they were native to a given land. Such a claim might be inflected in several ways. In Thebes, for example, a myth of immigration (Cadmus the founder of Thebes was said to have come to Greece from Phoenicia) could be combined with the tale of the "sown men", the *spartoi*, who were produced from the earth when Cadmus sowed it with the teeth of the local dragon, and whose descendants were thought to be part of the Theban elite. An alternative foundation story for Thebes ascribed its foundation to Amphion and Zethus, who were sons of a local river, and thus in some sense, autochthonous (Berman 2004; Kuhr 2006). In Athens the narrative of the relationship between the Athenians and their land became increasingly specified during the classical period. In a seminal article, Vincent Rosivach traced the development whereby an early belief that the primeval Athenian king Erechtheus, who may originally have been a god, was born from the earth (Homer, *Il.* 2.547–548) developed into the notion that the Athenians as a people were autochthonous, born from the earth and inhabitants of the land from time immemorial. It may only have been in the fifth century, when the Athenians became rivals to the Spartans (with their myths of migration and conquest), that they theorized the implications of being indigenous (Rosivach 1987: 294–297).

Athenian autochthony, conceived as birth from the soil of Attica and representing indigenous habitation, would become a staple of the Athenian Funeral Oration and form the bedrock for the Athenian imaginary (Loraux 1986: 148–150; 1993: 49–52, 65–66). It implied that the Athenians were naturally just. Their ancestors fought for justice because the beginning of their life was just; rather than settling the land after they had expelled others, the same land was both mother and fatherland to them (Lysias 2.17).

Although the autochthony theme may not have been well developed at the time the play was composed, the justice of autochthonous inhabitants seems to lie behind Athena's remark in Aeschylus' *Eumenides* (911–912): "Like a gardener, I love the griefless race of these just men" (Tyrrell and Brown 1991: 139). In his commentary on this passage, Alan Sommerstein concludes that the phrase "these just men" refers not to all Athenians but to the Areopagite jurors (Sommerstein 1989: 259). He is perfectly right to point out that not all Athenians are or will be just, but the broader context of the passage suggests that a general characterization is at issue here. Athena is asking the Furies to bestow blessings upon Attica, from heaven, the earth, and the sea, that gentle and sunny breezes blow, that there be abundant fruit from the earth and the flocks, that the *seed* of mortals may be preserved, and that the land may be *more productive* of pious men (although the text is uncertain here: Sommerstein 1989: 259). She then makes the comment quoted above. The bounty and fertility of the earth is closely tied to the production of Athenians, and pious and just ones at that. It is no accident that Athena compares herself to a *phitupoimēn*. This word is translated as "gardener," but literally means "shepherd of plants" (Sommerstein 1989: 259), a conceit that both brings to mind Athena as receiver and nurturer of autochthonous Athenians and stresses that the citizens are not mere plants, but animals (thus mobile and with independent motivation) as well. The relationship of the goddess to her citizens is complex and generates an evocative mixed metaphor; Plato will replicate this complexity when he discusses the relationship of the Athenians to Athena in his *Critias* (see below). For now, the important point is that divinity, earth, and people are tied together in an image that coheres closely with the concept of birth from the land.

Autochthony provided all Athenians with a noble birth, so that democracy took on an aristocratic flavor (Tyrrell and Brown 1991: 195–196). A further consequence was democratic equality; the natural justice of the Athenians led them to seek rule by consensus (Lysias 2.18–19, cf. Plato *Menex.* 239a) (Loraux 1986: 180–202; Rosivach 1987:

303–304; Lape 2010: 18–19). Isocrates sums up several of these themes when he writes in his *Panegyricus* that

> We inhabit this land not because we expelled others, nor did we seize it when it was deserted, nor have we been gathered together as a mixture of many races. Our birth is so noble and so legitimate that we have continued for all time in possession of the land from which we were produced. We are autochthonous and can address our city by the same names with which we address our closest relatives. For we alone of the Greeks can appropriately call the same land nurse and fatherland and mother. (4.24–25)

Racial purity, nobility, and legitimacy all combined to create a powerful vision which seized the moral high ground from lesser migratory peoples, one in which "social actors framed their identification as citizens in a language of birth and ancestry" (Lape 2010: 3).

Neither Herodotus nor Thucydides devotes much energy to the propagandistic possibilities of Athenian autochthony, rather the reverse. Herodotus (1.57–58) has been thought to undermine Athenian pretensions by calling the Athenians Pelasgians who later became Hellenized and learned to speak the language (Thomas 2001: 223–224; Lape 2010: 151–153). Thucydides (1.2) rationalizes autochthony by admitting on the one hand that the same people have always inhabited Attica, but attributing this to the poverty of the Attic soil that made Attica an unattractive target for invasion, and adding that the security of Attica made it popular with refugees. The resultant increase in population enabled Attica to colonize Ionia, but this undermines any claim to be an ethnically "pure" stock. Pericles' funeral oration in Book 2 nods to the notion of autochthony ("the same men always inhabiting the land" 2.36.1), but spends more time on the democratic mindset that forms the Athenian character (Lape 2010: 181: "With the funeral oration he attributes to Pericles, Thucydides does grant Athenian exceptionalism of a sort, but attributes it to culture rather than essence."). We might expect no less in a narrative that declares itself from the outset hostile to the "mythical element" (1.21.1).

Yet for all this intellectual austerity we still see evidence in Thucydides for a fundamental, though embattled, Athenian commitment to the land, albeit differently expressed than in the patriotic fantasies of autochthony. When the historian narrates the changes in Athenian life brought on by the Peloponnesian War, he comments that before the war many Athenians had lived in the countryside rather than the city (2.14–16). Regular invasions of Attica during the war meant that many citizens moved inside the city walls, causing no small hardship and disaffection among those who knew that their farms were being devastated by Peloponnesian forces (2.21, 2.59, 2.65). Pericles, as Thucydides presents him, urged the Athenians to stand fast and prioritize their sea power, considering their land and rural houses to be only a "garden and ornaments of wealth" (2.62.2–3). Whatever the advantages of this strategy, it forced an unwelcome reconceptualization of the relationship of a significant number of Athenians to Attica, separating an agrarian past from a present dependent on naval power. The ramifications of this tension inform Aristophanic comedy in the last part of the fifth-century and the fourth-century theorizing of Plato, Xenophon, and Isocrates.

The connection of farming with comic heroism in Aristophanes has long been recognized. Dicaeopolis in *Acharnians* and Trygaeus in *Peace* are both heroes who take drastic steps to end the Peloponnesian War so that they can return to life on the farm (Wilkins 2000: 103–155; Rosenbloom 2002: 320). *Acharnians* ends with the festive celebration of the rural Dionysia after the hero overcomes the doubts of a bellicose chorus enraged by the devastation of the countryside. *Peace* evinces a similar nostalgia for agrarian life. Not the least of the play's complexities is the way that a chorus initially said to be composed of Greeks from various cities (302), or farmers, merchants, artisans, workers, metics, foreigners, and islanders (296), ends up being characterized as farmers alone. When the chorus attempts to recover the play's eponymous goddess, Trygaeus comments that "the farmers are pulling it off, and nobody else" (Aristoph. *Peace* 511; trans. Henderson 1998), and the chorus subsequently exclaim in delight that they have had an amazing desire to creep back to the countryside (582) (Hanson 1999: 57). This slow focusing of identity has been thought to indicate a move away from the particular towards "a new social order in which a panhellenic chorus comes to accept a primary identity as farmers." On this reading, the chorus would not represent a particular interest group within the Athenian state, but anyone capable of understanding the advantages of peace (McGlew 2001: 87 [quote], 92–94, arguing against Hanson's claim [1999: 213] that the plays of Aristophanes are often anti-urban and anti-elite, and that they give a special status to farmers). It is right, I think, to resist the temptation to see an endorsement of particular groups and interests within the *polis*, but it still seems significant that it is farmers (rather than craftsmen or merchants) who are selected to create a successful identity for the recovery of peace. Comedy oversimplifies the opposition between town and country, trade and agriculture, war and peace, in order to produce a clear and attractive picture (Wilkins 2000: 104–106, 136–138).

One element at work here is surely an association of agriculture with truth-telling and authority that reaches back to Hesiod in the *Works and Days* (Murnaghan 2006: 100–107; see Hanson 1999: 212–216 for further enumeration of agrarian virtues in Greek literature). Theoreticians of the fourth century elaborated a model of the inherent virtue of the agrarian lifestyle. Aristotle declared that the best democracy is agriculturally based, and the best *dēmos* is composed of farmers (*geōrgikos*; *Pol.* 1318b), partly because they have the basics of life and are too busy to covet their neighbor's possessions. The pseudo-Aristotelian *Oeconomica* places agriculture first among occupations

> because it is just. It does not take from men—either willing ones, as trade and wage-earning occupations do, or unwilling ones, as occupations do that are connected with war. It is, in addition, natural, since everyone is naturally nurtured by their mother, as men are by the earth. (1.1343a25–b2)

The author goes on to say that agriculture is conducive to bravery because it produces strong bodies able to endure toil and willing to encounter the enemy (given that farms lie outside the city walls). Xenophon's Socrates too had expatiated on its advantages, labeling it a luxury as well as a way to increase one's estate and improve one's body (*Oec.* 5.1). He observes, additionally, that farming teaches justice (*Oec.* 5.12), and ends his eulogy by calling it the "mother and nurse" of the other arts (*Oec.* 5.17). When Socrates reports his conversation with Ischomachus, an idealized landed gentleman, we find that the earth itself has additional virtues, being open and truthful (*Oec.* 15.11, 20.13).

In her discussion of the ideological work done by this characterization of farming, Sheila Murnaghan (2006: 108) notes perceptively "the slippage between owning the land and working the land, by which the landowner acquires the virtues—and the distinction from other kinds of workers—of the farm laborer." Yet in addition to this generalization of agrarian virtue from the working farmer to the landowner, Xenophon's *Oeconomicus*, as well as the Aristotelian and pseudo-Aristotelian passages discussed here, presents us with an ideal that is profoundly complicit in the strategies of Athenian autochthony. Just as autochthonous Athenians are naturally just because they did not take the land from others, so farming (and farmers) in the pseudo-Aristotelian *Oeconomica* are just because they do not exploit other human beings, whether willingly or unwillingly. This characteristic does not, unfortunately, map onto Xenophon's picture of Ischomachus because the latter is a landowner and employer, yet even here the earth teaches justice because she does good in return to those who cultivate her well. We note also that the *Oeconomica*, although it does not speak of autochthony, takes for granted the metaphor of the earth as a nurse when arguing that farming is natural. Nor is it accidental that Socrates in the *Oeconomicus* calls the earth the "mother and nurse" of the arts, just as Isocrates' autochthonous Athenians in the *Panegyricus* are able to call the earth "nurse and fatherland and mother." The idealization of an agrarian lifestyle may thus be seen as an ideological counterpart to the theme of autochthony. If the first Athenians were sown in and produced from the earth it makes sense, by the operation of a subtle symmetry, to think of them as fundamentally sowers of the earth as well. Athenian ideology inherits and develops the Greek traditions that associate farming with truth-telling and virtue. We may see here a correspondence with the Roman agrarian idealism and commitment to working the land that are the focus of the following chapter.

The myth of Athenian autochthony, then, capitalized upon the moral and social implications of noble and primordial heritage and interacted profitably with the ideal of the virtuous farmer to generate enduring paradigms in classical political theory. As if this were not enough, we may see another reflection of primal connection with the fertile earth in another subject of Athenian self-congratulation, the invention of agriculture. After addressing Athenian autochthony in the passage of the *Panegyricus* quoted above, Isocrates goes on to celebrate Athens' contributions to the rest of Greece. First among these are the fruits of earth that are produced through agriculture, together with the Eleusinian Mysteries. Both were the gift of the goddess Demeter to the city, and Athens, because of her love of humanity, did not keep these gifts to herself, but communicated them to the rest of the world (4.28–29). Because of this, "the majority of Greek cities send to us first fruits of grain every year as a memorial of our ancient benefaction" (4.31). Isocrates is referring here to the practice specified in the Athenian decree concerning Eleusinian first-fruits (*IG* I^3 78), to be dated either to the years immediately preceding the Peloponnesian War, or to around 422 BCE (ML 217–223). The decree orders the contribution of first fruits (offerings from the grain harvest) by the Athenians and their subject allies, invites other Greek cities to do so as well, and cites as authority both ancestral custom and the Delphic oracle. Such an invitation to acknowledge cultural indebtedness would generate impressive symbolic capital whether before or during the Peloponnesian War. No wonder that the late Sicilian historian Diodorus Siculus (or his source) is at pains to emphasize that it was in Sicily that the rape of Persephone occurred and where the goddesses first shared corn with mankind. The Athenians were the first *after the Sicilians* to be given the fruit of wheat (Diod. Sic. 5.2.4, 5.4.3–5). In spite of Diodorus' revisionist attempts, we can see here a final element in a perfect storm of agrarian ideology. Not only were Athenians born from the land, with all that this implied, but they played a significant part in the development of a political identity closely associated with farming. To cap it all, they were the origin of agriculture for the rest of the Greeks and felt no compunction in demanding recognition for this singular service to humanity.

3 The Sea

Perhaps it is now time to counterbalance this impressively coherent picture. We can take our cue from Pericles' exhortation to the Athenians, referred to above, to consider Attica outside the walls of Athens to be an ornament and a garden and to focus primarily on the city as a sea power. For the growth of Athenian power in the fifth century was generated by its naval empire and depended on the participation of rowers, craftsmen, and others who may not have identified as hoplites and farmers. The Periclean citizenship law of 451 BCE (which restricted citizenship to those born of two citizen parents) reinforced an ideology of heredity and connection with the land at a time when the citizen body was less uniform than it had ever been. The same tension underlies the elaborate stress on autochthony in Isocrates, in Euripides' *Ion*, and in the funeral orations of Lysias (who was not himself a citizen of Athens) and others. It may have been the very diversity of Athenian citizens that encouraged so uniform an imaginary.

The Athenian relationship with the sea entailed a relationship with the divinity of the sea, Poseidon. The history of the cult of Poseidon in Attica is still a matter of scholarly debate. It has generally been thought that his cult on the Athenian acropolis postdates the battle of Salamis (480 BCE) and is connected with the rise of the Delian League; the west pediment of the Parthenon may then commemorate the founding of this cult (Binder 1984: 21–22 with further bibliography). On the pediment Athena was shown defeating Poseidon for patronage of Athens and gifting the first domesticated olive tree to Attica. The antiquity of the divine contest for Attica is also disputed; although the pediment is the first representation of the myth in monumental sculpture, it is possible that a vase painting of c.540 BCE may have presented it, and if so we cannot argue that the contest was entirely a mythological reflection of the fifth century naval empire (Marx 2011). Nevertheless, the prominence given to the struggle on the Parthenon suggests that the tension between land and sea was a structuring opposition from the second half of the fifth century onwards. We need not necessarily think that the pediment is intended to counteract the rise in popularity of Poseidon (Donald 1996: 210–220); the presence of both divinities on the pediment can signify that the Athenians had their mythological cake as well as eating it. The role of maritime Poseidon is made prominent by this quasi-erasure, and Aelius Aristides could later comment that, defeat notwithstanding, Poseidon still gave naval superiority to Athens (*Panath.* 42; Binder 1984: 22).

When the Socrates of Plato's *Gorgias* casts his jaundiced eye over the politicians who built up the empire, men like Pericles and Themistocles, he criticizes them for indulging the people rather than making them better (*Gor.* 519a): "they have filled the city with harbors and dockyards and walls and tribute and nonsense like this, but not with justice and moderation" (looking forward to the next chapter, one wonders whether Livy's localization of the farm of Cincinnatus, whence he is called to save the city, as "opposite the very place where the dockyards are now" [3.26] is pointed). The appurtenances of empire meant that "everything from the entire earth comes into the city, and we have the use of the good things that come from here with an enjoyment that is no more familiar than that with which we enjoy the products of the rest of mankind" (Thuc. 2.38).

Pericles' boast deconstructs the opposition between native and foreign that is at the heart of the autochthonic ideal.

The tensions in Athenian democracy in the second half of the fifth century shed further light on the prominence of Aristophanic farmers. David Rosenbloom (2002) has argued that the rise of a new political elite after the death of Pericles, an elite whose wealth derived from "production for exchange" rather than from land, created oppositional political identities in Attic drama, allying the citizen farmer with members of the old nobility against the new politicians (the commercial and industrial elite) and an "urban peasantry." Examples include Trygaeus and Dicaeopolis, mentioned above, but also the noble farmer of Euripides' *Electra*. In the *Orestes* (920) we are told that the farmer (*autourgos*) alone preserves the land. Rosenbloom observes that this play makes a coalition of elite and agrarian values explicit; we may add that the nobility of the one who works the land himself, the *autourgos*, resonates (even in the case of Euripides' Argive farmer) with the inherent nobility of the Athenian *autochthon*.

Rural conservatism, then, seems to reject the fripperies brought to Athens by the empire and the decadence of late fifth-century democracy. This may help to explain the puzzling tradition recorded in Plutarch's *Themistocles*. In discussing the achievements of Themistocles, Plutarch comments that he developed the Piraeus because he wished to fit the city to the sea. By so doing, he was opposing the policies of the "ancient kings of the Athenians," who,

> making it their business to detach the citizens from the sea and accustom them to live without sailing but rather by planting the land, transmitted the story about Athena, that when she contended with Poseidon over the land, she won the victory by showing to the jury the sacred olive. But Themistocles did not, as the comic poet says, "knead the Peiraeus for the city," but fastened the city to the Peiraeus and the land to the sea. So he increased the *dēmos* at the expense of the best people and filled it with boldness, since power came into the hands of sailors and boatswains and helmsmen. Accordingly later on the Thirty turned around towards the land the speaker's platform on the Pnyx, which had been constructed to look towards the sea, thinking that the maritime empire was the root of democracy and that farmers were less troubled by oligarchy. (*Them.* 19.3–4)

Although the orientation of the Pnyx did change at the end of the fifth century, a view of the sea was never in question, and it is doubtful that the Thirty engaged in building operations on the Pnyx. Yet so strong was the association between fifth-century democracy and the sea that this incorrect tradition found its way into Plutarch's sources, coupled to a retrojection of the land/sea tension onto the ancient kings of Athens that makes their conservative agrarianism the origin of the story about the contest of Athena and Poseidon for the city.

4 Plato and the Construction of the Past

We are fortunate to have in Plato both a thinker and a commentator who pondered deeply the issues at stake in the construction of the past, and a mythologizer in his own right. The second part of this essay will survey Plato's readings and re-creations of the myth of autochthony and his interventions on the issue of politics and the sea. We may start with his *Menexenus*: a parodic reimagination of the well-worn topoi of the funeral oration, clarifying them through exaggeration (Loraux 1986: 94). The oration that Socrates affects to report in this dialogue starts with autochthony (237b–c), continues with the quarrel of the gods (i.e. Athena and Poseidon) over patronage (proving that the land is dear to the gods, 237c), and then implies that it was in Attica that humankind was first produced by the earth. After emphasizing that wheat was first produced in Attica (237e–238a), Socrates passes on to constitutional matters, equating Athenian democracy with aristocracy (238c–d) and attributing this constitution to equality of birth ("all brothers from one mother"), which in turn leads to equality under the law: *isogonia* generates *isonomia* (238e–239a).

The intense packing of these patriotic commonplaces in the *Menexenus* confirms their interrelationship, yet a reading of the *Republic*, and in particular the "noble lie" of Book 3, shows that the specifically democratic thematic configuration we meet in the funeral oration was not the only possibility. The discussion of the ideal state in the *Republic* establishes early on that in a successful city there will have to be a principle of specialization: each citizen should do what he is good at. This principle leads to the idea that there will have to be a specialized fighting (and in the end, governing) class. In order to produce this ordered and hierarchical society, education will have to be of a particular sort, a requirement that leads to Socrates' famous strictures on the form and content of poetry. In the course of this discussion, when dealing with the topic of falsehood, Socrates makes an interesting concession. Sometimes a "falsehood in words" can be useful. One example is "in the mythical tales we were just now speaking about, because we do not know what the truth is about ancient matters, we make them useful by likening falsehood to truth" (2.382c–d). It seems that the "historical" reconstruction of ancient events is a matter of informed inference, ideally governed by principles of social and moral utility. This observation has obvious relevance for myths of Athenian origins and primacy and stands behind the generation of the noble lie (cf. Saxonhouse 1986). Autochthony and the contest of Athena and Poseidon over Athens are useful social fables, emphasizing social pride and cohesion. Even though the latter was included in the *Menexenus* it is unlikely that it would find a place in the ideal city of the *Republic*, since we learn in that dialogue that no poet should portray strife and contention among the gods (379d).

Autochthony is another matter. Belief in such a narrative is well suited to produce just the kind of citizen Socrates wants. After he has discussed the training of the guardian class, therefore, Socrates suggests that they devise a "noble falsehood"—one of the necessary ones they were just talking about (Schofield 2007: 149). He describes it as "a Phoenician tale, one that has previously occurred already in many places, as the poets say, and as they have persuaded people to believe, but never in our time, nor do I know whether it could happen" (*Rep.* 414b–c). The idea is to persuade the inhabitants of the city that their training and education were a dream, and that they were really being molded and nurtured within the earth, together with their weapons or tools. When they were completed, the earth released them. They must, therefore, think of the earth as their mother and nurse, defend her if attacked, and consider the rest of the citizens as their earthborn brothers. They will be told that the god who molded them mixed gold into some of them, the ones who were meant to rule. Others (the auxiliaries) were mixed with silver, while the famers and the rest of the craftsmen were mixed with iron and bronze respectively. Their children will for the most part be born admixed with the same metal as their parents; when anomalies happen (e.g. a gold child being born from iron parents or the reverse) the citizens must be vigilant and make sure that the child is assigned to the proper class for education. Although it seems unlikely to the interlocutors that the first citizens will believe this, they hope that subsequent generations may, and conclude that the myth will help them care for the city and for each other (414d–415d).

This "myth" is remarkable both for its similarities to and its differences from the Athenian autochthony narrative. By calling it a "Phoenician" tale, Socrates directs our attention away from Athens and toward Thebes, founded by the Phoenician Cadmus. Why Thebes? Because Socrates needs his citizens to be formed within the earth along with the characteristic implements they will use in life (weapons or tools). Like the Theban *spartoi*, then, who emerged from the earth fully armed, they are not born naked but with equipment. This will make it easier to assign them to the correct social class. Yet from another perspective, these earthborn citizens are not at all like the Thebans. In one version of the story found in the Athenian mythographer Pherecydes, Cadmus was afraid when the *spartoi* were born and threw a stone into their midst. Thinking that they were under attack from each other they immediately started fighting until only five were left. (In another less dominant version—perhaps from Hellanicus—only five *spartoi* emerged and there was no fight) (Gantz 1993: 468–469). Such internecine strife would be an unwelcome paradigm for Socrates' utopia, so Socrates is at pains to focus on love for the land and for one's fellow citizens. This aspect of reciprocal care is, as we have seen, one of the most prominent elements in the Athenian autochthony narrative as it developed in the later fifth century and after, where equality of birth from the land creates political equality and a strong connection to the earth. It is worth noting, however, that mutual respect and brotherhood were not necessary and permanent elements even of Athenian narrative. A body of tradition concerning early autochthonous kings of Athens preserved in Apollodorus (3.14–3.15) indicated that they had a tendency to die childless or fight amongst themselves (Tyrrell and Brown 1991: 142). Civic strife could thus easily find a place in the story line, although this is not an aspect on which the composers of funeral orations choose to linger. Perhaps, indeed, the need to insist on general brotherhood became more pressing in the fourth century precisely because of the faction that characterized Athenian political life at the end of the fifth. It is tempting, and probably correct, to suspect some irony in Socrates' mythologizing here. The Athenians are as gullible as the next Greek (at *Laws* 2.663e–664a the story of Cadmus and the birth of the armed men from the dragon's teeth is used to prove that the young can be persuaded of anything), but one thing they would never do is adopt a myth that entrenched a strong division of classes. It is not so much that the Athenians could never accept a story of earthborn men as that they could never accept that political and governing capacity is unequally distributed within the population.

The noble lie of the *Republic* is thus an amalgam of Theban and Athenian elements—not to mention Hesiod, whose myth of the five ages of man at *Works and Days* 106–201 (gold, silver, bronze, heroic, and iron) is another model, although Plato has adapted the story so that the different metal races do not succeed each other diachronically but exist synchronically within the same society (Adam 1902: 193; cf. Schofield 2007: 138; Pappas 2011: 69–71). This charter myth has been crafted to accommodate a structured society different from Athens and from Thebes as well. It is evident that Plato has theorized the function and manipulability of autochthonic myth. We may note particularly that his version is a thoroughgoing deconstruction of the thematic bundling discussed in the first part of this essay, where I associated agrarian virtue with Athenian autochthony and the primacy of Attic agriculture. By using Theban myth as his basis, Plato has presented the story through a military filter, where farm implements take second place to weapons. Farmers are only one class in the new society, and they are structurally equivalent to craftsmen. While Aristophanes' comic utopia may privilege the agrarian ideal, Plato's dethrones it.

This is not to say that Plato's myth of origins in the *Republic* envisages a non-agrarian basis for society, even though he acknowledges the need for trade and exchange. If we move on to the *Laws*, we can see that trade must be kept firmly in its place. When the interlocutors in that dialogue discuss founding a new city, the Athenian Stranger is adamant that it cannot be located too close to the sea, and is disappointed that a potential site has good harbors:

> It is a pleasant thing to have the sea nearby on a daily basis, but it is in truth a very salty and bitter neighbor. By filling it full of commerce and money-making through trade, and engendering psychic habits that are intrusive and suspicious, it makes the city suspicious and unfriendly to itself and towards the rest of mankind as well. (705a)

He takes comfort, however, in the ruggedness of the countryside, which means that there will not be too much to export. Export once again entails large amounts of currency, which would be a great impediment to the development of a noble and just character in the citizens (705a–b).

This anti-maritime ideology has fascinating implications for the Athenian's (re)construction of the Greek past in myth and history (as we might expect from the author of the *Gorgias* passage considered earlier). After his disapproving comments on the effects of too much trade, the Athenian is pleased to learn that the area of the future city is not particularly well equipped with the kind of wood necessary for shipbuilding. This will prevent the city from copying its military antagonists to its own detriment. As an example of what he means, he narrates how Minos of Crete once extracted a cruel tribute from Athens (the youths and maidens who became the victims of the Minotaur, until Theseus sailed with them and killed the monster). At that time, we learn, the Athenians did not have the navy they later had, nor did Attica produce much wood for shipbuilding. They could not, therefore, simply repel the Cretans (*Laws* 706a–b). Paradoxically, this was a good thing, since naval warfare accustoms men to retreat to their ships without dishonor (as opposed to hoplite warfare, where the soldier must bravely stand his ground). Cities whose power comes from their navy do not honor the noblest elements in their city; rather, they depend on helmsmen and captains and rowers and "all sorts of not very worthy men" (707a–b). To his credit, Clinias, the Cretan interlocutor, objects that the naval battle at Salamis saved Greece. But the Athenian will have none of it:

> I … say that the infantry battles that took place at Marathon and Plataea began and finished (respectively) the salvation of the Greeks. And they made the Greeks better, but the other battles did not—if we may speak like this about the battles that helped to save us at that time, for I will add the battle at Artemisium to the one at Salamis. We are now looking at the excellence of a constitution and are investigating the nature of the land and the arrangement of the laws, not considering safety to be the one most valuable thing for men, as the many do, but being as good as possible … (707c–d)

This is a startlingly tendentious interpretation of Minos' oppression of the Athenians and of the Persian Wars (cf. Hanson 1999: 328–329). Plato has taken Thucydides' hypothesis

(1.4) of Minoan sea power and a naval empire and used it to paint a moralizing picture of pre-maritime Athens with pointed implications for the present. Thucydides' reconstruction of the Greek past in his "Archaeology" had stressed the growth of naval power and the importance of financial capital. Plato reads Thucydides against the grain, so that the march of history becomes an increase in corruption; every reader would measure the Athenian's comments against Athenian naval history and present ambition. The interpretation of the battles of the Persian Wars is even more extreme. Not only does it fly explicitly in the face of popular tradition about what saved Greece in the early fifth century, but it suggests that defeat at the hands of the Persians might in some respects have been preferable to the development of a navy and its accompanying ethical decay. It could not be clearer that the moralizing politician can and should rewrite and reinterpret mythological or historical traditions.

The best example of this imperative is of course the famous narrative of Athens and Atlantis narrated in Plato's *Timaeus* and *Critias*, where we are presented with a story purportedly preserved through the ages by Egyptian priests and told in order to satisfy Socrates' desire to hear about the deeds and achievements of an ideal state composed along the lines laid down in the *Republic*. The narrative tells how ancient Athens, a virtuous and hierarchically ordered state, once opposed the mighty naval empire of Atlantis (a state that had declined from its ancient morality through greed and ambition). Detailed analysis (Morgan 1998) shows that the representation of Athens and Atlantis recycles many of the tropes of the funeral oration and other Athenian festival speeches in order to create a charter myth for fourth-century Athens. It will come as no surprise to read that Plato engineers the opposition to showcase the perils of a navally inflected polity. The state of Atlantis is sponsored by Poseidon. Its rulers are his direct descendants and they preside over a city glittering with precious metals and well equipped with dockyards of every kind. Initially, they are able to preserve their divine inheritance of virtue, but in the end their expansionism leads them to try to conquer Europe. Athens is the state that defeats them and ensures the freedom of the lands within the Pillars of Heracles.

This Athens is, however, in no way similar to the state that defeated the Persians, developed a naval empire, lost the Peloponnesian War, and spent the first half of the fourth century trying to regain its maritime influence. Indeed, it seems quite clear that it is Atlantis onto which classical Athens is mapped and thus depreciated (Vidal-Naquet 1964; Brisson 1970; Morgan 1998). Primeval Athens is characterized by a rich and fertile countryside—Plato's solution to inconsistent Athenian representations that sometimes stressed the fertility of Attica and sometimes (as in Thucydides' comments on Attic soil, considered above) the poverty of the soil and the need for imports (cf. Wilkins 2000: 108). The Acropolis used to be much larger and the rock that remains today is the mere skeleton of a much larger and better-endowed high ground. Of particular interest is the adaptation of the autochthony myth. At *Timaeus* 23e we are told that Athena received from the earth and from Hephaestus the "seed" of the Athenian race, and this is repeated at *Critias* 109d:

> Hephaestus and Athena, since they had a common nature, a fraternal one deriving from the same father, and since they had the same goals because of their love of wisdom and of skill, both took this land as one allotment, naturally fitted and suitable to excellence and intelligence as it was, and they created in it autochthonous and good men, and put in their minds the ordering of their state.

We note that the uncomfortable sexual background of the story of Athenian autochthony is elided. No longer does Hephaestus comically pursue Athena with erect phallus, only to ejaculate on her thigh. This means that, rather than the Athenians being generated from the seed of Hephaestus that Athena wiped off and threw to the earth, they are "created in" the earth, although the precise mechanism is vague. Given the general strictures Plato places on divine behavior, attempted rape seems out of the question; instead divine unanimity and kinship are emphasized. Once humans inhabit the land, the military class is separated off, while the land is worked by "men who were truly farmers and who practiced only this, well-shaped and lovers of the noble" (*Crit.* 111e). Autochthony and agrarian idealism are here mixed with the principle of occupational specialization to decidedly undemocratic effect. In this idealized Attica there is no conflict between city and countryside, nor between the effects of a land-based vs. sea-based polity. Athens' maritime trajectory and its disastrous results are projected onto Atlantis. Any thought that Poseidon could have been a contender for presiding honors in Athens is forestalled by Critias' pointed and programmatic assertion that it would be incorrect to suggest that the gods entered into any kind of strife concerning the lands that belonged to them (*Crit.* 109b).

Plato's treatment of the relationship of a polis to the land and the sea is, as we have seen, differently inflected in different dialogues. The self-consciousness with which he manipulates the traditions of autochthony and maritime destiny is neat confirmation (if any were needed) of their structuring role in the Athenian imagination. The agrarian ideal, which acts in Aristophanes as a symbol of a happier past and as a conceptual refuge in the present, sees its pragmatic value decreased in Plato even as its metaphorical valence continues (good citizens must treat the land as their mother and nurse). Before concluding this section, however, it is worth pondering briefly the place and symbolic power of pastoralism in the Platonic corpus as a complement to agrarian and marine ideologies. It seems that pastoralism was for Plato a kind of zero grade of human existence. When civilization is wiped out through periodic cataclysms in the narrative of the *Timaeus*, only herdsmen are left, illiterate and without culture (*Tim.* 23a–b); the *Laws* similarly envisions herding as the earliest stage of existence (3.677e–679a). There was, of course, no politics at this point. Indeed, Plato seems to like using the herdsman as an image of absolute control. In the *Statesman* in the course of the search for the ideal ruler, the interlocutors consider the life of mankind in the Age of Cronus, when divine spirits ruled men like herdsmen. There was no agriculture at this time; the earth brought forth food for men spontaneously. It seems evident that there was no political community and very little culture either. Even though the ideal lawgiver will have something of the herdsman about him (Merrill 2003; cf. Brock 2013: 43–52, 149–150), the relationship between the herder and his flock is an uncomfortable model for a participatory community (as its employment in the fraught discussion of *Republic* Book 1 proves). In *Critias* the gods are again herdsmen, but the combination of imagery here is surprising. The gods:

> peopled the lands, and when they had peopled them, they nurtured us as their possessions and creatures, like herdsmen do their flocks, except that they did not use physical force, like shepherds who drive their flocks to pasture with a blow, but they directed us from where an animal is most manageable, guiding us from the stern, fastening onto our souls with persuasion like a rudder in accordance with their intent. Leading us like this, they steered everything mortal. (*Crit.* 109b–c)

A few sentences later Athena and Hephaestus plant the Athenians like farmers. In the space of one page, then, the idealized relationship of humans to the gods is conceived in terms of pastoral, agrarian, and naval imagery. One might conclude from this the radical contingency of all systems of imagery when one is talking about the interaction of the human with the divine, whether retrojected into the past or anticipated in the future. With Athena in charge it does not matter whether one is a sheep, a seed, or a ship. When it comes to human politicians and leaders, however, all metaphor is imperfect.

5 Conclusion

In her contribution to this volume, Mary Jaeger (Chapter 5) presents a fascinating reading of the Roman idealization of agrarian self-sufficiency with particular reference to the story of the summoning of Cincinnatus from his plough to serve as dictator and to the connection of republican values with the production and consumption of food. She stresses repeated acts of commitment to the land and the personal choices that lead to these acts. It may be useful to conclude by noting briefly some continuities and discontinuities between the material presented in this chapter and what is shortly to follow. The idealization of agriculture is an obvious point of comparison. We have seen how various Greek authors engage with and theorize the agricultural way of life as a preferred alternative to a life of trade. If the myth of agrarian self-sufficiency has been viewed "as one, if not *the*, pillar of Roman *libertas*," it is no less the case that this self-sufficiency has been seen as fundamental to the *polis* in genres as diverse as Aristophanic comedy and Aristotelian philosophy, not to mention modern scholarship (Hanson 1999).

We have also encountered the contrast between virtuous rural simplicity and urban luxury and decadence. Although the Romans may have found it attractive to equate a simple meal with the preservation of republican freedom, in Athens things were somewhat more complicated. It is certainly true that the consumption of luxurious food, fish in particular, could be seen as a sign of decadence. Plato's and Xenophon's Socrates saw it as such, and John Wilkins has identified "a civic identity of abstemious eating and restraint" as one aspect of the Athenian ideology of food (Davidson 1997: 12–26; Wilkins 2000: 97, 153). The guardians in the *Republic* will not be allowed to eat fish or Attic pastries (404b–d), and no unregulated sex will be permitted. Yet when Socrates begins to design his idealized city in this dialogue, it does not take much to persuade him that he must design not just a simple and basic city, the "city of pigs," but a "luxurious" (*truphōsan*) city, with all modern dining conveniences such as couches, relishes, incense, and courtesans (372c–373a). This is what it takes to make the prospect of the city come alive in the minds of his interlocutors. They have, after all, grown up watching Attic comedy in which utopian fantasies of the Age of Cronus and other ideal situations presented the provision of automatic and often ready-cooked food (Wilkins 2000: 110–116). As James Davidson has argued in his political history of Athenian appetites, comedy's emphasis on food, drink, and sex is evidence of a certain "class unconsciousness"; even Aristophanes' agrarian heroes have an appetite for banquets and that slippery category of consumption, the relish (*opson*) (Davidson 1997: 234–238; cf. Wilkins 2000: 162: "Luxury, provided it is democratic, is ideologically desirable for the Athenian demos"). What was important was the ability to control one's appetite; inability to do so was the mark of a flawed citizen, one with a tendency toward tyrannical aspiration (Davidson 1997: 278–301).

A passion for luxurious food and for fish (the pre-eminent *opson*) returns us for a final time to Poseidon and Athens' naval hegemony and thence to the rich men in the comedy of Antiphanes who think that the whole point of a naval empire is to ensure the safe transportation of fish into Athens (Antiphanes fr. 188 *PCG*; Davidson 1997: 264–265). The Athenians' commitment to the land and to an agrarian ideal in the classical period was tempered by an enthusiasm for the perks of empire.

Even if Aristophanes' farmer chorus might be at home in a Roman setting it remains true that in Athens at least the commitment to the land of Attica was eventually conceived as a matter of quasi-biological destiny. Birth from the land and the complex of kinship metaphors associated with it tendentiously represent *ēthos* as a function of heredity. Plato exposes the underpinnings of this ideology, both implicitly and explicitly. Yet he also strikes at the heart of the fantasy that could proclaim a farmer to be a useful arbiter in civic government or that could call the famer from his plough to lead the city. Indeed, Cincinnatus' concern (as portrayed in Dionysius of Halicarnassus) that leaving his farm in order to be dictator will mean that his family will not have enough to eat is an interesting counterpoint to Plato's insistence on occupational specialization; *his* guardians will not be farmers, and the state in the *Republic* is organized precisely so that such a conflict of interest could never arise. Plato's stubbornness on this point probably reflects just how fundamental agrarian and political multi-tasking was to some segments of the ancient Greek imagination.

REFERENCES

Adam, J. 1902. *The Republic of Plato*. 2 vols. Cambridge.

Berman, Daniel. 2004. "The Double Foundation of Boiotian Thebes." *TAPA* 134: 1–22.

Binder, J. 1984. "The West Pediment of the Parthenon: Poseidon." In K. Riggsby, ed., *Studies Presented to Sterling Dow on his Eightieth Birthday*. Greek, Roman and Byzantine Monographs 10. Durham, NC, 15–22.

Brisson, L.P. 1970. "De la philosophie politique à l'épopée. Le 'Critias' de Platon." *RMM* 75: 402–438.

Brock, R. 2013. *Greek Political Imagery from Homer to Aristotle*. London.

Cohen, E. 2000. *The Athenian Nation*. Princeton.

Davidson, J. 1997. *Courtesans and Fishcakes: The Consuming Passions of Classical Athens*. London.

Donald, I.A. 1996. "Athena and Poseidon: The Contest for Athens." Diss. University of Alberta, Edmonton.

Gantz, T. N. 1993. *Early Greek Myth: A Guide to Literary and Artistic Sources*. Baltimore.

Hall, J. 1997. *Ethnic Identity in Greek Antiquity*. Cambridge.

Hall, J. 2002. *Hellenicity: Between Ethnicity and Culture*. Chicago.

Hanson, V.D. 1999. *The Other Greeks: The Family Farm and the Agrarian Roots of Western Civilization*. Berkeley.

Henderson, J.J., trans. 1998. *Aristophanes: Clouds. Wasps. Peace*. Cambridge, MA.

Konstan, D. 2001. "*To Hellēnikon Ethnos*: Ethnicity and the Construction of Ancient Greek Identity." In Irad Malkin, ed., *Ancient Perceptions of Greek Ethnicity*. Cambridge, MA, 29–50.

Kowalzig, B. 2007. *Singing for the Gods*. Oxford.

Kuhr, A. 2006. "Invading Boeotia. Polis and Ethnos in the Mirror of Theban Foundation Myths." *Hermes* 134: 367–372.

Lape, S. 2010. *Race and Citizen Identity in the Classical Athenian Democracy*. Cambridge.

Loraux, N. 1986. *The Invention of Athens: The Funeral Oration in the Classical City*. Trans. A. Sheridan. Cambridge.

Loraux, N. 1993. *The Children of Athena: Athenian Ideas about Citizenship and the Division between the Sexes.* Trans. C. Levine. Princeton.

Malkin, I. 1994. *Myth and Territory in the Spartan Mediterranean*. Cambridge.

Malkin, I. 1998. *The Returns of Odysseus: Colonization and Ethnicity*. Berkeley.

Marx, P. 2011. "Athens NM Acropolis 923 and the Contest between Athena and Poseidon for the Land of Attica." *Antike Kunst* 54: 21–40.

McGlew, J. 2001. "Identity and Ideology: The Farmer Chorus of Aristophanes' *Peace.*" *Syllecta Classica* 12: 74–97.

Merrill, J.P. 2003. "The Organization of Plato's *Statesman* and the Statesman's Rule as a Herdsman." *Phoenix* 57: 35–56.

Morgan, K. 1998. "Designer History. Plato's Atlantis Story and Fourth-Century Ideology." *JHS* 118: 101–118.

Murnaghan, S. 2006. "Farming, Authority, and Truth-Telling in the Greek Tradition." In Rosen and Sluiter 2006: 93–118.

Pappas, N. 2011. "Autochthony in Plato's *Menexenus.*" *Philosophical Inquiry* 34: 66–80.

Rosen R. and Sluiter, I., eds. 2006. *City, Countryside, and the Spatial Organization of Value in Classical Antiquity*. Mnemosyne Supplements 279. Leiden.

Rosenbloom, D. 2002. "From *Ponēros* to *Pharmakos*: Theater, Social Drama, and Revolution in Athens, 428–404 BCE." *ClAnt* 21: 283–346.

Rosivach, V.J. 1987. "Autochthony and the Athenians." *CQ* 37: 294–306.

Saïd, Suzanne. 2001. "The Discourse of Identity in Greek Rhetoric from Isocrates to Aristides." In I. Malkin, ed., *Ancient Perceptions of Greek Ethnicity*. Center for Hellenic Studies Colloquia 5. Cambridge, MA, 275–299.

Saxonhouse, A. 1986. "Myths and the Origins of Cities: Reflections on the Autochthony Theme in Euripides' *Ion.*" In P. Euben, ed., *Greek Tragedy and Political Theory*. Berkeley, 252–273.

Schofield, M. 2007. "The Noble Lie." In G.R.F. Ferrari, ed., *The Cambridge Companion to Plato's Republic*. Cambridge, 138–164.

Sommerstein, A. 1989. *Aeschylus. Eumenides*. Cambridge.

Thomas, R. 2001. "Ethnicity, Genealogy, and Hellenism in Herodotus." In I. Malkin, ed., *Ancient Perceptions of Greek Ethnicity*. Cambridge, MA, 213–233.

Tyrrell, Wm. and F. Brown. 1991. *Athenian Myths and Institutions*. Oxford.

Vidal-Naquet, P. 1964. "Athènes et l'Atlantide : Structure et signification d'un mythe platonicien." *REG* 77: 420–444.

Wilkins, J. 2000. *The Boastful Chef: The Discourse of Food in Ancient Greek Comedy*. Oxford.

FURTHER READING

For understanding the self-conception of Athens, Loraux (1986) is still fundamental; more recently see Lape 2010. A different take on Athenian identity is presented by Cohen (2000). For Hellenic identities more generally and their construction through myth (among other strategies), the work of Hall (1997 and 2002) is important. Malkin (1994) focuses on myth and Spartan identity, while his 1998 book turns to the significance of myths of return from the Trojan War for constructions of ethnicity in the Mediterranean. Kowalzig 2007 is a stimulating exploration of aetiological myth presented in choral performance in a variety of Greek locations. For the opposition between town and country in classical antiquity, see the essays in Rosen and Sluiter 2006), and on agrarian ideology Hanson's (controversial) book (1999).

CHAPTER 5

Agriculture and Identity in Roman Myth

Mary Jaeger

1 Introduction

Serere rem publicam, "to plant a commonwealth." The metaphor is Cicero's, from his overview of Rome's early history in *De re publica* 2 (Kronenberg 2009). Here the dialogue's central figure, Scipio Aemilianus, introduces Romulus' choice of the site for Rome (2.5):

> [h]e is said to be the first to have thought of founding a city with auspices and establishing the commonwealth. Moreover he chose an incredibly suitable location for the city, a matter to be looked to most carefully by anyone attempting to plant a commonwealth that will endure.

Scipio's words bring to mind an image of Romulus the farmer choosing agricultural land in the manner of Cato's ideal *agricola* selecting a farm. In fact Scipio has already pointed out (2.4) that the shepherds who rescued the infant Romulus brought him up "in rustic pursuits and labor" (*in agresti cultu laboreque*). Although taken out of context the expression *agresti cultu* is vague enough to encompass all aspects of a rural upbringing, the addition of *labor* and Cicero's metaphor together skew its meaning away from the pastoral towards the agrarian.

In these ideas of selection and cultivation the Roman foundation myth differs from, for example, the Athenian; for unlike the Athenians, the Romans had no myth of autochthony. Rather a combination of personal choice, divine intervention, the occasional participation of the landscape itself and, most of all, an insistence on repeated acts of commitment to the place, distinguish the story of Rome's origins.

Likewise, affirmations of a particularly Roman commitment to working the land characterize the writing of the middle, late, and collapsing Republic (e.g., Cato's *De agri*

A Companion to Greek Democracy and the Roman Republic, First Edition. Edited by Dean Hammer.

cultura; Cicero, *De rep.* 2.4–5; *Sen.* 51–64; Varro *RR*; and Virgil's *Georgics*, his song of the *Italian* earth; see also de Ligt, Chapter 21, on Roman economic attitudes and Stewart, Chapter 23, on slaves). A good example of such affirmation appears in Polybius when, praising Scipio Aemilianus' temperance, the historian sets it against the licentiousness of Scipio's contemporaries, wayward and corrupt lovers of luxury all (31.24.5 and 5a):

> For some had given themselves up to love affairs with boys and others to courtesans, and many to musical entertainments and drinking parties and the attendant extravagance, having during the war with Perseus swiftly taken up Greek licentiousness in this respect. And so great was the incontinence that had broken out among the young men in such matters, that many paid a talent for a boy lover and many three hundred drachmas for a jar of pickled fish from Pontus. In response to these things, Marcus [Cato] said once in a speech addressed to the people [πρὸς τὸν δῆμον] that one might particularly recognize the republic's progression towards the worse from the following [ὅτι μάλιστ' ἂν κατίδοιεν τὴν ἐπὶ (τὸ) χεῖρον προκοπὴν τῆς πολιτείας ἐκ τουτών]: when pretty boys fetch more than fields, and jars of pickled fish more than plowmen [ὅταν πωλούμενοι πλεῖον εὑρίσκωσιν οἱ μὲν εὐπρεπεῖς παῖδες τῶν ἀγρῶν, τὰ δὲ κεράμια τοῦ ταρίχου τῶν ζευγηλατῶν].[1]

If the reconstruction of this passage is correct (Walbank 1979: 501), Polybius uses Cato's comment on how to measure the deterioration of the Republic to reinforce his own remarks about the vices of young Romans. After all, what more authoritative critic of *mores* than the stern censor of 184 BCE? Polybius points out the Roman youth's "Greek licentiousness" and "incontinence"; Cato's speech echoes these criticisms down to the details, the outlay on pretty boys and expensive pickled fish.

Setting aside any discussion of the cost of pickled fish in the second century BCE, except to note that it was not yet a cheap and ubiquitous relish (Walbank 1979: 500), I want to make some observations that aim to defamiliarize slightly this apparently stock diatribe against luxury (Horsfall 2003: 30). In making these observations, I also aim to refocus attention on the production and consumption of food and its role in creating community. First, Cato's remark links the condition of the *politeia* to the relative value placed on agriculture. His specific examples (pretty boys and pickled fish, fields and plowmen) are not themselves the cause of decline; rather their prices provide the means by which one can assess decline: what caused the decline in the *politeia* was a shift in the location of value, from necessity to luxury, from the means of producing locally the staff of life to the cost of consuming imported relish. The passage's persuasive force, then, relies on Cato and the people, and Polybius and his readers, coming to an agreement about value, an agreement to place a premium on production, the local, sobriety, sexual restraint and maturity, over against consumption, the foreign, drunkenness, sexual indulgence, and youth. And the productive values endorsed are agrarian, not pastoral: Cato mentions field and plowman, not shepherd and sheep.

Second, Polybius says that Cato addressed his speech to the people. We know neither its context nor the people's response (Walbank 1979: 501); but Cato's examples appear to have been chosen for their potential effect on his listeners, many of whom owned only small amounts of farmland, if any, many of whom often did not get enough to eat (Garnsey 1999: 2–4; 34–61), and for whom 300 drachmas spent on pickled fish would be a considerable sum (Walbank 1979: 510). These agrarian images receive additional force from Cato's own self-proclaimed identity—and ostentatiously simple life—as farmer and as author of the *De agri cultura* (Astin 1978: 240–266). The people, as portrayed by Polybius, would be receptive, more perhaps because of Cato's status as farmer as well as censor, Polybius' readers, more perhaps because of Cato's status as author. Plain-spoken, as is evident from his own writing, plain-living too, if his later portrayal by Cicero and Plutarch and others reflects objective reality, a *nouus homo* (first of his family to reach the Senate), Cato, as Polybius shows him here, makes his point by invoking values consistent with both his way of life and that of the people.

Finally, Polybius' reference to drinking parties and Cato's to pickled fish and plowmen bring together the major components of an ancient Mediterranean meal: cereal of some kind, represented by field and plowman; drink, by the *symposia*; and the cereal's supplement, or relish, represented by the pickled fish (Davidson 1997; Purcell 2003). Thus the passage conjures up, albeit indirectly, the image of the community divided along the fault lines within a meal, with its more virtuous members gathered together around the staff of life. Let young aristocrats have their drinking parties and expensive, imported relish; Cato and the people know the worth of bread or porridge made from grain grown locally (Shaw 1982–83; Garnsey 1999: 17–19; Purcell 2003).

2 Ideology and Agrarian Writing: The Scholarship

The expression of cultural values by means of relative cost in the Polybius passage figures prominently in Cato's own writing on agriculture. Thomas Habinek's reading of the opening of the *De agri cultura* draws attention to the repetition of the verb *existimare* and related noun *existimatio* in both their original sense of placing a value on an item and the metaphorical sense of judging a person's worth. He argues that, as a literary intervention into the cultural politics of the middle Republic, the *De agri cultura* played an important role in the creation of Latin literature and conveyed the anxieties of an aristocracy whose nature was shifting. Accordingly, Cato uses these terms of evaluation to create an authoritative past that validates his own position as aristocrat and farmer: *maiores nostri* reckoned that farmers were more valuable than merchants and money-lenders; therefore Cato does too, and he expects readers to do so as well (Habinek 1998: 45–50; Reay 2005: 337). Cato expressed his evaluation quantitatively: *maiores nostri* fined thieves twice the usual indemnity and money-lenders four times. From these relative numbers, says Cato, in an expression that calls to mind his price comparisons in Polybius, one can reckon how much worse they considered the money-lender than the thief (*quanto peiorem ciuem existimarint foeneratorem quam furem hinc licet existimare*, pr. 1).

The Romans' idealization of agriculture is well known, as is their fetishization of virtuous poverty and simple living (e.g. Garnsey 1999: 72; Saller 1994: 3; Woolf 2006; Thibodeau 2010). Both topics have received increased attention during the past two decades, as scholars have examined the various political and cultural ideologies inherent in Roman agricultural discourse (e.g. Garnsey 1988, 1998, 1999; Habinek 1998; Reay 1998, 2005; Shaw 1982–83; Woolf 2006; Thibodeau 2011). Their work has shown how classical descriptions of meat-eaters and milk-drinkers from Homer on contributed to a general Graeco-Roman ideology that placed agriculture and the eating of grain at the center of civilization (Shaw 1982–83: 5–31). Attention to Roman self-consciousness about diet has shed light on the nature of Romanness (Purcell 2003); and close examination of discussions of grain from the early empire has both helped to identify "values that genuinely united Romans of different statuses" and shown how changes in diet and agriculture became a means of narrating historical change at Rome (Purcell 2003: 329–330). Other recent work has explored the ideology of agrarian literature as satire and has called into question how such texts as Xenophon's *Oeconomicus*, Varro's *De re rustica*, and Virgil's *Georgics* construct agriculture as an ideal version of politics (Kronenberg 2009). In sum, the scholarship of the past twenty years has demonstrated clearly that discussions of farming, and even brief references to food—farming's main product after all—are not neutral testimony to the farming and eating habits of the past; rather, they bear ideological weight and consequently deserve careful attention (Gowers 1993).

What follows responds to this work by re-examining how the figure of Cato, with his interest in relative economic values, participates in the construction of a republican myth. The myth is that of agrarian self-sufficiency as one, if not *the*, pillar of Roman *libertas*. Modeling the cohesion of community around the idea of the Roman meal, this myth of agrarian self-sufficiency constructs a past in which agreement about the relative value of various foodstuffs held the city together in times of constitutional crisis. Our re-examination of Cato involves rereading what appears to be a very old story about economics and food, an undervalued plowman, and a modest field, a story Polybius' Cato could—and very well may—have told.

3 The Cincinnatus Story and the Roman Meal

This is the story of L. Quinctius Cincinnatus, impoverished after paying bail for his son Caeso, who had been charged on a capital offense. Cincinnatus left Rome to farm his meager acreage, whence he was recalled from his plow to save his city in both military and political crises. Scholars have already commented on Cincinnatus' resemblance to the elder Cato (see especially Reay 2005: 335). The two figures and their sources have a complex and convoluted relationship: Cincinnatus' story is set in the fifth century BCE; Cato's in the second; Cato's own surviving works do not mention Cincinnatus; Cicero does, as part of his representation of Cato in *De senectute*, which comes from the 50s, in a brief fragment of the *De re publica*, also from the 50s, and in *De finibus* 2.12.15. Livy's extended narrative of the legend, one of two that survive (the other is that of Dionysius of Halicarnassus), appears about thirty years after Cicero's, on the cusp of the Augustan age. As is true of Roman historical legends generally, there is no "control" version of the story; whatever its kernel of truth, it comes to us refracted through the politics and ideologies of the middle and late Republic (Garnsey 1988: 170–171; Purcell 2003). But perhaps we can redirect our line of sight, so that Livy's account, especially when set against the fragments of that of Dionysius, sheds light on ways of imagining community in republican Rome.

Livy presents the famous scene as follows (3.26.7–11):

> It is worthwhile to hear [*operae pretium est audire*], all who scorn everything human except wealth [*prae diuitiis*], and think there is no place for great office or excellence, save where resources abound [*nisi ubi effuse afluant opes*]. The only hope of the Roman people's dominion, L. Quinctius, was on the far side of the Tiber cultivating four acres [*quattuor iugerum colebat agrum*], which are called the Quinctian Meadows, opposite the very place where the

> dockyards are now [*ubi nunc naualia sunt*]. There the legates found him either digging in the dirt and leaning on a shovel or while he was plowing—intent, it is certainly agreed, on some agrarian project [*seu fossam fodiens palae innixus, seu cum araret, operi certe, id quod constat, agresti intentus*]; greetings exchanged, he was asked (with the wish that it might it turn out well for himself and the Republic) to don his toga and hear the Senate's instructions. Wondering and asking, "is all well?" he orders his wife Racilia quickly to bring his toga from the hut. As soon as he comes forth clothed in it, all dust and sweat wiped off, the legates salute him as dictator, summon him into the city [*in urbem uocant*] and explain the army's fear. A ship was obtained for Quinctius at public expense; once he was borne across the river, his three sons came out and received him, as did other associates and friends, then the majority of the Senate. Thronged by this pack, and with lictors clearing the way, he was led home.

Celebrated in historical paintings and sculptures and familiar to Americans from its association with George Washington, Livy's image of Cincinnatus at plow (or spade) has focused attention on this part of the narrative, with the result that few have studied it in its entirety and in its context (two fine and relatively recent studies focus, respectively, on the events of either Book 3 [Vasaly 1999] or Book 4 [Lowrie 2010]). What follows attempts to do so as fully as space allows, and in doing so to show how the idea of cultivating the land extends itself to other forms of Roman endeavor, political and intellectual, and embraces the entire Roman community via the idea of the Roman meal.

4 The Context and Structure of the Cincinnatus Story

Livy's account unfolds in a context of political instability, its first events taking place about fifty years after monarchy ended at Rome. The causes of turmoil included debates about limits on consular and tribunician power, about the prorogation of magistrates including plebeian tribunes, and about limiting the power to imprison bodily a person accused of a crime. There were chronic problems with external enemies, epidemics, and prodigies; and the Sabine leader Appius Herdonius with a band of runaway slaves seized the very Capitoline. The decemvirs came, and went. Verginia perished, and famine almost caused sedition (Liou-Gille 2007). In this atmosphere of plebeian aggression, patrician push-back, and internal and external strife, two strands of Livy's narrative, that of L. Quinctius Cincinnatus and that of Appius Claudius, serve as foils to one another. The result is to emphasize the notorious Claudian arrogance and to recast the Quinctii as ideal aristocrats, whose ability to address effectively the *plebs* fosters *concordia* between the orders (Vasaly 1999: 513–515).

The Cincinnatus strand of the narrative falls into two sets of events about twenty years apart, the first in 461–458 BCE, which appears in Livy, Book 3 (Part I), Cincinnatus' "exile," and two of his returns, first as consul then as dictator. The second set takes place in 439–437 BCE, in Book 4 (Part II), Cincinnatus' execution as dictator of Sp. Maelius. Thus Cincinnatus' first dictatorship responds to an external threat (Part I), and his second to an internal one (Part II). Such, often complementary, repetition appears in a number of interrelated guises in Livy's Cincinnatus narrative: in his representation of Roman topography, of Cincinnatus' family, of the taking of human life. Together with repeated economic themes and images, this repetition bridges the divide between Books 3 and 4 and helps readers make sense of Cincinnatus' story as a whole.

5 Topography: *Rus et Urbs*

First, topographical references tie the two parts of the story together. The Tiber, which plays such an interactive role with the legendary figures of early Rome, plays an important one in the Cincinnatus story. In Part I, Cincinnatus moves across the Tiber (*trans Tiberim*) into his poverty-imposed exile from political life; properly togate and appointed dictator, he is conveyed back across it in a ship obtained *publice*, "at the public expense." Andrew Feldherr has observed that "Livy constructs the Cincinnatus episode… to emphasize particularly the passage into the public space, from which Cincinnatus' farm is symbolically separated by the Tiber river" (Feldherr 1998: 120). In Part II (at 4.12.11), the starving poor cover their heads ritually and jump into the Tiber to drown (Garnsey 1988: 175). (Interactions with the Tiber are frequent in Books 1–2: in Book 1, Tiberinus, Romulus and Remus, Hercules and his cattle; the building of the Pons Sublicius. In Book 2, the bridge's destruction, Horatius' defense and swim to safety; Mucius' crossing it to attack Lars Porsenna; Cloelia's swimming to freedom. Such interactions being much less frequent after Book 2, Cincinnatus' crossing and the suicides of the desperate poor stand out. On topography and narrative in Livy, see Jaeger 1997.)

What of this farm? Telling of Cincinnatus' exile, Livy says that he moves *trans Tiberim* to live in "some hut off the road" (3.26.8); telling of his recall, Livy says precisely where this hut is ("opposite the very place where the dockyards are now"), and how much land goes with it ("four acres, which are called the Quinctian Meadows"). Cincinnatus, then, has a very small farm, a modest dwelling, and a wife, Racilia, *trans Tiberim*. When he describes Cincinnatus' return at 3.26.11, Livy includes, for the first time, the information that Cincinnatus still has a house and three grown sons on the near side of the river, in the city. (None of *them* ever crosses the Tiber to farm. The only one of Cincinnatus' sons who crosses the river, and only by implication, is Caeso on his way to exile in Etruria (3.13.8).

On each side of the Tiber, then, is a complete household unit: the one recalls the model of economic self-sufficiency portrayed by Xenophon's *Oeconomicus*: husband and wife labor together—he works the land, she runs errands to and from the house (Saller 1994: 80–88); the other reflects the ideal of the Roman political dynasty: the great man escorted to his town house by lictors, three sons receiving him—a supply of sons sufficient to make one hopeful about the continuity of the generations, even with Caeso gone (Saller 1994: 88–95).

In Part I, in fact, Livy constructs Cincinnatus' return to public space so as to show that it is the transition from one kind of life to another (almost the reverse of a funeral and journey across the Styx). Indeed, the story's binary topography reflects the two sides of a Roman statesman's life: on the one side, the life of *negotium*, business, in public places, with lictors leading him and a crowd escorting him to his town house; on the other the life of *otium*, leisure, however unwelcome such a break from politics might be, and however hard and sweaty work it is to follow the plow. In Rome, *negotium*; across the Tiber, *otium*; *urbs et rus*, like the two sides of a coin. (The two parts of the Cincinnatus narrative include two kinds of *otium*, the enforced *otium* of virtual exile (he is *uelut relegatus*), which Cincinnatus endures in Part I, and the *otium* of old age, which he is reluctant to leave in Part II. See Cicero, *Att.* 2.3.4; *De orat.* 1.224, 2.57.)

A literary allusion reinforces this interpretation. Livy expresses uncertainty as to whether Cincinnatus was plowing or digging when he was called—a trivial detail. But expressing doubt allows the author to introduce variant versions, and to reconcile them: whether plowing or digging, Cincinnatus was "certainly, as is agreed, focused on an agrarian task," *operi certe, id quod constat, agresti intentus.* Reconciling these alternatives raises a question as to the range of activities indicated by the expression *opus agreste*: does it mean plowing, digging, or something else? Any time after the mid-second century BCE this phrase could call to mind a particular kind of *opus agreste*, that is, not agricultural work with spade or plow, but a work on agriculture, such as the *De agri cultura*; for writing is what a republican statesman did with his *otium*, enforced or not. (Consider, for example, not just Cato, but Cicero's *De re publica*, and his philosophical works of the mid-40s.) Indeed, Varro opens his agrarian work, *De re rustica*, with the word *otium*, saying that had he more of it, he would write about farming at greater length (Reay 2005). Livy's description of Cincinnatus' industry calls to mind Cicero's quotation of the words of Cato, whose figure is so strongly evoked by this story: "great and illustrious men owe an account of their leisure time no less than their time at work" (Cic. *Planc.* 66 = F 2 Peter: *Clarorum hominum atque magnorum non minus otii quam negotii rationem exstare oportere*; see André 1966: 28–33). As we shall see, these two sides of Cincinnatus' life, the agrarian *trans Tiberim* and the political Roman, so carefully opposed by Livy in Part I, work together in Part II, when Cincinnatus invokes his agrarian experience for political ends.

6 Farming, Food Production, and Economics

References to food as well as farming tie both parts of the story together. In Part I, the idea of food production is implicit in Cincinnatus' agrarian work. Digging or plowing, he is presumably working the land in order to raise food. Indeed, Dionysius of Halicarnassus mentions repeatedly and explicitly that Cincinnatus farms in order to eat:

> Quinctius happened, at the time, to be plowing a piece of land for sowing, following his lean oxen as they were breaking up the soil. … The insignia of office, the consular robe and fasces, were laid at his feet. And he, pausing for a moment and shedding tears, said only this: "So my field will go unsown this year and we shall run the risk of not having enough to live on." Then he kissed his wife, and charging her to take care of household affairs, went to the city.[2]

Dionysius also tells us that, having served his consulship, Cincinnatus "returned to that little cottage of his and lived, as before, the life of a farmer working his own land." Describing the second call, this time to the dictatorship, Dionysius says:

> It chanced that Quinctius was *on this occasion as well* engaged in *some work of husbandry*… [A magnificent horse is led up and the insignia of the dictator are placed before him] Quinctius, far from being pleased, was actually vexed and said, "this year's crop too shall be ruined then, because of my official duties, and we shall all go dreadfully hungry."

Unlike Dionysius, Livy never mentions Cincinnatus predicting starvation, not so much as a twinge of hunger; rather, he presents him as austere and self-sufficient always. Livy is, in fact, also interested in Cincinnatus' production of food; but he employs the idea differently, bringing a variety of food-related motifs into the narrative and using them to tie the two parts together. (We must, however, keep in mind that we do not have all Dionysius' version.)

In Part II, the lack of food, of course, nearly causes sedition and a return to monarchy. What causes the famine that gives Sp. Maelius his opportunity to grasp at kingship? The people's metaphorical sweet tooth: Livy calls the year noteworthy for, among other disasters, "the yoke of kingship nearly received on the people's necks through the sweetness of the dole [*per largitionis dulcedinem*]" (4. 12.7). He raises the possibility that the famine that made the dole so "sweet" was caused by the people's refusal to engage in food production. Moreover, this refusal might also be blamed on the people's sweet tooth: the famine, he says, "began from a severe dearth, either because the year was unfavorable to the crops or because the cultivation of the land had been abandoned [*deserto agrorum cultu*] on account of the *sweetness* of assemblies and of the city [*dulcedine contionum et urbis*]; for both stories are handed down" (4.12.7) Indeed, the very idea of *agricultura*, conveyed by the phrase *deserto agrorum cultu*, calls to mind the image of Cincinnatus cultivating his little plot in Part I, *quattuor iugerum colebat agrum* (3.26.8). By recalling the earlier image of Cincinnatus "intent on some agrarian work," the passage introducing the famine both helps connect the two parts of the story and, by recalling the image of Cincinnatus hard at work, leaves the impression that, while generally the fields have been deserted, his four *iugera* are still producing.

Economic ideas and motifs appear and resurface. Part I sees the introduction of the practice of pledging sureties. Caeso was, says Livy, the first person to give them (*hic primus uades publicos dedit*, 3.13.8); moreover, Livy says that Cincinnatus exhausted himself financially, having sold off *all* his property (*diuenditis omnibus bonis*, 3.13.10) to make good on the sureties. The pledge of money first took the place of Caeso being kept in chains; when Caeso did not appear on the day appointed for the trial that could have seen him executed, "the money" says Livy, "was exacted from his father, cruelly" (*pecunia a patre exacta crudeliter*, 3.13.10). The adverb, delayed and emphatic, conveys the idea of a physical penalty being transferred from son to father. Paying hurts, so much so that Cincinnatus gives up his political life in exchange for his son's freedom (Woolf 2006).

Livy introduces the plowing scene in Part I with economic metaphors (3.26), including one in which he, like Cato, reckons up value: "it is worthwhile to hear [*operae pretium est audire*], all who scorn everything human except riches [*prae diuitiis*], and think there is no place for great office or excellence, save where resources abound [*nisi ubi effuse afluant opes*]". Economic imagery resurfaces in Part II, when Cincinnatus accuses the plebeians of holding their freedom too cheap. Maelius, he says "a rich grain-dealer" (*frumentarium diuitem*), had expected to buy the *libertas* of his fellow-citizens for two pounds of wheat (*bilibris farris sperasse libertatem se ciuium suorum emisse*, 4.15.6). And Cincinnatus refers to Maelius' goods as "contaminated by trying to buy the throne" (*contacta pretiis regni mercandi*, 4.15.8). Part I of the story sees Caeso pledge money and his father pay, all he has, for Caeso's bail; Part II sees the people willing to exchange their freedom (all they have) for a couple measures of grain. Finally, the *bona*, "goods," of both Cincinnatus and Sp. Maelius are sold, those of Cincinnatus (Part I) to pay the sureties, those of Maelius (Part II) as expiation (4.15.8).

7 Farming, Authority, and Age

In addition, both parts of the story comment explicitly on age: the first sets the rashness (*temeritas*) of youth against the judgment (*consilium*) of maturity. Part I describes young men behaving wildly: Caeso and his aristocratic gang beat up plebeians and strip them bare (3.11.8). They are accused of roaming, *grassari*, the Subura and getting into brawls, *rixae* (3.13.1–2). The older patricians distance themselves from the young in their struggle with the tribunes, because it is clear that the young men are running the show and have little use for *consilium* (3.11.4–5). Finally, defending Caeso, both the ex-consul Lucretius and Cincinnatus himself apologize for his youth and promise that age will make him daily more steady (3.12–2–8). Part II raises the idea of the infirmities of old age before celebrating its wisdom: Cincinnatus is reluctant to take up the dictatorship because of his age, over 80 years old (*post octogesimum annum*). The senators tell him that there is more *consilium*, more *uirtus* in his aged mind (*illo senili animo*) than in everyone else. Cincinnatus prays that his old age not be harmful to the state (4.13.12–14). Of course it is not. It turns out to be a great advantage; for, as we shall see, in dealing with the crisis Cincinnatus draws upon a lifetime's accumulated experience. Like Polybius' Cato, he has been watching and reckoning.

Thus the story's progression, and its shift in emphasis from the disadvantages of youth to the advantages of old age, reflect the mythical progression of the Roman people from a society of bandits to one of farmers; for farmers, according to Roman myth, are *old*. Consider, for example, the portrait of Cato in *De senectute*. Cicero has Cato discuss the good points of old age, the joys it holds after the passions of youth are gone. One of them is farming (*Sen.* 51–60). Cicero's Cato says that one can farm until one is very old (indeed M. Valerius Corvinus farmed as a centenarian), and that the other great thing left to old men is their *auctoritas* ("the glory, moreover, of old age is *auctoritas*," *apex est autem senectutis auctoritas*). Thus Cicero links the two as benefits of old age. Moreover his Cato uses an agricultural metaphor when he says that a man has to lay the foundations of a fine old age earlier in life: "neither grey hairs nor wrinkles can suddenly snatch up *auctoritas*, but a life honorably lived picks its last fruits" (*cani nec rugae repente auctoritatem adripere possunt, sed honeste acta superior aetas fructus capit auctoritatis extremos*). The activities and character of the farmer—hard work, patience, and steady cultivation—produce *auctoritas*, Brilliance does not suffice: Caeso, who went about, says Livy, "*as if* bearing in his voice and might all consulships and dictatorships," never acquired the *auctoritas* his father had (3.11.7; in contrast, the end of the Cincinnatus narrative shows one of Caeso's more disciplined brothers acquiring it steadily, coming in second in an election after a man "of highest prestige," *summae dignitatis*, and proving himself "worthy of his father," *parente dignus* (4.16.8; 17.9).

8 How the Motifs and Values of Part I Affect the Interpretation of Part II

It is hard to discuss any of these ideas—sons, agriculture, households, topography, economics, and age—in isolation, because they are so interrelated. However, when we recognize that Livy has constructed his account so that the references to them in the two parts balance and complement one another, and that Livy uses the figure of Cato, derived from Polybius, Cicero, and Cato himself, as a lens through which to view this old Roman story, it becomes clear that we must consider the Cincinnatus narrative as a whole. Therefore, the explanation and even justification of the events of Cincinnatus' second dictatorship (Part II), or at least some justification of the way Livy presents the events of Part II, lies in the events of the first.

This is because the most important point of contact between the two parts of the story has to do with taking life, and both Parts I and II have at their core a set of economic agreements: in Part I, the Senate and tribunes agree on the magnitude and number of sureties to demand for Caeso's bail, that is, his supposedly temporary freedom from imprisonment—and possible execution—on a capital charge; in Part II, the dictator and the people decide the relative worth of the executed Maelius' life and their own liberty. Thus both halves of the story raise the important questions: how much is life worth? How much is *libertas* worth?

Now in making good Caeso's sureties, Cincinnatus pays for a murder he did not commit himself (nor, of course, did Caeso). In Part II as well, Cincinnatus takes responsibility for another death, again, one which he does not bring about—directly; but how very different in the telling is the death of Spurius Maelius in Part II from the fictitious death of Volscius Fictor's brother in Part I! Fictor's brother died, says Livy, well before Fictor ever accused Caeso; the accusation was a false one, made by a man appropriately named for falsehood (3.13.1–3). In contrast, Livy casts the death of Sp. Maelius before his readers' eyes in all its bloodiness, with simple syntax, and main verbs in the present tense (4.6.6: *Haec eum uociferantem adsecutus Ahala Seruilius obtruncat; respersusque cruore obtrucati, stipatus caterua patriciorum iuuenum, dictatori renuntiat*). When Ahala returns all spattered in gore, the dictator, in direct speech, says "'Well done, Gaius Servilius; you have saved the state'" (*"Macte uirtute," inquit, "C. Seruili, esto liberata re publica"*, 4.12.7).

Ahala's returning, spattered with gore (*respersus cruore*), to the dictator, exemplifies the motif of a victim's blood tracing the path of responsibility, as when, for example, Tullia drove through her father's body then home, and the bloodied chariot wheels reinforced the connection of the murder to the house of the Tarquins (also: Mettius Fufetius' body, dragged apart [1.28.10]; Lucretia's gory dagger [*manantem cruore*, 1.59.1]; Verginius' weapon, and himself "spattered with gore" [*respersusque ipse cruore*, 3.50.3]). After Ahala reaches the dictator, the dictator, by saying "*Macte uirtute*", endorses the execution and thus accepts responsibility for it. Ahala struck the blow, but Livy makes it clear that Cincinnatus is its *auctor*, the person who approves the act of another. (The image of spattered *cruor* provides another link between the two parts of the story by recalling the punishment for Caeso's failure to appear, which was enacted upon Cincinnatus *pater* in place of son; the money was exacted, "cruelly" (*crudeliter*, 3.13.10).

Cincinnatus' taking responsibility in paying for Caeso, and for Maelius' death, expresses his *auctoritas*, the quality that was so prominent in Augustus' presentation of himself as Rome's new leader (Galinsky 1996: 10–20). And it is his *auctoritas*, drawn from multiple sources, that Cincinnatus uses to calm the people after Maelius' death. When Cincinnatus addresses the crowd, it is "in an uproar" (*tumultuantem*), because it does not know what to think of Ahala's killing Maelius, "the assessment of the act being uncertain" (*incerta existimatione facti*, 4.15.1). The noun *existimatio* introduces the economic metaphor familiar from the opening of Cato's *De agri cultura*, because the first definition of *existimare* is to "evaluate, or assess" (Habinek 1998: 46; Reay 2005: 337). In fact, with his words to Ahala, Cincinnatus has already set a value on this deed: *Maelius obtruncatus* = *res publica liberata*. Now he guarantees that value by convincing the people to accept it.

Cincinnatus first points out that Maelius disregarded the dictator's command: obeying it would have won him a hearing; therefore Maelius' disobedience suffices to condemn him. Then he points out that Maelius, born in a state now free of kings, knew better than to aim at kingship. A series of *exempla* illustrates this point: the sons of Brutus, executed on their father's orders; Collatinus forced to abdicate and go into exile; Sp. Cassius, punished for seeking kingship, the decemvirs, driven into exile for "kingly arrogance" (4.15.3–5). Examined from the point of view of law, the speech so far raises a question: did Maelius die because he disobeyed the dictator, or because he tried to be king? As Michèle Lowrie points out, either one is cause enough (Lowrie 2010). But seen as dramatizing the multi-faceted nature of *auctoritas*, this "overdetermined" nature makes perfect sense, for *auctoritas* comes from a variety of sources, all of which reinforce one another (Galinsky 1996: 10–20). Many of them are at play in this speech, and all aim at bringing about an agreement as to value, namely that things are worth what Cincinnatus says they are.

In the first part of his speech, Cincinnatus uses the *auctoritas* inherent in his office, and stemming from the *maiestas* of the dictator—a dictator who was reluctant to take office, who left his office after fifteen days the first time he held it, who, when elected consul (*after* his exile and *before* his famous recall) and urged to run for another consecutive term, criticized the Senate, saying no wonder its *auctoritas* was empty, *uana*, since it did not abide by its own resolution (3.21.4); a man who closed his speech on that occasion by saying that his own glory would be increased (*auctam*) by his refusal (3.21.7). No one needs fear that this man *wants* high office for its own sake.

Cincinnatus also draws upon the *auctoritas* of a historian, using historical *exempla* reinforced by eyewitness (Marincola 1997): his listeners themselves had seen and experienced the decemvirs' "kingly arrogance" (some may have seen Verginia stabbed by her father). But Cincinnatus' *exempla* go farther back than that, to the first year of the Republic, to events most of his listeners had not seen. By Livy's reckoning, however, Cincinnatus was at least nine years old when the Tarquins were expelled and the Romans swore never to endure a king, eleven when Brutus executed his sons and Collatinus went into exile, and forty-three when the *people themselves* spurned Sp. Cassius' attempt to pay for grain, as if it were "a direct attempt to purchase kingship," *praesentem mercedem regni*. At over eighty years old, Cincinnatus was living history: he had seen the kings; he had witnessed the entire life of the Republic. (As a child Cincinnatus may have joined in taking the oath never to allow kings at Rome. Old men remember what they swore at age nine: in Book 21.1.4, Livy says that Hannibal, was "about nine years old" when his father made him swear to be an enemy to the Roman people. Other sources including Polybius have Hannibal himself tell this story in his old age as evidence of his unrelenting hatred of Rome.) He knew that commitment to *libertas* had cost Brutus two sons and Collatinus his life at Rome; he knew that in the past kingship could not be bought. His past spent watching these values in play reinforces his authority to set a value on life and liberty now.

In the rest of the speech, Cincinnatus continues to draw on his own experience for his *auctoritas.* He asks rhetorically, what kind of man was Maelius? Not one of lofty birth, like the examples above, but (4.15.6–7):

> Spurius Maelius, for whom the office of plebeian tribune was more to be hoped for than expected, a rich grain-dealer [*frumentarium diuitem*], had expected to buy the freedom of his own fellow-citizens for two pounds of emmer-wheat [*bilibris farris sperasse libertatem se ciuium suorum emisse*], and thought that by throwing it food [*ciboque obiciendo*] he could entice a people victorious over all the neighboring ones into slavery [*in seruitutem perlici*], so that the man it could scarcely stomach as a senator [*quem senatorem concoquere ciuitas uix posset*], it would endure as king, a king moreover wielding the power and insignia of Romulus, who was founder of the city, born from gods and to gods returned.

Note here the question raised by the economic metaphor: what is *libertas* worth? When Cincinnatus makes the speech that justifies the killing, he does it as one who knows the relative cost of things. He has already paid for a life: Caeso's life and freedom cost him Caeso, who never returns from exile; it cost him all his "goods"; and for a while it cost him his own political existence, forcing him into unwelcome, though productive, *otium.*

Cincinnatus also participated, however unwillingly, in an innovation. He paid a sum agreed upon by the warring parties in the state, after both the Senate and the representatives of the people, working independently, came to an agreement about value, the Senate determining the number of sureties Caeso should give, and the tribunes determining how much each surety should be (3.13.7–8). Livy says that Caeso's giving sureties was the first case of a person doing so, thus setting the precedent for the institution. However, although Caeso was the first to give sureties, his father was the first to *pay* them. Had he not done so, the practice would not have continued; thus by making good on his son's promise, Cincinnatus became the *auctor* of this practice. Cincinnatus stood behind his son's bond, even though his son left town; and Cincinnatus paid the bail, even though his son was innocent of the murder charge made by a false witness; and he did so at the cost of his own political life (Woolf 2006).

Finally, one more source of *auctoritas,* the one most likely to appeal to a hungry audience: in this period of famine, which Livy suggests may have been brought on by the neglect of agriculture, Cincinnatus speaks with the *auctoritas* of the farmer, the person who produces his own food. Unlike Dionysius' Cincinnatus, who repeatedly predicts his and his family's starvation, Livy's Cincinnatus is not concerned about what will or will not go into his own stomach; rather, he is concerned about what the people can stomach (*concoquere*), and they can barely stomach Maelius as senator. He will make an indigestible accompaniment for their dearly purchased *bilibris farris.* Having slaughtered Maelius, Cincinnatus has turned him into overpriced relish. Both parts of Cincinnatus' life, the agrarian and the political, come together here: Cincinnatus can persuade the people using the kind of language and imagery that Cato does in his speech on pickled fish, pretty boys, and plowmen, because he has lived the kind of life Cato has. He can give as good an account of his *otium* as of his *negotium.*

Afterwards, Cincinnatus continues to act as a historian (4.16.1–2): he has Maelius' house torn down to serve as a *monumentum.* Moreover, L. Minucius, the agent in charge of the grain supply, gets a statue of a gilded cow, *bos auratus,* at the Porta Trigemina; nor are the people unwilling, says Livy, because Municius sold them the "Maelian grain" priced, *aestimatum*, at an *as* per *modius*—a price which Livy's readers might think of as one from the "good old days" (Purcell 2003: 331). The word *aestimatum* brings us nicely back to where the speech started, with the *existimatio* of the deed (killing Maelius) being uncertain. And it brings us back to the figure of Cato, Polybius' Cato, Cicero's Cato, and Cato's own. The pillars of *auctoritas* are past virtuous deeds, offices held, age—and farming; and Livy had models to follow in presenting them. Paying up for Caeso gave Cincinnatus *auctoritas* (that of a father who guarantees—and pays up); refusing a second consulship increased it; his *otium* spent engaged in agricultural labor increased it still more. He also has the *auctoritas* of old age: he has seen everything, can guarantee his *exempla*, which have the potency of events known by eyewitness. He uses all of it to calm the crowd after endorsing the execution of a citizen without trial. Livy presents Cincinnatus, not staving off starvation pathetically, as Dionysius does, but as living a self-sufficient life, making responsible use of his *otium*, and laying down the foundations of *auctoritas* that later justified the execution of a potential king.

9 The Roman Meal as an Expression of Roman Values

An important element in producing this agreement about value is the idea, fostered by Livy throughout the narrative in Part II, and made credible by groundwork in Part I, that Cincinnatus and the people, like Cato and the people in Polybius, are engaged in a discussion about the elements of a Roman meal. In fact, the Maelian problem might be said to arise from all the parts of the Roman meal: grain is in short supply; metaphorical *dulcedo*, "sweetness," has led the people astray. That sweetness might be said to represent the drink accompanying a meal, because Livy uses *dulcedo* for that troublesome luxury, wine, and for associated metaphors. (Livy's only non-metaphorical use of the word blames the *dulcedo* of the Italian fruit for drawing the Gauls southward; see also, for example, Horace *Odes* 1.37.11–12 *fortunaque dulci ebria*. Tacitus may have been thinking of Livy's passage when he used the same metaphor in his outline of Augustus' rise to power at *Annals* 1.2.1: *ubi militem donis, populum annona, cunctos dulcedine otii pellexit*.... How about the relish? Well, again, metaphorically speaking, a very public sacrifice has just taken place, and the body of the freshly slaughtered Sp. Maelius is available; but as Cincinnatus points out, he is too expensive and simply indigestible. Something is wrong with the Roman meal: the central foodstuff, *far*, is missing and its enhancements threaten *libertas*. Thus in making the people agree on the *aestimatio* of Maelius' death, Cincinnatus brings them to the table as it were, to make them agree on a relative values, the value grain over against the value of luxuries, the value of liberty over against the value of grain.

Reading the entire Cincinnatus narrative in the light of its Catonian antecedents also brings into view some of the ironies of history, as constructed by Livy. One of them was to make Cincinnatus so strongly prefigure Cato (just as Dionysius' chronically weeping Cincinnatus does not). Cincinnatus was the sterling representative of the patrician *gens Quinctia* in its struggle against the advancement of the plebs; as a new man, Cato was closer in his antecedents to a Sp. Maelius than to a Cincinnatus, and yet, when it came to *uita* and *mores*, he was Cincinnatus' truest son (as Livy says at 39.40.4: *urbanas rusticaque res pariter callebat* [Reay 2005]). Another, related, irony is that, whereas Livy's Cincinnatus told the people that they could scarcely stomach Sp. Maelius as a senator,

Livy's Cato expelled from the Senate several men he felt the state could not stomach at all, most notably a member of the Quinctian *gens*, Lucius Quinctius Flamininus, consul 192, censor 189, who—at least according to Livy (citing Cato's speech on the event), over-indulged at a feast, over-valued a pretty boy, and *with his own hands* executed an innocent man, so that the blood splashed over the table (39.41.5–12). The motif of economic extravagance reinforces the moral corruption: Flamininus brought the boy to Gaul "with the expectation of great gifts," *spe ingentium donorum*; he complained that he was pulled away from the gladiatorial games, "so he might sell his services to his lover," *ut obsequium amatori uenditaret*.

Livy constructs the resemblance between Cato and Cincinnatus so as to make Cincinnatus a fundamental figure of authority, *auctoritas*, and to examine further how Cincinnatus uses that *auctoritas* to make the people agree on a set of values. Using Cato's image, one created and promoted by Cato himself, echoed by Polybius, and enhanced by Cicero, as a means of recasting the old republican myth, Livy links age, farming, and *auctoritas* in a comprehensive ideology that links the simple Roman meal to the preservation of republican freedom. This movement of virtue, from patrician to new man, but always remaining an attribute of the farmer, *who is by definition old*, aligns the myth of agrarian frugality and stolid independence with Rome's development from a community of pastoralists and shepherds (see also Varro *RR* 2 pr. 4); and incidentally, it makes the myth highly flexible.

It is hard to overemphasize the importance of the figure of Cato to Roman moral discourse: his image was so potent because he represented in one person the *auctoritas* of statesman and moralist, *and* historian, *and* farmer. Cato voiced the Roman aristocratic ideal of productive *otium*; Cicero and later Varro linked it to the discussion of the state, whether *res publica* or *res rustica*; but Livy, implicitly equating the acts of plowing and writing, placed the origins of that ideal earlier, as he did for so many cultural practices and institutions.

10 Conclusion

Divine intervention, chance, and human agency (motivated by desire and guided by foresight) flooded the Tiber, set Romulus and Remus adrift in the river, landed them below the Palatine, sent the she-wolf to suckle them there, caused a shepherd to find them and bring them up in the area, led Romulus to look for bird signs on the Palatine, and impelled him to defend the place by killing his own brother. In republican myth, expressions of commitment to Rome take a number of forms, whether working the land for crops or setting down its values with the pen. The agrarian metaphors increase opportunities for participation: not all Romans could farm; but they could all, figuratively speaking, gather together around an agreed-upon meal, one that placed a premium on the products of agrarian industry and confirmed their group identity as the cultivators of a particular place.

The mythmakers of the Roman Republic borrowed much from Hellenic tradition. Kathryn Morgan points out the antiquity of the connection between agriculture, truth-telling, and authority. Moreover Roman myth follows Athenian, both in positing a special relationship to the land and in generalizing agrarian virtue from the working farmer to the landowner. (Cincinnatus the plowman segues naturally into Cato the landowner and agrarian writer.) But in contrast to Athenian mythmakers, who saw their unique relationship to their land as the result of autochthony, the Roman mythmakers placed emphasis on repeated acts of selection and commitment. According to Cicero, Romulus *chose* the site of his future city; and the various versions of the Cincinnatus story show him repeatedly *choosing* to return to his family plot and his plow. The exemplary nature of Roman historical myth further distinguishes it from Athenian: Cato followed the example set by Cincinnatus, and the idealized late republican portraits of both men held them up as salutary models that could recall contemporary Romans to the virtues of their self-disciplined and frugal ancestors. In addition, although by the middle Republic Rome possessed a significant navy, Roman myth portrayed Rome's relationship with the sea as troubled, and inverted Pericles' boast that "everything from the entire earth comes into the city." For the sea offered a means of approach to enemy armies, luxury items, dangerous new ideas, and change. Indeed, distance from the sea was a virtue of the site Romulus chose for his city. Finally, whereas, as Morgan points out, Plato's insistence on occupational specialization brings to light the potential conflict of interest in those who both govern and farm, Roman republican myth insists on the opposite: the farmer produces: he produces his food; he produces texts; he produces the independence that guarantees his love of *patria* genuine and his motives pure.

NOTES

1 The English is mostly a modified version of W.R. Paton's Loeb translation, Polybius, *The Histories*, vol. 6 (London, 1927).

2 This and the other quotations from Dionysius are modified from E. Cary's Loeb translation, *Dionysius of Halicarnassus, Roman Antiquities*, vol. 6 (Cambridge, MA, 1947).

REFERENCES

André, J.-M. 1966. *L'Otium dans la vie morale et intellectuelle romaine*. Paris.

Astin, A.E. 1978. *Cato the Censor*. Oxford.

Davidson, J. 1997. *Courtesans and Fishcakes: The Consuming Passions of Classical Athens*. London.

Feldherr, A. 1998. *Spectacle and Society in Livy's* History. Berkeley and Los Angeles.

Galinsky, K. 1996. *Augustan Culture*. Princeton.

Garnsey, P. 1988. *Famine and Food Supply in the Graeco-Roman World: Responses to Risk and Crisis*. Cambridge.

Garnsey, P. 1998. *Cities, Peasants, and Food in Classical Antiquity: Essays in Social and Economic History*. Cambridge.

Garnsey, P. 1999. *Food and Society in Classical Antiquity*. Cambridge.

Gowers, E. 1993. *The Loaded Table: Representations of Food in Roman Literature*. Oxford.

Habinek, T.N. 1998. *The Politics of Latin Literature: Writing, Identity, and Empire in Ancient Rome*. Princeton.

Horsfall, N. 2003. *The Culture of the Roman Plebs*. Bristol.

Jaeger, M. 1997. *Livy's Written Rome*. Ann Arbor.

Kronenberg, L. 2009. *Allegories of Farming: from Greece and Rome*. Cambridge.

Liou-Gille, B. 2007. "Lucius Quinctius Cincinnatus et ses quatre arpents." *Latomus* 66(2): 301–326.

Lowrie, M. 2010. "Spurius Maelius: Homo Sacer and Dictatorship." In B. Breed, C. Damon, and A. Rossi, eds., *Citizens of Discord: Rome and its Civil Wars*. Oxford, 171–186.

Marincola, J. 1997. *Authority and Tradition in Ancient Historiography*. Cambridge.

Purcell, N. 2003. "The Way We Used to Eat: Diet, Community, and History at Rome." *AJP* 124(3): 329–358.

Reay, B. 1998. "Cultivating Romans: Republican Agricultural Writing and the Invention of the Agricola." Ph.D. Diss. Stanford University.

Reay, B. 2005. "Agriculture, Writing, and Cato's Aristocratic Self-Fashioning," *ClAnt* 24(2): 331–361.

Saller, R.P. 1994. *Patriarchy, Property, and Death in the Roman Family*. Cambridge.

Shaw, B. 1982–83. "'Eaters of Flesh, Drinkers of Milk': The Ancient Mediterranean Ideology of the Pastoral Nomad." *Ancient Society* 13–14: 5–31.

Thibodeau, P. 2010. *Playing the Farmer: Representations of Rural Life in Vergil's Georgics*. Berkeley, Los Angeles, and London.

Vasaly, A. 1999. "The Quinctii in Livy's First Pentad: The Rhetoric of Anti-Rhetoric." *CW* 92(6): 513–530.

Walbank, F. 1979. *A Historical Commentary on Polybius*. Oxford.

Woolf, G.D. 2006. "Writing Poverty in Rome." In M. Atkins and R. Osborne, eds., *Poverty in the Roman World*. Cambridge, 83–99.

FURTHER READING

The most important primary sources on agrarian ideology in republican Rome are Cato's *De agri cultura* and Varro's *De re rustica*, both conveniently available in W.D. Hooper's 1934 Loeb translation (revised by H.B. Ash). For discussion of the ideology of Cato's preface and Cato's role in the formation of Latin literature, see Habinek (1998); on the figure of Cato, see Reay (2005). Shaw (1982–83) shows how classical descriptions of meat-eaters and milk-drinkers contributed to a general Graeco-Roman ideology that placed agriculture and the eating of grain at the center of civilization. Purcell (2003) is interested in the light that Roman self-consciousness about diet sheds on the issue of Romanness. Peter Garnsay's work on food and famine is crucial reading for anyone interested in the Roman agrarian ideal. The early books of Livy are roughly contemporary with the composition of Virgil's *Georgics*, on which, see especially Kronenberg (2009) and Thibodeau (2010). On Livy's version of the Cincinnatus myth, see especially Reay (2005) and Vasaly (1999).

PART III

Dēmokratia and *Res Publica*

CHAPTER 6

Liberty, Equality, and Authority: A Political Discourse in Greek Participatory Communities

Vincent Farenga

At the start of her 1958 essay, "What Is Authority?" Hannah Arendt reminds her mid-twentieth-century readers how difficult it is for them to understand this concept. She tells them that, since traditional forms of authority have disappeared from the modern world, they—and, I presume, we today as well—no longer have an "authentic," common experience of it; consequently, the term confuses us and its nature no longer appears "self-evident or even comprehensible to everybody" (Arendt 1968: 91). Concerning authority, we are therefore left with only one recourse: to understand what it once was historically and what it once meant to the ancients and early moderns (1968: 92).

For Arendt authority is a force in society that "always demands obedience," although it must not be confused with power, violence, or any type of coercion. It is also a force that is inimical to the sorts of communication that flourish in egalitarian societies: persuasion and the use of argument. Instead it relies for its effectiveness on the hierarchical nature of a social order and on the mutual recognition, by those who wield it and by those who are subject to it, that this hierarchy is "righteous and legitimate" (1968: 92–93). Her essay then proceeds to explore in brilliant fashion what sort of forms and meanings authority acquired in Greek and Roman political thought. The student of archaic (c.800–500 BCE) and classical Greece (c.500–323 BCE) may, however, be startled to read that not all polities in history knew this concept. In fact, Arendt claims, in their political experience the Greeks (unlike the Romans) had "no knowledge of authority and the kind of rule it implies" (1968: 104 and 119).

What sense can we make of this sweeping statement? In Arendt's definition of the concept, authority cannot exist in any political society that is organized according to egalitarian principles; and so immediately we are compelled to recognize a relation between authority and equality. She also claims, "Authority implies an obedience in which men retain their freedom" (1968: 106), and so liberty joins authority and equality to form a triad worth pondering. Arendt of course assumes that we have a grasp of the development

A Companion to Greek Democracy and the Roman Republic, First Edition. Edited by Dean Hammer.

of the Greek *polis* and its institutions from the archaic to classical periods—in particular of citizenship and its privileged practices of open deliberation and decision-making. She also assumes our familiarity with tyranny or despotism, the anomalous and illicit form of monarchical authority that emerged in Greek city-states c.650 BCE (1968: 104–106) (On her argument that Greek political philosophy tried to fill the "authority gap" in Greek politics, see Rosler 2005: 89ff.) In what follows we shall first backtrack a bit historically to find out how and why Greek states originated and developed along lines that were more egalitarian than hierarchical. We shall then, *pace* Arendt, ask whether oligarchic and especially democratic city-states developed forms of authority that did seem "righteous and legitimate" to citizens. We'll complete the triad by considering the peculiar roles that freedom and equality played in relation to the authoritative acts democratic citizens had the privilege to perform. Here our objective is to see if there might be a unified principle linking the three concepts. Finally, we'll anticipate Malcolm Schofield's contribution to this volume (Chapter 7) by asking how the Greeks' experience of authority, freedom, and equality may have differed from that of the Romans.

1 Authority in Greek Communities before State Formation

In the early to middle geometric periods (c.900–760 BCE) pre-state communities in Greece entered a "formative era" characterized by modest settlements we can designate as autonomous hamlets and villages (Donlan and Thomas 1993). A key feature of these small-scale societies was their peculiar type of leader: the term *basileus* describes this figure not as a "king" but as what political anthropologists call a village "headman," a "big man," or for the few larger settlements a "chieftain" (see Farenga 2006: 37–45, with references; cf. Thalmann 1998: 249–255; Morris 2000: 201ff.; Whitley 2001: 80–101; and Hammer 2002: 29–43). Material evidence and ethnographic models suggest that: (1) he was a composite of these three anthropological types; and (2) he induced obedience in followers through a personally constructed authority that depended on exchange relations with kin and neighbors, military leadership, the adjudication of disputes, and organizing productive activities and religious ceremony (see Thomas and Conant 1999 and Johnson and Earle 2000: 33–34). Because there were no significant material differences in the lives of those who inhabited these pre-state village societies, we can characterize their social relations, including the leader–follower relationship, as predominantly egalitarian.

However, the larger of these pre-state communities (like Athens, Knossos, and Argos) were stratified between elites and commoners; and they relied on a social hierarchy that was simple rather than "elaborate" or "rigid" (Whitley 2001: 90; cf. Thalmann 1998: 250). Walter Donlan even sees communities like these three low-level chiefdoms as beset by a "fatal defect" in the form of an "underlying contradiction" based on "conflicting claims of egalitarianism and authoritarianism" (1989: 25; cf. Farenga 2006: 44–45). So there is a good possibility that on the eve of state formation these larger communities experienced a tension between elites who wished to reinforce hierarchy and other community members (including their rivals for leadership and commoners) who wished to resist it. The societies in the Homeric poems reflect different stages in this "formative" period of the Greek state, ranging from primitive to advanced, but the Greek army at Troy and Odysseus' Ithaca best dramatize the tension between authority and egalitarianism in low-level chiefdoms. *Basileis* like Agamemnon in the *Iliad* and Odysseus in the *Odyssey* certainly make claims to authority when it comes to redistributing plunder to rivals and followers or reclaiming their own wealth from predatory rivals—and the very struggles that beset them testify to how contestable and fragile were their claims to personal authority.

But on what concepts or practices do they make such claims? Pre-state authority relies on a three-part template consisting of: (1) *kratos* (*kratein*, *krateros*, *kratistos*), which can signify both physical or martial prowess as well as the ability to rule others by issuing commands they will obey without coercion; (2) *euboulia*, or the wisdom a *basileus* displays when dispensing advice at a council (*boulē*); and (3) an ability to adjudicate disputes by dispensing a justice (*themis*, *themistes*) acceptable to all parties. Once the city-state develops, however, this template will become the basis for the legitimate, authoritative acts of citizens who are *kurioi*, or entitled by the state, to perform these functions when they participate in both ruling (*archein*) and being ruled (*archesthai*) through the reciprocal sharing over time of state offices (*archai*) and of service as jurors in the law courts.

The quarrel between Agamemnon and Achilles in *Iliad* 1 is a contest over whose capacity to display *kratos* inspires a greater claim to voluntary obedience from the Achaeans. In addition to physical strength and martial prowess this term designates the capacity these attributes give a *basileus* to rule and command others to obey. When Achilles feels demeaned by Agamemnon, he puts to him the question, "How can any clear-thinking Achaean obey you either to go on a journey or fight powerfully against men in battle?" (*Il.* 1.149–151). Agamemnon concedes that Achilles is "very strong" in the physical or martial sense (*mala karteros*, 1.178), but he counters that he is nevertheless "superior" (*pherteros*, 1.186) as commander-in-chief of all the Achaeans at Troy, and he sarcastically invites Achilles to return to Phthia to rule as lord (*anasse*, 1.180) over his smaller contingent of Myrmidons.

When aged Nestor tries to end this quarrel, he concedes that Achilles is "strong" (*karteros*, 1.280), and he also echoes Agamemnon's claim to be "superior" (*pherteros*) because he rules as lord (*anassei*, 1.281) over a greater number of men—a scope of command meriting belief that Agamemnon is entitled to special honor (*kudos*) from Zeus (1.279). But Nestor also highlights how important wise counsel is to the authority of a *basileus*, reminding his listeners of how his success as a warrior alongside the "most powerful" of heroes in his day relied on this sort of cognitive talent: "And they (the great heroes) listened to my advice [*bouleōn*] and obeyed my words" (*muthoi*, 1.273; cf. 9.443). Using a later term, *euboulia* (wise counsel), Malcolm Schofield has demonstrated that this virtue enables Homer's deliberators and disputants to shift perspectives from personal to communal, and from the present to the past or future, in ways that express a "moral authority" essential to the heroic code (Schofield 1986: esp. 26–28). A related virtue of the *basileus* is his capacity to adjudicate formal disputes. In the midst of the quarrel Achilles alludes to this when he refers to the herald's scepter he holds—a "symbol of royal and indeed divine authority" (Kirk 1985: 77–78)—as an object the Achaean leaders bear in their hands when, as "dispensers of justice [*dikaspoloi*], they produce the *themistes* that come from Zeus" (1.237–239). *Themistes* are restricted to gods and *basileis*, and they refer to the cognitive and verbal actions a *basileus* performs when he consults Zeus or follows the god's directives for determining a just course of action that is in the communal interest and acceptable to all parties (see Farenga 2006: 161–168).

2 The Authority of Statute Law in Archaic Greece

City-states (*poleis*) and regionally federated states (*ethnē*) emerged in the early eighth century BCE when local village societies surrendered their autonomy and allowed their economic production, military actions, religious cults, and political governance to be organized within the confines of a clearly defined geographical territory. However, the authority of the *basileus* was a primary "casualty" of this new formula for state formation. Most of his privileges were denied to any one individual in the *polis* and were divided among several magistrates as well as a council of elders and a citizen assembly. So the emergence of the state rejected the concentration of personal authority in the hands of one individual and "refracted" it as a more impersonal capacity to call for obedience that was open to multiple groups and individuals. This does not mean, however, that the elite citizens who filled these civic offices in the first few generations of political life yielded to this egalitarian turn. Most states of the archaic period—at least until the sixth century BCE—were oligarchic, where elites formed blocs that manipulated the key magistracies, military offices, judicial procedures, and privileges of the council of elders that had been carved out of the *basileus*' pre-state authority. (Before the sixth century some states may well have had more popular, quasi-democratic regimes; see Robinson 1997.)

More specifically, it's clear that by the seventh century BCE wealthier citizens, comprising perhaps 25–35 percent of the citizen body, were demonstrating how ruthlessly they could marshal their superior resources into predatory weapons that increased their wealth at the expense of poorer citizens. In states like Athens this reached the point where elites were depriving the poor of livelihood, personal autonomy, and citizen participation, reducing them to utter ruin as long-term debtors and in some cases slaves who were sold abroad to repay debts (see [Arist.] *Ath. Pol.* 2–6). At least one unique cultural resource did, however, serve to stem the tide of oligarchic control—and in the process a novel form of authority was born. Soon after 650 BCE city-states and their citizens began to develop the practice of inscribing laws on stone or wood and displaying them on public buildings and *stelai* (see e.g. Gagarin 2005). Many (if not most) of these early laws were procedural, and their objectives included control over abuses by magistrates, some of whom inherited the judicial role of the *basileus*. Laws sometimes limited a magistrate's term of office, dictated his manner of appointment, indicated the type of proofs he could use when settling disputes, or the amount of fines that must be imposed on him for improper conduct in office (see Gagarin 1986: 86–96; 2005; Gehrke 1995: 16–180).

The most conspicuous and influential use of written statute law—and a paramount step in the development of the democratic constitution we know best—occurred in Athens c.594 BCE when an elite citizen, Solon, was chosen first to mediate the crisis of debt slavery described above and then to act as lawgiver in creating new statute laws (on Solon, also see Raaflaub, Chapter 2). In a single moment Solon dramatizes for us how the law possessed an authority even more effective than that of the pre-state *basileus*—but of an entirely different nature. Our sources concur that his first law immediately canceled the debts that were burdening the poor and costing many of them of their citizenship. At the same time it prevented any future incurring of such debt by forbidding use of a citizen's person as collateral ([Arist.] *Ath. Pol.* 6; Plut. *Sol.* 15). Since at a later point Solon composed songs to justify his decisions and actions, we have access to the kind of political intelligence and intention (*noos* in Solon's Greek) behind the novel authority wielded by the law. In trumpeting his decision to cancel debts and restore citizenship to the enslaved, he returns us to *kratos* and the three points of the triad "authority–freedom–equality":

> Those citizens who suffered shameful slavery right here in Athens, trembling in fear of their masters, I made free [*eleutherous*]. I did it through the authority of law [*kratei nomou*] by fashioning a joint linking coercion [*biēn*] and a just verdict [*dikēn*]—and I finished the job as promised. In the same way I wrote laws equally [*homoiōs*] for both wicked people and righteous by fashioning a joint linking each one to a verdict [*dikēn*] that was straight. ([Arist.] *Ath. Pol.* 12.4; fr. 36.13–20W; my trans.)

But Solon's new laws did not only "free" the citizens by enabling them to enjoy the produce of their own land and so escape dependency on others. They also guaranteed even the poorest a vote in the citizen assembly, the right to sit on juries, the right to bring a legal complaint against any other citizen (presumably including magistrates), and the right to appeal judicial decisions to a popular court, probably the citizen assembly itself ([Arist.] *Ath. Pol.* 9; Plut. *Sol.* 18; on the last right, see Rhodes 1981: 160–161). In a word Solon injected the notion of the law with a concrete sense of agency that wielded *kratos*—and that empowered citizens to enact a concrete and complex agency as well. This agency was "performative" in the sense that it sanctioned an individual's participation in the kinds of communication and decision-making typical of these legislative and judicial bodies and offices.

In describing Solon's law-making, both Aristotle (or his school) and Plutarch use a term that is not attested before the fifth century BCE and that speaks to this agency's "right" (or entitlement by the state) to perform these acts. For Plutarch the people of Athens were now "authorized to control the laws" (*tōn nomōn kurious*, *Sol.* 18), meaning that they could not only settle disputes but also determine punishment, for within the law's powers is the sanctioned use by the state of force or coercion (*bia*)—something without precedent in pre-state communities. As Aristotle puts it, "When the people [*dēmos*] is authorized to control [*kurios*] voting, it is authorized to control [*kurios*] the *polis*" ([Arist.] *Ath. Pol.* 9.1; cf. 41.2). So a citizen's freedom meant not only freedom from control by others but freedom to share in the triple privileges of the pre-state *basileus*: every citizen now contributed to a collective use of *kratos*, could exercise *euboulia* in deliberation, and help determine what is *themis* (just) through a law court version of *themistes*.

Kratos, *kurios*, and *archein* (and their cognates) demonstrate how city-state authority, sanctioned by statute law, is not a simple but a composite concept. These three terms also suggest that this authority cannot be understood apart from a citizen's experience of freedom and equality. *Kratos* signifies the cumulative or global effect of the authoritative power an individual or group can wield in the state, whether Greek or non-Greek. (It is obviously the operative term in naming a regime that gives power to the people [*dēmos*] a *dēmokratia*.) When, for example, Herodotus c.430 BCE reports a (probably fictional) debate over the best type of constitution, he puts it in the mouths of seven Persian elites almost a century earlier. One participant, Otanes, speaks glowingly of democracy as "turning power [*to kratos*] over to the majority [*to plēthos*]," and another, Megabyzos, counters that oligarchy will be superior if "we select a group of the best men and entrust power [*to kratos*] to them" (Hdt. 3.81.1 and 81.3).

Archein, however, returns to Solon's sense of citizen agency by designating the ability to perform various specific actions that constitute such power, and so Otanes can speak of what happens "when the majority rules" (*plēthos de archon*). This act of ruling depends on specific laws that define its scope, and so *archē* designates the office itself understood as the role an office-holder is permitted to play: in the case of democracy the majority "fulfills offices by lot" (*palōi men archas archei*) and "holds an office subject to scrutiny" (*hupeuthunon de archēn echei*). As we've seen, the law in a democratic state also insists that the people practice *euboulia*, and so it commands that "all proposals be referred to the public" (*bouleumata de panta es to koinon anapherei*). In Otanes' opinion, what results "has the most beautiful name of all, 'equality before the law'" (*isonomiē*, 3.80.6), a slogan that may have originated with aristocratic opposition to tyranny (see Raaflaub 2004: 94–95) but that in time characterized democracies.

At another point in his *History*, Herodotus uses another term linked to democracies, *isēgoriē*, the "equal right to speak in public," when he attributes to it the Athenians' growing military success in the early years of the democracy after they had rid themselves of the Peisistratid tyranny. Once again equality and freedom are tied tightly to the question of the kind of authority that induces citizen to obey commands and that defines for them a superior agency:

> At this point the Athenians grew in strength—and not just in one way but in every way it's clear that *isēgoriē* is a fine thing; for if the Athenians, living under tyranny, were no better in war than any of their neighbors, when they were released from the tyrants they became by far the best. This makes it clear that when held in check they deliberately weren't making much of an effort because they were working for a master, but once they were liberated [*eleutherōthentōn*], each citizen was eager to achieve something for himself. (Hdt. 5.78; my trans.)

3 Democratic Citizen Agency as a Performance of Freedom and Equality

But we can probe a bit more into the political reasoning that yokes a citizen's freedom to participate in politics, his legal equality with others, and the state's legitimate and righteous ability to command and demand obedience. One of the participants in Herodotus' constitutional debate, Otanes, the champion of democracy, makes an unanticipated move late in the discussion. Because he senses that the debate is going to favor monarchy over oligarchy or democracy (which is here called *isonomiē*, Hdt. 3.83.1), Otanes offers to withdraw from the contest, flatly declaring that he wishes "neither to rule over nor be ruled by" any one of the others. He does, however, place one condition on his withdrawal: that neither he nor his descendants ever be ruled by any of the others. His interlocutors agree to this decision. Herodotus then observes that Otanes' household remained the "only free [*eleutherē*] family among the Persians and is ruled [*archetai*] by another only insofar as it wishes, and without violating Persian law" (3.83.2–3).

Why does Otanes try to "cut this deal" with his competitors? It can only be motivated by the strength of his commitment to democracy and the conversely powerful repugnance he feels toward monarchy (or tyranny). Apparently the arch-democrat and the anti-monarchist are one and the same. Note, however, the reason Otanes gives for his withdrawal: he will not participate in the sort of contest that amounts to "ruling" as a monarch or "being ruled by" one (*oute gar archein oute archesthai*)—and at 3.83.2 he particularly emphasizes the latter as a fate he does not wish for himself and his descendants.

Conversely, as an arch-democrat he secures for himself (and his offspring) the right to live freely, which here means "as one wishes." This phrase anticipates by about a century Aristotle's more famous claims in *Politics* 6 that freedom is the basic principle (*hupothesis*) of democracy, and that being ruled and ruling in turn (through holding and vacating offices) is an important part of this freedom (1317a40–b3). At the same time Aristotle emphasizes how, in addition to having an equal share (*ison*) in this office holding, democratic liberty consists in "living as one wishes," which means not living as a slave (*doulou*) (1317b10–13). This "second characteristic" of democracy, he says, can be expressed as "not being ruled by anybody, or if this isn't possible, to rule and be ruled in turn [*kata meros*]" (1317b14–16). Living as one wishes is, then, what "contributes to the kind of freedom that conforms to an idea of equality" (*pros tēn eleutherian tēn kata ton ison*; 1317b16).

So Otanes' "special deal" underscores a dimension of freedom in citizen agency that is sometimes overlooked: ideally a democrat might wish to be ruled by no one, but he will settle for freedom defined as a *voluntary* participation in the exchange of offices (*archai*) over time, with its corresponding participation in the protocols of commanding (ruling) and obeying (being ruled). Along the same lines Thucydides has Pericles in part define democracy through the "fear" motivating citizens to obey those in office and the laws themselves, whether these be statute laws or the deep moral precepts whose violation would bring "shame" on any Athenian (2.37.3). Oligarchic regimes like Sparta's could also be characterized by a similar fear of law or moral precepts (*nomos* can mean both), as we hear when Herodotus has the ex-king of Sparta, Demaratos, explain to King Xerxes how Spartan freedom is qualified: "For though they [Spartan citizens] are free men, they are not entirely free: *nomos* is their master [*despotēs*], and they live in fear of it more than your subjects do of you" (7.104.4–5).

In Book 2 of the *Politics* Aristotle gives the name "reciprocal equality" (*to ison to antipeponthos*, 1261a31) to the exchange of offices, indicating that this is one important way to experience democratic freedom. In fact he claims this practice is vital to civic life (it "saves city-states," 1261a31–32) because it reintroduces to a democratic (or even oligarchic) state degrees of difference in the citizen body that the constitution may erase, particularly in a democracy, where citizens are legally "free and equal" (1261a32). Temporary office-holding therefore "imitates" (*mimeitai*, 1261b3) whatever original or natural differences citizens possess from a non-constitutional perspective (the text is, however, uncertain here); and so this particular way of experiencing freedom ensures that they will in some way "differ in kind," which enables a citizen body to be organized into a state constituting a unified whole (1261a17–24). Aristotle then suggests that this imitation of original differences among citizens has one additional effect: when citizens assume their offices for a year and then vacate them for others to fill, and when different citizens get to hold different offices, "it's as though they become different persons" (*hōsper an alloi genomenoi*, 1261b5). So the reciprocal equality experienced through the sort of free agency citizens enjoy when administering state authority through the laws seems to be mimetic in nature because it induces them to suspend temporarily one kind of civic identity (a citizen subject to the authority of magistrates and jurors) for another (a magistrate or juror who rules over citizens).

Another name for this mimetic activity is role-playing, and it invites us to consider citizenship as a repertoire of standardized roles and scripts into and out of which individuals cycle in the course of their political lives. Aristotle is thinking along these lines in *Politics* 3 when he concludes that the identity over time of a city-state depends on the sameness or difference of its constitution (*politeia*, 1276b1–2). And if a constitution is a "community" (*koinōnia*) of citizens, then changes in its form (*eidos*) over time can be compared to a chorus with a fixed group of performers who on one occasion present a comedy and on another become a tragic chorus because they perform a tragedy (1276b5–6). So, for example, when Syracuse passed in 466 BCE from the rule of tyrants to the rule of its *dēmos*, its citizens in one sense did not change their identities. But in another sense, as Diodorus describes it, they were transformed from being subjects who suffered unjust death, exile on trumped-up charges, and confiscation of their property, to becoming "one mass of people" (*pandēmei*) now "organized" (*suntakhthentes*) and able to "cling to their freedom" (*anteichonto tēs eleutherias*, 11.67.6–7). As liberators of Syracuse itself and other Sicilian cities (11.68.1–2), they then entered a sixty-year age of peace, growth, and prosperity as democrats (11.68.6). (Cf. Herodotus on Athens' similar transformation [5.78] and Robinson 2000 on classical democracies outside Athens.) Aristotle also represents citizens as role-players when he identifies the one virtue they all should share. In this regard, he says, they are like sailors who are members of the community we call a ship's crew. Just as individual sailors have various skills matching their roles on board—one is a rower, another a helmsman, a look-out, etc.—so are citizens unlike one another. But despite their different skills and roles, all the sailors must work toward the same goal, safe navigation. Likewise citizens must organize their differences so that they can all display the virtue that results in the welfare of the state (1276b20–31).

So perhaps "the authoritative role-playing of different citizen identities" or "the authoritative performance of different degrees of equality and freedom" is the glue that binds together each point of the triad "authority–freedom–equality." This accounts as well for the relative or conditional nature of the equality and freedom of citizens: they are "less free" and "less equal" when subject to the authority of a fellow citizen in office, and "more free" and "more than equal" when holding office themselves. The triad thus appears to be a dynamic structure that over time regulates citizen life as "sharing in the polis" by participating in a performance cycle displaying how citizens occupy different positions and assume different identities according to what Aristotle calls the "organizational plan" (*taxis*) of a given *politeia* (constitution) that regulates the holding of offices (cf. *Pol.* 1274b38–40).

4 Freedom and the Autonomy of Greek States

In his fundamental study of Greek freedom, Kurt Raaflaub concludes that the meaning of freedom underwent a series of specific changes over the course of about 150 years, from roughly 600 to 450 BCE. Its first political meaning, occurring at *Solon* 15, is one we've already considered: it refers to the need for a citizen to be a free, as opposed to enslaved or dependent, individual, especially in relation to his own land (2004: 45–57; also Raaflaub, Chapter 2). But it was not until the Persian invasion of 480–79 BCE that Greeks began describing their political communities using the adjective "free" (*eleutheros*); evidently they didn't see their states as communities in need of "liberation" from the threat of outside aggression. Soon after the invasion, however, the noun "freedom" (*eleutheria*) was coined, and as many states as possible boasted of their contribution to saving the freedom of Greece (2004: 58–65). Likewise Raaflaub argues that, when it came to their *internal* political interactions as citizens, it was not until the period of the Persian Wars (490–479) that the Greeks on the whole considered themselves "free" as opposed to "enslaved by a tyrant" (2004: 96–102). So freedom took on new meanings depending on which perspective Greeks took on their city-states. By 470 they could see themselves as "free" or "enslaved" in relation to an outside power (the Persian Empire), but they could also see themselves as "free" or "enslaved" in relation to performing citizenship within the *taxis* organizing their *politeia*.

These two senses of freedom, one looking outward and emphasizing freedom from foreign domination, the other looking inward and emphasizing freedom from internal constraint, allowed states as different as Athens and Sparta to identify themselves as champions of freedom. A new rhetoric of freedom vs. enslavement emerged, prompting the Athenians to represent themselves on one hand as agents of freedom when they drove out the last of the Peisistratids (cf. Hdt. 5.55.24 and 78.7) and on the other to press in 478 for establishment of the Delian League under their hegemony in order to secure Greek freedom from future Persian aggression (Raaflaub 2004: 87–88; cf. Thuc. 3.10.3). But the Spartans also identified themselves as protectors of freedom when their commander Pausanias dedicated an altar to Zeus Eleutherios after the battle of Plataea in 479 (Thuc. 2.71.2, cited by Raaflaub 2004: 300, n.11 and 102–103), but more dramatically throughout the Peloponnesian War by representing themselves as the guardians of Greek freedom against the tyranny of the Athenian empire (most notably when in 404 they celebrated the dismantling of Athens' defensive walls as "the day when freedom began for Greece" [Xen. *Hell.* 2.23]).

This same dual perspective, looking outward to a state's relation with other, more powerful, states, and looking inward toward the conditions of domestic politics, also generated a new concept and word, *autonomia* (autonomy). Building on studies by Bickerman (1958) and Ostwald (1982), Raaflaub argues that a state's freedom (*eleutheria*) characterized its outward perspective in a positive manner that resulted from a double negative, signifying non-domination by a foreign power (e.g., in a passive sense, "We are not unfree"). *Autonomia* on the other hand, while also a positive term, represented from an inward perspective a state's capacity for self-government and self-determination (e.g., in an active sense, "We are independent and able to determine our own laws and norms") (2004: 154). When and why did autonomy emerge as this particular expression of a state's freedom? It occurred in the middle of the fifth century, soon after 450, and under the tense relations between Athens and her subject allies. It became necessary to specify the kind of freedom some Athenian allies enjoyed in contrast to others, and to provide a more nuanced approximation of just how "equal" such states would be to Athens: where Athens agreed not to intervene in an ally's internal politics, that state retained its *autonomia* in the form of authoritative control over its own *politeia* (2004: 159).

We find an excellent example of such distinctions in the plea the Mytilenians made to the Spartans in 428 when, attempting to break from the Athenian empire, they sought both an alliance with and assistance from the Spartans. Note how the question of "alliance" (*summachia*) between Greek states provokes anxieties in interstate relations about the very positive and negative values we've been discussing *within* the *politeia* of one state or another (equality, freedom, enslavement, independence). The Mytileneans describe for the Spartans the history of their participation in Athens' hegemonic league this way: "[But] we allied ourselves with the Athenians not for the enslavement [*katadoulōsei*] of Greeks but with Greeks for our liberation [*eleutherōsei*] from the Mede. And so long as they led us on an equal basis [*apo tou isou*], we followed them eagerly. But ever since we've seen them relaxing their hostility toward the Mede and working to enslave [*doulōsin*] their allies, we've been no longer unperturbed" (Thuc. 3.10.2–4; my trans.). Because the Athenians interfered in the internal politics of all the allied states except Mytilene and Chios, the Mytilenians characterize these others allies as "enslaved" (*edoulōthēsan*). And with the hindsight provided by this troubling enslavement, they now see themselves as having campaigned alongside the Athenians as "people who were only supposedly [*dē*] independent [*autonomoi*] and free [*eleutheroi*] in name [*tōi onomati*]" (3.10.6; my trans.).

5 From Greece to Rome

I have tried to indicate how tightly intertwined were the points of the triad "authority–freedom–equality" in the political practice, history, and theory of archaic and classical Greece. At the same time I've tried to understand how, despite Arendt's claim, Greek states of this era did rely on forms of authority recognized as legitimate by "the one who commands and the one who obeys." Each of these role-players, I've argued, employed both "common reason" and "persuasion" to share in a hierarchy where they occupied "predetermined" places that were not, to use Arendt's word, "stable" but were instead reciprocally exchanged (1968: 93). In the next chapter of this volume Malcolm Schofield discusses the Roman experience with this triad of core values. His discussion points to an interrelation between freedom and equality that parallels the Greek experience in a number of ways, especially in: (1) the strong, productive tension linking freedom (*libertas*) to domination (*dominatio*) by a monarch or tyrant; (2) the tie between freedom and equality which induces both elites and the common citizens (*plebs*) to seek an "equal liberty" (*aequa libertas*) that seems to echo the democratizing tendency of *isonomia*; and (3) the role philosophical and historiographical texts (Cicero, Sallust, Livy) play in locating these tensions and demands within a reasoned discourse consistent with cultural tradition.

But Schofield clarifies for us, as Arendt also emphasized (1968: 120–124), how Roman authority (*auctoritas*) was anything but commensurate with the Greeks' experience of this value. The privileged status which the city of Rome occupied as both the paradigm and the unique expression of legitimate polity (the sole *res publica*) lent its foundation and its founders an authority that dwarfed anything the Greeks experienced in the archaic and classical periods. While the foundation of the Roman political community could never be replicated, the ancestral *auctoritas maiorum* of the fathers (*patres*) who were its founders and perpetuators was incessantly accessible to future generations of Romans. Its source or channel, however, was not the people (*populus*) themselves but only that portion of them who could be distinguished by displays of high worthiness (*dignitas*) and honor (*honos*). And the voice of this authority could most frequently be heard through the deliberations and counsels not of a popular assembly (*comitium*) but of the Senate itself as a unique assemblage of worthies, the *patres conscripti*.

REFERENCES

Arendt, Hannah. 1968. *Between Past and Future: Eight Exercises in Political Thought*. New York.

Aristotle. 1996a. "The Constitution of Athens." In *The Politics and the Constitution of Athens*. Trans. Stephen Everson. Cambridge.

Aristotle. 1996b. "The Politics." In *The Politics and the Constitution of Athens*. Trans. Stephen Everson. Cambridge.

Behrends, O. and W. Sellert, eds. 1995. *Nomos und Gesetz: Ursprunge und Wirkungen des griechischen Gesetzedenkens*. Göttingen.

Bickerman, Elias. 1958. "Autonomia: Sur un passage de Thucydide (1.144.2)." *RD*, 3rd ser. 5: 313–344.

Collins, S. 2006. *Aristotle and the Rediscovery of Citizenship*. Cambridge.

Diodorus Siculus. 1946. *The Library of History*, Books IX–XII.40. Trans. C.H. Oldfather. Cambridge, MA.

Donlan, Walter. 1989. The Pre-State Community in Greece." *SO* 64: 5–29.

Donlan, Walter and Carol G. Thomas. 1993. "The Village Community of Ancient Greece: Neolithic, Bronze, and Dark Ages." *SMEA* 31: 61–72.

Farenga, Vincent. 2006. *Citizen and Self in Ancient Greece: Individuals Performing Justice and the Law*. Cambridge.

Gagarin, M. 1986. *Early Greek Law*. Berkeley.

Gagarin, M. 2005. "The Unity of Greek Law" and "Early Greek Law." In Gagarin and Cohen 2005: 29–40 and 82–94.

Gagarin, M. and D. Cohen, eds. 2005. *The Cambridge Companion to Ancient Greek Law*. Cambridge.

Gehrke, H.-J. 1995. "Der Nomosbegriff der Polis." In Behrends and Sellert 1995: 13–35.

Goldhill, S. and R. Osborne, eds. 1999. *Performance Culture and Athenian Democracy*. Cambridge.

Hammer, D. 2002. *The* Iliad *as Politics: The Performance of Political Thought*. Norman, OK.

Herodotus. 1998. *The Histories*. Trans. Robin Waterfield. Oxford.

Johnson, A. and T. Earle. 2000. *The Evolution of Human Societies from Foraging Group to Agrarian State*. 2nd edn. Stanford, CA.

Kirk, G.S. 1985. *The Iliad: A Commentary*, vol. 1: *Books 1–4*. Cambridge.

Kraut, R. 2002. *Aristotle: Political Philosophy*. Oxford.

Lewis, J. 2006. *Solon the Thinker: Political Thought in Archaic Athens*. London.

Morris, I. 2000. *Archaeology as Cultural History: Words and Things in Iron Age Greece*. Oxford.

Ober, J. and C. Hedrick, eds. 1996. *Dēmokratia: A Conversation on Democracies, Ancient and Modern*. Princeton.

Ostwald, M. 1982. Autonomia: *Its Genesis and Early History*. American Classical Studies 11. Chico, CA.

Parker, R. 2005. "Law and Religion." In Gagarin and Cohen 2005: 61–81.

Plutarch. 1998. "Solon." In *Greek Lives*. Trans. Robin Waterfield. Oxford.

Raaflaub, K. 2004. *The Discovery of Freedom in Ancient Greece*. 1st English edn. rev. and updated from the German. Trans. Renate Franciscono (and revised by the author). Chicago.

Rhodes, P.J. 1981. *A Commentary on the Aristotelian Athenaion Politeia*. Oxford.

Robinson, E.W. 1997. *The First Democracies: Early Popular Government Outside Athens*. Stuttgart.

Robinson, E.W. 2000. Democracy in Syracuse, 466–412 BC. *HSPh* 100: 189–205; also in E.W.Robinson, ed., 2004. *Ancient Greek Democracy. Readings and Sources.* Oxford and Malden, MA, 140–151.

Rosler, A. 2005. *Political Authority and Obligation in Aristotle*. Oxford.

Schofield, M. 1986. "*Euboulia* in the *Iliad*." *CQ* 36: 6–31.

Solon. 1993. "Solon." In *Greek Lyric Poetry*. Trans. M.L. West. Oxford.

Thalmann, W.G. 1998. *The Swineherd and the Bow: Representations of Class in the* Odyssey. Ithaca. NY.

Thomas, C. and C. Conant. 1999. *Citadel to City-State: The Transformation of Greece, 1200–700 BCE*. Bloomington.

Thomas, R. 2005. "Writing, Law, and Written Law." In Gagarin and Cohen 2005: 41–60.

Wallace, R.W. 1996. "Law, Freedom, and the Concept of Citizens' Rights in Democratic Athens." In Ober and Hedrick 1996: 105–119.

Whitley, J. 2001. *The Archaeology of Ancient Greece*. Cambridge.

FURTHER READING

On changes and contradictions in the authority of the *basileus* during the pre-state era and in Homer, see Whitley's archaeologically based survey (2001); for this figure's relevance to later Greek citizenship, see Hammer 2002 (with a focus on the *Iliad*) and Farenga 2006 (on the pre-state era, the *Iliad*, and the *Odyssey*). The essays by Gagarin, Thomas, and Parker in Gagarin and Cohen 2005 provide an excellent introduction to research on early Greek law, and John Lewis (2006) discusses Solon's contribution as a mediator, lawgiver, and poet to early Greek political thought. On Greek citizenship in the archaic and classical periods as a kind of performance, see Farenga 2006 and, for democratic Athens alone, Goldhill and Osborne 1999. For a general introduction to Aristotle's political philosophy, see Kraut 2002. Recent work by Collins 2006 explores questions on Aristotle's concept of citizenship with a particular focus on its relevance as a paradigm in political philosophy today. For the question of whether Aristotle recognized the legitimacy of political authority, see chapter 3 in Rosler 2005. Raaflaub 2004 provides a magisterial inquiry into the changing nature of freedom in Greek politics and political thought, while Wallace 1996 explores the links in democratic Athens among law, freedom and "rights."

CHAPTER 7

Liberty, Equality, and Authority: A Political Discourse in the Later Roman Republic

Malcolm Schofield

This chapter presents—in relatively discursive mode—a sketch of the physiognomy of the concepts of liberty, equality, and (with more limited ambition) authority, as they functioned in interrelationship with each other in the political discourse of late republican Rome, and of some of the arguments that deployed or examined them, in historical and philosophical writing as well as oratory. The plan is to listen to the Romans themselves talking about *libertas*, *auctoritas*, and *ius aequum* (equal right), and to reflect on what we hear as we go along. Cicero's testimony will inevitably bulk large, but authors writing after him who share the same political vocabulary and reflect the same political culture, even if they write about earlier periods of Roman political history, will also join the conversation.

1 Liberty

In the British Museum are a couple of coins, evidently struck at Rome by Marcus Junius Brutus, and dated by the experts to 54 BCE, which tell us a great deal about Roman republican ideology (Crawford 1974: 455–456; Wiseman 2009: 17–18, 190). One has on the obverse an image of Brutus' great ancestor Lucius Junius Brutus, a leading figure in the overthrow of the last of the Roman kings, Tarquin the Proud, and one of the first two consuls (509 BCE), who would die a noble death in battle against the Tarquins' forces. On the reverse is an image of another of Brutus' ancestors, Gaius Servilius Ahala, who in 439 BCE on instructions from the dictator Cincinnatus killed Spurius Maelius, a populist politician suspected by the political establishment of harboring tyrannical ambitions. The other coin also shows an image of Lucius Junius Brutus, this time on the reverse. On the obverse is the head of a goddess, identified by the legend as LIBERTAS. In due course Marcus Brutus was himself to participate in the assassination of Julius Caesar, likewise regarded by him and his associates as a tyrant, and was later to pay for that with his

A Companion to Greek Democracy and the Roman Republic, First Edition. Edited by Dean Hammer.

own life. "Was it my authority [*auctoritas*, or authoritative influence]," asks Cicero in the second *Philippic* (*Phil.* 2.26), "that incited Brutus to liberate our country—Brutus who every day would see in his ancestral home images of Lucius Brutus and Ahala too, and had them as authorities [*auctores*, or authoritative models prompting emulation] enough?"

Liberation from tyranny was what the Roman Republic was all about: everybody agreed about that. But consensus ended there. For who were the tyrants, and who the liberators? Only a few years earlier than Brutus' coin issue, for example, popular sentiment turned against Cicero, who after suppressing the Catilinarian conspiracy in 63 BCE had been praised in senatorial circles as father of the country. In 58 BCE he was driven into exile, and as Dio reports in his matter-of-fact manner (Dio Cass. 38.17.6): "His property was confiscated, his house was razed to the ground as though he were a public enemy, and they dedicated its site for a temple of Liberty." By the next year the mood had swung again, and Cicero was back in Rome, suing—in the end successfully—for the restoration of his property. In one of the speeches he made in this connection, he waxes eloquent about the temple erected in the shell of his house (*Dom.* 110): "What is the goddess [i.e. to whom it is dedicated]? It's Liberty, he says ["he" being Publius Clodius, the populist politician close to Julius Caesar who as tribune had promoted the vote to have Cicero exiled]. So were *you* [Clodius, again] the person to install liberty in my house—something that you have abolished in the city as a whole? … Is it an image of liberty that you have installed in that house, the house which was itself a proof of the exceeding cruelty of your own domination [*dominatus*] and of the exceeding wretchedness of the servitude [*servitus*] of the Roman people?" To Clodius, it was Cicero who had behaved like a tyrant, when as consul he had had Catiline's leading associates executed without trial: hence the triumphalist consecration of the site of his house to Liberty. To Cicero, that got things exactly the wrong way round: Clodius' actions showed *him* to be the enemy of the people, intent on *depriving* them of their liberty by his attack on their savior in the critical days of 63 BCE.

That is just a glimpse of the way the idea of liberty saturated Roman self-identity, in their conception of the *res publica* (i.e. the Roman commonwealth), their sense of their own history, their political arguments, their propaganda, and their religion. Above all, liberty was an ideal and (it was hoped) a reality to fight for. Certainly this was the way it seemed to subsequent Roman historians as they looked back on the political development of the Republic through constant vicissitudes. Thus Sallust, accounting for the transition from monarchy to republic, explains it (*Cat.* 6.7) as a reaction to the degeneration of rule by kings, which had initially served to "preserve liberty and build up the commonwealth," i.e. promote the common good, into "arrogance and domination [*dominatio*]." By replacing the kings with two rulers (*imperatores*) subject to annual turnover, they thought "the human spirit would have least opportunity to grow above itself through having no constraints on it" (*per licentiam*: a word often used to denote the abuse of liberty, as when Livy talks of the young members of the nobility as "quite openly preferring their own *licentia* to the *libertas* of all" (3.37.8), following the coup staged by the decemvirs in 449 BCE).

The contrast between liberty and domination—*dominatio* always carries an echo of the power the master exercises over his slave—is something of a Sallustian leitmotif, often accompanied by reflection on the power liberty itself constitutes or enables. In the great speech by Gaius Memmius (111 BCE), Sallust's emblematic populist leader in his *Jugurthine War* (*Iug.* 31.11), for example, the popular assembly is reminded that slaves who have been purchased do not put up with unjust directions (*imperia*) from their masters: so will the people, "born in command [*imperium*], tolerate slavery with equanimity?" After quite a bit more in similar vein, he dismisses any thought of compromise with the nobility (*Iug.* 31.23): "Their desire is to be masters [*dominari*], yours to be free." Catiline in the *Catiline* tells those he urges to exercise their rights that they have been brought up to behave as slaves (*servire*) instead of exercising command (*imperare*): liberty and the exercise of *imperium* go hand in hand, and with liberty the prospect of riches, honor and glory—at present the exclusive preserve of those who lord it over them (*Cat.* 20.8, 14, 17). In a fragment of a speech by Scipio Aemilianus (a generation earlier than Memmius, but on the opposite side of the political fence) *imperium* is likewise represented as flowing from the *dignitas* which brings a man honor—and from *imperium libertas* in its turn (Malcovati, *ORF*, 3rd edn., 21.32).

The bottom line was independence from foreign rule. A popular assembly would hear Cicero conclude the sixth Philippic, speaking of the threat posed by the populist Mark Antony, with the words (*Phil.* 6.19): "Other nations can endure slavery: freedom is what is natural to the Roman people." In 41 CE the thought was still potent: Josephus has Gaius Chaerea, author of the successful plot to assassinate Caligula, talk of the way his "country, once unequaled in liberty, has been reduced to slavery" (*AJ* 19.57). At the very beginning of their history it was in this sense that the Romans defended with their arms "liberty, country, parents" (Sal. *Cat.* 6.5). This is the *libertas* which according to Cato the Censor motivated the Rhodians to hope that the Macedonians would not be completely crushed by the Romans, as they gradually brought the whole of the Mediterranean world under their single rule (Gell. 6.3.15). But in most political contexts it was popular sovereignty, and the constitutional guarantees and the legal rights which went with that, thanks to a long if often obscure sequence of political gains achieved over several centuries, which those who talked of liberty had in their sights. For Cicero and Clodius alike, the liberty of the *populus Romanus* is the rallying call, and by that each meant freedom from the arbitrary rule of a tyrant or would-be tyrant. Anyone might be perceived as a tyrant who was or could be seen as riding roughshod over fundamental citizen rights, or the proper procedures enshrined in the constitution (or, for a senior anti-populist politician like Cicero, "*libertas* in taking our part in public affairs": *Fam.* 1.8.3).

One favored way of making the point was to contrast liberty with kingship. Livy tells us that when the Romans were urged by a neighboring power to restore the Tarquins, they replied (2.15.3): "The Roman people exists not under kingship, but in liberty," a sentiment that in effect captures the theme of his second book as a whole. Tacitus famously begins the *Annals* with the sentence (*Ann.* 1.1.1): "The city of Rome was originally in the possession of kings; liberty and the consulate were instituted by Lucius Brutus." Another favored contrast carrying similar import was no less famously deployed by the emperor Augustus, in the opening sentence of his *Res gestae* (1.1): "I emancipated the commonwealth, oppressed as it was by the domination of a faction, into liberty." Here Augustus deliberately echoes a republican trope (Wirszubski 1950: 103–106) that had before him tripped off the tongues of Cicero and Sallust (and no doubt countless Roman politicians), most immediately in the form Julius Caesar had given it when he defended his return under arms from Gaul to Italy, thus triggering civil war. Caesar explained that he did so "to emancipate into liberty himself and the Roman people, oppressed as it was by the faction of a few" (*B Civ.* 1.22.5).

"People" in such contexts generally signifies "the citizen body." Of course, Cicero, a leading representative of the anti-populist senatorial "faction" in Caesar's eyes, would for his part see claims by a Catiline or a Clodius to be defending the liberty of the Roman people as masking an attempt to enlist the support of the common people—the *plebs*, the *multitudo*—in what was in reality a bid for tyranny. And although he sometimes allows use of the expression *popularis* to characterize someone who truly has the safety of the *populus* as the whole citizen body at heart (e.g. *Cat.* 4.9), something politicians who accepted the designation would no doubt have insisted (Brunt 1988: 32–35), he generally means "popularist" when he describes a political actor in these terms: i.e. someone who may talk of the interests of the citizen body, but is really aiming to please the masses—as in his classic distinction between those in public life who wish to be and to be considered *populares*, on the one hand, and *optimates*, "the best sort," on the other (*Sest.* 96). Gaius Gracchus he counted as the *popularis* or popularist *par excellence* (*Dom.* 24).

When Sallust applies the familiar emancipation trope to the Gracchi, he has no hesitation in saying approvingly that they "began to emancipate the *plebs*—the common people—into liberty, and to expose the crimes of the few," to the consternation of the nobility, conscious of their guilt (*Iug.* 42.1). His Memmius (a generation later) takes it for granted that it is the *plebs* who are the true representatives of the *populus* (people). In the context of the theory of the mixed constitution in the *De republica*, when Cicero refers to the *plebs* as the third element in the mixture he talks of keeping some matters "for the judgment and will of the masses [*multitudo*]," as contrasted with the *principes*, the leading citizens (*De rep.* 1.69), but also of the entitlement of the *populus* to liberty (*De rep.* 2.57): he means *plebs* both times round. One might say that this simply mirrors what had actually happened with the Roman constitution: *plebiscita*, resolutions of the *plebs*, initially required ratification by an assembly of the whole *populus* if they were to become law, but by Cicero's own day their validity (thanks to the *lex Hortensia* of 287 BCE) was unconditional. The double use of Greek *dēmos* is an obvious comparison; and as with *dēmos*, or with *plēthos* (the equivalent of *multitudo*) in Aristotle's *Politics*, it may sometimes be unclear which meaning of *populus* is being employed—perhaps to the writer himself.

In Cicero's *De republica*, his dialogue "on the best constitution for the citizen body and on the best citizen" (*Q. Fr.* 3.5.1), the sovereignty of the *populus* as citizen body is fundamental (Schofield 1995). The *res publica* is actually defined as the *res*, the affairs and interests, of the *populus* (*De rep.* 1.39), reflecting its original spelling as *res poplica* (Wiseman 2009: 1). That such a *populus* must be a people possessed of liberty is taken as a given by all participants to the conversation: with the possible exception of Spurius Mummius, a minor character, who in the fragmentary Book 3, apparently after advocating aristocracy as the best form of the commonwealth, and preferring it to kingship, ends by saying that even so he would rather have kingship than a "free people" (*liberum populum*)—this third kind of system makes for a most defective commonwealth (*De rep.* 3.46). Scipio, the leading speaker in the dialogue, notes Mummius' characteristic aversion to the *ratio popularis*, which I take to mean something like "the popularist scheme of things" or "the popularist program." But after querying Mummius' preference for aristocracy over kingship, he offers the sophisticated democratic constitution of Rhodes as a legitimate form of a commonwealth governed by the people (a *popularis res publica*: *De rep.* 3.47; for Rhodes under Roman rule, see Rhodes with Lewis 1997: 274–275):

here—however Mummius may have been conceiving of the reference of *populus*—the idea is government by the citizen body.

In the rarefied air breathed by participants in the fictitious representation of a philosophical debate, it was evidently possible to argue for monarchy or to express an aversion to the idea of popular liberty not to be risked in the public arena. The *De republica* invests quite a lot of energy into thinking out what might or might not need to be involved in talk of a *liber populus*. What Mummius assumes is that a *liber populus* means democracy, in undiluted form. Earlier in the discussion Philus, a weightier contributor to the debate, had articulated, but at the same time by implication queried, the same assumption (*De rep.* 3.23): "If the people has the greatest power, and everything is governed by its decision, that is called liberty, but is really *licentia* [license, absence of restraint]." In Book 2 of the dialogue Scipio has already offered his own answer to the question of the best form of constitution for a commonwealth. He proposes a mixed constitution, incorporating elements derived from each of the three basic forms: kingship, aristocracy, democracy. A mixed constitution of this sort, with "enough power in the magistracies, enough authority in the advice given by leading citizens, and enough liberty in the people," has "in a strong sense a kind of *aequabilitas* [equality], which is something free men are hardly able to do without for very long" (*De rep.* 2.57). That claim brings us inexorably to the issue of equality.

2 Equality

One recurring phenomenon in texts relating to republican Rome is the association of liberty with equality (Wirszubski 1950: 9–15). If we can trust Livy, when the common people or their advocates demanded more rights or a greater say in the government of the commonwealth, they frequently argued the case on the grounds of *aequa libertas*, equal liberty. Even if Livy is reconstructing events and arguments with little solid historical warrant, more important is what the way the reconstruction is done tells us about the Roman republican ideology that we have seen being echoed by the emperor Augustus, as well as permeating the writings of Cicero and Sallust. That appeal to *libertas* should have been made in such arguments should come as no surprise. What is significant for our immediate purposes is that such appeals take the necessary association of liberty with equality to be something nobody could deny—nor do we ever hear it being denied.

A key episode is Livy's account of how a proposal from the tribunes, after a long period of class struggle, led to the suspension of the constitution in the middle of the fifth century BCE, and the appointment of a board of ten (the decemvirs) to draw up fresh legal provisions—resulting in the drafting of the original Ten (later Twelve) Tables, whose distinctive feature seems to have been publication in written form of what had been for the most part customary law. The tribunes had asked for measures to be proposed by a panel of legislators, drawn from both the *plebs* and the patricians, which would be advantageous to both sides and would represent the equalizing of liberty (*aequandae libertatis*) (3.31.7). Their request succeeded (except that the panel appointed was exclusively patrician); and in due course the decemvirs in reporting on their proposals claimed that they had indeed equalized rights (*iura*) for all, high and low (3.34.3; something once achieved under the kings, according to Cicero: *De off.* 2.41). Evidently what they meant was that it was now incontrovertibly established that all citizens had the same rights where private law (as it would later be categorized) was concerned. And that does indeed seem to have been the case. Whether it was quite all the tribunes had in mind (as Livy represents them) is another matter.

When, though their work was done, the decemvirs tried to hang on in power, there followed some months of turbulence, brought to a temporary end by the election once again of two consuls (Lucius Valerius Potitus and Marcus Horatius Barbatus) in 449 BCE. Livy's narrative of the turbulence and his account of the legislation Valerius and Horatius are said to have promoted indicate what for the *plebs* remained unfinished in the business of equalizing liberty. The one thing that agitated the plebeians, he tells us, was how they could recover the power of the tribunes, their champions under the constitution and the "bulwark for liberty" (3.37.5)—but a function suspended like other elective offices for the duration of the decemvirate. Valerius and Horatius soon emerged as "leaders of the masses" (3.49.3), and following success in isolating the decemvirs from support in any quarter, were received by the *plebs* as "liberators" (3.53.2). The Senate duly resolved that the decemvirs must abdicate, and that there should be an election of tribunes of the *plebs* on the Aventine hill, where (the *plebs* are reminded) "you inaugurated the first beginnings of your liberty" (3.54.5–9: by secession from the city en masse, 2.32.1–3.3).

We now reach the moment critical for the issue of equality. Livy next tells us that Valerius and Horatius, now elected consuls, carried three laws, designed to safeguard "the liberty of the *plebs*," something the patricians saw as a threat to their own power, even though in reality they were subject thereby to no injustice (3.55.1–2): one making resolutions of the *plebs* in the *comitia tributa* binding on the Roman people; a second restoring the citizen's right of appeal to the people if impeached (*provocatio*), "a unique bastion of liberty" (it was also ordained that no magistracy should be created that was not subject to similar appeal); and a third giving the office of tribune (and some other functions intimately concerned with the rights of the *plebs*) the protection of religious sanction (3.55.3–7). Thus was "the power [*potestas*] of the tribunes and the liberty of the *plebs* firmly established" (3.56.1). "Equal liberty," as the *plebs* and their protagonists saw it, ought to mean not just that any individual citizen should have the same rights in the private sphere as any other, but that they as a body should have legally protected political rights, which would give them collectively powers balancing those of the patricians (as vested in the consulate and the senate) (on arrangements of power, see also Mouritsen, Chapter 9 and Tatum, Chapter 15).

Couching an argument in terms of equality elevates it above the appearance of mere sectional or factional interest. That point emerges with particular force and clarity as Livy's narrative moves on a few years, when he gives the tribune Gaius Canuleius a speech putting the case both for opening the consulship to plebeians and for allowing them to intermarry with patricians. "Does supreme power [*imperium*] belong to the Roman people or to you," he asks the patricians at the beginning of his peroration (4.5.1). "When the kings were forced out, did that produce domination for you or equal liberty for all?" Canuleius is here claiming the moral and political high ground. He is attacking the patricians for the kind of negation of liberty associated with kingship. And he makes the plebeian case the cause of the sovereignty of the Roman people itself as such, and represents that as equivalent to the liberty of all of them equally. The *plebs*' concern, he will go on to say, is the unity of the citizen body, hope of reward for virtue, and the basic principle that marks any political society, the key to equalizing liberty: obeying and ruling in turn in annual magistracies (4.5.5; cf. 3.39.8: "the sole key to equalizing liberty").

The commentators (Wirszubski 1950: 11n.1, Ogilvie 1965: 470) note that Canuleius' formulation of "the key to equalizing liberty" seems to echo Aristotle's treatment of rotation of offices as one of the indicative characteristics of freedom—which is the headline value democrats claim as special to democracy (*Pol.* 6.2.1317b2–3; it was actually widely regarded as a mark of any non-monarchical political system: *Pol.* 2.2.1261a37–b5, 3.6.1279a8–10; further texts as e.g. in Oakley 2005: 514–15). Is Livy implying that Canuleius himself was meaning to argue for democracy? Certainly he is going further than the position allegedly achieved by Valerius and Horatius, which was an equal liberty—or an equalizing of liberty—constituted by a balance between one set of political rights, secured for the *plebs*, and another, monopolized by the patricians. The equalization of liberty envisaged by Canuleius would do away with the monopoly, with the rotation of magistracies opened to plebeians as well as patricians. But it could still be argued that the division of powers and responsibilities as between consul and Senate, on the one hand, and the people, on the other, fell far short of democracy, and indeed of real liberty or real equality.

Precisely such an argument is put by Scipio in Book 1 of Cicero's *De republica*, when he develops (without endorsing) the case for what its advocates would recognize as democracy (*De rep.* 1.47, translation adapted from Zetzel 1999: 20–21):

> How can liberty be equal (I won't speak about kingship, in which slavery is not even hidden or ambiguous) in those states in which everyone is free in name only? They vote, they entrust commands and offices, they are canvassed and asked for their support, but they give what must be given even if they are unwilling, and they are asked to give to others what they do not have themselves. They have no share in power [*imperium*], in public deliberation, or in the panels of select judges, all of which are apportioned on the basis of pedigree or wealth.

Scipio then draws a contrast with a truly free people such as Rhodes or Athens—though unfortunately the detail of the contrast is lost. From what he has already said, together with what he will say about the Rhodians in Book 3 (*De rep.* 3.48), one might guess that the people of Scipio's Rhodes are seen as possessing a truer liberty inasmuch as its constitution provides that the assembly has as much power as the Senate, and especially because it is not just the magistracies that are subject to rotation, but membership of the Senate itself. In short, from the Rhodian perspective true liberty at Rome would require a much more radical reshaping of the basic structure of the constitution than anything attempted by Canuleius: one that really would ensure (in line with the idea of democracy now articulated by Scipio) that "the rights of those who are citizens in the same commonwealth" are "among themselves … equal"—even if talents and financial resources cannot be equalized (*De rep.* 1.49).

One might wonder whether what I have called the Rhodian perspective on liberty and equality captures or reflects anything Romans would recognize as at all authentically Roman. After all, the debate Cicero is staging at this point in *De republica*—about the comparative merits of monarchy, aristocracy, and democracy—is a thoroughly Greek debate, which we meet first in the pages of Herodotus (albeit represented in the form of a discussion between leading figures in the Persian nobility: Hdt. 3.80–82), but which is given classic expression in Book 3 of Aristotle's *Politics*, often seen as directly or indirectly, through Peripatetic reworkings, the main source Cicero must be supposed to be exploiting here (Solmsen 1933; Frede 1989). Whatever source material he used has, however, been comprehensively Romanized, particularly where the basic philosophical justification for democratic equality is concerned. Here is how the case is presented (*De rep.* 1.49):

> Since law is the bond of citizen association, and the justice [*ius*] of law is equal [*aequale*], then by what justice can an association of citizens be held together, when the status of citizens is not equal [*par*]? For even if making financial resources equal [*aequari*] is not appealing, even if everyone's mental capacities cannot be equal, definitely the rights [*iura*] of those who are citizens in the same commonwealth ought among themselves to be equal. For what is a citizen body [*civitas*] other than an association in justice?

This is a pregnant piece of argumentation, which will require some midwifery to deliver its significance.

The final clause, articulating the assumption governing the whole train of thought here, directly echoes Cicero's formulation a few pages earlier of one of the basic ingredients in his definition of *res publica* or commonwealth, as the *res* or "affairs and interests" of a *populus* (people) (Schofield 1995). A people, he says, is "an assemblage of some size which forms an association by virtue of agreement created by justice [or law as justice: *ius*] and sharing in advantage" (*De rep.* 1.39; later on that agreement is already being referred to as a *vinclum*, "bond": *De rep.* 1.42). The last sentence of the present passage recapitulates "association," but can omit everything else but "justice" as irrelevant to the thesis being advanced. But as well as reminding the reader of the original definition of a people, it serves also to draw attention to the opening move in the reasoning here—and to indicate that it was already implicit in the definition. For if we return to the "since … " clause at the beginning of the passage, we find Cicero unpacking the assumption underlying the argument, stated in such compressed form at the end, a bit more fully, distinguishing the law and the justice elements in *ius*.

First we get the claim that law is the bond of citizen association. This initial premise is not in the least unRoman. Indeed, as James Zetzel points out in his commentary on *De republica* (Zetzel 1995: 139), Cicero's formulation puts one in mind of a famous purple passage in a speech to the court of 66 BCE (over ten years earlier), when he says of the laws (*Clu.* 146): "This is the bond that secures the esteem [*dignitas*] we enjoy in this commonwealth, this is the foundation of liberty, this is the source of equity [*aequitas*]. The intellect and mind and thinking and judgement of the citizen body [*civitas*] are located in the laws." The second premise—that the justice (*ius*) of law is equal—is if anything still more Roman. *Pro Caecina*, a still earlier speech of Cicero's (dated to 69 BCE), but probably "his last effort before the civil bar" (Frier 1985: xi), is saturated with appeals to *aequitas*, which as he uses it has been analyzed (Frier 1989: 120) as "a concept of 'internal or immanent fairness' that mediates between an abstract general rule and the concrete, specific case"—precisely what in *De republica* he seems to have in mind by talking of the justice of or in the law. As Bruce Frier comments regarding *Pro Caecina* (Frier 1989: 122): "It is plain that Cicero enjoys the high ground of *aequitas* and the spirit of the law." He must have expected on that occasion that invoking them to counter more literalist and legalistic interpretation of legislation would do much to help sway the jury in his client's favor—as it probably did (Frier 1989: 231–232).

The adjectives that would ordinarily correspond to the noun *aequitas* are *aequabilis*, meaning "equal," when the focus is on *aequitas* as equality (e.g. Cic. *De off.* 2.41–42: "Equal justice is what people always seek [i.e. from laws embodying *aequitas*]—justice cannot be anything else"), or *aequus*, which is ambiguous as between "equal" and "fair." The note of fairness is probably the one struck more loudly when Cicero says of the private individual—evidently by way of an intended commonplace—that he ought to live *aequo et pari cum civibus iure*, "in fair and equal justice with the citizens" (*De off.* 1.124). But when Livy makes a speaker talk of *aequum ius* being impossible unless the *plebs* have, through access to power, (*imperium*) an equal (*par*) share with the patricians in the commonwealth (6.37.4), his point is plainly one about the terms on which equal justice or equal rights are possible. In the second premise of his argument here, however, Cicero makes the unusual choice of *aequalis* as epithet (again meaning "equal"). I suspect this is because, while still wanting to evoke all the powerful associations of *aequitas* and *ius aequum*, talking of *ius legis aequale* (with the adjective in the neuter) allows him to hint at a significant wordplay: fairness = equal law, *aequa le*[*x*].

However that may be, the consequence Cicero draws from his two premises, and then spells out further in terms of equal rights, is both entirely logical and again thoroughly Roman. If a citizen society is bonded by law enshrining equal justice, then it follows that its members—the citizens—must have an equal status if they are to receive justice: they must have equal rights. That is precisely what Cicero thinks himself—and indeed takes to be uncontroversial as applied to private individuals. They should live in fair and equal justice with other citizens (*De off.* 1.124). The Ten Tables may have done little to ensure that the *plebs* as a class had political rights that achieved a balance with those reserved for patricians. Nonetheless the decemvirs insisted that they had "equalized rights" (Livy 3.34.3), a claim Livy represents as endorsed by the plebeians' champion Valerius (3.61.6), and as accepted with regret by the patricians (3.67.9). Although reconstructing the style and content of the Ten Tables is a hazardous business, it seems clear that the main achievement was to give definitive written formulation to customary private law. That will presumably have counted as an equalization of laws inasmuch as it provided any citizen, rich or poor, plebeian or patrician, with the same access in principle to knowledge of an established corpus of laws that applied to all equally as citizens, and that did not discriminate in content between citizens—hence the outrage when the decemvirs added their two further tables of "*un*equal" (unfair) laws (*iniquarum legum*), including the notorious rule prohibiting intermarriage between plebeians and patricians (e.g. Cic. *De rep.* 2.62–63).

So Cicero makes the democratic argument for equal rights exploit his own definition of what makes a *res publica* a *res publica*, in terms entirely at home in Roman thought, to achieve a general formulation of citizen equality which at that level of generality would constitute not just a valid deduction, but one any contemporary Roman would be more than happy to embrace—as the very foundation of Roman civil order. But of course, to work as a rationale for democracy the argument has to be taken more specifically as appealing to a conception of what *political* justice consists in if it is to generate the conclusion that all citizens should have equal *political* rights. And that is something no longer uncontroversial. Cicero makes Scipio argue on his own account that where, as in a radical democracy, all political business is transacted by the people itself, this is an equality (*aequabilitas*: cf. Fantham 1973) that is *in*equitable (*inique*), because it provides for no distinctions in rank (*dignitas*) or honor (*honos*) (*De rep.* 1.43; cf. 1.53). His view is that the people will do better to entrust the management of what remain their interests and affairs to those with more capacity for deliberation and policy (*consilium*) (Schofield 1995: 77–81).

Elsewhere he introduces a different kind of argumentative maneuver, but one designed likewise to undermine the case for democracy. In *De legibus* he has his brother Quintus allege it to be universally appreciated that the law providing for the secret ballot at elections has "deprived the best sort [*optimates*] of all their authority [*auctoritas*]." This was something, he goes on, that "a free people [*populus liber*] never wanted—they asked for it only when oppressed by the domination and sway of leading citizens" (i.e. popularist politicians) (*De leg.* 3.34; Cicero's response at *De leg.* 3.38–39 is more nuanced, but he indicates that his own proposal on the subject is designed to present the form of *libertas* while preserving the *auctoritas* of "good men": Nicolet 1970). A very similar line of thought is developed at greater length in the *Pro Sestio* (56 BCE), Cicero's fullest political manifesto, where the general resistance of "the true people" (*verus populus*, *Sest.* 108, 114) to popularists and their causes is given extensive chapter and verse. It is the Senate that is the constitutional guardian, custodian, and champion of the *res publica*. Magistrates are to be guided by its authority (*auctoritas*), and it is its historic responsibility to protect and enlarge the liberty and interests of the *plebs* (*Sest.* 137). Authority—*auctoritas*—is the final main topic on our agenda.

3 Authority

Sallust passes a grim verdict on the last decades of the Roman Republic (*Cat.* 38.3):

> All who troubled the commonwealth pretended concern for the public good, with slogans that sounded honorable, some maintaining that they were defending the rights of the people, others that they were intent on maximizing the authority [*auctoritas*] of the Senate. But they were contending each for his own control of events [*potentia*].

The rights of the people (which have been getting the lion's share of the attention in this chapter so far) are contrasted by Sallust with the authority of the Senate. But these could also be represented as complementary—indeed Sallust himself is probably implying that there was a time when they actually were (cf. *Iug.* 41.2). By the time Cicero composed his *Philippics* (44–43 BCE), their pairing has become almost a mannerism when he wants to talk of the twinned fundamental political values anyone who cares for the *res publica* will commit himself to upholding and championing (*Phil.* 4.5, 10.23, 13.33, 47). Senate and people together gave Rome its constitutional identity, as the emperor Augustus recognized when he claimed to have restored the commonwealth from his own power to the *arbitrium* (decision-making) of the Senate and the Roman people (*Res gestae* 34.2)—and as was of course in the acronym SPQR (*Senatus Populusque Romanus*) given symbolic expression on countless coins and inscriptions as well as on military standards. There was a crucial difference in constitutional status, however (see Rhodes, Chapter 8).

The formal designation of the Roman state was *res publica populi Romani Quiritium*, "the commonwealth of the citizens of the Roman people" (Varro, *Ling.* 6.86). The people was the sovereign body, and its decisions (in legislation, trials, and elections) were needed to legitimize the outcomes of the processes in question. These and other powers, such as the Roman version of *habeas corpus* (*provocatio*), or again the powers of the tribunes to act on behalf of the *plebs*, were exercises of that sovereignty—of its liberty. What the Senate exercised, by contrast, was *auctoritas*: not the legally authorized exercise of *imperium*, but authority in the sense of authoritative influence, deriving formally from its constitutional role as the chief forum for deliberating public policy and for advising the consuls and other senior magistrates on the decisions they needed to take—executive decisions were for magistrates, not the Senate itself—in order to implement it (for the institutional context, see Mouritsen, Chapter 9).

This was undoubtedly a rather extraordinary form of "influence." The Senate was the one relatively cohesive and stable political entity at Rome, with descendants of the same wealthy landowning families appearing generation after generation, acculturated to a strong aristocratic military ethos. Its influence when at its height represented enormous power, even if formally speaking that remained "advice," or "leadership" (*hēgemonia*), as Livy's Greek contemporary Dionysius of Halicarnassus conceptualized it in his *Roman Antiquities* (e.g. *Ant. Rom.* 6.71.3, 6.74.3, 6.85.1, 7.50.4; cf. Plut. *Rom.* 13.4). That advice could be formally expressed in *senatus consulta*, which were conceived as resolutions magistrates would ignore at their peril, with the *senatus consultum ultimum* a resolution "of last resort," which would purportedly authorize emergency action (overriding the laws) to protect the commonwealth from unusual danger.

What the late Republic called the authority of the Senate was the descendant of what Livy when writing about the early Republic called "the authority of the fathers" (e.g. 3.21.1, 6.19.4), i.e. of the hereditary aristocracy known as "patricians" from their designation corporately as *patres*, "fathers." Quite why they were so designated is unclear. Likewise: "It is very uncertain precisely what the *auctoritas patrum* amounted to" (Cornell 1995: 341). The Roman *paterfamilias*' legal powers over his family and household and its properties, if not universally absolute, fell not far short of being so. His authority in this sphere by the same token constituted something very much stronger than paternalistic "advice," "leadership," or "influence" (although Plutarch guessed that Romulus called senators "fathers" precisely to encourage them to exercise paternal care and consideration, without inspiring fear or envy [Plut. *Rom.* 13.3]). It more resembled sovereignty. Yet, as everyone knew, sovereignty was *not* vested in the Senate, not even in the early largely patrician Senate. The associations of the expression "the authority of the fathers" perhaps occupied a more indeterminate (and thereby the more potent) hinterland between advice commanding respect on account of its source, and the powers vested by law in a *paterfamilias*. Did talk of "the authority of the Senate" convey something of the same indeterminate resonance, reassuring or threatening, depending on circumstance and one's place in the social and political order?

Certainly the dynamics of popular liberty and senatorial authority ran in opposite directions: broadly speaking, democratic and oligarchic respectively. Livy writes the entire history of the early Republic as an unceasing sequence of struggles between these countervailing forces. On the other hand, given the constitutional division of responsibilities between consuls, Senate, and people, there was obviously no theoretical incompatibility between the authority of the Senate and the liberty of the people. In Book 2 of *De republica* Cicero—here following Polybius and conceivably also Panaetius, Greek theorists of the mid-second century BCE (*De rep.* 1.34, 2.27; Polyb. 6.11–18)—represented the contemporaneous Roman Republic as having achieved a balance between consular power, senatorial authority, and popular rights that made for harmony, not conflict. Whether or not it really did do that, there is nothing intrinsically impossible in the idea of a mixed constitution that *could* achieve it: the ideal form of constitution is what Cicero takes as his formal objective in the dialogue (cf. *De rep.* 2.64–66).

But it appeared to observers that in the last decades of the Republic any such balance had been and was being progressively shattered. In their assessment there had been a fatal blurring of the distinction between defense of the authority of the Senate and the concern for their own *dignitas*, their deserved status or pre-eminence in the perception of the people and of their peers, on the part of its leading members—something not in itself illegitimate. Long ago, early in the second century BCE, Cato the Censor had said (Malcovati, *ORF*, 3rd edn., 8.252): "Justice, law, liberty, the commonwealth—these must be things we share. Glory and honor are to be enjoyed as each achieves for himself." Now, however, to quote Sallust again, "the nobility began to turn their *dignitas* and the people their liberty into unrestrained desire" (*Iug.* 41.5), perhaps echoed in Livy's observation on how different from the struggle between liberty and *dignitas* that has prevailed in his own times was the "moderation, fairness [*aequitas*], and elevation of spirit" of which the people as a whole showed themselves capable in the period following the turbulent episode of the decemvirate (4.6.11–12).

Cicero complained in a letter to Lentulus Spinther of 55 BCE that the great aim of men who had succeeded in public life—"*dignitas* in expressing our views and *libertas* in taking our part in public affairs"—was altogether lost under the dominance of "the few," i.e. the triumvirate of Crassus, Pompey, and Caesar (*Fam.* 1.8.3). In other words, in his evidently partisan perception the dynasts had crushed both the liberty of the people, which not merely gave the *plebs* their rights, but ensured senior statesmen their own place in public life, and the proper *dignitas* they could expect to have recognized when they fulfilled their public responsibilities. Nor was that *dignitas* just (as he saw it) their own. Two years later we find Cicero writing to the spirited young Curio urging him at a time of affliction for the commonwealth to "prepare, reflect, and think" so as to be able to emancipate it into its "old *dignitas* and *libertas*" (*Fam.* 2.5.2; cf. e.g. *Phil.* 3.19: "the *libertas* and *dignitas* of the Roman people," i.e. the freedom and respect it used to enjoy). Others might have thought that Cicero's confidence that the *dignitas* and *libertas* of his own political class and those of the Roman people survived or fell together simply illustrated the historical diagnosis Sallust and Livy were subsequently to articulate.

4 Concluding Reflections

Before the full Latin version of Augustus' *Res gestae* was reconstituted, it was generally supposed that Mommsen must have been right in thinking that the emperor had ended his testament with the unpersuasive claim that, while he outstripped everyone in *dignitas*, he had no more power than those who were his colleagues in the magistracies he held (*Res gestae* 34.3)—on the reasonable assumption that *axiōma* in the Greek version best translates into Latin as *dignitas*. In fact with the discovery of the Monumentum Antiochenum it transpired that the word in question was *auctoritas*, something that was indeed inherent in one's *dignitas* (Cicero in an early work actually defined *dignitas* as "*auctoritas* deserving of devotion, honor, and respect": *Inv.* 2.166).

Richard Heinze, author in 1925 of the foundational modern study of the concept of *auctoritas*, observed that while all societies have to have room for a notion of authority, there is something distinctively Roman in *auctoritas*, highlighted by the comparison with Greece. The word signified a mutually reinforcing union of social and political standing and of impressiveness in character and judgment, with a consequential power to exert influence which was often summed up as *gravitas* (Hellegouarc'h 1963: 299–300). *Axiōma* is in fact better fitted to render *dignitas* than *auctoritas* (for which there is no entirely obvious or satisfactory Greek equivalent), and neither *axiōma* nor any similar Greek concept represented—as did *auctoritas* at Rome—a value fundamental to the ideological basis supporting the operation of the political system and the apparatus of government (Heinze 1925: 363–364). Greek political thought, both theoretical and practical, respected wisdom and judgment, and of course in many Greek cities there was a council (*boulē*) to advise or prepare business for the popular assembly (see Rhodes, Chapter 8; cf. Rhodes with Lewis 1997: 475–497). But there was no expression yoked habitually to *boulē* as was *auctoritas* to *senatus*, to indicate the weight of its deliberation or the respect it carried or deserved to carry. *Timē* ("honor"), the most obvious Greek equivalent for *dignitas*, was no less important as a motivation to politics; and in Athens political offices were standardly called *timai* (honors). But the Greeks seemed to have lacked the intense sense of hierarchy that led the Romans to devise the rigid career ladder of the *cursus honorum*, or the various forms of gradation governing the composition and procedures of the centuriate assembly.

Although equality and liberty were by contrast concepts fully at home in Greek as in Roman political discourse, their role in Roman republican culture was significantly—and by now not unexpectedly—different. Henrik Mouritsen has written (Mouritsen 2001: 11; also Chapter 9):

> *Libertas* was the common ideal invoked by all Romans who aspired to power, no matter what their political views and methods might otherwise have been.… All political acts and arguments must be justified within the ideological framework of the liberty of the *res publica* and the *populus Romanus*. And precisely because it was such a fundamental tenet of the identity of the Roman state, all political agents could draw moral capital from it and exploit it for their own purposes.

Greek politicians and theorists of politics of course invoked the ideal of freedom a good deal, not least when celebrating their escape from Persian tyranny or warning against similar threats. But for the Greeks it never constituted the framework within which different factions competing for power and for the moral high ground had to develop their rhetoric. Similarly, whereas Greek *isonomia* usually meant equal individual political rights (though classical Greek had no developed vocabulary of rights), and is often virtually synonymous with democracy, Roman talk of *ius aequum* or *leges aequae* could be applied to classes as well as to individuals and their citizen rights, and once again was common ground for all Romans—it struck no distinctively democratic resonances (Wirszubski 1950: 13–15).

In Greece it looks as though the warring or potentially warring classes subscribed to quite different ideologies—which could indeed be nuanced to appropriate some of the opposition's rhetoric and lines of thinking, but remained in essence poles apart. At Rome things were different. It may never have achieved the harmony of the mixed constitution celebrated by Cicero's Scipio. Yet the liberty of the Roman people and the fundamental significance of the idea of the *res publica* constituted shared values, so that the struggles between the *plebs* and their champions and the Senate and its protagonists sound much more like family debates and fractures than ever was the case in Greece—as Greek observers themselves commented (Dionys. *Ant. Rom.* 7.66.4–5; App. *B. civ.* 1.1.1).

ACKNOWLEDGMENTS

Warmest thanks to Valentina Arena, Stephen Oakley, Peter Rhodes, and Peter Wiseman for comments, corrections, and suggestions.

REFERENCES

Arena, V. 2012. *Libertas and the Practice of Politics in the Late Roman Republic*. Cambridge.

Brunt, P.A. 1988. *The Fall of the Roman Republic and Related Essays*. Oxford.

Cornell, T.J. 1995. *The Beginnings of Rome: Italy and Rome from the Bronze Age to the Punic Wars (c.1000–264 BC)*. London.

Crawford, M.H. 1974. *Roman Republican Coinage*. Cambridge.

Fantham, E. 1973. "*Aequabilitas* in Cicero's Political Thought, and the Greek Tradition of Proportional Justice." *CQ* 23: 285–290.

Frede, D. 1989. "Constitution and Citizenship: Peripatetic Influence on Cicero's Political Conceptions in the *De re publica*." In W.W. Fortenbaugh and P. Steinmetz, eds., *Cicero's Knowledge of the Peripatos*. New Brunswick, 77–100.

Frier, B. 1985. *The Rise of the Roman Jurists. Studies in Cicero's* Pro Caecina. Princeton.

Heinze, R. 1925. "Auctoritas." *Hermes* 60: 348–366.

Hellegouarc'h, J. 1963. *Le Vocabulaire latin des relations et des parties politiques dans la République*. Paris. 2nd edn. 1972.

Nicolet, C. 1970. "Cicéron, Platon et le vote secret." *Historia* 19: 39–66.

Oakley, S.P. 2005. *A Commentary on Livy Books VI–X*, vol. 4. Oxford.

Ogilvie, R.M. 1965. *A Commentary on Livy Books 1–5*. Oxford.

Pettit, P. 1997. *Republicanism: A Theory of Freedom and Government*. Oxford.

Rhodes, P.J. with D.M. Lewis 1997. *The Decrees of the Greek States*. Oxford.

Schofield, M. 1995. "Cicero's Definition of *Res Publica*." In J.G.F. Powell, ed., *Cicero the Philosopher: Twelve Essays*. Oxford, 63–83.

Skinner, Q.R.D. 1998. *Liberty before Liberalism*. Cambridge.

Solmsen, F. 1933. "Die Theorie der Staatsformen bei Cicero *De re publica* I." *Philologus* 88: 326–341.

Wirszubski, C. 1950. Libertas *as a Political Idea at Rome during the Late Republic and Early Principate*. Cambridge.

Wiseman, T.P. 2009. *Remembering the Roman People. Essays on Late-Republican Politics and Literature* . Oxford.

Zetzel, J.E.G., ed. 1995. *Cicero De Re Publica. Selections*. Cambridge.

Zetzel, J.E.G., ed. 1999. *Cicero On the Commonwealth and On the Laws*. Cambridge.

FURTHER READING

There are two excellent well-established general studies of the subject matter of this chapter, each taking the idea of *libertas* as its main focus, and providing authoritative guidance on the whole topic. Wirszubski 1950 is an attractively written monograph, although readers whose Latin is not as fluent as they might wish will need to have translations or dictionaries to hand, since the frequent quotations are left in the original. The chapter in Brunt 1988 entitled "*Libertas* in the Republic" does not present the same problem. It engages with the historical realities in greater detail and depth, as well as offering acute discussion of many of the conceptual issues. A major new treatment (Arena 2012) highlights the Romans" common understanding of liberty as fundamentally non-domination, but argues that optimate and *popularis* appeals to *libertas* typically reflect two distinct, well-developed intellectual traditions.

For understanding the way the vocabulary of liberty, equality, and authority functioned in political discourse, a useful resource is Hellegouarc'h 1963. Cicero's political theory in *On the Commonwealth* (*De republica*) and *On the Laws* (*De legibus*) is best approached via Zetzel 1999, which as well as its translation supplies introduction, bibliography, synopsis, and notes on key terms. Cicero is inevitably a main source, though his voice as always needs counterbalancing with, for example, Sallust's. Viewpoints associated with more "popularist" political leaders, to whose ambitions, activity, and ultimately ascendancy Cicero was so bitterly opposed, are unearthed and sympathetically assessed in Wiseman 2009—which relates also to an ongoing scholarly debate about how much the people (whether in its powers as a formally constituted body or as the Roman *plebs*) really mattered in late republican politics.

The afterlife of the Roman ideal of *libertas* in the Western political tradition has received considerable attention in recent years: see, for example, Skinner 1998 (with bibliography). Contemporary political philosophers have developed and advocated a theory of "republican liberty," as what might be seen as a middle way between political philosophy in communitarian style and the prevailing individualistic political liberalism: see Pettit 1997.

PART IV

Institutions

CHAPTER 8

The Congruence of Power: Ruling and Being Ruled in Greek Participatory Communities

P.J. Rhodes

1 The Development of the Greeks' Institutions

After the dark age around 1000 BCE, there developed in the Greek world a very large number of separate political communities. The form of community which the Greeks came to think of as typical was the *polis* (city-state: I shall hereafter use the term "city"), which might be dependent on a more powerful state in external matters but had a considerable degree of independence in the running of its own internal affairs. However, particularly towards the north and west of mainland Greece, some Greeks lived in less developed communities which were grouped and had some of their power vested in regional bodies, and in some areas (such as Boeotia from the late sixth century onwards) cities too could be combined in a federal organization which conducted external business for the whole federation. Athens and some other large cities had their own subsidiary bodies ("demes" in the case of Athens) which were structured as cities in miniature, with their own members and institutions and the right to administer some local affairs, but bodies of this kind had less separate identity and power than the cities in a federation. The network of Greek political communities was not fixed unalterably, but over time there were changes as new entities were created (often by the equal or unequal combination of pre-existing smaller units) and existing entities were dissolved.

Leaving aside the less developed local units, it has been estimated that at any one time in the fifth and fourth centuries there were about 1,000 Greek cities, about 600 in the heartland of mainland Greece, the Aegean islands and the Aegean coast of Asia Minor, and 400 in settlements elsewhere around the Mediterranean and the Black Sea. Only four of these—Athens and Sparta in Greece, Syracuse in Sicily, and Panticapaeum in the Crimea—had with their surrounding territory an area of more than 2,000 km^2, and another nine between 1,000 and 2,000 km^2, while 80 percent had no more than 200 km^2. Athens in the third quarter of the fifth century had perhaps 60,000 adult

A Companion to Greek Democracy and the Roman Republic, First Edition. Edited by Dean Hammer.

male citizens and a total population of several hundred thousand, but many small cities had under 1,000 adult male citizens and under 5,000 total population (see in particular Hansen, in Hansen and Nielsen 2004: 53–54, 70–73, Hansen 2006: 73–84). No Greek city became so large in territory and in citizen population as to make the notion of participation in government by the citizens wholly unrealistic, as Rome did. The various cities came to occupy different points on the spectrum of oligarchy and democracy, but despite differences in emphasis they were constitutionally similar in their overall pattern, while varying in their particular details (and of course smaller states needed less elaborate machinery than larger states). However, in most cases we lack the detailed information which is available for Athens and to some extent for Sparta, so this chapter will inevitably have to concentrate on Athens and Sparta.

At first the cities seem to have been ruled by kings (of a far more modest kind than the grand despots of the near-eastern kingdoms), but before long these gave way to collective rule by an aristocracy of the families which had emerged from the dark age as the owners of the largest quantities of good agricultural land, and (while as in the *Iliad* and the *Odyssey* kings will on occasions have consulted other members of their communities) it was in this context that formal political institutions began to develop (see Raaflaub, Chapter 2). Fundamental were an assembly of all members of the community who had a share in political power (limited always to adult males, and in these aristocratic communities to those who belonged to the right families and/or owned sufficient property), and one or more officials appointed for a limited period, commonly a year. Our earliest surviving inscribed Greek law is from Dreros, in Crete, and is probably to be dated to the second half of the seventh century: it is presented as a decision of the *polis*, it prescribes that a man who has served as *kosmos* may not serve again for ten years (to protect the solidarity of the aristocracy against the risk that one of its members may step out of line), and an oath to uphold it is to be sworn (every year?) by the current *kosmoi*, the *damioi* (perhaps treasurers) and "the twenty of the *polis*" (perhaps a council: see below) (ML 2, trans. Fornara 11).

In the seventh and sixth centuries the growing pains of the cities often involved a period in which power was seized by a "tyrant," commonly an ambitious man on the fringes of the ruling aristocracy, who appealed to sections of the population which for any reason were disaffected, and who might rule either through existing institutions or autocratically. Tyrants in turn became a cause of disaffection, and their rule lasted at most for three generations, after which most cities came to have participatory regimes in which the landed aristocracy still tried to dominate but some political power, at any rate membership of the assembly which possessed the ultimate right to make major decisions, was shared, at any rate among all men rich enough to fight in the city's army as hoplites (heavy infantry).

Athens by the middle of the fifth century had taken the final steps towards democracy (*dēmokratia*, "people power," distinguished from *oligarchia*, "rule by a few"), in which even the poorest citizens, who did not fight in the army but rowed the navy's warships, were accepted as full members of the community (though they were admitted to office-holding only in the less populous Athens of the fourth century), and the balance was tipped so that the assembly and bodies representative of the citizens as a whole were powerful, the officials were comparatively weak, and there was no distinction between a ruling class and the remainder of the citizens (on the typical distinctions between democratic and oligarchic regimes notice Arist. *Pol.* 6.1317b17–1318a10). From the middle of the fifth century, Athens took to inscribing public documents on stone on an unusually large scale, and in the fifth and fourth centuries (but not earlier or later) most of the Greek literature which survives was written by Athenians or by non-Athenians in Athens, so in the classical period we are much more fully informed about Athens than about other cities. Nevertheless, while Athens was distinctive for its democracy, and for its size, which led to the development of an exceptionally elaborate governmental apparatus, it was not different in kind from other cities, whether democratic or oligarchic, but had its own embodiment of a pattern of institutions which was widespread across the Greek world. This chapter will therefore have to rely on Athens for much of the detail, but will be concerned with the general Greek pattern of participatory institutions.

2 The Body of Participants

The citizen bodies of a state were articulated in various ways. In several states including Athens new locally based "tribes" (*phylai*) were created some time before 500, beside or in place of older tribes based on imagined kinship, and membership of the new tribes itself became hereditary. In Athens the old tribes and smaller units known as "phratries" (*phratriai*, "brotherhoods") survived; but the new tribes became the basis of the city's political life, and they were each divided into three "thirds" (*trittyes*), each in a different part of Attica, and the thirds were in turn composed of varying numbers of the local units known as "demes" (a special use of the word *dēmos*, "people") (see Traill 1975). All of these had their own participatory institutions. There were also various other units within the state to which citizens might belong.

Sparta retained the three tribes which it shared with the other cities belonging to the Dorian strand of the Greek people, but in the reforms attributed to Lycurgus (probably to be placed in fact in the early seventh century) the citizens were also distributed over five local units known as "obes," corresponding to the four villages of Sparta proper and Amyclae, a short distance to the south (this has been much debated, but see the Great Rhetra in Plut. *Lyc.* 6.2 and MacDowell 1986: 26–27). In Sparta the full citizens, the Spartiates, were a minority among the native population: there were in addition a large number of *perioikoi* ("dwellers around"), free men living in their own cities and able to run the affairs of those cities but subordinate to the Spartan citizens in external affairs, and "helots" (a word which probably means "captives"), men in a servile condition required to work the land of the Spartan citizens who owned it (see MacDowell 1986: 27–37). Important among other units within Sparta were the messes (*syssitia* was the general Greek term, *pheiditia* perhaps the particular Spartan term): each citizen had to obtain admission to one of these (a single adverse vote excluded), and to contribute food to it and eat at it (see Michell 1952: 281–297).

3 Making Decisions

As noted above, a fundamental institution of Greek cities was the assembly (often called *ekklēsia*, but some cities used other words), open to all adult male citizens. In a democratic state that would mean all free men of native ancestry; in an oligarchic state there would commonly be a property qualification. Although the citizen body could be subdivided in various ways (see above), and in Rome different kinds of assembly were based on different subdivisions, and produced different kinds of block votes, in the Greek cities the subdivisions were irrelevant to membership of the assembly, which was an undifferentiated body of qualified citizens, who voted as individuals. An enactment of an assembly was known as a decree (*psēphisma*, "thing voted," or some other term).

Regularly, though perhaps not universally, the assembly's business would be prepared by a council (*boulē* or some other term), which could be recruited in various ways. In Athens this was a body of 500, fifty from each of the ten tribes, by lot from the candidates in the 139 demes, for one year at a time, with service limited until the end of the fourth century to two years in a man's life; on the abolition of the limit, perhaps in 307/6 when with the creation of two new tribes the membership of the council was increased from 500 to 600 (see Rhodes 2006: 33 and n.35, 38 and n.69; Byrne 2009). In Sparta there was a *gerousia* (council of *gerontes*, "elders"), comprising the two kings and twenty-eight men aged over 60, elected by the assembly from a privileged circle of families for what remained of their lives. Typically, the council would meet more often than the assembly; it had some decision-making powers of its own, and by the procedure known as *probouleusis* it chose the business to be discussed by the assembly. The relationship between the two bodies could vary. In Athens a great many decisions were taken by the assembly, in Sparta far fewer. In Athens the council could make a specific recommendation when it referred a matter to the assembly, but it did not always do so; and, while the assembly could not discuss matters not referred to it by the council, in the assembly's debate any citizen could speak, and could put forward a new proposal or an amendment to a proposal already under discussion. In the Spartan assembly only the ephors (see below), kings, and *gerontes* could make speeches or proposals, while the ordinary citizens listened to the debate and decided, but their power of decision was significant only when the ephors, kings, and *gerontes* were themselves divided. (This seems the best way to reconcile the emphasis on the power of the *gerousia* by Arist. *Pol.* 2.1273a6–13, cf. 1272a10–12 and the Great Rhetra as quoted and discussed in Plut. *Lyc.* 6, with the location of decision-making in the assembly and silence on the *gerousia* by Thucydides and Xenophon's *Hellenika*.) The formal relationship between council and assembly was strikingly different in the Greek cities from that in Rome, where the Senate and magistrates dominated the decision-making process in practice (as also, for instance, in Sparta) but in theory the Senate's function was simply to advise the magistrates.

In Athens votes were taken usually by show of hands, estimated rather than precisely counted, but ballots were used on motions affecting named individuals, to check that a quorum of 6,000 had been achieved; in Sparta voting was by acclamation, with men in a windowless hut deciding which was the louder shout. (See on the council and assembly in Athens [Arist.] *Ath. Pol.* 43.2–44; Hansen 1999: 125–160, 246–257; and, in more detail, Rhodes 1972; Hansen 1987; on the *gerousia* and assembly in Sparta, see Michell 1952: 135–148.)

In Athens the presidents of the council and assembly were perhaps at first the nine archons (see below), but from the middle of the fifth century were provided by the council: until c.380 the *prytaneis*, the fifty members of the council appointed from one of the ten tribes, serving as a standing committee and in this capacity for a tenth of the year; after that a separate sub-committee of nine *proedroi*, changing every day. In Sparta the ephors presided. There were various procedural safeguards: in Athens, at any rate by the late fifth century, an improper decree and its proposer could be challenged in a law court through a *graphē paranomōn* ("public prosecution for illegality":

see Hansen 1974); some major decisions in Athens were spread over two days; some decrees in Athens and elsewhere sought to protect themselves against subsequent change or annulment by including an entrenchment clause, forbidding annulment either absolutely or unless a previous meeting of the assembly passed a special vote of immunity (see Rhodes with Lewis 1997: 16–17, 521–526, 552). In the fourth century Athens distinguished between "laws" (*nomoi*), of higher status and validity, and decrees, of lower status and validity, and introduced an elaborate procedure for enacting laws in which the assembly was involved but the final decision was taken by a smaller body of *nomothetai* ("legislators"); improper laws, like improper decrees, could be challenged in a law court (see Hansen 1999: 161–177; many details remain uncertain).

In Rome the role of the assemblies in electing officials and making decisions was passive, but it was nevertheless important because the *populus* was considered the ultimate source of authority. In Greek cities, whether the citizens in assembly were active as in Athens or passive as in Sparta, the assembly was seen as the body which made at any rate the most important decisions, and allotted and elected officials were not above the citizens, as in Rome, but were agents given duties for a limited term by the citizens and accountable to the citizens (see below).

4 Implementing Decisions

In modern states representative institutions are used for making decisions, and government departments may be headed by representatives who have to make political decisions, but the carrying out of decisions is entrusted to professional administrators, who are expected to work with efficiency and political neutrality. In the Greek states, while the citizens were involved together in making decisions, they were involved in turn in carrying out the decisions, and this is what Aristotle was referring to when he wrote of a citizen as a man who would rule and be ruled in turn (Arist. *Pol.* 2.1261a30–b6). A few public slaves might be employed for low-level work: for Athens see [Arist.] *Ath. Pol.* 47.5–48.1 (keeping records of contracts and payments), 50.2 (removing the bodies of those who die in the streets), 54.1 (repairing the roads), 65 (assisting in the procedures for assigning jurors to courts). Otherwise there was a range of offices and boards to which citizens were appointed, usually for a limited term (often a year) and often with restrictions on reappointment (as in seventh-century Dreros, above). Some offices might be recognized as more important than others, but Greek states did not have a formal *cursus honorum* as Rome did. Many civilian appointments were made by allotment: this was often regarded as characteristic of democracy, but oligarchic regimes could use allotment also to share out positions among men considered equally eligible; in most cases the work did not require a high level of skill, and the principle of sharing out the work fairly among the citizens was considered more important than finding the best man for the job (allotment was considered characteristic of democracy [e.g. Arist. *Pol.* 4.1294b7–9], but was used for instance under the oligarchy in Athens in 411 [Thuc. 8.70.1, cf. the constitutional documents in [Arist.] *Ath. Pol.* 30–31]).

In early Athens the senior officials were the nine archons (*archontes*: a special sense of a word meaning "rulers"), three probably instituted earlier than the remaining six. They were appointed originally by election, for one year without repetition, and after the year were admitted to the Council of the Areopagus. By the middle of the fifth century they were routine officials, appointed by lot, and eventually a secretary was added to make ten, of whom one could come from each tribe; they still joined the Areopagus, but that council was no longer politically powerful apart from a resurgence between the 340s and 320s (see [Arist.] *Ath. Pol.* 3 [later reconstruction rather than attested history], 8.1–2, 22.5, 26.2, 55–59, 62.1, 3; and, on the reduction of the Areopagus' powers in 462/1, 25.1–2).

Athens made considerable use of boards of ten men (or occasionally multiples) based on the ten tribes; nearly all were appointed by lot, without repetition on the same board (for a selection see [Arist.] *Ath. Pol.* 46–48, 50–54, 60; the general principle, 43.1, 62.3). The Council of 500 had general oversight of the administration ([Arist.] *Ath. Pol.* 47.1, 49.5), and some of the particular boards were appointed from among the council's members. The generals and other military officials were elected (originally on a tribal basis, but for the generals, after a period in which one per tribe was normal but no longer universal, the link with the tribes was eventually abandoned) and could be re-elected (see [Arist.] *Ath. Pol.* 22.2, 61, 62.3; and, on the second half of the fifth century and first half of the fourth, Mitchell 2000). In the second and third quarters of the fifth century the leading politicians tended to be among the men elected as generals, but after that politicians tended to rely on their ability to make persuasive speeches in the assembly and law courts, and did not regularly (though they might still sometimes) hold any office. Although warfare was one of the major concerns of the Greek cities, as it was in Rome, and military commanders were important in Athens as in many cities, the highest positions in the state were not everywhere tied necessarily to military command as they were in Rome.

One civilian position which was seen as requiring skill and was filled by election (but still for a single year without repetition) was that of the secretary whose job it was to read out documents at meetings of the council and assembly ([Arist.] *Ath. Pol.* 54.5); but the principal secretary of the state was appointed until the 360s for one-tenth of the year by election from the fifty members of one tribe in the council, after that by allotment from volunteers among the citizens of one tribe for a year ([Arist.] *Ath. Pol.* 54.3, supplemented by the evidence of inscriptions). From the middle of the fourth century, after half a century of over-stretched finances, there were elected and powerful financial officials (theoric official/board, [Arist.] *Ath. Pol.* 43.1, 47.2; Aeschin. 3 *In Ctes.* 25; and on that and the office "in charge of administration" [*epi tēi dioikēsei*] see Rhodes 1972: 105–108, 235–240). Although the poorest citizens were excluded from office-holding until the fourth century, most offices were open to men of moderate means, and to make it easier for them to exercise their rights and for the state to fill its many offices modest stipends were introduced, probably between the 450s and the 430s (jury pay earliest, and probably 450s: [Arist.] *Ath. Pol.* 27.3–4; stipends in existence by 411: Thuc. 8.67.3, 69.4, 97.2; [Arist.] *Ath. Pol.* 29.5, 33.1). Some scholars believe (but on the basis of silence, not positive evidence, and I am not convinced) that many of the offices were not salaried in the fourth century: see Hansen 1979b, 1971–80 (offices unpaid); Gabrielsen 1981 (offices paid).

Officials were not merely appointed by and from the citizen body but (in the Greek cities in contrast to Rome) they were accountable to the citizen body. The Athenians were proud of their detailed procedures for accountability: an initial vetting, *dokimasia*, before the beginning of the year ([Arist.] *Ath. Pol.* 45.3, 55.2–4, 56.1, 59.4); an interim financial check ([Arist.] *Ath. Pol.* 48.3) and a vote of confidence ([Arist.] *Ath. Pol.* 43.4, 61.2) in each tenth of the year; a final examination, the financial *logos* ([Arist.] *Ath. Pol.* 54.3) and the general *euthynai* ("straightening": [Arist.] *Ath. Pol.* 48.4–5), after the end of the year. However, accountability was not limited to Athens or to democratic states, but was a general Greek principle, though with regard to who might take the initiative and who would pass the final judgment states of different complexions applied the principle in different ways (see Rhodes 2005: 1–7; what Arist. *Pol.* 3.1281b32–1282a41 and elsewhere considered democratic was the use of the whole body of citizens as the body which held officials to account).

The duty of holding officials to account was taken seriously, and in Athens and elsewhere there are many instances of men's being judged unsatisfactory. I give a few striking instances from Athens: Pericles was deposed from the generalship and fined in 431/30, but re-elected for 430/29 (Thuc. 2.59.2, 65.3–4, Diod. Sic. 12.45.4, Plut. *Per.* 35.4–5); Callistratus, a leading politician of the 370s–360s, was prosecuted and condemned in his absence in 361, and later risked returning to Athens but was put to death (Hyp. *Euxenippus* 1–2; Lycurg. *Leoc.* 93); some time in the fifth century the *hellenotamiai* (treasurers of Athens' Delian League) were judged guilty of embezzlement, and nine were executed, but the truth was discovered in time to save the tenth (Antiph. *Herodes* 69); in 344/3 the *thesmothetai* (the six junior archons) were deposed but acquitted and reinstated ([Dem.] *Theocrines* 27–28). There were various charges on which officials might be prosecuted, and it was a problem with Athens' orator-politicians of the late fifth century and after who did not necessarily hold any office that they could not be controlled as office-holders could. This led to such charges as the *graphē paranomōn* for proposing an improper decree (above), and to the clause in the fourth-century law on *eisangelia* (sometimes translated "impeachment": a special procedure for prosecuting major public offenses) specifying, "If any one, being a speaker [*rhētōr*, used of the men who spoke frequently in the assembly], says what is not best for the people of Athens, taking bribes" (Hyp. *Euxenippus* 8). Ostracism was instituted by Cleisthenes, first used in the 480s and still theoretically available in fourth century ([Arist.] *Ath. Pol.* 22.1.3–4, 43.5): it gave the citizens each year the opportunity to send one man into exile without finding him guilty of any offense, and came to be a way of letting them choose between rival political leaders. However, after the ostracism of (probably) 415 had led to the removal not of one of the rivals Alcibiades and Nicias but of its proposer Hyperbolus, it was judged to be too unreliable a weapon and was not used again (Plut. *Alc.* 13, *Nic.* 11, and, more briefly, *Arist.* 7.3–4; Thuc. 8.73.3 mentions Hyperbolus' murder and the fact that he had been ostracized; for discussion with further references see Rhodes 1994).

Sparta had not one hereditary king but two (probably as a result of the amalgamation of two neighboring communities). These were retained until the Hellenistic period, and remained powerful as commanders of the army and *ex officio* members of the *gerousia*, but not later than the 550s five ephors (*ephoroi*, "overseers") were created (Chilon in 555/4 is the first attested powerful ephor: Diog. Laert. 1.68), who were elected for one year without repetition from the whole body of citizens; by the mid-fourth century that body had become so small that one citizen in three or four must have served a year as ephor (Rhodes 1981b). They were the civilian heads of state, presiding in the *gerousia* and assembly and enjoying considerable executive power, especially over non-citizens. They were not always opposed to the kings or to one of them, but there was always a possibility of tension, and when a king had to be put under pressure or brought to trial that was their responsibility (on the kings and ephors see Michell 1952: 101–131, discussing various theories). In the sixth century Anaxandridas II was obliged to take a second wife when his first failed to bear him an heir (Hdt. 5.39–41); the trial of Cleomenes I after failing to follow up a victory over Argos at the beginning of the fifth century (Hdt. 6.81.2) is the first of a series of attested trials of kings and regents. Other officials of whom we hear (cf. Michell 1952: 233–280) are mostly military. More elaborately than in other states, there was within the Spartan army a hierarchy of units with their own commanding officers (Thuc. 5.66.3–4, 68.3; Xen. *Lac. Pol.* 11.4–6). Forces not consisting of full citizens could be commanded by men other than kings, and for these and for garrison commanders in cities the term "harmost" (*harmostēs*) came to be used: in Asia Minor in the 390s harmosts of the first kind were appointed annually, were subject to inspection and could be reappointed (harmosts with non-citizen army, e.g. Xen. *Hell.* 3.1.4, with garrison e.g. 3.1.9, inspection and reappointment e.g. 3.2.6). For the navy an admiral (*nauarchos*, "ship-commander") was appointed, originally perhaps for the duration of a campaign, but from the late fifth century annually without repetition (Sealey 1976), so that when the Spartans wanted to make further use in 405/4 of the successful Lysander they appointed another man as figurehead with Lysander as his secretary (Xen. *Hell.* 2.1.7).

5 Justice

The administration of justice in the Greek world was again based on citizen involvement rather than expertise. In Athens most lawsuits could be divided into *dikai* (also the generic term for lawsuits of any kind), private suits, in which only the injured party or his or her relatives could prosecute (this category included homicide), and *graphai* ("writings"), public suits, in which any citizen could prosecute. Officials and official bodies might become aware of offenses in the course of their duties, but publicly appointed prosecutors were rarely used. The final trial was held in a jury-court (*dikastērion*) and lasted not more than one day: one of the archons or another official presided, but did not provide expert guidance; litigants had to plead their own cases, but could employ speech-writers and could make over part of their time allowance to supporting speakers; verdicts were given and penalties were decided by a jury of several hundred citizens (for some offenses the laws prescribed a penalty, for others the jury had to choose between the penalties proposed by prosecutor and defendant). On Athens' judicial system in general see Hansen 1999: 178–224 (where the chapter title, "The People's Court," is misleading in that there is nothing in the Greek terminology—as there was, for instance, in the "Volkspolizei" of the erstwhile Deutsche Demokratische Republik—which expresses the notion of "People's"); we have a large number of Athenian law-court speeches from the century c.420–c.320, and there is an account of a day in the courts in [Arist.] *Ath. Pol.* 63–69. From 453/2 the smaller private suits were judged by traveling magistrates (*dikastai kata demous*, "justices by the demes": [Arist.] *Ath. Pol.* 16.5, referring to the sixth-century tyranny, 26.3, 53.1–2: from the last years of the Peloponnesian War they no longer traveled but worked in Athens), and from 399/8 the larger private suits were decided by an arbitrator, a 59-year-old man in his last year on the military registers ([Arist.] *Ath. Pol.* 53.2–6); these suits went to a jury only if there was an appeal.

There were special procedures for certain kinds of offense. In general, in a world in which powers of enforcement were weak, the Greeks did not believe in a separation of powers and therefore a separate judiciary, but believed that administrative bodies needed judicial power to reinforce their executive power: thus the Council of 500 was a court of first instance for various administrative matters, but its powers of punishment were limited and if it wanted to go beyond a fine of 500 drachmae it had to refer a case to a jury-court ([Dem.] *Evergus & Mnesibulus* 43; [Arist.] *Ath. Pol.* 45.1 reports the removal from the council of greater powers which I believe it never possessed: see Rhodes 1981a: 537–538). For some offenders there were procedures involving the taking of the offender to the authorities or of the authorities to the offender, and common criminals ("thieves, kidnappers and clothes-stealers") could be put to death without trial if they acknowledged their guilt (see Hansen 1976, and on common criminals [Arist.] *Ath. Pol.* 52.1).

The Athenians made heavy use of their judicial system: it has been estimated that in the fourth century, when no private suits went to a court except on appeal, there were sittings of the courts on 175–225 days a year (see Hansen 1979a). Each year there was a panel of 6,000 jurors (attested for the fifth century, e.g. [Arist.] *Ath. Pol.* 24.3, and presumed for the fourth), open to all citizens over the age of 30 including the poorest, and from probably the 450s paid on the days when they served (see above); and by the middle of the fourth century, in order to prevent bribery, jurors were assigned to courts day by day by an elaborate system which ensured that nobody could know in advance which men would try which case and no juror could know in advance which men would be his colleagues in his particular court. Through involvement in the enactment of laws and decrees, and in the judicial system as presiding officers, litigants, and jurors, many Athenians became familiar with the law and judicial procedures, but with the exception of a few specialists in sacred law (e.g. Andoc. *Mysteries* 116, Lys. *Andocides* 10) Athens had no legal experts; and although litigants might cite precedents which they hoped would support their cases there was no official record of precedents and interpretations: each jury started from scratch in deciding the application of the law to the case presented to it. Some scholars recently have seen an Athenian trial as a contest between the litigants for the favor of the people rather than an attempt to apply the law, but it is better to accept that the Athenian courts did genuinely attempt to apply the law (see the editors' introduction in Harris and Rubinstein 2004: 1–18) but had a more generous understanding of relevance than courts in our world (in particular, where the point legally at issue was one element in a larger dispute, speakers would tend to deal with the whole story of the larger dispute: Rhodes 2004). A more serious objection to Athenian justice from our point of view is that the Athenians did not distinguish as clearly as we should wish between unlawful behavior and unsuccessful or politically misjudged behavior.

For Sparta we have little information except on cases of major public importance (see in general MacDowell 1986: 123–150). The enactment of new laws in the classical period was by the usual decree-making procedure of the *gerousia* and assembly, and it may be that the ephors had to take the initiative (see MacDowell, 1986: 5–8; ephors' initiative, Plut. *Lys.* 17.2; *Agis* 5.3, 8.1—but the first two laws are probably fictitious: Hodkinson 2000: 25–29, 90–94). Cases against citizens in which the penalty was death, exile, or loss of rights were tried by the *gerousia* (Xen. *Lac. Pol.*, 10.2; Plut. *Lyc.* 26.2; cf. Arist. *Pol.* 4.1294b33–34); when a king was on trial the other king retained his vote and the ephors voted too (Paus. 3.5.2). Passages in which "the Spartans" decided the verdict (e.g. Hdt. 6.82; Thuc. 5.63.4) do not necessarily mean that the case was referred to the assembly, but the assembly does seem to have been involved on two occasions when who was to succeed to the throne was at issue (Hdt. 6.66.2, Xen. *Hell.* 3.3.4, but contrast Paus. 3.6.2, where in the third century the *gerousia* decided). The kings tried a few cases, in particular concerning heiresses and adoption, religious matters, and perhaps cases arising between citizens in the army on campaign. The ephors had considerable discretion; sometimes individually and sometimes jointly, they tried many cases, particularly private disputes, and their power over non-citizens perhaps extended to the death penalty. *Hellanodikai* ("Greek justices") perhaps dealt with cases involving non-Spartans (Xen. *Lac. Pol.* 13.11).

The extent to which we can speak of a "unity" of Greek law has been much disputed. Each state had its own local laws, with their own local details, and (for instance), when we compare the provisions for heiresses (daughters of a man who left no sons) in Athens, Sparta, and Gortyn (in Crete), we find three distinct sets of rules (for Gortyn see *IC* iv.72, vii.15–ix.24; text with translation and commentary Willetts 1967). On the other hand, although the details varied from place to place, the different Greek states confronted the same kinds of problems, and they came up with the same kinds of solutions to those problems, with regard both to substantive law and to the procedures for implementing the law. (In a recent study Gagarin 2005 argues for a procedural but not a substantive unity, but as Harris 2008: 215 remarks in reviewing that book, "there is much more evidence than he allows for shared principles in substantive law"; Todd 2012: 812 concluded that "Greek law, if it existed, was not a national legal system, but a family of systems like Islamic law today".) In the Hellenistic period, at times of crisis states often resorted to "foreign judges," i.e. judges invited from another state, to resolve their disputes, on the assumption that these men's understanding of the general principles and lack of personal involvement in the local disputes would outweigh their ignorance of the details of the local laws (see Spawforth 2012).

6 Religion

Religion was "embedded" in society and the state, as Christianity used to be embedded in Europe (but contrast Amendment I (1791) to the Constitution of the U.S.A.—"Congress shall make no law respecting an establishment of religion, or prohibiting the free exercise thereof"—though in its original intention this was only semi-detached: very probably the purpose was to take Christianity for granted but to make the state neutral between different forms of Christianity), and Islam is still embedded in some Muslim states. It was not a matter of private choice, from which the state kept at arm's length, but was one integral aspect of the life of the community; and, although the Greeks could distinguish between sacred and secular—they maintained separate sacred treasuries (in Athens, the treasury of Athena, [Arist.] *Ath. Pol.* 8.1, which refers simply to the "treasurers," 47.1; a consolidated treasury of the Other Gods was created probably in 434/3, ML 58 = *IG* I^3 52, trans. Fornara 119; over the next ninety years these were sometimes combined and sometimes reseparated), and prescribed that sacred business should have priority in meetings of the assembly ([Arist.] *Ath. Pol.* 43.6, and many inscriptions from Athens and elsewhere, e.g. *IG* II^2 1 = RO 2.73, 107 = 31.16 [the second mistranslated in Harding 53])—they were willing to use sacred treasuries for secular purposes, in their assemblies they made decisions on sacred matters as they made decisions on secular matters, and religious officials were state officials like any others (for Athens see Rhodes 2009). The embeddedness of religion in Rome was similar, but there favorable omens seem to have been required to authorize a range of public activities more often than in Greece.

In Athens, priests and some other functionaries of the older cults were appointed from specified families, while in the newer cults they were appointed from "all Athenians" (male or female as judged appropriate in each case), and when there were rival contenders the use of allotment gave the gods a say in the choice of their servants (see Lambert 2010). Other functionaries, such as *hieropoioi* (cult administrators), were regularly appointed by ordinary secular means ([Arist.] *Ath. Pol.* 54.6–7, cf. *IG* I^3 5, on *hieropoioi* of the Eleusinian cult appointed by and/or from the deme of Eleusis, 82, on *hieropoioi* for the Hephaestia). Decrees of the Athenian assembly regulate a wide range of religious matters (and, indeed, of the few surviving decrees earlier than c.450 the majority are religious): examples are the appointment of *athlothetai* (contest administrators) for games at Marathon in honor of Heracles (*IG* I^3 3); regulating the offering of first fruits at Eleusis, and commanding the members of Athens' alliance, the Delian League, to send offerings and inviting other Greeks to do so (ML 73 = *IG* I^3 78, trans. Fornara 140); winding up the Periclean building program on the acropolis, as the Peloponnesian War approached (no decree initiating the program survives, but the various works were supervised by publicly appointed boards) and creating the consolidated treasury of the Other Gods (ML 58 = *IG* I^3 52, trans. Fornara 119, with annual accounts of boards, *IG* I^3 433–466); arranging for the leasing of the *temenos* (sacred land) of Neleus, Basile, and Codrus (and involving the *poletai*, the secular officials responsible for making contracts, as well as the *basileus*, the archon with particular religious responsibilities) (*IG* I^3 84); consulting the Delphic oracle about land near Eleusis known as the sacred *orgas* (*IG* II^2 204 = RO 58).

One decree for the Eleusinian cult states that, as with the treasury of Athena, the people may use the funds as they wish (*IG* I^3 6). From 433/2 onwards, the Athenians took money from the sacred treasuries to help pay for the Peloponnesian War; this was treated as a loan, and an inscription gives details of sums taken and interest due for 426/5–423/2 with a summary for the previous seven years; after the Peace of Nicias in 421 repayment was authorized and some repayment may have been made, but the war resumed, Athens ended the war defeated and without funds, and in the end the sacred treasuries did not get their money back (record to 423/2, ML 72 = *IG* I^3 369; repayment after 421, Andoc. *Peace* 8, Aeschin. *Embassy* 175).

Since there was no ecumenical council, calendars listing the observances of different cults due on different dates (e.g. *IG* I^3 234, *SEG* xxxiii.147; from outside Athens, *LSCG* 151 = RO 62) must have been issued by the state and its subdivisions. Athens' compilation of an up-to-date code of laws which was begun in 410, interrupted by the regime of the Thirty and completed in 399 included the compilation of an up-to-date calendar of festivals, and Lysias' speech *Against Nicomachus* (one of the compilers) complains that he omitted some traditional observances and inserted some novel ones (Lys. *Nicomachus* 17–21). Greek religious festivals, both those of individual states and those of the great panhellenic sanctuaries, were major public occasions. They included activities which we should not regard as belonging to religious festivals, such as musical and athletic competitions; and they were also regarded as suitable occasions for what the Greeks too will have regarded as secular business. In 428, when Mytilene was planning to revolt against Athens and contacted Sparta, the Spartans instructed Mytilene and the members of the Peloponnesian League to send representatives to the Olympic festival, and "after the festival" they convened a meeting of the League at which the Mytilenaeans stated their case (Thuc. 3.8). The Great Dionysia at Athens included various items of civic business—among them the passing-out parade of the orphans of the war dead; in the time of the Delian League's treasury in Athens, the receipt of the tribute from the member states; and proclamations of honors decreed by the assembly—and this has attracted discussion recently in connection with the political interpretation of Athenian tragedy and the festivals at which it was performed (e.g. Goldhill 1987: 59–68, revised 1990: 98–114; Rhodes 2003: 111–113).

7 Smaller and Larger Entities

I end this chapter with some examples of public institutions in entities smaller and larger than the individual city (cf. Rhodes 1993). In Athens the tribes, thirds, and demes had institutions matching those of the whole city, and we are best informed about the demes. Each deme had its presiding official, the demarch (exceptionally, for the harbor deme of Piraeus, appointed not by its own members but by the city as a whole), and various other officials happen to be attested in one deme or another. There was a deme assembly, to transact the deme's business (which included keeping the deme's register of members up to date); some items of city business were transacted at deme level, such as the distribution (from the mid-fourth century) of "theoric" grants to cover the cost of members' tickets at major festivals; and demes had their religious observances, as the city did (see Whitehead 1986 and, less concerned with the institutions, Osborne 1985). After a single city of Rhodes was founded in 408/7, the three original cities on the island, Camirus, Ialysus, and Lindus, retained their separate physical existence and a degree of independence, and three neighboring islands, Carpathus, Chalce, and Syme, were also treated as parts of the city of Rhodes with their own institutions; these six communities were subdivided into demes; and there were further Rhodian dependencies on the Asiatic mainland (see T.H. Nielsen and V. Gabrielsen in Hansen and Nielsen 2004: 1196–1210, and Rhodes with Lewis 1997: 265–275).

Of larger units (on interstate relations and federal organizations, see Bolmarcich, Chapter 18), I mentioned at the beginning of this chapter the federal organization of Boeotia, where for most of the time from the late sixth century onwards there were major cities which were components formally represented in the federation and minor cities which were dependent on one or another of the major cities. In the late fifth and early fourth centuries the federal organization was based on eleven electoral units, with the largest component cities accounting for more than one and the smallest sharing one: each unit provided one of the principal federal officials, the boeotarchs, and sixty members of the federal council of 660; the council was divided into quarters, which took it in turn to act as the probouleutic body for the other three (Thuc. 5.38.1–3; *Hell. Oxy.* 19.3–4 Chambers; *Hell. Oxy.* 19.2 shows that the cities' citizen bodies were divided into quarters too). After the King's Peace in 386 the federation was dissolved, but it was re-created in and after 378: in its new form it had not a council but a federal assembly, which met in and was therefore dominated by Thebes; it had seven boeotarchs, who could perhaps in theory come from any component city but all the boeotarchs known to us until the destruction of Thebes by Alexander in 335 were Theban (*IG* VII 2407 = RO 43.2408; *SEG* xxxiv.355); and Thebes at least now had a council and an assembly (Xen. *Hell.* 7.3.5–12; Diod. Sic. 17.9.1). (See Larsen 1968: 26–40, 175–180.)

Of other larger units the earliest were religious, the best known of them being the Amphictyony ("league of neighbors") responsible for the sanctuaries of Apollo at Delphi and Demeter at Anthela (near Thermopylae). This body comprised twelve *ethnē* ("peoples"), most of them in central and northern Greece, but Athens was included in the Ionians and Sparta in the Dorians, and at some point two small peoples were combined and the vacant place was given to the city of Delphi. There was a *synedrion* (council) of twenty-four *hieromnēmones* ("sacred recorders"), two from each of the twelve peoples, with two regular meetings each year and the possibility of holding additional meetings; the peoples could also appoint *pylagoroi* ("speakers at [Thermo]pylae"), who could speak but usually not vote; there could also be an assembly of all the members of the Amphictyonic peoples who happened to be at Delphi. (Peoples are listed by Aeschin. *Embassy* 116 and inscriptions e.g. *Corpus Inscr. Delph.* ii.36 = RO 67; an account of a meeting, Aeschin. *In Ctes.* 115–124; see Sánchez 2001).

At the end of the sixth century Sparta organized its Peloponnesian allies in a league under its leadership which scholars refer to as the Peloponnesian League (see conveniently de Ste. Croix 1972: 101–124, 333–341; but the institutional arrangements were probably not as thoroughly worked out as he supposed); Athens in 477 organized the Delian League, primarily to continue fighting against the Persians, but the League became increasingly an Athenian empire and regular fighting against Persia was discontinued after c.450 (see Meiggs 1972, and in particular Thuc. 1.96–97); and in 378 it organized the Second Athenian League to champion the Greeks against abuses of the King's Peace by Sparta (see Cargill 1981, and in particular *IG* II^2 43 = RO 22; but Cargill was probably mistaken to argue that only the states listed in that inscription were members of the League; see Bolmarcich, Chapter 18, on the organization of these leagues). Sparta and Athens respectively provided the political and military leadership, and in the Delian League Athens provided the *Hellēnotamiai* ("Greek treasurers"), but there was a mechanism for consulting the allies about joint action (in the case of the Delian League, apparently abandoned after the treasury was moved from Delos to Athens in 454), and in the Second Athenian League the *synedrion* had a non-Athenian chairman (RO 29.15–16. Philip of Macedon after his victory at Chaeronea in 338 organized the mainland Greeks (except Sparta) in the League of Corinth (see Griffith in Hammond and Griffith 1979: 623–646, and in particular *IG* II^2 236 = RO 76); and in the Hellenistic period two leagues based on a region rather than a dominant city came to expand beyond their regions and to include much of mainland Greece, the Aetolian League north of the Gulf of Corinth and the Achaean League in the Peloponnese (see Larsen 1968: 195–215 and 215–240).

8 Conclusion

The many small states of the Greek world present variations on a theme. The poorest men might be included among the citizens with political rights or excluded, the assembly of qualified citizens might be strong or weak vis-à-vis the council and other authorities, but all embodied Aristotle's principle of ruling and being ruled in turn. Thus, while in the Greek world we may contrast "the authorities," as those holding office at a particular time, with "the people" at large, we cannot contrast "the government," as an ongoing body, with "the people," as a body of citizens permanently outside the government. The citizens took at least the most important decisions in their assembly; they took turns in holding a variety of short-term offices to implement the decisions; they dispensed justice in law courts which were not beholden to legal experts; religious decisions were made by the organs of the state in the same way as secular decisions. Larger states had subdivisions which functioned as the state writ small; federal organizations and leagues limited but never wholly suppressed the individual existence of their component states. While Rome absorbed more and more of the communities which came under its control, so that the theory of a city-state ruled by its citizens became increasingly detached from the reality, the Greek states remained citizen-states, with institutions which gave expression to that fundamental characteristic.

REFERENCES

Byrne, S.G. 2009. "*Agora* xv 112 and Iteration of Council Service in Hellenistic Athens." In A.A. Themos and N. Papazarkadas, eds., *'Αττικὰ 'Επιγραφικά … C. Habicht*. Athens, 215–223.

Cargill, J.L. 1981. *The Second Athenian League: Empire or Free Alliance?* Berkeley.

De Ste. Croix, G.E.M. 1972. *The Origins of the Peloponnesian War*. London.

Ehrenberg, V. 1969. *The Greek State*. 2nd edn. London.

Gabrielsen, V. 1981. *Remuneration of State Officials in Fourth-Century* B.C. *Athens*. Odense.

Gagarin, M. 2005. "The Unity of Greek Law" and "Early Greek Law." In Gagarin and Cohen 2005: 29–40 and 82–94.

Goldhill, S. 1987. "The Great Dionysia and Civic Ideology." *JHS* 107: 58–76.

Goldhill, S. 1990. "The Great Dionysia and Civic Ideology." Revised in J.J. Winkler and F.I. Zeitlin, eds., *Nothing to Do with Dionysos?* Princeton, 97–129.

Hammond, N.G.L. and G.T. Griffith. 1979. *A History of Macedonia*, vol. 2. Oxford.

Hansen, M.H. 1974. *The Sovereignty of the People's Court in Athens in the Fourth Century* B.C. *and the Public Action against Unconstitutional Proposals*. Odense.

Hansen, M.H. 1976. *Apagoge, Endeixis and Ephegesis against Kakourgoi, Atimoi and Pheugontes*. Odense.

Hansen, M.H. 1979a. "How Often did the Athenian *Dicasteria* Meet?" *GRBS* 20: 243–246.

Hansen, M.H. 1979b. "*Misthos* for Magistrates in Classical Athens." *SO* 54: 5–22.

Hansen, M.H. 1971–80. "Perquisites for Magistrates in Fourth-Century Athens." *C&M* 32: 105–125.

Hansen, M.H. 1987. *The Athenian Assembly in the Age of Demosthenes*. Oxford.

Hansen, M.H. 1999. *The Athenian Democracy in the Age of Demosthenes: Structure, Principles, and Ideology*. Expanded edn. Norman, OK.

Hansen, M.H. 2006. *Polis: An Introduction to the Ancient Greek City-State*. Oxford.

Hansen, M.H. and T.H. Nielsen, eds. 2004. *An Inventory of Archaic and Classical Poleis*. Oxford.

Harris, E.M. 2008. Review of Gagarin 2005. *JHS* 128: 215–216.

Harris, E.M. and L. Rubinstein, eds. 2004. *The Law and the Courts in Ancient Greece*. London.

Hodkinson, S. 2000. *Property and Wealth in Classical Sparta*. London.

Lambert, S.D. 2010. "A Polis and Its Priests: Athenian Priesthoods Before and After Pericles' Citizenship Law." *Historia* 59: 143–175.

Larsen, J.A.O. 1968. *Greek Federal States: Their Institutions and History*. Oxford.

MacDowell, D.M. 1986. *Spartan Law*. Edinburgh.

Meiggs, R. 1972. *The Athenian Empire*. Oxford.

Michell, H. 1952. *Sparta*. Cambridge.

Mitchell, L.G. 2000. "A New Look at the Election of Generals at Athens." *Klio* 82: 344–360.

Osborne, R. 1985. *Demos: The Discovery of Classical Attika*. Cambridge.
Rhodes, P.J. 1972. *The Athenian Boule*. Oxford.
Rhodes, P.J. 1981a. *A Commentary on the Aristotelian Athenaion Politeia*. Oxford.
Rhodes, P.J. 1981b. "The Selection of Ephors at Sparta." *Historia* 30: 498–502.
Rhodes, P.J. 1993. "The Greek *Poleis*: Demes, Cities and Leagues." In M.H. Hansen, ed. *The Ancient Greek City-State*. Copenhagen, 161–182.
Rhodes, P.J. 1994. "The Ostracism of Hyperbolus." In R. Osborne and S. Hornblower, eds. *Ritual, Finance, Politics… David Lewis*. Oxford, 85–98.
Rhodes, P.J. 2003. "Nothing To Do with Democracy: Athenian Drama and the *Polis*." *JHS* 123: 104–119.
Rhodes, P.J. 2004. "Keeping to the Point." In Harris and Rubinstein 2004: 137–158.
Rhodes, P.J. 2005. *Euthynai (Accounting)*. Durham.
Rhodes, P.J. 2006. "'Classical' and 'Hellenistic' in Athenian History." In E. Dębrowa, ed., *Greek and Hellenistic Studies*. Kraków, 27–43.
Rhodes, P.J. 2009. "State and Religion in Athenian Inscriptions." *G&R*[2] 56: 1–13.
Rhodes, P.J. with D.M. Lewis 1997. *The Decrees of the Greek States*. Oxford.
Sánchez, P. 2001. *L'Amphictionie des Pyles et de Delphes*. *Historia* Einzelschriften 148. Stuttgart.
Sealey, R. 1976. "Die spartanische Nauarchie." *Klio* 58: 335–358.
Sinclair, R.K. 1988. *Democracy and Participation in Athens*. Cambridge.
Spawforth, A.J.S. 2012. "Judges, Foreign." In *Oxford Classical Dictionary*. 4th edn. Oxford, 777.
Todd, S. 2012. "Law in Greece." In *Oxford Classical Dictionary*. 4th edn. Oxford, 811–812.
Traill, J.S. 1975. *The Political Organization of Attica: A Study of the Demes, Trittyes, and Phylai, and Their Representation in the Athenian Council*. Princeton.
Whitehead, D. 1986. *The Demes of Attica, 508/7–ca. 250 B.C.* Princeton.
Willetts, R.F., ed. 1967. *The Law Code of Gortyn*. Berlin. *Kadmos* suppl. 1 Berlin.

FURTHER READING

Ehrenberg 1969 is still valuable as a survey of the Greek states and their institutions; Hansen and Nielsen 2004 has a valuable general introduction and an annotated catalogue, arranged by regions, of all known Greek cities of the archaic and classical periods. On Athens see in general Hansen 1999, the culmination of a great deal of work which he has done on Athenian institutions (many of his conclusions are new and some controversial: see the "One Hundred and Sixty Theses about Athenian Democracy" included in this edition), and Sinclair 1988; on Athens' tribes, thirds, and demes see Traill 1975, and on the demes in particular see Whitehead 1986. On Sparta see Michell 1952 (which is old-fashioned, but convenient as a collection of basic material) and MacDowell 1986; recent work which has transformed our understanding of some aspects of Sparta but has not greatly affected the matters discussed in this chapter can be found in and through Hodkinson 2000. On federal institutions see Larsen 1968.

CHAPTER 9

The Incongruence of Power: The Roman Constitution in Theory and Practice

Henrik Mouritsen

A primary aim of historical comparisons is to distinguish the specific from the universal or, in other words, identify those aspects of a given community that set it apart from others and determined its particular trajectory. Before embarking on such an endeavor, it is worth briefly noting the difficulties a comparison of Greek and Roman institutions faces. At the most basic level we have to acknowledge the simple fact that we are contrasting a single city-state, and one as the previous chapter concludes that grew as it absorbed other cities, with an entire city-state culture. And within that culture only a few *poleis* are better documented—and not necessarily the most typical ones in terms of scale and structure. Another problem relates to the diachronic aspect of such a comparison. The Roman Republic lasted close to 500 years and did not remain static over this period, either in her institutional structures or in their practical articulation. Indeed, the Romans themselves saw the dynamic nature of their political system as one of its central qualities and strengths. Therefore, given the duration of the Roman Republic and the sheer number and variety of Greek *poleis* there is a risk that we end up comparing a "distillation" of the Roman Republic with a generalized "Greek *polis*."

While the difficulties raised by the uneven distribution of evidence for the Greek *poleis* are addressed in the companion chapter, this chapter will attempt to gauge the implications of the evolving nature of the Roman Republic. An added complication here derives from the fact that the surviving evidence makes it hard to compare Roman institutions at different stages of their development. Thus, early Rome cannot be viewed in isolation from the later periods, which produced almost all our evidence. We must also allow for the possibility that the Greek comparanda may themselves have influenced these late, retrospective accounts of the Roman past, causing a kind of "cross-contamination" between different periods, cultures, and traditions.

There is no obvious way of overcoming these fundamental problems, which largely prevents us from going much beyond the merest—essentially hypothetical—outline of

A Companion to Greek Democracy and the Roman Republic, First Edition. Edited by Dean Hammer.

early Roman institutions. Still, despite these limitations it is important that an attempt is made, not least because many of the distinctive features of the Republic can be traced back to its earliest beginnings and perhaps even to the monarchy that preceded it.

1 From Monarchy to *Res Publica*

According to the canonical chronology the city was ruled by kings from its mythical foundation until 510, when an aristocratic revolt led to the creation of a free polity where no one man was allowed to hold absolute power. The transition from monarchy to republic may have been considerably more complex than implied by this tradition and the date is itself suspicious, coinciding as it does with the overthrow of the Peisistratid tyranny in Athens. However, there is sufficient evidence to suggest that a change of this nature did take place and probably around this time. The new republican structures are the subject of much debate, but apparently they included the "standard" elements of assembly, magistrates, and council, making the system broadly comparable to those of the Greek *poleis*. The distribution of competencies also appears similar, with the assembly passing legislation and appointing magistrates, who held the executive power, above all military, and were advised by a council of elders. However, the articulation of these institutions seems to have differed in important respects from that typically found in the Greek world.

According to later tradition, two consuls were appointed immediately after the overthrow of the kings, but there are indications that during the earliest periods the Republic may have been led by a single chief magistrate. In that case it could be argued that the traditional version may be a retrojection of the system that emerged from the patricio-plebeian compromise, which accommodated the plebeian demand for an equal share of executive power by doubling the number of office-holders. Defined as *imperium* or "command" (derived from *imperare*), the authority of the chief magistrate was extensive and stands out as a defining aspect of the Roman political system. Effectively, it conferred supreme power at home and in the field, the centrality of the latter being underscored by the consuls' formal appointment in the military assembly. The powers of the magistrate were almost monarchical in nature, suggesting a degree of continuity between the *res publica* and the system that preceded it—although that does not imply that the consuls therefore embodied "kingship" in the sense later envisaged by Polybius, *History*, Book 6. The consuls may have "inherited" the powers of the kings along with the attendant symbols of *fasces* and *sella curulis*, but crucially they held them for only a short period of time, strictly limited to a single year. The brief tenure may thus have been the fundamental guarantee against excessive accumulation of power, collegiality being added only at a later stage.

The magistrates derived their mandate from the people, but the procedures surrounding this act—often described as "election"—as well as the relationship between the magistrate and the *populus* cast doubts on the original nature of the process. The people convened in assemblies, *comitia*, of which there existed a number of different versions defined by the types of unit into which the *populus* was subdivided. In all Roman assemblies citizens were represented only as members of a particular unit, which delivered a single verdict. We may therefore be dealing with an act of acclamation rather than election. The procedure did not allow for "mixed" messages, and revealingly the Latin word for vote, *suffragium*, only carries the positive meaning of support, which could be granted or withheld but not qualified. It has also been suggested the word may etymologically derive from the sound made by the banging of weapons as a—primitive—sign of approval (Vaathera 1993). On this interpretation the "election" of the consul(s?) would in effect have been the formal presentation of the new leader(s) before the assembled people, whose subdivisions each would come forward to express their loyalty and support. Such a procedure might explain the origins of the uniquely Roman practice of block voting, which is without parallel in the ancient world.

This line of interpretation might also cast light on the magistrate's position in relation to the assembly, which seems to have differed in important respects from that known in Greek *poleis*. The Roman magistrate was not merely the holder of a public office carrying certain responsibilities and remits; he was above the *populus* and exercised complete control over the assembly, which had no formal or practical existence without his leadership (see below). Moreover, when the appointment procedure was transformed into a genuine election, the people's role remained circumscribed. As it has been convincingly demonstrated, the people were neither "sovereign" nor active in the elective assemblies (Badian 1990). It was convened by a magistrate, who formally guided the *comitia*, and the technical language used for the appointment indicates that it happened through the joint action of the presiding magistrate and the *populus*. Without the guidance of a magistrate the *populus* could not appoint new leaders. It is significant too that the appointment was formally made only when the leader announced it. This feature gave the appointment of magistrates an element of internalized succession, with the appointee formally being "created" by the incumbent, rather than through the popular vote. When the chain between them was broken an *interrex* had to be appointed to carry out the ritual handing over of power to the successor. The procedure was one where the outgoing magistrate presented his successor to the assembly, asking it to give its approval, and it is generally assumed to have originated in the traditional acclamation of the new king by the *comitia curiata*. Supposedly, the kings had received their *imperium* through a *lex curiata de imperio*, which in effect was an oath of allegiance sworn to the new ruler, expressing the people's consent.

The Romans' willingness to invest extensive powers in their leaders is illustrated also by the institution of the dictatorship, which enabled the Senate to grant supreme authority to a single individual, usually to deal with a military emergency. Again, however, it was of strictly limited duration with a maximum tenure of six months. In addition, the dictator would appoint a *magister equitum*, who was not his colleague but second-in-command.

According to legend, Romulus first nominated 100 elders from the leading families to advise him in the governance of the state, perhaps indicating a fluctuating rather than permanent body. It is not clear at what point it developed into the stable institution known in later periods when access was formalized and largely reserved for former office-holders who in principle were appointed for life. Given the state of our evidence, the issue can probably never be settled, but considering the powers of the chief magistrates and the likelihood that they had been pre-selected through an internalized process it would seem plausible if the senate had established itself as an independent source of authority with a relatively well-defined membership already before the passing of the *lex Ovinia*, which formally constituted it as a council of former office-holders (Hölkeskamp 1987).

The senators became known as *patres*, fathers, closely associating them with the hereditary "caste" of patricians, whom the sources present as holding a monopoly on public office during the early Republic. The ascendancy of the patricians sparked a prolonged conflict between them and the so-called plebeians who were excluded from office, a conflict that would reshape the political system in fundamental respects.

2 The "Struggle of the Orders"

Virtually no contemporary evidence survives for this conflict and almost all aspects therefore remain open to dispute (Raaflaub 1986). At the most basic level the identity of the two parties involved is subject to debate. Moreover, it is not even certain that the conflict is best understood as a single "struggle," since we may be dealing with an extended series of loosely interrelated socio-economic and political issues which only in hindsight was conceptualized as the unified "Struggle of the Orders" we find in later sources. This brief summary will leave these issues aside and concentrate on the changes it brought to the political institutions (see also Fronda, Chapter 3).

Patricians are normally seen as a hereditary "caste," which asserted an exclusive right to magistracies and possibly also membership of the Senate. This monopoly on executive power appears to have been justified on religious grounds and associated with the patrician claim to the *auspicia*, the right to consult the gods on matters of state. In Rome modern distinctions between "politics" and "religion" did not apply, and any action which had an impact on the public weal—legislation, elections, declarations of war and peace, military engagements—required divine consent (for the Greek religious context, see Rhodes, Chapter 8). This in turn was ascertained through a complex system of divination, and it is therefore possible to argue that, in addition to the socio-economic resources that undoubtedly underpinned the patrician supremacy, their position rested on an exclusive entitlement to the *auspicia*, which precluded plebeian tenure of the highest office. It logically followed that only patricians could hold the state priesthoods and sit in the Senate, which itself acted as the highest authority in matters of cult and divination.

The plebeians reacted to their exclusion from state offices by creating a set of alternative institutions as a means of furthering their interests. An assembly was established, the *concilium plebis* or *comitia plebis tributa*, which issued its own resolutions, *plebiscita*, that were binding for the plebeian population. It also appointed its own officials, *tribuni plebis* (initial number uncertain, but later rising to ten), who were charged with the protection of individual plebeians and in return enjoyed their collective protection, and two *aediles plebis* who were responsible for celebrating specifically plebeian religious festivals.

Eventually the patricians made a series of concessions to the plebeian elite, which was then admitted to all magistracies and priesthoods through a succession of legal measures. The background for this retreat can only be conjectured, but key must have been the simple fact that the patricians constituted a small and shrinking minority, whose position became increasingly untenable as the plebeian elite harnessed wider social and economic grievances in support of their demand for political influence. The main breakthrough came in 367 with the passing of the *leges Liciniae-Sextiae*, which entitled the plebeians to one of the two consulships, although it does not appear to have come into effect until 342, from which point onwards at least one consul was always plebeian. These laws also admitted plebeians for the first time to one of the major state priesthoods, the *decemviri sacris faciundis* (later *quindecimviri*), although it was not until the *lex Ogulnia*, 300, that they gained access to the colleges of the *pontifices* and the *augures*. In 356 the first plebeian *dictator* was appointed, and four years later a plebeian first held the censorship.

The *lex Ovinia* (late fourth century) appears to have been closely linked to this process. As noted, it regulated the membership of the Senate and ensured former office-holders a seat irrespective of background and it has been suggested that by formulating objective criteria for admission it may have created a more independent political body (Cornell 2000).

The old distinctions between the two categories gradually became obsolete and an important consequence of these constitutional changes was the emergence of a new elite, known as the *nobilitas*, comprising both plebeians and patricians. Ideologically this class embraced a meritocratic ethos of office-holding and public service, while at the same time maintaining an element of hereditary entitlement based on ancestral achievement. Indeed the prestigious title *nobilis* came to refer to any descendant, however distant, of a holder of the consulship.

The most paradoxical outcome of the patricio-plebeian settlement was the continuation of the—formally redundant—plebeian institutions, which were given official recognition and incorporated into the Roman state. Plebeian tribunes continued to be appointed and were endowed with extensive powers to veto and propose laws and to exercise *intercessio*, intervention on behalf of citizens against state coercion. Moreover, the *lex Hortensia*, c.287, gave resolutions of the plebeian assembly the force of law and made them binding for the whole population—despite the fact that patricians could still not take part. The long process of accommodation thus left behind a highly complex constitutional legacy, which not only contained a number of paradoxes and contradictions but also made it difficult to identify precisely where political power was located.

3 Institutions in the "Classic" Roman Republic

The period between the end of the "Struggle of the Orders" and the re-emergence of political violence in 133 has long been seen as the "classic" Roman Republic, when the empire expanded and the constitution functioned at its best. This image may be somewhat idealized, conceived as it was under the influence of later events and the eventual collapse of the republican system. Thus, closer scrutiny of the surviving evidence suggests that the degree of stability may have been overestimated and that the political system also during this period frequently was put under considerable stress (Bleckmann 2002). Importantly however, it still managed to resolve political conflicts through negotiation and without the use of force. Rome's ability to deal with these challenges is therefore notable, and ever since Polybius first devoted a digression to Rome's political system the secret behind the relative stability that characterized the middle Republic has been sought in her political institutions and not least in their mutual interaction. These will therefore be considered in some detail (see also Fronda, Chapter 3).

The magistrates

During the Republic, Rome saw a steady increase in the range of public offices and in the number of appointees, which reflected the growing scale and complexity of Roman society as well as the incorporation of the plebeian institutions into the state. Every year the Romans filled a very considerable number of posts, reaching a total of forty-four magistracies in the late republic in addition to fifty lower officials. Most important were the two consuls, who served as eponymous heads of state, and originally may have been known as *praetores.* Their role was to a great extent defined in military terms, and their primary function was that of commander of the legions; hence their appointment in the military assembly, the *comitia centuriata.* Their *imperium* gave them wide-ranging powers "domi militiae," at home and in the field. Although their powers of life and death, symbolized by the axes in the *fasces,* no longer applied in civilian contexts after the *leges Porciae,* they still had sufficient authority to coerce citizens. Politically they had the right to propose legislation, convene the people, and preside over meetings of the Senate.

In 366 the first praetor was appointed to oversee the administration of justice and perform the consuls' political functions while these were away on campaign (Brennan 2000). He also held *imperium* and was therefore able to carry out military functions too. While in some respects similar to the consuls, the praetor remained subordinate and complex theories have been developed to explain the precise nature of this office and its place in the constitutional development of Rome; these inevitably contain a strong element of conjecture (e.g. Bunse 1998). The number of praetors increased gradually to cope with rising administrative demands, a second one being added around 242 to deal with disputes between Romans and foreigners, the *praetor inter peregrinos,* eventually reaching eight after Sulla's reform.

The *census* was an essential Roman institution that formed the basis for civic organization, military conscription and taxation. Already in the fifth century two censors had been appointed to oversee the quinquennial register of all citizens and revise the membership of the Senate.

To these posts were added two *curule aediles* (the term *curulis* derived from the insignia of senior state officials, the *sella curulis*) who performed various public functions, including the celebration of games and festivals, and had oversight of the grain supply to the city. They functioned alongside the two plebeian *aediles.*

As noted, plebeian tribunes continued to be appointed after the plebeian–patrician settlement, and as a result ten officials, still in the early stages of their careers, were granted extensive powers to propose and veto legislation throughout the classical period. Apparently they were also allowed to attend the Senate and from the third century they could convene meetings too. The *lex Atinia* (date is disputed but perhaps 149) gave them automatic membership of the Senate.

A steadily increasing number of *quaestores* were appointed to assist the consuls and perform administrative duties related to finance and provisions for the city of Rome. Below the magisterial level a substantial number of posts were filled by the assemblies, including *tribuni militum*, *tresviri monetales*, and *tresviri capitales.*

In 180 the *lex Villia annalis* for the first time created a formalized magisterial ladder, the *cursus honorum*, stipulating minimum age requirements for each office, regulating the order in which they should be held, and prescribing minimum intervals between offices as well as for the iteration of the consulship. This attempt to regulate the public career path was a response to increased competition within the elite and coincided with a spate of other initiatives to tackle a wide range of electoral malpractices. The existence of an official *cursus* stands in contrast to Greece and reflects the unique status of the Roman elite as an aristocracy defined by and articulated through the holding of public office.

As a rule, Roman office-holders had to meet a basic property requirement and qualify for membership of the highest census class. Offices were defined as *honores* and were therefore unremunerated. Indeed, they normally entailed considerable expenditure, the aedileship being particularly onerous. In addition, magistrates had access to a very limited "civil service" and relied on private staff to carry out many public duties.

The Senate

When a young man had taken his first step on the magisterial ladder and completed his year as *quaestor*, he could normally expect to be admitted to the Senate, which meant joining the official "political class." During the "classic" Republic the Senate counted around 300 members, although the five-year interval between censuses meant that the official figure often would have been lower. Sulla later doubled its membership as part of the judicial reform which granted the senators full control over the juries.

The internal structure of the Senate was strictly hierarchical, with members ranked according to offices held and seniority within each magisterial class (Bonnefond-Coudry 1989; Ryan 1998). The senator heading the list carried the honorific title of *princeps senatus*, which conferred prestige and the right to open the debates. The deliberations were highly formalized, with members being asked for their opinions, *sententiae*, in order of seniority, in practice leaving the majority of senators without any real opportunity to contribute—although there is no evidence that the lower ranks, sometimes described as *pedarii*, were not allowed to speak, as once assumed. Votes were rarely taken since the aim was to present unanimity and consensus rather than expose divisions.

The Senate could issue resolutions, *senatus consulta*, which served as advice to the consuls but had no binding force of law. In the late Republic the Senate introduced the so-called *senatus consultum ultimum*, a declaration of emergency instructing the consuls to take any action required to deal with the enemies of the Republic. The measure had no basis in law and its validity therefore remained a source of dispute.

The Senate's status as an advisory body and lack of formal powers may seem unusual from a Greek perspective but can be explained by two related factors: the formal equation of the state with the *populus* and the extensive powers of the magistrates who acted on their behalf. Although internally consistent and logical, this construction of the Roman state did not leave room for a council with autonomous powers. As a result we find a stark discrepancy between the Senate's constitutional role and its *de facto* position as the center of power; its membership comprised everybody with active political and military experience as well as the accumulated social influence and economic resources of the leading families.

The assemblies

In contrast to Greece, the "classic" Roman Republic had a variety of popular assemblies, the *comitia curiata*, *centuriata*, *tributa*, and the *concilium plebis*. They were created at different moments in Rome's history, and for different purposes. They did, however, share the same formal structure and procedures. While formally representing the Roman people, each assembly did so in a different configuration. Unlike Greek assemblies the Roman ones were defined according to the kind of unit into which the *populus* was divided.

The oldest assembly appears to have been the *comitia curiata*, which organized citizens in *curiae*. Little is known about its original functions, but in the classical period it was largely ceremonial, formally conferring *imperium* on holders of the highest offices. As an assembly it became practically redundant and was convened without any popular involvement, each *curia* being represented by a *lictor*.

The *comitia centuriata* represented the Roman people as an army and, reflecting the traditional link between property and military service, it was also the most overtly timocratic of the Roman assemblies. It was divided into 193 *centuriae*, basic military units, which in turn were grouped together into *classes*, defined according to a sliding scale of property ownership. Voting first were the eighteen equestrian centuries, which included the so-called *sex suffragia*, presumably senatorial centuries. They were followed by the five *classes* and four unarmed centuries and a single century reserved for those without any property, the *proletarii*. This arrangement was an elaboration of an older and simpler system that divided the citizens into those who served, *classis*, and those who did not, *infra classem*. The system of block voting allowed the weight of each vote to be carefully calibrated, reconciling the principle of equal citizenship with inequality of influence. Thus, the assembly was heavily tilted in favor of the propertied classes.

The assembly was the object of a little-known reform between 241 and 218, prior to which the first class held 80 centuries and the four remaining classes 20, 20, 20, and 30 respectively (Mouritsen 2011). After the reform the number of first-class centuries was reduced to 70. The background for this move is debated, but a primary objective appears to have been the coordination of the first class with the *tribus*, of which there were 35. This move reflects the increasing practical and ideological importance attached to the tribal units, which became so central to the identity of Roman citizens that they even entered into their nomenclature and became part of their name.

The origins of the *tribus* remain obscure. According to tradition the Roman people was in its earliest stages composed of three tribes, Ramnes, Tities, and Luceres, about which no reliable information survives. These were in turn divided into the *curiae*, which originally formed the basic unit for the assembly and the army. The *tribus* of the classical period appear to be different in nature, since they were regionally defined units that subdivided the citizen body according to domicile. In principle, this made them more socially representative, although distortions soon emerged as the rapidly growing urban population remained confined to just four *tribus*, which also became the default *tribus* of freed slaves. Political influence therefore came to lie with the rural *tribus*, to which landowners continued to belong irrespective of their place of residence.

The earliest assembly to be based on the *tribus* appears to have been the *concilium plebis*, also known as the *comitia plebis tributa*, which established an alternative source of authority among the plebeians. Modeled on the plebeian assembly, a *comitia tributa* was created, open to all citizens and presided over by state magistrates. As just noted, a tribal element was also added to the already complex structure of the *comitia centuriata*, as (at least) the first-class centuries were combined with the 35 *tribus*.

This reform strengthened the formal mandate delivered by the centuriate assembly since the centuries, following the introduction of the maniple as the operative military unit, were no longer essential subdivisions of the Roman people. But another objective seems to be the launch of a striking new feature, the so-called *centuria praerogativa*, which was a single century chosen by lot from amongst the first-class units to cast the first vote and thereby provide a lead to the rest of the assembled citizens. The sources suggest that the vote of the *centuria praerogativa* was considered an omen and routinely followed by the assembly. The implication is that the electoral process was given a strong element of lottery while still maintaining the fundamental principle of "popular" choice.

Magistrates and assemblies

All political gatherings require some degree of organization, but in Rome that role went far beyond the strictly practical. The presiding official was in full control of every aspect of the proceedings. The various assemblies and meetings could convene only when called by an authorized official. Thus, unlike classical Athens, there were no statutory assembly days in Rome, allowing the people to come together on a regular basis and debate current issues. An assembly came into being only through the initiative of an official, who could dismiss it again at any time, thereby preventing it from reaching a decision.

The fact that it was a magistrate who constituted the people politically also determined the workings of the *comitia*. Again the contrast to Athens is remarkable (although less so when compared with Sparta), since there was no possibility of popular initiatives or proposals emerging from the meetings, which were not even allowed an open debate. Discussions were formally separated from the decision-taking meetings (*comitia*), and relegated to so-called *contiones*. These non-decision-taking meetings also had to be convened by an official and did not offer the opportunity for free or open debate either. The proceedings were tightly regulated and remained under the direct control of the presiding official. It was he who decided time and place as well as the issue(s) to be debated and, crucially, who was permitted to speak—usually arranged in advance. The *contio* was therefore more an address to the people than a consultation of it. There was no formal interaction between speaker and *populus*, merely a one-way communication. It follows that the Roman people had no legitimate way of convening or expressing its views without formalized leadership (see Morstein-Marx, Chapter 17, for a discussion of rhetoric in the *contiones*; also O'Bryhim, Chapter 25, on the reluctance to create a permanent theater where people might assemble).

The essentially passive role of the *populus* is also reflected in the legislative procedure. The presiding magistrate would present proposals to the assembly, whose response was limited to yes or no without any opportunity to modify what was put before it. Given the lack of active input into policy-making, a legislative *comitia* may be best defined as an ad hoc meeting convened by a magistrate for the purpose of ratifying a specific proposal.

At elections we find a similar situation, for although the assemblies were offered a choice of candidates there is no evidence that the assembly was then free to vote for whomever it wanted. The presiding magistrate was still formally and in actual fact in charge of proceedings, and he could refuse to accept a vote by the *populus*, as happened on at least thirteen recorded occasions (Badian 1990).

The relationship between magistrate and assembly in Rome therefore differed in fundamental respects not just from that found in modern political systems, but also from that found in, for example, classical Athens. Unlike Athenian officials, the magistrates were not simply officials in charge of specific public functions and accountable to the *ekklēsia*. They were superior to the *populus*, and the power of the people was expressed via—and only via—the actions of its elected officials.

4 Popular Participation

Despite the growth of the Roman state and its citizen body, the political system continued to operate along the lines of a traditional city-state. The basic principle remained that of direct participation, and political influence could therefore be exercised only if citizens turned up in person at a given time and place. Needless to say, this constitutional fiction, which ignored the logistic realities of numbers and distance, imposed very strict limits on the proportion of citizens able take part in the proceedings. Any attempt at assessing the scale of participation possible at the various assemblies must by necessity remain conjectural. However, the archaeological and literary evidence for political venues does allow some cautious estimates (Mouritsen 2001).

The old Comitium in the northwestern corner of the Forum Romanum was in historical times used for the tribally structured assemblies. It was a relatively small space that would have been able to hold little more than c.3,800 voters, taking into account also the fact that they had to be separated physically into thirty-five groups. When the legislative assemblies were transferred to the Forum in 145, the rationale seems to have been ideological rather than practical. Still, the change of venue did allow considerably larger crowds to take part, but since voting procedures remained highly complex and time-consuming attendance levels are unlikely to have risen beyond 10,000 and realistically would have remained well below that figure.

In the late second century the elective tribal assemblies were moved to the Saepta on the Campus Martius, historically the venue of the centuriate assembly which as the people under arms convened outside the religious boundary of Rome, the Pomerium. This site was substantially larger than the Comitium and the Forum, but the layout suggests that it could not have accommodated more than a small section of the citizen body. Structurally it was split in into two spaces, a forecourt for the opening procedures and a central area which was further subdivided into thirty-five enclosures, one for each of the *tribus*. The size of the forecourt would suggest that the maximum attendance envisaged was around 25,000 voters, a figure that should be considered in relation to a total citizen population that exceeded a million in the late Republic.

Political venues could remain small and the procedures cumbersome despite the growth of the state and its citizen body, because no quorum was required for assemblies to be valid. Only in one respect did the system contain inflexible requirements of representation, but they concerned the participation of voting units rather than voters. Thus, for an assembly to be able to take legally binding decisions all units had to be represented, even if just by a handful of voters each (Cic. *Sest.* 109). A similar formalism is reflected in the rule that all *tribus* had to cast their vote in the—successively voting—legislative assemblies, even if a majority had already been found and the bill effectively was passed.

This emphasis on formality and procedure, combined with the essentially passive role played by the *populus*, raises the question: what in fact were the function and rationale of the assemblies? Given the magistrates' control over all aspects of the proceedings and their ability even to disallow electoral results, they were clearly not intended as vehicles for the free expression of the "popular will." Their key function appears to have been the conferral of formal legitimacy on those who were to exercise state authority.

The *populus* was the only true source of legitimacy in the Roman state, a fundamental principle that was apparently never contested even by the elite. The people and its best interests therefore remained the basis for all claims to political power and influence. The Romans saw no clear distinction between the state and the people; indeed the former was not conceptualized as a separate entity. Since the *res publica* in a very literal sense belonged to the *populus*, it followed that the people had to lend its approval to all public measures and office-holders. Importantly, however, this was a formal requirement, and the *populus* that gave its consent was a highly formalized version of the citizen body.

Thus, it was the people as represented by its more or less abstract subdivisions that offered its approval, not the sum of its citizens. Only the participation of these units counted, and for that reason the overall turnout mattered little from a constitutional point of view. No effort was made to facilitate or encourage large-scale popular participation, for example through remuneration for attendance, and as the territory and population grew the opportunity for taking part was correspondingly reduced.

How much choice the political crowds actually exercised is an open question. The procedures for passing laws seem to have been carefully designed to elicit a positive response, and rejections are hardly ever reported—not a single unambiguous instance is recorded in the first century. Still, the appointment of new magistrates obviously did involve a choice, and the open procedures and the electoral contests that preceded them had the potential to expose political divisions, internally within the elite and more broadly in society as a whole. In this context the introduction of the *centuria praerogativa* and the element of lottery it gave to the process may be seen as an attempt at streamlining the outcome and present an image of civic unity and consensus, the leaders of the Republic receiving strong and unanimous popular mandates (Mouritsen 2011).

The magistrates received their mandate from the *populus*. However, the magistrates (and pro-magistrates) were not formally accountable to the people, as a whole or to the specific assembly that had elected them. While their powers may have been restricted by the personal rights, which all citizens enjoyed, and by the tribunician veto and *intercessio*, they were answerable for their actions neither during nor after their tenure. In exceptional cases they might be prosecuted after the expiry of their term in office, but that required a specific initiative taken by the tribunes. This marks a sharp contrast to Greece, which may be explained by the particular Roman conceptualization of the people as "sovereign" (to use the modern anachronistic term) but also fundamentally responsive and passive, their interests being entirely entrusted to their appointed leaders.

5 Religion in the Roman Republic

The relationship between the *res publica* and its tutelary gods was the responsibility of a number of different priesthoods, which performed very specific roles as advisors on often highly technical matters of ritual. The most important were the *pontifices*, the *augures*, and the *quindecimviri sacris faciundis*. The *augures* played a particular role in public life since no collective action could be taken without the consultation of Jupiter, whose signs it was their task to interpret. The major priesthoods were all filled by members of the elite who would normally pursue public careers alongside their religious duties. The pontifices were originally appointed through co-option, but in 104 the *lex Domitia* transferred the election to the assembly (later rescinded by Sulla but restored in 63).

Supreme religious authority rested with the Senate, which had the final word in disputes, and would sanction new initiatives, such as the introduction of foreign deities or changes to cult practice. The integration of politics and religion (itself an anachronistic concept) was complete in Rome and affected not just the holding of assemblies but any public action. It therefore offered the elite another means of controlling public affairs, which became increasingly important during the political conflicts of the late Republic.

6 Justice and Law Courts

The pursuit of justice was in principle a private matter, and the state would only actively pursue cases of treason and other serious threats to the state, although the *tresviri capitales*, primarily responsible for organizing a fire brigade of public slaves, had some role to play in criminal cases. The role of the state was to provide a framework for citizens seeking justice. Criminal disputes were originally held in the centuriate assembly and, reflecting the importance and open nature of its decisions, this is the only context where we come across contemporary concerns about turnout and participation (Varro *Ling.* 6.90–93). Later public courts were introduced with magistrates presiding but jurors delivering the verdict. Gradually a more complex system was developed, with standing courts, *quaestiones*, that dealt with different types of crimes. The proceedings involved speakers from both sides of the dispute pleading their case before a panel of jurors who were all drawn from the propertied classes. Civil cases would be resolved by *iudices*, appointed by a magistrate. During the last centuries of the Republic the courts came to occupy an increasingly central role in the political process, with prosecutions for electoral malpractice, *ambitus*, and provincial extortion, *res repetundae*, becoming standard means of challenging opponents.

7 Power and Authority in the Roman Republic

The precise location of power in Rome has been the subject of long-standing debate, beginning with Polybius' attempt to explain her political system as the embodiment of the Greek ideal of the "mixed constitution," and recently revived by scholars arguing for a strong "democratic" component to Roman politics. However, the difficulties we face when trying to identify who really held the power in Rome may be best resolved by distinguishing between the formal allocation of powers and the practical functioning of the political institutions. From a purely constitutional point of view the Republic was indeed strikingly "democratic." The aristocratic council held limited powers, merely serving as advisors to the elected magistrates, while the *populus* was recognized as the fount of political legitimacy. In addition, we find in the Roman Republic a remarkably unified political discourse focused on the common good and the people's best interest, itself considered identical with that of the state.

The reality, however, was quite different, since the *populus* had few means of exercising the powers that were formally theirs. They could not act without the formalized leadership of a magistrate, their scope for shaping political initiatives was close to nil, and their choice of leaders was strictly limited and offered few political options. The people's power therefore had a distinct element of ritual to it, as is also underlined by the arcane procedures followed and the simple fact that the vast majority of the population could never take part.

The *de facto* disenfranchisement of the large majority of citizens did not mean that the political elite formed a self-sufficient oligarchy. Not only was it open to outsiders but, as importantly, there was a practical as well as an ideological imperative that leaders of state consider the views and interests of those outside their order. However, to understand this relationship simplistic notions of the "people" and the "will of the people" are better avoided; for despite the fact that the *populus* formed a single entity in the dyadic construction of the Senatus Populusque Romanus, the non-senatorial population was of course highly diverse, ranging from wealthy *equites* to impoverished *proletarii*, with landed gentry, traders, and craftsmen (mostly freedmen), and rural smallholders in between. Across this social spectrum individual groups and classes would have held different material and political interests and commanded different degrees of influence on policy-making, often evolving over time, as the emergence of the land and grain issues in the late Republic demonstrate. The question of the real "power of the people" is therefore too complex to be given a single, straightforward answer. Instead we have to look at the ways in which each constituent element was able (or unable) to enforce its interests at any given moment in time.

8 The Institutional Context of Rome's Expansion

The institutional structure of the Republic was in a sense a form of structured elite rivalry channeled into an ongoing competition for public *honores* and the power and prestige they conferred. The highest of these accolades was the triumph, the ceremonial procession through Rome awarded to victorious generals, and the extraordinary attraction of this honor illustrates the point often made that the Roman elite was in many respects a "warrior class," imbued with martial values and measuring status in terms of military achievement. Moreover, it is no coincidence that the *nobilitas* which emerged out of the "Struggle of the Orders" established itself during the period of Italian expansion in the fourth and third centuries, the spectacular military advances underpinning their claim to political leadership (Hölkeskamp 1993).

The expansion was further facilitated by a set of political institutions that revealed a striking integration of the civilian and military spheres. Military experience was required of all office-holders, and the primary role of the heads of state, the consuls, was that of commanders-in-chief; hence their election by the *comitia centuriata*. Similarly, the basic civic organization of society was in essence martial in nature, with citizens classified according to military rank or lack thereof, for example *equites*, *classes*, *seniores*, *iuniores*, and *proletarii*.

As the conquest of Italy progressed, Rome imposed a complex political structure on the peninsula. Substantial parts were incorporated into the Roman state and given Roman citizenship. As a result Rome soon outgrew the natural limits of a city-state, and her ability to expand both territory and citizen body is one of the most striking aspects of this polity. It was possible because Roman citizenship was defined primarily in terms of personal rights, for example legal protection, rather than active political participation. Therefore, while other city-states were restricted by the constraints of distance and scale, there were no natural limitations to the extension of Rome's citizen body, which could grow both internally through the enfranchisement of emancipated slaves and externally via the incorporation of neighboring communities. Whereas conventional political notions of citizenship were predicated on physical integration and geographical proximity, the Roman focus on personal status and individual rights enabled the transformation of their city into a territorial state.

According to tradition, the first significant conquest was that of the neighboring Etruscan city of Veii, which was destroyed and her territory taken over by Romans in 396. A different approach was followed in 381 when the Latin town of Tusculum was incorporated and her citizens given Roman citizenship. The number of *tribus* was steadily increased until it reached thirty-five in 241, at which point the process was discontinued for reasons that are not evident. Later incorporated communities would be allocated to existing *tribus*, which thereby lost their territorial integrity and became separated into multiple sections scattered across the peninsula. However, this *tribus* structure may have served an integrative function in relation to conscription, since recruitment was organized on a tribal basis, bringing together Roman citizens from different parts of her territory in single military units (Jehne 2006).

There was also a shift in policy toward treaties that bound the community politically to Rome and imposed military obligations. Occasionally allied communities would also receive elements of the Roman citizenship, but since they were not inscribed in *tribus*, the fundamental mark of the citizen, they remained formally outside her citizen body. Eventually the separation of citizenship from political participation became so complete that by the second century colonies of Roman citizens were founded in Cisalpine Gaul despite the fact that it was geographically cut off from Roman territory and located hundreds of kilometers from the mother city where all political activity continued to be concentrated.

9 The End of the Roman Republic

The main symptoms of the crisis are well known: a decline in consensual government and growing divisions within the elite; increased use of assemblies without senatorial approval; the accumulation of power and influence in the hands of a few leading men; the emergence of violence as a political weapon; and the growing involvement of the army. Several institutional factors may have contributed to the crisis, above all the weakening central control over office-holders and the availability of prolonged military commands and special powers through the popular assemblies. It could be argued that the relative ease with which laws could be passed in Rome may have played a critical role behind the growing instability. There were few if any restrictions on the kinds of laws the *populus* could pass; what regulations existed were largely concerned with legislative procedure rather than with content.

The most fundamental safeguard was the expectation that office-holders act in accordance with the majority view of the Senate and respect the principle of collegiality. However, after Tiberius Gracchus' tribunate in 133 both of these were fatally compromised and thereafter the system had few ways of protecting itself against non-consensual use of the magistrates' legislative powers. Sulla's response to this state of affairs and his attempt at restoring senatorial supremacy were quickly undone, since legal measures always could be revoked as easily as they had been passed. The Senate therefore faced real difficulty when trying to assert the collective interests of the elite against the ambitions of individual nobles; for while the importance of constitutional legitimacy never waned, even during the most tumultuous of times, formal mandates from the *populus* were at the same time also extraordinarily simple to obtain. All it required was a well-disposed magistrate willing to put a bill before the assembly, which—no matter how small and unrepresentative—could pass measures of immense scope and implication that might potentially threaten the very core of the republican system.

The events of this period exposed the weak points in the republican constitution, which, as we saw, was characterized by a peculiar incongruence between real and formal powers. They revealed the crucial importance of unwritten and non-formalized rules and conventions, whose observance ultimately relied on elite cohesion and group discipline, as well as ingrained respect for ancestral tradition and ancient custom (often summarized as *mos maiorum*). When these faded under the impact of increased competition and external pressures, the republican elite found itself with few means of enforcing its authority and upholding the existing political order.

It paved the way for extended military commands and veteran settlements which strengthened the bonds between generals and their troops that were to become crucial in the final stages of the Republic. In the end the absence of a formal constitution, as opposed to "custom," meant that the supremacy of an individual could be accommodated within the existing legal framework. Because the Republic relied on adherence to *mos*, it was left without effective safeguards against its own gradual abolition. The Republic could therefore be voted out of existence by perfectly lawful means, while those attempting to halt the process—somewhat ironically—had to resort to "unconstitutional" methods such as violence.

REFERENCES

Badian, E. 1990. "Kommentar: Magistratur und Gesellschaft." In Eder 1990: 458–475.

Badian, E. 1996. "*Tribuni plebis* and *res publica*." In Jerzy Linkerski, ed., *Imperium sine fine: T. Robert S. Broughton and the Roman Republic*. Stuttgart, 187–213

Beard, M., J. North, and S. Price. 1998. *Religions of Rome*. Cambridge.

Bleckmann, B. 2002. *Die römische Nobilität im Ersten Punischen Krieg: Untersuchungen zur aristokratischen Konkurrenz in der Republik*. *Klio* Beiheft 5. Berlin.

Bleicken, J. 1968. *Das Volkstribunat der klassischen Republik: Studien zu seiner Entwicklung zwischen 287 und 133 v. Chr*. Zetemata 13. Munich.

Bleicken, J. 1972. *Staatliche Ordnung und Freiheit in der römischen Republik*. FAS 6: Kallmünz.

Bleicken, J. 1975a. *Die Verfassung der römischen Republik*. Paderborn.

Bleicken, J. 1975b. *Lex Publica: Gesetz und Recht in der römischen Republik*. Berlin and New York.

Bonnefond-Coudry, M. 1989. *Le sénat de la république romaine de la guerre d'Hannibal à Auguste*. Paris and Rome.

Brennan, T.C. 2000. *The Praetorship in the Roman Republic*. Oxford.

Brunt, P.A. 1988. *The Fall of the Roman Republic and Related Essays*. Oxford.

Bunse, R. 1998. *Das römische Oberamt in der frühen Republik und das Problem der "Konsulartribunen."* Trier.

Cornell, T. 1995. *The Beginnings of Rome. Italy and Rome from the Bronze Age to the Punic Wars (c.1000–264 BC)*. London.

Cornell, T. 2000. "The lex Ovinia and the Emancipation of the Senate." In C. Bruun, ed., *The Roman Middle Republic: Religion, Politics, and Historiography c.400–133 B.C.* AIRF 23. Rome, 69–89.

De Martino, F. 1954–1972. *Storia della constituzione romana*. Naples.

Develin, R. 1985. *The Practice of Politics at Rome 366–167 B.C.* Coll. Latomus 188. Brussels.

Eder, W., ed. 1990. *Staat und Staatlichkeit in der frühen römischen Republik*. Stuttgart.

Eder, W. 1991. "Who Rules? Power and Participation in Athens and Rome." In K. Raaflaub, A. Molho, and J. Emlen, eds., *City States in Classical Antiquity and Medieval Italy*. Ann Arbor and Stuttgart, 169–196.

Eder, W. 1996. "Republicans and Sinners: The Decline of the Roman Republic and the End of a Provisional Arrangement." In R.W. Wallace and E.M. Harris, eds., *Transitions to Empire: Essays in Graeco-Roman History 360–146 B.C. in Honor of E. Badian*. Norman, OK, 439–461.

Finer, S.E. 1997. *The History of Government from the Earliest Times*, vol. 2: *The Intermediate Ages*. Oxford.

Finley, M.I. 1983. *Politics in the Ancient World*. Cambridge.

Flaig, E. 1995. "Entscheidung und Konsens. Zu den Feldern der politischen Kommunikation zwischen Aristokratie und Plebs." In M. Jehne, ed., *Demokratie in Rom? Zur Rolle des Volkes in der Politik der römischen Republik*. Stuttgart, 77–127.

Flaig, E. 2003. *Ritualisierte Politik: Zeichen, Gesten und Herrschaft in alten Rom*. Göttingen.

Flower, H. 2010. *Roman Republics*. Princeton.

Forsythe, G. 2005. *A Critical History of Early Rome*. Berkeley.

Gelzer, M. 1912. *Die Nobilitat der römischen Republik*. Leipzig and Berlin.

Giovannini, A. 1985. "*Auctoritas patrum*." *MH* 42: 28–36.

Giovannini, A. 1990. "Magistratur und Volk: Ein Beitrag zur Entstehungsgeschichte des Staatsrechts." In Eder 1990: 606–636.

Grieve, L. "The Reform of the *Comitia Centuriata*." *Historia* 34: 278–309.

Gruen, E.S. 1974. *The Last Generation of the Roman Republic*. Berkeley.

Gruen, E.S. 1991. "The Exercise of Power in the Roman Republic." In A. Molho, K. Raaflaub, and J. Emlen, eds., *City States in Classical Antiquity and Medieval Italy*. Ann Arbor, 252–267.

Hall, U. 1964. "Voting Procedure in Roman Assemblies." *Historia* 13: 267–306.

Hall, U. 1990. "Greeks and Romans and the Secret Ballot." In *"Owls to Athens": Essays on Classical Subjects Presented to Sir Kenneth Dover*. Oxford, 191–199.

Hall, U. 1998. "'Species libertatis': Voting Procedure in the Late Roman Republic." In *Modus Operandi: Essays in Honour of Geoffrey Rickman*. BICS suppl. 71. London, 15–30.

Harris, W.V. 1979. *War and Imperialism in Republican Rome, 327–70 BC*. Oxford.

Harris, W.V. 1990. "On Defining the Political Culture of the Roman Republic: Some Comments on Rosenstein, Williamson, and North." *CPh* 85: 288–294.

Hölkeskamp, K.-J. 1987. *Die Entstehung der Nobilität*. Stuttgart.

Hölkeskamp, K.-J. 1993. "Conquest, Competition and Consensus: Roman Expansion in Italy and the Rise of the Nobilitas." *Historia* 42: 12–39.

Hölkeskamp, K.-J. 2010. *Reconstructing the Roman Republic: An Ancient Political Culture and Modern Research*. Princeton.

Jehne, M. 2000. "Jovialität und Freiheit. Zur Institutionalität der Beziehungen zwischen Ober- und Unterschichten in der römischen Republik." In B. Linke and M. Stemmler, eds., *Mos Maiorum. Untersuchungen zu den Formen der Identitätsstiftung und Stabilisierung in der römischen Republik. Historia* Einzelschriften 141. Stuttgart, 207–235.

Jehne, M. 2006. "Römer, Latiner und Bundesgenossen im Krieg. Zu Formen und Ausmaß der Integration in der republikanischen Armee." In M. Jehne and R. Pfeilschifter, eds., *Herrschaft ohne integration? Rom und Italien in republikanischer Zeit*. Frankfurt am Main, 243–267.

Linke, B. 1995. *Von der Verwandtschaft zum Staat: die Entstehung politischer Organisationsformen in der frührömischen Geschichte*. Stuttgart.

Lintott, A.W. 1997. "The Theory of the Mixed Constitution at Rome." In J. Barnes and M. Griffin, eds., *Philosophia Togata II: Plato and Aristotle at Rome*. Oxford, 70–85.

Lintott, A.W. 1999. *The Constitution of the Roman Republic*. Oxford.

MacMullen, R. 1980. "How Many Romans Voted?" *Ath* 58: 454–457.

Meier, C. 1956. "Praerogativa centuria." *RE* suppl. 8: 567–598.

Meier, C. 1980. *Res publica amissa*. Wiesbaden. (1st edn 1966, Frankfurt am Main).

Meier, C. 1997. "Der griechische und der römische Bürger. Gemeinsamkeiten und Unterschiede im Ensemble gesellschaftlicher Bedingungen." In E.G. Schmidt, ed., *Griechenland und*

Rom. Vergleichende Untersuchungen zu Entwicklungstendenzen und –höhepunkten der antiken Geschichte, Kunst und Literatur. Tbilissi, Erlangen, and Jena, 41–66.

Meyer, E. 1961. *Römischer Staat und Staatsgedanke*. 2nd edn. Zurich and Stuttgart.

Millar, F. 1984. "The Political Character of the Classical Roman Republic, 200–151 B.C." *JRS* 74: 1–19.

Millar, F. 1986. "Politics, Persuasion and the People before the Social War (150–90 B.C.)." *JRS* 76: 1–11.

Millar, F. 1989. "Political Power in Mid-Republican Rome: Curia or Comitium?" *JRS* 79: 138–150.

Millar, F. 1998. The Crowd in Rome in the Late Republic. Ann Arbor.

Mommsen, Th. 1887. *Römisches Staatsrecht*. Leipzig.

Morstein-Marx, R. 2004. *Mass Oratory and Political Power in the Late Roman Republic*. Cambridge.

Mouritsen, H. 1987. *Elections, Magistrates and Municipal Élite: Studies in Pompeian Epigraphy*. Rome.

Mouritsen, H. 1998. *Italian Unification: A Study in Ancient and Modern Historiography*. BICS suppl. 70. London.

Mouritsen, H. 2001. *Plebs and Politics in the late Roman Republic*. Cambridge.

Mouritsen, H. 2007. "The Civitas Sine Suffragio: Ancient Concepts and Modern Ideology." *Historia* 56: 141–158.

Mouritsen, H. 2011. "Lottery and Elections: Containing Elite Competition in Venice and Rome." In N. Fisher and H. van Wees, eds., *Competition in the Ancient World*. Swansea, 221–238.

Nicolet, C. 1980. *The World of the Citizen in Republican Rome*. London.

Nippel, W. 1980. *Mischverfassungstheorie und Verfassungsrealität in antike und früher Neuzeit*. Stuttgart.

Nippel, W. 1995. *Public Order in Ancient Rome*. Cambridge.

North, J.A. 1981. "The Development of Roman Imperialism." *JRS* 71: 1–9.

North, J.A. 1990. "Politics and Aristocracy in the Roman Republic." *P&P* 126: 3–21.

North, J.A. 2002. "Introduction: Pursuing Democracy." In A.K. Bowman et al., eds. *Representations of Empire: Rome and the Mediterranean World*. Oxford, 1–12.

Paananen, U. 1993. "Legislation in the *Comitia Centuriata*." In *Senatus populusque Romanus. Studies in Roman Republican Legislation*. AIRF 13. Rome, 9–73.

Pani, M. 1997. *La politica in Roma antica: cultura e prassi*. Rome.

Patterson, J.R. 1999. *Political Life in the City of Rome*. London.

Pina Polo, F. 2011. *The Consul at Rome: The Civil Functions of the Consuls in the Roman Republic*. Cambridge.

Raaflaub, K.A., ed. 1986. *Social Struggles in Archaic Rome: New Perspectives on the Conflict of the Orders*. Berkeley.

Raaflaub, K.A. 1993. "Politics and Society in Fifth-Century Rome." In *Bilancio critico su Roma arcaica fra monarchia e repubblica. In memoria di Ferdinando Castagnoli*. Atti dei convegni Lincei 100. Rome, 129–157.

Rieger, M. 2007. *Tribus und Stadt: Die Entstehung der römischen Wahlbezirke im urbanen und mediterranen Kontext ca. 750–450 v. Chr*. Göttingen.

Rüpke, J. 1990. *Domi militiae: Die religiöse Konstruktion des Krieges in Rom*. Stuttgart.

Ryan, F.X. 1998. *Rank and Participation in the Republican Senate*. Stuttgart.

Sandberg, K. 2001. *Magistrates and Assemblies: A Study of Legislative Practice in Republican Rome*. AIRF 24. Rome.

Scheid, J. 2003. *An Introduction to Roman Religion*. Edinburgh.

Sherwin-White, A.N. 1973 (2001). *The Roman Citizenship*. 2nd edn. Oxford.

Stemmler, M. 1997. *Eques Romanus—Reiter und Ritter. Begriffsgeschichtliche Untersuchungen zu den Entstehungsbedingungen einer römischen Adelskategorie im Heer und in den comitia centuriata*. Prismata 8. Frankfurt am Main.

Stewart, R. 1998. *Public Office in Early Rome: Ritual Procedure and Political Practice.* Ann Arbor.
Taylor, L.R. 1960. *The Voting Districts of the Roman Republic.* Rome.
Taylor, L.R. 1966. *Roman Voting Assemblies.* Ann Arbor.
Vaathera, J. 1993. "The Origin of Latin *Suffragium.*" *Glotta* 71: 6–8.
Wirszubski, C. 1950. Libertas *as a Political Idea at Rome during the Late Republic and Early Principate.* Cambridge.
Wiseman, T.P. 1971. *New Men in the Roman Senate 139 BC–AD 14.* Oxford.

FURTHER READING

The fundamental study of Roman political institutions remains Mommsen's *Römisches Staatsrecht* (1887). A convenient summary of the constitution can be found in Lintott 1999. On the assemblies Taylor 1966 is still valuable, as is her work on the *tribus* (1960). Hölkeskamp's work (1987, 1993, 2010) has greatly enhanced our understanding of the middle Republic and Roman political culture. For the role of the people in politics see e.g. Mouritsen 2001, responding to Millar 1998. For the early development of the Roman state Raaflaub 1986 is valuable. On the two highest magistracies see now Brennan 2000 and Pina Polo 2011. On the army, state and society Harris 1979 and North 1981 are important, while Beard, North, and Price 1998, along with Rüpke 1990 and Scheid 2003, are essential on Roman religion. Aspects of the Roman expansion in Italy are explored in Mouritsen 1998 and 2007. The fundamental discussions of the end of the Republic remain Meier 1980, Gruen 1974, and Brunt 1988.

PART V

Law

CHAPTER 10

Tyranny or the Rule of Law? Democratic Participation in Legal Institutions in Athens

David Cohen

1 Introduction

We may begin by distinguishing formal from informal modes of participation in the governance of the Athenian *polis*. Formal participation is defined by the constitution and laws of the Athenian democracy. Although many of the details are far from clear, the evolution of Athenian democracy to the system of "radical democracy" of the fifth and fourth centuries is the story of the gradual expansion of popular participation in the key areas of law-making, judicial decision-making, political deliberation, accountability of magistrates, and civic offices. It is precisely that expansion of popular participation that excites the criticism of oligarchs and opponents of Athenian democracy, and their opposition is often directed at the vagaries of the courts and the arbitrary legislative activity of the assembly.

By informal participation I mean the attempts by individuals to gain influence greater than that which the formal system grants them (see Fisher, Chapter 12, and Wallace, Chapter 14, on informal practices). In the absence of elections the paths to leadership found in representative democracies were not available. Because of the direct nature of democratic institutions in Athens, and because participation in most of those institutions was determined by a random method of selection (by lot), informal means were the only path to political leadership apart from the one major public office that was not determined in a random manner: the *strategoi* who commanded Athenian armed forces. Success as a general could provide the basis of claims of leadership, but also great risks should popular opinion turn against them, as it did with the prosecution and condemnation of Alcibiades and of the generals after the defeat at Arginusae. Informal participation is important not only in politics but in law and legislation as well. Those vying for leadership and pre-eminence might measure their success in part by their success in persuading the assembly to pass decrees that they proposed or supported. Elites also used the law courts

A Companion to Greek Democracy and the Roman Republic, First Edition. Edited by Dean Hammer.

in their competition for influence and for harming their rivals and enemies. Demosthenes, for example, could build his political career on the foundation of his own litigation and his prominence as a rhetor.

There were no jurists, not even a rough equivalent of jurists, at Athens, but the rhetors come closest and many used the courts as an arena and springboard for wider aspirations (see also Rhodes, Chapter 8; on juries, compare to Mouritsen, Chapter 9, and Williamson, Chapter 11). The participatory nature of the process by which officials and leaders were held accountable at Athens also offered opportunities for rivalry and ambition. In Athens the non-professional, participatory nature of the administration of justice, and particularly the private initiation of criminal prosecutions, enhanced the opportunities for individuals to manipulate legal institutions to serve their private purposes. The ability for any citizen to bring a criminal prosecution before a mass lay court for bribery, malfeasance, treason, impiety, having engaged in prostitution, introducing an unconstitutional measure, and so on, was both a means for the mass of citizens to hold leaders, generals, or officials accountable, but also a weapon that those individuals could seek to employ, though not without risk, against their rivals.

In analyzing the nature of the participatory institutional framework at Athens we must thus keep both the formal and informal dimensions in view, the constitutional framework of laws as it should work and the ways in which that system was actually experienced by Athenians. In pursuing this abbreviated inquiry into participation, two strands guide us: (1) What are the legal arenas which defined the participatory functions? (2) Who was entitled to participate and what was the nature and meaning of that participation?

As a preliminary we should note that reliable evidence is only available for the fifth and fourth centuries. In earlier periods there is no doubt that through Solonian and other innovations there was a response to civic pressures that resulted in a series of changes in institutional arrangements, increasing participation in every aspect of civic governance (see Farenga, Chapter 6). There is, however, little reliable evidence about the details, and scholarship in this area has produced scores of learned treatises debating at length the meaning, reliability, and authenticity of the fragmentary evidence. For present purposes these interminable debates are irrelevant. In the period for which we have substantial evidence, citizen participation is fully established and the legal system is almost entirely driven through this participation. Of course Athenians inherited the legacy of the previous period in the form of some legislation such as Draco's homicide laws and some institutions that had survived constitutional changes, such as the Areopagus. Rather than attempting to provide a chronological account of the evolution of Athenian institutions with the concomitant growth of popular participation that led to the peculiar form of direct democracy which Plato and Aristotle criticized as the tyranny of the *dēmos*, this chapter will focus on the period for which we have the greatest evidence and in which full citizen participation had become contested (on the tyranny of the *dēmos* see, e.g., Arist. *Pol.* 1292a 24–34).

2 Legal and Judicial Functions: Lawmaking, Litigation, Judgment

Our knowledge of the overall picture of Athenian substantive and procedural law is fragmentary and incomplete. Whether there ever was a comprehensive legal codification is doubtful, and in any event no code, comprehensive or otherwise, has survived. Our knowledge of Athenian laws (*nomoi*) is based upon quotations or paraphrase from later authors and fragmentary legal inscriptions. Much is made of the lawmaking activities of Solon (c.590) and Draco (c.630), but we really have no idea of the overall structure or content of Athenian laws until down into the fifth-century literary sources, and even then our knowledge, as already noted, is sorely incomplete. With the evidence in such a state, to speak of the nature of the more than two centuries of "legal evolution" at Athens is illusory.

What we do know with some certainty is that there was a major attempt at law reform in 403/2 at the end of the Peloponnesian War. This reform was apparently intended to address perceived problems in the Athenian legislative process. These problems, as judged from the nature of what we know about the reform process, seem to have centered on the chaotic nature of Athenian legislation and the way in which laws were created, memorialized, and accessed. There was apparently no centralized public archiving of laws, which seem to have been placed on *stelai* around the city as they were passed. There also seems to have been little attention to how new legislation fit in with previously enacted laws. The result was a legal corpus of uncertain content, difficult to access, potentially riven with contradictory or overlapping legislation, and with no authoritative mechanism or body of officials to deal with these problems.

This situation was probably in large part due to the participatory nature of the process of law creation at Athens. The Athenian assembly was an amateur body whose composition could change from session to session depending on which of around 6,000 citizens might happen to show up to attend on a given day. Until 403/2 they had virtually unrestricted legislative authority to enact laws (*nomoi*) or decrees (*psēphismata*) by majority vote. There was no "Supreme Court" or "Constitutional Court" of legal experts or jurists to review such legislation. In this way the legislative authority of the assembly may be seen to be virtually absolute, as even the ability to successfully challenge the constitutionality of a law depended upon a decision of the assembly. Even if business was prepared for the assembly by the Council of 500 (*boulē*) that body was also amateur and its composition changed annually. This unfettered amateurism of lawmaking and decision-making was one of the principal participatory features that led critics like Aristotle or Plato to deny that the rule of law obtained under the Athenian democracy. It was those same features which led proponents of the "radical" democracy to claim that they were the bedrock of a free citizenry protected by their laws and by their popular courts (see e.g. Aeschin. 1.5: "Autocracies and oligarchies are administered according to the temper of their masters, but democracies according to the established law… In a democracy it is the laws that guard the person of the citizen and the constitution of the state"; see also Dem. 24.75–76).

The law reform of the late fifth century was supposed to address the perceived problems of this system through a comprehensive review of the laws to ensure their uniformity, through initiating a system of public archiving, and through the role of officials known as *thesmothetēs*, about whose actual work we know very little. The reform establishes, at least in theory, the priority of laws over decrees, and restricted the legislative activity of the assembly to the passing of decrees. About how this reform actually played out we have relatively little information, which is in itself telling. For present purposes what matters more is that from a modern perspective the law reform would have been the occasion to create a specialized body of individuals with expert knowledge or training to undertake the mandated continuing oversight that was to ensure uniformity and eliminate contradictory laws.

The problem at Athens was that because of the structure and nature of participatory democracy as embodied in the legal system there was no institution that could have trained or constituted such a body. It was essential to the notion of the "radical democracy" that "the laws" were the property of the people, of the *dēmos* whose rule was instantiated in the very name *dēmokratia*.

What Athenian democratic ideologues implicitly understood was that the "rule of law" is a legal fiction. "Laws" do not rule but certain institutions may be empowered with ensuring the primacy of the law over arbitrary decisions (for a fuller account of Athenian debates about the rule of law, and classical scholarship on this issue, see Cohen 1995: ch. 3). But because those institutions are composed of human beings, the issue is who controls the creation and operation of those institutions and who is entitled to participate in them. It behooves us to remember, as Richard Posner has forcefully reminded us, that modern American democracy is built around a system of "checks and balances" in which the highest judicial authority is relegated to an elite body that once appointed is not accountable to the people or to any other branch of government (Posner 2003: chs. 4–6, 9). Such an institution is abhorrent to the very nature of Athenian participatory democracy.

Demosthenes (21.224–225) points out the democratic understanding of the rule of law by identifying the laws with the Athenian citizenry themselves (for Aristotle's very different view of the rule of law and his criticism of Athenian democracy as lawless, see e.g. *Pol.* 1292a4, 1292a29–35, 1298a31–34). He exposes the fiction that it is the laws that rule, and not the *dēmos* that rules through the law, when addressing a court of hundreds of randomly selected lay judges that embody the citizens of Athens. He asks the judges to consider, "And what is the strength of the laws? If one of you is wronged and cries aloud will the laws run up and stand at his side to assist him? No. They are only letters [*grammata*] and incapable of such action. Wherein resides their power? In yourselves, if only you support them and make them all powerful to help him who needs them. So the laws are strong through you and you through the laws." In this litigation where he purports to be defending the rights and security of ordinary citizens against hubristic and violent elites, Demosthenes argues that the strength of the Athenian democratic conception of the "sovereignty" of the laws resided in the fact that behind the laws stood the *dēmos,* and that it was only through the commitment of the *dēmos* to the rule of law that this "sovereignty" had any meaning.

Athenian reluctance to entrust that domain of the law to any institution that was not an instantiation of the people themselves, selected in a purely random manner from the body of the citizenry, resulted in a system that was maximally participatory and maximally amateurish, with all the potential problems that amateurism brings with it. Knowledge of the law was acquired on an ad hoc basis by those who needed it either to represent themselves in court or by the rhetors who made a living through litigation. Decisions as to which litigant prevailed, however, were, with the exception of homicide cases, left to panels of 101, 201, 501, or even more, untrained citizens randomly selected through an elaborate procedure from a pool of 6,000 volunteers, to sit on that one case for that one day. (Homicide cases and related prosecutions were the domain of specialized courts. Intentional homicide cases were heard by the Areopagus, a body composed of archons. While the Areopagus had in earlier periods enjoyed much greater powers as part of the rise of the popular [dikastic] courts, its jurisdiction was curtailed. It should be noted, however, that in the last decades of Athenian independence, as part of a movement to restrict some of the features of the radical democracy, the Areopagus seems to have acquired a somewhat larger role. See Wallace 1989: 174–206.)

Even at the critical juncture where the necessity of creating a more coherent and uniform legal environment seems to have been recognized, the principle of direct participation seems to have held sway (For a brief overview of the Athenian judges, see Todd 1993: 82–91). The legal reform of 403/2 aimed to promote coherence by ensuring the repealing of previous laws that contradicted new ones, but the determination was left to lay persons drawn from the same citizen pool as the judges. In litigation, the responsibility for adducing the law was left to the citizen-litigants themselves rather than to judges or jurists.

Reflection upon what this meant in legal practice reveals the depth of the attachment to participatory democracy as embodied in the legal system. Imagine the following: Litigant A in his speech to the mass body of lay judges argues that the case is governed by Statute X. He has that statute read to the court and explains why he thinks that under this statute he should prevail. Litigant B in his speech to the court produces a different statute and has it read to the court. This statute directly contradicts the provision in Statute X (that such scenarios are not far-fetched, see for example the contradictory accounts of who is entitled to inherit under the law in certain inheritance cases as seen in the almost hopeless situations in Isaeus, *On the Estate of Hagnias* and [Demosthenes] *Against Macartatus*, on which, see Cohen 1995: ch. 8). The entire trial consists of these two speeches. The judges do not speak or ask questions. The judges have nothing more to base their decision on than the two speeches citing two different laws that may or may not have been designed to govern such cases. It is perfectly possible that in fact the case should have been brought under a different statute altogether, which neither of the litigants has referred to, whether out of ignorance or because it didn't suit their interests to do so. There is no further evidence before the court. The judges have no special knowledge of the law and they have neither the time, authority, nor resources to research the law. They may not understand anything about the legal issues before the court or what statues exist in this area. They have no recourse to expert advice. Even if the panel of some hundreds of citizens included individuals that had some experience of similar cases they could not share that with the other judges as deliberation was forbidden. The case is complicated further by the fact that the statutes themselves typically offer little or no guidance in the form of definitions or explanations. As the impetus to law reform indicates, the decision to leave matters in this state is not a matter of "ignorance" or Athens' position on some imaginary scale of "legal evolution" where ideas of professionalism had not occurred to them, but rather a choice determined by the nature of the participatory governance that was their pride.

This mode of operation of the courts fits in perfectly with the operation of other Athenian institutions where the many hundreds of public officials were selected randomly by lot, regardless of aptitude, education, or expertise, and where the highest and most authoritative deliberative body was also no more than a selection of citizens that happened to show up on a given day to enter the assembly and vote on the business at hand (see Rhodes, Chapter 8). That the most important legal reform process that we know of in the classical period did not touch upon the "democratic" quality of participation in the justice process, and, indeed, in law-making (differentiating only the part of the *dēmos* that would be involved in the two different kinds of legislation) tells how central the commitment of direct participation was embedded in Athenian democratic thinking about the law.

It cannot be emphasized enough that this situation was not due to the "primitive" nature of the Athenian system but rather to a willingness to pay the price for, and enjoy the benefits of, participatory amateurism. Because the laws had no technical definitions or authoritative commentaries, the interpretation of a statute arose from the collective decision of a body of citizens deciding a particular case. That is, it was necessarily based upon their collective normative consciousness. In its application, law, then, was no more and no less than the lay judgment of ordinary citizens, informed by the values, expectations, and interests they each brought to the court, aggregated through an anonymous voting procedure that allowed no discussion between the judges. In Athens there was quite literally no means of telling what the law and facts were in a given case on a given day other than what the judges believed it to be after listening *only* to what the two litigants chose to tell them. Given the absence of *any* means of accurately ascertaining either the most basic facts or law governing the case, it is not surprising that the judges who watched the *agon* of the law court looked not to the niceties of legal doctrine, but to a collective sense of what would serve the interests of their city, which was arguably their ultimate benchmark of what justice was. (Litigation, not surprisingly in such an agonistic society, was considered, like athletic and dramatic performances, a competitive struggle, like warfare, an *agon*. For the implications and importance of this for Athenian governance and democracy, see Ober 1989.)

3 Legal and Judicial Functions: Prosecution, Self-Help, Accountability

At Athens the operation of what we today would call the system of criminal justice was participatory to its core. This is not necessarily surprising in that the development of public prosecution services is relatively modern. In England, for example, private prosecution was the norm until well into the nineteenth century. Needless to say, in small-scale traditional societies informal justice mechanisms and self-help tend to be the rule rather than the exception. Nonetheless, one must still inquire why Athens remained so invested in criminal prosecution through private initiative. There was in fact a body of something like police magistrates, the Eleven, and they did, as we will see, have a function that included summary trial and execution. But their activities were largely limited in this sphere to citizens who approached them with an accused person they alleged had been caught in the act of committing certain specified crimes. The Eleven had no power to initiate public prosecutions on their own, nor were they the mechanism through which criminal prosecutions were vetted and initiated. I would suggest that one reason why the institution of the Eleven never developed further into something like investigating magistrates has squarely to do with the close connection between participatory democracy and participatory justice.

As already noted above, the democratic formulation of the rule of law aimed to protect citizens from overreaching by the state. In oligarchies and autocracies the law and the power of prosecution and punishment were the preserve of the elite that monopolized the power of the state and used it to serve their own private interests.

This protection afforded by participatory democracy had as one of its central pillars the reservation to the citizens as a whole of the exclusive right to prosecute and judge public and private cases. Any Athenian who enjoyed full citizen rights (see below) could prosecute any other citizen, including public officials, by bringing criminal charges against them. The advantages that accrue to the wealthy and influential in a modern society were curtailed as much as was realistically possible through the nature of such prosecutions. The accuser had no need to fear that the accused would appear in court protected by a phalanx of the best lawyers money could buy. In theory, only the accused and the accuser addressed the judges and, as remarked above, a trial consisted only of their two speeches. The employment of speechwriters and rhetors later skewed this process in favor of the wealthy and may have in practice provided a disincentive for "ordinary" Athenians to prosecute members of the economic or political elites (see Wallace, Chapter 14). Rhetorical tropes, such as those employed by Demosthenes in his prosecution of the wealthy Meidias, provide a self-serving example of how judges might view the socio-economic disparity between litigants. Our sample of surviving lawsuits and prosecutions is also not representative of what the "typical" prosecution was like because they are preserved in the works of the orators who were part of and represented those with means. We have no trial records for prosecutions between citizens who were not themselves rhetors and who genuinely represented themselves.

Nonetheless, it can be said that democratic Athens relied upon the initiative of private citizens to prosecute wrongdoing rather than a body of officials, and upon mass courts of lay citizens chosen by lot to serve as judges. In Athenian literature the reign of the Thirty Tyrants (404–403 BCE) represents the antithesis of the democratic administration of justice and the democratic rule of law. The Thirty are used in fourth-century texts to epitomize the way in which an elite group can use the prosecutorial power for its own interests at the expense of the lives and property of the citizenry. Their abuse of the legal process to murder thousands of citizens and expropriate their property for private gain provided the paradigm of the dangers of allowing the coercive power of legal institutions to be captured by any individual or group. Lysias' speech *Against Eratosthenes* and Xenophon's account of the sham trial of Theramenes (2.3.24–51) forcefully make this point.

The overthrow of the Thirty by democratic forces was followed not by mass revenge of the kind Thucydides described as the Greek norm in his account of civil war in Corcyra (3.69–85) but by remarkable reconciliation. (See e.g. Isocrates' [18.31–32] celebration of the amnesty: "It is worthy or remembrance that although our forefathers performed many glorious deeds in war not the least of our city's esteem has come from these agreements of reconciliation." On reconciliation see Elster 2004 and Wolpert 2002). The terms of the amnesty that formed the foundation of the reconciliation are significant. What the victims of the Thirty solemnly promised was not to prosecute those who fell under the terms of the amnesty. According to Andocides, what they swore was "not to hold a grudge (*mnēsikakein*) against any citizen, except the 30, the 10, and the 11, and even of them against none who will submit to *euthunai*" (on *euthunai* see below). The term *mnēsikakein* connotes harboring the desire to seek revenge, and in the participatory legal system of Athens this would have meant directly initiating and pursuing a prosecution. The terms of the reconciliation thus reflect the understanding that the legal system provides the mechanism for individual citizens to pursue justice on their own terms through their own initiative. There is no other institutional means.

The one great exception to these reconciliatory provisions of the amnesty also indicates the place of private initiative and self-help in Athens. A clause of the amnesty provided that citizens could bring prosecutions in the case of murder or physical injury if that violence had been perpetrated "with the accused's own hand" (*autocheir*). The executions carried out by the Eleven (or others) on behalf of the Thirty would thus not qualify under this provision. There was a religious duty at Athens to prosecute the murder of kin, and the failure to do so could be considered impiety (which was itself a serious crime). The mandate for kin to pursue revenge for homicide through the legal system was so strong that it could not be excluded from the amnesty but was instead limited through the provision that the accused had to have murdered with his own hand.

As noted above, there were other features of direct self-help in the Athenian legal system and they also reflected the limitation of the intrusion of the legal sphere into the family. For certain kinds of crimes where the accused was caught in the very act (*ep' autophōrō*), such as theft or adultery, the accuser could either kill him in the act or take him immediately, with witnesses, to the Eleven, who would execute him on the spot if he did not plausibly deny the charges. (There is considerable controversy about specific details of this procedure but they are well beyond the scope of this chapter. I have used a formulation that attempts to strike a balance between the various quibbles about the exact procedure.) In the latter case he would be held for trial and the accuser would make the case against him before the panel of citizens serving as judges on that day.

A final feature of citizen participation in the legal system can be briefly noted. This has to do with the provisions for holding public officials accountable. There were a variety of means for citizens to do so, including bringing various kinds of actions before the court or directly to the assembly. This procedure, *eisangelia*, allowed for the prosecution by any citizen of officials for malfeasance in office at any time. This kind of prosecution was typically heard by the assembly as a whole. This allows an extraordinary amount of latitude to citizens to call officials to account and reflects both the Athenian fear of corruption or betrayal as well as the commitment to direct participation in prosecution of even the most important political cases (on *eisangelia* see Hansen 1975 and Rhodes, Chapter 8). The other main mechanism for popular intervention to hold officials accountable was the procedure known as *euthunai*, referred to above in the amnesty provision. Without going into details, *euthunai* were a kind of audit procedure that took place at the end of an official's term of office. There were many hundreds of public officials at Athens, selected by lot for everything from inspecting the harbors to tax or grain-supply officials. Each of them had to undergo this procedure. The salient point for our purposes is that any citizen could appear at the audit and accuse the official of malfeasance. We see again that the officials charged with conducting the audit did not have a monopoly on the process, but any citizen could appear before them and bring charges that had to be heard. (Aristotle's critique of democracy focuses on the way in which it allows too much participation by citizens in governance and specifically in holding magistrates accountable. He regards the democratic practice of holding officials accountable as "the overturning of all the magistracies" [*Pol.* 1292a30, 1298a29–35] and an undermining of the very notion of constitutional government [1292a31–34].)

We have seen, then, through a whole range of legal and judicial functions that the Athenian system operates to maximize direct citizen participation. Whether in legislating, judging, prosecuting, defending, seeking accountability of officials, or engaging in self-help, the Athenian legal system was one driven by a conviction that the interests of a democratic society were best served by engaging randomly selected amateur citizens in almost every aspect of the justice process and civic governance. The question that remains, however, was who fell into this charmed circle of participation and who was excluded. The final section of this chapter now turns to that question.

4 Citizenship and Participation

The issue of citizenship and participation is a vexed one for several reasons. First there is the problem of the legal requirements for citizenship. How was citizenship defined in Athenian law? How did that law develop in relation to the profound changes that occurred as the Athenian population grew, the empire emerged and was lost in a prolonged war that decimated the male population, and independence ended? Next there is the issue of what citizenship entitled one to. What did "citizenship" actually mean at Athens and how were the boundaries of participation drawn? A full answer to any one of these questions would require very lengthy treatment. The issue of development is outside the scope of this chapter, which confines itself to the classical period. We may then take Pericles' law of citizenship of 451/50 as our starting point.

A great deal has been written about the Periclean law in relation to its antecedents, and those learned disquisitions cannot be dealt with here (see Patterson 1981 for monographic treatment and review of all of the earlier scholarship; Patterson 2005 is the best article-length treatment and considerably updates Patterson's previous views). What is clear is that Pericles' law limited citizenship to individuals born of two Athenian parents (*astoi*). This raises the question of whether both of these *astoi*, male and female, were viewed as citizens. That question is not answered by Pericles' law because it does not define citizenship. It simply sets out a basic qualification that must be met. Implicitly it covers men and women, despite the fact that the conventional view until fairly recently has been that women were excluded from citizenship. In order to illuminate this issue we must return to the question of what citizenship meant at Athens.

As Cynthia Patterson, the leading authority, rightly notes, citizenship was thought of as "having a share" in the city (Patterson 2005: 279). What seems quite clear is that "to have a share" (*metechien*) in its essence meant participating in civic institutions. At its core, the *polis* is a partnership/community (*koinōnia*) of those qualified to "have a share" (that is, children of two *astoi* under Pericles' law). What those shares were, or how equal they were, varied and was defined by the constitution (*politeia*) of each Greek *polis*—democracy, oligarchy, monarchy, tyranny, or aristocracy.

What is without question at Athens is that foreigners, permanent alien residents, and slaves did not qualify "to have a share" (see also Balot and Atkison, Chapter 22). These groups vastly outnumbered those who did participate. When praising the participatory nature of Athenian democratic institutions, and no institution was more essentially participatory than the law courts, it is always important to remember that participation of the exclusive club of male citizens who could sit in judgment in the courts or assembly might have made up some 10–20 percent of the total population. (Estimates of Athenian population in the classical period are controversial so I have given a range that would fairly easily encompass most models of the population, which of course expanded and contracted in the course of the fifth and fourth centuries.) We will return to the question of

Athenian women as citizens in a moment, but first further discussion of the relationship of citizenship and participation is required.

As Aristotle notes, different political communities will adopt different principles of organization, or constitutions. These will in turn define the contours and content of citizenship (*Pol.* 1275b, 1278a). The constitution (*politeia*) thus reflects the distribution of power in society and the laws will be formulated accordingly (1279a22ff., 1291b7–i3;1296a22–b3). Under an oligarchic constitution citizens will have different shares according to the property qualifications provided in the constitution, and full participation will be limited to the oligarchs. As Aristotle says, citizens are those who are qualified "to have a share" in civic judgment, that is to participate in the courts, decision-making bodies, and magistracies, that is, in the central functions of governance (*Pol.* 1275a23–25). In the Athenian democracy in the classical period this in principle meant the entire body of male citizens, those adult males born of two citizen parents. A democracy in the Athenian understanding is a political community ruled by the *dēmos* that constitutes the citizenry and who share in its governance. For the adult males this means full and equal participation in all of the essential institutions of civic governance, where all have an equal right, to use Aristotle's phrase, to rule and be ruled in turn. (In the classical period citizens, male or female, could be punished with various forms of *atimia*, or loss of specified civic rights. For women this meant being barred from holding religious offices or participating in civic religious life [see below].) Citizenship, unlike in modern democracies, is not just an equal right to vote but rather a right to govern. It follows that governance in the realm of the law is participatory in nature and equally shared.

Were, then, women born of two Athenian *astoi* citizens? It is obviously true that they did not share in the governance that Aristotle used to define citizenship, but they nonetheless "had a share" in the *polis*. Patterson provides the best summary of why this was the case:

> The expression of citizenship as "shareholding" is notable for its concrete yet unrestricted expression of an active citizenship not limited to any one area of polis life—religion, law, economy, and so on—or any one gender. The nature of the share might differ in different spheres of polis life ... Contrary to those who see Periclean Athens as the exclusive domain of the male citizen, I suggest that the language of Pericles' law expresses a sort of imperial citizenship that could be enjoyed by both male and female—over, against, or above the allies or other *xenoi*. (Patterson 2005: 279–280)

The sphere of participation where women indubitably "had a share" in the *polis*, and a major share, was civic religion. Priests and priestesses of the civic and deme cults were considered as office-holders, public officials who were part of the general body of public officials referred to above. Women served as priestesses, including head priestess, in some of the most important civic religious cults in Athens, such as that of Athena Polias. They presided over public ceremonies, some of which were exclusively for women, like the Thesmaphoria, some of which were shared by men and women (see also Rhodes, Chapter 8, on the role of women in religion). As such, they were public officials subject to the same kinds of official scrutiny and audits as were other officials. This distinguished them from the many women in the population of Athens who were not born of two citizen parents and who were thus not qualified to hold such office. Women, thus, had that share in the *polis* that was defined and limited by the Athenian *politeia*. It was a grossly unequal share, but it was a participatory share limited to citizens nonetheless.

The participatory nature of the Athenian legal system also opened avenues by which claims to citizenship of both men and women could be contested (see Balot and Atkison, Chapter 22, on challenges to Greek participatory practices). There are surviving orations that accuse women of not being entitled to hold the office of priestess on this basis (see Dem. *Against Neaera*). There are also orations that revolve around periodic attempts in the fourth century to purge the citizen ranks of those accused of not being entitled by birth to "share in the *polis*." Cases such as Demosthenes' *Against Eubulides* provide good examples of what the participatory nature of legal institutions at Athens meant in practice. Here a man who appears to present more than ample evidence of his birth to qualify him for citizenship has been struck from the citizen register of his deme. He claims that this is due to his ongoing enmity with a fellow demesman, and he attempts to explain how it could happen that the members of his own deme community could have voted the way they did. He has appealed against this decision, and in doing so he incurs a very great risk, for the law provided that those who fail in such appeals were sold into slavery by the city.

Athenian direct participation in civic life and in legal institutions in particular was a great strength of Athens and doubtless contributed to the relative stability that the democracy enjoyed. On the other hand, such direct participation in a legal system inhabited by amateurs at every stage also brought with it risks that litigation would become an arena in which social, political, and economic rivalries could be played out and judged by the community. As Ober has argued, this doubtless contributed to the relative lack of serious civic disorder in Athens because it mediated the relationship between the *dēmos* as a whole and the elites who strove to be its most prominent leaders. It is also because of its participatory and amateur nature that Athenian law, particularly in comparison with its Roman counterpart, makes little contribution to jurisprudence or the Western tradition of substantive law. The situation in regard to legal theory and legal philosophy is entirely different, of course, but that is because Plato and Aristotle developed their own realm of inquiry into law and politics outside of the messy agonistic world of the amateur law courts and the assembly (for this philosophic context, see Morgan, Chapter 4 and Balot and Atkison, Chapter 22).

REFERENCES

Cohen, D. 1995. *Law, Violence, and Community.* Cambridge.

Elster, J. 2004. *Closing the Books: Transitional Justice in Historical Perspective.* Cambridge.

Gagarin, M. 2008. *Writing Greek Law.* Cambridge.

Gagarin, M. and D. Cohen, eds. 2005. *The Cambridge Companion to Greek Law.* Cambridge.

Hansen, M.H. 1975. *Eisangelia.* Odense.

Ober, J. 1989. *Mass and Elite in Democratic Athens.* Princeton.

Ober, J. 2008. *Democracy and Knowledge: Innovation and Learning in Classical Athens.* Princeton.

Patterson, C. 1981. *Pericles' Citizenship Law of 451–50 B.C.* New York.

Patterson, C. 2005. "Athenian Citizenship Law." In M. Gagarin and D. Cohen, eds., *The Cambridge Companion to Ancient Greek Law.* Cambridge, 267–289.

Posner, R. 2003. *Law, Pragmatism, and Democracy.* Cambridge, MA.

Sinclair, R.K. 1988. *Democracy and Participation in Athens.* Cambridge.

Todd, S. 1993. *The Shape of Athenian Law*. Oxford.
Wallace, R.W. 1989. *The Areopagos Council, to 307 B.C.* Baltimore.
Wolpert, A. 2002. *Remembering Defeat*. Baltimore
Yunis, H. 1996. *Taming Democracy: Models of Political Rhetoric in Classical Athens*. Ithaca, NY.

FURTHER READING

For further discussions of law in ancient Greece see Ober 1989, 2008; Sinclair 1988; Cohen 1995; Yunis 1996; Gagarin 2008; and Gagarin and Cohen 2005.

CHAPTER 11

The Evolution of Law and Legal Procedures in the Roman Participatory Context

Callie Williamson

1 Introduction

It is generally held that a body of laws, understood as the accepted rules delineating the varied relationships and interactions between and among citizens, slaves, foreigners, and the gods, already existed when the Roman Republic began in c.509 BCE. It is also conceded that legal knowledge, legal interpretation, and the implementation of remedies of the law were the exclusive purview of the highest priests of Rome, members of the same patrician clans providing the political leaders of Rome. In early Rome, however, this system and more broadly the origins of law and procedure are obscured by the absence of written records. With the advent of writing in Rome, at least by the seventh century BCE, and the gradually widening application of the tool of writing to render a degree of permanence and accessibility to fundamental community norms, we are on more certain ground. The laws and legal procedures of Rome were first written down in the middle of the fifth century BCE. From now on, as measured by both permanence and accessibility, the law was among the most deep-seated of those norms deemed important to the Roman community throughout the Republic (c.509–44 BCE) and beyond.

Central to the further development of the law and legal procedure was the territorial expansion of Rome and the increase in numbers of the Roman citizen population as well as the eventual dispersal of Romans across all of Italy (see Fronda, Chapter 3). The corresponding change in scale in the Roman world was unprecedented in the ancient Mediterranean region. Between the fourth and second centuries, Roman citizens and Latins settled in colonies scattered across Italy and individually on conquered land. New Roman tribes, territorial districts in which citizens were organized based on land holdings, and which formed voting units of the tribal assemblies, were created. Roads were built that facilitated movement to and from Rome by a highly mobile population of citizens and foreigners. The citizen population grew, in part because the Romans began to

A Companion to Greek Democracy and the Roman Republic, First Edition. Edited by Dean Hammer.

grant citizenship to Italians and others. The inhabitants of the city of Rome may have numbered almost one million eventually, requiring an infrastructure to accommodate permanent and transient residents. Rome was also the destination of revenues in the form of cash, slaves, rich material assets, and grain, produced by newly established provinces outside Italy (see de Ligt, Chapter 21). The increase in the people and resources coming to Rome necessitated increased administrative and judicial capacities both within and outside Rome. These developments were unique in the Mediterranean world, and presented unique challenges to the Romans. But over the course of the Roman expansion, the contours of the Roman legal system were continuously shaped by the carefully maintained balance between the Roman people and the Senate, arguably the most unique feature of the Roman participatory community.

2 Beginnings

Roman law formally begins with the laws of the Twelve Tables, in Latin the *leges duodecim tabularum*, the first (and only) compilation of law and procedure in republican Rome, made in the mid-fifth century BCE. The Twelve Tables were produced by a select committee of ten men, the *decemviri*, charged with collecting and writing down the rules and prohibitions that defined socio-economic relationships among Romans of differing ranks and gender, foreigners, slaves, and gods. Included were the ritualized forms of dispute resolution already in use, the *legis actiones* or actions of the law, discussed in a later section. The end-product of this effort, comprising a set of twelve tablets, was presented to the Roman people for their endorsement and set on public display in the Forum—probably on wood tablets, though this is debatable, as the regular practice of engraving statutes on bronze appears to begin later (Williamson 2005: 312–314, 396–397). Although the surviving remnants of the actual words of these laws fill only three modern pages (Crawford 1996: 578–583), their contemporary impact was momentous and their importance enduring. Over the long span of the Republic, the Twelve Tables are at the center of almost every aspect of further developments in Rome's legal institutions in a way that Greek codes never were (see Cohen, Chapter 10).

The Twelve Tables owe their composition to the internal conflicts in early Rome. At this time, Rome, like Greek city-states in earlier centuries, was in the early stages of a long period of social and political turmoil, as the Romans worked to shape the framework of society and government. From their first manifestation in the Twelve Tables, Rome's laws and procedures were an important part of this struggle, known as the conflict of the orders. From the inception of the Republic at the end of the sixth century BCE until the third century BCE, Romans citizens were divided in a struggle between patricians and plebeians. The patrician clans, a small, traditional aristocracy, were Rome's political leaders, controlling the Senate and Rome's chief magistracy, the consulate. The plebs were ordinary citizens, including the Romans who fought as infantrymen and voted in the primary voting assembly, *comitia centuriata* (centuriate assembly). Among them were also a growing number of wealthy plebeian clans whose members sought to share political leadership with the patricians. The plebs sought to participate fully in the voting assembly and seek protection from the power of the consuls, the chief magistrates and military commanders of Rome, derived from the consuls' *imperium* (power of command) to summarily punish, even execute, citizens. In addition to *imperium*, the consuls also had *iurisdictio*, the "authority to administer justice" in the *Oxford Latin Dictionary* definition, as well as *coercitio*, the authority to enforce compliance with their decisions.

At a critical juncture in the fifth century BCE, patricians and plebeians found the middle ground in the gradual construction of a balanced but parallel political structure. Fundamental to this balance was the codification of law in the Twelve Tables, heretofore the special purview of the consuls as gatekeepers of the law and the priests as guardians of the ritual language and acts of the *legis actiones*. Now the laws of Rome were written and set on public display, a step that reified not only the laws of the day but the social relationships enshrined within them. The publication of the laws in the mid-fifth century BCE has been seen as a popularizing move ensuring access to legal process for all citizens. In a city whose inhabitants were of limited literacy, however, publication best served the newer aristocracy in Rome, members of high-status plebeian clans with political aspirations. In either case, the production of the Twelve Tables signals both a widespread demand for the tools of participation in leadership and the central position of the law in Rome.

Fundamental also was the decision to divide official authority between patricians and plebeians by opening one of the two offices of consul to plebeians. More important, the Romans created a voting assembly for the plebs alone called the *concilium plebis* (plebeian tribal assembly), based on the tribes in which all citizens were registered, to balance the centuriate assembly (see Mouritsen, Chapter 9). A new state office, the tribunate, held only by men from plebeian clans, was created to convene the plebeian assembly and serve the interest of the people. Tribunes protected citizens against the consuls' authority to unilaterally punish and execute citizens. Tribunes also had the authority to veto the actions of other magistrates, including other tribunes. In short, the resolution of the conflict of the orders resulted not only in the plebeian and patrician clans sharing power but also in establishing a workable structure which in turn provided a dynamic balance between the people and the Senate.

The momentum toward the separation and balance of powers between different groups visible in these developments on a large scale was repeated time and again in the further development of political institutions and by extension legal institutions (see also Fronda, Chapter 3, and Mouritsen, Chapter 9). In 367 the office of praetor was created in a series of laws enacted in the plebeian tribal assembly, the Licinian Sextian laws (*leges Licinae-Sextiae*). The new magistrate took on most of the judicial functions of the consuls; like the consuls the praetor held the powers of *iurisdictio*, *imperium*, and *coercitio*. While the consuls retained *iurisdictio*, they tended to exercise it in matters relating to state security, presiding over special commissions established by Senate decree or vote of the Roman people to adjudicate these matters (Pina Polo 2011: 122–134). In the same year two low-level magistrates were created, the curule aediles. Like the two plebeian aediles created at the same time as the tribunes, the duties of curule aediles included record-keeping. All four aediles supervised city maintenance, the city markets and grain supply, and public order. In 339 the censorship was opened to plebeians, and in the same year plebeians entered the Senate. Of greater magnitude, and the terminus of the "conflict of the orders," were the advancements around the turn of the century which deepened the participation of the Roman people as a whole.

The first development was the affirmation, at the end of the fourth century, of *provocatio* (calling out), the chief guarantee of civil liberties (Livy 10.9). *Provocatio* gave citizens the right of appeal to the plebeian assembly against the summary justice of magistrates. Roughly contemporary, around 300 BCE, was the contentious publication of the *legis actiones*, still largely controlled by priests, and the calendar of days on which legal action was permissible by a "new man" Cn. Flavius, tribune and aedile (Livy 9.46.5). Finally, in 287, decisions of the plebeian tribal assembly were made binding on the entire population (Livy *Periochae* 11). By now, the plebeian tribal assembly was the primary lawmaking assembly in Rome. Tribunes convened the Roman people in judicial voting assemblies (*iudicia populi*) to pass judgment in matters that affected public security and safety and carried the penalty of money fines or even death. Very much in evidence in these developments are the continuing impulses of separation and balance that underlay the formation of all Rome's political institutions and shaped further developments in Rome's legal institutions.

3 Effects of Expansion on Law and Legal Procedure

During the peak centuries of Roman expansion in Italy, the third and second centuries BCE, modifications in law and procedure were inevitable as more offices were created to administer the growing state. Significantly, all these changes adhered to patterns already set. The division of legal authority continued in the allocation of specific issues among more than one magistrate. Around 244 BCE, the single praetor was supplemented by another, the praetor who came to be known as the *praetor inter peregrinos* (peregrine praetor), created to administer the first of Rome's overseas possessions, Sicily, a major source of grain for the population of Rome and Italy (Brennan 2000: 85–91, 95–97). Eventually this praetor moved into the resolution of commercial disputes between Romans and foreigners when in Rome. But the original praetor, now called the *praetor urbanus* (urban praetor) had the primary responsibility for all litigation in Rome. In addition to the judicial needs of Rome, the settlement of Roman citizens on Roman territory across Italy also extended the reach of the urban praetor. Using his authority to delegate judicial functions, the urban praetor selected "deputies," the *praefecti* who traveled to Roman communities around Italy to handle litigation between citizens.

In Rome, the urban center of a growing empire, the legal needs of a more varied, rapidly expanding city population were also growing (see also Champion, Chapter 19). A trading hub, Rome's market areas welcomed traders from across the Mediterranean region. As administrative hub of a vast land area, initially in Italy and after the Punic Wars abroad, Rome was the destination of citizens and foreigners with complaints to be resolved. Administrators with a wider range of responsibilities were needed to manage and public order was an area of concern. The four elected aediles, generally charged with city maintenance, including the upkeep of roads, water, markets, and festivals, were joined by a board of "three men for night-time crime" (*tresviri nocturni,* later *capitales*). The *tresviri* summarily resolved complaints of petty crime during the night and supervised Rome's holding cell, the *carcer* (Nippel 1995: 22–26). A board of "five men for this and that side of the Tiber" (*quinqueviri cis uls Tiberim*) of uncertain date had a similar purview—order in the marketplace—in areas along the banks of the Tiber River. The *tresviri* and *quinqueviri* were not elected at this time, but selected by the praetor.

Not unlike these panels and the special commissions of investigation created on an ad hoc basis by the Roman people in lawmaking assemblies or by Senate decree, were the permanent courts of inquiry (*quaestiones*) of the second and first centuries BCE. These were panels of judges, (*iudices*; more commonly referred to as jurors), chaired by the praetor whose members were drawn by the praetor from a list of senators and/or equestrians—the composition of the list was a point of contention addressed in lawmaking assemblies almost from the beginning—to adjudicate a growing number of newly defined crimes committed primarily by political leaders or other Romans of high status. The first of these was the crime of extortion (generally the extortion of money or property from provincials) and next was treason. Both could also be, and were, used in politically motivated contests among Roman aristocrats, especially in the first century BCE. The crime of bribery (*ambitus*) was similarly adaptable. By the end of the Republic there were other courts to address criminal matters, including a court to investigate poisonings, which were generally attributed to women and viewed with great alarm. As the number of *quaestiones* grew—and as the need for commanders in the provinces increased—the Romans added still more praetors who, in addition to their military duties, chaired proceedings. By the mid-first century there were six praetors in addition to the urban praetor and the peregrine praetor.

4 Legal Process, Formal Legal Structures, and Informal Mechanisms

Over the 465 years of the Republic (c.509–44 BCE) the Roman legal process presents a dynamic patchwork of ritualized and rationalized procedure and an array of courts (more precisely, panels of judges or a single judge) of specific focus. Setting these courts in motion was a rudimentary judiciary comprising, in the fifth and fourth centuries, the consuls and praetor, and from the third century to the end of the Republic, largely the praetors. Litigation began when a complainant approached one of these magistrates. In operation, the praetor determined whether there were issues to be adjudged between two parties. This was called the *in iure* stage of proceedings, from the language of the Twelve Tables (Crawford 1996: 2.578: XII Tabulae I,1) By delegation of the praetor's authority, a *iudex*, a private citizen, then decided the facts and passed judgment. This was the *apud iudicem* stage. Already in the early Republic, depending on the nature of the issues, the *iudex* might be a single individual or a panel. Matters involving the recovery of property were decided by a panel of men called *recuperatores*. Matters involving inheritance or adoption were given to the court of 100 men, the *centumviri*. There may have been other constellations of fact-finders in the early Republic, as there were later.

Despite the appearance of regularization in the courts, there was no uniform procedural basis for the application of either civil law (*ius civile*, or private law) or criminal law. In the fourth and third centuries BCE, when a citizen sought legal redress, the consul or praetor stated whether the right at question accorded with one of the *legis actiones* which were few in number, limited in application, and highly ritualized. With the *legis actiones*, we are in murky waters. The term *actio*, translated in English as "action," takes in the whole legal process by means of which a Roman plaintiff and defendant asserted their rights in a dispute. The meaning of *lex* in combination with *actio*, however, is unclear. Our main informant, the first century CE jurist Gaius, provides two explanations, that actions (*actiones*) were enacted by statute (*lex*) or that actions unfolded in rigid accordance with the precise wording of a statute (Gaius 4.11). Given the known inflexibility in the wording of the actions and the absence of statutory procedures prior to the Twelve Tables, the second of these is the more likely (though not fully embraced) explanation. Accordingly, Greenidge suggests the Romans understood *legis actiones* to be "actions of the law" (Greenidge 1901: 51, Schiller 1978: 213–218). Perhaps not surprisingly, the term *legis actiones* is seldom translated in modern studies on Roman law. The process itself was at some point no less troublesome to the Romans.

Over time the praetors began to devise case-specific forms of action. Probably before the second century BCE, it was becoming possible to litigate without using the ritual words and acts of the *legis actiones.* Instead, at the initial stage of litigation the plaintiff and defendant could come to an agreement jointly with the praetor on a statement of the issues in dispute that the praetor would formulate in writing and give to the *iudex* selected for the judgment stage of the proceeding. The *formulae* as they were called—leading to the phrase "formulary procedure" to describe the process—were eventually collected and each praetor, at the beginning of his year of office, would post them as the praetor's edict. The praetors' *formulae* represent the most important development in legal procedure during the period of expansion.

Visible, though obscurely so, during the third and second centuries BCE, then, is the gradual replacement of the *legis actiones* with more flexible statements of rules and consequences devised by the praetor. The simplest, historical explanation for the change is practical: the *legis actiones* were too rigid and too few in number to accommodate the kinds and numbers of complaints brought to the praetor. By the time the praetorship was divided between two men during the First Punic War (264–241 BCE), there were more citizens both in Rome and abroad, more foreigners in Rome or dealing with Romans outside of Rome, and new foreign holdings to administer. Hence the formulary procedure is probably owed to the recognition by the annual praetors over time that more efficiency and flexibility was needed in the procedures leading to the resolution of cases at law.

Alongside this formally structured judiciary the traditional mechanisms of a culture conspicuous for the pre-eminence of family and social ties continued to be used. Indeed for most forms of complaint, such mechanisms were routine. While substantive law encompassed a wide range of social and economic relationships between individuals or between individuals and the state, and pertaining to citizens, slaves, foreigners, women, and the gods, legal remedies achievable through process were not necessarily available for every set of circumstances. The workings of the extra-legal judicial process in Rome, in an episode called the Bacchanalian conspiracy, shows the degree to which legal process, social relationships, political institutions, and citizens interacted to transform a low-level, personal complaint to a historical movement, memorialized on the bronze tablet engraved with the *SC de Bacchanalibus* (Senate Decree on the Bacchanalia).

As reported by Livy (39.8–19), a young man of high status, Aebutius, son of a deceased *eques equo public* (holder of a public horse: a signal honor among equestrians) and himself an equestrian, approached the consul Sp. Postumius Albinus in the year 186 BCE with a personal complaint. Specifically, his mother and stepfather intended to offer him to the cult of Bacchus as a young initiate in order to remove him as heir to his father's estate. The sequence of events leading Aebutius to the consul was circuitous. After discussing the matter with his lover, a courtesan and a former slave from Campania where the cult was prominent, Aebutius had refused to become an initiate, whereupon his mother evicted him from the house. Aebutius had then approached his paternal aunt, Aebutia, and the aunt had urged him to go to the consul. In response to Aebutius' story, the consul's first step was to utilize a family resource of his own, his mother-in-law, to verify the reputations of the aunt, Aebutia, as well as the courtesan, Hispala Faecenia. Assured of the women's credibility, Postumius then enlisted his mother-in-law to summon Hispala to her house for an interview with the consul. There, Hispala Faecenia relayed her fears about her lover's involvement in the cult of Bacchus. The informal resources of Rome's highest elected official are unmistakable in the episode to this point.

That women were visible and influential actors in public matters is obvious not only in the actions of all the women involved in the episode to this point, but in the intuitive reliance of both the young equestrian and the consul on the judgment of a female relative. That men and women nonetheless operated in separate spheres emerges from the preliminary investigation, in which the consul's mother-in-law collected necessary information about witness credibility, arranged and supervised the consul's interview with the ex-slave woman, and installed her in her own apartment for protection. Clear also in the preliminary stage of the Bacchanalian conspiracy is the availability of Rome's highest officials, consuls, when they were in the city, to Roman citizens. Other aspects are less clear, however. In particular, if this was at bottom an estate matter, there was a court in existence to handle it, the *centumviri*, and the magistrate to approach was the praetor. Yet the aunt of Aebutius appears to have believed more was at stake than the boy's inheritance. As well she might, for the safety of Rome was tied firmly to the gods of the Romans, and the care and keeping of the gods was the closely held responsibility of the Senate and magistrates of Rome. Unless they were brought under the same umbrella of responsibility, foreign cults were viewed with suspicion. At the end of the preliminary investigation the consul took action.

Recognizing a serious threat to the stability of Rome in the popularity of a cult which was not managed by elite members of the community, the consul summoned the Senate and presented his discoveries to them. The Senate issued a decree instituting a court of inquiry, headed by both consuls. The consuls directed the judicial panels and low-ranking magistrates operating most directly with ordinary people in Rome to round up people in the city who were involved in the cult of Bacchus. These were the *tresviri capitales* and the *quinqueviri cis uls Tiberim*, both created about forty years earlier, and also the four aediles. The *tresviri* and *quinqueviri* were also instructed to break up any meetings taking place during the night and be on guard against fire-starting, a reasonably obsessive fear in a city constructed primarily of flammable material. Thousands were said to be implicated in the cult. Eventually hundreds of men and women of all stations were arrested and executed in Rome and in Roman towns. The consul Postumius marched an army to the south of Italy, an expedition resulting in the execution of several thousand slave herders. Thus was the crisis resolved.

5 Separation of Legal Functions, Non-Professional Judiciary, Legal Knowledge

A unique feature in the evolution of law and legal procedure that finds parallels in the Roman political system is the principle of separating the authority to state the law or the cause of action from the process of fact-finding and judgment. Just as the division of the highest office, the consulate, between two men was an important feature of Roman government, so the principle of separating the authority to state the law or cause of action held by the praetor from the process of fact-finding and judgment conducted by the judge(s), the separation of legal authority was an important feature of Rome's legal system. Likewise, just as the creation of the office of praetor purposely divested the consuls of the routine uses of their judicial power, so the separation of the functions of deciding the law and deciding the facts in any given case prevented the magistrate with the considerable powers of *iurisdictio*, *coercitio*, and *imperium* from abusing his position in matters of law. The delegation of fact-finding and judgment to a *iudex*, already in operation at the beginning of Republic, has been seen as a significant "popularizing" feature in the Roman legal process (Greenidge 1901: 16). More precisely, the practice disseminated judicial duties among a larger number of high-status Romans than those relatively few men holding high office in Rome. This division between more than one individual of critical parts of legal function or focus continued into the middle and late Republic and was terminated only by the *cognitio* process of the imperial period.

Also unique in the evolution of Roman law and legal procedure is the absence of legal professionals. There was no professional judiciary in Rome. Rather, Rome's praetors and judges were all men from the highest-status groups and property classes, the senators and equestrians, from whose ranks came the elected office-holders. Such men were elected to office based on reputation and performance in a range of areas from military to political, and on personal associations extending from the level of tribe to that of the Senate. The corollary is that a man elected as praetor might have specialized knowledge of the law, or he might not. His election to office was not based on such knowledge alone. Similarly, the *iudex* and all other judges were private citizens of high status with no specialized knowledge. Conversely, the absence of legal professionals, in combination with the annual turnover in magistrates with *iurisdictio* and the need for more men to act as judges, served to diffuse knowledge of the rules and practices involved in conducting litigation among the men who were potential office-holders. By the second century BCE, the political elite was not a narrow set of old families but a widening number of newer families. Not only were the mechanics of the legal process included in the baggage of Rome's political leaders or potential political leaders, but also a general level of knowledge of the various facets of the law.

To be sure there were men with specialized knowledge of the law. An early expert, Sextus Aelius Paetus, consul in 198 BCE, was a scholar of the laws of the Twelve Tables and their interpretation, and also of the forms of litigation, *legis actiones* (Watson 1974: 135–136). Other jurists of the second and early first century BCE were, like Aelius Paetus, knowledgeable about and interpreters of the Twelve Tables and like Aelius Paetus were highly placed Romans. While the focus of late Republican jurists extended beyond the Twelve Tables to matters of law and procedure characteristic of the period, the jurists themselves were still Romans of high status (Frier 1987). Some of these men were jurisconsults, consulted by their peers as specialists in the law. They did not, however, occupy formal positions in Rome's functioning judiciary.

Despite the absence of legal specialists in presenting or deciding cases at law, Romans show an impressive range of legal knowledge. Orators who argued cases in support or defense of clients facing judgment, or in support of or opposition to proposed laws, had a firm command of the tools of rhetoric but also a command of the substantive laws and procedures of Rome (Williamson 1990: 268–271). The audiences for whom forensic speeches were originally, that is in their public versions, intended—and given the public nature of the proceedings these were made up of people from all backgrounds and social groups—had an expectation of or appreciation for law-based argument. The speeches of

Cicero from the last forty years of the Republic are replete with examples. No other orator's speeches survive in the same volume as do the speeches of Cicero, but the recorded fragments of forensic argument from the same and earlier times corroborate a widely held knowledge of Rome's laws on the part, certainly, of elite Romans. This is not surprising when the education of young Romans included the Twelve Tables which, as late as the first century BCE, were publicly posted in Rome, the language of the original tablets presumably regularly modernized (Crawford 1996: 2.556–557, 571).

6 Citizen Participation in the Formation of Law and Procedure

There are two ways of looking at citizen participation in this context: the diffusion of legal experience among growing numbers of potential leaders and leaders, discussed above, and the involvement of all Romans in making and using law. In this section I focus on the Roman people. For, looking beyond areas dominated by elite Romans, it is also true that law and procedure evolved as both products and supports of citizen participation in the civic life of Rome.

Underlying the formal developments in Sections 2 and 3 is the essential though unacknowledged role of the Roman people. Most if not all of the official changes in Rome's judiciary noted above were made or modified by Roman citizens voting in lawmaking assemblies (Williamson 2005: 277–278). A law enacted by the people, between 287 and 218, added the supervision of weights and measures in Rome's markets and resolution of related disputes to other duties of Rome's four aediles. The tribune Papirius, sometime between 241 and 123 (Festus 347), carried a measure that removed the selection of the *tresviri capitales* from the praetor and gave the people the right to elect them in a tribal assembly. In addition to their regular duties, the *tresviri capitales* were also made responsible for collecting the money fines required in the *legis actio sacramento*, an action used to get title to something or to assert an obligation agreed upon by two people. The involvement of the people indicates the importance of these matters to the Romans. It was the Roman people also who, in this period and later, increased the number of praetors. After the *praetor inter peregrinos* in c.244 BCE, two more praetorships were added after 227, and two more again after 197, initially to command armies and administer Roman justice in Rome's overseas territories. In 81, a further two praetors were created, for a total of eight praetors, six of whom chaired the *quaestiones* in addition to commanding armies and governing provinces. All these offices filled a need.

So too did the special commissions of inquiry. When matters arose, specifically matters involving foreign states that did not fall under any existing legal procedure or action, a more and more frequent occurrence after the Second Punic War (218–201 BCE), the Romans instituted commissions of investigation. While sometimes these commissions were set up by Senate decree, in response to outside request or inside concern (witness the Bacchanalian affair above), sometimes, too, the commissions were instituted by decision of the Roman people in a legislative assembly (Williamson 2005: 277–278).

Other judges and courts that became part of the regular administrative and legal apparatus of the Roman state noted in earlier sections were subject to creation, regulation, or attempted regulation by public lawmaking assemblies (Williamson 2005: 277–278). By direction of the Roman people in 210, the Senate established the *quattuorviri praefecti*

Capuam Cumas, a commission of four men selected by the praetor to administer justice in the districts of Campania. In this way were penalties imposed on Capua for failing to support Rome during the Second Punic War. In 124 BCE, another public law directed that the *quattuorviri* be elected in the tribal assembly. More enduring than the special commissions of inquiry were the permanent courts or *quaestiones*, also products of Rome's lawmaking process, beginning with the *lex Calpurnia de repetundiis* of 149 and followed by a range of others. All were initially created and then modified, often repeatedly, by decision of the Roman people (Williamson 2005: 318–319).

While the magistrates, panels and commissions in the previous paragraph are matters of public law, that is law as between citizens and the state, Roman lawmaking assemblies also addressed matters of private law. To be sure, these are relatively few in the surviving accounts. Of 541 proposed or enacted public laws reported by ancient recorders between 350 and 44 BCE, only thirty address private law issues (Williamson 2005: 452–473). It is reasonable to ask why, then, private law matters were presented to the Roman people.

Looking at the group as a whole a common thread appears to runs through all of them, leading ultimately back to the Twelve Tables. Some statutes address practices previously codified in the Twelve Tables. The institution of nexus or debt-bondage, for instance, included among the laws of the Twelve Tables, was terminated by statute. A few statutes, about nine of the thirty public laws dealing with private law matters, deal specifically with *legis actiones*, the ritualized forms of action of the early and middle Republic. This very small group provides a key to understanding why Roman lawmaking assemblies addressed private law matters at all.

The original *legis actiones* were five in number, whose description and history is recorded by the jurist Gaius (*Institutes* 4.10–20). Four were already in existence or introduced in the laws of the Twelve Tables and one, an action to enforce claims for a fixed amount of money, is later than the Twelve Tables, introduced perhaps in the third century—presumably after the Romans began to formalize a money economy by minting their own coins—by a *lex Silia* (Gaius 4.19). Only one of the actions, the *legis actio sacramento*, antedated the Twelve Tables (and continued in use throughout the republican period in the centumviral court). Of these five *legis actiones*, four were modified at some point between the fourth and second centuries BCE by lawmaking assemblies, the modifications taking the shape generally of an extension of the action to other sets of circumstances. The *legis actio* created by the *lex Silia*, for example, was later extended by a *lex Calpurnia* to cover also claims for a specific item (Gaius 4.19).

Attested in these statutory modifications are the limitations of Rome's traditional *legis actiones* in the more complex economic and social environment from the mid-third century BCE onwards. The modifications made to some of the *legis actiones* during the long period of their use served to widen their scope, an indicator of the recognition by Rome's lawmakers that the *legis actiones* were too limited. Since the *legis actiones* envision the possibility of a limited set of issues at law, that is, the precise words and rituals of the *legis actiones* restricted legal action, it is easy to understand the changes introduced by statute. The need for such modifications reinforces the idea that not all matters in dispute among people in Rome could conform to the ritual words and actions of one of these procedures and other procedures simply did not exist. Correction of this system was unavoidable.

Hence, the statutory modifications of the *legis actiones* appear to move the evolution of legal procedure along in a direction it was already going in practice: they are stages on the way to creating a different way of seeking legal redress. Most indicative of the ongoing and dynamic adjustments in this series of public laws was a *lex Aebutia*, reported in passing by only two sources (Aulus Gellius, *Noctes Atticae* 16.10.8; Gaius 4.30). Much uncertainty and even more scholarly discussion continues to surround the *lex Aebutia*. It is generally conceded that the law was most likely enacted in the second half of the second century BCE and that it in some way addressed the substitution in litigation of the praetor's *formulae*, statements of the cause of action, for one or more of the *legis actiones*. Thus the statute appears to confirm the critical shift from the uses of *legis actiones* to the formulary procedure. The practice, now formalized by statute, confirmed the urban praetor in an important role in making law by articulating the legal issues of a case in *formulae* before the facts were adjudged by a *iudex* or *iudices*. Such statements formed the basis for model rules, which were written down and posted at the urban praetor's tribunal. Every year the next elected praetor added or removed *formulae* as he saw fit. The praetor's ability to create new rules of procedure and the praetor's edict published on tablets giving them concrete form are regarded as one of the most important sources of law in republican Rome. That the development was formally endorsed by the Roman people is significant.

Although we do not know the full content of the Twelve Tables, it appears that every significant change in substantive law or procedure enacted as law by the Roman people was a change specifically in something previously codified in the Twelve Tables. Conversely, matters contained in the Twelve Tables originally endorsed by the people were subject to modification only by the Roman people. And just as the Twelve Tables constituted a major turning point, changes with momentous consequences for the direction of Roman law were always presented to the Roman people. In sum, based on even a small number of public laws dealing with matters of private law, such matters are to be counted among the issues Roman lawmakers deemed of sufficient importance to bring to the Roman people, that is to say issues that were fundamental in Roman eyes to sustaining the continued stability of Roman society.

7 Access

The details of routine access to legal process by ordinary Romans in the republican period are virtually undocumented. We have nothing like the petitions, for example, from Roman Egypt or Syria under the Empire showing the extensive recourse by provincials and Roman citizens to legal channels of redress. Comparable information for the Republic is harder to come by. We have a few forensic speeches by Cicero, defending Romans of high status or clients of wealthy patrons, and fragments of speeches by other orators. We have allusions in rhetorical writings of the period and later, as well as references to issues at law by jurists of the period, preserved by Gaius and later jurists of the imperial period (see also Morstein-Marx, Chapter 17, on the role of orations, including forensic orations). Consequently, some would say that litigation in Rome only ever involved a narrow swathe of the population because only a small number of citizens had resources that might put them in situations where they needed to assert a right to something or make a claim against another (Frier 1987: 273).

It is not possible to say how many Romans, or even which Romans, made use, over the course of their lives, of the growing body of civil and criminal laws and procedures that emerged during the Republic. Yet the many manifestations of law and legal procedure in Roman society, and the very public character of the law in the city of Rome, whether in its physical manifestations, inscribed like the Twelve Tables on wood tablets or engraved on bronze, provide compelling evidence of the predominance of law in everyday life. The visibility of legal institutions no less than the attention paid to them suggests their utilization was common in Roman society throughout the Republic. The legal documents from the imperial period, surviving in large quantities, show that people from all social and economic levels had access to and used the available legal mechanisms. Perhaps the single largest coherent group across the Empire was composed of Roman soldiers and military dependents. As noted, no comparable body of documents exists for the republican period. Nonetheless, the central position of the Roman army in Roman society and the role of military service as catalyst for economic and civic advancement provide sufficient grounds for thinking that ordinary Romans made similar use of the mechanisms of the law in the earlier period. Indeed, the most active private law court in Rome, the centumviral court, was not beyond reach of ordinary Romans if we accept the fluidity inherent in the Roman population, especially in terms of land ownership and devolution of title to property (Williamson 2005: 215–220, 421–422).

The same court points to tribes as the point of entry into the legal system (see also Fronda, Chapter 3, and Mouritsen, Chapter 9). The mechanisms of justice, the courts and their officers, were enmeshed in Rome's social structure via tribes, the territorial and voting districts to which all citizens belonged. A tribe was a community within the state that embraced aristocrats and non-aristocrats alike. Within their tribes, Romans exhibit the vertical ties of the larger population characterized by the deference of ordinary Romans to high-status Romans. Tribes were also somewhat egalitarian due to the leveling features of tribal activities. Within the tribe, aristocrats and ordinary Romans came face to face to conduct the business of the tribe. As tribesmen, they voted and assembled every five years to be counted and placed in property classes. Tribal relationships underlay networks linking family, friends, and neighbors, patrons and clients, soldiers and officers, people and leaders. These small-scale networks at the tribal level connected Romans to the Roman state during the Roman Republic.

The plebeian tribal assembly was the chief lawmaking assembly in Rome (see Fronda, Chapter 3, and Mouritsen, Chapter 9). The tribes were more important than property classes as bases of political action, perhaps due to the intermix of Romans of all wealth and status groups which gave full rein to the mutual deference of aristocrats and ordinary citizens in determining the tribal vote. Ordinary tribesmen deferred to the vote of their aristocratic neighbors as they deferred to aristocrats generally. In turn, aristocrats deferred to ordinary tribesmen. As tribesmen themselves, the most effective political leaders were attuned to the wishes of fellow tribesmen and correspondingly to the people as a whole.

It is apparent that tribal affiliation came into play in the changing legal procedures of the second and first centuries, although how precisely it did is unclear. In the surviving clauses of the extortion law (*lex repetundarum*) dated c.133–121 and engraved on a bronze tablet, we read that the names of the 450 men on the annual album of *iudices* shall be written in full, to include their father's name, their tribe and their cognomen, suggesting that parties to a complaint, when selecting judges from the panel, paid attention to tribal affiliation (Crawford 1996: 1.66–67, 98–99, *lex repetundarum* lines 12–18) Corroboration comes from the special tribal elections established by the *lex Plautia* in 89, in which the tribesmen from each tribe selected fifteen judges from the tribe for the standing court instituted by another statute, the *lex Varia* to judge cases of treason. Similar elections were conducted in 81, following the decimation of the Senate in the civil war, to choose 300 equestrians for Sulla's expanded Senate, and again in 70 to select the judges of the three panels of senators, equestrians, and *tribuni aerarii* instituted by the *lex Aurelia*. Finally, the tribes selected the 105 men—three from each tribe—who sat as the centumviral court. Clearly the Romans were mindful of the tribal voice and tribal loyalties in matters of law.

8 Comparison

With its popular assemblies, Senate, and magistrates, republican Rome presents on the surface a governing structure similar to that of Athens and other Greek participatory communities in the fifth and fourth centuries. Likewise, the Roman legal system, like the Greek legal system, is rooted in the governing structure. Dig deeper, and the similarities disappear. There was more than one popular assembly in Rome. Magistrates were elected, not selected by lot. The Roman people did not participate directly in the articulation of policies or laws in any public forum. Another layer down, where law is concerned, the differences between Rome and Athens are especially profound. The Roman legal system, like the Greek, evolved as both a product and reinforcement of citizen participation in the civic life of Rome. Notwithstanding differing degrees of involvement, determined by social standing, in the making and implementing of law, Roman citizens at all levels had a very real impact on the development of the laws and legal procedures deemed necessary for community stability. Indeed, the adaptability of the Roman legal system to the enormous changes in Roman society over the period is no small measure of its success. Overall, the Roman system seems far more dynamic than the Greek in both operation and development throughout the Republic.

Conversely, at the heart of Roman law and procedure in the republican period is the fifth century BCE compilation of laws written on twelve tablets, the Twelve Tables. Modeled, in Roman tradition, on Greek codes, specifically the sixth century BCE Athenian Code of Solon, the Twelve Tables are certainly artifacts of that same impulse of social and political creativity that characterized the early development of the Greek city-states. In Rome, however, the Twelve Tables occupied a central place far longer than did the Greek codes, playing a pivotal role in the evolution of law and procedure throughout the 465-year period of the Republic when the Romans expanded from small city-state to world empire.

REFERENCES

Bagnall, R.S., K. Brodersen, C.B. Champion, A. Erskine, and S.R. Huebner, eds. 2012. *The Encyclopedia of Ancient History*. 13 vols. Malden, MA.

Brennan, T.C. 2000. *The Praetorship in the Roman Republic*. Oxford.

Crawford, M.H., ed. 1996. *Roman Statutes*. BICS suppl. 64. 2 vols. London.

du Plessis, P. 2010. *Borkowski's Textbook on Roman Law*. Oxford.

Frier, B. 1987. *The Rise of the Roman Jurists*. Princeton.

Greenidge, A.H.J. 1901. *The Legal Procedure of Cicero's Time*. Oxford.

Kelly, J.M. 1976. *Studies in the Civil Judicature of the Roman Republic*. Oxford

Kunkel, W. 1972. *An Introduction to Roman Legal and Constitutional History*. Oxford.

Metzger, E. 2005. *Litigation in Roman Law*. Oxford.

Metzger, E. 2013. "An Outline of Roman Civil Procedure." *Roman Legal Tradition* 9: 1–30.
Nippel, W., 1995. *Public Order in Ancient Rome.* Cambridge.
Pina Polo, F. 2011. *The Consul at Rome: The Civil Functions of the Consuls in the Roman Republic.* Cambridge.
Schiller, A.A. 1978. *Roman law. The Mechanisms of Its Development.* New York, The Hague, and Paris.
Watson, A. 1974. *Law Making in the Later Roman Republic.* Oxford.
Williamson, C. 1990. "The Roman Aristocracy and Positive Law." *CPh* 85: 266–276.
Williamson, C. 2005. *The Laws of the Roman People: Public Law in the Expansion and Decline of the Roman Republic.* Ann Arbor.

FURTHER READING

The starting point for the text and development of the Twelve Tables, and all other surviving statutes is Crawford 1996. On the important role of public lawmaking in the Roman Republic see Williamson 2005, which includes a listing of reliably reported proposals of law and enacted law. Watson 1974 devotes a chapter to public lawmaking assemblies as sources of private law.

The available information on legal procedure in the Republic is scanty and subject to interpretation. Greenidge 1901 is essential reading for its depth of understanding, as is Kelly 1976. To put both authors and their subject-matter in perspective, Metzger 2005 and 2013 are also essential. Frier 1987 is a dynamic account of the republican jurists and the praetor's edict. On the office of praetor whose functions were military as well as judicial see Brennan 2000.

Among the many handbooks and textbooks on Roman law across the ages, du Plessis 2010 is comprehensible and also includes online resources. Kunkel 1972 presents a thorough survey of the historical context of Roman legal developments. Schiller 1978 contains the most important primary sources (in English translation) for the development of legal mechanisms from the early Republic to the late Empire as well as the viewpoints of scholars.

Finally, comprehensive accounts of the various judicial offices, judicial panels and laws in this chapter are provided in the eponymous articles in Blackwell's *Encyclopedia of Ancient History* (Bagnall et al. 2012), available in print and online, if not in earlier chapters of this volume.

PART VI

Social Values

CHAPTER 12

Informal Norms, Values, and Social Control in Greek Participatory Communities

Nick Fisher

1 Introduction

Many Greek states in the classical period encouraged widespread citizen participation in political and judicial bodies, and the extent of participation naturally increased with the adoption of more democratic governmental systems (see Rhodes, Chapter 8, and Mouritsen, Chapter 9). Athens, which had the fullest democratic system known to us, achieved the involvement of a remarkably high proportion of middling or poorer citizens as voters in the assembly, as jurors (6,000 a year), and as members of the probouleutic council (500 a year) or other administrative boards (in contrast with popular participation in the Roman Republic, see Mouritsen, Chapter 9). The process of selection for the council and many boards of officials involved the lot and representation from all the ten tribes; in total, not counting the jurors, well over a thousand citizens had to be found annually to fulfill important and time-consuming functions, many of which were remunerated (Hansen 1991: 232–233). All would be held to account at the end of their year of office (the *euthuna*). Participation in trials or in legal arbitration procedures, whether as defendants, self-help prosecutors, witnesses, arbitrators, or jurors was part of the lives of very many citizens, bringing them into direct contact with the operation of the laws.

Defenders of Athens' democratic system greatly valued the ideal of the individual freedom of male citizens (see Pericles' funeral speech, Thuc. 2. 37, Lysias 2.13, Arist. *Pol.* 1317a40–1318a3), including the freedom of action ("living as one wishes") and freedom of speech (*parrhēsia*). This ideal was not seen as absolute, but had to be held in a delicate balance with the citizens' acceptance of the democratically determined laws, and of the obligations to participate, appropriately according to their property qualifications, in the defense, management and well being of the state (see Liddel 2007). Sparta, a much less democratic system, none the less demanded high levels of civic participation of its citizens (the "Spartiates"), but in a more restricted and regimented way.

A Companion to Greek Democracy and the Roman Republic, First Edition. Edited by Dean Hammer.

In this chapter the focus is on how the socialization, informal interactions, and participation in festivals all contributed to political consensus and the commitment to make individual contributions to the state: it explores how far Athens, Sparta, and other cities developed institutions and practices which encouraged acceptance of basic social and political norms, and how far these institutions and practices were also designed to encourage critical debate on these values. It is divided into two halves. First, I consider how civic instructions, knowledge, and advice, instilling awareness of civic laws and norms and the duties and responsibilities of citizens, were delivered to the young, in schools and gymnasia, as part of the induction into the constituent sub-units of the *polis* (such as tribes, demes, or phratries) or by other interactions. Second, I consider how widespread participation in major festivals, with their athletic and cultural competitions, enhanced awareness of the community's history and ideals, and explored the coherence or contradictions of its values, traditions, and ambitions.

2 Education and Socialization

Schools and democracy

The earliest evidence for schools in Greek cities comes in anecdotes dated to the early fifth century. Herodotus (6.27) reports that on Chios c.496 two supernatural warnings were given of the impending battle of Lade which ended the Ionian revolt: first, out of a chorus of a hundred young men sent to perform at Delphi ninety-eight died of the plague, and second, the roof of a school collapsed, and only one of the 120 boys learning their letters survived. At about the same time Cleomedes the boxer, maddened by a disqualification at Olympia, returned to his small island of Astypalaea and destroyed a school and the sixty children inside (Pausanias 6.9.6–8). Later, Thucydides (7.29) reports that in 413 Thracian mercenaries on the rampage carried out a massacre in Mycalessos, a small Boeotian city, including the killing of all the boys in the largest school. These casual references, all referring to small cities, suggest that schools offering basic literacy skills become widely available by at least the early fifth century across the Greek world. As the democracy developed, in Athens, especially after the reforms of 462–450 (and to some extent in other cities), public documents, both on paper stored in public buildings, and monumentally on stone or bronze inscriptions, were used to give essential information to citizens, to demonstrate the accountability of their institutions or to make impressive statements of Athens' power. Ordinary citizens who served on the Council of 500, or on many of the boards of officials concerned with finance or overseeing major projects, would find themselves expected to have a minimal level of literacy and numeracy skills; participation by large numbers of boys in the many performances and contests in choral singing (see below) will have enhanced the literacy skills of many who may have had little or no schooling (see Missiou 2011). From the late fifth and early fourth centuries written records came to be required in commercial and property agreements, as evidence for the courts.

Attendance at Athens' schools was encouraged. In his *Crito* (50d–e) Plato gives a speech to the personified Laws which makes them claim—exaggeratedly—that they "required" Socrates' father to "educate his sons in *mousike* and *gymnastike*"; in the later fourth century, Aeschines claimed that Solon passed laws (i.e. in the early sixth century) regulating opening hours and teachers at schools and *gymnasia*, to protect the boys from abuse (Aeschin. 1. 9–10). The attribution to Solon is doubtful, but it is likely that at least some of these laws were established during the late sixth or early fifth century. But there was no state financial support for schools and they were not compulsory (Arist. *Pol.* 1337a 5–25). Some fifth-century archaeological evidence for schooling in Athens is provided by a small building, inside the hero shrine to Academos (later the site of Plato's Academy), where a number of slate-like stones with letters scratched on them have been found, apparently schoolboys' writing slates (Vanderpool 1959: 279–280; Travlos 1971: 43); some Athenian vases show boys learning their letters together or engaged in singing or gymnastics (Morgan 1998: 19).

Primary education had three basic elements, usually taught in different establishments: there were teachers of *grammata* (letters), *mousike* (singing and learning instruments, especially the lyre), and *gymnastike* (athletics). Schoolteachers did not enjoy wealth or high status, as is demonstrated by Demosthenes' abuse of his enemy Aeschines' social origins, allegedly the son of an ex-slave and poverty-stricken schoolteacher (Dem. 19. 249, 281; 18. 129–130, 258). Surviving figures for teachers' salaries, from inscriptions detailing the foundation of schools and *gymnasia* at Miletos (200/199 BCE, Austin 1981: no. 119) and Teos (second century BCE, Austin 1981: no. 120), suggest that fees were moderate. Even so, as "Protagoras" says in the speech given to him in Plato's dialogue, wealthy fathers were able to keep their sons at schools and *gymnasia* for longer than the poor (Plato *Prot.* 323d–e: see Harris 1989; Pritchard 2003: 206–218).

These schools taught more than basic literacy and numeracy (see Morgan 1998, 1999). Our sources suggest their aims were not so much the teaching of useful skills (taken for granted) as the instilling of discipline, good order, and the moral values suitable for "good men" (Plato *Prot.* 325d–326e; Aristoph. *Clouds* 961–1062). There is little sign, however, that they did this by formal teaching of the institutions, laws, or history of their city. The literacy teacher (*grammatistes*) would support the learning of letters with reading, learning by heart, and reciting poetic texts, above all the Homeric epics and choral songs (Plato *Prot.* 325d–e; Aristoph. *Frogs* 1054–1055). The conservative "Right Argument" in Aristophanes' *Clouds*, defending the "Old Education," focuses on the decency, health, courage, and respect for parents instilled by discipline, gymnastics, and the choral singing of traditional songs. Competitive recitations of epic poetry at festivals such as the Panathenaia, and informally by traveling rhapsodes, kept awareness of such material alive. In Plato's *Laws* Book 2 it is agreed by all that singing in a chorus throughout one's life was the right and proper way to learn and maintain the values of the community; an uneducated man was an *achoreutos*, one not part of a chorus (654a; Swift 2010). It was believed that the content of Homeric and other poetry would encourage preparedness to fight for their city and sound political and moral principles, while choral songs would impart awareness of their city's traditions, gods and religious rituals, and highlights of their mythical and historical past (cf. Plato *Ion*; Xen. *Symposium* 3.4–6; Lycurgus 1.102–104; Ford 1999). Further, performing and listening to the rhythms and tunes of music and song were thought to have the power to stir emotions and to instil moral character; see the discussions in Plato (*Rep.* 398–400) and Aristotle (*Pol.* 8), with Ford 2003. Discussions and memories inside the family no doubt reinforced some basic awareness of their political culture and the fundamental social values, above all those associated with honor, shame, and reciprocity.

Phratries, demes, and the ephebeia *in Athens*

After Cleisthenes' reforms of 508/7 BCE, sons of Athenian citizens had to be accepted as new members into two distinct sets of sub-groups of the *polis*; both had a local origin, but membership was based on inheritance. The earlier organization was the phratry: a citizen's son would be accepted at about 16 into his father's phratry at its major festival (*Apatouria*), accompanied by animal sacrifices, feasting, and the performance of appropriate songs (Lambert 1993). A couple of years later he would also be accepted into one of the 139 demes established by Cleisthenes, the rural or urban "villages," linked to the ten new tribes and thirty new *trittyes* in complex ways which broke down local loyalties by "mixing up" Athenians across the whole territory of Attica. Tribes and phratries and similar pseudo-kinship organizations occurred very widely across Greece, and were often subject to radical reorganization and redefinition; one such change in southern Sicily also provides evidence for the use of writing to define membership: fifth-century lead tablets recently discovered in the temple of Athena at Camarina were inscribed with a citizen's name with his patronymic on one side, and a number indicating his phratry on the other (Murray 1997).

At Athens, after deme enrolment had been ratified by the Council of 500, c.18-year-olds were taken round the sanctuaries and had to swear a solemn collective oath, declaring their commitment to fight for the *polis*, honor its gods and rituals, and obey its laws and magistrates. They then spent some time together, acquiring skills and knowledge relevant for their future roles.

The form of this quasi-initiatory process changed over time, and details of the earlier stages are very uncertain. It is clear that a major reform took place c.335/4, after the military defeat of Chaironea in 338, when many measures were taken to renew Athenian military and financial efficiency and civic pride. Henceforth 18–19-year-olds spent two years engaged in a well-organized program (now called the *ephebeia*) of military training, frontier-guarding, and performance of a good many rituals ([Arist.] *Ath. Pol.* 42). Before 335 a few elements of this probably existed, including some training at *gymnasia*, competing in the tribal torch-races (at least three a year), guarding of frontiers, and performing duties at other festivals. (Aeschin. 2. 167; Xen. *Ways and Means* 51–52; and *IG* II^2 1250). It is unfortunately uncertain whether these programs were compulsory for all new citizens, or voluntary and undertaken mostly by the better-off. The personified Laws in Plato's *Crito*, urging Socrates not to flee Athens to avoid the death penalty, claim that all citizens are bound by contract to obey the laws, and that each one, when he passes his registration before the council (*dokimasia*) and sees the city's business and the laws, has the choice of leaving; if he stays, this constitutes a binding commitment (*Crito* 50a–52d). This may suggest that there was already in the early fourth century some general discussion of the laws and the political constitution, though detailed knowledge of all the laws was certainly not expected; in later life individuals sought out the laws as and when they needed them.

More importantly, the solemnity of the ceremonial tours, oath, rituals, and contests, at least after the reform of 335/4, would have done much to create cohesion and commitment to the state; this is emphasized by Lycurgus, *Against Leocrates* 76–80, who cited the text of the ancient "ephebic" oath (of which we also have a version on an inscription from Acharnai of the same period, Rhodes and Osborne 2003: no. 88; see e.g. Ober

2008: 178–179). Lycurgus, who delivered this intensely patriotic prosecution speech in a treason trial in 330, was a leading figure in Athens' revival after 338. Each new citizen recognized two "eponymous heroes" as his divine patrons and models; his "tribal hero," as each of the ten tribes was named after an early Attic mythological king or warrior, and his "age-class hero," as each of the forty-two year-classes of militarily active Athenians was represented by forty-two other heroes, covering the ages from 18 to 60. Very little is known of the latter; only three names survive (see [Arist.] *Ath. Pol.* 21.5, 42, 53.4–5; Davidson 2006, 2007; Steinbock 2011). Comparable organizations of new adults, also commonly called *ephebeiai*, spread across the Greek world, probably on the Athenian model, but, as at Athens, then tended to provide a form of military training and higher education for the sons of the elite.

These Athenian patriotic narratives, some situated in legendary periods, such as the deeds of Theseus and the eponymous heroes, and some in historical times such as the Persian Wars, were regularly retold in the official speeches delivered, every year in which Athenians died in battle, at the honorific state funeral (see also Hölsher, Chapter 26). Tribal heroes feature regularly in these speeches, as the dead were honored in their tribal groups, and listed in the official casualty lists (see e.g. Dem. *Funeral Speech* 60.27–31; Loraux 1986).

Informal socialization and homoerotic relationships

Much informal instruction would have taken place at the *gymnasia*, at drinking parties (*symposia*), and at festivals to which boys and youths might be taken. In particular, the accepted practice of homosexual pursuit located at *gymnasia* and *symposia* offered to some adolescents relationships with older males outside the family, which might bring, in addition to excitement and affection, useful contacts and valuable guidance in appropriate behavior in political and social life. They also brought some risk of social disgrace or psychological damage. The complex norms of these relationships in Athens imposed on adolescents delicate decisions concerning which (or how many) lovers to entertain, and what to permit them to do (norms and problems are set out most fully in the speeches in Plato's *Symposium* and *Phaedrus*). Gossip and disapproval might attend youths thought to be too flirtatious or too promiscuous, and especially any believed to have accepted money, excessive gifts, or lavish lifestyles from lovers; laws introduced at least by 424 BCE meant that any citizens thought to have so "prostituted" themselves ran the risk of being prosecuted if (but only if) they engaged in public life, by speaking in the assembly, standing for public office, or the like (Aeschin. 1.20–32; Aristoph. *Knights* 876–879). Acceptance of anal or oral penetration seems not to have incurred guilt as such under these laws, but suspicion of having engaged in such "shameful," "servile," or "womanish" sex seems to have increased the chances of being held to have "prostituted" oneself (Aeschin. 1, esp. 185–187). Prosecution under these was very rare; the only case we know anything about, Aeschines' prosecution of Timarchos in 345/4, was successful, despite the blatant fact that Aeschines had no good evidence to present (see Fisher 2001: 36–67).

How far participation in these practices extended beyond the leisured elites is a matter of dispute. In my view, the way Aeschines presents his case against Timarchos to the popular jury, arguing that the youthful Timarchos' promiscuity was a shameful betrayal of the noble and valuable institution of the love of boys, in which he himself still indulged

(1.132–140), is strong evidence that it was not restricted to an elite, but had become quite widely practiced among middling Athenians (Fisher 2001: 58–62; against see Hubbard 1998; Pritchard 2003; 2013: 80–83, 130–133). It can further be argued that it was precisely because the Athenians observed large numbers of their young men engaging in these pursuits and then going into active democratic politics, that they passed these laws directed at those in the political classes; Athenians feared that those who had disobeyed the proper rules of friendship and reciprocity in sexual relations would be equally unreliable in public life (see Fisher 2008). Other cities no doubt encouraged or restricted such practices in many different ways. Pausanias' speech in Plato's *Symposium* (189c–185c) suggests that at Sparta, as at Athens, the picture was complex, while in Elis and Boeotia approval was granted uncomplicatedly to boys who accepted lovers, but in Ionia this was held to be shameful (cf. also Xen. *Symposium* 8.34; *Lac. Pol.* 2). But we lack details of any specific regulations.

Higher education—the Sophists

Forms of higher education, and the concomitant invitation to take critical attitudes to political and moral values, began in Greece around the middle of the fifth century; they helped to create social tensions and a generation gap, dramatized at its starkest by the contest in Aristophanes' *Clouds* between Right and Wrong Argument. Leading intellectuals, who came collectively to be known as the Sophists (skilled or wise men), traveled around the Greek world teaching the wealthy young for substantial fees: subjects included mathematics, astronomy, history, religion, linguistics, and music, but the most successful courses covered rhetoric, politics, and morality, advertised with the prospect of subsequent fame and wealth. Men like Protagoras of Abdera, Hippias of Elis, Prodicos of Cos, or Gorgias of Leontini were serious thinkers and educators, but it is hard to free them completely from the critique found in the "Socratic" dialogues of Plato and elsewhere that the amorality of their ideas had a harmful impact on the young. Their teaching, delivered both by public lectures and seminars, encouraged the young to apply rational arguments and critical skepticism to the most important issues; but Thucydides' presentation of the brutal rhetoric and imperial policies of politicians suggests that many Greeks, as a result both of "sophistic" education and the pressures of the Peloponnesian War, adopted immoral attitudes; and it emerges from Aristophanes' *Clouds* that young Athenians reveled in the excitement of unconventional ideas which justified the selfish pursuit of pleasure and power. After Athens' defeat in the war, and the harsh rule of the oligarchic junta (the "Thirty Tyrants"), the restored democracy held their own citizen Socrates to be one of the Sophists who had morally corrupted politicians such as Critias, and he was condemned to death in 399 BCE (see Guthrie 1969).

During the next century the explosion of demand and the spread of new disciplines led to the creation of more permanent associations, which operated as institutions of "higher education." Athens remained the main center of intellectual development and attracted students from everywhere: Plato's Academy, and in the next generation Aristotle's Lyceum, were centers for research in sciences, mathematics, philosophy, and other subjects, while Isocrates' school focused on rhetoric, history, and politics. Those unable to afford their fees might have learned about politics and morality by listening to discussions in the *agora* and by attending the assembly and the law courts; the many citizens who chose to serve on boards, juries, and the council will have found this a way to acquire understanding of the institutions and ability to handle arguments from basic norms, as well as practice in the basic skills of literacy and numeracy (cf. Ober 2008).

The idea that citizens came to understand their city's values through practical experiences is given memorable expression in the funeral speech given to Pericles by Thucydides, where he urges the citizens to "gaze on the power of the city and become its *erastai*" (Thuc. 2.39). This metaphor derives its power from the idealized pederastic relationship between a lover and his boyfriend; here the good citizen observes and feels passion for his city's power and policies and the beauty of its monuments, as a lover does for the goodness and beauty of the noble youth. There is the further implication of an ideal reciprocity, that the city knows how to reward the citizens who fight for it with love and devotion by returning to them due honor in life and in death (cf. Aristoph. *Frogs* 1020–1022, below; and see Monoson 2000: 64–87; Wohl 2002: 30–72).

Education and socialization in Sparta

Classical Sparta had the most elaborate system of education of any Greek state. In its complete form (at the latest by the early fifth century) a complex progression took Spartan boys from c.7 to c.20, providing extensive training in physical and military skills, endurance, and song and dance, all aimed at the inculcation of political and social values designed to make them effective in war. This much is certain, but our knowledge of the details is problematic, because our limited evidence comes from non-Spartans writers, many of them antiquarians from the Hellenistic and Roman periods such as Plutarch. Fifth- and fourth-century authors say that Spartans had little use for writings, though in speech their famous "laconism" (Hdt. 3.46; also Thuc. 1.86; Plato *Prot.* 342b–c; Plut. *Lyc.* 19–20) enabled them to present their case with sharp wit and to deceive their enemies, especially through carefully phrased oaths (Thuc. 2.39–40; Isocrates *Panathenaikos* 209, 251; Cartledge 2001: 49–51; Bayliss 2009). Some functional literacy seems to have been expected of all Spartans (Plut. *Lyc.* 16), though it remained far more of an oral society than Athens or many other cities; the elite who held the major public offices no doubt had greater capacities (Cartledge 2001: 39–54). An important issue on which there is no direct evidence is whether teaching letters and music was delivered as part of the official system through the age-class sets, with teachers paid by the state, or through private teachers, as elsewhere in Greece. Since basic *mousike*, leading to an elaborate program of choral singing and dancing for both males and females, was a vital part of Spartan culture, one can argue that it, and with it some teaching of letters, was part of state provision (e.g. Cartledge 2001: 85–86; Hansen 2009: 477–478). On the other hand, the absence of any mention of state teaching of literacy, for example in Xenophon's *Constitution of the Spartans*, leads some to suggest that, under the general supervision of the *paidonomos* (cf. Xen. *Lac. Pol.* 2), this was provided privately by teachers paid by the fathers (e.g. Ducat, 2006a: 119–137, Hodkinson 2009: 446–447, 485–488).

The distinctive feature of the compulsory educational system was the prolonged physical training designed to produce uniformly tough soldiers, committed to defend the state's power and institutions (see Xen. *Lac. Pol.* 2). Boys up to c.12 were organized in small sets, supervised by older youths, in an unremitting life of competitions, fights, and beatings, kept shoeless, on short rations, and encouraged to steal. From c.12 until c.18 they were organized in annual age-classes with their own peculiar names; intensified training came to include public displays of endurance at festivals, for example being whipped at the rite of Artemis Orthia and dancing all day in the heat of midsummer at the Gymnopaedia.

Homosexual relationships between older and younger youths were an approved part of the boys' upbringing (see Xen. *Lac. Pol.* 2.12–13, claiming that if based on admiration for the boy's character it was "pure" and the "finest education," but if focused on the youth's beauty it was condemned). Though this was probably not a compulsory part of the age-classes system, a boy from c.12 was invited to form a lasting relationship with an older "lover" (*erastes*), who was to act as his role-model, develop his character, and encourage his adherence to the disciplined lifestyle. State approval is indicated by the rule that a lover might be fined by magistrates if his boyfriend showed insufficient endurance (Plut. *Lyc.* 18; see Cartledge 2001: 91–105; Ducat 2006a: 196–201; Davidson 2007: 315–343). Up until c.20, youths would eat their austere and limited food collectively, under supervision; but lovers might occasionally introduce their adolescent boyfriends into their adult common messes (*syssitia*), for them to get a taste of them as continuing "schools of self-discipline," to hear political discussions, and see entertainments appropriate for free men (Plut. *Lyc.* 12). The expectation was that in due course a boyfriend would be admitted to his lover's mess, when, at c.20, they would also be admitted into the army (possibly mess-members served in the same army units).

Membership of such messes, each apparently small in number, remained the basis of citizens' political and social life. As members were men of all ages, the atmosphere was supposedly set by the older and more experienced, restraining drunkenness or shameful behavior and encouraging discussions of great deeds for the state (Xen. *Lac. Pol.* 5.5). Friendships emerging from the pederastic relationships and continuing in the messes could often be of political importance. The centrality of courage and discipline as primary virtues (asserted at Hdt. 7.104) was reinforced by shaming procedures; a Spartan who showed cowardice in battle might be labeled a "trembler" (*tresas*) and subjected to a number of dishonoring sanctions, designed to make life not worth living. In practice this penalty seems have been applied rarely, and decreasingly from the later fifth century, when Spartan citizen manpower was in sharp decline (see Ducat 2006b).

At the end of the upbringing every year, three leading men of the 20–30 sets (*hippagretai*) selected 300 "knights" (*hippeis*)—though they were no longer cavalry—for specific military and political duties; and it may have been from these that members of the mysterious "Secret Service" (*krypteia*) were chosen for the specific policing functions, whereby, according to Plutarch (*Lyc.* 28), bands of young men armed with daggers would patrol the countryside, killing any helots out at night or thought to be dangerously brave. Unfortunately, the origins of this practice and the frequency of helot-killing are unclear and disputed. Many see it as an re-institutionalized adaptation, of the sixth or early fifth century, of old initiation practices (e.g. Cartledge 2001: 87–88, 98–102, 129–30; Ducat 2006a: 281–332); others see the helot-killing as a more recent response to Spartan crises, for example after the earthquake and helot revolt c.465 (Whitby 1994) or the defeat at Leuctra and the creation of the independent Messenia in 369 (Christien 2006: 175–177). Thucydides said (4.80), "most Spartan institutions have always been designed with a view to security against the Helots"; and most scholars agree that the need to control and derive agricultural surpluses from this large "serf-like" population, most of whom preserved (or acquired) a political identity as "Messenians" and harbored dreams of independence (finally to be achieved in 469), best explains many aspects of the Spartan political and social system, its uniform values, and the upbringing designed to instill them (e.g. de Ste. Croix 1972: 89–94; Cartledge 2001: 127–152).

Finally it should be emphasized that the description given here of Spartan educational and social institutions is based on the idealized and simplified picture given by non-Spartan sources such as Xenophon and Plutarch. Many sources, however, also agree that from the mid-fifth century Sparta went into a long-term crisis, as numbers in the citizen class of Spartiates began to decline, and under economic pressures the regulations imposing a uniform and austere lifestyle were increasingly ignored (see e.g. Xen. *Lac. Pol.* 14; Arist. *Pol.* 1269a29–71b19; see Hodkinson 2000).

While Spartan musical and poetic culture was full and varied, independent thought and free intellectual life were relatively undeveloped, in contrast to Athens and other cities. Spartan festivals demanded high levels of performance of choral singing and dancing, and there were famous Spartan poets in the archaic period whose works became models for citizens; Tyrtaeus' patriotic and exhortatory poems (c.600?) were apparently recited regularly after dinner on campaigns and probably also at *syssitia* at home (Philochorus *FGH* 328F216 = Athenaeus 640f., Lycurgus 1.107; Bowie 1990). But according to Plato (*Prot.* 342a–c; Hippias *Major* 283–287), Spartan education remained conservative, and the authorities discouraged new ideas from visiting "sophists"; Hippias, from nearby Elis, was permitted to give lectures there, but only on antiquarian history and the principles of education, not on science, mathematics, or rhetoric. Nor did Sparta develop or import any cultural forms comparable to the challenging drama fostered at and exported from Athens.

3 Festivals, Civic Norms, and Cohesion

Festivals in honor of their gods were central to the civic life of citizens in all Greek cities. They might occupy one day, or be spread over several days and contain diverse events: many smaller rites were managed by sub-groups such as demes or phratries, or private associations, but the most lavish were those organized by the *polis,* such as the Great Panathenaia at Athens or the Carneia at Sparta. The central ritual act was the sacrifice, the killing of domestic animals witnessed by all participants, and the offering, with prayers, of inedible parts to the deity while the humans shared the meat in a collective feast. Large festivals (*heortai*) also included processions, choral singing and dancing, athletic, song-dance or dramatic contests, and all-night singing and dancing (*pannychides*). Festivals were recognized as serving important religious purposes, designed to thank the gods, or to win or maintain their approval, by acts believed to give them honor and pleasure (see e.g. Lysias 30, 17–19); it was equally believed that festivals served a wide variety of political and social purposes, including the provision of recreation and respite from work, the cementing of the shared identity of the community, and the offering of artistic or athletic stimulation and entertainment (see e.g. Ps.-Xenophon *Ath. Pol.* 2.9, 3.1–2; Plato *Laws* 653d–e; Arist. *NE* 1160a18–30). Greeks often claimed that such contests were a major cause of political stability and social harmony. A striking expression of this comes in Polybius' account of how song-dance culture gave cohesion to all the Arcadian *poleis,* with the exception of Cinaitha (4.20–21). The connections may be formally recognized in public documents: at Eretria on Euboea, for example, in c.340 BCE, the restored democracy announced enhanced and more expensive competitions for their major festival for Artemis Amarysia, in the hope that "as many people as possible may share the sacrifices," "so that the sacrifice and the music for Artemis shall be performed in this way for all time, as long as the Eretrians are free, prosperous and autonomous" (RO 73.41–45). These connections between song-dance and cohesion are explored extensively by the philosophers, for example in Plato's *Laws*, Books 1–2, and Arist. *Pol.* Book 8.

As a central ideal of festivals was large-scale participation and inclusiveness, many cities spent very large amounts of public money on them. The Athenians developed an ingenious system (the *leiturgia*), whereby rich citizens were compelled or encouraged to contribute their own money and organize aspects of the festivals (e.g. by paying for and managing a chorus for a play or a dithyramb, the *choregia*), and they expected to win gratitude and honor from the community in return. There are suggestions that there were similar ways of involving rich men in the festivals in other cities, perhaps many of them fifth-century allies of Athens (see Wilson 2000: 279–302). All cities developed their festivals in their individual ways, featuring the gods and heroes and their mythical stories most relevant to them, and emphasizing their particular institutions and norms; we can, as always, understand this best in relation to Athens and Sparta. For festivals and choruses in less well-documented cities, see essays in Murray and Wilson 2003 and Wilson 2008 and also Kowalzig 2007, 2008; Fisher 2010.

Athenian festivals and civic ideals

Athenians believed, probably rightly, that their city stood out for the number and extravagance of its *polis* festivals (e.g. Lysias 30.13), nearly thirty spread throughout the year. A number of important issues are currently the subject of interesting debates, and will be briefly surveyed here: the levels of participation achieved in the festivals, both those performing in the contests and those attending; the levels of public and private finance involved, and the social and political consequences of the procedures adopted; the intellectual and emotional impact on audiences of the songs and plays; and the general appeal of the dramas and their spread across the wider Greek world

The two most important were the Greater Panathenaia and the City Dionysia. The Greater Panathenaia was celebrated every four years in midsummer, with several days of athletic and other contests, an all-night rite (*pannychis*), an ephebes' torch-race, and a large-scale procession culminating in the offering of a new embroidered robe for Athena and a huge oxen sacrifice and feast. The City Dionysia occurred every year in spring, with a procession bringing Dionysos back to his sanctuary on the south slopes of the Acropolis, followed by preliminary presentations for the contests, another procession with a feast, some opening patriotic ceremonies, receiving tribute from their allies, presenting the sons of the war-dead as they came of age, and honoring citizens who had done great service (on the importance of these, see Goldhill 1990), and then five days of contests of dithyrambs, tragedies, comedies, and satyr plays. Both offered participation, sustenance, and entertainment to most groups present in the city, defined by gender or civic status; this broad inclusiveness was offset by hierarchical divisions. The all-night rite permitted women and especially unmarried girls to dance and sing together (as did at least eleven other festivals), while men watched and all also consumed wine and food.

In the procession at the Panathenaia a representative selection of different groups gathered in the Ceramicus, and processed slowly through the Agora and up to the

Acropolis where the robe was presented: officials, infantry soldiers (hoplites) and cavalry, perhaps some ephebes, and a selection of other groups: handsome old citizens, well-born citizen girls as basket carriers (*kanephoroi*), metics carrying trays and metic girls holding parasols. Presumably the rest of the citizens followed along, in their deme-groups, and others could watch along the route. Of the contests, the torch race, a relay between teams from the ten "tribes," probably needed at least 100 young runners; other events limited to citizens were dithyrambic choruses, the warlike dances (*pyrrhikai*), teams of boys, beardless youths and men, perhaps involving c.100, and a boat race, a tribal contest between ten triremes each crewed by up to 200 of the poorer citizens. Most of the athletic contests were open events, attracting skilled competitors from across the Greek world.

The Greater Dionysia had two processions accompanied by much drinking and merriment, dressing up, and licensed abuse (Aeschin. *Against Timarchos* 1.43); again there were many official participants, including officials, girl basket-carriers, metic tray-carriers, and general throngs of citizens and foreigners running around. The dithyrambic and dramatic competitions demanded very large numbers of participants; 500 boys and 500 men for the dithyrambs, 120 chorus men for the comedies and forty-five for the tragedies (and there were in addition other choral contests at other state festivals and at the Dionysia held in winter in many of the rural demes). In total, there was an annual need for approximately 5,000 citizens of various ages to learn complex songs and perform them collectively as a chorus in the theater. The performances also needed smaller numbers of specialists—poets, composers, musicians, solo singers, and actors—who did not need to be, and increasingly were not, from Athens. These figures, rough and uncertain though they are, suggest that the athletic and musical/dramatic contests demanded the participation of very large numbers of boys, youths, and adults, considerably more than could be supplied by the families of the top 4–5 percent of rich men who were defined by their membership of the liturgical class; there were probably 50,000–60,000 adult citizens between the Persian and Peloponnesian wars, and, after the losses during the Peloponnesian War, closer to 30,000 through the fourth century (for these numbers, see Osborne 1993; Fisher 1998, 2011; Christesen 2012; but for more restricted participation see Pritchard 2003, 2004, 2013).

The dithyrambs and plays were performed to large audiences. Numbers in the theater of Dionysos in the fifth century and the first half of the fourth have been reduced by recent archaeological research; rather than the 15,000 previously thought, there were probably closer to 6,000–7,000 sitting on wooden bleachers in a rectilinear space, with perhaps some more sitting on the ground higher up (numbers were thus comparable to those able to attend the assembly on the Pnyx in the same period). After the rebuilding in the 340s and 330s BCE, capacity in the semi-circular stone auditorium visible today was increased to c.17,000 (cf. Csapo 2007: 87–115 with Goette 2007: 116–121; Csapo 2010: 83). Of these, the large majority were no doubt citizens. It is disputed whether citizen women could attend, but even if they could, as I think more likely, they were unlikely to have been numerous (see e.g. Goldhill 1994: 347–369, against, and Sourvinou-Inwood 2003: 177–184, for). There will also have been a fair number of foreigners, including official representatives of colonists and allies; during the fifth century allies presented their tribute (and a ceremonial phallos) as part of the opening ceremonies at the City Dionysia in March. The lesser dramatic festival, the Lenaia, held in midwinter, attracted few if any foreigners (see Aristoph. *Acharnians* 503–508). It is likely that a very large number of the spectators of the plays and dithyrambs had themselves been at some time members of a chorus or had family members who had been (see Revermann 2006).

Already in the fifth century the Athenians showed that they viewed choral and theatrical performances as serious entertainment as much as part of a religious festival: they took the radical decision to charge a daily fee for attendance (see Sidwell, Chapter 24). It seems that the state leased the right to erect the temporary wooden seating to private contractors, "*theatron*-buyers," who sold seats and kept the difference between their lease-payment and their takings (see Csapo 2007: 87–115). But the Athenians remained concerned that the audience should remain predominantly composed of citizens, and decided not to leave it entirely to the market, but to make cash payments to enable poorer citizens to buy tickets. Uncovering how this system operated through the fifth and fourth centuries from the small number of statements in late authors is very difficult. It seems likely that one-off distributions of surplus income occurred occasionally in the fifth century and continued rather more regularly in the fourth, down to about 350; at that point, as the plans for a new stone theater took shape, and the expense of providing wooden seating would be phased out, an annual system of payments to citizens was instituted, and a new fund created, significantly labeled the "theater fund" (*theōrikon*), which received any surplus revenue and either distributed it to citizens at festival times or spent it on other public works (Wilson 2008: 91–96). This signaled the symbolic importance of the plays to the democracy by connecting the *theōrikon* fund responsible for the main "handouts" for the poor, and with it the main financial committee responsible for the city's public works, so closely to the ideal of citizen attendance at the Dionysia and other festivals. The institution and its title testify to the cohesive power the festival was believed to possess.

Overall these festivals cost a great deal. At the City Dionysia, apart from the provision of the venue, the state paid for 1,000–1,200 oxen for the great feast; vessels, jewelry, and the phallos-pole and its wagon for the procession; and prizes for the victors and pay for the poets, actors, and musicians: a rough calculation suggests perhaps total state expenditure of c.13 talents. Similarly, the Panathenaia consumed perhaps about 10 talents. Comparable contributions came from private individuals, the liturgists and the overseers in charge of running the festivals. At the City Dionysia, twenty-eight rich *choregoi* each contributed something between 1,000 to 4,000 drachmai for the costumes and other expenses for a dithyrambic or dramatic chorus, and at the Panathenaia, forty or so liturgists spent something between 500 and 3,000 drachmai as sponsors of dithyrambic choruses, pyrrhic dancers, and teams for the manhood contests or the boat race (see Wilson 2008).

This form of super-tax imposed on the richest Athenians naturally caused some resentment (e.g. Xen. *Oec.* 2.4–8). In the fourth century it could be claimed in public speeches that festival liturgies were of less importance to the community than expenditure on trierarchies, *eisphorai*, and voluntary contributions to fortifications (e.g. Dem. 1.19, 4.4, 20.18–20; Aeschin. 3. 240; Lycurg. 1. 139–141); and some philosophers saw such expenditure on the less "useful" festival contests as unjustifiable extravagance (see Arist. *Pol.* 1309a17–20; Theophrastus *Characters* 26.6). But there was a strong alternative view. Co-operation to win the competitions often created strong bonds and community spirit between the rich liturgists and the more moderately-off performers. Xenophon recognized the high value of collective work between liturgists and their teams more often than he presents the grumbles of the rich (*Mem* 3.3.11–12, 3.4.4–5, 3.5.5–6, 18–19;

Oeconomicus 8.3–15). Liturgists could then claim the "symbolic capital" of social and political gratitude and enhanced prestige from their fellow-tribesmen or the people as a whole, which could take practical forms such as electoral support for their political careers and favorable consideration when they appeared in the law courts. In fact many of the elite voluntarily performed many more liturgies than were required by the law (e.g. Lysias 21.1–21). This reciprocal relationship between the elite and the people may be seen as a rational choice designed to increase social harmony by involving the rich in these activities which increased the quality of life for all (see slightly divergent views in Wilson 2000 and Fisher 2003, 2010).

Athenian drama: purposes and diffusion

Vigorous debates are currently raging on the target audiences of these dramas, and on the nature of their political impact (see also Sidwell, Chapter 24). Many scholars in the 1980s and 1990s, viewing the festival procedures as essentially democratic and aimed at citizens, debated whether the plays—painful tragedies or hard-hitting topical comedies—might have been received more as patriotic representations of the city's greatness or as critical questioning of Athenian practices (see e.g. Winkler and Zeitlin 1990; Cartledge 1997). More recent research, however, has brought out that many of the elements of these Dionysos festivals should be seen as typical of the Greek *polis* in general (e.g. Rhodes 2003), and that the plays appealed to many who were not Athenians. There were many foreigners present at the City Dionysia; many plays received subsequent productions both in the smaller deme theaters across Attica and also in Macedonia, Thessaly, south Italy, and Sicily (cf. Plato *Rep.* 475d, on theater-lovers attending Dionysia "missing out none of those in the cities or the country villages," with Whitehead 1986: 212–222; Taplin 1999: 38–39). There were also home-grown dramatic traditions elsewhere, again especially in Sicily and south Italy. We know much less about the conditions of performance and the roles of *choregoi* outside Athens, but the spread of dramatic productions, with its increasing professionalism and international fame of the poets, actors, and musicians, was a major cultural phenomenon of classical Greece, and the dominance of Athenian drama put it at the center of this international art form (see Easterling 1999; Wilson 2000, 2007; Kowalzig 2007, 2008; Taplin 1999, 2007; Csapo 2010).

Athenians believed that the plays performed valuable social functions for their community in representing, or challenging, their values, as well as contributing to the city's international reputation. Surviving statements of these purposes are interesting, though they do not cover the full range of possibilities. In the contest in Aristophanes' *Frogs* (405 BCE) to determine which of the two great dead poets, Aeschylus or Euripides, was the cleverest poet who would be the most useful for Athens if brought back at a crucial final stage of the Peloponnesian War, "Aeschylus" states (and "Euripides" agrees) that poets should make people better: "boys have teachers to tell them things, but adults have poets" (1054–1055), and he argues that his plays such as the *Seven against Thebes* or *The Persians*, like Homer's poems, taught men to love war and be brave (1020–1036); at the end it is he who is picked, as he gives the best political advice. The play suggests, however, that pleasure at the poet's cleverness and skillful use of language, music, and ideas, are as highly valued by audiences as is giving "good advice"; it also suggests (largely through the humorous comments of "Dionysos") that the impact of plays is unpredictable, and that Athenians could argue, as does "Euripides" (971–979), that poets who (like the Sophists) challenge existing ideas and provoke critical thought might be more useful than those whose plays are held to reinforce conventional morality. It would be unsafe to conclude from the decision to restore Aeschylus that Aristophanes wished the audience to conclude that he was the better and more valuable poet (see Dover 1993: 10–37); and while "Aeschylus" argues that Euripides' plain style encouraged the audience to identify with immoral characters and their arguments, the chorus presents the audience as sophisticated enough not to be so easily influenced (1109–1118; see Rosen 2008).

Aristophanes also asserts that comedies can be useful as well as funny, and like tragedy "it knows what is just" (e.g. *Acharnians* 496–501; *Frogs* 686–688; *Ecclesiazusai* 1154–1162). Old Comedy presented a confusing amalgam of fantastical plots, caricatured characters, and all types of jokes. Comic writers enjoyed much freedom to abuse prominent individuals and to satirize state policies (e.g. the Peloponnesian War in *Acharnians* and *Lysistrata*), new-style politicians (e.g. Cleon in *Knights*), the operations of political institutions (e.g. the law courts in *Wasps*), or new moral or educational ideas (e.g. philosophers and poets in *Clouds* and *Frogs*); but they stopped short of challenging the basic principles of democratic government. There was not an absolute law guaranteeing this freedom, but legal challenges were very rare. The case successfully brought against the early tragedy by Phrynichos on *The Capture of Miletos* (c.490), because the play had reduced the audience to tears by "reminding them of their sorrows close to home" (Hdt. 6.21), had the effect of ruling out tragedies based on Greek disasters from recent history. But when Cleon brought Aristophanes before the Council of 500 for defaming the city in his second play, *The Babylonians*, of 426 BCE, while there may have been an out-of-court settlement (*Acharnians* 370–382, 496–519, 628–632; *Wasps* 1284–1291), Aristophanes' criticisms of Cleon's malign influence on Athenian politics were intensified, above all in his *Knights*. Other suggestions in the ancient commentators on Aristophanes of legal bans on personal abuse are probably inventions (sources in Csapo and Slater 1995: 165–185; see Halliwell 1991, but also Sidwell, Chapter 24). Down to the early fourth century, the Athenians valued this form of comedy, and, as we now know, it was also successfully exported to south Italy (see Taplin 2007). Most Athenians must have believed its license to arouse legitimate indignation at powerful individuals and state policies in front of a large citizen audience was a beneficial safety-valve which should in principle be protected (see Carey 1994; Rosenbloom 2012; Konstan 2013). On one occasion, ancient commentators report that the Athenians passed a decree praising a comic poet for his excellent political advice, and the play was restaged within a few years at the theater of Dionysos: this was Aristophanes' *Frogs* (spring 405 BCE), which contains what is by far the most serious and "straight" passage of political advice (lines 674–737), delivered by the chorus in support of reconciliation and civic harmony at a time of great danger.

Gradually, however, comedy changed; topical issues and specifically Athenian political comments decreased, whereas mythological comedies remained popular, and moralizing family-based comedies (such as those of Menander) won out; these featured complex plots and usually a happy ending in a marriage for a young couple. The reasons for these changes are far from clear, but probably included the awareness that the wider public across the Greek world would prefer less Atheno-centric themes, a lessening in confidence in the democracy (and after 322 serious threats to democracy itself), and a greater pleasure taken in romantic comedy.

A relatively simple view of the moral purposes of tragedy can be found in law court speeches. Especially in the period c.346–330, when the three fifth-century tragedians had gained the status of classics, some competing politicians argued that tragedies (like Homer) provided useful moral lessons for young citizens about leadership, courage, sacrifice for the city, or noble love, and quoted extracts from tragic speeches (and Homer) out of context to suit their rhetorical needs (e.g. Aeschin. 1.141–153; Dem. 21.149–150, 19.246–267; Lycurg. 1.98–104: see Wilson 1996). Philosophers debated more intelligently the educational and social value of such performances of imaginative fictions. Plato questioned the truth and usefulness of the poets' presentations of human experience, arguing (*Rep.* Books 3 and 10) that artistic representations were two stages removed from the realities discoverable by philosophy, that tragedy's presentations of divine injustice or indifference were untrue and dangerous, and that portrayals of human suffering (or, in comedy, of absurdity), as well as the looser and more emotional styles of music popular in tragedy and dithyramb from the 420s on (Csapo 2004, 2011), aroused extreme emotions among the popular audiences which were better controlled. An underlying source of his rejection of tragedy (emotionally difficult for him, given his evident appreciation of its power, see *Rep.* 607b–8a), was that the open-ended uncertainties of the tragic world's concentration on human suffering and death were incompatible with the positive answers to the questions of reality and morality provided by his theory of Forms (cf. also *Laws* 816–817, and Gould 2001: 304–318; Halliwell 1996; Taplin 1999). Aristotle defended the poets, suggesting that their fictions could offer a more generalized and truthful picture of life than the particularities of history, and their arousal of emotions such as pity and fear "purified" emotions (*katharsis*) and harmonized them with their perceptions of the world (*Poetics* chs. 6–9 with Halliwell 1998). Neither engaged explicitly with the issues of how the plays may have encouraged approval or criticism of Athenian political institutions, practices, or policies; one reason was probably that, as we saw above, they were more concerned with the lasting appeal across the wider Greek world of the now classic plays than with their impact in Athens (see Hall 1996).

Modern interpretations of the effects which surviving tragedies may have had on the first audiences vary greatly (see Sidwell, Chapter 24). Explicit criticism of Athens as a *polis* or a democracy is avoided, and Athens often appears, under King Theseus, the supposed founder of democracy, as a just community, in contrast to cities such as Thebes or Argos, where conflicts among ruling families engendered chains of horrific crimes and wars. Examples include Aeschylus' *Oresteia*, when the new institution of the Areopagus as a homicide court resolves the problem of revenge killings at Argos; Euripides' *Suppliants*, where the "democrat" Theseus intervenes to prevent the Thebans' denial of burial for the dead of the Seven, or Sophocles' *Oedipus at Colonus*, where Theseus again protects the exiled Oedipus and Antigone against Creon's attempt to reclaim them for Thebes.

But many plays probably raised doubts among the audience about ideologies, policies, and practices found in contemporary Athens. The issue of denial of burial to enemies or traitors is central to Sophocles' *Ajax* and *Antigone* and to Euripides' *Suppliants*, which was produced c.424–423 BCE at a time when Athenians and Thebans were locked in mutual recriminations over a refusal to return bodies for burial after the battle of Delion (Thuc. 4.97–101; cf. Bowie 1997). All these plays suggest that complete denial of burial contradicts a "Panhellenic law" respecting human dignity and is an offense to the gods; this is aligned with the praise in the official rhetoric in Athenian funeral speeches for cases when Athens went to war to insist on burial in other states. But this might be held to conflict with the Athenian official policy to deny burial within the state's frontiers to traitors and to cast their bodies out, as was carried out on condemned oligarchs in 410 (Lycurg. *Leoc.* 1.112–115). Gender tensions are also very prominent. In *Frogs* Euripides is represented as relentlessly portraying evil and sex-mad women, while Aeschylus avoided presenting women in love; in fact both playwrights offer complex pictures of powerful women (such as Clytemnestra and Medea) who challenge the male rhetoric of power and dominance before themselves responding to their husbands' betrayals and contempt by committing revenge murders.

The sophistic and hypocritical rhetoric found in many tragedies will have reminded Athenian citizens of their own politicians' speeches in the assembly or the law courts. The patriotic principles of rule are set out in Creon's opening speech as king in Sophocles' *Antigone* (lines 162–192) (cited approvingly by Dem. 19. 246–249); but in the play Creon uses these arguments speciously to justify his misguided law banning the burial of the traitor Polyneices. Some of the most damning representations of deceitful rhetoric come in Euripides' plays put on during the Peloponnesian War, especially in the debate between Eteocles and Polyneices in Euripides' *Phoenician Women* and in the trial of Orestes before a popular jury at Argos in his *Orestes* (Hall 1993). Most disturbing of all, perhaps, was the presentation in Euripides' *Hecuba* (late 420s BCE) and *Trojan Women* (415 BCE) of the atrocities committed by the Greeks at the end of the Trojan War, the killing of the adult males and selected royal children (Astyanax and Polyxena), and rape and enslavement of the women. Both plays radically challenge standard Greek beliefs in their moral superiority over "barbarians" such as the Trojans (Hall 1989). While the *Trojan Women* was being composed, the Athenians besieged the small Aegean island of Melos, and, on its surrender, killed the adult males and enslaved the women and children, and then planned the disastrous expedition to Sicily (cf. Thuc. 5.5.82–6.31). It is difficult not to believe that this play would be seen as challenging current Athenian policies and beliefs about their conduct of the war and their treatment of their subject allies (see Vickers 1973; Goldhill 1986; Croally 1994; Mills 2010 has doubts).

Festivals, choruses and civic ideals at Sparta

Religion was heavily "embedded" at Sparta, perhaps even more so than elsewhere, and official religious events and activities largely encouraged conformity to the state's values, and did not support opportunities for intellectual challenges and reflection. One indication of the connection between Sparta's emphasis on military prowess and its religion may be that most statues of gods in Spartan territory were displayed with armor and weapons, including normally "softer" deities like Dionysos and Aphrodite (see Flower 2009: 202–205; but also Hodkinson 2006: 141–142); another is the frequency with which Spartans used the religious scruple of a current festival to refuse to send military assistance (e.g. Hdt. 6.106, 7.206, 9.7; Xen. *Hell.* 4.5.11), or made the most of a religious offense to take action (e.g. Hdt. 75.63; see Flower 2009: 196–201).

As indicated above, major festivals at Sparta, with their contests displaying the results of boys' training, were essential proving points in the upbringing of future citizens; they remained equally important for Spartiates throughout their adult lives, encouraged to test their athleticism and endurance and participate in the assertion of Spartan values. Four festivals stand out. At the sanctuary of Artemis Orthia, outside the city by the marshy Eurotas, older boys (*paidiskoi*) attempted to steal cheeses from the altar while avoiding the assaults of young adults with whips (Xen. *Lac. Pol.* 2.8–9; cf. Plato *Laws* 633b; Ducat 2006a: 253–256). The other important festivals were all associated with Apollo. The *Gymnopaidiai* ("naked dancings"), held in the *agora* in the midsummer heat, featured singing and dancing competitions of three teams of choruses, boys, active adults, and old men, each claiming to be valiant (Hdt. 6.67; Xen. *Hell.* 6.4.16; Plato *Laws* 633; Plut. *Ages.* 29.3; Plut. *Lyc.* 21; Athenaeus 630d–631b). The report that early archaic poets like Thaletas and Alcman composed songs for the festival suggests it began no later than c.600 BCE (Sosibius *FGH* 595F5 = Athenaeus 678b–c; see Parker 1989: 150; Ducat 2006a: 265–274; Flower 2009: 207–211).

The second Apollo festival, the Carneia, which lasted nine days, featured young men's races held along the running track (*dromos*) in the city (Pausanias 3.14.6–7), and a scape-goat ritual, and feasting under tents (Demetrios of Scepsis, Athenaeus 141f). The last Apollo festival, the Hyacinthia, based at the sanctuary at Amyclai, lasted at least three days, and involved the whole community, male and female. The dead hero Hyacinthos, Apollo's beloved whom he killed accidentally, was mourned, and then Apollo was celebrated with processions, sacrifices, and feasts, and many contests: for boys (*paides*) in lyre-playing, singing, and horseback parades; for the older youths (*paidiskoi*) in choral singing and dancing; for girls *parthenoi*) parading on wagons and chariots (Hdt. 9.7–14; Polycrates *FGH* 588F1 in Athenaeus 139c–f: see Richer 2004: 80–81; Ducat 2006a: 262–264).

Thus the essential elements in the upbringing of Spartans and through the rest of their lives, athletic training and choral dancing and singing, were celebrated in regular contests at the festivals; a Spartan was defined by a fifth-century poet as "a cicada ready for a chorus" (Pratinas, quoted by Athenaeus 633a). As far as our late and brief sources allow us to see, their festivals were developed in distinctive ways designed to maintain the ideological principle that the citizens, who were all "similars" (*homoioi*), were united in their devotion to constant competitions that preserved a high level of physical fitness and discipline.

4 Conclusion

As with the Roman Republic and its set of key values connected under the label of the *mos maiorum* (see Arena, Chapter 13), Greek political communities conceived their systems as functioning because of the acceptance by most citizens of certain guiding values: these included courage, freedom, piety, self-control, honor, and reciprocity. Roman *mos maiorum* suggested a deep conservatism and respect for tradition, which, as Arena shows, in fact masked a readiness to negotiate change; the Spartans' constant concern to protect their economic and political system dependent on the domination of their helots similarly encouraged images of unchanging tradition and rigidity which were in some respects invented or exaggerated. At Athens, and probably at most other Greek *poleis*, innovation and challenges to existing practices were far more ideologically acceptable. In all these communities, these core values should not be seen as exclusively or predominantly the property of the nobility or the elite.

At Sparta, core skills and awareness of traditions were instilled in young citizens by a compulsory and tightly regimented educational program, which centered on military, athletic, and choral training and may not have included much if any schooling in literacy. This training was reinforced throughout their lives by performance in warfare, at the *syssitia* and at the many festivals. Criticism of tradition and open debate were discouraged. Athens, on the other hand, led the way for other Greek states in the encouragement of private education and relative openness to the new ideas of scientists and philosophers (both outsiders and home-grown). Formal instruction in political values and traditions might be part of the youths' inductions into their phratries and demes, and enhanced by attendance at festivals, assemblies, and patriotic occasions such as the annual state funeral, though the systematic two-year program of the *ephebeia* was only introduced in the mid-330s BCE.

Festivals were absolutely central to community life, and were democratically managed; their many contests demanded widespread citizen participation and encouraged the rich elite to contribute money and leadership to these community events in exchange for greater honors and prestige. The contests in tragedy, comedy, and dithyramb at the dramatic festivals produced forms of highbrow entertainment popular with mass audiences; they offered gifted poets the opportunity not only to reinforce the city's ideals of freedom and democracy, but also to criticize leading individuals, policies and practices, and to pose fundamental, unsettling, and unanswerable questions about political conflict, human suffering, and the justice of the gods (see O'Bryhim, Chapter 25, for the Roman contrast). These innovative forms had remarkably wide appeal and spread throughout the Greek world, both in places where forms of drama already existed and far beyond. Their impact is still powerfully felt today.

REFERENCES

Austin, M. 1981. *The Hellenistic World from Alexander to the Roman Conquest: A Selection of Ancient Sources in Translation*. Cambridge.

Bayliss, A. 2009. "Using Few Words Wisely? Laconic Swearing and Spartan Duplicity." In S. Hodkinson, ed., *Sparta: Comparative Approaches*. Swansea, 231–260.

Bowie, A. 1997. "Tragic Filters for History." In C. Pelling, ed., *Greek Tragedy and the Historian*. Oxford, 39–62.

Bowie, E. 1990. "Miles Ludens? The Problem of Martial Exhortation in Early Greek Poetry." In O. Murray, ed., *Sympotica: A Symposium on the* Symposion. Oxford, 221–229.

Carey, C. 1994. "Comic Ridicule and Democracy." In S. Hornblower and R. Osborne, eds., *Ritual, Finance, Politics: Athenian Democratic Accounts Presented to David Lewis*. Oxford, 69–83.

Cartledge, P. 1997. "'Deep Plays': Theatre as Process in Greek Civic Life." In P. Easterling, ed., *The Cambridge Companion to Greek Tragedy*. Cambridge, 3–35.

Cartledge, P. 2001. *Spartan Reflections*. London and Berkeley.

Christesen P. 2012. *Sport and Democracy in the Ancient and Modern Worlds*. Cambridge.

Christien, J. 2006. "The Lacedaemonian State: Fortifications, Frontiers and Historical Problems." In S. Hodkinson and A. Powell, eds., *Sparta and War*. Swansea, 163–183.

Croally, N. 1994. *Euripidean Polemic: The Trojan Women and the Function of Tragedy*. Cambridge.

Csapo, E. 2004 "The Politics of the New Music." In P. Murray and P. Wilson, eds., *Music and the Muses*. Oxford, 207–248.

Csapo, E. 2007 "The Men who Built the Theatres: *Theatropolai*, *Theatronai* and *Architecktones*." In P. Wilson, ed., *Greek Theatre and Festivals: Documentary Studies*. Oxford, 87–115.

Csapo, E. 2010. *Actors and Icons of the Ancient Theatre*. Chichester.

Csapo, E. 2011. "The Economics, Poetics, Politics, Metaphysics and Ethics of the 'New Music.'" In D. Yatromanolakis, ed., *Music and Cultural Politics in Greek and Chinese Societies*, vol. 1. Cambridge, MA, 65–132.

Csapo, E. and W. Slater, eds., 1995. *The Context of Ancient Drama*. Ann Arbor.

Davidson, J. 2006. "Revolutions in Human Time." In S. Goldhill and R. Osborne, eds., *Rethinking Revolutions through Ancient Greece*. Cambridge, 29–67.

Davidson, J. 2007. *The Greeks and Greek Love: A Radical Reappraisal of Homosexuality in Ancient Greece*. London.

De Ste. Croix, G.E.M. 1972. *The Origins of the Peloponnesian War*. London.

Dover, K. 1988. *The Greeks and their Legacy*. Oxford.

Dover, K. 1989. *Greek Homosexuality*. 2nd. edn. London.

Dover, K. 1993. *Aristophanes Frogs*. Oxford.

Ducat, Jean. 2006a. *Spartan Education*. Swansea.

Ducat, Jean. 2006b. "The Spartan 'Tremblers.'" In S. Hodkinson and A. Powell, eds., *Sparta and War*. Swansea, 1–56.

Easterling, P. 1997. "From Repertoire to Canon." In P. Easterling, ed., *The Cambridge Companion to Greek Tragedy*. Cambridge, 211–227.

Fisher, N. 1998. "Gymnasia and the Democratic Values of Leisure." In P. Cartledge, P. Millett, and S. von Reden, eds., *Kosmos: Essays in Order, Conflict and Community in Classical Athens*. Cambridge, 84–104.

Fisher, N. 2001. *Aeschines, Against Timarchos*. Oxford.

Fisher, N. 2003. "'Let envy be absent': Envy, Liturgies and Reciprocity in Athens." In D. Konstan and K. Rutter, eds., *Envy in the Ancient World*. Edinburgh, 181–215.

Fisher, N. 2008. "The Bad Boyfriend, The Flatterer and the Sykophant: Related Forms of the '*Kakos*' in Democratic Athens." In I. Sluiter and R. Rosen, eds., *KAKOS, Badness and Anti-Value in Classical Antiquity*. Leiden, 185–231.

Fisher, N. 2010. "*Charis, Charites*, Festivals, and Social Peace in the Classical Greek City." In I. Sluiter and R. Rosen, eds., *Valuing Others in Classical Antiquity*. Leiden, 71–112.

Fisher, N. 2011. "Competitive Delights: The Social Effects of the Expanded Programme of Contests in Post-Kleisthenic Athens." In N. Fisher and H. van Wees, eds., *Competition in the Ancient World*. Swansea, 175–219.

Flower, M. 2009. "Spartan 'Religion' and Greek "Religion."" In S. Hodkinson, ed., *Sparta: Comparative Approaches*. Swansea, 193–230.

Ford, A. 1999. "Reading Homer from the Rostrum: Poems and Laws in Aeschines' *Timarchus*." In S. Goldhill and R. Osborne, eds., *Performance Culture and Athenian Democracy*. Cambridge, 231–256.

Ford, A. 2003. "Catharsis: The Power of Music in Aristotle's Politics." In P. Murray and P. Wilson, eds., *Music and the Muses*. Oxford, 309–362.

Goette, H.-R. 2007. "An Archaeological Appendix (to Csapo 2007)." In P. Wilson, ed., *Greek Theatre and Festivals: Documentary Studies*. Oxford, 116–121.

Goldhill, S. 1986. *Reading Greek Tragedy*. Cambridge.

Goldhill, S. 1990. "The Great Dionysia and Civic Ideology." Revised in J.J. Winkler and F.I. Zeitlin, eds., *Nothing to Do with Dionysos?* Princeton, 97–129.

Goldhill, S. 1994. "Representing Democracy: Women at the Great Dionysia." In S. Hornblower and R. Osborne, eds., *Ritual, Finance, Politics: Athenian Democratic Accounts presented to David Lewis*. Oxford, 347–370.

Gould, J. 2001. *Myth, Ritual, Memory and Exchange: Essays in Greek Literature and Culture*, Oxford.

Guthrie, W. 1969. *A History of Greek Philosophy*, vol. 3: *The Fifth-Century Enlightenment*. Cambridge.

Hall, E. 1989. *Inventing the Barbarian: Greek Self-Definition through Tragedy*. Oxford.

Hall, E. 1993. "Political and Comic Turbulence in Euripides' *Orestes*." In A. Sommerstein et al., eds., *Tragedy, Comedy and the Polis*. Bari, 263–286.
Hall, E. 1996. "Is There a *Polis* in Aristotle's *Poetics*?" In Michael Silk, ed., *Tragedy and the Tragic*. Oxford, 295–309.
Halliwell, F.S. 1991. "Comic Satire and Freedom of Speech in Classical Athens." *JHS* 111: 48–70.
Halliwell, F.S. 1996. "Plato's Repudiation of the Tragic." In Michael Silk, ed., *Tragedy and the Tragic*. Oxford, 332–350.
Halliwell, F.S. 1998. *Aristotle's Poetics*. London.
Hansen, M.H. 1991. *The Athenian Democracy in the Time of Demosthenes*. Oxford.
Hansen, M.H. 2009. "Was Sparta a Normal or an Exceptional Polis?" In S. Hodkinson, ed., *Sparta: Comparative Approaches*. Swansea, 385–416.
Hansen, M.H. and S. Hodkinson. 2009. "Spartan Exceptionalism: Continuing the Debate." In S. Hodkinson, ed., *Sparta: Comparative Approaches*. Swansea, 473–498.
Harris, W.V. 1989. *Ancient Literacy*. Cambridge.
Hodkinson, S. 2000. *Property and Wealth in Classical Sparta*. London.
Hodkinson, S. 2006. "Was Classical Sparta a Military Society?" In S. Hodkinson and A. Powell, eds., *Sparta and War*. Swansea, 111–162.
Hodkinson, S. 2009. "Was Sparta an Exceptional Polis?" In S. Hodkinson, ed., *Sparta: Comparative Approaches*. Swansea, 417–498.
Hubbard, T.K. 1998. "Popular Perceptions of Elite Homosexuality in Classical Athens." *Arion* 6, 48–78.
Konstan, D. 2013. "Old Comedy and Militarism in Classical Athens." In D.M. Pritchard, ed., *War, Democracy and Culture in Classical Athens*. Cambridge, 184–199.
Kowalzig, B. 2004. "Changing Choral Worlds: Song-Dance and Society in Athens and Beyond." In P. Murray and P. Wilson, eds., *Music and the Muses*. Oxford, 39–66.
Kowalzig, B. 2007. *Singing for the Gods*. Oxford.
Kowalzig, B. 2008. "Nothing To Do with Demeter? Something To Do with Sicily! Theatre and Society in the Early Fifth-Century West." In M. Revermann and P. Wilson, eds., *Performance, Iconography, Reception: Studies in Honour of Oliver Taplin*. Oxford, 128–160.
Lambert, S.D. 1993. *The Phratries of Attica*. Ann Arbor.
Liddel, P. 2007. *Civic Obligation and Individual Liberty in Ancient Athens*. Oxford.
Loraux, N. 1986. *The Invention of Athens The Funeral Oration in the Classical City*. Trans. A. Sheridan. Cambridge.
Mills, S. 2010. "Affirming Athenian Action: Euripides' Portrayal of Military Action and the Limits of Tragic Instruction." In D.M. Pritchard, ed., *War, Democracy and Culture in Classical Athens*. Cambridge, 163–183.
Missiou, A. 2011. *Literacy and Democracy in Fifth-Century Athens*. Cambridge.
Monoson, S. 2000. *Plato's Democratic Entanglements*. Princeton.
Morgan, T. 1998. *Literate Education in the Hellenistic and Roman Worlds*. Cambridge.
Morgan, T. 1999. "Literate Education in Classical Athens." *CQ* 49: 46–61.
Murray, O. 1997. "Rationality and the Greek City: The Evidence from Kamarina." In M.H. Hansen, ed., *The Polis as an Urban Centre and as a Political Community*: *Acts of the Copenhagen Polis Centre 4*. Copenhagen, 493–504.
Murray, P. and P. Wilson, eds. 2003. *Music and the Muses*. Oxford.
Ober, J. 2008. *Democracy and Knowledge: Innovation and Learning in Classical Athens*. Princeton.
Osborne, R. 1993. "Competitive Festivals and the Polis: A Context for Dramatic Festivals at Athens." In A. Sommerstein et al., eds., *Tragedy, Comedy and the Polis*. Bari, 21–37.
Parker, R. 1989. "Spartan Religion." In A. Powell, ed., *Classical Sparta: Techniques Behind Her Success*. London, 142–172.
Phillips, D. and D. Pritchard, eds. 2003. *Sport and Festival in the Ancient Greek World*. Swansea.

Pritchard, D. 2003. "Athletics, Education and Participation in Classical Athens." In Phillips and Pritchard 2003: 293–350.

Pritchard, D. 2004. "Kleisthenes, Participation and the Dithyrambic Contests of Late Archaic and Classical Athens." *Phoenix* 58: 208–228.

Pritchard, D. 2013. *Sport, Democracy and War in Classical Athens.* Cambridge.

Revermann, M. 2006. "The Competence of Theatre Audiences in Fifth- and Fourth-Century Athens." *JHS* 126: 99–124.

Rhodes, P.J. 2003. "Nothing To Do with Democracy: Athenian Drama and the *Polis.*" *JHS* 123: 104–19.

Rhodes, P.J. and R. Osborne. 2003. *Greek Historical Inscriptions 404–323 BC*. Oxford.

Richer, N. 2004. "The Hyakinthia at Sparta." In T. Figueira, ed., *Spartan Society*. Swansea, 77–102.

Rosen, R. 2008. "Badness and Intentionality in Aristophanes' *Frogs.*" In I. Sluiter and R. Rosen, eds., *KAKOS, Badness and Anti-Value in Classical Antiquity*. Leiden, 143–168.

Rosenbloom, D. 2012. "Athenian Drama and Democratic Political Culture." In D. Rosenbloom and J. Davidson, eds., *Greek Drama IV, Texts, Contexts, Performance*. Oxford, 270–299.

Sourvinou-Inwood, C. 2003. *Greek Tragedy and Religion*. Lanham, MD.

Steinbock, B. 2011. "A Lesson in Patriotism: Lycurgus' *Against Leocrates*, the Ideology of the *Ephebeia*, and Athenian Social Memory." *ClAnt* 30: 279–317.

Swift, L. A. 2010. *The Hidden Chorus: Echoes of Genre in Tragic Lyric*. Oxford.

Taplin, O. 1999. "Spreading the Word through Performance." In S. Goldhill and R. Osborne, eds., *Performance Culture and Athenian Democracy*. Cambridge, 33–57.

Taplin, O. 2007. *Pots and Plays: Interactions between Tragedy and Greek Vase-Paintings of the Fourth Century*. Los Angeles.

Travlos, J. 1971. *Pictorial Dictionary of Ancient Athens*. London.

Vanderpool, E. 1959. "News from Greece." *AJA* 63: 279–280.

Vickers, B. 1973. *Towards Greek Tragedy: Drama, Myth, Society*. London.

Wallace, R.W. 1997 "Poet, Public and Theatrocracy: Audience Performance in Classical Athens." In L. Edmonds and R.W. Wallace, eds., *Poet, Public and Performance in Ancient Greece*. Baltimore, 97–111.

Whitby, M. 1994. "Two Shadows: Images of Spartans and Helots." In A. Powell and S. Hodkinson, eds., *The Shadow of Sparta*. London and New York, 87–126.

Whitehead, D. 1986. *The Demes of Attica*, Princeton.

Wilson, P. 1996. "Tragic Rhetoric: The Use of Tragedy and the Tragic in the Fourth Century." In M. Silk, ed., *Tragedy and the Tragic*. Oxford, 310–331.

Wilson, P. 2000. *The Athenian Institution of the* Khoregia: *The Chorus, the City and the Stage*. Cambridge.

Wilson, P. 2003. "The Politics of Dance: Dithyrambic Contest and Social Order in Ancient Greece." In Phillips and Pritchard 2003: 163–196.

Wilson, P., ed. 2007. *Greek Theatre and Festivals: Documentary Studies*. Oxford.

Wilson, P. 2008. "Costing the Dionysia." In M. Revermann and P. Wilson, eds., *Performance, Iconography, Reception: Studies in Honour of Oliver Taplin*. Oxford, 88–127.

Winkler, J. and F. Zeitlin, eds., 1990. *Nothing To Do with Dionysos?: Athenian Drama in its Social Context*. Princeton.

Wohl, V. 2002. *Love among the Ruins: The Erotics of Democracy in Classical Athens*. Princeton.

FURTHER READING

On the details of participatory systems in Athens, see Hansen 1991, and for democratic ideals and the acceptance of reciprocal obligations see Liddel 2007; for the Spartan systems, see

Cartledge 2001, Hodkinson 2000. On education and literacy in Athens and elsewhere, Morgan 1998, Missiou 2011; on phratries, demes, and ephebes, Lambert 1993, Liddel 2007, 290–293. For debates over socialization and homoerotic relationships, see Dover 1988, Fisher 2001, 25–67, Davidson 2007; on sophists, Guthrie 1969. On education in Sparta, Ducat 2006a, Cartledge 2001, Hansen 2009, Hodkinson 2009. On the importance of festivals and song-dance and athletic contests throughout Greece, essays in Murray and Wilson 2003 and Phillips and Pritchard 2003, and Kowalzig 2007. For debates on levels of participation in Athenian contests, see Pritchard 2003, 2004, 2013, Fisher 2011, Christesen 2012; on Athenian dramatic festivals, Wilson 2000, Csapo 2010, and essays in Wilson 2007; and on the export of Athenian drama to the wider Greek world, Taplin 1999, 2007, and other essays in Wilson 2007. For the political and moral purposes and effects of Athenian tragedy, see for example the varied debates in Goldhill 1986, essays in Winkler and Zeitlin 1990, and in Easterling 1997, Pritchard 2013, and Rhodes 2003; and for those of comedy, Carey 1994, Rosenbloom 2012, Konstan 2013. On Spartan festivals and contests, see Parker 1989, Ducat 2006b, Flower 2009.

CHAPTER 13

Informal Norms, Values, and Social Control in the Roman Participatory Context

Valentina Arena

1 Introduction

For a long time, in the tradition of Theodor Mommsen's *Staatsrecht* (1887), most scholars of Roman political structures identified the history of republican institutions and their procedures formalized through statutory law and/or legally binding conventions, as the object of their study (Nippel 2005). Reacting against this form of constitutional history, subsequent studies have focused not only on the cultural and social contexts in which republican institutions were embedded, but also on the flexibility and adaptability of the Roman "organic constitution" (Meier 1980; Mommsen's view was strongly criticized in Magdelain 1968: 5–6). Conceiving this as a cluster of formalized rules and institutions resulting from a continual political process (Lintott 1999; North 2006), recent studies of Roman political culture addressed the factors that allowed such a process to occur and continually evolve. One such factor, which has attracted a considerable degree of scholarly attention, is the set of moral rules, or code of behavior, applicable to both private as well as public life, centered around essential values such as *auctoritas*, *dignitas*, *libertas*, *gratia*, *honos*, and often subsumed under the encompassing label of *mos maiorum* (ancestral customs) (Wieacker 1988; Hölkeskamp 2010).

Emphasizing the exceptionally flexible nature of the *mos maiorum*, such studies are united by the conviction that by acting as an equivalent of statutory law and formal regulations at least until the middle Republic, this set of values guaranteed the actual working of the political and social life of the whole community. The *mos* was composed of principles central to the normative vocabulary of the Republic, incorporating traditional models of behavior in both private life and the public sphere and including everything from institutional conventions to the military system and state religion, and as such provided the socio-cultural fabric that allowed the Republic to flourish. With the breakdown of political and social consensus in the second century BCE, however, a series of rules

A Companion to Greek Democracy and the Roman Republic, First Edition. Edited by Dean Hammer.

and procedures which had previously been "regulated" or, better, sustained by the *mos maiorum* (so it is argued) became the object of a series of legislative acts that progressively transformed the *mos* into law, a process Bleicken called the '"jurification of the *mos*" (Bleicken 1975: 387–393). The actual enactment of the so-called *leges tabellariae*, which introduced the secret ballot progressively into the electoral, judicial, and legislative assemblies, of the *leges de ambitu*, which attempted to curb political corruption in various ways, and of the so-called *leges annales*, which established a fixed structure for Roman political careers, has been interpreted as a process directly related to the actual failing of the *mos maiorum* to fulfill its original function (however, see Jehne 2012 on "*mos*-ification of the law" in the first century BCE). In the words of Hölkeskamp (2010: 22–23), "it was a growing disregard or disrespect for, and increasingly wide-spread abuse of, the rules of the *mos maiorum* that seems to have overstrained the considerable flexibility and adaptability of these rules and brought about an erosion of its traditional binding force." Rather than attesting an increase in the importance of popular assemblies, such a need to formulate social and political norms into rules, it is claimed, demonstrates the decline of traditional consensus amongst the ruling elite.

However, the fragmentation of consensus in the second century, and the parallel increase in legislative activity, have also been interpreted as the most visible manifestation of disputes about the identity of the most legitimate source of political power between the Senate and the people. "The mechanisms that traditionally ensured political and social cohesion seem to have no longer been sufficient: alongside the *mos maiorum*, coined principally by the *nobilitas*, comitial law would now also be cited as a source of authority. Refuge in the law, which implies a degree of belief in the efficacy of the legislative procedures and in the political will that they express as well as in the source of power from which they originate (the *comitia*), is a sign of the time" (Duplá 2011: 296).

Although these readings of Roman republican politics reach opposite conclusions, they are based on two identical assumptions: first, that the *mos maiorum*, and those central values of Roman political vocabulary such as *auctoritas*, *dignitas*, *virtus*, *libertas* (to mention just a few), were solely expressed and elaborated by the nobility; second, that however flexible the *mos maiorum* was, at least as far as the public sphere was concerned it was constituted by a core of unwritten rules and principles that could be overstrained and lose its cohesive force. Even studies that affirm the vitality of *mos* in the public sphere after the second century BCE conclude that those appeals to the ways of the past are "only a moralistic invitation. The speaker appeals to people's character and sense for normal values and justice" whilst the laws, instruments of so-called "social technology," were a much more effective means to guarantee the efficient running of the commonwealth (Jehne 2012: 428). Even in this kind of reading, the *mos maiorum* (and related values) is not only the exclusive preserve of the nobility, who alone engaged in public speaking at Rome, but also seems to be relegated to the world of rhetoric, a world that is apparently completely detached from the actual course of politics.

In what follows, however, I wish to emphasize the fluid, flexible, and diverse nature of the *mos maiorum*. Far from being that stable and permanent entity that our sources portray it to be, it was open to continuous variations and interpretations, which at times were even diametrically opposed to one another. More specifically, what I wish to show is that, in virtue of its flexible nature, the *mos maiorum* and those principles at the core of republican normative vocabulary (such as *virtus*, *dignitas*, *auctoritas*, *libertas*) consistently acted as a legitimizing factor throughout the Republic (Beetham 1991: 2001).

Despite its conservative façade, the *mos maiorum* and the great Roman values seen as upheld from a mythical past, acted as a force for change during the Republic as well as later (Wallace-Hadrill 2008).

Understanding the nature of this normative vocabulary allows us to see appeals to the *mos maiorum* and other Roman core values not simply as instances of manipulation, which no doubt they were in part, but also as strategies possessing a perlocutionary linguistic function that permitted the conferral of legitimacy to new circumstances (Bettini 2011: 121). It follows that a proper appreciation of the function of republican normative vocabulary in Roman society will lead to an appreciation of the *mos maiorum* and those related principles as one of the engines of historical change.

By analyzing the phenomenology of the *mos maiorum* in the terms theorized by the ancients themselves, it will become apparent that, in their opinion, for an action to become a custom of legitimizing power, or for a value to increase its performative force within republican society, the consensus of the people at large (and not just that of a restricted elite) was an essential and necessary factor. Judging by the efforts that the elite invested in controlling the social process by which Roman values were socially disseminated and transmitted from one generation to the next, it appears that the Roman nobility was well aware of the role the people fulfilled in the elaboration of a new *mos* (the expression *novum mos* is attributed to Varro by Gellius 14.7.9), as well as of the potential power of this *mos*—hence their need to steer such elaborations towards ends and aims that were congenial to them. Although the elite was mostly successful in this operation, at times the people—understood as those Romans outside any established circle of power—had the possibility of making their voice heard, and, operating within the discursive framework elaborated by those in power, question the elite's system of values (see also Tatum, Chapter 15).

I argue that since, according to the ancient theorists, the people at large played an essential function in the shaping of these values as well as of the language in which they were articulated, the people themselves played an important, and often obscured, role as a legitimizing force during the Republic. Contrary to the idea that people wished to be led by the elite and that the *mos maiorum* and its related values fulfilled this function (Jehne 2000; Flaig 2003), my claim is that appreciating the phenomenology of these principles allows us to see the Roman people not as more or less active participants in the dynamics of power-sharing (currently subject of intense debate amongst scholars), but rather as one of the essential factors for the establishment of values, that, in turn, possessed the power to legitimate a new course of action.

2 Roman Discourse on *Mos*

Comparing Roman *mores* with the Greek way of life, Cicero finds himself forced to admit the superiority of Greece in the sphere of *doctrina*, but only because, he claims, this is a field in which the Romans decided not to compete (Cic. *Tusc.* 1.2.4). In his opinion, the pre-eminence of Rome over Greece is patently obvious: "our ways and practices of living, our domestic and private affairs are both better conducted and more polished; our public life has been regulated by our ancestors through institutions and laws that are clearly superior. Need I mention military life, in which we have always been strong both in virtue and even more in discipline?" (Cic. *Tusc.* 1.1.2; Gildenhard 2007; Baraz 2012).

Referring to the ways of the ancestors as a means to validate the superiority of the Romans, Cicero clearly draws a picture that distinguishes Greek values and ways of life from the Roman *mores*—the constitutive trait, he implicitly argues, of Roman identity. A close friend of Cicero, Cornelius Nepos, in his *De excellentibus ducibus* (*praefatio* 1) writes to Atticus stating that:

> they will probably be people who, ignorant of Greek culture, will believe that they should only approve what conforms to their own customs (*nisi quod ipsorum moribus conveniat*). When they learn, however, that the criterion for judging what is good and decent or reprehensible (*honesta atque turpia*) is not the same for everyone and that each thing has to be judged according to the traditions of its own ancestors (*omnia maiorum institutis iudicari*), they will not be surprised that in treating the virtues of the Greeks I conformed with their customs (*mōres*).

It follows, Cornelius Nepos continues, that those customs which for the Romans are defamatory, humiliating, and contrary to decent behavior—such as, for example, taking part in sport or acting on stage—are common, and often acclaimed practice amongst the Greeks. By the same token, some Roman customs may appear to the eyes of the Greek as highly reprehensible (for a comprehensive analysis of Nepos' text see La Penna 1981).

As these passages show, appeals to the *mos maiorum* in Roman social discourse act as a defining factor and clearly distinguish what is inherently Roman from what is not. By so doing, they create artificial boundaries between Greece and Rome to preserve the "Roman" way as different from the rest (on the artificiality of this distinction, see Wallace-Hadrill 2008). Such passages, and many others of similar tenor, assign a role of absolute pre-eminence to the *instituta maiorum* as a judging factor in the societies under scrutiny, Greece or Rome alike. The "traditions of the ancestors" appear to function as the measure according to which moral judgment on that society is expressed: whilst adherence gives rise to appreciation, departure from them inevitably leads to profound disapproval. The *mos maiorum*, according to the Romans, thereby plays a central role in defining collective behavior, its axiomatic force being so patent that it is also applied when passing judgment on other cultures (cf. Cat. *Orig.* fr. 31 Peter; Plaut. *Cas.* 963; Nepos, *De excel. duc.*, preface 6–7). Furthermore, these statements are based on a more subtle and important assumption. As each society construes its model of behavior on the *mores atque instituta maiorum*, which have to be understood in their own right, it follows that each culture is entitled to maintain and preserve its own customs unaltered. This Roman attitude indicates a profound conservatism that upholds the centrality of ancestral customs and apparently rejects the introduction of *mores novi* (Cic. *Leg. Man.* 9.60.2; Bettini 2011).

However, whilst the *mos* was typically portrayed as a static set of "purely" Roman practices and values, it was in fact characterized by a high degree of fluidity and diversity. Even when qualified by the genitive *maiorum*, which apparently (but as we shall see, only apparently) provides *mos* with specific boundaries, its actual content is very hard to define. Despite its normative function, it was not constituted by a prescriptive series of rules and regulations, but included the most disparate customs (for a collection of these references see Rech 1936 and Roloff 1967). It was invoked, for example, to support the principle that it was necessary to obtain *auctoritas patrum* before presenting a measure to be voted on before the people (Cic. *Corn.* I fr. 24Cr), or to regulate social behavior in the theater, both for the audience—in its customary duty of applauding at the end of a play (Plaut. *Cist.* 787)—and for the actors, who were reminded of the traditional custom of wearing undergarments (Cic. *De off.* 1.129). It was also invoked in matters of religion, military discipline, and education, and played an essential part in Roman law (see Quintilian's famous remark: "the greater part of *ius* depends on *mores*, not on *leges*" in *Inst. or.* 55.10.13. See also Cic. *Part. or.* 130 and Berger 1953: s.v. *mos*).

The fluidity of the *mos maiorum* is perhaps best expressed in the anecdote reported by Cicero in the *De legibus* (2.16.40; cf. Xen. *Mem.* 4.3.15). When the Athenians asked the oracle of Delphi which sacred rites they should have practiced above all, the oracle replied, "those which conform to the customs of the ancestors" (*eas quae essent in more maiorum*). However, Cicero recalls, the Athenians "returned a second time and, affirming that the customs of the ancestors had changed many times, asked what custom specifically they should attend to among the many different ones. The oracle responded 'the best one'" (it is most revealing that Cicero renders *nomos poleōs* of Xenophon's passage not with *lex civitatis*, but rather with *mos maiorum*, and adds the sequel of the Pythia's answer; see *comm.* ad loc. Dyck 2004). Even for the ancients, then, there was not a single *mos maiorum* which functioned as a normative measure of what was acceptable in society. Rather, it was a fluid notion that could even support opposed courses of action. The answer of the oracle highlights such potential ambiguity, indicating that behind the appearance of a codified cultural paradigm providing behavioral norms, the *mos mairoum* contained numerous models often in competition with one another. The oracle suggests that individuals should exercise their own good judgment in discerning the behavior most appropriate to the current situation, according to the shared criteria of the value most appropriate to the circumstance (Bettini 2011).

The adaptability of the *mos maiorum* as a domain of contention and negotiation is also attested in the contest between Q. Lutatius Catulus and M. Tullius Cicero over the conferral of extraordinary powers to Pompey to fight against Mithridates in 66 BCE (Rech 1936: 37, who however appears to consider *mos* as a permanent and stable form of behavior that may function as precedent for political and juridical innovations). Catulus, who himself supported the conferral of exceptional powers against Lepidus, opposed the bestowing of such powers to Pompey with a variety of arguments, claiming not only that this measure would have deprived the *res publica* of its liberty, but also that it would have contravened Roman custom: and "nothing new," he argues, "should be done against the examples and institutions of our forefathers" (Cic. *Leg. Man.* 60; Dio 36.35; Cic. *Phil.* 11.17–18; for a reconstruction of this whole debate see Steel 2001; Lintott 2008; and Arena 2012). In his response, Cicero—who in 43 BCE would not hesitate to hold the opposite view against the conferral of extraordinary powers to P. Servilius Isauricus—rebuked Catulus' argument by advancing two interesting claims. First, he underlined how the whole of Pompey's career was signposted by exceptionality. This contravention of the *mos maiorum* was permissible, therefore, because there was nothing that was so *inusitatum*, so *inauditum* that Pompey had not already experienced: "all the unusual circumstances which in the memory of man have ever happened to all other men put together, are not so many as these which we see have occurred in the history of one man"; and on none of these occasions had the *mos maiorum* been advocated to prevent him from gaining access to his new office (Cic. *Leg. Man.* 60). The present circumstances, in Cicero's opinion, with Rome being under threat from Mithridates, did not feature anything different from the previous cases. More importantly for the present argument, Cicero also claims that by their own behavior the ancestors validated Pompey's transgression of the *mos maiorum*. "If, in matters of peace, our forefathers always obeyed usage, in war they minded utility, and always adapted the parameters of innovative plans to the circumstances produced by new events" (Cic. *Leg. Man.* 60). Corroborating his point by citing a number of examples from the careers of Scipio and Marius, Cicero explicitly elaborates the idea of a *mos* that is not fixed but open to negotiation. The ancestors establish the *mos*, but they also authorize its alteration.

Sallust deployed a not dissimilar argument in the speech assigned to Julius Caesar in his account of the famous debate about the fate of the Catilinarians. The first to speak up against capital punishment for the arrested, Caesar is made the advocate of the argument that tradition is expected to change. Advocating life imprisonment for the culprits, Caesar describes the *mos maiorum* as an entity of changeable nature and legitimating force:

> Our ancestors, fathers of the Senate, were never lacking in wisdom or courage, and yet pride did not keep them from adopting foreign institutions, provided they were honorable. They took their offensive and defensive weapon from the Samnites, the badges of their magistrates for the most part from the Etruscans. To sum up, whatever they found suitable among allies or foes, they put in practice at home with the greatest enthusiasm, preferring to imitate rather than envy the successful. (Sal. *Cat.* 51.37–38)

After having followed the Greek example that inflicted the supreme penalty upon those found guilty, the ancestors, Caesar continues, devised a series of laws that provided the condemned with the alternative of exile. This is the *mos maiorum* that, according to Caesar, the senators should follow: "this seems to me, fathers of the Senate, a particularly cogent reason why we should not adopt a new policy (*novum consilium*). Surely there was greater merit and wisdom in those men who, from slight resources, created this mighty empire, than in us, who can barely hold what they gloriously won" (51.41–42).

However, just as Caesar could appeal to the virtue and example of the ancestors in support of *lenitas* towards the conspirators, so when Marcus Porcius Cato was called upon to express his opinion, in Sallust's account, he could also refer to the *mos maiorum* in support of the opposite course of action. Speaking in favor of capital punishment, Cato recapitulates a recurrent theme in Roman discourse by distinguishing the present wretched times from the glorious past, when *virtus* used to reign sovereign. The qualities that made the ancestors great, he claims, are those "that we do not possess: efficiency at home, a just rule abroad, in counsel an independent spirit free from guilt or passion. In place of these we have extravagance and greed, public poverty and private opulence. We extol wealth and foster idleness. We make no distinction between good and bad men, and ambition appropriates all the prizes of merit" (52.21–22). Following the example of the *maiores nostri*, Cato argues, we should adopt the most severe course of action: if Aulus Manlius Torquatus, whilst fighting against the Gauls, ordered the execution of his own son because he had fought against the enemy contrary to orders, how could there be any doubt about what punishment to inflict upon the most ruthless traitors (52.30–22)? Although the reader knew that Cato's view prevailed in the end, he also knew that his model of ancestral behavior and the value of *severitas* that it propelled were later superseded by the rival model, and that Cicero, consul at the time and responsible for the executions of the conspirators, was for this very reason driven into exile (only to be recalled later). It follows that these discrepancies, which attributed diametrically opposed models of both wisdom and actions to the *maiores* of the past, were not generated from some conflict within the tradition, or from a rupture between past and present; they were the product of a conflict for power in the present.

Such appeals to the ancestors, and the principles embodied by their actions, were based on the widely recognized authority of the *maiores nostri*. These *maiores* could be members of individual families as well as the whole community from earlier times, who in the past had formulated *boni mores*, collective good customs around which consensus was formed (there are also references to the *mores* of subgroups within the community, often defined in opposition to one another: the *mores* of the young versus those of the elderly, the *mores* of women versus those of men and so on; see Bettini 2011: 123–126). Belonging to the past, the *maiores* possessed the quality of "antiquity," so to speak, that rendered them closer to the gods (Cic. *De leg.* 2.27) and provided them with the power to grant legitimacy to a new circumstance (for a different approach to the identification of the *maiores* see Blösel 2000). So strong was the legitimating power of these appeals that even the rhetorical treatises of the first century BCE suggest that, whatever side a speaker takes on a specific issue, he must refer to the ways of the ancestors and related values if he wishes to entertain any serious hope of winning the case (Cic. *Inv.* 1.101, 2.133; *De orat.* 2.335; *Part. or.* 118).

3 The Elaboration of the *Mos*

The *auctoritas* of the Roman ancestors, then, was at the foundation of the establishment of a new *mos* as well as the emergence of a new value or the variation in the evaluative force of an existing notion (on *auctoritas* as factor determining social relationships see Lincoln 2000 and Bettini 2000). The principles at work in the elaboration of a new *mos* and related values can be found discussed by analogy in those texts focusing on language (on which Bettini 2011 and, more recently, Arena 2012). Quintilian makes the parallel explicit when, discussing the importance of *consuetudo* as "the surest guide by far in speaking," he goes on to state that "I will define custom in speech as the consensus of educated men, just as custom in living I define as the consensus of good men (*consuetudinem sermonis vocabo consensum eruditorum, sicut vivendi consensus bonorum*)" (Quint. *Inst. or.* 1.6.3; 45).

Varro also emphasizes *consuetudo* as the central factor involved in the elaboration of a new *mos*. According to Macrobius, Varro stated that "*mos* consists of a personal judgment (a judgment of the spirit), and *consuetudo* must follow" (*morem esse in iudicio animi, quem sequi debeat consuetudo*) (Macr. *Sat.* 3.8.9 ff. = Var. *Log.* fr. 74 Bolisani). This idea of *mos* as an individual disposition was already formulated in the second century BCE, as the famous saying cited by Terence attests: "there are as many opinions as there are men: each has his own *mos*" (*quot homines tot sententiae, suos cuique mos*) (Ter. *Phorm.* 454). As the proverbial and universalistic form of the saying suggests, in this century there seems to have been a shared understanding of *mos* as something residing in an internal disposition of the individual: namely, his personal judgment, of which there was a multiplicity of specimens, attested also in the various qualifications *meo more*, *tuo more*, *suo more* found in Latin texts (*ThlL* 8.15526.30ff.). A century later, Varro states that, in order to establish a collective *mos*, it is necessary that the judgment expressed by an individual is first shared by the whole community, and later transformed into a *consuetudo*, a common usage, hence a custom.

As Bettini lucidly shows, it is Varro who provides the clearest description of how *mores*, originating in an individual choice, come to gain a collective dimension. According to Servius, Varro stated that "*mos* is based on the consensus of all those who live together, which, once it is established in time, creates a habit" (*Varro vult morem esse commune consensus omnium simul habitantium, qui inveteratus consuetudinem facit*, Serv. in *Aen.* 7.601). It follows that from Varro's point of view, which is echoed in Ulpian's words ("the *mores* are the tacit consent of the people, which has been consolidated with time through long habit," Ulp. *Reg.* 1.4), the *mos* of an individual, in order to become part of the *mores atque instituta* of the whole people, first must be embraced by the whole community, and then should be repeated through time. For Varro there are therefore three essential passages for the establishment of a collective *mos*, that is of the *mos maiorum*. First, as a result of a personal choice, an individual should adopt a new custom, which by virtue of his personal authority may be considered for adoption by others. It then has to be embraced by the wider community, so as to be supported by general consensus, which will confer its legitimacy. Finally, it has to be repeated over and over again to be consolidated over time and become publicly acknowledged as a *consuetudo*. As Macrobius states, paraphrasing Varro, "so *mos* came first and the observance of the *mos* followed, which corresponds to habit" (Macr. *Sat.* 3.8.12; Bettini 2011; cf. Lind 1979). This transformation of a personal *mos* into a collective one is well illustrated by the example of Caesar recalled by Pliny the Elder. "The dictator Caesar, after a particularly serious fall from a chariot, was accustomed to repeat a magical formula three times before getting onto a chariot, in order to guarantee that the trip would be favorable: something that now, we know, a great part of the population does (*plerosque nunc facere scimus*)" (Pliny *NH* 28.21). Caesar's individual choice, originating in his personal misfortune, had acquired a wider consensus by virtue of his *auctoritas*, and being repeated through time until Pliny's own age, had become a widely shared *consuetudo*. An individual *mos* had been transformed into a distinctive custom of a whole cultural group.

In order to appreciate fully the dynamics at work in the establishment of Roman custom according to the ancient theorists, it will be useful to turn to their understanding of *consuetudo* as best attested in linguistic theories. In his analysis of the dynamics of linguistic changes that, by admission of the same authors, govern also the changes of customs, Varro assigns a prominent role to *consuetudo*, understood as the common usage derived from the agreement of a large number of people. However, Varro claims, if an orator was allowed to implement a linguistic innovation because of his *auctoritas*, his definitive success could be sanctioned only by the people as a whole, understood as the language users. Varro expresses this notion in the powerful metaphor of the *gubernator*. "As a helmsman (*gubernator*) ought to obey reason (*ratio*), and each one in the ship (*unusquisque in navi*) ought to obey the helmsman, so the people ought to obey reason, and we individuals ought to obey the people (*nos singuli populo*)." Whilst the use of language on the part of the *populus* should be anchored to *ratio* (within the limits deemed acceptable) in order to preserve it from mistakes, so individuals, chiefly orators and poets, should follow *consuetudo*, the way language is used by the speaking community: "the people has power over itself (*populus enim in sua potestate*)," Varro claims, "but individuals are in its power (*singuli in illius*) … I [the individual] am not the master—so to speak—of the people's usage, but it is of mine (*ego populi consuetudinis non sum ut dominus, at ille meae est*)" (Var. *Ling.* 9.6. A similar analysis is in Cic. *De orat.* 3.152–153 and 170; cf. Quint. *Inst. or.* 1.6.2–3; cf. 9.3.3 and Arena 2012 on the different stances amongst these authors).

According to these authors, the way language is used by the speaking community—and so the way customs are adopted—derives its force not from its conformity to *ratio*, but rather from the *consensus multorum* (Bettini 2011). Varro identifies these *multi*, in whose hands the power of sanctioning the use of new words and customs resided, as the people who, although completely uneducated, possessed that *medius loquendi usus*, that allowed them to understand the constituent parts of compound names immediately. Their consensus was regarded by ancient authors as the ultimate engine of linguistic change.

Consequently, if, on the one hand, the successful affirmation of a custom will primarily depend on the power of the groups or individuals who make appeal to the *mos maiorum*, on the other, such success will also be determined by these groups' or individuals' ability to choose the custom that the wider community will find most plausibly suitable to the parameters required by any given circumstance (Bettini 2011: 118; cf. Smelser 1962. On the legitimating role of the *mos maiorum* based on a degree of popular assent, and ultimately the support of the existing power structure, see Morstein-Marx 2012; Beetham 1991, 2001).

By prompting a different view of present circumstances, the application of a specific model of behavior and its related values favored the elaboration of a different (although not necessarily new) social perception, and by so doing it legitimated actions that were not previously accepted or had attracted criticism (see, for example, the discussion over the so-called "*senatus consultum ultimum*" in Arena 2012).

As the ancient theorists argue, the affirmation of a specific model of ancestral behavior depended both on the *auctoritas* of those who proposed it and, decisively, on the people (understood as the largest section of society), who bestowed a degree of consensus and transformed that model into *consuetudo*. It was therefore the people at large who, embracing rhetorical description by means of normative language, eventually prompted or rejected a modification of a social and political perception.

4 Ways of Transmission and Control

In their constant struggle for power to increase their personal "symbolic capital," the members of the Roman elite reinvented, transmitted, and proposed models of past behavior (and related value systems) to the wider community. In 56 BCE, restoring the Fornix Fabianus, an arch built by his grandfather in 121 BCE at the intersection of the Via Sacra and the Forum (Chioffi 1995; *LTUR* 2.264–266), Fabius Maximus added a portrait gallery of family statues, attested by an inscription (*CIL* 6 1303–1304, 31593 = 1² 762–763; see Coarelli 1985: 172–180). In doing so, he added both Aemilius Paullus and Scipio Aemilianus, who were only remotely linked to the family and even so only through adoption (Wallace-Hadrill 2008: 220). In the process of manipulating his lineage in an attempt of self-promotion, Fabius Maximus had also reinvented the *mos maiorum* of the Fabii as well as of the community at large. Similarly, in 52 BCE, the consul Metellus Scipio set up a large collection of gilded statues on the Capitoline, several of them equestrian, with the intention to increase his "symbolic capital" through an exaltation of the

Scipiones. However, as Cicero did not miss the opportunity to ridicule, he attached the label "Sarapio" to the wrong Scipio and mistakenly attributed a censorship to Africanus (Cic. *Att.* 6.1.17; Flower 1996: 73–74; an analogous process of self-promotion based on family ethnicity is identified by Farney 2007).

In Rome this kind of re-elaboration, which sometimes took the form of outright invention, was possible thanks to the absence of any written codification of the custom of the ancestors. As Isidore put it, "*mos* is a custom that has withstood the test of time, or an unwritten law. In fact, the law is called so from the act of reading (*a legendo*), because it is written (*mos est vetustate probata consuetudo, sive lex non scripta. Nam lex a legendo vocata, quia scripts est*)", (Isid. *Etym.* 2.10.1–2; cf. 5.3.2–3). In the *Partitiones oratoriae* (130) Cicero himself identifies the difference between *lex* and *mos* in the written codification of the first: "both the written rules and those that are conserved not in alphabetic characters but by the right of the peoples and by the custom of the ancestors are part of law" (*propria lgis et ea quae scripta sunt et ea quae sine litteris aut gentium iure aut maiorum more retinentur*; cf. Serv. *in Aen.* 6.316). It follows that the transmission of *mos* was entrusted to a wide variety of practices that, by virtue of their repetitive nature, preserved or perhaps forged the customs of the ancestors in the collective memory of the Romans (for the *mos maiorum* as a central element of the "cultural memory" as well as of "social memory" of Roman society see Flaig 2004; Hölkeskamp 2005, 2006a; Bettini 2011: 11; for these labels see Assmann 1992 and Fentress and Wickham 1992).

This process took place through a variety of means, including the use of *exempla* in public speeches and historiography, education, the topography of the city, and other practices that can be conveniently described as public spectacles—such as funerals, triumphs, theater, religious festivals, and so on (a list can be found in Rech 1936). On the one hand, such public spectacles were an expression of the values of the political elite, but on the other they "served as a vehicle for communication between all citizens, as all participated together in celebrating and reaffirming the common values, shared goals, and political institutions of the community" (Flower 2004: 322). They forged a sense of identity and tradition not only for the members of the elite, but also for the whole community, and permitted the *mos maiorum* to function as a paradigm as a term of reference that both united the people who identified with these *mores* (Quint. *Inst. or.* 5.10.13), and separated them from others who cherished their own *mos* or from the members of their own community who could be said to be following a different *mos.*

The great deeds of the past and the actors who performed them were enshrined in the *exempla* present in Roman historiography as well as in poetry, deployed in deliberative oratory, and present in the topographical and social spaces that marked such memorable locations, the urban landscape of Roman historical memory (on the latter, see Hölkeskamp 1987, 1996, 2001 as well as 2006a; on exemplarity in historiography see the splendid work by Roller 2004, 2009). Through these means, some of which were truly public in nature, moral principles and models for actions were transmitted and, in turn, evaluated by the members of the community, who accepted or rejected them as normative (Roller 2009). In discussing the function of *exempla* in oratory, Quintilian encourages the use of example from the past as form of proof: adduce, he states, "some past action real or assumed ... to persuade the audience of the truth of the point which we are trying to make" (*Inst. or.* 5.11.6–7), implicitly claiming that, in his opinion, *exempla* do not fulfill a narrative function, but rather by operating as "signs" to evoke "cultural memory" play a commemorative role (Bettini 2011: 115).

This function of exemplarity was perceived by the ancient themselves. As the Greek Polybius observed in the second century BCE, Roman funerals were one of the most prominent means by which the Romans forged and transmitted the values that functioned as a connective force throughout the social fabric of republican Rome. In his attempt to identify the reasons behind Roman success as a world power, Polybius famously noted that although the Italians might appear to be generally gifted with an extraordinary bodily strength and personal courage, it should nevertheless be observed that "they do much to foster a spirit of bravery in the young men by way of their institutions" (*Hist.* 6.52). He proceeds to illustrate this case by referring to Roman funerary practices, which were celebrated with an extraordinary splendor and in a highly public manner:

> Whenever any illustrious man dies [that is a Roman magistrate], he is carried at his funeral into the Forum to the so-called rostra, sometimes conspicuous in an upright posture and more rarely reclined. Here with all the people standing round, a grown-up son, if he has left one who happens to be present, or if not some other relative mounts the rostra and discourses on the virtues and successful achievements of the dead. As a consequence the multitude and not only those who had a part in these achievements, but those also who had none, when the facts are recalled to their minds and brought before their eyes, are moved to such sympathy that the loss seems to be not confined to the mourners, but a public one affecting the whole people. (*Hist.* 6.53)

The spectacular dimension of the funeral is further emphasized by the participation of actors, who, representing the ancestors of the deceased, wear wax masks that closely resemble their faces, as well as the garb and attributes (from the number of lictors to the rods and fasces) of the highest political office the individual had held in his lifetime. They precede the bier in chariots, and once at the rostra they all sit in a row on ivory chairs according to the highest office held in their lifetime. "There could not easily be a more ennobling spectacle for a young man who aspires to fame and virtue. For who would not be inspired by the sight of the images of men renowned for their excellence, all together and as if alive and breathing? What spectacle could be more glorious than this?" (*Hist.* 6. 53). The "ancestors" functioned at the same time as a special audience to the eulogy, ensuring that the deceased was worthy to be counted amongst the members of their family, and as the subject of the eulogy itself, since after the life and achievement of the deceased the speaker exalted their deeds and exploits. "By this means," Polybius comments, "by this constant renewal of the good report of brave men, the celebrity of those who performed noble deeds is rendered immortal, while at the same time the fame of those who did good service to their country becomes known to the people and a heritage for future generations. But the most important result is that young men are thus inspired to endure every suffering for public welfare in the hope of winning the glory that attends on brave men" (*Hist.* 6.53–54; on the relation between the aristocratic funerals and ancient *mores* see also Cic. *De orat.* 2.225; Flower 1996, 2004). Adding gladiatorial shows, plays, and even banquets to public funerals could enhance the occasion as an opportunity for families to deploy their "symbolic capital" to advance their claims to power by showing its strength across different generations at the moment when a member of their family had died. At the same time, however, for the public who had hastened at the herald's announcement of the funeral they also recalled, as well as re-created, the heroic past of Rome, thereby forging, in the process, the identity and the values of the whole community.

The material for funeral *laudationes* was constituted by family traditions, publicly rehearsed, and most probably transmitted orally from one generation to the next. Some families kept records of the *laudationes* given by the relative of the deceased, and some others even composed *commentarii* that provided summaries of family trees and careers (Gell. *NA* 13.20 with regard to the Porcii). Although there is no certainty of the extent to which the custom of keeping "family records" was adopted, it seems that, at least from the middle Republic onwards, they constituted the basis for the sepulchral *elogia* (tomb inscriptions that recapitulated the merits of the deceased) and the *tituli* (inscriptions that listed the career of the ancestor to which they were attached) of the *imagines* displayed in the *atrium*, which they provided with the selective information the inscriptions highlighted (Flower 1996: 160–183).

Although the inscriptions on tombs were not specifically designed for a public audience, but rather functioned as a more private form of self-image, their connection with the *laudationes*, whose public dimension was one of the defining traits, allows us to use them as a window on those values that the Roman elite promoted as well as on the history of their family that they elaborated ultimately to the benefit and on behalf of the whole community.

The best-attested example (although the exception rather than the rule) is provided by the tomb of the Scipiones situated on the via Appia, just outside the porta Capena. Distancing themselves from the common practice of cremation, in the third century BCE, the Scipiones built a family tomb, where on the Etruscan model inhumed bodies, deposed in sarcophagi and distinguished by inscriptions, were arranged hierarchically around the founding figure of Barabtus (Coarelli 1996; Flower 1996: 166–180; on the exceptionality see Cic. *De leg.* 2.56; Pliny *NH* 7.187). In the mid-second century, an architectural façade of Hellenistic style was added to the tomb, providing it with impressive grandeur as well as a number of portrait statues, including those of Publius Scipio Africanus and Lucius Scipio Asiaticus as well as the poet Ennius (Livy 38.56; on the actual identity of these statues see Coarelli 2002).

The *elogium* of L. Cornelius Scipio Barbatus (consul 298 BCE), dated probably to the 250s (Wachter 1987: 301–342, *contra* Zevi 1999), reads as follows:

> Lucius Cornelius Scipio Barbatus
> born to his father Gnaeus, a brave and sagacious man (*fortis vir sapiensque*)
> whose fine looks were equal to his virtus (*quoius forma virtutei parisuma fuit*)
> consul, censor, aedile he was among you.
> he captures Taurisia and Cisauna in Samnium,
> he reduces all of Lucania and leads away hostages
> (*ILLRP* 309 = *CIL* 1^2 6–7)

It is interesting to observe that this inscription is characterized by a distinctive Hellenistic flavor often associated with elitist attitudes. Mirrored in the form of the sarcophagus as altar, the phrases *fortis vir sapiensque* and *quoius forma virtutei parisuma fuit* appar to reflect the Greek ideal of *kalokagatia* (for discussion see McDonnell 2006: 33–34). Fifty years or so later, the same association of *forma* with *virtus* is also found in Plautus' *Miles gloriosus* (12, 57, 1027, 1042, 1327), where it is attributed to Pyrgopolynices. Although probably present in the Greek model adopted by Plautus, this association of values, formulated by the Roman elite, was propagated to the wider echelons of society through the means of theater. The association of physical beauty and *virtus* became such a current part of those values informing Roman society that it is revealingly found in one of Publius Syrius' *sententiae* composed, if not compiled, in the first century BCE (Flamerie de Lachapelle 2011). It recites "a beautiful appearance is a silent recommendatio" (*formosa facies muta commendatio est*, F4 FdeL). Most likely originally a line in one of Publius Syrius' mimes (a very popular and somewhat crude form of theater), this *sententia* represented as well as informed the widespread attitude of all social groups in Rome: "*sententiae*," the author of the *Rhetorica ad Herennium* states, "are maxims extracted from real life, that express in few words what happens or should happen in life" (*sententia est oratio sumpta de vita, quae aut quid sit aut quid esse oporteat in vita, breviter ostendit, Rhet. Her.* 4.24).

The elite succeeded in formulating and affirming a framework of values and norms that, strengthening their collective identity as well as their claim to legitimate power, could be (and, in their view, should be) also espoused by the rest of the community (on popular morality in the early Empire see Morgan 2007). As far as our sources attest, the wider Roman community does not seem to have resisted the nobility by attempting to enact and impose alternative values. However, within the institutions and political and conceptual discourse of the society they lived in, the people gave expression, borrowing Thompson's phrase, to their antagonistic interests and correspondingly dialectic culture (Thompson 1978; Roseberry 1994). This is illustrated by the appearance of a graffito on the temple of Concordia in 121 BCE. In the aftermath of the killing of Gaius Gracchus and his supporters during the fight on the Aventine hill in 121 BCE, the city was cleansed by lustration of the bloodshed and the Senate decreed that Lucius Opimius should build a new temple of Concordia in the Forum (App. *B. civ.* 1.26.120; Plut. *C. Gracch.* 17.6–7). According to Plutarch, "what vexed the multitude (*tous pollous*) more than this or anything else," that is, more than seeing the head of Gaius hunted and paid for in gold, his body and those of his followers denied burial and thrown into the Tiber, and their widows forbidden to mourn, "was the erection of a temple of Concord by Opimius," who appeared to be celebrating a triumph for the slaughter of so many citizens. "Therefore at night, beneath the inscription on the temple, somebody carved this verse: 'A work of mad discord produces a temple of Concord'" (Plut. *C. Gracch.* 17.6). Plutarch seemingly regards this graffito as a manifestation of popular thought, of the view of the many (*oi polloi*) (Plut. *C. Gracch.* 17.8 and 18.2; cf. App. 2.133 and Plut. *Caes.* 62.6 preserving "the default assumption" that graffiti were indeed the preserve of shopkeepers and artisans, Hillard 2013: 113–114; see also Cic. *De orat.* 2.240; Zadorojnyi 2011: 123n.37). However, rather than an example of sharp dissent from the dominant discourse and an attempt at popular resistance against the senatorial perpetrators (Morstein-Marx 2012: 198 and 201), this graffito shows how even within a context of public opposition, the people (or at least the author of the graffito) manifest their dissatisfaction with the elite within the same ideological framework and discourse elaborated by the elite. As the defacing of the temple of Concordia shows, the graffito "appropriated the very language of the monument hijacked" (Hillard 2013: 110). The members of the elite and the author of the graffito disagreed on the understanding of the notion of *concordia* or, at least, on the means to achieve it, rather than on its place amongst Roman values. Adopting a formula that parodies the standard dedicatory formula for temples (most likely *Discordia fecit* probably being a derisory alternative to *L. Opimius fecit*, see Morstein-Marx 2004: 102–103n.159), the unknown author, giving (according to Plutarch) expression to the voice of the majority, does not claim that *concordia* is not a value that the community should uphold, but rather that Lucius Opimius' actions did not support this ideal central to the *res publica* as a whole. The emphasis of the graffito appears to be on the civic rights violated by those who suppressed Gaius Gracchus and other 3,000 citizens. Opposing a senatorial ideal of *concordia*, often associated with senatorial concessions to plebeian demands and implying the plebeian deference to the senatorial elite in the name of the common good (see Morstein-Marx 2004: 54–56, 102–103, 268–269), the graffitist presents a notion of this value conceived in such a way that the rights of all members of the community should be upheld in a balance and, possibly, in equal measure. The graffito does appear as a "hidden transcript," to adopt Scott's terms (1990; see also Morstein-Marx 2012), by which the people (or at least those who opposed the elite's violent action) talked about and questioned the elite's domination. However, this hidden and public transcript exists within the elite's discursive framework that grants the graffito meaning. As such, it adopts the form and language of domination in order to be heard, and thus recognizes power as it protests it, whereby implicitly acknowledging its legitimacy (Roseberry 1994: 364).

A similarly controversial understanding of *concordia* is also attested in Roman fables. Described as a simple form of speech, of servile origins, that appeals to rough and uneducated minds (Livy 2.39.9; Ph. 3 prol. 43–47; Quint. 11.19–21), fables represent an attestation of norms and values held also amongst the lowers social groups in Rome (on the mutual permeability of popular and elite culture with particular reference to fables see Morgan 2007). The Aesopic fable of the limbs and belly, whose co-operation is essential to the functioning of the body, was adopted, according to Livy and Dionysius of Halicarnassus (Livy 2.32.9–11 and Dionys. 6.86.1–3), by Menenius Agrippa to convince the plebeians to collaborate with the patricians. It implied the granting of certain powers to the people as well as the acceptance of the leadership of the Senate and its prominent role in distributing resources in the name of the common good. At the beginning of the first century CE, Babrius composed a fable that presented the very same understanding of social harmony: when a snake's tail decided it wished to lead for a change, rather than follow, without eyes or nose, it ended up dragging the rest of the body in a pit and hurt itself. Aware of the mistake made, the tail apologized and promised to subject itself to be led again (B134). However, at the very end of the first century BCE, Phaedrus gave expression to a different notion of *concordia* in the fable of the dog and the wolf (3.7). When a hungry wolf saw a well-fed dog and inquired about it, the dog replied that he was so well treated because he watched the house of his owners and did as he was told, and they, in turn, fed and looked after him. However, looking closely, the wolf noticed that the dog carried the signs of a chain around his neck: this form of social harmony as realized in the household between the dog and his owners required the loss of freedom.

5 Censors

In order to preserve these values, the Romans assigned the censors the control of the so-called *regimen morum*, loosely translatable as "lifestyle" referring to neither formal nor legal prescriptions (Livy 4.8.2; Astin 1988). The censors were in charge of the *mores* of the whole community, so in legal terms, all citizens were subject to their authority. Their sphere of intervention was so extensive that, alongside military discipline and magisterial abuse, it included the sphere of private life: so that the censors, in the words of the

Greek observer Dionysius of Halicarnassus, seemed to exercise their authority even in the bedroom of Roman citizens.

> The Athenians gained repute because they punished as harmful to the state the indolent and idle who followed no useful pursuits, and the Lacedaemonians because they permitted their oldest men to beat with their canes such of the citizens as were disorderly in any public place whatever; but for what took place in the homes they took no thought or precaution, holding that each man's house-door marked the boundary within which he was free to live as he pleased. But the Romans, throwing open every house and extending the authority of the censors even to the bed-chamber, made that office the overseer and guardian of everything that took place in the homes; for they believed that neither should a master be cruel in the punishments meted out to his slaves, nor a father unduly harsh or lenient in the training of his children, nor a husband unjust in his partnership with his lawfully wedded wife, nor children disobedient toward their aged parents, nor should own brothers strive for more than their equal share, and they thought there should be no banquets and revels lasting all night long, no wantonness and corrupting of youthful comrades, no neglect of the ancestral honors of sacrifices and funerals, nor any other of the things that are done contrary to propriety and the advantage of the state. (Dionys. 20.13.2–3)

As Dionysius perceptively emphasizes, although the censors did not act according to an established list of prescribed acts, they intervened against any act that seemed against "the advantage of the state" and the well-being of the whole community, as was also attested by the oath they took at the beginning of their mandate (Zon. 7.19).

The censors did not impose a monetary sanction, just a blush on the condemned person, a mark on his good name (*ignominia*), as Cicero says (Cic. *De rep.* 4.6). The sanctions they imposed on those who, in their opinion, had infringed Roman customs involved demotion in the citizens' classification of census:

> one who was a senator was expelled from the Senate; one who was an *eques* was deprived of his public horse; one who was a plebeian [in its later sense of a member of a lower order] was transferred to the list of *Caerites* and was made *aerarius*, and in consequence was not in the register of his own century but remained a citizen only in the sense that in accordance with his personal liability he paid the *tributum*. (Ps-Asc. 189St)

It follows that by affecting the *lectio senatus*, the *recognitio equitum*, and the census itself, the censors' evaluation of someone's *mores* was more than a judgment on his behavior per se, as it assessed the fitness of an individual to be a member of the citizen body (Astin 1988: 16). By exercising the *regimen morum*, the censors provided the role that each citizen played within society with a moral justification and, as a result, the *mores* functioned as a criterion at the foundation of the political structure of republican society.

The censors' assessment of the citizens' *mores* was theoretically and legally applicable to all members of the community (for examples of people of humbler origins: see Livy 24.18.7–8, 27.11.15; Cic. *De orat.* 2.272; *Clu.* 126). However, it seems most probable that, as a matter of fact, they could not and did not concern themselves with the *mores* of the ever-growing population of Rome in a sustained and significant manner. Not only were the punishments the censors inflicted conceived in such a way as to have their strongest repercussions on those of wealth and high status, but also, at least from the mid-third century BCE, the actual logistics of the census operation would not have granted them enough time to deal with all individual declarations (Astin 1988: 18 n.22), even if these had all been released in Rome—which from the first century BCE was no longer the case, as the Tabula Heracleensis attests (Crawford 1996: I, n.24, ll. 142–158). Although the senators and the *equites equo publico* were most probably the primary focus of their judgment, in practice the censors must have been able to deal with a limited number of cases brought purposefully to their attention either by hearsay, personal observation, or a third party.

However, beyond the censors' ability to carry out the *cura morum*, the deepest significance of their function consisted in providing the Roman elite with a mechanism of self-restraint by publicly excluding those deemed unfit for their role from the very position that, within the censorial organization, provided them with power. The practice of relegation of those condemned to the lowest category of citizens acted as a demarcating line between those who were part of the elite and those who were not. Crucially, this sense of the elite's identity was forged on the basis of informal, ever-changing, values, that thereby came to be one of the cornerstones of the Roman elite's coherence.

Although the origins of the censorship are rather obscure, it seems that the censors gained the *cura morum* of the Roman *cives* by virtue of the *plebiscitum Ovinium* (dated either to 339/4 BCE or 312 BCE), which extended their powers to the *lectio senatus* (Festus s.v. *praeteriti* 209L). Although fraught with numerous problems, the general gist is clear: the *lex Ovinia* established that the Senate had to be composed of those members whom the censors considered *optimi*, that is, wealthy men, who had held a magistracy and were morally fit as conforming to the *cura morum* (Cornell 2000; Clemente 2016). It follows that, at the end of the fourth century BCE, contrary to the Greek system, the *cura morum* acted as a self-defining factor of the senatorial elite and a legitimating force of its own power. In the Greek city-states, according to their political regime, there was a system of checks on the magistrates' exercise of power that involved the *boulē* and some dedicated officials (for Athens see MacDowell 1978: 167–174), while in Rome until the second half of the second century BCE there were no specific courts to judge a magistrate's exercise of powers. The only judgment he might have incurred was that exercised by his peers, the censors, endowed with considerable discretionary powers in this regard, which would have subjected him to a *nota censoria*.

However, as Cicero put it, the censorial mark did not cause permanent damage to one's career. Its effect did not last longer than the next censorship, as the new censors could reinstate those who had been affected by it or, as in 115 and 70 BCE, those expelled by censorial action could find their way back into the Senate by securing election to a magistracy. As Cicero emphasizes in the *Pro Cluentio* (119–121), differing from the *infamia* procured by a *iudicium publicum*, the *nota censoria* was not supported by any legal sanction, which would transform its effects into a permanent sentence, but, rather, was based on the consensus of the wider community. If the community at large had not acknowledged the complex of civic norms applied by the censors as core values of the society, the censors' action would have been devoid of force (Clemente 2016).

This role of the wider community became, so to speak, institutionalized from the second half of the second century onwards. Despite the constant reference to the *cura maiorum* amongst the censors' prerogatives, from the *lex Calpurnia* of 149 BCE and the Gracchan *lex repetundarum* of 122(?) onwards, it is apparent that a new principle had progressively established itself: a conviction in the *iudicia publica* of the *quaestiones* or even in *iudicia populi* (although the latter were more and more rare) would deprive the condemned senator of his senatorial *dignitas*. No longer exclusively subjected to the arbitrary decision of the censors and their interpretation of the community's values, the magistrates' behavior was judged according to the rule of law. Even in Cicero's ideal code of the *De legibus* (3.7), composed in the 50s, the Senate has to be composed solely of ex-magistrates, that is of those chosen by the people to hold a magistracy without the interference of censorial co-optation. The censors had to make sure that the Senate was free from faults and were assigned the role, borrowed from the Greeks, of reviewing the conduct of the magistrates at the very end of their term of office (3.28 and 46) (on Cicero's passage and Clodius' attempt to curb the censors' powers see Tatum 1990; Clemente 2010; and Arena 2012).

A degree of fear amongst the Roman elite concerning their loss of control over the supervision of Roman *mores* is discernible in the affair of the rhetorical school of Plotius Gallus, which also exemplifies their effort to tighten their grip on the means by which these values were propagated. In 92 BCE the censors issued an edict of firm disapproval against the innovative methods of this school, opened in Rome by a rather obscure rhetorician, Plotius Gallus. According to our sources, Gallus' school inaugurated (although it may not have been strictly the case) the practice of training advanced students to make speeches directly in Latin without recourse to Greek practice speeches or Greek study material (on this see Bloomer 2011: 37–52). In condemning this kind of teaching at Rome, the censors Gnaeus Domitius Ahenobarbus and Lucius Licinius Crassus are reported to have stated that

> it has been brought to our attention that some persons have instituted at Rome a new type of instruction … our forefathers have already decided what our children should learn and what schools they should attend. We do not like these innovations, which go against all habits and customs of the ancestors, nor do they seem just. Therefore we have determined to make our judgment plain both to those who preside over these schools and to those who have become accustomed to attending them: we do not approve. (Suet. *De rhet.* 25.1; Gell. *NA* 15.11.2)

Although the reasons behind this closure are still the subject of debate, it seems that Gallus' school upset the traditional system of education, opening up a dangerous breach in the control of new generations and the transmission of values. The school appears to have been open to students at a later stage of their education, at which stage *tirocinium fori* was generally the norm. Rather than attending a practicing orator in the Forum in a relationship of *clientela*/friendship, the students of Plotius paid a fee to attend a school, a custom inconceivable in the standard practice, that subverted the existing social relations of power within the elite. In addition, Plotius offered, or at least was perceived to offer, short-cuts. Bypassing expensive and, in this sense, exclusive years of studies of Greek in the privacy of great homes and later in the company of renowned orators, he gave immediate access to the secrets of rhetorical composition and performance in Latin, setting exercises modeled on contemporary speeches (Quint. *Inst. or.* 2.4.5). The resultant form of oratory was of a very different nature from that fostered by traditional training. Members of the elite, such as Crassus the orator, but also Varro, rejected it on a social as well as stylistic level. In a fragment of the *Saturae Menippeae* (157 Riese) a student at Plotius' school is described as someone who *bubulcitarat*, that is as someone who "had brayed like an ox-driver," and in another fragment Varro ridicules him by making fun of his name: "this *gallus* [cock]," the fragment reads, "who stirs up a tribe of brawlers" (186 Riese). Such orators were perceived as vulgar, speaking too loudly, and moving too swiftly, in essence as low-class demagogic speakers. This new school was thereby seen to remove new potential politicians from the control of the traditional elite, whose system of the *tirocinium fori* had long guaranteed the secure transmission of those values at the core of Roman identity.

6 Conclusion

In the Roman Republic as well as in classical Greek city-states, in order to fulfill their social and political function informal norms and values had to be accepted and shared by all—or nearly all—members of the community. Behind the facade of traditionalism and conservatism, these values were of a very flexible nature and open to negotiation, and indeed could act, at least in Rome, as a vehicle for social and political change. As the Roman theorists argue, the affirmation of a specific model of ancestral behavior and its related values depended, on the one hand, on the *auctoritas* of the individual or group who proposed it and, on the other, on the people, understood as the wider section of society, who assented to this model. By doing so, it was the people at large who, embracing the rhetorical description by means of normative language, eventually prompted or rejected a modification of a social and political perception.

However, contrary to Greek customs, in the Roman Republic the *mores* regulated all aspects of a citizen's life including his private behavior in his bedroom, as Dionysius of Halicarnassus put it. Assessed by magistrates, adherence to these values functioned as a justification for the hierarchical political structure of the whole society. It was with the *plebiscitum Ovinium* that, contrary to contemporary Greek customs of election (differing according to political regimes), the *mos maiorum* as interpreted by Roman magistrates came first to act as one of the factors defining the senatorial elite. And again contrary to the Greek practice of institutional checks on the magistrates' exercise of power, *regimen morum*, as arbitrarily interpreted by the censors, provided the Roman elite with a mechanism of self- restraint as well as, ultimately, with a legitimation of its power.

Although the success of any social and political value as normative within society resided ultimately in its acceptance by the people, in Rome the means of transmission and control of these informal norms and ideals were regulated by the elite. Contrary to Greek practice, education, public speeches, use of *exempla*, funerals, triumphs, and even festivals paid for extensively by the aediles who oversaw even the choice of theater performances (Manuwald 2011), were conceived and regulated by members of the elite. Towards the end of the Republic, however, the institutionalized forms of control of the *mos maiorum* progressively lost their effectiveness, creating the perception amongst contemporaries, as well as some modern observers, that it was the disintegration of political and moral consensus that caused the end of the Republic.

REFERENCES

Anderson, W.S. 1979. "Plautus' 'Trinummus': The Absurdity of Officious Morality." *Traditio* 35: 333–345.

Arena, V. 2012. *Libertas and the Practice of Politics in the Late Roman Republic.* Cambridge.

Assmann, J. 1992. *Das Kulturelle Gedächtnis: Schrift, Erinnerung und Politische Identität in frühen Hochkulturen*. Munich.
Astin, A.E. 1978. *Cato the Censor*. Oxford.
Astin, A.E. 1985. "Cicero and the Censorship." *CPh* 80: 233–239.
Astin, A.E. 1988. "Regimen morum." *JRS* 78: 14–34.
Baird, J.A. and C. Taylor, eds. 2011. *Ancient Graffiti in Context*. New York and London.
Baltrusch, E. 1989. *Regimen morum: Die Reglementierung des Privatlebens der Senatoren und Ritter in der römischen Republik und frühen Kaiserzeit*. Munich.
Baraz, Y. 2012. *A Written Republic: Cicero's Philosophical Politics*. Princeton.
Beard, M. 2007. *The Roman Triumph*. Cambridge, MA.
Beetham, D. 1991. *The Legitimation of Power*. London.
Beetham, D. 2001. "Political Legitimacy." In K. Nash and A. Scott, eds., *The Blackwell Companion to Political Sociology*. Oxford, 107–116.
Berger, A. 1953. *Encyclopaedic Dictionary of Roman Law*. Philadelphia.
Bettini, M. 2000. "Alle soglie dell'autorità." In B. Lincoln, ed., *L'autorità: Costruzione e corrosione*. Turin, vii–xxxiv
Bettini, M. 2011. "*Mos, Mores,* and *Mos Mairoum*: The Invention of Morality in Roman Culture." In M. Bettini, ed., *The Ears of Hermes: Communication, Images, and Identity in the Classical World*. Trans. W. Short. Columbus, 87–130.
Bleicken, J. 1975. *Lex Publica: Gesetz und Recht in der römischen Republik*. Berlin and New York.
Bloomer, W.M. 2011. *The School of Rome: Latin Studies and the Origins of Liberal Education*. Berkley, Los Angeles, and London.
Blösel, W. 2000. "Die Geschichte des Begriffes mos maiorum von den Anfängen bis zu Cicero." In B. Linke and M. Stemmler, eds., *Mos Maiorum*. Stuttgart, 25–97.
Buchwald, W. 1964. "Morem gerere." *MH* 21: 180–182.
Chaplin, J.D. 2000. *Livy's Exemplary History*. Oxford.
Chioffi, L. 1995. "Fornix Fabianus." In E.M. Steinby, ed., *Lexicon Topographicum Urbis Romae*. Rome, 2.264–266.
Clemente, G. 1990. "Tradizioni familiari e prassi politica nella repubblica romana: tra mos maiorum e individualismo." In J. Andreau and H. Bruhns, eds., *Parenté et stratégies familiales dans l'antiquité romaine*. Rome, 595–608.
Clemente, G. 2010. "Cicero, Clodio e la censura: la politica e l'ideale." In E. Dovre, ed., *Munuscula : Scritti in ricordo di Luigi Amirante*. Naples, 51–74.
Clemente, G. 2016. "I censori e il senato: i mores e la legge." *Athenaeum*.
Coarelli, F. 1985. *Il foro romano I: Periodo arcaico*. Rome.
Coarelli, F. 1996. *Il Sepolcro degli Scipioni a Roma*. Rome.
Coarelli, F. 2002. "I ritratti di 'Mario' e 'Silla' a Monaco e il sepolcro degli Scipioni." *Eutopia* 2: 47–76.
Cornell, T. 2000. "The Lex Ovinia and the Emancipation of the Senate." In C. Bruun, ed., *The Roman Middle Republic: Religion, Politics, and Historiography c.400–133 B.C.* AIRF 23. Rome, 69–89.
Crawford, M.H., ed. 1996. *Roman Statutes*. BICS suppl. 64. 2 vols. London.
David, J.-M. 1981. "*Maiorum exempla sequi*: L'exemplum historique dans les discours judiciaires de Cicéron." In *Rhétorique et Histoire. Table ronde organise par l' École Française de Rome le 18 mai 1979*. MEFRM 92, 1980, I. Rome, 67–86.
Duplá, A.A. 2011. "*Consules Populares.*" In H. Beck, A.A. Duplá, M. Jehene, and F. Pina Polo, eds., *Consuls and Res Publica: Holding High Office in the Roman Republic*. Cambridge, 279–98.
Dyck, A.R. 2004. *A Commentary on Cicero,* De Legibus. Ann Arbor.
Fantham, E. 1977. "Censorship, Roman Style." *EMC* 21: 41–53.
Farney, G.D. 2007. *Ethnic Identity and Aristocratic Competition in Republican Rome*. Cambridge.
Fentress, J. and C. Wickham. 1992. *Social Memory*. Oxford.

Flaig, E. 1993. "Politisierte Lebensführung und ästhetische Kultur: Eine semiotische Untersuschung am römischen Adel." *Historische Anthropologie* 1: 193–217.

Flaig, E. 1995. "Die Pompa Funebris. Adlige Konkurrenz und annalistische Erinnerung in der Römischen Republik." In O.G. Oexle, ed., *Memoria als Kultur*. Göttingen, 115–148.

Flaig, E. 2003. *Ritualisierte Politik: Zeichen, Gesten und Herrschaft in alten Rom*. Göttingen.

Flaig, E. 2004. "Habitus, Mentalitäten und die Frage des Subjkts: Kulturelle Orientierungen sozialen Handelns." In F. Jaeger, B. Liebsch, J. Rüsen, and J. Straub, eds., *Handbuch der Kulturwissenschaften*. Stuttgart, 3, 356–371.

Flamerie de Lachapelle, G., ed. 2011. *Publius Syrus. Sentences*. Paris.

Flobert, P. 1973. "Mos." *Latomus* 32: 567–569.

Flower, H. 1996. *Ancestor Masks and Aristocratic Power in Roman Culture*. Oxford.

Flower, H. 2004. "Spectacle and Political Culture in the Roman Republic." In H. Flower, ed., *The Cambridge Companion to the Roman Republic*. Cambridge, 322–343.

Gehrke, H.-J. 1994. "Römischer mos und griechische Ethik: Überlegungen zum Zusammenhang von Akkulturation und politischer Ordunung im Hellenismus." *HZ* 258: 593–622.

Gildenhard, I. 2007. *Paideia Romana: Cicero's* Tusculan Disputations. Cambridge.

Habinek, T.N. 1998. *The Politics of Latin Literature: Writing, Identity, and Empire in Ancient Rome*. Princeton.

Hellegouarc'h, J. 1963. *Le Vocabulaire latin des relations et des parties politiques dans la République*. Paris. (2nd edn. 1972.)

Hillard, T. 2013. "Graffiti's Engagement. Political Graffiti of the Late Roman Republic." In G. Sears, P. Keegan, and R. Laurence, eds., *Written Space in the Latin West 200 BC– AD 300*. London.

Hoffmann, Z. 1982. "The Parody of the Idea of *Mos Maiorum* in Plautus." *Oikumene* 3: 217–223.

Hölkeskamp, K.-J. 1987. *Die Entstehung der Nobilität*. Stuttgart.

Hölkeskamp, K.-J. 1996. "*Exempla* und *mos maiorum*: Überlegungen zum kollektive Gedächtnis der Nobilität." In H.-J. Gehrke and A. Möller, eds., *Vergangenheit und Lebenswelt: Soziale Kommunikation, Traditionsbildung und historisches Bewußtsein*. Tübingen, 301–338.

Hölkeskamp, K.-J. 2001. "Capitol, Comitium und Forum. Öffentliche Räume, sakrale Topographie und Erinnerungslandschaften der röischen Republik." In S. Faller, ed., *Studien zu antiken Identitäten*. Würzburg, 97–132.

Hölkeskamp, K.-J. 2005. "Images of Power: Memory, Myth, and Monuments in the Roman Republic." (Review of P. Holliday, *The Origins of Roman Historical Commemoration in the Visual Arts*, Cambridge 2002.) *SCI* 24: 249–271.

Hölkeskamp, K.-J. 2006a. "History and Collective Memory in the Middle Republic." In N. Rosenstein and R. Morstein-Marx, eds., *A Companion to the Roman Republic*. Oxford, 478–495.

Hölkeskamp, K.-J. 2006b. "Rituali e prospettive 'alla romana'. Nuove prospettive sulla cultura politica dell'eta repubblicana." *StStor* 47: 319–363.

Hölkeskamp, K.-J. 2010. *Reconstructing the Roman Republic: An Ancient Political Culture and Modern Research*. Princeton.

Horsfall, N. 2003. *The Culture of the Roman Plebs*. Bristol.

Jehne, M. 2000. "Jovialität und Freiheit: Zur Institutionalität der Beziehungen zwischen Ober- und Unterschichten in der römischen Republik." In B. Linke and M. Stemmler, eds., *Mos maiorum: Untersuchungen zu den Formen der Identitätsstiftung und Stabilisierung in der römischen Republik. Historia* Einzelschriften 141. Stuttgart, 207–235.

Jehne, M. 2012. "Statutes on Public Powers and Their Relationship to *Mos*." In J.-L. Ferrary, ed., *Leges Publica: La legge nell'esperienza giuridica romana*. Pavia, 405–428.

La Penna, A. 1981. "'Mobilita' dei modelli etici e relativismo dei valori: Da Cornelio Nepote a Valerio Massimo e alla Laus Pisonis." In A. Giardina and A. Schiavone, eds., *Modelli etici, diritto e trasformazioni sociali*. Rome, 83–206.

Lincoln, B. 2000. *L'autorità: Costruzione e corrosione*. Turin.

Lind, L.R. 1979. "The Tradition of Roman Moral Conservatism." In C. Deroux, ed., *Studies in Latin Literature and Roman History 1*. Brussels, 7–37.

Linke, B. and M. Stemmler, eds. 2000. *Mos maiorum: Untersuchungen zu den Formen der Identitätsstiftung und Stabilisierung in der römischen Republik*. Stuttgart.

Lintott, A.W. 1999. *The Constitution of the Roman Republic*. Oxford.

Lintott, A.W. 2008. *Cicero as Evidence: A Historian's Companion*. Oxford.

Litchfield, H.W. 1914. "National *Exempla Virtutis* in Roman Literature." *HSPh* 25: 1–71.

MacDowell, D.M. 1978. *The Law in Classical Athens*. London.

McDonnell, M. 2006. *Roman Manliness: Virtus and the Roman Republic*. Cambridge.

Madgelain, A. 1968. *Recherches sur l'‘imperium’: La loi curiate et auspices d'investiture*. Paris.

Manfedrini, A. 1976. "L'editto, ‘de coercendibus rhetoribus Latinis’ del 92 a.C." *SDHI* 42: 99–148.

Manuwald, G. 2011. *Roman Republican Theatre*. Cambridge.

Meier, C. 1980. *Res publica amissa*. Wiesbaden. (1st edn. 1966, Frankfurt am Main; repr. 1980 with new introduction.)

Miles, G.B. 1988. "*Maiores, Conditores*, and Livy's Perspective on the Past." *TAPA* 118: 185–208.

Mommsen, T. 1887. *Römisches Staatsrecht*. Leipzig.

Morgan, T. 2007. *Popular Morality in the Early Roman Empire*. Oxford.

Morstein-Marx, R. 2004. *Mass Oratory and Political Power in the Late Roman Republic*. Cambridge.

Morstein-Marx, R. 2012. "Political Graffiti in the Late Roman Republic: ‘Hidden Transcripts’ and ‘Common Knowledge.’" In C. Kuhn, ed., *Politische Kommunikation und öffentliche Meinung in der antiken Welt*. Stuttgart, 191–217.

Nicolet, C. 1976. *Le Métier de citoyen dans la Rome républicaine*. Paris.

Nippel, W. 2005. "Das *Staatsrecht* in der Diskussion—von 1871 bis heute." In W. Nippel and B. Seidensticker, eds., *Theodor Mommsens langr Shatten: Das römische Staatsrecht als bleibende Herausforderung für die Forschung*. Hildesheim, 9–60.

North, J.A. 2006. "The Constitution of the Roman Republic." In N. Rosentein and R. Morstein-Marx, eds., *Companion of the Roman Republic*. Oxford, 256–277.

Östenberg, I. 2009. *Staging the World: Spoils, Captives, and Representations in the Roman Triumphal Procession*. Oxford.

Pieri, G. 1968. *L'Histoire du cens jusqu'à la fin de la République romaine*. Paris.

Plumpe, J. 1932. *Wesen und Wirkung der auctoritas maiorum bei Cicero*. Bochum.

Rech, H. 1936. *Mos maiorum: Das Wesen der Tradition im alten Rom*. Diss. Marburg.

Rodolf, H. 1938. *Maiores bei Cicero*. Göttingen.

Roller, M. 2004. "Exemplarity in Roman Culture: The Cases of Horatius Cocles and Cloelia." *CPh* 99: 1–56.

Roller, M. 2009. "The Exemplary Past in Roman Historiography and Culture." In A. Feldherr, ed., *The Cambridge Companion to the Roman Historians*. Cambridge, 214–230.

Roloff, H. 1967. "Maiores bei Cicero." (Diss. Göttingen 1938.) In H. Oppermann, ed., *Romische Wertbegriffe*. Darmstadt, 274–322.

Roseberry, W. 1994. "Hegemony and the Language of Contention." In G.M. Joseph and N. Nugent, eds., *Everyday Forms of State Formation: Revolution and the Negotiation of Rule in Modern Mexico*. London, 355–366.

Scott, J. 1990. *Domination and the Arts of Resistance: Hidden Transcripts*. New Haven.

Scott, J. 1994. "Foreword." In G.M. Joseph and D. Nugent, eds., *Everyday Forms of State Formation. Revolution nd the Negotiation of Rule in Modern Mexico*. London, vii–xii.

Smelser, N. 1962. *Theory of Collective Behaviour*. New York.

Solin, H. 2008. "Introduzione allo studio dei graffiti parietali." In O. Brandt, ed., *Unexpected Voices: The Graffiti in the Cryptoporticus of the Horti sallustiani and Papers from a Conference on Graffiti at the Swedish Institute in Rome 7 March 2003*. Stockholm, 99–124.

Steel, C. 2001. *Cicero, Rhetoric, and Empire.* Oxford.
Steinwenter, A. 1933. "Mores." *RE* 16(1): 290–298.
Suolahti, J. 1963. *The Roman Censors: A Study on Social Structure.* Helsinki.
Tatum, W.J. 1990. "The *Lex Clodia de Censoria Notione.*" *CPh* 85: 34–43.
Thompson, E.P. 1978. "Eighteenth-Century English Society: Class Struggle without Class?" *Social History* 3(2): 133–165.
Toner, J. 2009. *Popular Culture in Ancient Rome.* Cambridge.
van der Blom, H. 2010. *Cicero's Role Models: The Political Strategy of a Newcomer.* Oxford.
Versnel, H.S. 1970. *Triumphus: An Inquiry into the Origin, Development and Meaning of the Roman Triumph.* Leiden.
Wachter, R. 1987. *Altlateinische Inschriften: sprachliche und epigraphische Untersuchungen zu den Dokumenten bis etwa 150 v. Chr.* Bern.
Wallace-Hadrill, A. 1997. "*Mutatio morum*: The Idea of a Cultural Revolution." In T. Habinek and A. Schiesaro, eds., *The Roman Cultural Revolution.* Cambridge, 3–22.
Wallace-Hadrill, A. 2008. *Rome's Cultural Revolution.* Cambridge.
Walter, U. 2004. *Memoria und Res publica: Zur Geschichtskultur im republikanischen Rom.* Frankfurt am Main.
Wieacker, F. 1988. *Römische Rechtsgeschichte.* Munich.
Zadorojnyi, A.V. 2011. "Transcripts of Dissent? Political Graffiti and Elite Ideology under the Principate." In Baird and Taylor 2011, 110–133.
Zafiropoulos, C.A. 2001. *Ethics in Aesop's Fables: The Augustana Collection.* Leiden.
Zevi, F. 1968/9 "Considerazioni sull'elogio di Scipione Barbato." *Studi Miscellanei* 15: 65–73.
Zevi, F. 1999. "Sepulcrum Scipionum." In E.M. Steinby, ed., *Lexicon Topographicum Urbis Romae* 4: 85.

FURTHER READING

In particular for the collection of passages on the *mos,* the best starting point are Rech 1936 and Roloff 1967, both in German. The latter focuses on Cicero's usage of the term, on which more recently H. van der Blom 2010 (in English). Useful also the entry *mores* in *RE* 16(1): 290–298 (in German).

For the normative function exercised by the *mos maiorum* the most illuminating accounts are Wallace-Hadrill 2008 and Bettini 2011 the latter, an English translation from Italian.

On the function fulfilled by the *mos* in Roman society, Bleicken 1975; Wieacker 1988; Flaig 2003; Hölkeskamp 2010 (only the latter in English) as well as the collection of essays in Linke and Stemmler (2000), of which of particular interest are the contributions by Blösel, Stemmler, and Jehne (all in German).

On cultural and social memory in Roman context, Flaig 2004; Hölkeskamp 2005 and 2006a; Bettini 2011. For these labels see Assmann 1992 and Fentress and Wickham 1992. On Roman popular culture and morality, Horsfall 2003 and Morgan 2007; with specific reference to graffiti Zadorojnyi 2011; Morstein-Marx 2012 and Hillard 2013.

On *exempla* as means of transmission of values see Hölkeskamp 1996; Roller 2004 and 2009, on funerary practices Flower 1996 and on Roman public spectacles more in general Flower 2004 and Hölkeskamp 2006b; on triumphs Versnel 1970; Beard 2007 and Östenberg 2009; on education Bloomer 2011; on the topography of the city Hölkeskamp 2001, 2005, and 2006a; on literature and *mos* most penetrating is Habinek 1998; on the censors Suolahti 1963 (in English); Baltrusch 1989 (in German), Astin 1988 (in English); Clemente 2016 (in Italian).

PART VII

Power Relations and Political Groups

CHAPTER 14

The Practice of Politics in Classical Athens, and the Paradox of Democratic Leadership

Robert W. Wallace

1 Politics in Post-Cleisthenic Athens

Classical Athens is the only *polis* where evidence permits some understanding of politics as practiced, and as politics evolved, within and outside of a Greek democratic constitution. From Cleisthenes' foundation of the classical democracy in 508/7 BCE down to 442 (the first and least well documented of three distinct periods of democratic politics), Athens' hereditary aristocracy remained important, as did sometimes violent aristocratic factions, links between great families, elite ideologies, wealth, regionalism, local patronage, local cults, and *philoi*, friends and kin as political allies (see Connor 1971; Bicknell 1972; and Davies 1981, with Rhodes' helpful summations at 1986: 132–136). In these ways Athenian politics of this period shared qualities with the politics of republican Rome, important differences being the greater fragmentation of Athens' elite class, and the ever more dominant role of its *dēmos* (Rauflaub, Ober, and Wallace 2007; Fronda, Chapter 3). We may compare the tradition (Plut. *Them.* 5.6) that in the 480s Themistocles, who "knew every citizen by name," grew powerful by being an impartial arbitrator and thus pleasing the masses, and so got his rival aristocrat Aristeides ostracized (banished for ten years). In these years the assembly ostracized other aristocrats once it decided on directions that they continued to oppose.

In the first of two better-attested episodes of this early period, in the later 460s Athenians divided on questions of enmity with Sparta and expanding democracy by depoliticizing the Areopagus Council, which the Aristotelian *Ath. Pol.* 23 says had come to dominate government. These reforms were promoted by Ephialtes, Pericles, and other progressives, but contested by conservatives including the wealthy aristocrat Cimon, whose politics included generosity to the residents of his "deme" or civic ward (e.g. [Arist.] *Ath. Pol.* 27.3), and whose father Miltiades had won at Marathon. The progressives prevailed, but the struggle was brutal and prolonged. Cimon was prosecuted

A Companion to Greek Democracy and the Roman Republic, First Edition. Edited by Dean Hammer.

by Pericles and Ephialtes and then ostracized, war broke out with Sparta, Ephialtes was murdered, in 458 Aeschylus' *Eumenides* counseled Athenians against civil violence in favor of the rule of law (Wallace 1989: 87–93), and in 457 some aristocrats conspired to overthrow the democracy (Thuc. 1.107.4, 6, 108.1; Plut. *Arist.* 13 reports another such conspiracy in 479).

Between 447 and 443 politics divided again, when Pericles' Acropolis building program was challenged by Thucydides, son of Melesias (not the historian), Athens' last conservative aristocratic leader and Cimon's relative by marriage ([Arist.] *Ath. Pol.* 28.1). According to Plutarch (*Per.* 11.2), Thucydides "did not allow the aristocrats to be scattered and mixed up with the masses [in the Assembly] as before … but by separating and grouping them in a single body he concentrated their strength." (Some scholars believe that Plutarch's source said only that in the assembly Thucydides was surrounded by his friends: see Hansen 1991: 137–138 and 1987: 72–86.) In *Ajax* (444) and *Antigone* (442), Sophocles, himself an aristocrat unfriendly to Pericles, for the only time in classical Athenian drama or rhetoric publicly defended aristocrats—Ajax and Polyneices—who had tried to destroy their own communities. *Ajax* includes harsh words against the corrupt and irrational masses (lines 440–449, 1135–1137, 1247; Wallace 2010), while *Antigone* champions elite *philoi* (family members) ahead of the city and condemns civic laws (e.g. lines 450–457, 522–523, cf. 182–190; Wallace 2013), which conservatives considered tools of the democracy (Wallace 2007b). In 443 Thucydides was ostracized, followed in 442 by Pericles' counselor Damon (Wallace 2004b).

2 "The ruling hand of the *dēmos*" (Aeschylus, *Suppliants* 604)

While inadequate sources obscure much of the history of post-Cleisthenic politics, from the 430s (when we are better informed) the aristocracy, aristocratic ties (Davies 1981: 119–120), *philoi* (Plut. *Per.* 7.5; Connor 1971: 91–101), private wealth (Rhodes 1986: 137–138), local patronage, and factionalism all greatly diminish in importance, and direct democracy has strengthened. What were the ideals and practices of this second period of democratic politics, down to 350 when politics shifted back toward greater authoritarianism, with newly powerful officials and greater authority by the Areopagus Council, which the *dēmos* now mistrusted? (On this brief period of more limited democracy, see Wallace 1989: ch. 7.)

Already from 508/7, the core principle and practice of Athens' *dēmokratia* ("people-rule") was that the assembled citizens govern, freely, equally, and when they felt like it noisily, through majority voting by a show of hands, and with the authority to decide almost every important question facing the community (see e.g. Arist. *Pol.* 1317b5–18a3, and on assembly hubbub Tacon 2001; Wallace 2004a). Assembly speeches dominate the pages of Thucydides, keenest analyst of later fifth-century politics. The Aristotelian *Ath. Pol.* thus summarizes Athens' post-403 polity: "the people have made themselves supreme in all fields; they run everything by decrees of the assembly and by decisions of the courts in which the people are supreme" (41.2). Before assembly meetings—at a minimum, every nine days throughout the year—public slaves dragged ropes dripping with red paint through the *agora*, driving citizens up to the Pnyx where the *dēmos* gathered (Aristoph. *Ach.* 22, 54–57, etc.). Notices of special assemblies (*kataklesiai*) were disseminated through the countryside. Fourth-century Athens compensated thousands of assembly-goers for time away from work, as it had compensated 6,000 jurors since the 450s. True, the Pnyx itself held only some 6,000 people, while adult male citizens numbered 30,000–40,000. Factors affecting assembly participation included individuals' interest in politics and how far they lived from town, farming schedules, and military campaigns, naval or land (compare to Mouritsen, Chapter 9). When progressives voted against the Areopagus in 462/1, Cimon was away helping Sparta with 4,000 middlingly prosperous hoplites. In 411 when the assembly voted to abolish democracy, Athens' fleet, manned by poorer citizens, was at Samos (Thuc. 8.53–54). If older citizens and urban non-farming residents were typically well represented among assembly attendees, the political implications of this are unclear, and the assembly's composition changed every meeting, not least during the Peloponnesian War (431–404 BCE) when the entire population might be within city walls. After political leadership opened to non-aristocrats in the 430s, many elites disdained political engagement (Carter 1986; see below).

Yet notwithstanding the assembly's limited size and shifting composition, Athens was a direct not a representative democracy. Except when electing generals and treasurers (offices respectively requiring competence and honesty), assemblies voted on proposals, not people. Political leaders there were, called *rhētores*, "speakers," *hoi politeuomenoi*, "politicians," or *symbouloi*, "counselors" (see below). However, leadership meant persuading the assembly on each issue. Many ordinary citizens participated actively in assemblies, following democratic ideals of "equal" and "frank speech" (*isēgoria*, *parrhēsia*: Hansen 1984; Rhodes 1995: 159–160; Wallace 2004a). Every assembly opened with the herald's call, "Who wishes to speak?" Isocrates notes that sometimes the wisest speakers miss the point and an ordinary citizen, "deemed of little account and generally ignored," comes up with a good idea and is judged to speak the best (12.248). The Demosthenic *exordia*—model openings of assembly speeches—show how ordinary Athenians might address their peers. *Exordion* 13 begins:

> Perhaps it might seem offensive, Athenians, if a private citizen and one of the many like you, should come forward after others who are eminent for long political experience and reputation have already stated their opinions, and say that he thinks the others are not only wrong but not even close to discerning what ought to be done. Nevertheless, I feel so confident that I shall give more profitable counsel than theirs that I shall not hesitate to declare all they have said to be worthless.

For the *dēmos*, shouting speakers down, even having them dragged off the speaker's platform, was democratic freedom. Demosthenes mentions that when he tried to counter his rival Aeschines in an assembly in 346, "Aeschines and Philocrates posted themselves on either side of me and kept shouting and interrupting, and finally jeering at me. You were all laughing, you would not listen to me … and by the gods I think your feelings were quite natural" (19.23–24). The opening scene of Aristophanes' *Acharnians* echoes the rowdiness of democratic assemblies. All citizens could speak, but none could demand to be heard through, a tyrant's pleasure (Soph. *Ant.* 690–92; Thuc. 8.66.1; Lys. 12.73–75), when the public had enough of him.

Then, having voted, citizens rallied behind their decisions, even if Demosthenes complains that they did not always act on them (e.g. 4.19, 20, 30; Mader 2006) and Aeschines protests that illegitimate *proedroi* presiding over assemblies put illegal motions to a vote (3.3). Greek peoples had long hated violent conflicts by rival aristocrats, beginning with *Iliad*'s dispute over prestige (*timē*) between Agamemnon and Achilles, "which put pains thousandfold upon the Achaeans" (*Il.* 1.2). From the 430s Athenian politics was largely free of the ongoing corrosive public discord typical of Greek elite (and contemporary representative) governments, where politicians remain in permanent opposition until retaking power. Political violence now disappears, except by anti-democratic aristocrats at the end of the fifth century. Ostracisms also largely disappear, and after late fifth-century elite violence, the democracy embraced and mostly lived by the ideology of *homonoia*, "concord" (Funke 1980), although certainly major issues roiled fourth-century Athens, including navy finance and foreign relations with Persia, other *poleis*, and the rising power of Macedon. Assembly decisions began, "It seemed best to the people," not "to a majority." Thucydides seems to imply that assembly-goers did not sit in organized groups (6.13.1: see Dover in Gomme, Andrewes, and Dover 1970, ad loc.). If later assemblies reopened an issue for further debate (e.g. Thuc. 3.16.4–49.2; 6.14), the community rallied behind any new decision. Decisions reflected and furthered not competing factions but community interests, a dominant ideology (e.g. Sinclair 1988: 188–190).

It is therefore judged "uncontroversial" that democratic Athens "pushed to the limit" the principle that assemblies govern. "Smaller bodies had extremely little power of decision, and men in an official position had very little power to direct the assembly; so there was nothing that could be called 'the government', in contrast to the citizen body" (Rhodes 1995: 154). If "canvassing, persuasion, exchange of services, rewards and benefits, alliances and deals are the essential techniques of politics in real life, in every known political society" (Finley 1983: 51, in a chapter called "Politics"), direct popular government explains why most of these techniques were far less visible and important in democratic Athens. From the 420s, dissent from democracy mostly happened in private, and in written texts not for public dissemination (Ober 1998). Finley's comment better suits the practices of republican Rome, as Jeffrey Tatum shows in Chapter 15 of this volume. Whatever the power of *contiones*, Rome was always far from democratic.

3 Politics Outside the Assembly

Within the framework of assembly primacy, other elements of Athens' democratic polity, formal and informal, affected the practice of politics. Of political institutions, most important were the Council of 500 and city officials. The Council of 500 was chosen each year by lot, from men over 30 who had not served more than twice (most served only once), from across Attica. It met every non-festival day, and most meetings were open to non-members. Addressing "complaints that it is impossible to get a matter dealt with by the council or assembly although one waits for a year," the "Old Oligarch" (Ps.-Xenophon, *Ath. Pol.*) details some of the council's busy schedule. In addition to organizing festivals, conducting numerous private and public lawsuits, and scrutinizing archons (chief officials) and incoming councilors, "it has multifarious business to deal with, concerning war, revenue, legislation, the day-to-day affairs of the city and matters affecting the allies, receiving the tribute, and looking after the dockyards and shrines" (3.1–2). The council conducted much of the daily administration of *polis* affairs (Rhodes 1972: 88–207), a year-long, full-time job for 500 citizens, although Demosthenes (22.35–36) distinguishes between more and less active councilors, and attendance was not mandatory. Although we hear few details about council meetings, these too may sometimes have been rowdy. In the fifth century, Scythian archers (Athens' police) maintained order (Aristoph. *Knights* 665), and the Council House had a hearth where people could flee for safety (Rhodes 1972: 32).

Although the "Old Oligarch" ignores it, a major council task was debating and fixing the assembly's agenda. Politicians and foreign ambassadors often addressed it. Council decisions had a marked impact on assembly votes (Sinclair 1988: 84–105, a superb discussion). However, no source indicates that it was thought to compromise assembly government, or that it opposed assembly decisions once made (Hansen 1991: 138–140; Rhodes 1972: 82–85; Sinclair 1988: 84–105). Thucydides barely mentions the council (Hornblower 2008: 23–31). Assemblies could amend council motions; they could direct the council to discuss any issue; and they decided. Councilors will normally have had a good sense of public attitudes. In addition, serving in the council taught thousands of citizens about governing, useful for lifelong assembly participation.

Was the council subject to improper influence? Only weak evidence indicates that individual councilors or *prytaneis* (the council's executive committee) might be bribed to introduce measures to the council or assembly (Hdt. 9.5 [479 BCE]: a possibility; [Lys.] 6.29: an accusation; cf. [Lys.] 20.7). In Aristophanes' *Peace* 905–908 (a comedy), probably the chairman of the *prytaneis* took money to introduce something to the council (see also Aristoph. *Thesm.* 936–938). Addressing complaints that the council was too busy "to settle everyone's business," the "Old Oligarch" continues the passage I have quoted: "Some say that if you approach the council or assembly with money, you will transact your business. I would agree that money plays a considerable part in getting things done in Athens, and it would be even more influential if more people employed it. However, I am absolutely sure that the city could not deal with all the requests that come before it, however much gold or silver was offered" (3.3). Many think this passage alludes to bribery (e.g. Rhodes 1972: 112), and a law at Dem. 46.26 criminalizes bribing the assembly, council, or courts. A word for bribing, *dekazein* meaning "to ten," may refer to bribing groups of ten (such as boards of officials, see below) or larger groups (Harvey 1985: 88–89). Yet while hostile to Athens' democracy, the "Old Oligarch" does not suggest that bribing councilors was a serious problem. A council decree specifies that any honor and must have spoken and acted "without taking bribes" (*IG* II^2 A 5, cf. 11). In Aristophanes' *Knights* 615–682, the Sausage-Seller ends by bribing the councilors with coriander and onions (a joke). Neither passage need reflect much more than the Athenians' ready fear of corruption.

Although citizens who volunteered to stand for membership in the council were chosen by lot, some major politicians managed to become councilors in politically important years: Cleon in 427/6 when the fate of Mytilene was debated; Hyperbolus in 421/20 after Cleon died; Demosthenes in 347/6 (Aeschines 3.62 alleges by a bribe) when Athens made a peace treaty with Philip of Macedon. On the other hand, while local demes superintended council appointments, [Arist.] *Ath. Pol.* 62.1 is evidence that these appointments were not thought corrupt. In 410 after the collapse of a brief aristocratic junta, the Athenians legislated that seating in the council be determined by lot (Philochorus *FGH* 324 fr. 140). This suggests that under the junta, seating had been politicized. Nothing indicates such politicization for democratic councils.

Athens' hundreds of officials were called *archai*, "powers," and some *archai* were very powerful indeed. Notably, prison officials called "the Eleven"—ordinary citizens chosen by lot—were obligated to execute certain types of criminals on the spot if they confessed, even to the offense of cloak-stealing. Above all, Athens' ten elected generals were powerful, and could be re-elected. Many fifth-century politicians were generals, seeking to exploit this ongoing public platform and the glory of military command, although many generals were politically unimportant (Hansen 1991: 268–271). In principle and fact, the generals' main task was carrying out assembly instructions.

All *archai* were protected against physical violence and verbal abuse in the performance of their duties. At the same time, as a danger to "people-rule," most"powers" were carefully constituted to be politically insignificant (Wallace 2005). Athens filled most *archai* by lot (a hallmark of Greek democracies [Arist. *Rhet.* 1365b30–31] and on which see Farrar 2010), most *archai* were annual and constituted in boards (often of ten), and iteration was mostly forbidden. *Archai* swore to obey the laws, and many laws consisted of instructions specifying what *archai* could do. They were subject to scrutinies, before, during, and after their terms of office, and they could be prosecuted by *eisangelia*, "summoning," before the assembly or council. Penalties could be severe (for generals see Knox 1985; Hamel 1998: ch. 8; and Hansen 1975, also for other *archai*). Several speeches stress that *archai* should not oppress the people but treat citizens "gently," *praōs* (e.g. Dem. 22.51).

According to Thucydides (8.54.4), "groups bound by oath" (*xunōmosiai*) existed in and before 415, "for lawsuits and offices [*archai*]." Plato (*Tht.* 173d) mentions *hetaireiai* (secret societies) "for offices." Lysias 19.57 claims that some men spent money to gain office, hoping "to carry off twice as much." As the generalship was Athens' most important elected office, generals' elections may have been subject to manipulation by private groups, possibly by discouraging some men from seeking office, or by generating negative publicity. The significance of any such activities is uncertain. Already in the Peloponnesian War (when these groups were active) most politicians were not generals, now necessarily professionalized (B. Mitchell 1991: 172–173, 185–189), although politicians and generals often collaborated. For fourth-century generalships Athens' great families retained an importance which they had lost in politics, because private wealth was needed now to perform this office properly, when the state was comparatively poor (Davies 1981: 124–131; Hansen 1983: 49–52).

Citizens were divided into ten tribes and 139 demes; trainee soldiers (ephebes) and later the army were mobilized by age groups. Rhodes (1986: 135–136) collects the evidence that fellow tribesmen, fellow demesmen, and "contemporaries" (*hēlikiōtai*, men of the same age), might normally support each other in court. Nothing shows that they did so in politics, except during the aristocratic junta of 404 (Lys. 12.43–44, 20.11–12). Nothing indicates that phratries or *genē* ("clans"), to which most citizens belonged, had any political importance.

For Athens, political "parties" still haunt the pages of translated Greek. The Greeks had nothing like modern political parties, with party leaders and long-term policies that registered members are expected to support (Connor 1971: 5–9). According to Thucydides and others, during the Peloponnesian War various *poleis* were divided into factions, democrats favoring Athens and oligarchs Sparta (Thuc. 1.19, 126, 3.82.1, 8.64–65; "Old Oligarch" 1.14, 16, 3.10–11; Arist. *Pol.* 1307b; Diod. Sic. 13.47.8). At Athens, except during two aristocrat-led juntas, pro-Spartan oligarchs played no role in politics.

In the 340s, Demosthenes complained that Philip of Macedon "forced" his Athenian supporters to have friends and enemies "as seems best to him" (19.225–226). Demosthenes also complained to the assembly, "you conduct your politics by companies. Each company has a *rhētōr* as leader, a general under him, and 300 men to shout" (2.29 = 13.20). The reality behind these complaints is uncertain. Mitchell (Mitchell and Rhodes 1996: 11–20) describes the shifting, fractured nature of fourth-century political ties. Although conservatives including the "Old Oligarch" (1.1–9) complained that poor men dominated the assembly, Athenian government was mostly free of class conflict, mainly because everyone politically active played democracy's game (Ober 1989). Most times, each person voted on issues as seemed best to him, free from direct pressures by polarized groups. The alternative was *stasis*, literally "standing" or "position," and meaning faction and civil war.

As I have mentioned, from the 420s some elites ignored city politics. During the Peloponnesian War, anti-democratic dissent was linked to *hetaireiai* which rejected democratic politics, not least because defeating commoners—or being defeated by them—brought no prestige (*timē*), and the *dēmos* was fed up with aristocratic rivalries. These groups' conspiracies against Athens' democracy ([Arist.] *Ath. Pol.* 34.3) led to two brief and violent juntas, in 411 and 404. The restored democracy forgave most of these oligarchs but banned anti-democratic *hetaireiai* (Hyp. 4.7–8; [Dem.] 46.26; Pecorella Longo 1971). Henceforth, anti-democrats in public mostly ceased criticizing democracy. Only Socrates, teacher of some of Athens' murderous oligarchs and apparently himself aristocratic (his sons and wife Xanthippe had aristocratic names), continued to condemn democracy when such talk was dangerous treason.

From the 430s, elite families were of minimal political importance. Instead, contemporary texts show families fractured along generational lines (Strauss 1993: 132–136, and generally 130–178; Forrest 1975), as with *Antigone*'s Creon and Haimon, or *Clouds*' Strepsiades and Pheidippides. Pericles' relations with his sons were fraught (Plut. *Per.* 16.4, 36.1–6). After Plato *Apology* 41e, we never hear again of Socrates' three sons. In addition, Athens or Greece never had anything like Roman *clientela* or patronage by elite citizens, as Greeks would not be subordinate to richer or more powerful men (Millett 1989: 43; de Ste. Croix 1981: 181–186; Xen. *Mem.* 2.8; Arist. *Rhet.* 1367a 32; Isaeus 5.39, Isocr. 14.48; Dem. 57.45).

How far did Athens' courts assume political functions? Laws were administered in courts staffed by hundreds of *dikastai*, lay judges/jurors both chosen and assigned by lot to court cases. Dikasts took laws seriously, but verdicts, unrecorded, could not serve as precedent and no judge instructed the dikasts as to what laws meant or which were relevant: no individual should exercise so much power. Discussion among dikasts was forbidden, to prevent corruption. Case by case, each dikast judged as "seemed most just" to him, often in the light of community interests. Recent scholarship on how far Athens respected the rule of law has been contentious. My belief is that courts wanted to enforce laws while also guarding the community of citizens, law's purpose (Wallace 2007a). In the fourth century, many legal cases were political or politically motivated. *Graphai paranomōn*, indictments for illegal measures, were often deployed against political enemies. The fourth-century politician Aristophon's acquittal seventy-five times in such cases suggests that courts did not wish to contravene assembly decisions.

Many Athenians participated in assemblies and deme governments, served in the council, courts, and public offices, and fought in Athens' army and navy across Greece and beyond. Conservative charges that they were ignorant (e.g. Thuc. 6.1; Plato *Crit.* 47a–48a) are largely unfounded.

4 Athens' Democratic Paradox

The assembly was at the center of Athens' democracy, and the assembly mostly voted on proposals, not individuals. However, proposals were advanced or opposed by individuals, some of whom spoke sufficiently often that in the fourth century they were formally and legally designated *rhētores*. Beginning with seventh-century tyrants, the Greeks had long recognized the dangers of powerful individuals. Already in the early sixth century Solon warned the Athenians, "exalted men portend the city's death: the folk in innocence fall slave to tyranny. Raise them too high, and it's not easy afterward to hold them" (fr. 9 and trans. West). In 508/7 the new democracy introduced ostracism, to banish overly potent individuals who threatened popular rule. Its first victim was Hipparchus, a relative of Athens' tyrant Peisistratus. In 489 Miltiades voided democratic control by convincing the assembly to let him command an independent fleet. He was later prosecuted for "deceiving the people" by Pericles' father Xanthippus, and heavily fined (Hdt. 6.132–136). In the 480s the *dēmos* began choosing archons by lot, not election, partly to prevent ambitious men from controlling important offices.

It is therefore paradoxical that from the 430s, precisely when Athens' democracy was most fully developed, assemblies sometimes followed leaders whose opinions carried weight and so could sometimes mislead them.

The terms *prostatēs tou dēmou* and *dēmagōgos*, both meaning "leader of the people," epitomize and date this democratic paradox. In panhellenic contexts, *prostatēs tou dēmou* first occurs in Herodotus' constitutional debate (3.82.4), written perhaps in the 430s, where Darius says that in democracies cliques arise until "some leader of the people" (*prostas tis tou dēmou*) makes himself tyrant. The term becomes common in Thucydides during the Peloponnesian War: in 3.75.2 and 4.46.4 at Corcyra, 3.82.1 in Greece generally, 4.66.3 at Megara, 6.35.2 for Athenagoras at Syracuse, 8.89.4, cf. 6.89.4, where Alcibiades says that his family has long held the *prostasia* at Athens. Thucydides presents post-Periclean Athenian politics as a contest for *prostasia* of the people (2.65.11, 6.28.2, 8.89.3: see Connor 1971: 111–115). "Leading the *dēmos*" was limited to progressive democrats including Pericles and Cleon, the arch-"demagogue" of the 420s for Thucydides and Aristophanes. *Prostatai* of the *gnōrimoi* ("notables," conservatives) are first attested in the Aristotelian *Ath. Pol.* of the 320s. Earlier fourth-century sources (e.g. Plato) make the conservative democrat Cimon a *prostatēs* of the people (Rhodes 1993: 345), although he is too early and conservative for that title. Conservatives among themselves tolerated no *prostatēs*, because as both Herodotus (3.82.3) and Thucydides (8.89) explain, elite conservatives each wanted to be top dog and fought violently with rivals if he was not (compare Themistocles and Aristeides earlier in this chapter, and Militades and Xanthippus). The masses supported *prostatai* and demagogues partly as a counterweight to powerful conservatives and oligarchs, just as they had supported early tyrants (Wallace 2009).

Democratic politicians gained power and influence in the assembly through skillful speaking; hence, the designation *rhētores*. Thucydides calls both Cleon and Athenagoras "most persuasive" with the masses (3.36.6, 4.21.3, 6.35.20). In 424, targeting Cleon,

Aristophanes' *Knights* 626–629 confirms rhetoric's political importance. Starting in the second half of the fifth century, some politicians trained in the new art of rhetoric, gaining advantage over rival speakers.

To protect and divert attention from their influence in the assembly, leading politicians often used surrogates, something the *dēmos* disliked. According to Plutarch (*Arist.* 3), Aristeides often "introduced his assembly measures through other men, so that Themistocles might not be driven by the spirit of rivalry to oppose what was advantageous." At the turn of the century Andocides complained that politicians do not dare to "stand in the middle, fearing refutation," but "send others who are shameless" (2.4).

As Athens lacked a civil service, politicians' administrative and financial skills may have been a further source of assembly influence. Rhodes (1986: 141 with n. 119) and Hornblower (1991: 344–347) discuss the argument by Andrewes, Finley, and others, how far Pericles and the "demagogues" owed their success to the "mastery of finance and administration." Aristophanes attributes to demagogues a preoccupation in collecting the tribute from Athens' allies (e.g. *Knights* 312; *Wasps* 671). Plutarch notes that after Pericles' death the demagogues succeeded in raising the tribute (*Arist.* 24). Later, in Xenophon's *Memorabilia* (3.6.2–18), Socrates says that *prostatai* need to know how to increase the city's revenue and reduce excessive expenditures, to understand the city's and its enemies' strengths, and to maintain Athens' silver mines and the grain supply. Rhodes argues that such expertise represents a change from the fifth century.

Wealth continued to help build political influence, through private loans, liturgies (trierarchies and choruses), and possibly also prestigious, costly victories in panhellenic games (but compare Rhodes 1986: 137). Many Athenian leaders were wealthy. Our sources also mention individual canvassing by politicians. According to Plutarch (*Nic.* 9.5), Nicias canvassed individuals to support his peace with Sparta. According to Thucydides (8.53.2), Peisander solicited individuals to support Alcibiades' recall (Xen. *Hell.* 2.3.23).

Although the Athenians sometimes followed political leaders, they were aware of their dangers, especially through "clever speech" (see e.g. Eur. *Supp.* 417–425; Ober 1989: 165–174; above all Hesk 2000). Assemblies began with a curse against "deceiving the people" (Aristoph. *Thesm.* 356–367; Dem. 18.282, 23.97). In what is itself a brilliantly clever, often perverse speech, Thucydides has Cleon praise "ignorance with temperance" over "skillfulness with license," warning the assembly that more intelligent people seek to dominate public debates but bring ruin on cities; cleverness (*deinotēs*) can be inconsistent with good judgment (3.37.3–5). Thucydides later says that the sophist Antiphon never spoke in public because he was mistrusted for cleverness (8.68.1). In the fourth century Aeschines calls Demosthenes "the pirate of politics, who sails on his craft of words over the sea of state" (3.253, cf. 35.40–43). Demosthenes retorts that Aeschines "bids you be on your guard against me, for fear that I should mislead and deceive you, calling me a clever speaker, a mountebank, a sophist and so forth." Demosthenes admits his *deinotēs*, which he calls "experience" and says he uses it only to benefit the *dēmos* (18.276–277).

Assemblies sometimes punished those who gave "bad advice" (see the "Old Oligarch" 2.17; Thuc. 8.1.1 after Sicily; Xen. *Hell.* 1.7.35 after Arginousai). Athens' democracy was (and still is) criticized for such punishments, because the *dēmos* had voted for the advice given. The *dēmos* wants to share the credit when things turn out well, but not the blame when things turn out badly: Thuc. 2.60.4, 61.2, 64.1. However, for the *dēmos* these men had harmed the community, Athens' most serious offense. The speaker of [Lysias] 20.20

observes, "Even when one of our citizens here persuades you with mischievous advice, it is not you who are to blame, but your deceiver."

The *dēmos* enacted various legal measures to punish bad politicians, most powerfully *eisangelia*, a "summoning" before assembly or council especially on charges of bribery. According to Hypereides 4 *Euxenippos* 7–8, someone might be "summoned" who, "being a *rhētor*, does not speak what is best for the people of Athens, taking money and gifts from those acting contrary to the people." According to Aeschines (3.214), if anyone made a profit from addressing the assembly, he might be prosecuted by *eisangelia* or *probolē* (another type of summons) or *graphē* (public indictment) to the *thesmothetai*, a board of six archons (see also Hyp. 3.7–8; [Arist.] *Ath. Pol.* 43.5; Dem. 46.26). If a *rhētor* said something judged not to be in Athens' best interest, why should he have done so, unless some dastardly foreigner had paid him? However, bribery was complicated not least because gift-giving was traditional, especially among the upper classes. Gabriel Herman's book on ritualized friendship shows how *dora*, gifts between friends (both terms were often construed politically) could be viewed as bribes (1987: chs. 4–5). *Xenia*, "guest friendship," formalized assisting foreigners with ties to elite families, sometimes in war when such conduct could seem treasonous (Harvey 1985:106–111; Herman 1987; L. Mitchell 1997; Sinclair 1988: 179–186). Ambassadors were frequently accused of treason for corruption or other misconduct (*parapresbeia*), although again ancestral ties of *xenia* and gift-giving could be misunderstood (Perlman 1976; Herman 1987: ch. 4 and 156–161; L. Mitchell 1997). We may compare Hypereides 5.24–25 (cf. 1.24–25) that the *dēmos* tolerated generals and *rhētores* "making large personal profits" provided the money was spent in the *dēmos*' interest. Finally, as noted, anyone proposing a law or decree was subject to a *graphē paranomōn*, if someone attacked his proposal as inconsistent with current law.

Despite concerns, however, assemblies might follow the judgment of persuasive leaders, rather than their own. The dangers of doing so are best illustrated not by Cleon, who has long been redeemed (see e.g. B. Mitchell 1991 and Woodhead 1960), but by Athens' most famous *prostatēs tou dēmou*, Pericles, whose favorable reputation (we shall see) partly reflects Thucydides' elitist, anti-democratic admiration and attraction for strong generals. At once "of the foremost family and lineage on both sides" (Plut. *Per.* 3.1) and by birth and ideology democratic (his mother was Cleisthenes' niece), Pericles, powerful since the later 460s, was elected general and dominated Athens' government for fifteen years from 443 to his death in 429. The scholarly consensus regarding Pericles' power in this later period appears to be that, while he could not count on prevailing in any particular assembly, he generally guided the direction of Athenian public policy. Although Thucydides sharply contrasts him with later "demagogues," [Aristotle] followed by Finley notes that Pericles "first acquired political influence by prosecuting Cimon for malfeasance in office; he energetically pursued a policy of naval power, 'which gave the lower classes the audacity to take over the leadership in politics more and more'; and he introduced pay for jury service, thus bribing the people with their own money" ([Arist.] *Ath. Pol.* 27, quoted and paraphrased by Finley 1974: 3). Plutarch writes that unlike Thucydides, "many others [including Plato] say that the *dēmos* was first led on by [Pericles] into allotments of public lands, festival grants, and distributions of pay for public services, thereby falling into bad habits, and becoming luxurious and unbridled under the influence of his public measures, instead of temperate and self-sufficing" (*Per.* 9.1). While different prejudices drive all these ancient judgments, Pericles probably led Athens' transition from old- to new-style democratic politics by giving up his *philoi* (Plut. *Per.* 7.5) and *xenia* ties with Sparta's king Archidamos (Plut. *Per.* 33.1–3; Thuc. 2.13.1), by cultivating the *dēmos* as a whole and not his local deme (Plut. *Per.* 9.2–3 and esp. 11.4–6, 34.2), and by improving his oratorical skills for assembly debates (Thuc. 1.139.4). According to Plato (who scorned democracy), he acquired from the philosopher Anaxagoras' "idle prattling" (*adoleschia*) the mental elevation and finished execution needed for success in rhetoric (*Phdr.* 269e–270a; cf. Plut. *Per.* 5, 8). The comic poet Eupolis' *Demes* of 412 BCE (fr. 102 *PCG*) remembered the power of Pericles' oratory: "Speed marked his words, and persuasion sat upon his lips. Thus he charmed, and alone among the *rhētores* he left his sting behind in his hearers."

Plutarch also notes how frequently Pericles used associates in the assembly. "He did not choose to speak on every question, but reserved himself … for great occasions, and allowed his friends and other *rhētores* to deal with other matters" (*Per.* 7.7–8, also 9.5). In *Precepts of Statecraft* 811c–813a he quotes from a contemporary comedy criticizing the architect Metiochos, who is a "general" and "inspects the roads," "the bread," "the flour," and "takes care of all things," and "who will come to grief" (Adesp. 741 *PCG*). Plutarch comments, "He was one of Pericles' *hetairoi*, and used the power he got through him, it seems, in such a way as to arouse odium and disgust."

In Thucydides' judgment, Pericles, by his abilities, reputation, and incorruptibility, "held down the masses freely and led them rather than they led him." Hence, Athens "was in name a democracy but in fact rule by the first man" (2.65.8–9). Others put a darker spin on Pericles' regime. After 443, comic playwrights accused Pericles and his *hetairoi* of being *Peisistratidai*, "sons" of Athens' tyrant Peisistratus, and "urged Pericles to swear not to become a tyrant, because his pre-eminence was too oppressive and incommensurate with democracy" (Plut. *Per.* 16.1). Plutarch quotes Telecleides that "the Athenians had handed over" to Pericles control of the empire. In *Cheirones* Cratinus labeled Pericles the "greatest tyrant" and son of civil strife, *stasis* (fr. 258 *PCG*). In 442 Sophocles' *Antigone* features Creon, a general (*stratēgos*, line 8) who becomes increasingly tyrannical (506–507, 739, 757) during the course of the play. Creon's opening speech, "I could never make that man a friend [*philos*] who is hostile to our country, knowing this, that our country *is* our safety. Only when it sails upright can we establish true friendships" (187–190, see also 182–183), many have thought echoes Thucydides' Pericles: "when the whole *polis* is upright it is a better thing for each individual than when personal interests are satisfied but the *polis* as a whole is going downhill" (2.60.2; see Wallace 2013: 16 and references). Sophocles' Oedipus in *Oedipus the Tyrant* similarly becomes a tyrannical ruler in the course of that play, and is like Pericles both highly intelligent and skeptical of religion. Working in Athens in these years and himself anti-democratic, Herodotus also seems to consider Pericles a tyrant (see e.g. Moles 2002: 41–42). According to Plutarch (*Per.* 7.1), the young Pericles seemed to resemble Peisistratus the tyrant, "and as his voice was sweet and his tongue glib and speedy in speaking, old men were amazed at the resemblance." Pericles was the first man "able to do what he liked [another tyrant's pleasure] in the city and all over Greece and among many great nations of the barbarians" (Plut. I *Alc.* 104b). So too, in historical fact beautifying cities by public works as Pericles did on the Acropolis, was characteristic of Greek tyrants.

To assess the consequences of Pericles' persuasive leadership, we may briefly consider his role in bringing on the Peloponnesian War. After thirty years fighting Persians and Spartans followed by Cimon's death in 450, Athens made peace with Persia in 449 and with Sparta in 446. Plutarch (*Per.* 19–28) sketches out Pericles' many later military actions, against the Chersonese, against a revolt in Euboea, and against Samos from 440 to 437, a war against Greeks for which he wrote the authorizing decree and many thought he had personal reasons, as his long-time companion Aspasia came from Samos' enemy, Miletos. Around 436 he led an expedition to the Black Sea with 600 colonists. For reasons we shall see, Thucydides ignores or minimizes Pericles' role in these conflicts.

For the Peloponnesian War, Thucydides narrates two immediate causes at length: Athens' military engagements with Sparta's ally Corinth first over Corcyra (1.24–55) and then over Potidaea (1.56–65). He does not mention, as Plutarch does, that Pericles spoke in support of helping Corcyra against Corinth, and then was much criticized for sending Corcyra only ten ships, which gave Athens' enemies "a great pretext for war" (*Per.* 29.1–2). By contrast, other sources, including Aristophanes' *Acharnians* (515–556) and Plutarch (*Per.* 29–31), say that the most important cause of the war was Athens' Megarian Decree, which excluded Sparta's ally Megara from most commercial activity and which most sources, including *Acharnians* 532, attribute to Pericles. Later in Book 1 Thucydides agrees about Megara. As he writes in 1.139.1, the Spartans repeatedly sent embassies to Athens asking the Athenians to withdraw from Potidaea and give Aegina its independence. "Above all they declared in plainest terms that they could avoid war only by rescinding the decree about the Megarians ... But the Athenians paid no heed." Plutarch is more specific about Pericles' role. Because of Sparta's many embassies, as King Archidamus

> tried to resolve most of the accusations of Sparta's allies and to soften their anger, it does not seem probable that the war would have come upon the Athenians for any remaining reasons, if only they had been persuaded to rescind the Megarian Decree and be reconciled with them. And therefore, since Pericles was most opposed to this and incited the *dēmos* to abide by their contention with the Megarians, he alone was held responsible for the war... All writers agree that Pericles was responsible for not revoking this decree. (*Per.* 29, 31)

The Spartans tried to have Pericles expelled, "thinking that if he were banished, it would be easier for them to gain concessions from the Athenians" (Thuc. 1.126.2–127.2). In 1.127 Thucydides states in his own voice that Pericles "opposed the Spartans in everything and would have no concessions, but ever urged the Athenians on to war."

In the final episode of Thucydides' first book (139–145), the Athenians held an assembly where various points of view for and against the war were expressed. Then Pericles spoke, saying among other points, "Let none of you think we should be going to war for a trifle if we refuse to revoke the Megarian Decree. It is a point they make much of, and say that war need not take place if we revoke this decree" (1.141). The Athenians followed Pericles' advice to go to war. However, Thucydides' Corinthians had already addressed each of his arguments why Athens would win.

Finally, when the war began and was not going well for Athens, Pericles refused to convoke an assembly, lest the *dēmos* "commit some error" (Thuc. 2.22.1), or as Plutarch writes (*Per.* 33.6), lest he be constrained to act against his better judgment. By way of soothing the many who in spite of Sparta's departure from Attica were distressed over the war, he won their favor by distributions of money (*Per.* 34.2). Later that year the *dēmos* again "held Pericles to blame because he had persuaded them to go to war," and actually sent envoys to make peace with Sparta (Thuc. 2.59.2). Pericles persuaded them not to (2.65.2). "You are holding me to blame, who urged you to go to war, and yourselves, who joined in the decision" (2.60.4). Nonetheless they fined him and deposed him from office, until they realized (Thucydides says) that the city was more important than their private sufferings (2.65.3–4). Thucydides is proud that Pericles' rhetoric could cow or cheer the masses (2.65.9).

Although for much of Book 1 (and then 2.65) Thucydides shielded Pericles from blame for the cataclysmic error of provoking this disastrous war, his later comments in Book 1 face facts. Neither the Spartans nor the Athenians wanted to fight. Long aggressive militarily, Pericles provoked the Peloponnesian War by outraging Sparta's allies and then dominating Athens' assembly debates by his formidable rhetorical skills. Accurately but too kindly, Plutarch writes (*Per.* 15.1–2), "He led the *dēmos*, for the most part willingly, by persuading and teaching. And yet there were times when they were most unhappy with him, and then he tightened the reins and forced them into what was advantageous … He showed that rhetoric is, in Plato's words, 'an enchantment of the soul.'" Later Western democracies, too, would come to know such leaders.

5 Conclusions

For the most part Athens' citizen community came together in open debate, to govern their city. They then went out and did what they had voted for, learning from the consequences of their decisions. Every year they watched and discussed nine new tragedies and five new comedies, all highly sophisticated and often political, questioning, challenging, and occasionally celebrating different aspects of Athens' politics and values. At a minimum every nine days they heard major issues debated in the assembly, by thoughtful, articulate speakers, and then they had the power to decide what Athens would do. Over nearly two centuries Athens' democratic government proved remarkably successful, and improved over time. In the end some decisions did not work out; that happens. Some actions have been misrepresented by anti-democratic sources, beginning with Thucydides. Exhibit A for critics is always the Sicilian expedition of 415–413, which worked out poorly. Yet, free of military commitments elsewhere and at the request of Sicilian allies, Athens prudently sent a large and therefore (as they thought) safe expedition guided by three experienced generals with differing strengths and opinions, asking them only to do what was in the city's best interests. Thucydides' assertions that Athens wanted to conquer all Sicily and move against Carthage are contradicted in his own text (e.g. 6.8.4). He complains that Pericles' successors, "being more on a level with each other and each wanting to be first", were ready to surrender to the people "even the conduct of public affairs to suit their pleasures" (2.65.10). Yet so democracy is run—minus Thucydides' anti-democratic inflammatory word (a leitmotif) "pleasure," *hēdonē* (compare 2.53.1 in the plague, and 2.37.2 said by Pericles). The Athenians would have been far better off following their own judgments, without Pericles.

If under Pericles Athens' main troubles lay in the paradox of democratic leadership, later politicians had not his hold over the *dēmos*. Cleon's assembly recommendation in the Mytilenean debate was defeated by the otherwise unknown Diodotus (Thuc. 3.41ff.). No fourth-century *rhētor* achieved any comparable position of dominance (Hansen 1991: 268–271). Central factors in the success of Athens' democracy were its citizens' energy, intelligence, hard work, dedication to others including Athens' allies (cleruchies, promoted by Pericles, were partly an exception), and learning from what had not worked out. Public honor, civic glory, and virtue (*aretē*) were more important to them than individual success, political or financial, when at the expense of others.

Jeffrey Tatum's fine essay (Chapter 15) sets out the basic data to compare and contrast Rome's basically oligarchic government with politics in Athens' post-440 democracy. While the importance at Rome of martial fame, public service, and oratorical brilliance is paralleled in democratic Athens, the accomplishments of ancestors or family, noble status, clients, patronage, *amici*, marriage ties, the exclusion of "new men," and urban violence are mostly not found in post-440 Athens. Although Tatum stresses the importance of popular assemblies in electing magistrates and voting on laws—residue from the debate now ended whether Rome had some kind of democracy—he is clear that magistrates were elected as leaders rather than representing the people (also, the votes of the lower classes were mostly inconsequential, and few people voted); that so far from deciding policy Roman popular assemblies were especially concerned with benefits to the masses such as land or grain; that *contiones* were controlled by magistrates; and that "most of the time," the Senate governed. No Greek government, democratic or oligarchic, had any equivalent to the Roman Senate.

REFERENCES

Bicknell, P.J. 1972. *Studies in Athenian Politics and Genealogy*. Historia Einzelschrift 19. Stuttgart.

Carter, L.B. 1986. *The Quiet Athenian*. Oxford.

Connor, W.R. 1971. *The New Politicians of Fifth-Century Athens*. Princeton.

Davies, J.K. 1981. *Wealth and the Power of Wealth in Classical Athens*. New York.

De Ste. Croix, G.E.M. 1981. *The Class Struggle in the Ancient Greek World: From the Archaic Age to the Arab Conquests*. Ithaca, NY.

Farrar, C. 2010. "Taking our Chances with the Athenians." In M. H. Hansen, ed., *Démocratie athénienne—démocratie moderne: tradition et influences*. Entretiens sur l'Antiquité Classique 56. Vandoeuvres and Geneva.

Finley, M.I. 1973. *Democracy Ancient and Modern*. London.

Finley, M.I. 1974. "Athenian Demagogues." In *Studies in Ancient Society*. London, 1–25; repr. from *P&P* 21 (1962).

Finley, M.I. 1983. *Politics in the Ancient World*. Cambridge.

Forrest, W.G. 1975. "An Athenian Generation Gap." *YCS* 24: 37–52.

Funke, P. 1980. *Homonoia und Arche: Athen und die griechische Staatenwelt vom Ende des Peloponnesischen Krieges bis zum Koenigsfrieden (404/3–387/6 v. Chr.). Historia* Einzelschrift 37. Wiesbaden.

Gomme, A.W., A. Andrewes, and K.J. Dover. 1970. *A Historical Commentary on Thucydides*, vol. 4: *Books V 25–VII*. Oxford.

Hamel, D. 1998. *Athenian Generals. Military Authority in the Classical Period*. Leiden.

Hansen, M.H. 1975. *Eisangelia*. Odense.

Hansen, M.H. 1983. "The Athenian 'Politicians,' 403–322 B.C." *GRBS* 24: 33–55.

Hansen, M.H. 1984. "The Number of *Rhetores* in the Athenian *Ekklesia*, 355–322." *GRBS* 25: 123–155; repr. in *The Athenian Ekklesia II: A Collection of Articles 1983–1989* (Copenhagen, 1989), 93–125.

Hansen, M.H. 1987. *The Athenian Assembly in the Age of Demosthenes*. Oxford.

Hansen, M.H. 1991. *The Athenian Democracy in the Age of Demosthenes: Structures, Principles and Ideology*. Oxford.

Harvey, F.D. 1985. "Dona Ferentes: Some Aspects of Bribery in Greek Politics." In P. Cartledge and F.D. Harvey, eds., *Essays in Greek History Presented to G.E.M. de Ste. Croix*. London, 76–117.

Herman, G. 1987. *Ritualised Friendship and the Greek City*. Cambridge.

Hesk, J. 2000. *Deception and Democracy in Classical Athens*. Cambridge.

Hornblower, S. 1991, 1996, 2008. *A Commentary on Thucydides*, vol. 1: *Books I–III*, vol. 2: *Books IV–V.24*, vol. 3: *Books V.25–VIII*. Oxford.

Knox, R.A. 1985. "'So mischievous a beaste'? The Athenian 'Demos' and its Treatment of its Politicians." *G&R*^{2} 32: 132–161.

Mader, G. 2006. "Fighting Philip with Decrees: Demosthenes and the Syndrome of Symbolic Action." *AJP* 127: 367–386.

Millett, P.C. 1989. "Patronage and its Avoidance in Classical Athens." In A. Wallace-Hadrill, ed., *Patronage in Ancient Society*. London and New York, 15–48.

Mitchell, B. 1991. "Kleon's Amphipolitan Campaign: Aims and Results." *Historia* 40: 170–192.

Mitchell, L.G. 1997. *Greeks Bearing Gifts: the Public Use of Private Relationships in the Greek World, 435–323 B.C.* Cambridge.

Mitchell L.G. and P.J. Rhodes. 1996. "Friends and Enemies in Athenian Politics." *G&R*^{2} 43: 11–30.

Moles, J. 2002. "Herodotus and Athens." In E. Bakker et al., eds., *Brill's Companion to Herodotus*. Leiden, 45–48.

Ober, J. 1989. *Mass and Elite in Democratic Athens*. Princeton.

Ober, J. 1998. *Political Dissent in Democratic Athens: Intellectual Critics of Popular Rule*. Princeton.

Pecorella Longo, C. 1971. *"Eterie" e gruppi politici nell'Atene del IV sec. a.C.* Florence.

Perlman, S. 1976. "On Bribing Athenian Ambassadors." *GRBS* 17: 223–233.

Raaflaub, K.A., J. Ober, and R.W. Wallace. 2007. *Origins of Democracy in Ancient Greece*. Berkeley and Los Angeles.

Rhodes, P.J. 1972. *The Athenian Boule*. Oxford.

Rhodes, P.J. 1986. "Political Activity in Classical Athens," *JHS* 106: 132–144; repr. in Rhodes, ed., *Athenian Democracy* (Edinburgh, 2004), 185–206.

Rhodes, P.J. 1993. *A Commentary on the Aristotelian* Athenaion Politeia. Oxford.

Rhodes, P.J. 1995. "The 'Acephalous' Polis." *Historia* 44: 153–167.

Rhodes, P.J. 2000a. "Who Ran Democratic Athens?" In *Polis and Politics, Studies in Ancient Greek History Presented to M.H. Hansen*. Copenhagen, 465–477.

Rhodes, P.J. 2000b. "Oligarchs in Athens." In P. Flensted-Jensen, R. Brock and S. Hodkinson, eds., *Alternatives to Athens: Varieties of Political Organization and Community in Ancient Greece*. Oxford, 119–136.

Sinclair, R.K. 1988. *Democracy and Participation in Athens*. Cambridge.

Strauss, B. 1993. *Fathers and Sons in Athens: Ideology and Society in the Era of the Peloponnesian War*. London and New York.

Tacon, J. 2001. "Ecclesiastic *Thorubos*: Interventions, Interruptions, and Popular Involvement in the Athenian Assembly." *G&R*^{2} 48(2): 173–192.

Wallace, R.W. 1989. *The Areopagos Council, to 307 B.C.* Baltimore.

Wallace, R.W. 2004a. "The Power to Speak—and Not to Listen—in Ancient Athens." In I. Sluiter and R.M. Rosen, eds., *Free Speech in Classical Antiquity*. Leiden, 221–232.

Wallace, R.W. 2004b. "Damon of Oa—a Music Theorist Ostracized?" In P. Wilson and P. Murray, eds., *Music and the Muses in Ancient Greece*. Oxford, 249–268.

Wallace, R.W. 2005. "'Listening' to the *Archai* in Democratic Athens." In R.W. Wallace and M. Gagarin, eds., *Symposion 2001*. Vienna, 147–158.

Wallace, R.W. 2007a. "Law and Rhetoric: Community Justice in Athenian Courts." In K. Kinzl, ed., *Blackwell Companion to Ancient Greece*. Oxford, 416–431.

Wallace, R.W. 2007b. "Law's Enemies in Ancient Athens." In E. Cantarella and G. Thür, eds., *Symposion 2005, Vorträge zur griechischen und hellenistischen Rechtsgeschichte*. Vienna, 183–196.
Wallace, R.W. 2009. "Charismatic Leaders." In K.A. Raaflaub and H. van Wees, eds., *A Companion to Archaic Greece*. Oxford and Malden, MA, 411–426.
Wallace, R.W. 2010. "Tecmessa's Legacy: Valuing Outsiders in Athens' Democracy." In I. Sluiter and R. Rosen, eds., *Valuing Others in Classical Athens*. Leiden, 137–154.
Wallace, R.W. 2013. "Sophokles' Lucky Day: *Antigone*." *Erga-Logoi* 1: 7–22.
Woodhead, A.G. 1960. "Thucydides' Portrait of Cleon." *Mnesmosyne IV* 13: 289–317.

FURTHER READING

Recommendations for further reading partly depend on readers' tastes. Sinclair 1988 is fine on both politics and institutions. On the Athenian constitution (written only and partly in laws), see above all M. Hansen's monographs, articles, and overview (Hansen 1991). Hansen tends to discount exceptions or irregularities when inconsistent with what other sources (especially Aristotle) set out as rules. M. Finley's essays and books (Finley 1973, 1983) are brilliant, concise to dogmatic (but not to Marxism), and driven by an unparalleled breadth of knowledge and historical vision. Not least on issues pertaining to this chapter, Rhodes' scholarship is superbly documented and judicious, if typically shy of bold new ideas or conclusions. Ober is well worth reading and has been influential, especially for those interested in the less historical field of political science.

CHAPTER 15

The Practice of Politics and the Unpredictable Dynamics of Clout in the Roman Republic

W. Jeffrey Tatum

Whence clout? The Romans' answer, notwithstanding its appearance in different contexts and genres, remained consistent and clear: reputation, not least the distinction conferred by a glorious ancestry, wealth, and extensive personal connections. Our earliest texts celebrate martial fame, public service in high offices, oratorical brilliance, and the devotion of an accomplished family—and of loyal friends and followers (Earl 1967: 11–43; Hölkeskamp 1987; Flower 1996: 91–184). By the late Republic, these constituents of power are at some times catalogued by way of complaint, at others in praise or commendation, but their efficacy is never denied (e.g. *Rhet. Her.* 8; Cic. *Att.* 1.29.7; *Caec.* 57; *Clu.* 94; *Mur.* 69; *Parad.* 46; *Part. or.* 87; *Q. fr.* 1.2.16; *Red. pop.* 3; *Red. sen.* 20; *Sest.* 10; *De rep.* 2.11.3). Esteem continued to be founded on achievement and lineage: *gloria* ("military fame") and *honor* ("high office and honor"), *dignitas* ("prestige") and *nobilitas* ("noble birth"). Wealth enabled its owner to devote himself entirely to duty and gave him the means to lavish benefits and favors on individuals, at every social level, as well as on his community. The resources of a grand family—*cognatorum et adfinium opes, multae clientelae* ("the might of their kindred and relations, the multitude of their clients")—were unassailable advantages to the man who possessed them, as Sallust's Marius resentfully grumbled (*Iug.* 85.4), and a great man's alliances were extensive in their reach: in standard descriptions they include, in addition to clients and freedmen, friends (*amici*), foreign connections (*hospites*), aristocratic fraternities (*sodalitates*), the companies and partnerships of rich equestrians (*societates*), fellow tribesmen (*tribules*), and neighbors (*vicini*). The man who could command and deploy these assets was able, by doing good to others, to shackle them with inevasible debts of gratitude. Indeed, *gratia* ("gratitude") is clout—in its purest form.

A Companion to Greek Democracy and the Roman Republic, First Edition. Edited by Dean Hammer.

1 Politics and Power

Roman government consisted in the official exertions of the Senate, the people, and their magistrates, the three formal elements of the city's constitution. The exhibition of influence, however, was by no means limited to these institutions. The courts, for instance, were frequently venues for political conflict (Epstein 1987: 90–126; Riggsby 1999; Lintott 2008: 43–125). Here eloquence took center stage and was often more potent than any evidence. Still, shrewd advocates freighted each defense with every ounce of a defendant's prestige, nor did they fail to marshal his kin and associates. In desperate cases, juries could be suborned by illicit payments, an illegal tactic sometimes necessitated in the cut and thrust of partisan prosecutions. Forceful indictments earned prosecutors respect as redoubtable men, even if they failed to eliminate their rivals, and advocates, by taking a public stand in behalf of a targeted figure, amplified their reserves of *gratia*, obligating their client and their client's connections. Political competition, this single example suffices to make clear, pervaded Roman society. Still, nothing mattered more than the magistracies, the assemblies, or the deliberations of the Senate.

The Roman aristocracy was fundamentally political in its origins and nature. Senators were deemed by all to be *optimi*, the best men (Festus 290L), a status they claimed owing to their accomplishments as aediles, praetors, or consuls—or, by the late Republic, as quaestors or tribunes of the *plebs* (Lintott 1999: 68–72). From the beginning, Rome's best men boasted of the achievements *as magistrates* (Hölkeskamp 1987). A magistracy was a *honor*, an honor awarded to the man who merited it at the time of his election to it. To take only a single if perhaps glamorous example, before he stood for the quaestorship in 70 BCE Julius Caesar had served as a diplomatic envoy and as a military officer, won a civic crown for valor, gained appointment to a priesthood, conducted public prosecutions in Rome, and won election as military tribune. Admittedly Caesar's energies and talents were exceptional, but his early accumulation of military and civilian service was far from unique.

In electing their magistrates, the Romans did not believe that they were selecting representatives, even if they expected their magistrates, especially the tribunes, to respect popular rights and to preserve popular entitlements. Instead, the people chose *leaders*, men who merited confidence and deference, who could command Rome's armies and ably govern the city. In Rome there were no political parties. Candidates did not offer the public programs or policy statements, nor were elections ordinarily viewed as contests of conflicting political philosophies. Instead, each election was a competition in and for prestige, a *contentio dignitatis*, in which the public made a judgment about the excellence, the *virtus*, of rival candidates (Cic. *Mur.* 14; *Planc.* 8; *De off.* 1.38; see Meier 1980: 163–174; Brunt 1988: 35–39). Success was a glorious personal achievement, just as failure at the polls was a disgrace. Advancement proceeded by way of an obligatory sequence of magistracies, the *cursus honorum*: the first obligatory *honor* was the quaestorship, followed by a praetorship and, ultimately for a worthy few, a consulship, the *summa laus* ("supreme glory", see Cic. *Cat.* 4.21; *Phil.* 2.20, 8.30) that conferred dignity on its holder and nobility on his posterity.

Thus it is clear why men of consular status, the *consulares*, enjoyed the highest dignity in the state and, by virtue of their achievements and successes, the greatest influence (Jehne 2011a). It was, after all, praetors and consuls who received the military commands that led to real *gloria*—in a society that prized military valor as the finest of virtues (Harris 1979: 10–41, with Rosenstein 2006). The exalted position of the *consulares*, like the standing of all the others in the Senate whom they had excelled, was, from the Romans' perspective, established and legitimated by the will of the people. The senators constituted, then, not an aristocracy of birth, though lineage was far from irrelevant to political success in Rome, but rather an aristocracy of office, attained through service and accomplishment (Hölkeskamp 2004: 32–38; 2010: 89–95).

2 The Nobility

Special grandeur belonged to those families that had given Rome its past consuls. These men were the *nobiles* (for a discussion of rival views on the meaning of *nobilitas*, see Burkhardt 1990), who inherited abundant assets in wealth, associations, and especially in fame, assets so vast that they were at once admired and resented. The assumption was prevalent that *virtus* was hereditary, which meant that a man whose ancestors had served Rome brilliantly was likely to do the same. The sincerity of this belief can be gauged in the nearly unrelenting success of the *nobilitas*: during the last two centuries of the Republic the vast majority of consulships went to nobles and only rarely to a newcomer in politics, a *novus homo* or new man (Badian 1990). Jealous rivals sometimes painted a portrait of the nobility as an inert class whose abundant legacies rendered its predominance inevitable (Wiseman 1971: 107–116). As Cicero put it of the noble Domitius Ahenobarbus, the man had spent the whole of his life as consul-designate (*Att.* 4.8A.2). This, however, was less than entirely fair: *nobilitas* was not and must not become a magic word, and in fact Roman history is littered with noble failures (e.g. Broughton 1991). It was actually quite rare for a noble family to preserve its place at the top over several generations, a reality that naturally enhanced the reputation and influence of the very few who did. And it was little consolation to any failed noble that, collectively, his class excelled the rest. Success in Rome was success in the teeth of intense competition: every noble and every aristocrat who aspired to nobility for his family was a contender for *dignitas*, for *gratia*, and for the all-important consulship. The superiority of the leading nobles, like the success of any aristocratic family in Rome, demanded constant industry (Cic. *Planc.* 15; Hopkins 1983: 31–119).

Still, the nobility possessed real advantages over their competitors. Foremost of these, according to a long tradition of historical analysis, were *clientela* and family alliances (e.g. Münzer 1920; Syme 1939; Scullard 1973). In a society marked by extensive poverty and lacking institutions concerned with public welfare, many of Rome's poor, and sometimes also more prosperous members of the lower orders, relied for their maintenance, at least in part, on the generosity of the wealthy. Which was customarily forthcoming. Even the affairs of the well-to-do could frequently benefit from the involvement or at least the advice of an influential man. It was through actions like these that a senator added to his *gratia* by obligating men of every social rank. Whereas in modern societies inaccessibility often signals importance, Roman grandees made themselves available: *comitas* ("affability and obligingness") was an aristocratic virtue (Heuer 1941; Deniaux 1993: 264–265), manifested most conspicuously in the routines of the morning greeting, the *salutatio*, when the mansions of great men were opened to all and sundry seeking advice or assistance, including material assistance (Goldbeck 2010).

One important means whereby the elite offered aid to their inferiors was through the institution of *clientela*: Roman patrons accumulated clients, who repaid their patron's help by placing themselves in his *fides*, that is by making a formal gesture of confidence in their patron, and by way of whatever modest tokens of gratitude they could offer (Gell. 5.13.2). So pervasive, and so socially significant, was *clientela* that the second century BCE comic poet Plautus could mock the eagerness of patrons to assemble clients in bulk:

> All the best men [*optumi*] make this their main habit: they crave many clients, and they don't bother asking whether they're good or bad men. (*Men.* 572–575)

The Romans believed *clientela* was an ancient institution, and for them it provided an ideological template for the broader aristocratic practice of exchanging favors for *gratia* with the multitude.

The possession of crowds of clients was associated with the nobility, and abundant *clientela* was routinely listed amongst the nobility's advantages over their rivals, as we have seen already in the case of Sallust's Marius (see also *Rhet. Her.* 8; Cic. *Cluent.* 94; *Part. or.* 87). The first century BCE historian Dionysius of Halicarnassus provides our only detailed account of *clientela*, and his is an idealizing one (*Ant. Rom.* 2.10.4). But it underscores how *clientela* was not a static affair: patrons *competed* with one another to acquire clients, and it required real effort to hang on to them. Patronage on a large scale, according to Dionysius, brought widespread fame—because the actions of a patron were an expression of his excellence, his *aretē* (or, in Latin, his *virtus*). Now *clientela* was certainly a social and therefore a political advantage, and it remained a potent symbol of righteous clout. But in political conflicts clients were hardly unflinching partisans, and in elections, so far as we can tell, the effect of *clientela* was negligible (Brunt 1988: 382–442; Morstein-Marx 1998; Mouritsen 2001: 67–79; Yakobson 1999: 66–111).

Clientela was a relationship between unequals. Men of the same, or nearly the same, status were joined in friendship (*amicitia*). Romans thought of friendship in two distinct but not entirely unrelated ways. On the one hand, there was ideal friendship, predicated on affection and goodwill. On the other hand, *amicitia* could describe relationships entered into mostly for reasons of utility, that is, ties that were based primarily on the exchange of beneficial services (Brunt 1988: 351–381; Konstan 1997: 122–148; Verboven 2002). Amongst aristocrats, ties could be formed, and obligations imposed, by generously lending large sums of money, or providing welcome assistance in political or financial transactions, or through forensic efforts, that is, by aiding a friend's defense in court either as a witness or an advocate. Friendship of either variety incurred debts of gratitude, which, *gratia* being no mere abstraction, exercised considerable moral and practical force. Few lapses in character were more shameful or destructive to one's reputation than ingratitude (Saller 1982: 17–39; Verboven 2002: 35–41). As Cicero put it, "no duty is more necessary than that of expressing gratitude" (*De off.* 1.47): "everyone hates a man who ignores a favor" (*De off.* 2.63).

Ambitious men endeavored to secure a wide circle of influential friends, and great houses were routinely linked by ties of marriage. These ties were serious ones—few expressions of friendship in Rome were more profound than the relationship between a father-in-law and his son-in-law—but their effect on politics is easily exaggerated. Even within a single family, political co-operation could not always be counted on—outside of critical moments like trials or elections. For these reasons, it is misleading to conceptualize

Roman politics as a contest between enduring or stable groups defined by family alliances and their network of friends, that is, as a competition between factions (Meier 1980: 7–63; Brunt 1988: 443–502; Hölkeskamp 2001–2). In the rough and tumble of politics, every aristocrat pursued his own success. Although everyone could be expected to help his friends and harm his enemies, nothing was ever mechanical or entirely predictable in Roman politics.

After all, it was not all sharp practice or preferential politics in the Senate and in the assemblies: issues also mattered, as, of course, did the personalities of their proponents or critics. Here again, however, it is dangerous to look for too much in the way of stable or lasting organization. Some Roman politicians, for instance, at least at certain moments in their careers, championed causes that were deemed relevant to upholding the freedom or sovereignty or comfort of the Roman people: such a figure could, in the moment, be labelled a *popularis* ("a supporter of a popular cause"). Similarly, when in any controversy a senator espoused the traditional influence of the Senate, he was counted amongst the *optimates* ("supporters of the best causes"). For some modern historians, *optimates* and *populares* represent ideological dispositions that defined enduring political configurations (e.g. Wiseman 2009: 5–32). This, however, is probably an error: during his tribunate, Marcus Porcius Cato brought in legislation vastly enhancing the grain subsidy for common citizens (Broughton 1952): 175), but because no one imagines describing him as a *popularis*, his measure is typically viewed as an insincere ruse placating popular resentment in the aftermath of the Catilinarian conspiracy (Fehrle 1983: 98–100). Examples of senators whose careers exhibit *popularis* gestures and senatorial sympathies alike could be multiplied. The reality is that the people's sovereignty and the Senate's authority coexisted as legitimate political motivations, and most senators were influenced, in different ways at different times, by both principles (Tatum 1999: 7–16; 2009). In reality, senators exhibited a striking tendency in any debate or controversy to converge into *ad hoc* alignments (Meier 1980: 163–190). We should not detect in the rhetoric of the *popularis* or the *optimates* references to political movements or anything resembling a modern party (Tatum 1999: 1–16; Kaster 2006: 31–37; Robb 2010).

It was more characteristic of Roman politics that, in any specific situation, political figures were confronted by conflicting obligations. During his consular candidature, for example, Cicero was compelled to seek the pardon of his intimate and valuable friend, Atticus, for refusing to represent his uncle, who was engaged in a private suit against a certain Caninius Satyrus. This Satyrus, however, though not a significant personage in his own right, was closely connected with the young noble Domitius Ahenobarbus, who was canvassing on Cicero's behalf. Cicero had asked Atticus' uncle to appreciate how his indebtedness to Domitius made it impossible for him to act against Satyrus' interests, but the man had refused and was instead deploying his nephew, and his nephew's friendship with Cicero, to trump Domitius' hold on the orator (*Att.* 1.1.3–4). A similar but far weightier dilemma confronted Cicero at the outbreak of the civil war between Pompey and Caesar. In his deliberations over which side to join, and even though his ideological instincts were plainly against Caesar, Cicero fretted over the debts of *gratia* he owed to both men, including a loan from Caesar amounting to 800,000 sesterces that inhibited Cicero's freedom to follow his natural inclinations (Brunt 1988: 363–365, collecting the sources). Caesar was naturally well aware of these claims, and in an extant letter he aggressively presses Cicero to refuse to join Pompey by appealing to the demands of their friendship (*Att.* 10.8B).

The predominance of the nobility derived from the same sources as the influence belonging to any aristocrat. But, at least most of the time, nobles enjoyed an advantage in the sheer scale of their assets. This edge, however, was not sufficient to exempt the nobility from the incessant exactions of political competition (Meier 1980: 175). It is no accident that, in aristocratic commendations, ***industria*** ("hard work") and its synonyms recur so frequently (***industria*** was a constituent of ***virtus***: see Hellegouarc'h 1963: 248–254 and McDonnell 2006: 335–378). Politics remained a struggle, and its constantly shifting circumstances necessitated vigilance as well as energy. This was especially the case in the essential and unavoidable scramble for magistracies.

3 The People's Choice

The Roman people elected their magistrates. Quaestors, aediles, and tribunes were elected by assemblies that organized the citizenry into thirty-five tribes (***tribus***), which were essentially voting districts. By the first century, when the franchise had been extended to all Italians, these districts extended up and down the peninsula. However, because elections took place only on specific days and only in Rome itself, these assemblies tended to be dominated by the votes of the urban masses. By contrast, praetors and consuls were chosen by the centuriate assembly, which distributed citizens into voting units called centuries. This distribution was based on each voter's economic class and therefore was grossly unequal: its result was that the votes of the rich literally counted for more than the votes of the poor (Lintott 1999: 40–64; Feig Vishnia 2012). The plutocratic quality of this assembly was not accidental: according to Cicero, King Servius structured the centuriate assembly "in such a way that the greatest number of votes lies in the power, not of the multitude, but of the rich" (*De rep.* 2.39), or, as Livy put it, "levels were designed so that no one appeared to be excluded from an election and yet all of the clout resided with the leading men" (Livy 1.43.10). Candidates for the highest offices, then, very much needed the support of the rich. Indeed, they could not hope to be elected without it.

It would be a mistake, however, to conclude that the role of the masses was negligible in the election of praetors or consuls. It is obvious that no one could become a candidate for the praetorship without first having been vetted by one of the tribal assemblies. Furthermore, the combined votes of the rich were not enough to secure election in the centuriate assembly. Even if there were unity on their part, the process required that a candidate win over voters amongst the more prosperous of the common citizenry. And in elections in which the competition was strong or the pool of viable candidates deep, and therefore the votes of the elite were divided, the votes of the lower classes would determine the outcome. It appears that this happened only rarely, but even that was enough to oblige candidates to make a habit of soliciting voters of all classes (Yakobson 1999: 20–64). It was beside the point that the actual number of voters each year was relatively small, even amongst the lower orders (Mouritsen 2001: 32–37), especially when it was impossible to know in advance who would actually attend the assembly on the day inasmuch as in different years different voters turned out (Tatum 1999: 29–30).

But it was not primarily for their votes in the centuriate assembly that men from the lower orders were canvassed. In Rome, campaigning for office during the final and crucial weeks before the election took the shape of three traditional, highly visible, and indispensable daily rituals: the morning greeting at a candidate's house (*salutatio*), his descent to the Forum (*deductio*), and his circulation throughout the Forum during the day, seeing and being seen by the public (*adsectatio*). The pageantry of these rites required the occasional presence of distinguished supporters (Q. Cic. *Comm. pet.* 18; 36–38) but what most mattered was a massive retinue, which was assembled primarily out of voters from the poorest classes. Indeed, it was by offering themselves to candidates as attendants that the humble endeavored to repay their debts of *gratia* to the men who were standing for office (Cic. *Mur.* 70–71). And it was a worthwhile exchange: popularity at these moments conferred prestige (*dignitas*: Q. Cic. *Comm. pet.* 36; 50; cf. Cic. *Mur.* 45–50; *Planc.* 21; *De orat.* 1.200) that was vital in winning over voters of *all* classes.

It must be remembered that in Roman society, the awesome powers of its magistrates notwithstanding, there was very little of the apparatus of any modern police state (Nippel 1995). Stability was secured, not by the ever-present threat of official force, but by the personal as well as the legal authority of the people's magistrates. In this respect, then, popularity was a significant predictor of a candidate's practical utility once in office. In the illogic of pageants and their impressions, massive attendance during his canvass signified a candidate's popular favor and lent him the aura of reliability—so long as in other aspects he remained attractive to voters in the upper classes: here, one could conclude, was a man the people could count on (thus the popular inference, or why else should so many follow him?), and here was a man whose capacity for commanding deference amongst the masses could maintain order and the status quo (thus the elite inference). Roman society was in many ways very much *de haut en bas*, but its elite were aware of the public's potential combustibility, which is why they could not sensibly support a candidate who was incompetent in his dealings with the multitude. This is why the *Commentariolum petitionis*, a text in which Quintus Cicero describes for his brother the best practices pertaining to a successful run for the consulship, describes the ideal candidate as someone whom the Senate deems a guardian of its authority, the equestrians and prosperous classes believe is devoted to peace and stability, and the masses trust to be favorably disposed to their entitlements (*Comm. pet.* 52).

In the absence of political programs and party structures, how did candidates win votes? In the *Commentariolum petitionis*, we find a useful analysis of the individuals and groups whose influence could most effectively assist Cicero in his candidature (Morstein-Marx 1998; Tatum 2007). There it is recognized that by the time anyone stood for the consulship, he had for more than a decade exerted himself in shaping his public reputation (in Cicero's case, by way of his performances as an orator) and in developing and sustaining useful social alliances. Quintus urges his brother to put on display his vast network of connections, which existed at every social level and constituted the best evidence of his accessibility, his readiness to be of service, and his capacity for delivering practical aid to those in need of it. The list of Cicero's supporters is a long one, ranging from young nobles and rich equestrians to members of the urban *collegia*, which were neighborhood societies composed of modest craftsmen and shopkeepers.

Naturally it was important to enjoy the support or at least the approval of the nobility and of the *consulares*. Similarly, the goodwill of the sitting consuls and tribunes was beneficial (*Comm. pet.* 18). But it is the mobilization of the residue of the electorate that receives the most attention in the *Commentariolum petitionis*, which stresses the necessity of cultivating, personally and through intermediaries, Cicero's fellow tribesmen and his neighbors both in Rome and throughout Italy, where he possessed several strategically located estates.

Each of Rome's thirty-five tribes had its headquarters in Rome, which candidates were expected to visit as part of their canvass (on tribes, see Taylor 1960). Each tribe's officers, the *curatores*, commanded followings of their own, which means that it was important to convert these men to one's cause. Carrying one's own tribe was deemed essential, and personal generosity in that cause was a hallowed practice: a candidate was expected to distribute gifts, including banquets and seats at the games, to the men of his own tribe, an undertaking so extensive that he routinely turned to experts, *divisores*, who organized the candidate's legitimate generosity toward his tribesmen. Tribesmen could also be solicited by way of the influence of others, through the efforts of wealthy equestrians or members of aristocratic fraternities (*sodalitates*): Cicero had been conspicuous in defending the interests of such men, and in the *Commentariolum petitionis* Quintus reminds him of the importance of reminding these men of their obligations (*Comm. pet.* 19).

The role played by intermediaries in winning mass support is obvious, and Cicero was also advised to court local figures, men who, though far from grand, were influential in their *collegia* or district (*pagus*) or neighborhood (*vicus*) (on local associations, see Tarpin 2002; Lott 2004). By cultivating these men, Cicero enhanced their own local status—a senatorial grandee was a connection that elevated a humble man's prestige—and they, in their turn, would endeavor to deliver the votes of their colleagues and neighbors, as well as, and often more importantly, their attendance in the daily business of canvassing for office. Naturally there was competition for the attentions of these men, and doubtless, within each *collegium* or neighborhood, there was more than one individual contending for local prestige and for senatorial contacts. The contest for influence, then, obtained at more than one social level, and it was incumbent upon a savvy senator to remain sensitive to the dignities of small fry (Tatum 1999: 118–119, 146–148).

The public was hardly passive in all this. Canvassing in Rome included posting placards that registered the support for candidates on the part of individuals and groups. If the evidence of Pompeii is anything to go by, even modest citizens, a client or a *collegium*, took part in these advertisements. So, too, did women (Mouritsen 1987; Savunen 1997). Graffiti presented the people with another means of making its voice heard (Morstein-Marx 2012). Elections coincided with annual games at Rome, a conspicuous feature of which were the cheers, jeers, and silences that greeted distinguished men on their arrival (Vanderbroeck 1987: 77–81; Tatum 1990; Laser 1997). These popular reactions were taken very seriously. And of course the public could exhibit its preferences and aversions by way of attending or avoiding candidates: an empty or only partially filled atrium was a humiliating sign of unpopularity (on the symbolism of a packed atrium see Goldbeck 2010: 240–246).

Elections were meant to be decided by *gratia*, in what the Romans approvingly described as *gratuita comitia* ("elections based on *gratia*" but normally used to mean uncorrupted elections: Cic. *Att.* 4.15.8; *Q. fr.* 2.15.4). Generosity past and present naturally and appropriately played a central role, as we have seen. But certain emoluments were immoral, at least in principle, and, were ultimately made illegal. Gifts to one's fellow tribesmen, for instance, were good and proper—and more or less obligatory. Similar gifts outside one's own tribe, however, were deemed objectionable: these were not considered traditional *gratia*-earning benefactions but were thought of, by the aristocracy at least, as bribes. Yet there were few candidates for office who neglected such pay-offs, which were directed at all classes of society, transactions that were facilitated by existing institutions like *divisores* and *sodalitates*. The crime of electoral corruption, *ambitus*, extended further. In view of the reality that massive attendance boosted the prospects of any candidature, candidates often resorted to paying the masses to follow them about during their canvassing. This was a clear distortion of the symbolism the rituals of a campaign were meant to project and so this, too, was opposed—in principle. *Ambitus* was a routine target for moralizing oratory, and the Romans passed numerous and increasingly punitive measures against it. But in vain. These practices remained robust so long as the Republic existed, not least because, despite protestations to the contrary, most Romans were keen to receive and the aristocracy (a few exceptions notwithstanding) all too willing to bestow this irregular baksheesh (Yakobson 1999: 140–147; Feig Vishnia 2012: 139–146). Prosecutions for *ambitus* were rarely crusades against vice: they were, instead, often last-ditch efforts by unsuccessful candidates straining to salvage a lost election (Adamietz 1986; *contra* Riggsby 1999: 47–48).

Elections were annual events, and the various activities essential to campaigning were a fundamental and pervasive aspect of everyday political life in Rome. Competition for office was a constant, which meant that the electorate, in its various guises and subdivisions, was always, at least in some manner, the object of solicitation by the political class. Candidates sought office. Their fellow aristocrats sought to exhibit and increase their influence by way of their endorsements. Intermediary political figures, leaders of *collegia* or neighborhoods, also worked to expand their local prestige through their connections to grand personages. And the whole of the citizenry literally profited from the profusion of generosity that was indispensable for every competitor.

4 Senatorial Clout

The Senate met only when summoned by a competent magistrate (a consul, praetor, or tribune), who presided over any meeting's agenda and debate. Senators were asked their opinions in a fixed order of rank, in which men of consular and praetorian status predominated. The presiding magistrate determined whether any motion should be put to a vote and, if it were carried, he oversaw the precise formulation of the resulting decree (*senatus consultum*). In principle and in legal reality, the Senate existed solely to tender its advice to sitting magistrates, but these were expected to comply with the Senate's advice. As were the Roman people, when senatorial decrees urged or forbade specific actions or undertakings. The Senate lacked any powers of coercion: even in emergencies it could only authorize magistrates to resort to exceptional measures through what is generally referred to as the ultimate decree (*senatus consultum ultimum*). And yet, by dint of its overwhelming prestige (*auctoritas*), the Senate managed to direct public affairs in Rome (Lintott 1999: 65–93). At least most of the time.

Acquiring authority within the institution of the Senate, then, was clearly an important, indeed crucial, matter for ambitious men. Within the Senate, as in Rome generally, reputation, wealth, and connections mattered most, not least because these were key factors, as we have seen, in winning the highest offices. The sharply stratified nature of the Senate itself meant that ex-consuls and ex-praetors had greater opportunities for shaping policy than did lesser men (Jehne 2000), and by now it is clear that the ranks of the *consulares* were largely filled by the *nobilitas*. Still, competition as well as honest divergences in opinion often divided the Senate's leading figures.

How, then, did rival senators win over their colleagues? One answer, once again, is by way of *gratia*. Some figures, and Marcus Licinius Crassus is a prominent example, won over less exalted senators through generous loans and through his constant exertions on behalf of many in the courts, each activity a laudable expression of *amicitia* (Meier 1980: 180). It naturally helped matters that Crassus was noble and had earned his share of military glory, which made him, by Roman standards, admirable. Crassus was not alone. His rival, Pompey the Great, was richer still, enjoyed greater military glory, and also endeavored to garner senatorial *gratia* on a grand scale.

These dimensions of senatorial clout are too often obscured from us. During the 70s, anyone hopeful of securing a command or province—including the distinguished consul of 74, Lucius Licinius Lucullus—was obliged to pay court to a certain Publius Cornelius Cethegus (Cic. *Parad.* 40; *Brut.* 178; Plut. *Luc.* 5.4; Ps.-Asc. 259St.). Who was he? A patrician and an early partisan of Marius, he eventually transferred his allegiance to Sulla and became a valued if unsavory associate. Presumably he reached the praetorship, though the office is unattested, and presumably he enriched himself during Sulla's proscriptions, though it is never mentioned even by hostile sources. His clout was apparently limited to the Senate (Plut. *Luc.* 5.4—*pace* Münzer 1900: 1281, and Meier 1980: 180—does *not* indicate popular favor), where, according to Cicero, he enjoyed the *auctoritas* of an ex-consul on account of his consummate expertise in public affairs. But Cicero's explanation seems sanitized or at least incomplete, and it remains far from obvious to us how this shadowy senator imposed his will on his more illustrious colleagues.

It was not always the case that senatorial policy was dictated by the views of the *consulares* or by obscure machinations (Ryan 1998: 13–133). When the Senate convened to debate the fate of Catilinarian conspirators, the consul-elect, Decimus Junius Silanus, the first to be asked his opinion, proposed the death penalty. The next fifteen speakers, the most distinguished men in the house, concurred. Only when the deliberation reached Julius Caesar, who was then praetor-elect, was there dissent: Caesar spoke in favor of life imprisonment, warning his colleagues of the dangers inherent in executing citizens without trial, and in doing so persuaded many to reconsider, including Silanus. Eventually Cato, merely a tribune-elect, addressed the body. Invoking the severity of the Romans' forefathers, he urged the house to embrace Silanus' original motion and was much applauded by the whole house. Then the presiding consul, Cicero, who also spoke, elaborating his own assessment of the propositions that had been advanced, instructed the Senate to vote for or against executing the conspirators. Cato's speech carried the day (Drummond 1995).

In this debate, the issue was determined by the speeches of non-consular men, one of whom had not even reached a praetorship. Admittedly, each was a noble. In the case of Cato, the speaker was wealthy and of truly splendid heritage, resources he had already amplified through brilliant ties of friendship and kinship. He was also admired for his moral rectitude, by a senatorial order whose moralizing sensibilities inclined to the censorial and warmed to old-fashioned strictness (Fehrle 1983: 49–82). Still, the oratory of Caesar and its earnest evocation of the legal and traditional rights of Roman citizens very nearly decided the outcome. Eloquence, then, and a sound application of Roman values mattered very much in senatorial politics. Senatorial debate was not, like its modern counterparts, a mere formality: well-expressed arguments could shape the views of others, and sway their votes. Hence the recurring emphasis on oratorical skill.

5 The Popular Assemblies

Oratory also played a central role in legislation. Like the selection of magistrates, the carrying of laws was an exclusive right of the Roman people, exercised through their assemblies. Most legislation was passed by the tribal or plebeian assemblies, which were, in ordinary circumstances, dominated by the urban masses. In these assemblies, unlike the centuriate assembly, the wealthy enjoyed no advantages. Consequently, the success or failure of legislative proposals was decided by the votes of ordinary citizens, or at least by the votes of those ordinary citizens who chose to participate.

A legislative proposal was called a *rogatio*: each one commenced with the formula *velitis iubeatis* ("is it your will and is it your command?"), thereby making clear the relationship between the magistrate who offered a bill—and in Rome only a consul, praetor, or tribune could do so—and the assembly that accepted or rejected it. Although it was not necessary to do so, proposals were often debated by the Senate and amended as a result of that body's deliberations (Nicolet 1958). Every *rogatio* was published in the Forum and its text was available to anyone who cared to inspect it. Between its promulgation and its coming to a vote, a specified period of time, three market days (a *trinundinum*), had to elapse, during which time interested parties could arrange to be present in Rome for voting—and during which time the proponents and opponents of the *rogatio* could exert themselves in trying to persuade the people.

Doubtless, in cases of controversial legislation, political figures employed their every available resource in *gratia* in order to sway voters, and it would be a mistake to ignore these crucial avenues to the hearts and minds of the Roman people. But a *rogatio*, unlike a candidate for office, could not be judged on the basis of its pedigree or achievements, nor even on the pedigree or achievements of its author. Legislative proposals were measures the effect of which often had a significant bearing on the lives of the voters themselves. This is most obvious in legislation that expanded the very modest entitlements of ordinary citizens, laws, for instance, that established or increased public subsidies for grain. There were also proposals whose attraction was ideological as well as practical: in 123 BCE, to take a single example, Gaius Gracchus proposed a law reaffirming every citizen's fundamental right to appeal to the people in capital cases. It is obvious how the very content of such proposals will have mattered to some voters every bit as much as the prestige of its advocates or detractors.

But the language of Roman legislation was technical, complex, and difficult to understand, a state of affairs that opened the door to varying interpretations. Naturally the public had to rely on the views of experts, who were mostly men from the senatorial order (Jehne 2011b). The setting for the ventilation of views on the merits or failings of any *rogatio* was the *contio*, an unorganized assembly summoned by a magistrate at which he, or anyone he invited, could address the public (on the role of the theater in gauging public opinion, see O'Bryhim, Chapter 25). In Rome, there was no universal right to address the people: that was a privilege belonging only to the magistrates and those whom they explicitly permitted to address a *contio*.

The importance of the *contio* can hardly be overestimated (Pina Polo 1996; Morstein-Marx 1998). It provided a setting in which politicians could offer explanations, tendentious or otherwise, of the likely effects of any bill. And an opportunity for the public to react, with applause or catcalls, or by simply refusing to attend in the first place—or by walking away at any point during a *contio* (a humiliation: Morstein-Marx 1998: 38). It was not a requirement or even an expectation that a *contio* would involve an exchange of conflicting views—although some did, and occasionally bills were revised in response to the reactions they encountered in *contiones* (Moreau 2005; Hollard 2010: 45–46). But it is clear how vital it was for a speaker in such an environment to command public respect and be equipped with a high level of oratorical skill. Eloquence was not the only factor in the success of a *contio*, to be sure. Some speakers were careful to pack a *contio* with supporters, transforming the event into a rally. Conversely, it was possible to infiltrate an opponent's *contio* with a cohort of one's own adherents, whose disruptive behavior could then be characterized as an expression of the people's true sentiments. No *contio* involved more than a tiny percentage of Rome's eligible voters, or even of the urban population, but every audience was routinely addressed as if it were the Roman people, and the responses of these assemblies could be claimed to be representative of the popular will.

There was nothing inconsequential about the *contio*'s role in shaping Roman government. During his consulship, Cicero delivered a series of speeches denigrating a *rogatio* introduced by the tribune Publius Servilius Rullus (on the rhetorical context of this episode, see also Morstein-Marx, Chapter 17). His measure proposed establishing a commission empowered to establish colonies and to distribute lands to the poor (Broughton 1952: 168; Crawford 1996: 757–760). Similar legislation had been proposed and passed before (Roselaar 2010), and so, at first blush, it is hard to imagine how Rullus' proposal could possibly have failed. Thus it is no surprise to us that its opponents in the Senate felt constrained to resort to the services of another tribune, Lucius Caecilius Rufus, who promised that he would veto the bill should it ever come to a vote. But Caecilius' intervention was unnecessary, because Cicero was able to make the case that Rullus' measure, should it pass, would in fact be damaging to public interests: the commission it created, he insisted, would be a danger to republican values, and the whole undertaking would undermine the prestige of the popular hero Pompey the Great, whose return from the east was imminent. There can be little doubt that Rullus' bill was comprehensively distorted in Cicero's rhetoric: but he was believed, nor did Rullus or his supporters possess the platform or persuasiveness to overcome Cicero's consular eloquence (Morstein-Marx 1998: 190–203; Jehne 2011a).

Cicero's achievement was all the more remarkable because the people were perfectly capable, when presented with a *rogatio* that plainly worked to its advantage, of rejecting the arguments of even the most distinguished consular authorities (Morstein-Marx 2013). This was the case with Tiberius' legislation in 133 BCE, and on numerous other occasions. Now it is true that the Roman people rarely said no to measures that had the positive endorsement of the bulk of the Senate's leadership. But that did not mean that the people were willing to vote against their own interests simply because a majority of the elite urged them to do so. There was, after all, nothing revolutionary in siding, on a specific issue, with one element in the aristocracy against another (Jehne 2011a). Persuading the populace was a magisterial responsibility that was hallowed by tradition. It was also, in legislative matters, a vital means of reaching consensus.

6 Violence

The operations of the assemblies could be disrupted by violence. Rome lacked anything in the way of a policing force. As a consequence, and in despite of all their conditioning for deference and obedience, the urban masses sometimes demonstrated or even rioted, apparently spontaneously, especially when foodstuffs became scarce or expensive. The urgings of charismatic leaders, or controversies over issues of genuine relevance to their daily lives, could also stimulate the people's turbulence. At times, meetings of the Senate took place against a backdrop of angry demonstrations, and politicians were not above directing political violence against their opponents, as the fates of the brothers Gracchus attest, although these deployments of violence remained unsettling. Violence did not have to become lethal, however, in order to be useful—or vexatious. Caesar, for instance, in passing his law distributing land to Pompey's veterans and to the needy, resorted to proletarian muscle to bar opponents from making their way into his legislative assembly. Although effective, this violence was enough to repulse significant numbers of the citizenry, and Caesar found himself snubbed by the audience when he appeared at the games. He took it badly (Cic. *Att.* 2.19.3).

Political violence reached new levels in the 50s BCE. After securing the devotion of the urban masses through legislation providing free grain and rehabilitating cherished *collegia*, Publius Clodius Pulcher organized many in the lower orders into a ready source of demonstrations, riots, and even physical attacks on his enemies. By constantly exploiting and expanding his connections with the *collegia* and with their leaders, through appeals to *gratia* not unlike the solicitations of a candidate for office, Clodius was soon able to close the city's shops and rally a rowdy crowd whenever it suited his purposes. These were forces that enabled him to remain a major and intimidating political figure until he was murdered in 52 BCE. Clodius' gangs did not, however, enjoy a monopoly on violence: they were soon countered by organized violence on the part of his opponents, and during the Republic's final decade their clashes remained a dangerous aspect of political life (Tatum 1999: 140–149, 166–186, 211–225).

7 Concluding Uncertainties

A medley of factors determined the winner in any political conflict, the outcome of which was rarely calculable in any mechanical way. One need only consider the perturbations of the year 133 BCE (sources assembled in Broughton 1951: 493–494). Whatever the idealistic or philosophical sensibilities motivating Tiberius Gracchus, his proposed agrarian law, which regulated and restricted longstanding occupations of public land on the part of the wealthy in order to distribute small farms to the needy, was also a response both to distinguished encouragement (his father-in-law, Appius Claudius Pulcher, was not the only eminent senator who favored reform) and popular agitation, visibly inscribed in graffiti. At the same time, Tiberius' nobility and the opportunities afforded him by the powers of his office combined to concentrate attention on his ambitions as well as on his actual proposal.

His senatorial esteem, however, was diminished when he rebuffed that body's authority by taking his measure directly to the people, who predictably found its provisions as attractive to themselves as they were unwelcome to significant numbers of senators and equestrians. No opposition, however, could overcome Tiberius' inspiring oratory, nor did the collective prestige of senatorial grandees overwhelm the public. The veto interposed by Marcus Octavius was undone by Tiberius through provocative if constitutional means: he passed legislation that removed Octavius from office, an unprecedented assertion of popular sovereignty that cleared the way for the agrarian law's ratification. Yet before the year was out, when his exertions to win re-election as tribune led to disturbances in the streets and consternation in the Senate, a distinguished private citizen, Publius Scipio Nasica, incited that body, or at the very least a sizeable portion of it, to take the law into its own hands: senators, equestrians, and their retainers and supporters, lynched Tiberius. Not only were there no consequences for this action, the Senate went on to establish a tribunal to look into the dangers posed by Tiberius' associates (Broughton 1951: 498). Nevertheless, Tiberius' legislation remained unaltered. Even the most reactionary of the senators knew their limits: the people may have acquiesced in the death of their champion but would not have endured the abrogation of the agrarian law.

Tiberius' tribunate was a cataclysmic episode in Roman history, but its political elements, although volatile and destructive in their mixture, were typical. What obtrudes is the uncertainty, at any moment in this episode, of the outcome whenever these elements combined or came into conflict: prestige was trumped, for a time, by an ideology of popular sovereignty amply bolstered by popular and material benefits—but only for a time, for soon Tiberius' adversaries found the resources to prevail, at least up to a point. It is not the constituents of clout, then, that elude modern historians so much as their effective application in specific circumstances. One final example will illustrate our difficulties in perceiving the discrete and practical operations of power.

In a letter of June 44, Cicero reports to Atticus about a meeting held by friends and family of Cassius and Brutus to discuss whether or not the two liberators should undertake the special commissions, proposed by Antony and confirmed by a decree of the Senate, which assigned them the organization of the grain supply from Sicily and Asia. Cicero urged acceptance, but the tenor of the conference was against it. Cicero responded with a lengthy rehearsal of the political situation, at which point Brutus' mother, Servilia, interrupted the orator to bring matters to a decision. She then promised that *she* would see to it that the grain commissions were expunged from the Senate's original decree (*Att.* 15.11.2). It is remarkable that Cicero did not find her promise remarkable. In executing it, she presumably employed her lofty reputation, her wealth, and her connections, but exactly how this woman—who could never be a senator and enjoyed neither martial glory nor fame as an orator—finally altered the policy of the Senate—and of Mark Antony—must remain anybody's guess. Although the foundations of Roman clout are obvious, even unmistakable, there is much in the actualities of the Romans' *arcana imperii* that remains undiscovered.

In Rome and Athens alike, individuals, not political parties, endeavored to have things their way in politics. In both cities, persuading the sovereign people was essential: consequently, oratory was crucial. But Rome remained aristocratic in outlook and design—clout in the Senate could and did challenge clout in the assemblies—hence the enduring importance of the family and its reputation, of military glory, of personal fame, and of the practical cultivation of others summed up in the word *gratia*. Social practices reinforced Roman inequalities, thereby conditioning the people to defer to their superiors in most, though not all, matters. And there was even a place for women, at least wealthy or aristocratic women, in the unofficial spaces of political influence.

REFERENCES

Adamietz, J. 1986. "Ciceros Verfahren in den Ambitus-Prozessen gegen Murena und Plancius." *Gymnasium* 93: 102–117.

Badian, E. 1990. 'The Consuls, 179–49 BC." *Chiron* 20: 371–343.

Balot, R.K., ed. 2009. *A Companion to Greek and Roman Political Thought*. Oxford.

Beck, H., A. Duplá, M. Jehne, and F. Pina Polo, eds. 2011. *Consuls and Res Publica: Holding High Office in the Roman Republic*. Cambridge.

Broughton. T.R.S. 1951. *The Magistrates of the Roman Republic*, vol. 1. New York.

Broughton. T.R.S. 1952. *The Magistrates of the Roman Republic*, vol. 2. New York.

Broughton. T.R.S. 1991. *Candidates Defeated in Roman Elections: Some Ancient Roman "Also-Rans."* Philadelphia.

Brunt, P.A. 1988. *The Fall of the Roman Republic and Related Essays*. Oxford.

Burckhardt, L.A. 1990. "The Political Elite of the Roman Republic: Comments on Recent Discussions of the Concepts Nobilitas and Homo Novus." *Historia* 39: 89–98.

Crawford, M.H., ed. 1996. *Roman Statutes*. BICS suppl. 64. 2 vols. London.

Deniaux, E. 1993. *Clientèles et pouvoir à l'époque de Cicéron*. Paris and Rome.

Drummond, A. 1995. *Law, Politics and Power: Sallust and the Execution of the Catilinarian Conspirators*. Stuttgart.

Earl, D. 1967. *The Moral and Political Tradition of Rome*. Ithaca, NY.

Epstein, D.F. 1987. *Personal Enmity in Roman Politics, 218–43 BC*. London.

Feig Vishnia, R. 2012. *Roman Elections in the Age of Cicero: Society, Government, and Voting*. London.

Fehrle, R. 1983. *Cato Uticensis*. Darmstadt.

Flower, H. 1996. *Ancestor Masks and Aristocratic Power in Roman Culture*. Oxford.

Goldbeck, F. 2010. *Salutationes: Die Morgenbegrüßungen in Rom in der Republik und der frühen Kaiserzeit*. Berlin.

Harris, W.V. 1979. *War and Imperialism in Republican Rome, 327–70 BC*. Oxford.

Hellegouarc'h, J. 1963. *Vocabulaire latin des relations et des parties politiques sous la république*. Paris.

Heuer, K.H. 1941. *Comitas-facilitas-liberalitas*. Münster.

Hollard, V. 2010. *Le rituel du vote: les assemblées du peuple romain*. Paris.

Hölkeskamp, K.-J. 1987. *Die Enstehung der Nobilität: Studien zur sozialen und politischen Geschichte der römischen Republik im 4. Jhdt. V. Chr.* Stuttgart.

Hölkeskamp, K.-J. 2001–2. "Fact(ions) or Fiction? Friedrich Münzer and the Aristocracy of the Roman Republic—Then and Now." *International Journal of the Classical Tradition* 8: 92–105.

Hölkeskamp, K.-J. 2004. *Senatus Populusque Romanus: Die politische Kultur der Republik—Dimensionen und Deutungen*. Stuttgart.

Hölkeskamp, K.-J. 2010. *Reconstructing the Roman Republic: An Ancient Political Culture and Modern Research*. Princeton.

Hopkins, K. 1983. *Death and Renewal*. Cambridge.

Ioannatou, M. 2006. *Affaires d'argent dans la correspondence de Cicéron: l'aristocratie sénatoriale face à ses dettes*. Paris.

Jehne, M. 2000. "Rednertätigkeit und Statusdissonanzen in der späten römischen Republik," In Neumeister and Raeck 2000: 167–189.

Jehne, M. 2011a. "Blaming the People in Front of the People: Restraint and Outbursts of Orators in Roman *Contiones*." In Smith and Covino 2011: 111–126.

Jehne, M. 2011b. "The Rise of the Consular as a Social Type in the Third and Second Centuries BC." In Beck et al. 2011: 211–231.
Kaster, R.A. 2006. *Cicero: Speech on Behalf of Publius Sestius.* Oxford.
Konstan, D. 1997. *Friendship in the Classical World.* Cambridge.
Kuhn, C., ed. 2012. *Politische Kommunikation und öffentliche Meinung in der antiken Welt.* Stuttgart.
Laser, G. 1997. *Populo et scaenae serviendum est: Die Bedeutung der städtischen Masse in der späten römischen Republik.* Trier.
Lintott, A. 1999. *The Constitution of the Roman Republic.* Oxford.
Lintott, A. 2008. *Cicero as Evidence: A Historian's Companion.* Oxford.
Lott, J.B. 2004. *The Neighborhoods of Augustan Rome.* Cambridge.
McDonnell, M. 2006. *Roman Manliness: Virtus and the Roman Republic.* Cambridge.
Meier, C. 1980. *Res Publica Amissa: Eine Studie zu Verfassung und Geschichte der späten römischen Republik.* 2nd edn. Wiesbaden.
Moreau, P. 2005. '*Sublata priore Lege*: le retrait des *rogationes* comme mode d'amendement aux propositions de loi, à la fin de la république." In Sineux 2005: 201–214.
Morstein-Marx, R. 1998. "Publicity, Popularity and Patronage in the *Commentariolum Petitionis.*" *CA* 17: 258–288.
Morstein-Marx, R. 2012. "Political Graffiti in the Late Roman Republic: 'Hidden Transcripts' and 'Common Knowledge.'" In Kuhn 2012: 191–217.
Morstein-Marx, R. 2013. "'Cultural Hegemony' and the Communicative Power of the Roman Elite." In Steel and van der Blom 2013: 29–47.
Mouritsen, H. 1987. *Elections, Magistrates and Municipal Élite: Studies in Pompeian Epigraphy.* Rome.
Mouritsen, H. 2001. *Plebs and Politics in the Late Roman Republic.* Cambridge.
Münzer, F. 1900. "Publius Cornelius Cethegus." *RE* 7: 1281.
Münzer, F. 1920. *Römische Adelsparteien und Adelsfamilien.* Stuttgart.
Neumeister, C. and W. Raeck, eds. 2000. *Rede und Redner: Bewertung und Darstellung in den antiken Kulturen.* Möhnesse.
Nicolet, C. 1958. "Le sénat et les amendments aux lois à la fin de la république." *REL* 36: 260–275.
Nippel, W. 1995. *Public Order in Ancient Rome.* Cambridge.
Pina Polo, F. 1996. *Contra arma verbis: Der Redner vor dem Volk in der späten römischen Republik.* Stuttgart.
Riggsby, A.M. 1999. *Crime and Community in Ciceronian Rome.* Austin.
Robb, M.A. 2010. *Beyond Populares and Optimates: Political Language in the Late Republic.* Stuttgart.
Roselaar, S.T. 2010. *Public Land in the Roman Republic: A Social and Economic History of Ager Publicus in Italy, 396–89 BC.* Oxford.
Rosenstein, N. 2006, "Aristocratic Values." In Rosenstein and Morstein-Marx 2006: 365–382.
Rosenstein, N. and R. Morstein-Marx, eds. 2006. *A Companion to the Roman Republic.* Oxford and Malden, MA.
Ryan, F.X. 1998. *Rank and Participation in the Republican Senate.* Stuttgart.
Saller, R.P. 1982. *Personal Patronage under the Early Roman Empire.* Cambridge.
Savunen, L. 1997. *Women in the Urban Texture of Pompeii.* Helsinki.
Scullard, H.H. 1973. *Roman Politics 220–150 BC.* 2nd edn. Oxford.
Shatzman, I. 1975. *Senatorial Wealth and Roman Politics.* Brussels.
Sineux, P., ed. 2005. *Le législateur et la loi dans l'Antiquité: hommage à Françoise Ruzé.* Caen.
Smith, C. and R. Covino, eds. 2011. *Praise and Blame in Roman Republican Rhetoric.* Swansea.
Steel, C. and H. van der Blom, eds. 2013. *Community and Communication: Oratory and Politics in Republican Rome.* Oxford.

Syme, R. 1939. *The Roman Revolution*. Oxford.
Tarpin, M. 2002. *Vici et Pagi dans l'Occident Romain*. Paris and Rome.
Tatum, W.J. 1990. "Another Look at the Spectators at the Roman Games." *AHB* 4: 104–107.
Tatum, W.J. 1999. *The Patrician Tribune: Publius Clodius Pulcher*. Chapel Hill.
Tatum, W.J. 2007. "*Alterum est tamen boni viri, alterum boni petitoris*: The Good Man Canvasses." *Phoenix* 61: 109–135.
Tatum, W.J. 2009. "Roman Democracy?" In Balot 2009: 214–228.
Taylor, L.R. 1960. *The Voting Districts of the Roman Republic*. Rome.
Vanderbroeck, P.J.J. 1987. *Popular Leadership and Collective Behavior in the Late Roman Republic (ca. 80–50 BC)*. Amsterdam.
Verboven, K. 2002. *The Economy of Friends: Economic Aspects of Amicitia and Patronage in the Late Republic*. Brussels.
Wiseman, T.P. 1971. *New Men in the Roman Senate, 139 BC–AD 14*. Oxford.
Wiseman, T.P. 2009. *Remembering the Roman People: Essays on Late-Republican Politics and Literature*. Oxford.
Yakobson, A. 1999. *Elections and Electioneering in Rome: A Study in the Political System of the Late Republic*. Stuttgart.

FURTHER READING

Syme 1939: 11–27, and Meier 1980: 174–190, remain fundamental, but these should be read against the extensive critical re-evaluation by Brunt 1988: 351–502. Wealth and its consequences are discussed by Shatzman 1975 and Ioannatou 2006. Although focused on imperial Rome, Saller 1982 is an admirable examination of Rome's culture of reciprocity. Hölkeskamp 2010 elucidates the sheer complexity of Roman political competition.

PART VIII

Rhetoric

CHAPTER 16

Persuading the People in Greek Participatory Communities

Joseph Roisman

The need to persuade an audience was not unique to democracy, but rhetoric was most significant in participatory states with a sovereign *dēmos*. The corpus of Attic Orators, a collection of speeches delivered for the most part in fourth-century Athens, contains the best evidence for the use of rhetoric in a democratic city (see MacDowell 2009: 7–9 for the question of the speeches' authenticity). I shall focus on Athenian rhetoric because of the unique value of this source, and because classical Athenian democracy was the most enduring and participatory of all Greek political systems. Rhetoric had similar uses in other Greek democracies, which will be touched on in this chapter, and even in non- or proto-democratic communities described by Kurt Raaflaub in Chapter 2. My exposition, however, focuses on the means of persuasion that Athenian speakers used in different civic situations and the historical, political, and cultural environments that influenced them, with special attention given to the way rhetoric related to the participatory aspects of membership in the community.

Athenian democracy resembled other systems in barring women, aliens, slaves, and minors from active participation in politics. The two features of participation and exclusiveness contributed to the Athenians' self-perception as a community of male citizens with largely equal rights and duties (but not abilities) who were expected to take an active part in the public sphere of the *polis*. This involvement included office-holding, decision-making, military service, religious activity, and a score of other duties (see Rhodes, Chapter 8). Rhetoric was highly relevant to almost all of these activities. Public speakers delineated communal expectations of participatory conduct and commented on whether these expectations were met. The audience could turn a meeting into an interactive experience by vocally endorsing, criticizing, or heckling a speaker or even dragging him off the podium (below). To illustrate these points I shall follow Aristotle's division of public speaking into three genres: epideictic, for praise or blame; forensic, for judicial settings; and deliberative, for convincing a governmental body to support a motion

A Companion to Greek Democracy and the Roman Republic, First Edition. Edited by Dean Hammer.

or policy. In his *Rhetoric* Aristotle identifies the subject matter of each genre as follows: matters of the present for epideictic oratory, matters of the past for courts, and matters of the future for deliberative sessions. As we shall see, his division is much too neat: all three genres shared common motifs and techniques, and all three crossed temporal boundaries. Focusing on themes rather than time frames, I have chosen to examine one representative oration from each genre, all dealing largely with perceptions of citizenship and military service and all informed by the ideology of a participatory community.

1 In Praise of Athens: Rhetoric, Patriotism, and Civic Ideology

The best-known examples of Athenian epideictic oratory are funeral orations (*epitaphioi*) at the public funerals given by the city to its fallen soldiers (Ziolkowski 1981 and Loraux 1986 offer the most comprehensive investigations of the subject; see also Carey 2007: 240–244 and Balot and Atkison, Chapter 22). The ceremonies took place in the public space of the Kerameikos, and the burial of the dead in a common grave, instead of individually and by the family, reflected a civic ideology that flattened individual and class distinctions in favor of collective excellence and merit (Hyperides 6 *Funeral oration* of 323–322 BCE deviated from the norm, but only to a degree, by adding to the communal eulogy praises of the dead general Leosthenes; see Herrman 2009). In general, the funeral oration was a patriotic speech that praised the dead and the living for their courage and other civic virtues. In addition to positioning itself in its historical context, it used or manipulated motifs from past eulogies. A public figure was elected by the city to deliver the speech, and the audience consisted of male citizens (to whom the speech was primarily directed), female relatives, as well as foreigners and resident aliens.

In 338 BCE the famous orator Demosthenes delivered a speech in honor of the Athenian dead in the battle of Chaeronea (Dem. 60 *Funeral Oration*), a battle in which Philip II of Macedonia and his allies defeated a Greek coalition led by Athens and Thebes (see also Balot, Chapter 22). Demosthenes' main rhetorical challenges were twofold (on the question of the authorship, see MacDowell 2009: 376–377; for the historical background of the speech, see Ryder 2000: 79–84; Herrman 2008: 3–10). He sought to maintain a balance between innovation and the use of traditional, stock themes. He also needed to help the Athenians overcome sorrow, restore national pride, and suppress self-doubts engendered by the defeat. Because the hearers wished to feel good about themselves (cf. Plato *Menex.* 235b–c), these challenges were not overwhelming. But as Demosthenes suggests, his success still depended on the hearers' goodwill (Dem. 60.14). Thus the funeral oration was a participatory experience, communally and rhetorically.

The speech says much about relations between speaker and audience, and about their shared ideologies and values. The etiquette of public eulogies required the speaker to subordinate his personality and status to the greater goal of celebrating Athenian merit. Nevertheless, Demosthenes managed to draw attention to himself with his use of the first person singular, which only Pericles' funeral oration (Thuc. 2.35–46), among extant eulogies, uses more frequently. Demosthenes tells the audience what he intends to do, shares with them his rhetorical difficulties, explains his reasoning for speaking as he does, and so forth (Dem. 60.1–3, 6, 9–10, 12–13, 15, 27, 31, 35, 37). Apart from stylistic considerations and Demosthenes' sense of self-importance, these self-references may result from the historical circumstances of the speech. Though his anti-Macedonian stand enjoyed popular support, there were some Athenians who felt the defeat proved the failure of his confrontational policy. By directing attention to himself and making the speech a collaborative project, Demosthenes reminds the audience of what he would claim explicitly in a later speech, namely, that his election to deliver the speech was a proof of the city's approval of his policy and its preference for him over his critics (*On the Crown* 18.285–288). In the funeral oration he interprets the election of a speaker as a sure sign that the city cares about the dead, and he defines the speech as the highest form of honoring them (60.2). Demosthenes also ranks his undertaking as more difficult and more collaborative than other performances (60.13–14). His appeal to the agonistic and democratic ethos of his audience combines self-promotion and granting his hearers a share in this public enterprise (Roisman 2007: 393–400).

At the end of the speech, Demosthenes returns to the subject of the speaker–audience relationship, stating that his mission has been to speak the truth (60.37). Speakers claim veracity in all types of speech, but its meaning could change from one genre to another. In the epideictic oratory of praise, the speaker's truth was uncontested and represented the consensus. Forensic truth, however, sought to prevail upon the opposition's alleged lies that aimed to mislead the court, while deliberative truth allowed the speaker to speak his mind to a misguided *dēmos* and to distinguish himself from his deceptive rivals. Undoubtedly, the meaning of epideictic truth reflected the more co-operative interaction between speaker and audience during a state funeral.

A major theme in this speech, found also in other eulogies, is the link between Athenian courage and democracy (see Balot 2004a: 246–257; 2010; Roisman 2005: esp. 69, 77, 110–113; Christ 2006: esp. 11–13, 64, 114–116, 124–142). True to the agonistic spirit of the funeral oration, the speaker tells the audience that the courage displayed by their dead compatriots was superior to other forms of courage. Their courage was both thoughtful and manly, because they understood the danger but faced it nonetheless. Oligarchy produced bad citizens who were more fearful than dutiful and who could use bribery to avoid punishment or shame. In Athenian democracy, however, freedom of speech encouraged prosecution of cowards in a judicial system immune to bribery and administered by the people. This makes the evaluation of courage and cowardice a communal affair in which the Athenians watch fellow citizens' performance in battle and reward or punish it accordingly (60.17, 25–26, 37). Demosthenes' novelty in 60.27–31 lies in his attaching a particular meaning of courage to each of the ten Athenian tribes or citizen groups. Perhaps he looked for originality in a speech otherwise heavy with commonplaces. (Herrman 2008: 176–177 ties the passage to what he identifies as Athenian traditionalism at this time. On Athenian tribes see Rhodes, Chapter 8 above.)

In the speech, the Athenians' noble origin matched their noble character. They wanted fame, strove for virtue (*aretē*), and, thanks to Athenian education, displayed manly self-control (60.2–3, 15). Because in Greece virtue often means superiority to others, the speaker keeps returning to the theme of the Athenians' pre-eminence. They are more ancient, more intelligent, more alert, and more active than other Greeks, and especially better in war. They defeated a number of invading armies that others had failed to repel, outdid the heroes of the Trojan War in accomplishment and challenge, and prevailed over and exacted punishment from enemies mightier than they, both in mythical and in historical times (60.3–5, 8–11, 18). All these compliments fostered in the audience a sense of shared superiority that contributed to communal solidarity.

Athens' glorious military record helped also to put the recent defeat at Chaeronea in historical perspective as a temporary setback.

The Athenians, who regarded themselves as having a first claim to Greek leadership, often justified it by claims to selflessly aiding or benefiting fellow Greeks. Demosthenes accordingly violates Aristotle's rule that epideictic speeches deal with the present, producing past examples that prove the Athenians' altruism. (For oratorical use of the past as evidence for or in support of policy and ideology, see e.g. Nouhaud 1982; Worthington 1994; Grethlein 2010: 105–146.) They helped the weak and always fought on the side of justice or in self-defense (60.5, 7–8, 11, 18). The presentation is clearly one-sided, but it is more than an exercise in patriotic make-believe. Justice and moral considerations also played an important part in deliberative speeches such as those on whether Athens should make an alliance with Corcyra in spite of Corinth's objections in 433, or what was the right punishment for the rebel Mytilenians in 427 BCE (Thuc. 1.132–144, 3.26–49). The funeral oration highlights Athens' moral superiority, but it was based on the idea that disinterested justice and aid should guide citizen conduct at home and abroad.

Although the speaker was preaching to the converted, he did face one demanding rhetorical task: accounting for Athens' defeat (see Roisman 2005: 67–71; cf. Low 2010). The loss at Chaeronea posed a problem for both speaker and audience in that it was not easily reconcilable with Athens' self-image of superior manliness, martial excellence, or fighting a just war. Demosthenes helps the Athenians deal with the incongruity and with their possible self-doubts by undermining the significance of the loss. He claims that anyone (including the enemy) who stood his ground and died at his post was victorious regardless of the final result. The emphasis on performance rather than outcome worked to the advantage of the defeated, and the audience, who were brought up in the Athenian tradition of facing the enemy regardless of the odds, would have agreed (Demosthenes and presumably his public would hold on to this thought in *On the Crown* of 330 (esp. 18.199–205), where he defended his policy and the decision to go to battle: Yunis 2000). Concomitantly, Demosthenes argues that the outcome was decided by fate, absolving the vanquished of the crime of cowardice (The idea is hardly original: cf. Lys. 2.59–60; Lycurg. 1.47–49). He even makes the Macedonians hypothetically concede that their victory was not due to their superior valor, and tendentiously interprets Philip's decision not to invade Athens as a proof of his fear to re-engage an enemy as courageous as the dead of Chaeronea (60.19–21). Finally, Demosthenes deals with problem of culpability for the defeat in a way that is both patriotic and democratic, blaming the outcome on the Theban commanders and thereby shifting responsibility from Athens to Thebes and from the masses to the elite (60.23–24). Because living in a participatory community meant sharing danger, it was necessary to sustain a spirited attitude toward war by denying defeat or making individuals responsible for it. (In fact, the Athenians condemned one of their generals at Chaeronea to death: Diod. Sic. 16.88.1. The last part of the speech is devoted to consoling the relatives and friends of the dead: 60.32–37.)

In rituals such as state funerals, the Athenian speakers rearticulated the city's self-identity, its democratic ideology, and the values that sustained state and community. The following example shows that rhetoric served similar purposes in other participatory communities and venues. Around 370 BCE, two Theban politicians, Pelopidas and Menecleides, were engaged in a nasty political contest, during which Pelopidas prosecuted Menecleides for moving to honor the Theban general Charon for a victory against Sparta (Plut. *Pelopidas* 25). Pelopidas claimed in his speech that the Thebans did not traditionally honor individuals but credited victories to the entire people, going on to suggest that voting for his opponent would be tantamount to the Thebans' admitting that they deserved no credit. The anxiety that individual honors might detract from collective worth can be gleaned also from Demosthenes' funeral oration, which contains a refusal to identify acts of individual heroism. Like Demosthenes, Pelopidas equated true excellence with communal effort, and, in true democratic fashion, appropriated for the people all claims to fame. Speakers in deliberative or forensic speeches often appealed to this belief in shared virtue, but their purpose was more utilitarian and their audience often less sympathetic.

2 Exhorting the Athenians: The Rhetoric of Betrayed Ideals

Before discussing the function of rhetoric in the assembly setting of participatory communities, a few general observations on the nature of Athenian political oratory are in order. In Athenian democracy, as in many other participatory communities, formal political deliberations took place in the courts, the council, and, especially, in the popular assembly. In the absence of political parties in the modern sense of the word, speakers had to rely on rhetoric to garner support for their position. As in Rome, the people attending the meeting did not establish its agenda. Yet in contrast to the Roman hierarchical system, Athenian politicians did not control the process. Councilmen and office-holders chosen by lot from among the citizens predetermined and advertised the agenda before submitting it to the assembly for consideration and decision-making. In the case of a disagreement, rival speakers used rhetoric to influence the vote. Descriptions of deliberative assemblies in historians such as Thucydides, Xenophon, or Diodorus often show how a speaker carried the day. Yet the power of rhetoric only went so far because the audience could interrupt the speaker or even silence him (see below). The people's direct participation in the debate and their power to accept, amend, or reject a proposal illustrates the limitations of the art of persuasion in the political process (see Rhodes, Chapter 8, for the Athenian assembly and its procedures).

When Demosthenes delivered his funeral oration in 338 BCE, he was a senior politician whose greatest glory was, in fact, behind him. The assembly speech commonly entitled the *First Philippic*, on the other hand, was given fairly early in his career (351 BCE), a circumstance that influenced both its style and content (for the speech and its background, see Pearson 1976: 123–127; Karvounis 2002: 223–260; MacDowell 2009: 210–218; for the rhetoric: Wooten 2008; cf. Mader 2006). The historical context also shaped the interaction between the speaker and his audience.

Demosthenes' *First Philippic* focused on Athens' relations with Philip II, king of Macedonia. Since c.357 BCE, Philip had succeeded in driving the Athenians from several places in the Strymon valley and Chalcidice in northern Greece. He also controlled much of Thessaly, intervened in Thrace as far as the Propontis, and attempted to invade central Greece before being stopped by Athenian and Phocian forces at Thermopylae. Demosthenes probably exaggerated the ineffectiveness of the Athenians' countermeasures, but he was surely right in saying they were less than wholehearted. In addition to their reluctance to embark on costly campaigns, many Athenians did not consider the king effectively dangerous, and Philip himself did not seek a direct confrontation. News of his withdrawal from an eastern campaign and of his illness made him seem a smaller threat. All of this increased Demosthenes' difficulties in persuading the assembly to act promptly and earnestly against what he saw as the real danger posed by Philip.

His strategy involves the creation of four rhetorical portraits—of the Athenians, of Philip, of his rival speakers, and of himself (see Mader 2003)—all with pre-existing identities that he refashioned to his purposes. Demosthenes makes these "characters" travel freely in time: to the past, which provides examples of both good and bad Athenian conduct; to the present, which is almost always bad; and to the future, which can be good or bad, depending on the result of the debate.

The most salient portrait is that of the erring Athenians. Their apathy lost opportunities to contain Philip, making them their own worst enemies and helping Philip to achieve his present power (4.2–12). Demosthenes uses a variety of means, including mockery and irony, to depict his audience as men guilty of their own misfortune (both Rowe 1968 and Mader 2003 argue that Demosthenes depicts Athens as an upside-down, perverted world). He contends that they reacted to Philip's encroachments with empty decrees, with underfunded and ineffective operations, or with belated and hence useless measures. He even compares them to a barbarian boxer (a comic, derided figure) who grabs or defends his body where he has already been hit (4.19, 40). The people know how to run state festivals on time and in good order, but in war everything is badly arranged, badly managed, badly defined. At the core of the negative portrait are the Athenians' violations of civic standards and manly ideals. Their passiveness, their reacting rather than acting, their following rather than leading, their allowing Philip to win, and their failure to seize opportunities are both defeatist and unmanly. Demosthenes also appeals to the Athenians' national pride when he portrays Philip's actions as insulting and their own inaction and self-deception as disgraceful and cowardly (4.10, 37–38, 42).

The idea that underlies both this speech and the *Funeral Oration* is that citizens are judged by the way they enact their membership in the community, especially in the military sphere; this performance establishes their character and reputation and those of their city. That is why the Athenians of the *First Philippic* are described as the antithesis of the ideal citizens of the *Funeral Oration*. But the speaker is careful not to carry his reproof too far. He wishes to motivate but not to antagonize his audience, and for his proposal to pass, he has to give them hope. Hence he portrays the Athenians' conduct more as an aberration than as the norm. From their past he selects examples not only of failure but also of military success that show they can win. In short, the Athenians have what it takes, and they can reverse their fortunes if only they adopt his plan (4.2–8, 24, 30, 39–40, 50). Such an attitude brings the Athens of the *First Philippic* closer to that of the *Funeral Oration*, because it restores the connection of communal effort to courage, energy, and a rightful position of leadership.

Demosthenes portrays Philip as the opposite of the Athenians in order to arouse their fear and rivalry. While they are lethargic, Philip is full of energy; if they are negligent and passive, he is proactive, opportunistic, and willing to face risks and toil (4.2–5, 31). They are losing power and respect as he feeds on their weaknesses and dishonors them (4.37, 42, 50). Demosthenes then warns that if they refuse to face reality, they may have to fight Philip in Attica (4.50) (see Mader 2003: esp. 60–69, for the resemblance of Philip's portrait to Thucydides' depiction of the Athenians, especially in 1.70). Yet Philip is never too formidable to be unbeatable. He is overreaching and overactive, and if the Athenians take the right steps, he can be defeated or intimidated (4.7, 9, 49).

The least developed portrait in the speech is that of Demosthenes' political rivals, whom he depicts as more misguided than malevolent, probably because he was a junior speaker who did not wish to antagonize his seniors. At the beginning of the speech, his criticism of rivals for failing to give needful advice is quite muted (4.1; cf. 4.18; *Proem* 1.1, and below). But elsewhere he tries to forestall potential criticism of his proposed plan, suggesting that those who are unwilling to criticize the people are ignoring reality and causing the city harm (4.28–29, 38). He also implies that competing plans are part of the usual political rivalry and name-calling that led to the present bad situation (4.44–50). Speakers in a participatory democracy confronted an active opposition and audience, but in the *Funeral Oration* Demosthenes was free of such concerns.

His self-presentation was designed to promote both his military plan and Demosthenes himself (see below). The details of his scheme cannot be discussed here, but some of its components illustrate his appeal to the city as a participatory community. He recommends sending against Philip a land force consisting of three-quarters mercenaries and the rest citizens. His greatest challenge, presumably, was to persuade the latter that they should serve in person, and he meets it primarily by deploring their inaction and past use of noncitizen troops as the root of their problem. The background of his urging every citizen to become "useful for the *polis*"—the rich paying the war tax and the able man serving in the army (4.7)—was the civic ethos of shared effort and sacrifice that informs the *Funeral Oration*. Elsewhere he notes that the citizens who will serve in the force could watch their commanding officers and bring them to justice for wrongdoing. The same precepts of accountability and active citizenship are supposed to prevent cowardice in battle and neglect of duty in the *Funeral Oration* (60.25–26).

It would be naive to assume that the presumed merits of the plan alone were sufficient to persuade the audience. In Athens a proposer and his proposal were linked both legally and politically, with each telling on the other. At the time of the speech, Demosthenes was about 33 years old and somewhat disadvantaged by his junior status as speaker and statesman. Hence at the beginning of the speech he half-apologizes for speaking ahead of his elders (a probably no longer enforced rule gave the privilege of speaking first in the assembly to citizens over 50 years old: Kapparis 1998), but goes on to reconstruct his identity and authority as that of an expert advisor and a better man than the assembled Athenians, going on to blame and even belittle the *dēmos*. He also displays detailed and presumably unique knowledge of the enemy and the theater of war (e.g. 4.31–32). Even his use of rhetorical questions is designed not just to keep the audience's interest but also to establish his authority as a man who knows better than the ignorant or misguided audience (e.g. 4.20). He also compares his role as advisor to that of a general who is expected to foresee and manage events rather than react to them (4.38–39). In his own way, then, Demosthenes resembled the eulogized Athenians who before Chaeronea faced a danger that threatened all Greeks but "were first to recognize it, and so often they exhorted everyone to save the situation, which is an illustration of purpose and right thinking" (60.18, trans. Worthington 2006; see Mader 2003: 62–64 on anticipation and leadership). At one point Demosthenes anticipates the criticism that the troops will be underpaid, promising in that case to volunteer for the expedition himself and to suffer the worst (4.29). Whether or not his promise is sincere, it draws a clear contrast between him and the audience, who refused to serve, take a risk, or make a sacrifice.

Demosthenes concludes the speech by reaffirming his rhetorical identity as a dedicated public speaker. He has never tried to flatter his audience, has said only what was good for them, and has spoken candidly (4.51). The last assertion claims for him the possession of truth and a better understanding of the situation than is offered by competing views and analyses. He adds that he is risking unpopularity or prosecution by advising the people, but that communal good should prevail over all other considerations (4.51). These statements are formulaic and answer popular expectations of leaders to be courageous and self-sacrificing (see, for example, Dem. 1.15–16, 3.30–32; Ober 1989: 318–332). But they also imply that he was meeting communal standards and ideals betrayed by the audience, such as those elaborated in the *Funeral Oration*.

Demosthenes, thus, depicts a polity undermined and endangered by citizens who shirk or fulfill halfheartedly the responsibilities that living in a participatory community entails. By branding them with an identity that stands in contrast to the model Athenians of the *Funeral Oration*, he hopes to provoke the people to prove him wrong and mend their ways. The other three identities in the speech also relate to his idealized model. Philip alarmingly resembles it, the rival politicians obstruct it, and Demosthenes follows it more loyally than anyone else.

Demosthenes' proposal was voted down, and not for frivolous reasons. The evidence shows that Athenian citizens did not evade their military duty as a matter of course but served in person when they themselves thought it necessary (Burckhardt 1996: 181–223). In addition, assemblymen attentive to the details of his plan might have found some of it too exacting in manpower, finance, and terms of service. And the audience was probably reluctant to accept the identity of passive, simple-minded, unmanly citizens that Demosthenes assigned them. Rightly or wrongly, they believed they were the same meritorious Athenians of the funeral orations, no matter how they dealt with Philip.

Thucydides' depiction of a debate in democratic Syracuse in 415 provides a useful comparison to Demosthenes' speech and its circumstances (6.32.3–41.2; for democratic Syracuse and the speeches discussed here, see, conveniently, Robinson 2000; Hornblower 1991–2008: 3: esp. 395–397, 405–407). At that time Athens had made preparations to invade Sicily but, according to the historian, not everyone in Syracuse believed the news, and even those who did thought that Syracuse could handle the threat. Like Demosthenes, the Syracusan leader Hermocrates urged his fellow citizens to recognize the danger, put an end to their apathy, and display courage. He too offered a detailed military plan to deal with the enemy, describing himself as a knowledgeable and courageous man. Thucydides depicts his political opponent, Athenagoras, as a misleading and/or misguided demagogue, who accused Hermocrates and his supporters of trying to establish an oligarchy in the city by scaring the people with unfounded reports of the invasion, which, even if it happened, would be easily repelled. (Conspiratorial charges were also common in Athenian oratory, including in Demosthenes' speeches. For Athenagoras' manipulation of democratic ideology and conspiratorial charges, see Andrewes 2009; on orators and conspiracy see Roisman 2006: esp. 66–94.) Athenagoras also defended democracy as a more inclusive and wiser form of government than oligarchy. His tribute to democracy had the same purpose as Demosthenes' criticism of the Athenians' failure to meet their ideals, in that both validated for their respective audiences their political systems and their supporting values. Explicitly or implicitly, both speakers also acknowledge the difficulties citizens had in sustaining these systems.

3 The Rhetoric of Good Citizenship

We turn now to forensic oratory. The Athenian law courts were run and manned by the same citizens who listened to the funeral orations and to speakers in the assembly (for the Athenian courts and laws, see Rhodes, Chapter 8). The litigants were citizens who delivered their own speeches, but they could be aided by supporting speakers. It was believed that speaking skills, legal knowledge, or expert representation constituted an unfair advantage that was especially available to the rich. Those who could afford it, however, might hire a ghostwriter to prepare their speech.

Our case in point is a speech that Lysias wrote, presumably for a fee, for an Athenian defendant most likely named Mantitheus (Lys. 16 *For Mantitheus*; see Roisman 2005's discussion of Mantitheus' depiction as a young man, esp. 23–25. For the speech see also Weissenberger 1987: 24–83). Sometime after 395 BCE, Mantitheus faced a *dokimasia* or review, a procedure that tested a candidate's legal qualification for public office (see Rhodes, Chapter 8, for the institutional context). Such reviews were often done *pro forma*, but at times interested citizens could question the eligibility of the candidate, either because they genuinely suspected it or, as was equally likely, they wished to harm him and his image. Mantitheus likely was one of 500 annual candidates for the council who were reviewed by its serving members (for *dokimasia* of councilmen, see Rhodes 1981: 542–543). Although he addressed the council, his speech was not deliberative, because the procedure resembled a judicial process. The speech shares themes with Demosthenes' *Funeral Oration* and *First Philippic*, allowing us to see how different genres, structures, and circumstances shaped rhetorical use of the Athenian participatory community. (We do not know the outcome of the case.)

Mantitheus' review took place during the Corinthian War, fought by Athens and her allies against Sparta. Domestically, the city had by now presumably recovered from the tyrannical rule of the Thirty, the oligarchs who in 404–403 BCE had oppressed, robbed, and killed their fellow Athenians. Democracy was restored in 403 BCE, and the so-called amnesty agreement stipulated that supporters or beneficiaries of the Thirty's regime, with a few exceptions, would not be prosecuted. Yet memories, antagonism, and opportunism kept the experience of the Thirty alive, both in politics and in the courts. Mantitheus' speech suggests that he was charged with serving in the cavalry under the Thirty and suspected of oligarchic sympathies. Neither charge appears to have been legally sufficient to disqualify him, but the accusation may have aimed to embarrass him and, if successful, to make him vulnerable to subsequent political or judicial attacks. There seems to have been little risk to the accuser or accusers, except for the chagrin of defeat. (Mantitheus, however, might have appealed the verdict or retaliated with charges of perjury against hostile witnesses.)

Lysias is known for his skillful construction of characters, and Mantitheus' self-depiction is no exception. He portrays himself as a man who meets and even exceeds the expectations of male citizens in private and public. More than other genres, forensic oratory foregrounded the personality of the speaker, often by demonstrating his conformity to the city's norms and values. Lysias designs Mantitheus' account of his career to refute not only specific accusations but also prejudices against his wealth, age, and even appearance.

Aiming to show that he did not threaten the city and its regime, as his accusers probably suggested, Mantitheus declares that he is loyal to the democratic government and was obliged to share in "your dangers" (16.3). The last reference is to his military service, which occupies a prominent role in his defense, serving to show his adherence to the ideology of citizenship as partnership in war (legally speaking, one of the review questions concerned the candidate's military service: Hansen 1991: 219). Demosthenes uses the same idea in the *Funeral Oration* to extol the Athenian dead and in the *First Philippic* to motivate the living through rebukes. Thus both speakers suggest not just the versatility of Athenian oratory but also how this communal ideal was communicated and reinforced in different public arenas. To complement his portrait, Mantitheus depicts himself as a *metrios*, a moderate man who conforms to civic and societal expectations (16.3; for the *metrios*, see Ober 1989: 162, 257–259). In this way he assures the audience that they have nothing to fear from him.

Mantitheus then turns to disproving the charge that he was part of the Thirty's government and that he served in their cavalry, who were viewed as their supporters. He first argues that he was not in Athens during much of the Thirty's time in power. He then uses probability to show that he was not the kind of man who supported the Thirty or whom they were likely to co-opt. Next he tries to refute written evidence of his service in their cavalry by producing contradictory and allegedly more accurate records (16.5–7). His reasoning and evidence demonstrate the kind of rhetoric used to persuade an audience asked to choose between conflicting "truths" (the speaker argues that the other side is lying: 16.8). One means of deciding the question was to evaluate the entire personality of the speaker through his contribution to the city. This is why Mantitheus dwells on his performance of military duties (see below).

At first, Mantitheus crafts for himself the identity of desirable family man and citizen. Character attestation in Athenian trials was meant to tell the jurors if the defendant was the sort of man who would do the kind of things he was charged with and if the city would benefit or be harmed by his conviction. Mantitheus presents his private conduct as that of a dutiful head of a household (*kyrios*). Although he did not get a big inheritance (his word), he married off his sisters with generous dowries. He even took less of his patrimony than his brother (16.10). His self-sacrifice and failure to pursue wealth reflected, in private life, the spirit of the dead Athenian warriors who nobly spurned wealth and pleasures (Dem. 60.2). It was important for the well-to-do Mantitheus to distance himself from the Athenian stereotype of the rich as self-indulgent men who shirked familial and civic obligations in favor of more selfish ends (for the image and the question of its validity, see Christ 2006: 143–204). Mantitheus then portrays himself as not litigious, elaborating his self-characterization as an unmeddlesome *metrios*, or a moderate, conforming man. He was never involved in "shameful" litigation, that is, in using the courts for personal gain or to harm other citizens and the public (sycophancy; for Athenian sycophancy, see Christ 1998). The class of the litigious may have been thought to include young men, and Mantitheus accordingly insists that he is not one of those (stereotypical) young men who waste their time in gambling, drinking, and disorderly behavior (16.11–12).

Much of Mantitheus' public identity revolves around his military service about eight years after the fall of the Thirty, an episode irrelevant, in legal terms, to his history under their rule. His aim here is ethical: to prove his loyalty to the ideal of the fearless, self-sacrificing citizen-soldier. He does it by manipulating two themes that are found in Demosthenes' *Funeral Oration* and *First Philippic*. Like the Athenian dead, or those who should fight Philip, Mantitheus the soldier placed others' welfare before his own (just as he did in private) and displayed his excellence against a background of often less worthy men. (If Mantitheus' tribal unit was charged with cowardice in the battle of Nemea, as Christ 2006: 107–109, suggests, he would have had an additional incentive to highlight his courage. He may even have been singled out as a coward.)

Mantitheus says he was assigned to the cavalry when the Athenians mobilized forces for a military campaign in Boeotia in 395 BCE. Everyone thought it was a safer service than fighting among the hoplites, and there were even men who joined the cavalry illegally. He, in contrast, asked his commanding officer (who testifies on his behalf in the review) to strike his name from the list of cavalrymen. It was shameful, he says, to care for his personal safety when many faced danger as infantrymen (16.12–13). About sixty years later Demosthenes would use this sentiment in the *Funeral Oration* to commend the dead of Chaeronea for scorning the passion for life (60.1). The difference between the two tributes to courage was that Demosthenes' tribute was given to anonymous citizens by a representative of the community, while Mantitheus' tribute was self-proclaimed. Indeed, one hopes that Mantitheus did not turn his discharge from cavalry service into a virtue and that his failure to mention that he fought as a hoplite in the campaign was a mere oversight. Taken at face value, his statements confirm that he shared danger with other citizens and even exceeded expectations by actively seeking it.

In addition to being courageous, Mantitheus was also a useful citizen. Both Pericles' and Demosthenes' eulogies praise Athens as a city served by its citizens according to their abilities and means (Thuc. 2.37.1; Dem. 4.7). The same participatory principle guided Mantitheus' contribution to the war effort, which Lysias clearly overstates. The speaker says that when the men of his deme (township) reported to duty, they included good but poor citizens who had no provisions. Observing the situation, Mantitheus urged men of means in the deme to provide for the needy, setting a personal example by giving two soldiers 30 drachmas each (16.14; according to one modern estimate, 30 drachmas might get a hoplite a shield and a spear or a month's wage: van Wees 2002: 63). The speaker foregrounds his generosity to show that he met the democratic expectation that rich men share their wealth with the public instead of spending it on themselves. In short, he was a valuable citizen whom the city would do well to protect from his accusers.

Returning to his military performance, Mantitheus mentions a later campaign at Nemea in 394 BCE against a Peloponnesian alliance, in which Athens lost the battle and many men. The most dangerous position in the hoplite phalanx was the front line, where Mantitheus volunteered to stand. He also notes that people knew the entire mission was dangerous. Like the dead of Chaeronea, the speaker measured up to the highest standards of Athenian manly courage, facing danger in full knowledge of the risk. He accentuates his performance by contrasting it with the cowardice of those who were retreating while he stood in the front rank, fought in a tribal unit that suffered many casualties, and was late to depart (16.15; cf. 16.19). In the *Funeral Oration* Demosthenes insists that the results of the battle are not as important as how it was fought, and Mantitheus' contention reflects this view.

Not long after Nemea there was another mission to Corinth, and the speaker describes the general fear that attended it as fully understandable. By now the council should have gotten the idea that universal fear leads Mantitheus to court danger. He went to the commanding officer and asked that his hoplite unit be sent to the front without using the lottery (16.16). He does not report if the officer accepted his offer or if he was sent to Corinth, but the incident reinforces the image of a patriotic citizen-warrior of the kind Demosthenes would have liked to send against Philip.

The city, for its part, was expected to reciprocate such services from its citizens. In the *Funeral Oration* Athens rewarded the dead warriors with lasting honor and memory, while in the *First Philippic* the presumed reward was the restoration of Athens' security and prestige. Mantitheus asks for a more modest and personal recompense when he states that the purpose of his displays of courage was to be treated favorably if he were ever put on trial (16.17). Other litigants in the oratorical corpus make similar pleas for leniency from the court in return for good citizenry, financial contributions, or other benefits to the city (see Isae. 7.41; Lys. 25.12–13; Roisman 2005: 153–155). However, reports of services or gifts rendered the city in the orations far surpass requests (explicit or implicit) for recompense. The Athenians who sat in judgment were much more interested in "the take" than in "the give" of the reciprocal relationship between the citizen and the state.

The last part of Mantitheus' speech discusses his political reputation and activity. He was apparently accused of harboring oligarchic sympathies, although the only charge he quotes was probably the easiest to deflect. The prosecution referred to his long hair, which suggested philo-Spartan views and conduct, a suspicion lent plausibility by his condition as a well-off young man. In response he resorts to the common wisdom of "appearances can be deceiving" in the hope that the councilmen will rise above their prejudices and adopt his functional approach to citizenship (16.18–19). Mantitheus also addresses a complaint related to his speaking in the assembly. Its exact nature is obscured by his incomplete allusion: he mentions annoying others by speaking in public at too young an age, but omits the possibly damaging content of this early speech. But while Demosthenes alludes to his youth only briefly in the *First Philippic* (see above), Mantitheus ingeniously uses his age both to excuse his conduct and to throw the accusation of speaking prematurely back at the opposition and even the public. While confessing that he may have been more ambitious (*philotimoteron*) than necessary in addressing the assembly, he says he did it because he felt it was expected of him (16.20). The notion of *philotimia*, or pursuit of personal honor, had a positive meaning when it served the common good, but negative connotations when it led to individual prestige and ambition at the expense of others or the city. The young were especially known for a competitive pursuit of honor that could result in conflicts and violations of the norm. Mantitheus accordingly seeks understanding for his ambition in youth, stressing that it drove him to benefit the city. In short, his political *philotimia* complemented his military pursuit of honor (for *philotimia*, see Whitehead 1983 and 1993; compare the Athenian warriors who were full of *philotimia* when they marched to the battlefield of Chaeronea: Dem. 60.22). Finally, he spoke because "you" (the jurors) regard only men who do so as worthy (16.20). Here Mantitheus is citing the Athenian participatory ideals of political engagement and harnessing individual pursuit of honor to public benefit. As in all genres of speech, the speaker acknowledges the power of the popular audience to decide his performance and its consequences.

4 The Speaker and His Public: Feedback and its Problems

Our discussion so far has focused on the rhetorical means speakers used to persuade their different audiences. Especially in the assembly, many took advantage of the democratic entitlement of *isēgoria* (equal right to speak) and *parrhēsia* (the right to speak one's mind), which allowed any citizen to voice his opinion, advise the city, or criticize other speakers and even the people as a whole. Furthermore, the consumers of rhetoric in the assembly, council, or court were not shy of expressing their opinions about the speakers and the subject at hand. By means of a so-called "clamorous din" (*thorybos*), the hearers might interrupt or even stop a speaker, thus becoming active players in the democratic communication process.

The extant speeches of the Attic orators are full of references to assembly meetings, in particular where heckling, raising objections, mocking, shouting down, and other forms of reacting to a speaker took place, some spontaneous and others provoked by adversarial speakers (for discussions of the evidence on the audience's behavior, see Wallace 2004; Balot 2004b: 242–246; Roisman 2004: 264–268). Rather than revisiting this familiar scholarly ground, however, I wish to return to democratic Syracuse in order to show that the audience's active role in political deliberations belonged more to the nature of participatory community than to a certain locale. The Syracusans were debating the fate of the Athenian prisoners of war, and especially their generals, who had surrendered at the end of their failed invasion of Sicily (413 BCE). The historian Diodorus of Sicily gives the fullest description of the deliberations, and although he, or his sources, might have confused the speakers and their positions and composed for them excessively long speeches, the account is still valuable to our topic (Diod. Sic. 13. 19.4–33.1; for Diodorus' narrative, see Ambaglio 2008: 37–56; Hau 2009: 190–191).

In Diodorus' version, the popular leader Diocles opened the debate with a proposal to imprison the troops and execute their generals. When the more conservative Hermocrates suggested treating the captives more humanely, the people vociferously objected, refusing to let him continue his speech (so also Plut. *Nicias* 28). They only stopped clamoring when a father who had lost two sons in the war asked to speak, because they thought, says Diodorus, that he would call for condemning the prisoners (Diod. Sic. 13.19.4–6). However, the old man advocated leniency and won the people's sympathy. Then the Spartan Gylippus, who had helped the Syracusans fight the invaders, spoke in favor of the original proposal of executing the enemy generals, with Diodorus, like a playwright, inserting into his speech the audience's acclamations to his rhetorical questions. Gylippus won the day, and Diodorus, as he was wont to do, stressed the people's volatility in making decisions (Diod. Sic. 13. 28.4–6, 33.1; according to Thuc. 7.85.1–86.5 and Plut. *Nicias* 27–28, Gylippus actually wanted the generals spared so he could take them triumphantly to Sparta).

The unflattering description of the *dēmos*' behavior reflects an elitist view of their role in the deliberation process and is akin to criticism of speakers that they cater to the people's whim (e.g. Aristophanes *Knights* or Plato *Gorgias*, *passim*.). Yet in a democracy the people had both the right and power to make the speaker tell them what they thought was proper or desirable. The clamoring and silencing of speakers were means of ensuring that they and the people would be like-minded. It informed speakers of public opinion, moved them to adjust their proposals to popular expectations, and even allowed them to benefit from the people's collective wisdom, and if they disagreed, they had to exit the stage (for wisdom found among the many: Thuc. 6.39.1; Arist. *Pol.* 1281a42–b5). The speaker was not powerless in the interaction because he had the right to free and frank speech, occupied center stage, and often outranked his listeners in status and expertise. He also had all the powers of the art of persuasion at his disposal. Nevertheless, making a commotion and silencing him showed him who the real boss was. The sources even suggest that it was improper for a speaker to ignore attempts to interrupt him (e.g. Aeschin. 1.34; Dem. *Exordia* 10.1, 56; see also Wallace 2004: 227).

The audience's active participation in the democratic discourse was thus full of tensions. Clamoring or silencing a speaker could prevent the city from getting good advice, or benefit from hearing both sides, as speakers seeking to calm the audience argued (Dem. *Exordia* 4, 10.1, 45.6). It antagonized orators and hearers, and discouraged contributions from men fearful of facing the crowd. It also raised the question of accountability and fairness. By law, speakers and proposers were liable to prosecution for the way they executed their role, while the people were not accountable (Hansen 1991: 204, 208, 267). Who, then, should have been held responsible for the consequences of a vote: the speaker-advisor or the public who guided him with friendly or hostile input and then approved his motion? Critics of democracy complained that proposers and other individuals were punished for decisions made by the people (e.g. [Xen.] *Ath. Pol.* 2.17). In the Syracusan debate involving the Athenian captives, "Gylippus" twists this complaint in one of the most (unintentionally?) ironic parts of his speech. He asserts that all Athenians, rather than their advisors alone, were guilty of their decisions, thereby exonerating him from responsibility for the decision, and making the Syracusans culpable for following his advice.

> We shall find, however, that in most cases their [i.e. the Athenians'] advisors pay every attention to the wishes of their audience, so that the voter suggests to the speaker words that suit his own purpose. For the speaker is not the master of the multitude, but the people, by adopting measures that are honest, train the orator to propose what is best. If we shall pardon men guilty of irrevocable injustices when they lay the responsibility upon their advisors, we shall indeed be providing the wicked with an easy defense! (Diod. Sic. 13.31.2–3, trans. Oldfather)

Democratic rhetoric, thus, was a product of a dialogue between speakers and their audience rather than a one-way communicative process. It was not always an easy dialogue, and there were consequences for which credit or blame could be subjectively assigned. Yet the interaction between a speaker and his listeners illustrates the participatory dimension of ancient democracy.

5 Conclusion

The above discussion does not aim to be exhaustive. The rhetoric of participatory community dealt with a range of military and nonmilitary matters as well, and the ideology that informed it could be inconsistent. I have tried, however, to show the endurance of key participatory ideals and the ways in which speakers communicated and manipulated them as they interacted with their audience in different institutions and historical settings. In Rome too, as Chapter 17 shows, each venue had its distinctive functions and audience that affected the rhetoric of the speaker and his means of asserting control over hearers who actively tested it. Similarly, in both communities elite speakers articulated common ideals in way that served collective and self-interest, only that in Athens such an enactment of political authority contributed more to the hegemony of the *dēmos* than to that of the elite. With that said, the relationship between rhetoric and communal ideals in Athens might have also had a darker side, as the following example shows. In 331 BCE Lycurgus, a politician with a considerable legal bloodlust, charged the Athenian Leocrates with treason. Leocrates had left Athens after the battle of Chaeronea, as the city was taking steps to defend itself against Philip. He returned home about seven years later, when Lycurgus sought in a forensic speech to portray his departure and absence as so harmful to the city that he deserved to die (for a recent discussion of the trial and possible reasons for its outcome, see Whitehead 2006). At one point Lycurgus tries to answer the defense's reasonable counter-argument that one man should not be held responsible for national security or the consequences of defeat. Lycurgus' rebuttal includes an assertion familiar from other speeches: "the city's safety was this man's responsibility. Every individual has his own personal share in managing and protecting the city, and when someone neglects his duty in one way, he may not realize it, but he neglects it in all ways… This man therefore deserves to suffer greater penalty, since he alone of all the rest of the citizens wanted safety for himself, not for the city" (Lycurg. 1.64–67, trans. Harris). Lycurgus' statements, inaccurate in substance and depending on the worst form of "slippery-slope" argument, aimed at condemnation of a man who decided, for whatever reason, that the pact between a citizen and his city was voluntary rather than compulsory and that sharing danger should not be so broadly defined. It was to the Athenians' credit that Leocrates escaped punishment. But it is an indication of the dangers of a participatory community and its rhetoric that he was acquitted on a tie vote (Aeschin. 3.252).

REFERENCES

Ambaglio, D., ed., 2008. *Diodoro Siculo: Biblioteca storica: libro XIII: commento storico. Storia. Ricerche*. Milan.

Andrewes, J.A. 2009. "Athenagoras, *Stasis*, and Factional Rhetoric (Thucydides 6.36–40)." *CPh* 104(1): 1–12.

Balot, R. 2004a. "Courage in the Democratic *Polis*." *CQ* 54: 406–423.

Balot, R. 2004b. Free Speech, Courage, and Democratic Deliberation. In I. Sluiter and R.M. Rosen, eds., *Free Speech in Classical Antiquity*. Leiden, 233–259.

Balot, R. 2010. "Democratizing Courage in Classical Athens." In D.M. Pritchard, ed., *War, Democracy and Culture in Classical Athens*. Cambridge, 88–108.

Bers, V. 1985. "Dikastic Thorubos." In P.A. Cartledge and F.D. Harvey, eds., *Crux: Essays in Greek History Presented to G.E.M. de Ste. Croix on his 75th Birthday*. Exeter, 1–15.

Burckhardt, L. 1996. *Bürger Und Soldaten: Aspekte der Politischen und Militärischen Rolle Athenischer Bürger im Kriegswesen Des 4. Jahrhunderts V. Chr.* Stuttgart.

Carey, C. 2007. "Epideictic Oratory." In I. Worthington, ed., *A Companion to Greek Rhetoric*. Oxford and Malden, MA, 236–252.

Christ, M.R. 1998. *The Litigious Athenian*. Baltimore.
Christ, M.R. 2006. *The Bad Citizen in Classical Athens*. Cambridge.
Grethlein, J. 2010. *The Greeks and Their Past: Poetry, Oratory and History in the Fifth Century* BCE. Cambridge.
Hansen, M.H. 1991. *The Athenian Democracy in the Age of Demosthenes: Structure, Principles, Ideology*. Trans. J.A. Crook. Oxford.
Hau, L.I. 2009. "The Burden of Good Fortune in Diodorus of Sicily: a Case for Originality?" *Historia* 58(2): 171–197.
Herrman, J. 2008. "The Authenticity of the Demosthenic *Funeral Oration*." *Acta Antiqua* 48(1–2): 171–178.
Herrman, J. ed. 2009. *Hyperides. Funeral Oration*. Oxford.
Hornblower, S. 1991–2008. *A Commentary on Thucydides*. 3 vols. Oxford.
Kapparis, K.A. 1998. "The Law on the Age of Speakers in the Athenian Assembly." *RhM* 141: 255–259.
Karvounis, C. 2002. *Demosthenes: Studien zu den Demegorien orr. XIV, XVI, XV, I II, III*. Tübingen.
Loraux, N. 1986. *The Invention of Athens: The Funeral Oration in the Classical City*. Trans. A. Sheridan. Cambridge, MA.
Low, P. 2010. "Commemoration of the War Dead in Classical Athens: Remembering Defeat and Victory." In D.M. Pritchard, ed., *War, Democracy and Culture in Classical Athens*. Cambridge, 341–358.
MacDowell, D.M. 2009. *Demosthenes the Orator*. Oxford.
Mader, G. 2003. "*Quantum mutati ab illis*...: Satire and Displaced Identity in Demosthenes' *First Philippic*." *Philologus* 147: 56–69.
Mader, G. 2006. "Fighting Philip with Decrees: Demosthenes and the Syndrome of Symbolic Action." *AJP* 127(3): 367–386.
Nouhaud, M. 1982. *L'utilisation de l'histoire par les orateurs attiques*. Paris.
Ober, J. 1989. *Mass and Elite in Democratic Athens*. Princeton.
Pearson, L. 1976. *The Art of Demosthenes*. Meisenheim am Glan.
Pritchard, D.M., ed. 2010. *War, Democracy and Culture in Classical Athens*. Cambridge.
Rhodes, P.J. 1981. *A Commentary on the Aristotelian* Athenaion Politeia. Oxford.
Robinson, E.W. 2000. "Democracy in Syracuse, 466–412 BC." *HSPh* 100: 189–205; repr. in E.W. Robinson, ed., *Ancient Greek Democracy. Readings and Sources*. Oxford and Malden, MA (2004), 140–151.
Roisman, J. 2004. "Speaker–Audience Interaction in Athens: A Power Struggle." In I. Sluiter and R.M. Rosen, eds., *Free Speech in Classical Antiquity*. Leiden, 261–278.
Roisman, J. 2005. *The Rhetoric of Manhood: Masculinity According to the Attic Orators*. Berkeley.
Roisman, J. 2006. *The Rhetoric of Conspiracy in Ancient Athens*. Berkeley.
Roisman, J. 2007. "Rhetoric, Manliness and Contest." In I. Worthington, ed., *A Companion to Greek Rhetoric*. Oxford and Malden, MA, 393–410.
Rowe, G., 1968. "Demosthenes' *First Philippic*: The Satiric Mode." *TAPA* 99: 361–374.
Ryder, T.T.B. 2000. "Demosthenes and Philip II." In I. Worthington, ed., *Demosthenes: Statesman and Orator*. London, 45–89.
Tacon, J. 2001. "Ecclesiastic *Thorubos*: Interventions, Interruptions, and Popular Involvement in the Athenian Assembly." *G&R*^{2} 48(2): 173–192.
van Wees, H. 2002. "Tyrants, Oligarchs and Citizen Militias." In A. Chaniotis and P. Ducrey, eds., *Army and Power in the Ancient World*. Stuttgart, 61–82.
Wallace, R.W. 2004. "The Power to Speak—and Not to Listen—in Ancient Athens." In I. Sluiter and R.M. Rosen, eds., *Free Speech in Classical Antiquity*. Leiden, 221–232.
Weissenberger, M. 1987. *Die Dokimasiereden des Lysias (orr. 16, 25, 26, 31)*. Frankfurt am Main.

Whitehead, D. 1983. "Competitive Outlay and Community Profit: φιλοτιμία in Democratic Athens." *Classica & Mediaevalia* 34: 55–74.

Whitehead, D. 1993. "Cardinal Virtues: The Language of Public Approbation in Democratic Athens." *Classica & Mediaevalia* 44: 37–75.

Whitehead, D. 2006. "Absentee Athenians: Lysias Against Philon and Lycurgus Against Leocrates." *MH* 63(3): 132–151.

Wooten, C. 2008. *A Commentary on Demosthenes'* Philippic I *with Rhetorical Analysis of* Philippics II *and* III. Oxford.

Worthington, I. 1994. "History and Oratorical Exploitation." In I. Worthington, ed., *Persuasion: Greek Rhetoric in Action*. London, 109–129.

Worthington, I., ed. 2006. *Demosthenes, Speeches 60 and 61, Prologues, Letters*. Austin, TX.

Worthington, I., ed. 2007. *A Companion to Greek Rhetoric*. Oxford and Malden, MA.

Yunis, H. 2000. Politics as Literature: Demosthenes and the Burden of the Past. *Arion*. 8(1): 97–118.

Ziolkowski, J.E. 1981. *Thucydides and the Tradition of Funeral Speeches at Athens*. New York.

FURTHER READING

Worthington 2007 edited a highly useful collection of chapters on various aspects of Greek rhetoric and its different genres, including the ones discussed here. Ober 1989 is a groundbreaking study of the relationship between masses and elite in Athenian democracy and of Athenian democratic values and rhetoric. Several authors in Pritchard's 2010 anthology discuss the Athenian culture of war and its martial ideals, while Christ 2006 investigates the ways by which many avoided or subverted the city's military expectations of its citizens. Athenian courage, cowardice and their rhetoric are examined by Roisman 2005 *passim*, and Balot 2004a and 2010. Of the individual speeches examined here, see Loraux 1986, esp. 8–10 and Herrman 2008 for Demosthenes' *Funeral Oration*; Wooten 2008 for Demosthenes' *First Philippic*; and Weissenberger 1987: 27–83 for Lysias' *For Mantitheus*. The audience's unruly behavior is the focus of Wallace 2004, and in greater details: Bers 1985 and Tacon 2001.

CHAPTER 17

Persuading the People in the Roman Participatory Context

Robert Morstein-Marx

Communication is central to a republican political system worthy of the name: if the people have votes that can decide major issues of their own governance, then these votes must be informed by adequate prior discussion and deliberation in order to fulfill this role. What constitutes "adequate" will depend crucially on the role voters are expected to play: the requirements for truly autonomous self-governance worthy of the name would be far more stringent than those implied by a narrow, elitist version of popular input (much like that of contemporary representative "democracies" and republics) restricted more or less to a periodic choice of leaders to represent us in political decision-making that actually takes place elsewhere. This touches immediately therefore on a basic question that pervades this chapter as a whole, that is: What kind of role *was* in fact implicitly envisioned for Roman citizens not of the senatorial order? For the moment we shall note simply that certain practices surrounding public deliberation clearly imply that Romans in the last two centuries BCE did have a conception of at least a minimal standard of adequate deliberation. Before a legislative proposal's fate was sealed by a vote or a veto it was expected to be read out and discussed by some of the leading men of the Senate over a period of roughly three weeks in open, public assemblies (*contiones*)—not just current magistrates, but other senators as well (*privati*) who might possess even greater personal authority (on Roman assemblies, see Mouritsen, Chapter 9). After these discussions the final vote would also be immediately preceded by a final set of speeches both "pro" and "con," with emphasis again on the advice of *privati*. Since all legislation had to be passed by the Roman people, quite a lot of open, public deliberation of this minimal standard was built into the political system.

As in all classical polities, oral communication was central to the functioning of Rome's Republic. Not that the written word was neglected: magistrates' edicts were written out on whitened boards, and the text of a law was usually (perhaps always) required to be posted "where it could be read rightly from the ground" (Crawford 1996: 19–20),

A Companion to Greek Democracy and the Roman Republic, First Edition. Edited by Dean Hammer.

apparently around the Rostra in the Forum or on the Capitol. Yet the primacy of the spoken word in a world of limited literacy and no news media is clear enough. We have just noted that proposed laws had to be presented to the people orally over three successive market-days from their formal promulgation, and magistrates' edicts seem to have been written down above all as a *safeguard*, so that those who were not present when they were read aloud in a public meeting could learn of their content (Morstein-Marx 2004: 8, 70, 249–251). So in the civic context speech-making was a key manifestation of political leadership and a fundamental enactment of political authority.

Up to about the middle of the second century BCE, traditional methods of training the scions of the political elite appear to have sufficed in the rhetorical realm: hearing Rome's great men speak in assemblies or trials, observing deliberations of the Senate from the forecourt of the Curia, perhaps also attending the general's council during military service. But as Roman senators came into closer contact with the Greek intellectual world in the course of the second century, and coincidentally their own domestic politics broadened to reach wider segments of a growing urban population and even distant communities of citizens in Italy who might come to the city for a vote, some members of this elite seized upon the rule-based technical skill of academic rhetoric refined in Greece from the days of the Sophists and Aristotle. Such training was originally available only from Greek tutors and thus demanded fluency in the Hellenic tongue as well as considerable family resources, putting it "safely" beyond the reach of the merely ambitious. But by 92 BCE the rise in demand for training in the *ars rhetorica* had induced some teachers of rhetoric to open schools offering tuition in Latin, vastly increasing access to what might now be seen as a merely technical skill. This was regarded by traditionalists as an intolerable incitement to "shamelessness" (*impudentia*: Cic. *De orat.* 93–94)—or social mobility—and a backlash came in that year in the form of a sharply disapproving edict from the censors L. Crassus and Cn. Domitius which probably induced both the "Latin rhetoricians" and their pupils temporarily to take a low profile. This strong pronouncement makes clear what was at stake for the nobility; but if rhetorical training were indissolubly linked to a broad Hellenic education, which was available to a relatively privileged few, then its social and moral effects could be managed in the interests of the elite. In fact, the Latin rhetorical schools must soon have reopened, but advanced rhetorical training under Greek masters in Rome and sometimes abroad (Athens or Rhodes) became a common form of preparation for aspiring members of Rome's political elite in the time of Cicero. The privileged access to formal rhetorical training that senators and *equites* enjoyed must have continued to play a large role in maintaining their ideological dominance over Roman public life, though it surely also loosened the grip traditionally held by the nobility (a narrow subset of the senatorial order) on recruitment to high office.

1 Typology, Venues, Audiences

Political speech was ubiquitous in the Forum, the great quasi-rectangular square, ringed by temples and the most storied hills of Rome, that constituted the topographical center of republican public life. A visitor in the 50s BCE must have stood a good chance of joining the rings of spectators (*corona*) around one or more criminal trials in session in different sectors of the Forum featuring some of the leading men of the state as defendants, plaintiffs, or counsel. (See David 1992: 44–45 for a speculative but interesting attempt to locate the courts within the Forum.) The judicial business of the Forum might have to compete with a magistrate addressing a public meeting from the Rostra in front of the Senate House. If the House was meeting that day, our imaginary visitor would have had difficulty approaching the densely crowded forecourt of the Curia to hear what was being said, but if he was patient the presiding magistrate and others might well emerge to report publicly from the Rostra on the nature of any decree. Although the growth of the scale of public business had largely banished commerce to the periphery of the ancient square by the second century, "artisans and shopkeepers" are often mentioned as the denizens of the Forum, and one can easily suppose that the endemic under-employment of an ancient metropolis gave the orators who performed there a regular audience, sometimes converted by indignant speakers into a riotous crowd. Great political controversies, legislative proposals of wide public interest, or indeed star performers such as Cicero and popular heroes such as Publius Clodius drew considerably greater and more diverse crowds to hear speakers in the Forum, and often to respond loudly with their own voices and hands (*clamor*, *admurmuratio*, *plausus*).

Political activity in the Roman Republic was oriented around two poles: the Senate and People of Rome (Senatus Populusque Romanus—SPQR—according to an ancient formula, whose order, incidentally, could be inverted). The dyadic structure of the state was reflected also in oratory, since speeches delivered before the Senate and before the people naturally differed to accommodate their differing audiences and rhetorical setting, with obvious effects upon the style of argument and ideology characteristic to each.

The orator's "greatest stage" was the *contio* or public meeting (Cic. *De orat.* 2.338), which merits special prominence for our purposes because it constituted the crucial point of discursive exchange between individual senators and the citizenry and thereby performed the crucial function of stitching together a potentially divided community. Most important, it was in *contiones* that magistrates seeking to further a legislative campaign needed to make their case to audiences of citizens who, whatever their numbers and precise constituents, could claim to embody at that moment "the Roman people." At times of high political excitement, tribunes might summon "daily *contiones*" and virtually live on the Rostra (Cic. *Brut.* 305–306), especially when they were seeking to rally public support in order to overcome resistance located in the Senate.

All magistrates had the right to summon a *contio*, but in practice tribunes held more than half of all the meetings whose presiding officer is recorded (Pina Polo 1996: 52); consuls come a distant second in frequency, usually acting in their capacity as (in effect) the executive arm of the Senate rather than as oppositional critic, as was more frequently the role of tribunes. The presiding magistrate could speak himself or hand "his" *contio* over to another, usually a senior senator of high authority who did not currently hold a magistracy (*privatus*) but whose opinion would hold great weight with the citizenry. Another variant of the practice occurred when the presiding magistrate "invited" an adversary to defend his position before a *contio*; to judge from known examples, in which the audience is typically hostile, this was actually a kind of pressure tactic rather than an idealistic concession to fairness in debate. These relatively informal meetings were not restricted to speech-making: an enormous variety of public announcements and legal acts were required, or expected, to take place before a *contio* for the sake of publicity. But the *contio* was so closely identified with public speeches that the word came to denote both the meeting itself *and* a speech delivered at such a meeting.

Audiences of *contiones* were self-selected, and as such can be shown to have been often quite partisan, usually in favor of the magistrate who summoned the meeting. The possibilities enjoyed by the magistrate for strategically manipulating the makeup of the audience were enhanced by the fact that public meetings were not called far in advance—typically for the same day, it seems. This, together with thoughtful reimbursement of expected supporters for time lost from their daily pursuit of life's necessities, could produce a crowd which was much more likely to applaud or echo the magistrate's words (or those of his allies) than drown them out or shout them down. This was symbolically useful for at least two reasons above all. Contional audiences claimed to stand in for the Roman people as a whole: thus their responses, positive and negative, were apt to be interpreted by interested politicians as clear signs of the will of the *populus Romanus* itself (see also Tatum, Chapter 15, on the role of the people). If on the other hand one did not like what they "said," then one could of course deny their representativeness, as famously did Scipio Aemilianus when he responded to the shouts of a crowd angered by his assertion that Tiberius Gracchus may have been justly killed by denouncing it as a rabble of foreign-born war-captives, and thus not really Roman at all (Malcovati 1976: 31–32). A second reason why conspicuous audience responses were useful is that they might have a kind of bandwagon effect influencing future "turnout" for further *contiones* and voting assemblies, making a legislative debate more and more one-sided until there was only one surviving contender in the Forum. The rarity of occasions on which a legislative proposal was actually *voted down* is, in my view, a measure of the strength of this tendency.

There has been some debate about the social makeup of contional audiences. It does seem clear (as is indeed implied by the foregoing) that it varied widely, so that phrases in the ancient sources such as *plebs contionalis* should not be understood as attesting to the uniformity of audiences but simply refers to the fact that crowds in the business center of a city where employment was sporadic were somewhat distinctive, with "artisans and shopkeepers" making up a regular and recognizable constituent. Depending on circumstances, these men might constitute a minority or a majority of a given *contio*—which of the two, we are rarely in a position to judge from the evidence. (In the nature of things, this was probably rarely clear even to eyewitness observers.) However, a view recently espoused would make the contional audience one that was on the whole "well-to-do," with time on its hands and no need to be more productively occupied (Mouritsen 2001: 38–62). This seems highly unlikely, however, given the tendency of all of our sources to treat these audiences as "popular" in social terms and expressive of views that often diverged sharply from those of the Senate and the most respected elements of the social hierarchy (Morstein-Marx 2004: 122–123; Jehne 2006c: 229–232).

Estimates of the size of audiences at public meetings must remain very rough. No one counted, and size itself was often a tendentious issue, as also today, when the media report divergent partisan estimates of the size of demonstrations. Calculations based on the capacity of the available space to the south and east of the Rostra have ranged from 6,000 to 20,000, but this can give only a broad sense of the order of magnitude since so little is actually known about the actual dimensions and details of the use of the available space. It is important to understand that the audience at a public meeting stood, and nothing prevented it from drifting away if its attention were not held. A speaker in a *contio* had to get to the point quickly, not drone on, and if he wanted to propel action he was well advised to seize his listeners' attention with strong emotionalism, frequently by arousing fear and indignation. Since ordinary citizens were excluded from direct observation of senatorial debates (see below) that often were the subject of a *contio*, or had already dealt with matters that were the subject of a *contio*, a speaker often was a mediator of communication between Senate and people. This allowed him to characterize senators in a certain light and to represent himself as also a peculiarly authoritative guide in the people's deliberations. This position astride the main line of communication between Senate and people was a valuable source of power both for individual senators who temporarily controlled access to it and, of course, for the political elite as a whole, which collectively monopolized this crucial node.

The rhetorical setting of the Senate, a body of some 600 men from the time of Sulla (half that number previously), was very different. Senatorial audiences were much smaller: a meeting of 400 was considered "full" (*frequens*). These few hundred, wealthy men all, had ostensibly devoted their lives to public affairs (the *res publica*) and consequently had a strong corporate sense, especially at their core, the nobility. Here, then, the audience consisted of the speaker's own rivals for honor, indeed normally many superiors, and the speaker's place in the hierarchy was reinforced by protocol which dictated that ex-consuls spoke first (consuls-elect if the annual election had already been held), then ex-praetors and so on, down to back-benchers who were not expected to speak—the *pedarii* or "foot-men," so called (according to the most widely accepted etymology) because their main function was to show support for others of superior rank by walking to join them at their benches. The distinctive character of the council was reinforced by its sitting in an enclosed space: the Curia in the Forum or one of the temples in the area of the great square, most often the Temple of Concord near the Rostra, the Temple of Castor in the upper Forum, and the Temple of Jupiter Best and Greatest on the Capitol. This was an aspect in which the senatorial setting was sharply differentiated from the other venues of Roman political oratory: onlookers were not allowed, and debate took place shielded from the people's monitoring gaze—though not entirely protected from expressions of popular feeling such as shouts and uproar that could penetrate the walls and the open door of the meeting-place (see Cic. *Cat.* 4.14–17 and, more explicitly, App. *B. civ.* 2.130–132).

In a senatorial debate, of course, not all spoke at any length. The clear order of hierarchy according to which the consul (or other presiding magistrate) called upon members of the House seems to imply a clear expectation that the opinions of those near the top of that hierarchy, with the longest experience of public affairs, were expected to set the parameters of subsequent debate. Even so, proper speeches were normally reserved for proposing a motion; otherwise, one usually expressed agreement in a few words with what another had said and resumed one's seat. Thus, even at the top of the hierarchy, many of the ex-consuls would simply agree with a given motion rather than deliver a speech seconding it. In a meeting of several hundred, to accept the consul's invitation to speak was in itself to assert a claim on the attention of one's social superiors and peers, some of whom still awaited their turn to address the issue. A speaker was therefore well advised to be brief, even though unlike the *contio*, his audience was seated and more or less captive.

Interestingly, despite these pressures upon those lower down in the hierarchy of status, debate in the Senate was probably not as top-heavy as the procedural rules seem to imply (Ryan 1998). In one famous debate about which we are unusually well informed, that on the punishment of the so-called "Catilinarian conspirators" of December 5, 63, *all* fifteen men of consular rank had assented to the motion for the death penalty proposed by the first speaker, a consul-elect, when C. Julius Caesar, only a praetor-elect, stood to propose life imprisonment instead. (On the terms of Caesar's proposal, see now Pelling 2011: 165–166.) Caesar's speech so stirred the House that the consul-elect humiliatingly backed away from the obvious meaning of his own motion. But that is not all. Caesar's proposal continued to garner support as the consul called upon those of lower rank in sequence, until a mere *tribune-designate*, M. Porcius Cato, revived the original motion and delivered a memorable oration that swung the Fathers overwhelmingly back to the death penalty (Sal. *Cat.* 50–53; cf. Cic. *Att.* 12.21.1). The depth of this debate was doubtless exceptional, but it shows both that those relatively low in the hierarchy of *dignitas* were by no means robbed of a voice and also that the Curia was a place for genuine debate that could change minds, in contrast to what appears generally to have happened in the *contio*.

Speeches in public meetings and in the Senate were central to the deliberative process of the Republic, but forensic oratory in the various criminal "courts" that were laid out in the open air around the Forum represented the pinnacle of the rhetorical art, with its various "stars" such as Marcus Cicero or Quintus Hortensius who would draw substantial crowds ringing (thus: *corona*) the jurors' benches and the magistrate's tribunal (see also Williamson, Chapter 11). Quite apart from the illustrious orators involved, these cases typically concerned the lives and reputations of senators and *equites*, not uncommonly leading men of the state, and the charges, including electoral bribery, political violence, and extortion from allies, were often intensely political in their background and nature. (See, for instance, Cicero's defenses of Roscius of Ameria in 80 BCE, Sestius in 56, or Milo in 52.) For such speeches one must envision *two* distinct audiences: the primary audience of well-to-do, though only partly senatorial, jurors (from 70 BCE, jurors were drawn equally from senators, *equites*, and a somewhat unclear group of well-off citizens called "tribunes of the treasury"), but also a secondary, mixed, audience of citizens who made up the *corona* and at times (depending no doubt on the nature of the case) might behave rather like a contional audience. The secondary audience of forensic speeches must inevitably have influenced jurors' decisions as they cast their vote under its gaze, perhaps even harassed by its shouts (Ascon. 40C). While the sentiments expressed in forensic orations were clearly designed chiefly to appeal to the senatorial, equestrian, and other well-off jurors, who alone directly decided the defendant's fate, they could hardly be entirely hidden from the ears of a wider public. This must in turn have had some effect on what a speaker ventured to say. The interruptions that spoiled Cicero's delivery at the trial of Milo (Ascon. 41–42C etc.) and, on the other hand, his lowering of his voice at the trial of Flaccus so that the surrounding *corona* could not hear his anti-Semitic remarks (Cic. *Flac.* 66), offer a sense of such pressures, though they also suggest that a speaker would after all say what needed to be said to further his case among the judges rather than be deterred by an impassioned crowd of spectators. He might even gain stature and sympathy by standing firm (Cic. *Q. fr.* 2.3.2).

Examples of speeches of all three types survive among the fifty-eight extant orations of Cicero, the sole rhetorical corpus that survives from the period, and numerous short "fragments" of speeches by others have been preserved in the works of other authors (Malcovati 1976). Although published orations cannot be regarded as verbatim records of the delivered speech, there is general agreement that they provide an accurate picture of the effective use of rhetoric in their implied context and thus may be used to inform us about actual rhetorical practice in the various types of setting that are represented. (Manuwald 2007: 54–58 offers a recent summary of this much-discussed problem.) The greater part of Cicero's surviving orations are forensic, as befits the prominence of the genre in rhetorical training, but there are also nine published *contiones* and twenty senatorial speeches (including twelve out of the fourteen *Philippics*). When assessing or interpreting a given speech or passage it is crucially important to keep clearly in mind the distinctiveness of these different venues, with their differing audiences. Before the Roman people assembled in front of the Rostra, Cicero will praise the Gracchi and fit himself into a tradition of "Friends of the People," championing the cause of land redistribution, deploring the duplicity of some senators who say one thing from the Rostra and another in the Curia, and declaring his readiness to cross swords with the powerful in his zeal to defend the people's interest as they choose to define it by their response to his arguments. In the Senate and the courts, on the other hand, Cicero declares that the Gracchi were justly killed for their manipulative use of state largesse to amass personal power, regards land redistribution as at best merely demagogic bribery, and sees the consensus of all "respectable" citizens (*boni*), meaning in practice those who constitute or take their cue from the *auctoritas* of the Senate, as the bedrock of resistance to aspiring "tyrants"—that is, the long string of popular heroes beginning with the Gracchi and reaching down to P. Clodius in Cicero's own day.

The very fact that Cicero could actually maintain two such divergent, even contradictory personae in the two main venues for public deliberation is in itself extremely important and worthy of our closer attention. This was possible only because of the high degree of "insulation" that protected senatorial speech: the general public was, as we have seen, shut out of meetings of the Senate and therefore unable to monitor directly proceedings in what was therefore for them a mysterious locus of power. True, senators frequently did not form a united front, and in opposition to the official public announcement of the Senate's transactions (normally in a *contio* immediately following) any magistrate had the right to summon a public meeting in order to provide an alternative, perhaps even subversive, version of what had transpired outside the public gaze. Yet there were strong disincentives against breaking ranks with one's senatorial peers quite so dramatically (it did not bode well for future hopes of collaboration), so this seems to have happened relatively rarely. Moreover, there was no guarantee to the public that the information such a discordant voice conveyed was in fact the truth rather than self-serving cant seeking to exploit public indignation. Citizens in the *contio* were not fools, and knew well—and were sometimes warned by *other* speakers—not to be duped by those who pretended to be *populares*, "Friends of the People," but in fact sought only self-aggrandizement. This was in fact a perfectly reasonable concern, as we shall see.

The result, then, was a grave lack of transparency at the very heart of the Republic that heavily influenced the whole process of public deliberation in a quite distinctive way. When combined with the fact that longstanding tradition and cultural norms of respect for *dignitas* ("worthiness" or stature) and *auctoritas* ensured that in open, public deliberation, those who spoke were senators while ordinary citizens were reduced strictly to listening and reacting to what they heard, one can readily see how the balance of "communicative power" was tilted heavily toward senators and toward the collective perspective of the Senate.

2 The Problem Exemplified: Cicero against the Agrarian Law

A particular case may provide a helpful illustration of the core problem. As a consul taking up his duties at the beginning of 63 BCE, Cicero immediately faced the challenge of a land reform bill proposed by one of the tribunes for that year, P. Servilius Rullus (on this episode, see also Tatum, Chapter 15; on land distribution in Roman history, see de Ligt, Chapter 21). Land redistribution schemes had been a continual source of political controversy since Tiberius Gracchus in 133 BCE, and it seems clear that the growth of indebtedness and poverty, both urban and rural, that followed the civil war and further violent disruptions of the Sullan era (88–78 BCE) made demand for an agrarian bill particularly acute at this time, quite apart from the fact that Gnaeus Pompey's victorious army was soon to return from the east with a reasonable expectation of long-deferred rewards for their service. Rullus' bill was drafted carefully to avoid old, polarizing pitfalls such as forced purchase or even confiscation, and modern scholarship has tended to vindicate the measure as a serious and well-considered effort at much-needed land reform (Gruen 1974: 389–394). Perhaps Cicero's "popular" persona thus far, and his interest in staying on the right side of Pompey, induced Rullus to think that the consul would not put up a fight, or might even be supportive of moderate land reform, as indeed he was to represent himself in the event. As a rule, conservatives had in the past found that public argument against land reform was pretty much useless and resorted instead to obstructive measures to stop or undermine them (below), so Rullus may have not have expected much of a contest in the sphere of public deliberation, despite Cicero's renown as an orator.

If that was his thinking, however, he was woefully mistaken. Cicero came out swinging even on the celebratory first day of his consulship, delivering sharp, detailed denunciations of the measure both in the Senate and immediately afterwards in a *contio* (Cic. *Leg. agr.* 1–2). Rullus tried to rebut the consul's objections in his own public meeting by painting him as the front man for those who had profited from Sulla's expropriations, but Cicero simply threw the charge back at him (Cic. *Leg. agr.* 3)—and in the contional audience, who was to say? Rullus' bill began to stall, and a tribune signaled his readiness to deliver the *coup de grâce* by means of a veto. We do not strictly know whether the proposal limped along to go down in defeat at the polls or whether in the face of inevitable failure it was simply withdrawn, as was customary. Either way, it is probable that Cicero's powerful rhetorical counter-attack over several *contiones* was in fact the deciding factor.

If so, then the nature of Cicero's rhetoric against the bill in his *contiones* is worth examining more closely, since it was evidently successful with its audiences. We should note first of all that Cicero starts by claiming in strikingly bad faith that he was in truth a *consul popularis*, a consul who, exceptionally, did not shun the people's gaze but was in fact eager to come before them and consult their wisdom at the Rostra (Cic. *Leg. agr.* 2.6–10). Nay more (he says), he was an ardent supporter of agrarian laws—provided, of course, that they were in fact honestly intended to aid the Roman people. However, *this* was no agrarian law in the true sense but a confidence scheme, a trap designed to seduce good, upstanding citizens into handing over dictatorial power to a shadowy, anonymous clique to be headed by Rullus himself (*Leg. agr.* §§10–15)! He promises to demonstrate the truth of this shocking assertion and disarmingly pledges to follow his audience's own conclusions if he fails to convince them (*Leg. agr.* §16). There follows an overpowering, apparently point-by-point demolition of the bill as tendentiously selective and relentlessly distorted as it is voluminous and detailed, containing a multitude of explicit quotation from the text of the proposal itself that gives the impression of incontrovertible accuracy while leaving the overwhelming mass of the bill altogether unremarked.

Some highlights of Cicero's rhetorical strategy of misinformation might be noted (if that does not seem too redolent of his own tactics on this occasion). Cicero makes much of the idea that Rullus was in fact robbing the Roman people of their prized right of suffrage by stipulating that the land commissioners would be elected by just short of a majority of the voting-units ("tribes") selected by lot, (*Leg. agr.* §26). In fact this was the traditional procedure used for election of the chief pontiff and recently extended to all priesthoods; it may have been intended to contain bribery, and anyway can hardly have been used by Rullus to impose his will on the tribes. Cicero goes on to predict that Rome and indeed the whole Roman Empire were going to be subjugated for five long years to the domination of the ten commissioners thus elected, "tyrants in the city," whose powers would be arbitrary, unrestrained even by any right of appeal (*Leg. agr.* §33). Yet, as emerges elsewhere, their *imperium* (power of command) would be merely propraetorian, ranking therefore under the (regularly elected) consuls and praetors. As one scholar has drily noted, "A land commission was not really a suitable instrument for ruling the Roman Empire" (Sumner 1966: 576). Cicero tries mightily to exploit some of the provisions of the law that seem in fact to have been designed to put the strife of the Sullan era firmly in the past to suggest that the whole scheme was designed to bail out the bankrupt beneficiaries of Sulla's victory who were eager to unload their ill-gotten swamps and deserts. (Sulla's name was clearly hated among the urban plebs of Rome, so this was potentially a promising path to take; but two could play at that game, as Cicero found out at Rullus' own *contio* [*Leg. agr.* 3].) Cicero also spends a considerable part of his speech arousing suspicion that the law was also in part a cunning plot to seize in advance all of the fruits of Pompey's new conquests so that the great man, currently riding a wave of popularity for his victories over the pirates and Mithridates, would be insultingly deprived of any say in their disposition. This invidious "anti-Pompey" interpretation seems to have "had its origin solely in Cicero's fertile and inventive brain" (Sumner 1966: 578), although of all Cicero's misrepresentations and diversions this one has had the most success among modern scholars.

Yet Cicero "won" this debate, a result that seems to speak volumes about the pathologies of mass public deliberation in republican Rome. Arguing in bad faith is of course common enough in any rhetorical setting, modern as well as ancient. The key point, however, is whether within a particular institutional context the temptation to do so (strong as it is for an interested party) is on the whole adequately restrained by transparency and therefore by the risks and potential costs of being "found out" and revealed. Only in the face of such risks and costs can self-interested parties to debate be obliged to address the common good (however imperfectly), whatever the true motivational springs of their action. Here, to put it simply, Cicero could successfully argue in bad faith because he could get away with it. That he *could* get away with it was in turn a product of the effective exclusion of the people from the alternative, but equally important, site of political speech, and of the traditions of deference to authority that this very fact engendered.

If Cicero could get away in this way with playing the *consul popularis*, the advocate of agrarian laws and of the people's *commoda* (benefits/interests) generally, then this relieved him of any need to contest the principle of agrarian distribution explicitly and directly, which would after all have led him onto very unfavorable terrain. Hence what I have called the "ideological monotony" of contional rhetoric: the outright avoidance by speakers in public meetings, even the strongest opponents of "popular" politicians, of any unambiguous sign that they adhered to a contrary, "optimate" vision of the public good (as in fact they often did) when they spoke to the Roman people from the Rostra. This does not imply that the competitive dynamic that so characterized republican politics was somehow suppressed in public deliberation under a warm glow of consensus, a notion that a glance at most extant *contiones* would immediately dispel. Rather, those whose political positions put them at a serious disadvantage in the popular forum of the *contio* still had a choice of viable strategies available to them that allowed them to avoid exposing their real views to public scrutiny and criticism. They could forfeit political argument altogether and resort instead to forms of obstructionism (veto threats or filibusters, for example) that were designed to turn the tide of public opinion by ultimately provoking their opponents to a seeming violation of republican norms, such as Tiberius Gracchus' abrogation of Octavius' tribunate, or Caesar's strong-arm responses to Bibulus and Cato. Or, like Cicero, they could pretend to agree with the "popular" goals of their opponents while raising a drumbeat of doubts about their opponents' motives, typically construed as tyrannical aspirations, thereby moving the basis of the argument onto the plane of personal trust and *dignitas*. Since those leading the "anti-popular" side of a contest were typically consuls or leading men in the senatorial hierarchy (*principes civitatis*), they had passed many tests of popular trust in the sequence of elections that got them where they were; tribunes, on the other hand—typically the ones to push a popular agenda—were relatively young, untested faces on the political scene, even if they did sometimes bear a noble name (the Gracchi, for example, or Publius Clodius for that matter). This move to an *ad hominem* plane of argument (in rhetorical terms, to "ethical" [*ethos*] in preference to "logical" proof [*logos*]) was therefore a very congenial one, far better than attempting to meet popular arguments for land distribution head-on in a naturally popular venue like the *contio*. And it could work, as Cicero demonstrates in the agrarian debate of 63.

3 The Rhetorical Construction of Ideology

Roman public oratory, above all in its largest venue, the *contio*, played a central role in verbally articulating the fundamental norms and values of the Republic and propagating them among the citizenry. It may fairly be viewed as the crucible in which "republican ideology" was forged. Since the speakers were (overwhelmingly) senators, this privileged position in the line of communication both buttressed the traditional authority of political elite and gave them the means to shape that ideology in ways that served their collective interest. Contional oratory, despite the disingenuous, ingratiating aspects just noted, is clearly marked by the aristocratic tenor of Roman republican values: the great emphasis on the *dignitas* of morally superior individuals, the conception of election as an *honor* awarded by the grateful citizenry in exchange for outstanding *virtus* in the service of the Republic, a tradition of deference to the *auctoritas* of men better qualified and better placed than the common citizen to discern what was truly the public good. It is hard to imagine that this relatively coherent ideological system could have come to dominate public speech before popular audiences if the senatorial order had not enjoyed a privileged place as speakers within the communicative hierarchy.

It is tempting therefore to apply the Marxist theorist Antonio Gramsci's concept of "cultural hegemony," according to which a ruling class exploits its authoritative position to persuade the "subaltern" (subordinate) orders of the essential and universal rightness of its own class-based moral and political perspective (Gramsci 1971 and 1975; Ives 2004 is helpful). The subaltern class, on this view, is not mindless or bereft of its own morality based on its concrete experience of life; yet the power of ideological production that can be mobilized by the dominant class is typically overwhelming, so that (if only by default) the subaltern ends up "voluntarily" collaborating in his own subjugation. The complementary (though not overtly Marxist) view of sociologist Steven Lukes clarifies how such ideological power can be employed to narrow the range of possibilities for deliberation in an interested way (Lukes 2005). According to Lukes, power has three notable "dimensions": outright control of another's actions is its bluntest and most blatant form, but power may also be exerted to control the agenda (thereby limiting the parameters of debate and possible outcomes) and further, more insidiously, to *shape in advance* the preferences that will determine any subsequent choice. It can be plausibly argued that Roman mass oratory did important work in Lukes' second and third dimensions to limit the self-determination of the Roman people despite the fact that *institutionally speaking* they possessed ultimate sovereignty over the Republic through their rights directly to elect all magistrates, to pass all legislation, and to judge or authorize all criminal trials. (Millar 1995: 94 indeed provocatively described the republican "constitution" as a "direct democracy"; but cf. Hölkeskamp 2010: 12–22.)

Yet this cannot be the whole story. "Dominant ideology" theses have a reductive tendency even if they are not utterly flawed. (See Scott 1990 for a bracing attack on Gramsci, Morstein-Marx 2012 and 2013 for an attempt to find a balanced position with specific application to the late Republic.) A historian in any case always must attend to specific local conditions. In the Roman context, then, we might ask why there was an "ideological monotony" of a broadly popular stamp in the *contio* if members of the senatorial elite could pretty much say whatever they wanted. Obviously the discourse of the *contio* was *in some sense* a negotiated compromise between speaker and audience, between elite and mass, even if, as I have argued, the balance of communicative power was tilted significantly toward the ones doing the speaking. Even if one views the *contio* as an occasion designed to construct the impression of a unanimous Popular Will, it becomes all the more important for the audience to respond actively with applause (*plausus*) and cries (*clamor*) of support (or hostile to the opposition). Various techniques were clearly used by orators to prompt such manifestations (*significationes*) of the "judgment and will of the Roman people" (Cic. *Sest.* 106–112)—bribery, claquers, and rhetorical devices for eliciting vocal audience response such as "call-and-response," anaphora, tricolon, and antithesis (Morstein-Marx 2004: 128–150)—yet the degree of control an orator could thus exert over audience responses was hardly total. Following the political scientist James C. Scott, we need also to be alert to the possibility that the picture of political leadership and rhetorical mastery that our sources convey may itself be a congenial ideological artifact, an idealizing construct meant to instruct, to inspire, and to hide unpleasant truths about the reality of domination beneath the benign surface of the "public transcript."

With weighty considerations pulling us in both directions, a relatively concrete, empirical test of plebeian docility in deliberation may help us to reach a balanced perspective on the phenomenon. When the deliberating was over and the voting assembly met, how obedient were the Roman people to the collective wisdom of the Senate? For pragmatic reasons, the question is best turned around: How "insubordinate" were the Roman people, that is, how often did voters *reject* the majority will of the Senate? The number of such "successful assertions of popular sovereignty" may be somewhat surprising: a *minimum* of 32 to 36 cases over the ninety-odd years that span the late Republic (expanded slightly to begin with the passage of the *lex Gabinia* in 139). That is, the popular assembly exercised its full sovereignty by *rejecting* the clear sentiment of the majority of the Senate on a legislative proposal on average more than once every three years—rather more frequent, on the whole, than the modern analog of "throwing the bums out" in an election. Indeed, if we set aside as unrepresentative the periods of unaccustomed legislative quiescence in the 90s followed by civil war and Sullan repression down to 70 BCE, the rate increases to about once every other year, with some periods (104–99, 70–66, 61–52 BCE) reaching an average frequency of roughly once a year. All of this reveals a higher degree of popular "insubordination" than one might have supposed simply on the basis of elite domination of political rhetoric. Evidently Roman voters, and therefore (one must suppose) Roman audiences, were more resistant to the authority of the collective will of the elite than a model based on Gramscian "cultural hegemony" alone would suggest.

We must recognize, of course, that all these examples of "successful assertion of popular sovereignty" were also simultaneously examples of successful leadership by individual magistrates willing to break ranks with their colleagues in the Senate by "playing the popular card" (Yakobson 2006: 392–396). Such was the competitive dynamic in Roman republican politics that a strong popular demand was apt to stretch senatorial solidarity to the breaking point. An ambitious individual senator might be induced by popular pressure to take up a cause that set him at odds with the will of the majority of the Senate and of its most authoritative leaders. Plutarch's account (*Ti. Gracch.* 8.10) of how popular graffiti on the "walls, porticoes and tombs" across the city provided the strongest stimulus of all to Tiberius Gracchus is a particularly interesting example of how a political agenda might be imposed on a member of the political elite rather than the other way around. Sometimes, as also in the case of the Gracchi (or Scipio Aemilianus, or Caesar) senators who thus crossed over to the "popular" side (however temporarily) were nobles from the core of the aristocracy. In such instances, then, with such men of the nobility as their leaders, audiences and voters could presumably enter into direct conflict with the collective will of the Senate without being unduly anxious that what they sought was in any serious sense "seditious" or contrary to the traditions of the Republic (Yakobson 2010: 288–291). As a matter of fact, even "sedition" could be justified in traditional terms, citing the ancient Secessions of the Plebs as historical precedents for a necessary defense of the freedom of the Roman people (Cic. *De orat.* 2.197–203; *Corn.* 1.48).

It is equally important to observe that popular "insubordination" remained within certain broadly defined limits. Even the fiery tribunician harangues re-created by Sallust in his histories (esp. *Iug.* 31; *Hist.* 3.48) turn out on closer examination not to be attacks on the hallowed institution of the Senate but on the allegedly unworthy cliques (*pauci potentes*, the "powerful few") who "dominated" it at any one time. Despite the impressive institutional powers of the people and a conception of popular sovereignty, before the Caesarian civil war no proposal was even made, so far as we can tell, to alter significantly the foundations of the political system and to make it a more effective and transparent instrument of the will of the people. (Contrast the incremental but irresistible expansion of the suffrage that has taken place by a self-generating process in the U.S. and U.K. from the nineteenth century to the present.) This fact must be explained by the control exerted by members of the elite over ideological production, above all in the form of political speech, as we have seen. All *popularis* "agitation" still remained within the parameters of an essentially paternalistic vision of republican governance, according to which leading senators were normally understood to advise what was best for the people on the basis of their superior experience and insight, while being at the same time susceptible to sometimes sharp "correction" when necessary by the people themselves, whose simple common sense on exceptional occasions reasonably prevailed over senatorial *auctoritas.* (This is, for example, more or less just what Cicero himself says while advocating as praetor acceptance of the popular Manilian Law, which would confer additional powers on Gnaeus Pompey, over the authoritative objections of two pillars of the Senate, Quintus Hortensius and Lucius Catulus [*Leg. Man.* 51–60].) The paternalism that is characteristic of the republican ideology of the *contio* was tempered in practice by productive discord emanating from below in a manner reminiscent of Machiavelli's famous observations in his *Discourses on the First Decade of Livy* (1.4).

Certain broad similarities link the institutions in Rome and Greece that generated the forms of public rhetoric examined in this chapter and the last. Deliberation took place in mass assemblies that preceded decision by voting by the (male) citizen body, and this took the form of orations by authoritative, well-practiced speakers who took on the role of faithful counselors of the people. Here the popular audience—however randomly or studiously a particular audience was constituted on a given occasion—impersonated the Roman people, and by its responses to speakers on the Rostra inevitably conditioned to some extent what could successfully be said to it. Speeches in the law courts reinforced dominant political ideology and to a significant extent policed the behavior of the political elite, helping to ensure its conformity to ideals of service to the community. Even the Roman tradition of funeral oratory, the *laudatio funebris* performed at aristocratic obsequies (see Polyb. 6.52.11–54.3, and Flower 1996), which on its face differs so sharply from the Athenian funeral oration in its glorification of distinguished ancestry and its focus on the individual family rather than the *polis*, also served the function of stimulating the citizenry to virtue in the service of the Republic (so at least Polybius). It is true that nothing surviving from Athens corresponds to the relatively closed setting of the Roman Senate, and this is clearly important. Yet it could also be argued that *oratory* in the Senate was actually fairly constrained, and therefore the least important of the major rhetorical genres of republican Rome.

When we turn to how the speeches construct the relationship between elite speaker and popular audiences we seem to have moved into a rather different civic world from that of Athens or other democratic Greek states. Roman senators can say all manner of ingratiating things to the people—praising their practical intelligence, claiming to be prepared to carry out whatever role they wished to impose, rhetorically subordinating themselves entirely not merely to their *interests* but to their *wishes*—but in fact the rhetorical stance they assume toward a popular audience is broadly characterized by authority. This authority is in turn constructed on the basis of eminent men's privileged insight into the often deceptive political realm and, if possible, an illustrious record of prior service to the Republic, perhaps bolstered by the achievements of their ancestors. As in Athens, Roman speakers might be subjected to heckling and uproar, spontaneous or organized, even physical intimidation (Sal. *Iug.* 34.1; Dio 36.39.3, Plut. *Pomp.* 25.9), but it is impossible to imagine a senator being tried for giving bad advice to the people, as an Athenian *rhētōr* might be (Roisman, Chapter 16). Despite the privileged position held by senators in the communication of political information, however, it was not impossible in the late Republic, or even particularly rare, for the Roman people to reject the collective wisdom of the Senate by the use of their ballots. A steeply hierarchical speech-situation did not suppress all plebeian autonomy and agency: Roman republican rhetoric was still recognizably the rhetoric of a republic.

REFERENCES

Berry, D.H. 2000. *Cicero: Defense Speeches.* Oxford.

Blom, H. van der, 2010. *Cicero's Role Models. The Political Strategy of a Newcomer.* Oxford.

Connolly, J. 2007. *The State of Speech: Rhetoric and Political Thought in Ancient Rome.* Princeton.

Crawford, M.H., ed. 1996. *Roman Statutes.* BICS suppl. 64. 2 vols. London.

David, J.-M. 1992. *Le patronat judiciaire au dernier siècle de la République Romaine.* BEFAR 277. Rome.

David, J.-M. 2006. "Rhetoric and Public Life." In Rosenstein and Morstein-Marx 2006: 421–438.

Dominik, W. and J. Hall, eds. 2007. *A Companion to Roman Rhetoric.* Oxford and Malden, MA.

Dugan, J. 2005. *Making a New Man: Ciceronian Self-Fashioning in the Rhetorical Works.* Oxford.

Fantham, E. 2004. *The Roman World of Cicero's* De Oratore. Oxford.

Flower, H.I. 1996. *Ancestor Masks and Aristocratic Power in Roman Culture.* Oxford.

Gildenhard, I. 2011. *Creative Eloquence: The Construction of Reality in Cicero's Speeches.* Oxford.

Gramsci, A. 1971. *Selections from the Prison Notebooks of Antonio Gramsci.* Ed. Q. Hoare and G. Nowell-Smith. New York.

Gramsci , 1975. *Quaderni del Carcere.* Ed. V. Gerratuna. 4 vols. Turin.

Gruen, E.S. 1974. *The Last Generation of the Roman Republic.* Berkeley and Los Angeles.

Gruen, E.S. 1990. *Studies in Greek Culture and Roman Policy.* Berkeley and Los Angeles.

Hölkeskamp, K.-J. 1995. "*Oratoris maxima scaena*: Reden vor dem Volk in der politischen Kultur der Republik." In M. Jehne, ed., *Demokratie in Rom? Die Rolle des Volkes in der Politik der römischen Republik. Historia* Einzelschriften 96. Stuttgart, 11–49.

Hölkeskamp, K.-J. 2010. *Reconstructing the Roman Republic: An Ancient Political Culture and Modern Research.* Princeton.

Hopwood, K. 2007. "Smear and Spin: Ciceronian Tactics in *De Lege Agraria II.*" In J. Booth, ed., *Cicero on the Attack: Invective and Subversion in the Orations and Beyond.* Swansea, 71–103.

Ives, P. 2004. *Language and Hegemony in Gramsci.* London.

Jehne, M. 2006a. "Methods, Models, and Historiography." In Rosenstein and Morstein-Marx 2006: 3–28.

Jehne, M. 2006b. "Römer, Latiner und Bundesgenossen im Krieg. Zu Formen und Ausmaß der Integration in der republikanischen Armee." In M. Jehne and R. Pfeilschifter, eds., *Herrschaft ohne integration? Rom und Italien in republikanischer Zeit.* Frankfurt am Main, 243–267.

Jehne, M. 2006c. "Who Attended Roman Assemblies? Some Remarks on Political Participation in the Roman Republic." In F. Marco Simón, F. Pina Polo, and J. Remesal Rodríguez, eds., *Repúblicas y ciudadanos: Modeles de participación cívica en el mundo antiguo.* Barcelona, 221–234.

Kaster, R.A. 2006. *Cicero: Speech on Behalf of Publius Sestius.* Oxford.

Lintott, A. 2008. *Cicero as Evidence: A Historian's Companion.* Oxford.

Lukes, S. 2005. *Power: A Radical View.* 2nd edn. New York.

Malcovati, H. 1976. *Oratorum Romanorum fragmenta liberae rei publicae.* 4th edn. 2 vols. Turin.

Manuwald, G. 2007. *Cicero,* Philippics *3–9.* 2 vols. Berlin.
May, J., ed. 2002. *Brill's Companion to Cicero: Oratory and Rhetoric.* Leiden.
May, J. and J. Wisse. 2001. *Cicero*: On the Ideal Orator. Oxford.
Millar, F. 1986. "Politics, Persuasion and the People before the Social War (150–90 B.C.)." *JRS* 76: 1–11.
Millar, F. 1995. "Popular Politics at Rome in the Late Republic." In I. Malkin and Z.W. Rubinsohn, eds., *Leaders and Masses in the Roman World: Studies in Honor of Zvi Yavetz.* Leiden, 91–113.
Morstein-Marx, R. 2004. *Mass Oratory and Political Power in the Late Roman Republic.* Cambridge.
Morstein-Marx, R. 2012. "Political Graffiti in the Late Roman Republic: 'Hidden Transcripts' and 'Common Knowledge.'" In C. Kuhn, ed., *Politische Kommunikation und öffentliche Meinung in der antiken Welt.* Stuttgart, 191–217.
Morstein-Marx, R. 2013. "'Cultural Hegemony' and the Communicative Power of the Roman Elite." In C. Steel and H. van der Blom, eds., *Community and Communication: Oratory and Politics in Republican Rome.* Oxford, 29–47.
Mouritsen, H. 2001. *Plebs and Politics in the Late Roman Republic.* Cambridge.
Pelling, C. 2011. *Plutarch*: Caesar. Oxford.
Pina Polo, F. 1996. Contra arma verbis*: Der Redner vor dem Volk in der späten römischen Republik.* Stuttgart.
Rosenstein, N. and R. Morstein-Marx, eds. 2006. *A Companion to the Roman Republic.* Oxford and Malden, MA.
Ryan, F.X. 1998. *Rank and Participation in the Republican Senate.* Stuttgart.
Scott, J.C. 1990. *Domination and the Arts of Resistance: Hidden Transcripts.* New Haven.
Smith, C. and R. Covino, eds. 2011. *Praise and Blame in Roman Republican Rhetoric.* Swansea.
Steel, C. 2006. *Roman Oratory.* Greece & Rome. New Surveys in the Classics 36. Cambridge.
Sumner, G. 1966. "Cicero, Pompeius, and Rullus," *TAPA* 97: 569–582.
Tan, J. 2008. "*Contiones* in the Age of Cicero," *ClAnt* 27: 163–201.
Yakobson, A. 2006. "Popular Power in the Roman Republic." In Rosenstein and Morstein-Marx 2006: 383–400.
Yakobson, A. 2010. "Traditional Political Culture and the People's Role in the Roman Republic." *Historia* 59: 283–302.

FURTHER READING

For elaboration and details of the arguments sketched in brief above, see Morstein-Marx 2004, 2012, and 2013. Millar 1986 opened the debate about the implications of mass oratory for the character of the Roman Republic, which may be traced further in Hölkeskamp 1995, Pina Polo 1996, Mouritsen 2001, Jehne 2006a, Tan 2008, and Yakobson 2010. On Cicero's strategies of misinformation in *On the Agrarian Law* 2, see also Hopwood 2007, Lintott 2008: 137–142, and, less pessimistically, Yakobson 2010: 297–300. An excellent sketch of the central place of oratory in public life is offered by David 2006. On rhetorical education in the Republic, see also now the contributions by Stroup, Corbeill, and McNelis in Dominik and Hall 2007; on the censorial edict of 92, Gruen 1990: 179–192 is stimulating. May 2002, Steel 2006, and Dominik and Hall 2007 offer useful entrées to Ciceronian or Roman oratory in general, while Fantham 2004 is an informative introduction to Roman rhetorical culture by way of Cicero's rhetorical dialogue *On the Ideal Orator.* The fully annotated translation of that work by May and Wisse (2001) provides an intriguing look into the orator's laboratory. Further investigation of late republican rhetorical culture might proceed through the stimulating recent books by Dugan 2005, Connolly 2007 (especially strong on links to modern republican political theory), van der Blom 2010, Gildenhard 2011, and a conference volume edited by Smith and Covino (2012). For a taste of the thing itself, Cicero's

On the Agrarian Law 2 and *In Support of the Manilian Law* are thought-provoking samples of the rhetoric of the *contio*, but one or two tribunician orations imaginatively re-created by Sallust (*Iug.* 31; *Hist.* 3.48) should be thrown in for seasoning. Senatorial oratory might be well represented by Cicero's *Fourth Catilinarian* and *On the Consular Provinces*, while his defense speeches for Sestius (Kaster 2006) and for Milo (Berry 2000) are politically charged examples of forensic oratory.

PART IX

Global Contexts

CHAPTER 18

Interstate Relations, Colonization, and Empire among Greek Participatory Communities

Sarah Bolmarcich

We read in our sources—Xenophon (*Oec.* 9.14–15), Plato (*Rep.* 449a–457e), Aristotle (*Pol.* 1253b1–14, *EE* 1242a40–b2)—that the Greek city-state was not only composed of individual *oikoi*, it was itself a larger version of the *oikos*. We hear something similar today during the budget crises of various countries, American and European: if individual households must live within their means, why can't their governments? At the civic level, it is easy to make comparisons between households and *poleis*. At the international level, the same type of "participatory community" simply could not exist, at least not in ancient Greece. (In Rome, as Craige Champion demonstrates in his companion chapter, circumstances were quite different.) While the terminology of Greek interstate relations was closely linked to that used to describe relations between the citizens of a *polis* (Low 2007: 129–174), the relations between states did not necessarily mimic those between fellow citizens. In many ways the Greek international community was extremely democratic, even if the states participating were not: interstate relations were based upon a premise of equality with other states (even if this was not true in fact) and reciprocity was expected between states in an alliance with one another. But when an imbalance of power was created between states and had to be acknowledged, the language of interstate relations tended to transform into a vocabulary used to express power and domination, not equality. Greek attempts to preserve their international system in the face of such threats ultimately weakened the participatory states themselves: the emphasis on an equal say in interstate affairs and on freedom and autonomy (as each city-state defined it) led to the collapse of Greece in the fourth century.

In this chapter, I first consider what a "participatory community" might have meant to the Greeks on an international stage, and then consider specific types of interstate relationship: colonization, interstate leagues, and imperialism.

A Companion to Greek Democracy and the Roman Republic, First Edition. Edited by Dean Hammer.

1 A Greek International Community?

The question of whether the Greeks had anything that resembles our international community of today is a long-standing one. Even today, the term "international community" is difficult to define; *Foreign Policy* devoted an entire special report to defining the term in September 2002, suggesting that "This feel-good phrase evokes a benevolent, omniscient entity that makes decisions and takes action for the benefit of all countries and peoples." If that is our standard, the Greeks certainly had no international community. But Greek states did certainly participate in life on the international stage; how did they do so, and what kind of participatory community did they create or envision for themselves? There are three areas at which we can look for answers: panhellenism, especially religious; international law; and the application of terms of individual and civic relationships or terms of civic approbation in the international sphere.

Panhellenism as a religious ideal was facilitated by the foundations of the earliest panhellenic sanctuaries, Olympia and Delphi, in the eighth century BCE, although when we can identify those sanctuaries as panhellenic is an open question (most recently, Morgan 1990; Rolley 1983; Scott 2010). At these sanctuaries, all Greeks were (usually) welcome, although the oracle at Delphi was occasionally under the influence of one or another Greek state or one of its factions (cf. Hdt. 5.63–65), and an Amphictyonic League oversaw affairs at Delphi and in the region (Lefevre 1998; Sanchez 2001). At Delphi, participation in the Pythian Games and access to the oracle were theoretically open to all, although certain states and individuals had right of access (*promanteia*) to the oracle on par with the Delphians, who always had first access (Bowden 2005: 17–18). City-states erected monuments and treasuries along the Sacred Way, although we do not know the procedures for getting permission to build at the site, and these monuments often not only served as a glorification of all Greeks, but also redounded to the glory of the sponsoring city-state. Placement of the monuments was important: for instance, the large Spartan monument to Lysander's crushing defeat of the Athenians at Aegospotami in 403, at the very entrance to the sanctuary, neighbored a smaller Athenian offering to the memory of their victorious general at Marathon in 490, Miltiades, while a few more steps down the Sacred Way, would have led one to a monument to the kings of Argos, Sparta's great rival in the Peloponnesus.

At Olympia, states erected buildings and treasuries along similar lines as at Delphi. The Olympic Games, held at the sanctuary every fifth year to celebrate Zeus, were open to all free men unless their state had committed some infraction (e.g. Thuc. 5.50), and during the time of the games, an "Olympic truce" extended to all Greek states (Thuc. 5.49, Arist. fr. 533; for a similar truce at Isthmia, Paus. 5.2.1). Victors were usually richly feted by their home state (Miller 2006), and so a strong individualistic and nationalistic component came to be attached to the games, whose prestige came from the fact that a victor had defeated not only other athletes, but the representatives of other city-states. As at Delphi, votive offerings at Olympia came from all over the Greek world (Morgan 1993). Additionally, the sanctuaries of Nemea and Isthmia also hosted panhellenic games that were open to all. This practice extended even to some "local" festivals, such as the Panathenaic Games at Athens, which, judging by the number of Panathenaic amphorae found all over the Greek world (Bentz 1998), were attended by athletes from all over the Mediterranean. And a number of sanctuaries throughout the

Greek world offer archaeological evidence of significant numbers of visitors from other city-states (Morgan 1993).

Religious panhellenism is unlikely to have existed before the eighth century BCE (Sourvinou-Inwood 1990). It provided less a sense of "Greek" than a sense of shared religion and ritual, as did several early interstate leagues, particularly the mysterious Kalaurian League (Kelly 1966) and the Ionian *koinon* (Roebuck 1955). Furthermore, most of the participants in the panhellenic rituals at these sites would have belonged to the aristocratic elite of the city-states. For this chapter, this is not so much a problem, since Greek interstate relations were heavily influenced by aristocrats with a good network of connections in other city-states (Herman 1987; Mitchell 1997), but it does suggest a very limited participatory community on the international stage, and there is no evidence that suggests that the panhellenic festivals were important occasions for establishing amity between states, beyond the fact that occasionally copies of treaty-texts were inscribed publicly at Olympia (e.g. Thuc. 5.22, 47). States did not always observe the Olympic truce, and representatives of states could behave quite badly towards each at the festivals, as when the judges whipped a Spartan competitor fraudulently enrolled as a Boeotian (Thuc. 5.50). Insofar as the presence of such sanctuaries facilitated communication and a sense of shared culture between states, they contributed to the *idea* of an international community, but they certainly did not establish one, just as the Olympics today may bring nations together—but largely to compete with one another, sometimes in politically-fraught contests, as victories like the 1980s "Miracle on Ice" demonstrate.

Panhellenism did not apply only to Greek religion, although it appears to have lacked any extra-religious aspect until the Persian Wars. After the defeat of the Persians by the Athenians (assisted only by the Plataeans) at Marathon in 490 (Hdt. 6.109–117), the Greeks took the impending threat of a second Persian invasion in 481 more seriously and formed the Hellenic League, the first panhellenic alliance. Virtually every Greek city-state on the mainland that had not already medized (gone over to the Persians) was a member, as were a large number of the Aegean islands not under the control of Persia, and at one point the Greeks in Sicily were potential members (Hdt. 7.158–160). The success of the Greek city-states in forming this league, given all the tensions between individual states, is surprising, but their dedication is attested by such early actions of the League as the willingness of the Athenians and the Aeginetans to put aside their long-standing war for the good of Greece (Hdt. 7.145), or the Athenian willingness to grant the Spartans leadership of the League since they recognized their own unpopularity among their fellow city-states (Hdt. 8.3).

After the Persians were rebuffed, however, the Greeks showed little inclination to pursue further unity. A serious dispute arose over how to treat the Ionian states, which had formerly belonged to Persia; the Athenians, who identified themselves as Ionian, insisted on their admission into the Hellenic League, while the other Greeks advocated that Ionia be forcibly depopulated and abandoned to the Persians. In 478, the Spartans slowly withdrew from League activities and allowed the Athenians to form the Delian League, largely composed of Ionian and seafaring states. Panhellenism as a political philosophy was at an end until the fourth century, when a number of orators—Lysias (Lys. 33), Gorgias (in his Olympic Oration), and Isocrates (Isoc. 4, 12)—urged that the Greeks unite, put aside their own petty disputes, and march against Persia. It was that dream that Philip II and Alexander the Great embraced, but to achieve it they first had to conquer the cantankerous Greeks and force them into unity via the League of Corinth (*IG* II[2] 236). Political panhellenism left no legacy of a strong international participatory community in Greece.

The Greeks had no equivalent of today's United Nations. The oracle at Delphi might be consulted on interstate questions, but its advice was easily ignored or misunderstood (e.g. Thuc. 7.18). The Amphictyonic League had a limited range of actions, and it too could turn into a tool of a state's ambition (cf. Dem. 5). Arbitration between states became increasingly popular in the Hellenistic world (Ager 1996: xiii), but was much less popular and successful in the archaic and classical periods.

It is sometimes suggested that the Greeks, despite having no formal bodies for its enforcement, did recognize an international law. The evidence for this largely rests upon a statement in Thucydides by the Corinthians that the Athenians do not act *kata tous Hellenon nomous* (Thuc. 1.41), a clear reference to their imperialism (see below). States are occasionally described as acting *nomimos*, lawfully, or with *paranomia*, outside the law (Low 2007: 97–102). This does not mean that the Greeks had a formal system of international law to which each state had signed on, like the Geneva Convention, but that in their dealings with other states they followed a set of recognized but unwritten rules, significantly different from the Roman approach. The problem lies, of course, with the lack of definition; the Corinthians accuse the Athenians of acting *kata nomous* (Thuc. 1.41), but Isocrates praises similar hegemonic behavior by calling it *nomimos* (cf. Isoc. 4.123). The meaning of international law shifted from speaker to speaker and state to state.

Perhaps the *nomoi* to which the Corinthians refer are simply the treaties and alliances the Greek states had made with one another. Although these could certainly be construed as *nomoi*, they do not present a coherent picture of anything we might call international law, a body of rules and regulations that states followed in their dealings with each other. Treaty language can differ significantly from document to document. So too can the efficacy and success of the alliances made, and due to the paucity of our sources we often have no way of knowing whether alliances established by treaty were maintained and adhered to as they were supposed to be.

It is true, however, that Greek alliances made between independent states clearly adhered to certain principles, although they may not have been formally expressed. One important characteristic of alliances between independent states is that the terms sworn to tended to be equal and reciprocal. For instance, in an agreement of 395 BCE between the Boeotians and the Athenians:

> [Go]ds.
> *vacat*
> [All]iance of the Boeo[tians and the Athenians for]
> all time. *vacat?*
> [If an]yone should make [war against the Athenians, either]
> [by] land or b[y sea, the Boeot]ians [will give aid]
> with [a]ll their stren[gth however the] Atheni[ans ask],
> [as best they are able. And if]
> anyone should m]ake [war against the Boeotians either by]
> [land or] b[y sea, the Athenians will give aid ——]
> (*IG* II[2] 14)

Although large portions of the text have been restored, and it breaks off before it concludes, the formulae used here are so common and well attested that the restorations are near-certain. Note the absolute reciprocity and equality in the terms: the Boeotians will help the Athenians when they are attacked, either by land or by sea, and do so to their utmost, and the Athenians undertake to do the exact same for the Boeotians. During this period—the Corinthian War—Athens was still in the process of recovering from her defeat in the Peloponnesian War and the Boeotians were a group of city-states in central Greece, organized into a league and led by Thebes (see below), who would later in the fourth century become quite powerful and hold hegemony over Greece. The two city-states were roughly but not precisely equal, yet the wording of the treaty makes it clear that to all intents and purposes they were equals and engaged on a purely reciprocal relationship with each other. These bedrock principles of equality and reciprocity are found in virtually every other alliance between independent states in classical Greece, and it is hardly a stretch to argue that, if the Greeks did conceive of some form of international law, this was it. This also explains why the Corinthians could condemn the Athenians for violating "the laws of the Greeks" before the Peloponnesian War (see also below).

The terminology that was used to describe relationships formed between states supports the idea that reciprocity and equality were the foundation of Greek interstate relations. The Greek word for alliance was *summachia*, which can be translated literally as "a fighting together." By the end of the fifth century, Greek states regularly made agreements of *philia kai summachia*, "friendship and alliance," in an apparent attempt to introduce an affective element into a diplomatic relationship, perhaps for enforcement purposes (Bolmarcich 2010; Mitchell 1997). In the *Rhetoricum ad Alexandrum*, Aristotle even identifies past reciprocity (or lack thereof) as a basis for arguing for or against an alliance, respectively (1424b39, 1425a4).

The evidence suggests that to a Greek a participatory community on an international level would be quite alien. Greek city-states might participate in panhellenic politics and religious rituals, they might make alliances with one another or join federal leagues, they might speak of an ill-defined international law and formally treat their allies as though they were equals and capable of giving as much as they got, but ultimately any idea of an international community among the Greeks remained quite fuzzy. Instead, we must focus on the individual actors on the Greek international stage—the city-states—to gain any sense of how they carried out interstate relations with one another.

2 Colonization

If any interstate relationship in the ancient Greek world could be expected to show a sufficiently close relationship between two disparate states that we might call it a participatory community, it is that of colony and mother-city (*metropolis*). Colonies, after all, consisted of citizens sent out from the metropolis for a variety of possible reasons (cf. Wilson 2006), who would naturally keep, if not their citizenship (Graham 1999: 111), an affinity for the mother-city and their kin there. Some of the foundation decrees for Greek colonies are still extant, and they stress the closeness of the relationship. Timaeus of Tauromenium, for instance, claims that the decree at Locris on the foundation of Epizephyrian Locri began by defining the relationship between the two as one of "parents towards children" (Polyb. 12.9).

Other foundation decrees lay out the nature of the relationship between colony and mother-city. Some state upfront that the colonists will cease to be citizens of the metropolis (ML 20.1, 6, 22), but a relationship between former citizen and mother-city is still envisaged; in some agreements, colonists could still inherit property left to them in the mother-city (Graham 1999: 57–59), and if they returned to their *metropolis* they could reclaim their previously surrendered citizenship (ML 20.6–10). Citizens of the mother-city could join the colony at any time and become citizens of the colony (ML 5.4–8). Other decrees make the dependence of colony on metropolis clear, as in provisions establishing that colonists (citizens or not) continue to pay taxes to the *metropolis* (Graham 1999: 51–52), oaths of loyalty from the colonists (ML 20.11–14), or guarantees granting religious privileges to the mother-city in the colony (*IG* I^3 46.11–13; Thuc. 1.25.3–4; cf. RO 93.2–6). Still others make the obligations of the mother-city to the colony clear, for instance in providing defense to the colony (*IG* I^3 46.13–17; Graham 1999: 73), or in allowing colonists to celebrate religious rites in the metropolis (Graham 1999: 49–51; *IG* I^3 46.11–13).

In theory, the relationship between colony and mother-city was quite close, or was ideally envisaged to be so. In practice, the story was sometimes different. Many colonies, especially those in the west or north, were far from their *metropoleis.* A.J. Graham has shown that relations between the mother-city of Paros and the colony of Thasos were much closer than we would otherwise expect, probably because the two were relatively close to one another in the Aegean (Graham 1999: 71–97). Thasos in her turn became the metropolis of a number of colonies founded on the mainland opposite her island shores and also appears to have established an extremely close relationship with them, perhaps even directly controlling local political and economic affairs. Other mother-cities, like Miletus, went further and even granted shared citizenship (*sympoliteia*) to the members of their colonies (RO 93; Graham 1999: 98–117).

Such close relations were not always the case, of course; often it depended on the attitude of the mother-city or the purpose for which the colony was founded. Argos, for instance, was in one tradition held to be the metropolis of the classical Cretan cities (*RE* s.v. Tylissos), and a decree involving a dispute between Knossos and Tylissos, with Argos as arbitrator, suggests that her relationship with her Cretan colonies was one of mutual friendship (ML 42). While Argives had privileges in Knossos and Tylissos, so too did the citizens of those city-states have privileges in Argos, such as exemption from taxes on foreigners or guaranteed religious rights in the mother-city. Argos does not appear to have interfered much in the life of her colonies, other than an expectation that they recognize her status as mother-city and act accordingly.

Some mother-cities founded colonies to assist to their imperial ambitions. The prime example is Athens (see also below), who founded colonies at Brea (*IG* I^3 46) and Amphipolis (Thuc. 1.100.3) during the fifth century BCE. Corinth was one of the most active *metropoleis* during the archaic period of Greek colonization, founding a number of colonies in Sicily, Magna Graecia, and along the Adriatic coast. Corinth's goal was not so much geographic as economic domination, and she achieved that with well-positioned colonies along the major trade routes west of Greece. While many of her colonies were far distant from Corinth, Corinth's large navy allowed for easy communication between—and control of—them. Although Corinth's colonies were autonomous in name, they had to tolerate a great deal of interference from Corinth, who saw the colonies not simply as outposts throughout the Mediterranean, but as key to her continued economic success.

It is in this context that the most famous dispute between colony and mother-city in Greek history occurred. One of Corinth's earliest colonies, Corcyra, had from the very beginning a tense relationship with her; the two fought the first naval battle in Greek history (Thuc. 1.13.4). In 435–433, hostilities erupted again over Corcyra's treatment of her own colony Epidamnus, at that time riven by civil war. Corcyra refused assistance. Epidamnus turned to Corinth for aid, and was welcomed, in large part because the Corcyraeans refused to give due honors to their mother-city (Thuc. 1.25.4), and the Corinthians resented the local pride of the Corcyraeans, who were proud of their own navy, wealth, and their island, supposedly Phaeacia in Homer's *Odyssey*. After losing a battle at sea to Corcyra, the Corinthians prepared a second attack; in response, the Corcyraeans appealed to Athens, who promised them aid, and, when it was delivered, started the first in a series of encounters that were to begin the Peloponnesian War in 431 (Thuc. 1.24–55). Another of those encounters concerned Corinth's colony Potidaea, which remained loyal to the mother-city but had been forced into tributary status in their empire by the Athenians.

Most colony/mother-city relationships in ancient Greece appear to have been harmonious, either because of distance (and lack of easy communication) or because of shared cultural affinities and mutual rights and respect. The exception appears to have been colonies like Corcyra that rose to a position of sufficient prominence to challenge and resent the authority of their mother-city. With colonization, the Greeks succeeded for a time in some locales in establishing a "community" that crossed interstate borders, but the unique circumstances of colony/mother-city were what made that possible, not any model for a Greek interstate community that colonists were following.

3 Interstate Leagues

Colonization presents us with a case of an interstate relationship that we would expect to be very close, but which could become fraught despite the ties that bound the city-states involved. Similarly, the existence of Greek interstate leagues in the archaic and classical periods attests to the potential for strong collaborative relationships between states on the basis of perceived similarities in ethnicity or culture, but the evidence also suggests an equally strong potential for conflict even in leagues formed with a common interest in mind. While several of these leagues were religious in nature (the Kalaurian League, based in the Saronic Gulf area, and the Ionian *koinon*), here I focus on those that served a military purpose: the Peloponnesian League, the Hellenic League (see also above), the Delian League, and the Boeotian League (for a discussion of the institutional context of these leagues, see Rhodes, Chapter 8).

Sparta's Peloponnesian League is the oldest of these interstate organizations. Its early history is murky, but most historians recognize its existence by the mid-sixth century BCE. Unlike some of the later Greek leagues, it lacked any formal charter or constitution (cf. Bolmarcich 2005, with bibliography in n.1), although some scholars argue for a detailed constitution that laid out provisions, such as regular League assemblies in which a majority vote carried the day, and provisions that member states not attack each other. Recent scholarship generally does not recognize the "constitution of the Peloponnesian League" and instead defines the League as a loosely organized defensive alliance centered around Sparta (Kagan 1969; Lendon 1994; Bolmarcich 2005; Yates 2005). Instead of having relationships with each other as well as Sparta, as a true interstate league would, all the member states had a relationship with Sparta alone. For instance, Corinth and Megara, both members of the League, were allies of Sparta, but not of each other—quite the opposite, in fact (cf. Thuc. 1.105.3–5). As hegemon, Sparta determined the courses of action the League would take. Often she was under the influence of her allies, but they were not always in agreement with each other or with Sparta.

The Peloponnesian League presents what encapsulates the result for Greek interstate leagues in creating an international participatory community: it simply didn't happen. The longstanding attempts by scholars to force the Peloponnesian League into a constitutional model in which member states had given rights and were a united whole represents a desire to see in the ancient world participatory international communities as we have today. In the case of the Peloponnesian League, this desire was fueled by the similarities of the member states: virtually all members were located within the Peloponnesus (Thebes was the major exception), virtually all identified themselves as ethnically Dorian, virtually all had strong oligarchic elements in their governments, and virtually all were landlocked states that practiced hoplite warfare (Corinth was the major exception). If states with so much in common could not form an international community in ancient Greece, what states could?

Instead, what united the members of the Peloponnesian League was Spartan power. Sparta was acknowledged to be the most powerful state in the League, and it was in her interests that the League was founded, as a protection against the Helots in the event of a slave revolt, or even against the one state in the Peloponnesus that did not recognize Spartan dominance, Argos. It was Sparta's needs that dictated the needs of the League, and members often complained of Spartan inaction when she was not directly affected by a current crisis (cf. Thuc. 1.68–71).

However, members were also quite free to opt out of League campaigns or decisions. Another aspect of Peloponnesian League scholarship that has now been superseded is the belief that all members of the Peloponnesian League swore an oath to Sparta "to have the same friends and enemies as the Spartans, and to follow the Spartan whithersoever they may lead" (De Ste. Croix 1972; Bolmarcich 2005, 2007; Yates 2005). If one cannot on the basis of either historical fact or the existence of a League constitution find a true participatory community in the League, an oath like this is the best evidence for the idea that there was such a community, by making Spartan desires the focal point of League activities—and thus the source of any international community in the ancient Peloponnesus. But there is no evidence that this oath was ever that of the Peloponnesian League; instead, it appears—when it does appear in the historical record—as an oath the Spartans exacted from those states that they had conquered, with or without the assistance of the League; it is an oath of individual loyalty to Sparta sworn by the subjugated (Bolmarcich 2005).

It was Spartan domination of the Peloponnesus that gave her hegemony over the Hellenic League. As hegemon of the Hellenic League, Sparta never suffered the resistance she encountered from states within her own Peloponnesian League. An early dispute over the hegemony—Athens, Gelon, or Sparta? (Hdt. 7.157–162)—was quickly resolved in her favor. Spartan policy as leader of the Hellenic League, however, did not consider Greece as a whole: her plan to move south when the Persians sacked Athens and fortify the Isthmus of Corinth would have been disastrous, given the strength and size of the Persian navy (Hdt. 8.57), and Themistocles of Athens had to resort to the utmost persuasion to get the Greeks to fight at Salamis and defeat the Persians (Hdt. 8.58–64). The Spartans may have been leaders of all Greece, but they were not thinking of themselves as such, with the corresponding obligations that would have entailed avoiding their usual isolationist, Peloponnesus-centered policies. Although the Greeks managed to repel the Persians and the Hellenic League did a great deal to create a sense of community among the Greeks, that sentiment was not only brief but also shallow.

This is demonstrated by events after the final defeat of the Persians at the battle of Plataea in 479 (Hdt. 9.106). A dispute arose over how to treat the Ionian Greeks who had formerly been under Persian control (and who had given the Great King assistance in his invasion of Greece). The Ionian-identified Athenians took up the Ionian cause, while the Dorian-identified Spartans were not eager to invite the Ionians into the Hellenic League (and thus increase the Athenians' base of support). A dispute also arose over how aggressively the Greeks should pursue the Persians; once again, the Ionians, the Greeks most in danger from a renascent Persia, and the Athenians supported a Hellenic League that would remain active against Persia, while the Spartans did not (Thuc. 1.89). Once the tyrannical behavior of the Spartan regent Pausanias alienated the Ionians and the Athenians still further, the Spartans essentially shut down all Hellenic League operations in Asia Minor and along the coast of Ionia (Thuc. 1.94–95).

As an immediate consequence of the policy disputes between Athens and Sparta over the Ionians and Persia, the Athenians formed the Delian League. Initially this was done at the request of the Ionians themselves, who felt that the Athenians were more trustworthy than the Spartans on grounds of their kinship to them (Thuc. 1.95). The initial basis for the Delian League, then, like that for the Peloponnesian League, was a shared ethnic identity, although in the case of the Delian League it was not at first the hegemon that stood to benefit the most from the formation of the League, but rather the Ionian allies. Athens was tasked with defending Ionia against Persia, and so the burden of leadership and administration of the League fell upon her (cf. Thuc. 1.98). And like the Peloponnesian League, Athens and her new allies tended to be states whose economy and military prowess were intimately linked to sea power.

Unlike the Peloponnesian League, however, the relationships between the allies in the Delian League did not depend upon an ally's relationships with the hegemon; rather, it appears that all states were not only in alliance with Athens, but with each other. As in the Peloponnesian League, this did not preclude conflict between the allies—later, for instance, the Chians and Mytilenaeans helped Athens against the Samian rebels (Thuc. 1.116–17.2), and the other Euboean cities did not aid Carystus in her revolt against Athens, although they were neutral (Thuc. 1.98.3)—but it did create a far more "united" League. The initial assessment of tribute—either in the form of money or of ships—by Athens does not seem to have been problematic; the League treasury was held in common at Delos as well (Thuc. 1.97). Furthermore, Delos' central location in the Aegean made it accessible to all allies and made it "neutral" ground, an area dominated by no single one of the allies or her hegemon, in contrast to Peloponnesian League assemblies, which almost always were held at Sparta.

Things were to change quickly, however. The Athenians held the allies to the tribute of money or ships that had initially been agreed upon, with the result that allies either revolted (and were easily subdued by Athens) or switched from making a contribution in kind—ships—to money (Thuc. 1.99.3). This second path was fatal to any sense of equality within the Delian League; the Athenians, who already held the hegemony, now also assumed military supremacy within the alliance, until only Athens and Samos, Lesbos, and Chios supplied any ships to League campaigns (Plut. *Cim.* 12.3–4; Thuc. 1.100.1, 3.10.5). This military acumen served Athens well in putting down revolts of allies who no longer wanted to pay tribute in any form and to return to their previous autonomy (Thuc. 1.99.3); and such revolts had to be put down so that the Athenians could maintain their undisputed control of the Delian League and the Aegean Sea. As a result, the Delian League shifted from an equal relationship between states with the same goals to an equivalent relationship between states whose purpose now was to assist the hegemon in maintaining her rule (*archē*) of the sea. The switch from ships to money as tribute gave Athens every reason to become interested in the domestic policies and infrastructure of her allies, since that directly affected their ability to pay her tribute. The three allies that remained largely autonomous throughout much of the fifth century, Samos, Lesbos, and Chios, managed to retain that autonomy only by retaining their own navies.

This cycle of Athenian demands-allied revolts-allied subjection continued throughout the fifth century until the defeat of Athens by Sparta in 404/3 BCE. What is striking about the Delian League is how little sense of community existed between the allies. Alliance, even between allies with such marked similarities, was worth little as a guarantee of communal feeling on the Greek international stage; by contrast, the Romans took the approach of granting Roman citizenship to loyal allies. I shall return to the Athenian Empire and how exactly it thwarted any possible conception of an international Greek participatory community in the following section.

After the fall of Athens, the Spartans tried their hand at imperialism, a failed experiment (again, see the next section). Their post-Athenian domination of Greece did not last long, effectively ending with the King's Peace and the end of the Corinthian War in 386, although they still remained a power to reckon with in the Peloponnesus. The fourth century saw two other Greek interstate leagues dominate interstate affairs in Greece without becoming imperial powers: the Theban hegemony of Boeotian states (the Boeotian League), and the Second Athenian Maritime League.

Unlike the Peloponnesian and Delian Leagues, the Boeotian League did have a formal constitution, an account of which survives today (*Hell. Oxy.* 16.2–4). This was a more federated organization than either Athens and Sparta had with their respective leagues. Membership in the League was limited to cities located in Boeotia, who therefore shared a closer geographical kinship than did the other leagues. Boeotia was organized into eleven groups of cities and their surrounding districts, each of which elected a boeotarch and sent sixty delegates to a federal assembly that met at Thebes. The eleven each also supplied the same number (1,000 infantry and 100 horse) to the Boeotian army. Power did not reside in the federal assembly alone, but each of the cities also ratified federal policy. On paper, Thebes, the hegemon, had slightly more power with two boeotarchs, but by 395, when the Oxyrhynchus Historian was writing, Thebes held four of those offices, because she had subjected to herself two of the other cities, including her longtime enemy Plataea (*Hell. Oxy.* 16.3). Of the other cities in the League, three each supplied one boeotarch; three more shared two between them; and the remaining six were divided into two groups of three, each of which took turns sending one boeotarch to the assembly (*Hell. Oxy.* 16.3). By the early fourth century, then, the Boeotian League was very much the province of Thebes. Even the League coinage demonstrates this: the obverse of each city's coin bore the symbol of Thebes, the Boeotian figure-eight shield, while the reverse bore each individual city's symbol (Kraay 1976: 114).

Boeotian subordination to Thebes is demonstrated by the brief period of the Theban hegemony over Greece from 371 to 362, during which the Thebans defeated the Spartans twice at the battles of Leuctra and Second Mantinea, and freed the Spartan helots, actions which effectively ended Spartan domination of the Peloponnesus and limited her to the southeastern Peloponnesus. Epaminondas and Pelopidas, the Theban leaders, organized and led the hegemony; the other cities' job was largely to follow Theban leadership. Despite Theban dominance, the Boeotian League demonstrates a greater sense of a participatory community than the other Greek leagues do. The federal assembly, with initial local autonomy and equal contributions to Boeotia's military efforts mimics the political infrastructure of some *poleis*, including Athens. This was only practical because of the limited geographical area of Boeotia, and it did not ensure that all city-states would participate equally or that all city-states would feel a part of the "group"—throughout her history, for instance, Plataea associated herself much more closely with Athens than with her fellow Boeotians. Following a federated structure for a league on a larger scale would have been impractical in Greece's geopolitical climate.

The final major Greek interstate league prior to the Macedonian conquest was the Second Athenian Maritime League. Its members had been members of the old Delian League, with the (initial) exception of Thebes, and so the ties of ethnic identity and affiliation with the sea still held true. Athens was again the hegemon, but she was a chastened one, very different from her incarnation during the Delian League. The "new tone" is evident in the Charter of the League (*IG* II^2 43). Athens promises not to establish cleruchies (forced settlements of Athenian citizens, displacing locals) in the lands of allied members and to give up all Athenian property there, not to exact tribute, and not to establish garrisons or governors in allied territory. Although the League treasury and assembly were based at Athens, the assembly appears to have been bicameral, with one house the Athenian assembly and the other composed of allied representatives. This meant that without unity between the two houses, no proposed League policy could go into effect. This arrangement gave both power to Athens as hegemon and protection to the allies.

The set-up of the League was also different from that of the Delian League. Although all members had their names inscribed upon the stele of the charter, several of them made individual alliances with Athens herself, suggesting that allies could have both a relationship with Athens and with the League as a whole. The purpose of the League was to resist Spartan imperialism, and once that threat had vanished, to protect against threats from Thebes. Despite some rhetorical shenanigans, such as imposing tribute (*phoros*) under the name of contributions (*syntaxeis*), the Athenians of the fourth century were far more popular as hegemon than those of the fifth century until the Social War of the 350s BCE. After the Social War, the Second League was largely toothless (Sealey 1955; Cawkwell 1981), but remained one of the few viable tools in the Greek resistance to Macedon (see below). There is insufficient evidence to judge the nature of the "participatory community" of the Second League, but so long as a basis of equality was maintained, it appears to have functioned relatively well as an instrument of interstate action.

4 Athenian and Spartan Imperialism

Imperialism, although it often brings untold economic and political benefits to both the imperialists and their subjects as well as their neighbors, is usually viewed critically today by other states and/or by opposition parties within the imperialist state. Ancient Greece was no exception; the Persian Empire was anathema to the Greeks since rule under the Great King represented slavery, and correspondingly they saw the Persians as not only effete barbarians, but, even worse, as slaves. When the Athenians and then the Spartans in the wake of the Peloponnesian War demonstrated imperialist behavior, Greek reaction was similar. The Peloponnesian War was fought against the increasing power of Athens, the Corinthian War against Spartan encroachment. Whatever economic benefits the Athenian Empire brought in terms of making trade routes safe and generally boosting the economic strength of the Greek world, these mattered little when she was also seen as infringing on the freedom and autonomy of the Greeks. Even imperial power, which under the Persian Empire created a forced interstate community that ranged in territory from Bactria to Nubia, and under Athens ranged from Ionia to Italy, could not impose upon its subjects a true community. More was needed.

In 428, the Mytilenaeans, on the eve of their revolt from Athens, mourned to the assembled Peloponnesian League at Olympia that:

> Justice and honesty will be the first topics of our speech, especially as we are asking for alliance; because we know that there can never be any solid friendship between individuals, or union between communities that is worth the name, unless the parties be persuaded of each other's honesty, and be generally congenial the one to the other; since from difference in feeling springs also difference in conduct ... as long as the Athenians led us fairly we followed them loyally; but when we saw them relax their hostility to the Mede, and try to make the allies their subject, then our apprehensions began. (Thuc. 3.10.1, 4, trans. Crawley)

If the sentiments the Mytilenaeans express here can be taken as a relatively accurate expression of ancient Greek attitudes in general, then the Delian League/Athenian Empire failed for a lack of shared values and goals, i.e. when the Athenians became less interested in leading a league of their Ionian kinsmen (see above) and more in the benefits of imperialism to themselves and their city-state. The Greek city-states also lacked the developed institutional mechanisms that the Romans had for the integration of non-Roman states into the larger Roman community, perhaps because of the Greek stress on each city-state's freedom and autonomy.

The foundation of the Delian League as an equal alliance and its transformation into an equitable one have been discussed in the previous section. But as the Athenians subdued more revolts, exacted more tribute, and infringed upon the "territory" of other Greek states like Corinth, they became increasingly unpopular. At the first conference at Sparta, addressing the complaints of the Peloponnesian League allies and Sparta, they offer an apologia for their empire by arguing that they did not ask for empire, but it was thrust upon them (Thuc. 1.76.2); that they now had to maintain it in self-defense; and that their past service to Greece in the Persian Wars had been essential to the survival of Greece. This last should have been a powerful argument: the Athenian service to Greece would not have been taken lightly, and indeed it saved the Athenians after their final defeat in the Peloponnesian War, when the Spartans resisted Corinthian and Theban calls for the extermination of Athens (Xen. *Hell.* 2.2.19–20). But, as the ephor Sthenelaidas pointed out (Thuc. 1.86), it did not matter whether the Athenians had been good for Greece fifty years before if they were bad now, and in this sentiment he agrees with the Mytilenaeans at Olympia. Once Athens was seen to have abandoned the interest of the other Greeks in favor of her own, she became the enemy.

A similar fate would befall Sparta in the years after the Peloponnesian War. Under the rule of a series of kings and leaders (e.g. Lysander and Agesilaus) who were more aggressive abroad than was the Spartan norm, she attempted to control the remnants of Athens' old empire, even going so far as to campaign in Ionia against the Persians in the years immediately following the Peloponnesian War (Xen. *Hell.* 3.4). While she did not exact formal tribute as Athens had, she does appear to have imposed decarchies (governing boards of ten) on some states to ensure their compliance (Xen. *Hell.* 3.4.2; Diod. Sic. 14.13.1; Plut. *Lys.* 3). The decarchs tended to be friends of Sparta and Lysander, and shared her oligarchic sympathies. Indeed, the establishment or encouragement of oligarchies in her subject states and friends appears to have been a standard Spartan policy (Thuc. 1.19.1; Arist. *Pol.* 1307b22). Athens is sometimes said to have done the same with democracies (Arist. *Pol.* 1307b22), but the evidence is sketchier (see most recently Brock 2009). During the Peloponnesian War we see oligarchs and democrats in conflict in the Greek cities turning for support to Sparta and Athens, respectively. This was an attempt to create communal feeling between states on the basis of shared political sympathies, yet this was by no means a guarantee of harmony between city-states; it was democratic Syracuse, for instance, that defeated Athens in Sicily (Thuc. 8.96.5).

With the example of Athens fresh before them, the rest of the Greek city-states counterattacked Sparta in 395, beginning the Corinthian War, ultimately resolved by the King's Peace in 386, which included the key guarantee of freedom and autonomy to all the Greek states (Xen. *Hell.* 5.1.31). With the passage of the King's Peace, the age of empires in Greece passed; from then on, the Greek states clung fiercely to the principles of freedom and autonomy for their cities, and while a few powerful interstate leagues arose in fourth-century Greece (see above), they did not approach the power of imperial Athens and Sparta.

5 Conclusions: The "Failure" of Greek Interstate Relations

It is in this stress on freedom and autonomy that the true problem of achieving an international participatory community lay for the Greeks; the Romans, as Craige Champion demonstrates (Chapter 19), had no such problems and were correspondingly more successful (see below). Any participatory community requires the surrender of some individuality and autonomy; think of "quiet hours" in a college dorm. The value placed on freedom and autonomy in post-Persian Wars Greece was ultimately a stumbling block for the creation of a Greek international community. Whether the Greeks were confronted with an imperial power, or simply a neighboring state with which they had a disagreement, or a mother-city whose demands on her colony had become intrusive, the stress on freedom and autonomy meant that for a state to give way under such circumstances, unless under compulsion, was highly unlikely. Correspondingly, any attempt to form an international community only got so far.

An insistence on freedom and autonomy, however, could be simultaneously a strength in domestic affairs and a weakness internationally. In 481, facing a second Persian invasion, the Greeks managed to put aside their differences and unite into the Hellenic League to meet the threat. But Herodotus makes clear how unusual this was for them (see above), and Thucydides how short the life expectancy of any such interstate co-operation among the Greeks was. After the Persian Wars, the Greeks faced no significant external threat for 150 years until Macedon under Philip II began to conquer Greek cities. Although the Greeks had united against Athenian and Spartan imperialism previously, a successful opposition to Philip would have required a sustained resistance to him both diplomatically and militarily, and this did not happen. Not only were the Greeks slow to recognize the threat from Philip (as we see in Demosthenes' speeches), but Greek states made individual alliances with him and even allowed him onto the Amphictyonic Council, from which he could and did unite some Greek states against other Greek cities such as Thebes. Former powers like Sparta had withdrawn from international affairs, and finally only Athens and Thebes were left to stand against Philip, a late alliance that did not succeed.

The Greeks had few signs of what we would consider today an international, participatory community. There was no United Nations, no NATO, nothing in place to facilitate communications and negotiation between states. There were institutions that had international standing but whose sense of community was limited or transitory, such as interstate leagues or panhellenic sanctuaries, and there were connections between colony and mother-city and artificial communities between the hegemon and subjects of an imperialist state. Beyond these, there was little in the nature of an interstate "community" in the ancient Greek world.

Throughout history, in fact, forming a true interstate "community" has been problematic. Craige Champion's companion chapter on Roman attempts to create a sense of international community with all members participating to some degree in Roman affairs illustrates this well. Romans were less interested in creating community by actually granting citizens of the territories they acquired full rights or say in Roman affairs than they were in incorporating new territories into the existing Roman aristocratic social structure by applying to them such domestic practices as patronage. The reflection of their social organization in their interstate relations was an attempt to create a strongly hierarchized international community, with Rome as the ultimate patron state, surrounded by client states of varying degrees of influence and importance. While this approach was effective for the Romans, Rome's political, social, and even geopolitical differences from Greece made it impossible for the latter. The Greek city-states' insistence on their own independence and autonomy, even when it was not in their best interests, scotched any attempt to form a true international community in the Aegean world. Athens came the closest to such an approach, and her power was relatively short-lived compared to the Romans. Instead, the Greek city-states operated upon an assumption of equality between participant city-states. In this basic distinction between their approaches to interstate relations, one can see as well the basic difference between Rome and Greece, between a culture predicated on hierarchy and a culture based on more individual values like freedom.

REFERENCES

Adcock, F. and D. Mosley. 1975. *Diplomacy in Ancient Greece*. London.

Ager, S. 1996. *Interstate Arbitrations in the Greek World, 337–90* BC. Berkeley.

Bentz, M., ed. 1998. *Panathenaika: Symposion zu den Panathenäischen Preisamphoren*. Mainz am Rhein.

Boardman, J. 1999. *The Greeks Overseas: The Early Colonies and Trade*. 4th edn. London.

Bolmarcich, S. 2003. "Thucydidean Explanations: Diplomacy and Historiography in Archaic and Classical Greece." Ph.D. Dissertation, University of Virginia.

Bolmarcich, S. 2005. "Thucydides 1.19.1 and the Peloponnesian League." *GRBS* 45: 5–34.

Bolmarcich, S. 2007. "The Date of the 'Oath of the Peloponnesian League.'" *Historia* 30: 1–14.

Bolmarcich, S. 2010. "Communal Values in Ancient Diplomacy." In R. Rosen and I. Sluiter, eds., *Valuing Others in Classical Antiquity*. Leiden.

Bowden, H. 2005. *Classical Athens and the Delphic Oracle: Divination and Democracy*. Cambridge.

Brock, R. 2009. "Did the Athenian Empire Promote Democracy?" In J. Ma, N. Papazardakas, and R. Parker, eds., *Interpreting the Athenian Empire*. London.

Cawkwell, G.L. 1981. "Notes on the Failure of the Second Athenian Confederacy." *JHS* 101: 40–55.

De Ste. Croix, G.E.M. 1972. *The Origins of the Peloponnesian War*. London.

Fornara, C.W., ed. and trans. 1983. *Archaic Times to the End of the Peloponnesian War: Translated Documents of Greece and Rome, 1*. 2nd edn. Cambridge.

Graham, A.J. 1999. *Colony and Mother-City in Ancient Greece*. Manchester.

Graham, A.J. 2001. *Collected Papers on Greek Colonization*. Leiden.

Hall, J. 2007. *A History of the Archaic Greek World*. Oxford and Malden, MA.

Herman, G. 1987. *Ritualised Friendship and the Greek City*. Cambridge.

Kagan, D. 1969. *The Outbreak of the Peloponnesian War*. Ithaca, NY.

Kagan, D. 1974. *The Archidamian War*. Ithaca, NY.

Kagan, D. 1981. *The Peace of Nicias and the Sicilian Expedition*. Ithaca, NY.

Kagan, D. 1991. *The Fall of the Athenian Empire*. Ithaca, NY.

Kelly, T. 1966. "The Calaurian Amphictyony." *AJA* 70: 113–121.

Kraay, C.M. 1976. *Archaic and Classical Greek Coins*. London.

Lefevre, F. 1998. *L'Amphictyonie Pyléo-Delphique histoire et institutions*. Athens.

Lendon, J.E. 1994. "Thucydides and the Constitution of the Peloponnesian League." *GRBS* 35: 159–178.

Low, P. 2007. *Interstate Relations in Classical Greece: Morality and Power*. Cambridge.

Meiggs, R. 1972. *The Athenian Empire*. Oxford.

Meiggs, R. and D. Lewis. 1999. *Greek Historical Inscriptions to the End of the Fifth Century* BC. Oxford.

Miller, S. 2006. *Ancient Greek Athletics*. New Haven.

Mitchell, L. 1997. *Greeks Bearing Gifts: The Public Use of Private Relationships in the Greek World, 435–323* BC. Cambridge.

Morgan, C. 1990. *Athletes and Oracles: The Transformation of Olympia and Delphi in the Eighth Century* BC. Cambridge.

Morgan, C. 1993. "The Origins of Pan-Hellenism." In R. Hägg and N. Marinatos, eds., *Greek Sanctuaries: New Approaches*. London, 14–33.

Osborne, R. 1996. *Greece in the Making, 1200–479* BC. London.

Rhodes, P.J. and R. Osborne. 2004. *Greek Historical Inscriptions, 404–323* BC. Oxford.

Roebuck, C. 1955. "The Early Ionian League." *CPh* 50: 26–40.

Rolley, C. 1983. "Les grands sanctuaires panhelléniques." In R. Hägg, ed., *The Greek Renaissance of the Eighth Century* BC: *Tradition and Innovation*. Stockholm.

Sanchez, P. 2001. *L'Amphictyonie des Pyles et des Delphes: recherches sur son role historique des origins au IIe siècle de notre ère*. Stuttgart.

Scott, M. 2010. *Delphi and Olympia: The Spatial Politics of Panhellenism in the Archaic and Classical Periods*. Cambridge.

Sealey, R. 1955. "Athens after the Social War." *JHS* 75: 74–81.

Sourvinou-Inwood, C. 1990. "What Is Polis Religion?" In O. Murray and S. Price, eds., *The Greek City*. Oxford.

Tritle, L., ed. 1997. *The Greek World in the Fourth Century* BC: *From the Fall of the Athenian Empire to the Successors of Alexander* London.

Wilson, J.-P. 2006. "'Ideologies' of Greek Colonization." In G.J. Bradley, ed., *Greek and Roman Colonisation: Origins, Ideologies, and Interactions*. Swansea.

Yates, D. 2005. "The Archaic Treaties between the Spartans and Their Allies." *CQ* 55: 65–76.

Yester, K. 2002. "What Is the International Community?" *Foreign Policy*. Available online at http://www.foreignpolicy.com/articles/2002/09/01/what_is_the_international_community. Accessed Apr. 2, 2014.

FURTHER READING

The time periods and topics covered in this chapter range widely enough that it is difficult to recommend works that speak to them all. On Greek interstate relations in general, Adcock and Mosley's *Diplomacy in Ancient Greece* is a good starting point, although it has been superseded by recent work like Low 2007. A.J. Graham 1999, 2001 and John Boardman 1999 on Greek colonization are irreplaceable. Russell Meiggs' *The Athenian Empire* and Paul Cartledge's *Agesilaus and the Crisis of Sparta* offer good backgrounds to Athenian and Spartan imperialism, respectively.

Students interested in the specific periods of Greek history and their related diplomatic phenomena that this chapter covers may find these more general works useful. Archaic Greece, the age of colonization, is detailed in Jonathan Hall's *A History of the Archaic Greek World* and Robin Osborne's *Greece in the Making*. The Peloponnesian War period and the growth of Athenian imperialism that led up to it are well documented in Donald Kagan's four-book series *The Outbreak of the Peloponnesian War*, *The Archidamian War*, *The Peace of Nicias and the Sicilian Expedition*, and *The Fall of the Athenian Empire*. The fourth century BCE and the fall of free Greece are covered in Lawrence Tritle's *The Greek World in the Fourth Century* BC.

Surviving ancient sources rarely deal explicitly with Greek diplomatic theory and practice, but the major historical authors all mention treaties, conquests, colonies, and so on. Students are advised to read through Herodotus, Thucydides, and Xenophon for excellent primary account of Greek history from the Persian Wars to the fall of Sparta in the middle of the fourth century BCE. Inscriptions are another important source: try Charles Fornara's *Archaic Times to the End of the Peloponnesian War*.

CHAPTER 19

Interstate Relations, Federal States, Colonization, and Empire during the Roman Republic

Craige B. Champion

In Memoriam Ernst Badian

Roman aristocratic, anti-egalitarian social values cast a long shadow—first in Rome itself; then throughout peninsular Italy; and finally across a vast geographical expanse encompassing the Mediterranean basin and Near East. The vehicle for their dissemination during the time of the Republic was territorial extension of arms and political domination; a dynamic evolution in power relations at the interstate level which we commonly call imperialism.

How did imperial expansion affect the *populus Romanus* in terms of participatory self-government during republican times? Can we say that imperial citizenship in the capital city had meaningful non-elite, democratic components? To what degree and by what processes were newly enfranchised citizens of subjected states, at first in Italy and thereafter throughout the Mediterranean, admitted into the *imperium Romanum*? Conversely, were citizens of long standing living away from Rome—for example, soldiers on military service abroad over several campaigning seasons or members of colonial foundations—in any sense active citizens in Roman politics?

There are similar problems at the interstate level. Were there any concrete principles of equality and reciprocity (as there were in the Greek world, as discussed by Sarah Bolmarcich in the companion chapter), underlying the Republic's relations with other states, so that they continued to exercise some autonomy in their foreign relations? Was there such a thing as an international public sphere, whereby polities in Rome's Italian Confederation, and later throughout its extra-Italian hegemony, could critique and ultimately modify imperial governance? At the ideological level, how was the fact of Roman political and military predominance articulated in the language of foreign diplomacy?

These are big questions, comprehensive answers to any of which are beyond the scope of a single essay. But this chapter will at least touch on each of them, arguing that Roman aristocratic social values constitute a thread that connects and helps us to understand

A Companion to Greek Democracy and the Roman Republic, First Edition. Edited by Dean Hammer.

them all. The first section assesses the heated scholarly controversy over the question of "democratic Rome"; that is, the extent to which non-elite citizens in the popular assemblies may have exercised independent political power in the operations of the state. It then considers the growth in the number of citizens, both in the capital and throughout Italy, which was concomitant with expanding imperial domination, and what this meant for active, participatory citizenship of non-elites.

The second section looks at republican Rome as a federal state and its relations with other city-states and state-confederations. Much like classical Sparta in the Peloponnesus, in Italy the Republic took a dim view of other states acting independently, outside of its own orbit of direct political influence. Rome could not tolerate a rival, whether it was a powerful, independent city-state or another federal state. All rival federal states were eventually broken up and their individual constituents incorporated in one way or another into the Roman Italian Confederation. Within its Italian hegemony, regardless of status—from states granted full citizenship (*civitas optimo iure*), to citizens without voting rights (*civitas sine iure suffragii*), to allies (*socii*), to peoples who submitted unconditionally (*dediticii*)—everyone had a place in the hierarchy of the Roman dispensation, with the incentive of moving up in status for demonstrated allegiance; and all provided an annual quota of troops to fuel the Republic's military operations. As a patron in relation to his client, Rome expected obedience, deference, and respect on the part of its Italian "allies."

The third section discusses Roman imperialism and its effects in the wider Mediterranean world and Near East. It begins with an examination of the nature and motivations of Roman imperial expansion, a fiercely contested topic among modern scholars. Can anything be said in support of the old view of "defensive imperialism"? In other words, were the Romans in any sense reluctant imperialists, who had an empire thrust upon them as a result of the realities of international affairs? Or was Rome rather exceptional in its militarism, exhibiting a pathological will to power? To what extent can political scientists help us to answer these questions?

International relations theories, and in particular those of the so-called Realist school pioneered by Kenneth Waltz (1979), offer fresh and exciting perspectives on the development of Roman imperialism, and they provide salutary warnings against neglecting to place Roman imperial developments within the larger context of the ancient Mediterranean interstate system in which the Republic existed. But the closing section also argues (drawing on Ernst Badian's classic study, *Foreign Clientelae*), that an important distinguishing—and exceptional—feature of Roman culture was the nature of its social relations, and that underlying social prescriptions left their imprint on the Republic's interactions with external powers and colored the diplomatic language it used to express those relationships. Much as the case in the ancient Greek world (see Bolmarcich, Chapter 18), but with radically different conceptual underpinnings, Rome's behavior in the international sphere was modeled on its social conceptions, which constitute the warp into which questions on popular political participation in the capital, the dynamics of Rome as a federal state in Italy, and the Republic's extra-Italian imperial ventures are interwoven.

1 "Democratic Rome" and the Extension of Roman Citizenship

One of the liveliest discussions in the study of the Republic in recent years has focused on the degree to which the average, non-elite citizen participated meaningfully in political processes at Rome (see Williamson, Chapter 11, Tatum, Chapter 15, and Morstein-Marx, Chapter 17). Fergus Millar (1984, 1986, 1989, 1998; cf. North 1990; Jehne 1995: 1–9; Tatum 2009) reinvigorated the long-dormant debate on this aspect of republican political culture, strongly arguing that Polybius' analysis of the Roman "mixed constitution," with equally balanced democratic, aristocratic, and monarchical elements, was essentially correct (though Polybius [6.51.5–8; cf. 6.11.1–2; 23.14.1–2] maintained that at the time of Rome's acme the aristocratic element in the republican polity was paramount; Millar and his followers have given insufficient attention to these Polybian passages). The objective of Millar's studies was to restore a significant and dynamically active democratic element in modern scholarship on Roman republican political life.

Millar challenged a long-standing, nearly unanimous scholarly consensus according to which the senatorial aristocracy had a stranglehold on political processes throughout all of republican history (see Gelzer [1912] 1969; Münzer [1920] 1999; Syme 1939, 1991). In launching his argument, he posed a simple question: How are we to account for elite preoccupation with rhetorical training and oratorical skill? Surely this concern indicates that elites believed their public image mattered and that stakes in the oratorical arena were high. Popular approval, renown, and political ascendancy through the *cursus honorum*, leading to a military command, which perhaps would culminate in the public spectacle of a triumph (although formally granted by the Senate, symbolically the quintessential manifestation of the people's will), were all at stake. Moreover, legislation against electoral bribery (*ambitus*) and the politics of largesse (*largitio*) seem to be impossible to understand if the people's political powers had been negligible (cf. Lintott 1990). Informal political gatherings (*contiones*, on which see Morstein-Marx 2004; also Morstein-Marx, Chapter 17), the popular assemblies, public games (*ludi*), and gladiatorial displays (*munera*) provided stages for expression of popular will and were barometers of public opinion, which the senatorial aristocracy could ill afford to ignore. And then, of course, there was the wild card of the political system, the tribunate, whose formal purpose was to serve as the watchdog of plebeian rights, possessing considerable powers of obstruction to political processes (Polyb. 6.16.4–5, though Polybius' statement that the tribunes were always beholden to act as the people decreed and to attend to their every wish is certainly idealized). In light of considerations such as these, Millar called for a radical reappraisal of republican political culture, refueling what had before seemed to be a worn-out scholarly cul-de-sac: the question on "democratic Rome."

It is easy to be misled by these considerations and to overestimate the extent to which the *populus Romanus* participated in political life. Ancient sources, such as Cicero's references to the "forensic mob" and the entire Roman people assembled on the Capitol, can contribute to the misunderstanding (see, for example, Cicero, *De orat.*, 1.26.118: *haec turba et barbaria forensis*). Passages such as these beg an important question: What proportion of the entire adult male citizen population could actually have attended informal political gatherings (*contiones*), voted in elections, or passed legislation? Since republican political culture never developed formal institutions for representative government, the citizen's ability to participate in political life was tied to his ability to be present in Rome. This was in turn dependent on the spatial proximity of his domicile to the city and its political spaces, or his privileged socio-economic position, which would have provided leisure time and means to travel to the imperial metropole in order to attend the popular political assemblies, or *comitia* (cf. Gabba 1976: 74–75; also Mouritsen, Chapter 9).

Roman demography (to the degree that we can know about it) has an important bearing on the question of citizens' active political participation (see also Williamson,

Chapter 11). By the last third of the second century BCE[1] the urban population in Rome itself may have reached a quarter-million (rapidly growing to perhaps one million by the time of Augustus), not to mention citizens outside the city and throughout Italy (Brunt 1971: 384; and the more conservative population estimates of Garnsey, Gallant, and Rathbone 1984: 40; cf. the recent survey of Scheidel 2008). The city population was increased in part by extension of *ius migrationis*, which allowed people (usually those enjoying Latin rights) to gain citizenship by moving to Rome. The number of citizens away from Rome was increased by the foundation of citizen colonies and the full enfranchisement of other states (see Sherwin-White [1973] 2001, *passim*), soldiers serving and living abroad for long periods (see Brunt 1971, *passim*), and individual land grants (most famously in the use of "public land," or *ager publicus*, in the social legislation of Tiberius and Gaius Gracchus).

Expansion of Roman military power and territorial extension of the citizen franchise away from Rome increased the number of "paper citizens" in the census returns, but decreased the percentage of the citizenry who actually participated in political processes in Rome on a regular basis. For an example of citizens removed from political processes permanently, already in 171 there were significant numbers of *hybridae*, offspring of Roman soldiers, who seem to have settled in the province, and indigenous women, in Spain (Livy 43.3.1–4); and according to Strabo (3.5.1), in 123 the consul Q. Caecilius Metellus settled 3,000 "Romans," who were in Spain, on Mallorca (see Broughton 1951: 513 for additional sources). By the late Republic the scale of such "paper citizens" was staggering: some 80,000 Romans joined Caesar's colonial foundations (Suetonius, *Divine Julius*, 42.1, with Brunt 1971: 234–265; see MacMullen 2000 for a concise account of colonization under Caesar and Augustus).

Communities of Roman citizens removed from the capital were firmly under Roman surveillance and control. By the beginning of the third century, states throughout the Italian peninsula were connected to Rome by formal treaty in a hierarchical system, with Rome at the top of the pyramid. Roman citizen colonies theoretically shared the pinnacle of this hierarchy with Rome itself, as did states granted the most favored status, *civitas optimo iure* (which we can loosely translate as "citizenship with full rights"). Incorporated states ultimately became Roman municipalities in their own right, with constitutions provided by Roman prescriptions (*praefectura*, *quattuorviri iure dicundo*, *duoviri*, etc.)

Roman overlordship in colonial foundations was a given from the very beginning. The case of Antium is a prime example. Surviving inhabitants of the city, which the Romans had conquered in 468, were enrolled in a new colony along with Romans, Latins, Hernici, and Volsci (Livy 3.1.7; Dionys. *Ant. Rom.* 9.59). In 338, after the Latin rebellion, Rome sent out another colony to Antium, but it permitted its former citizens to enroll in it (Livy 8.14.8), and in 317 Roman citizen colonists were again sent out there, some of whom acted as "patrons" who incorporated Antiates into a rejuvenated colonial foundation, for whom they established laws (Livy 9.20.10, *dati ab senatu ad iura statuenda ipsius coloniae patroni*, with Sherwin-White [1973] 2001: 81). Livy concludes that already by this time not only Roman arms, but also Roman law, began to exert influence throughout Italy. His use of the word *patroni* in describing the Roman arrangements at Antium is significant, as it encapsulates the Republic's political disposition at the level of imperial capital, Italian peninsula, and Mediterranean-wide hegemony.

Let us return to the city. Millar himself maintained that political power at Rome was located on the Rostra, or speaker's platform, but he did so with no emphasis on the relatively small audiences political arenas could accommodate (one need only think of the crammed Campus Martius on the day of C. Gracchus' election to his first tribunate, or the unwieldy electoral assembly on the Capitol on the day of Ti. Gracchus' murder). In an important study, Mouritsen (2001), stressing the distinction between the ideologically important, symbolic *populus Romanus* and the "people" as "the sum of individuals making up the citizen-body" (2001: 16–17), argued for a general alienation of the *plebs* from official politics (see Mouritsen, Chapter 9, with a different view by Tatum, Chapter 15). The former was vital to political discourse and had extensive formal powers; the vast majority of the latter never took part in politics. MacMullen (1980) had already forcefully asserted this point, estimating that at the very end of the republican period as little as 2 percent of enfranchised citizens actually cast ballots at elections. And even among those who did, various forms of elite pressure compromised the popular assemblies' decision-making powers (Champion 1997).

It is a matter of "the relative importance of formal and substantial, symbolic and practical, political participation" (Hölkeskamp 2010: 23). Concerning formal political participation, the structure of the popular assemblies curbed the potential for a strong popular element in political life: the centuriate assembly was weighted so that the wealthier classes voting unanimously could reach a majority, with the result that the lower classes would not even be called upon to vote (see Cic., *De rep.* 2.22.39–40; Livy 1.43.10–12); in the tribal assembly poor city-dwellers were collected into the four urban tribes, whose political voice could easily be overcome by the votes of the thirty-one rural tribes, usually represented by the well-to-do landowners, who could also enlist or bribe their poorer tribal members—some of whom may have been living in the city—to vote as they directed (see Taylor 1966: 59–83). Attempts to modify this picture (see e.g. Yakobson 1992, 1999), have not shaken the basic fact that the popular assemblies, and Roman political institutions in general, were structured to ensure the domination of the nobility and to stifle any radical manifestations of "people power," or *dēmokratia*, as the Greeks conceived it (cf. De Ste. Croix 1981: 300–326, 337–350, 518–537).

Concerning practical political participation, there is no reason to think that citizens' political involvement would have been much different from what we have come to expect from electorates in modern democratic nation-states. But at Rome, unwritten social codes and status hierarchies were far more important than the formal structures of institutions for the actual workings of politics. Those who participated by exercising their right to vote formed a minority of those who were eligible to do so, many of whom had to be mobilized in some way by the resources of those with a direct and vested interest in the outcome. The men with such a vested interest were members of the great aristocratic families, who could exert their enormous financial and social pressure upon vast numbers of subordinates to cast votes according to their wishes (it is well to remember in this context that the secret ballot was not introduced until the 130s; see Taylor 1966: 125n.2). To be sure, this was not a closed, hereditary ruling class, but rather a highly competitive, aristocratic meritocracy (cf. Hopkins 1983: 31–119). But it was no accident that during the Republic members of a rather small number of aristocratic clans, such as the Aemilii, Caecilii, Calpurnii, Claudii, Cornelii, Fabii, Fulvii, and Sulpicii, dominated election to high political offices (Badian 1990; on the Roman clan, or *gens*, see Smith 2006).

The growth of empire expanded the citizen base, but for reasons we have surveyed, political processes at Rome were not affected by this as much as we might expect. After the Social War early in the first century, non-elite citizens still lived within a social system that was built on verticality and inequality, which was the social bedrock of political institutions, including the popular assemblies with their formal powers of electing magistrates and passing legislation. While Quintus Cicero's "Handbook on Electioneering" (*Commentariolum petitionis*) certainly shows us that in the late Republic the aspiring politician could not ignore an anonymous and relatively independent electoral multitude, it also stresses the personal relationships that the candidate must forge, based on the creation of retinues of supporters, indebtedness, gratitude, and favor (Morstein-Marx 1998). While this is not patronage in the strict sense (see Brunt 1988: 382–442)—since frequently these relationships were not permanent; they could indeed be mercurial and fleeting—nevertheless the politician could not succeed without building up an image of himself as a socially superior, great man with the ability to benefit many. Scholars debate whether we should call this a patron–client social system, and in this debate much of course depends on how we choose to define patronage. In any event, networks of such personal relationships certainly became more unwieldy as citizenship grew outside of Rome, ultimately spinning a web throughout peninsular Italy, with one man's benefactor perhaps being another man's dependent. But each strand of that web would lead back to Rome, and there to one of the relatively few super-patrons who sat in the Senate.

2 Rome and Italy: City-States and Federal States

In this section we shall consider the interstate level; relations between Rome and federal states, and between Rome and individual city-states in Italy. Regarding rival federal states in Italy, the early religious leagues, such as the Thirty Peoples of the Lucus Ferentinae and the League of Diana at Aricia, are shrouded in the mists of prehistory and can be passed over without further comment. Our focus will be on the leagues or confederations of the Etruscans, Latins, Samnites, and the rebellious Italian allies during the Social War.

We can dispose of the Etruscan "League" quickly. According to tradition, there were twelve powerful Etruscan cities to the north and northwest of Rome, and these may have been joined in some sort of federal arrangement. Certainly during the course of the sixth century, Rome had fallen into the Etruscan cultural orbit, and it was perhaps dominated politically by Etruscan rulers by the end of the century. But as far as we can tell the Etruscan "League" (if it is not too historically distorting to call some sort of common Etruscan interstate understanding that) was rather weak and ineffectual, incapable of sustained collective enterprises, and Rome's struggles with Etruscans at the end of the monarchy and beginning of the Republic were against individual Etruscan city-states, as in the famous siege and sacking in 396 of neighboring Veii, across the Tiber River (Cornell 1995: 151–172, and 309–313 on the conquest of Veii).

Veii's territory was directly absorbed into the republican polity as Roman territory (*ager Romanus*), and its tutelary goddess, Juno, was extracted from her former abode through the religious ritual of *evocatio* and ceremonially escorted to her new home at Rome (Livy 5.22.3–7). Such incorporation was not new, but it wasn't always so violent. We find the Roman policy of incorporation of neighboring states already in the time of the monarchy, if we are to believe the accounts of Livy (1.54.10) and Dionysius of Halicarnassus (*Ant. Rom.* 4.57–58). According to them, the city of Gabii willingly entered the Roman commonwealth; Dionysius (4.58.3) even says that Gabii retained its city and territory, entering into a juridical status of "isopolity" with Rome. But much more frequent was employment of the instrument of the "unequal treaty" (*foedus iniquum*), according to which the lesser partner pledged "to preserve the greatness of Rome amicably." This type of treaty mirrored a basic notion of the patron–client relationship, as the inferior state placed itself into Rome's trust, *in fidem* (Badian 1958: 1–14; Sherwin-White [1973] 2001: 121–122). It is also worth noting that this basic type of "unequal treaty" was starkly different from the language of Greek interstate treaties, which stressed reciprocity and equality (see Low 2007; Bolmarcich, Chapter 18).

In the early fifth century, the Republic formed a bilateral agreement with nearby Latin states, known as the Cassian treaty (traditionally dated to 493 and named after the consul who arranged it), which was a mutual defensive alliance against raiders from the surrounding hills. The Latins formed a ring around Rome, and they took on the brunt of these raids. Their interest in forming this understanding with Rome was therefore based on their need for protection, while Rome gained recognition of its primacy in Latium. According to Livy (1.52.6), already in the time of Tarquinius Superbus, Romans and Latins contributed equal numbers of troops to an allied army, but under an exclusively Roman command structure. The Cassian treaty ensured that there would be peace among Romans and Latins, but it did not guarantee truce among Latin communities themselves (Dionys. *Ant. Rom.* 6.95.1–3; Livy 2.33.4–9; cf. Cic. *Balb.* 23.53). The agreement seems initially to have been an "equal treaty" (*foedus aequum*) between Rome and the Latins. Soon thereafter (in 486), however, this same man as consul, Sp. Cassius, cowed the non-Latin tribe of the Hernici with the threat of his army and brokered a treaty with them modeled on his prior terms with the Latins (Dionys. *Ant. Rom.* 8.68.1–69.4). As a result, the Republic became suzerain of a triple alliance. Both Latins and Hernici thereafter had to send troops annually to Rome, and the allied army was under a unified Roman command.

By the early fourth century, Rome had extended its power beyond Latium; threats from the neighboring hill tribesmen had been subdued; and the Latins became restive over an alliance that was no longer in practice by any means one among equals. The Republic now began to prefer treaties and alliances with individual Latin states, rather than abiding by the terms of the Cassian treaty and negotiating with the Latin League. Certainly the shock of the infamous Gallic sack and ransoming of Rome c.390 tarnished the Republic's international reputation, yet it rapidly recovered and continued its expansionist program (Cornell 1995: 318–322). In 358 the treaty with the Latins was renewed (Livy 7.12.7), but a decade later they revolted. The ensuing struggle was long and hard-fought. It was only in 338 that the Romans finally succeeded in extinguishing the rebellion's final embers (Livy 8.13.1–14.12). At that point the Latin League was once and for all dissolved, and Latin states could not conduct foreign relations independently of Rome. Thereafter the Romans dealt with Latin cities individually, and Rome's Italian Confederation was born, in which each state was joined to Rome by separate sets of rights and obligations. Just as a Roman patron would reward dutiful and loyal clients and punish disrespectful and disobedient ones, so the Republic raised the Campanian aristocracy, which had not participated in the rebellion, to a privileged status (Livy 8.11.16; cf. 8.14.10); while it inflicted harsh reprisals against the Veliterni, Antiates, Tiburtes, and Praenestini, who had been leaders of the uprising (Livy 8.14.5–10). Capua would in time experience a complete reversal of fortune: it paid the price for disloyalty more than a century later, suffering the harshest of punishments for having backed the wrong horse in Hannibal (Broughton 1951: 274; Toynbee 1965: 2.121–128).

The rebellion that led to the destruction of the Latin League arose within the context of looming hostilities with the Samnite Confederation. The Samnites were a non-Latin people who spoke Oscan, a language of the Sabellian linguistic grouping, and they lived as rugged mountaineers in the Apennine range of central and southern Italy. Their confederation was comprised of four tribes: the Caraceni, Pentri, Caudini, and Hirpini. They had a mixed economy of subsistence farming, stock-breeding, and transhumant pastoralism (Dench 1995: 111–153). They seem to have had a tribal confederation somewhat like the Latin League, with annually elected magistrates, periodic federal meetings, a council and assembly, and a commander-in-chief. By the 340s, when their expansion reached the Liris valley, Rome became wary of them, and war between the two federal states was probably by then inevitable (Salmon 1967: 187–213).

The Samnite Wars (343–341, 327–321, 316–304, 298–290) were unlike any earlier Roman warfare. These conflicts were of greater scale, intensity, and duration than what went before (Livy 7.29.1, with Cornell 1995: 345–363; Salmon 1967 for the standard account). They encompassed nearly all of peninsular Italy and its peoples, many of whom were eventually drawn into the strife on one side or the other. The climactic battle in 295 at Sentinum on the eastern slopes of the Apennines in Umbria resulted in an overwhelming Roman victory. Thereafter Samnites continued to resist the Romans' advance, but their backs were broken by that battle, and as a consequence their total submission was simply a matter of time. Between 292 and 290 the Romans took possession of large areas in the southeast of Samnium; there they established a colony at Venusia in 291. In 290 the Samnites became "allies" of the Romans, and some were even granted the "citizenship without the vote" (*civitas sine suffragio*). But the important point for our discussion is that the Samnite Confederation disappeared.

Some 200 years later, in 91, rebellion of its Italian allies convulsed the Republic in the Social War (see Gabba 1994). The rebels formed a short-lived federal state, with a capital at Corfinium—renamed Italia—and a separatist coinage, provocatively showing on its obverse the Italian bull gouging the Roman wolf. By this time allied cities were supplying—according to a formal quota system, the *formula togatorum*—more than half of the Roman armed forces, at the least; and perhaps as much as two-thirds of Rome's soldiers (Brunt 1971: 545–548, 677–686; cf. Vell. Pat. 2.15.2; Polyb. 6.21.4). The strain on allied manpower was therefore considerable. Already in 209, for example, twelve Latin communities refused to furnish contingents (Livy 27.9.7–8, 10.10), and in 177 Latins and incorporated Samnites and Paeligni complained that they were held to the same military manpower contribution as in the past, even though they had suffered massive emigrations (Livy 41.8.6–12).

Another cause for discontent was the confiscation of the Italians' land for the Gracchan resettlement program in the late 130s and 120s. At the time of the Italian revolt, proposals for agrarian laws at Rome undoubtedly continued to be a concern (cf. App. *B. Civ.* 1.5.36), but a more important cause of disaffection seems to have been the allies' unsatisfied demand for the Roman citizenship, and the murder of the tribune M. Livius Drusus, who had championed that cause. The senators' motivation for Drusus' assassination may have been their fear that such an extension of citizenship would create an intolerably large body of dependent supporters for the tribune and thereby upset the equilibrium of Roman politics (cf. the Italian oath of allegiance to Drusus at Diodorus, 37.11). In any event, while non-elite Italians had serious grievances concerning unequal treatment vis-à-vis Roman *cives* in terms of their compulsory military service and its compensation, for the reasons discussed in Section 1 most Italians living away from Rome would not have benefited much in any political sense from gaining the citizen franchise; and they certainly would not have been able to participate in the political life of the city on a regular basis.

Local Italian aristocracies, through whom Rome controlled Italian affairs, were another matter. Magistrates in Latin states already had access to citizenship (probably shortly after 125), but it was most likely of a type that required them to remain in their own communities (cf. Sherwin-White [1973] 2001: 112). Italian aristocrats, large landholders, and businessmen wanted a citizenship that would allow them to enter the high political arena at Rome, and it is reasonable to think that they instigated and mobilized the rebellion (Gabba 1976: 74–77; but see Sherwin-White [1973] 2001: 134–149 for another view). After the revolt was snuffed out, its ringleaders were killed, and loyal factions were rewarded—just as we would expect of a patron chastising and rewarding his clients (cf. already the reward to loyal elements of rebellious Fregellae in 125: Fregellae itself was destroyed, but those who had been loyal were included in the foundation of a new colony nearby, Fabrateria Nova: see Broughton 1951: 510, and Vell. Pat. 1.15.4 for the colony). The ephemeral rebel Italian federal state was of course extinguished, and in the aftermath of the Romans' granting *ius civitatis* throughout Italy, members of the most powerful Italian aristocratic families eventually made their way into the Senate, and as senators in Rome they acted as patrons of their communities of origin, with their own extensive networks of dependents back in their hometowns. Cicero's relationship with his municipal compatriots, the Arpinates, is a good example of the phenomenon (cf. *Fam.* 13.11.3 [Shackleton Bailey no. 278], for Cicero's oversight of affairs in his hometown and the role he hoped his son would play in the local government at Arpinum).

Independent federal states of the Etruscans, Latins, Samnites, and Italians had therefore all vanished by the early first century. In the decades after the Social War, all communities in Italy would become municipalities and formally part of Roman territory (Bispham 2007). By then Roman grandees would command extensive personal constituencies throughout the Italian peninsula. Dramatic examples are ready at hand. In 89, for example, as the civil war ground down to a conclusion, Cn. Pompeius Strabo personally granted citizenship to a group of loyal Spanish cavalrymen (Degrassi 1963: 28–29 [no. 515]); on the eve of his showdown against Caesar at Pharsalus in 48, Cn. Pompeius Magnus boasted that all he need do was stamp his foot on the ground in Italy and an army of his supporters would appear (App. *B. Civ.* 2.5.37; Plut. *Pomp.* 60.4–5); and of course ultimately Octavian would emerge from the next round of civil war as the super-patron and father of all Romans, *pater patriae* (Augustus *Res gestae* 6.35, with Syme 1939: 313–330, 369–386).

Let us leave the history of the Republic's relations with non-Roman federal states in Italy and consider other aspects of the nature and workings of Rome's Italian Confederation before the Social War. As Sherwin-White ([1973] 2001: 80) observed, "The creation of a wholly artificial community by the removal of a chosen number of the citizen body to another place, and the necessary growth of certain powers of self-government, corresponding to the duties which this isolated body must fulfill, are ideas that originated in the earlier days of the Republic" (cf. Salmon 1970; Gargola 1995). In relation to its colonies and incorporated states, Rome acted as the superior partner in so far as it took unilateral decisions affecting their autonomy and recognized rights. For example, in 193 the Senate enforced Roman laws against usury on allied financiers, which was a technical violation of their guaranteed commercial freedoms, or *ius commercii* (Livy 35.7.4–5); and in 187 the praetor Q. Terentius Culleo was ordered to force Latins living in Rome who had been enrolled in Latin cities in 204 or later to return to their hometowns; 12,000 Latins were expelled from the city (Livy 39.3.4–6; cf. Livy 41.9.9–12 [177]). Military exigency forced this latter measure because Latin cities could not meet their mandatory military manpower contributions with the exodus of so many of their male citizens to the capital. This ruling, however, was a violation of the Latin right to obtain Roman citizenship by moving to Rome (*ius migrationis*).

The Senate's extraordinary, self-assumed authority over all of peninsular Italy is perhaps best illustrated in the witch-hunt of the worshippers of Bacchus in 186. This event has perplexed modern scholars, as the Roman authorities lashed out against the worship of the Greek god Dionysus, who was known as Bacchus or Liber by his adherents in Italy. As Gruen (1990: 34) has noted, "The action came like a thunderbolt, scattering the faithful and terrifying sympathizers. Devotees of the cult can only have felt shock and horror at a policy that seemed incomprehensible." This was a Roman policing activity, which the senators deemed important enough for public security to justify running roughshod over the jurisdictional autonomy of the Italian states (McDonald 1944: 26–33). These selected examples show that in its relations with the Italian allies, the Senate expected absolute obedience and acquiescence, somewhat as a haughty patron over a submissive client.

3 International Anarchy and Roman Exceptionalism

Most modern scholars have subscribed to one of two competing interpretations of the origins and development of Rome's empire. Theodor Mommsen argued in the mid-nineteenth century that Roman imperial expansion was the direct result of security concerns, as Rome acted defensively against aggressive neighboring states. Mommsen's towering authority ensured that his interpretation would have lasting influence. In the early twentieth century, the American Tenney Frank expounded the idea for anglophone scholars, and shortly afterwards in France Maurice Holleaux argued that Rome was uninterested in Greek affairs but nonetheless drawn into a series of conflicts that resulted in empire. In strong opposition to this idea of defensive imperialism, the early twentieth-century Italian historian Gaetano DeSanctis and his followers maintained that Rome was uniquely militaristic and pathologically aggressive, driven by an insatiable will to power. In more recent times, William V. Harris (1979; cf. Raaflaub 1996) forcefully made the case for an incorrigibly bellicose Rome; his influential book demolished older views of defensive imperialism and has held sway as the single most influential account of the rise of Roman interstate power for over a generation. These are diametrically opposed reconstructions—Romans as reluctant, just-minded imperialists or relentlessly grasping predators—but they both operate within what political scientists call a metrocentric paradigm: Rome and its culture are the primary focus of analysis.

International relations theorists have suggested other models for understanding imperialism, and recently ancient historians have begun to employ these alternative perspectives, loosening somewhat the grip of the metrocentric paradigm for the study of Roman imperialism. One such alternative is the so-called pericentric approach, which explains imperial expansion by focusing on fringe areas in relation to imperial centers and on influences on imperial processes of people who eventually become subjected (see Champion

2007 for an example). The basic idea here is that conditions on the periphery often arise that practically invite the intervention of a powerful center and an extension of its power.

A third avenue for research offers a broader perspective, enlarging the analytical canvas to encompass both imperial metropoles and peripheries; it includes all players involved in interstate relations through politics, diplomacy, and warfare as integral units in a system of states. Eschewing explanations based on dispositions of individual states, scholars working in this tradition, who call themselves "Realists," or "Neo-Realists," see the default condition of such systems as one of anarchy, with frequent wars and the rise of empires as natural results of interstate conditions. In competitive anarchic systems, all states seek to maximize their own power and security within general conditions of violence and potential violence. Warfare is therefore a normal occurrence; that is, a normative way of settling crises in foreign relations, especially in the absence of effective international peace-keeping agencies.

To use a rough analogy, systemic approaches to empire are somewhat like social psychology or sociology in so far as the system is determinative of individual conduct, strongly encouraging certain types of behavior (in this case, militarism). The metrocentric and pericentric paradigms, on the other hand, are more like individual psychology in their orientations (see Waltz 1979; cf. Doyle 1986: 22–30). Eckstein (2006, 2008) has recently employed a systemic approach to the study of the ancient Mediterranean world in general and the rise of the Roman Republic in particular. As he convincingly argues, Rome certainly existed in an environment conforming to the bleakest paradigms of state behavior proposed by international-systems theoreticians: after all, the Romans suffered *ninety* severe defeats on the battlefield during the Republic (Rosenstein 1990: 179–204).

The systemic approach allows us to see that Roman imperialism took root in a brutal and hostile interstate environment: every state was aggressively militaristic because basic security and even survival demanded such behavior. The danger of this approach, however, is to reduce the Republic to a unit aggregate, an interchangeable player in a determinative system, and thereby to downplay or even disregard its unique features. One such feature was the political reorganization of Italy, which we have considered in the preceding section. This allowed Rome to exploit the vast military manpower reserves of Italy more efficiently than any one of its competitors was able to do in its domain. Unlike all other ancient empires, the Republic thereby created what I have elsewhere called an "empire of inclusion" (Champion 2004b: 208); indeed, the Romans' policy of liberally extending their citizen franchise to non-Romans was even celebrated in their foundation myths (Champion 2009).

Another exceptional characteristic of Roman imperial governance was the Republic's uniquely authoritarian and paternalistic style of relating to its subjects; a style that frequently took on domineering, arrogant, and even supercilious overtones (but see Burton 2011 for another view). Abuses by individual magistrates in the provinces led to the creation of an extortion court (*quaestio de rebus repetundis*) by the *lex Calpurnia* of 149, but relatively few were convicted by juries manned by their fellow senators (see Gruen 1968: 8–44); and the acquisition of a vast empire stimulated Roman lawyers to conceive of a law of nations (*ius gentium*), but this did not have significant practical consequences during the period under consideration here (cf. Bederman 2001: 48–87). Rather, the Republic's actual behavior towards subordinates followed a by now familiar pattern.

At the Isthmian Games at Corinth in 196, the proconsul Titus Quinctius Flamininus stunned the Greeks in the aftermath of the Roman victory in Greece over the Macedonian king Philip V. The throng of Greeks in attendance feared for their collective fate, but through a herald Flamininus declared that the Greeks were to be free and independent (as a decided philhellene, Flamininus' rhetoric was most likely influenced by the discourse of Greek international diplomacy, which stressed freedom and autonomy, as studied by Sarah Bolmarcich in the companion chapter). In disbelief the auditors asked the herald to repeat the proconsul's pronouncement, so unexpected were the good tidings (see Gruen 1984: 132–157 for discussion and sources). But there was a catch to Roman freedom, as Rome expected subjected states to behave as obedient subordinates and to consult the Senate on all matters of foreign policy. The Greek states tragically misunderstood this.

During the course of the First Macedonian War, in 212 or 211, Rome made an alliance with the Aetolian Confederation, King Philip's inveterate enemy. From a Roman perspective, the Aetolians later in 206 had had the effrontery to conclude a peace with Philip without consulting the Senate, and this act in the senators' view invalidated the treaty. From an Aetolian perspective, Flamininus' Isthmian Declaration violated the terms of the Roman–Aetolian alliance, which stipulated that cities taken in Greece were to be admitted into the Aetolian Confederation (Champion 2004b: 87). The disgruntled Aetolians later invited the Seleucid king Antiochus III to liberate Greece from Roman control, and after the Roman defeat of this coalition, the Aetolians were forced to submit to a treaty as subjects of Rome, their territorial possessions were diminished, and their influence at Delphi was extinguished.

In 191 the Aetolians surrendered to the Roman commander M.' Acilius Glabrio, after the Roman victory at the battle at Thermopylae. The Aetolian general Phaineas pointed out that the Aetolians had not placed themselves into slavery, but rather had entrusted themselves to Roman good faith (*eis tēn Rōmaiōn pistin*; *in fidem*). He objected to the orders Glabrio had given to the Aetolians, since they were contrary to Greek custom. The consul responded that he did not care about Greek protocols; he was acting in the Roman manner. Glabrio asserted that he was dealing with a people who had been conquered by force and had surrendered themselves into his power. And then he threatened that if the Aetolians did not immediately obey his commands, he would throw them into chains (Polyb. 20.9.1–10.9; Livy 36.28.1–6; Eckstein 1995).

Concerning the famous incident of Glabrio's imperious, chain-rattling threats in the face of an Aetolian statesman, Gruen (1982) argued that Polybius himself read too much into the affair; that Phaineas and the Aetolians must have understood the fine points of Roman diplomatic terminology by this time; and that indeed Greek *pistis* and Roman *fides* were not all that far apart conceptually. The important point for our discussion, however, is that Greeks were at the mercy of individual Roman potentates and their idiosyncratic and perhaps arbitrary interpretations of what constituted international fair practice. Perhaps Glabrio was singularly brutish, extraordinarily churlish, and anomalously hot-headed, but we have many other examples to make the point: in 171 the consul P. Licinius Crassus and the unscrupulous praetor C. Lucretius Gallus allowed their troops to commit outrages in Greece (Livy 42.63.3–12; 43.4.5–12; 43.7.5–8.10), as did the praetor L. Hortensius in the following year (Livy 43.4.8–13, 7.8–8.8); in 168 the legate C. Popillius Laenas arrogantly commanded a Hellenistic king to do his bidding (discussed below); and in 167 L. Aemilius Paullus somewhat randomly enslaved 150,000 people on his march through Epirus (Livy 45.34.1–6; Polyb. 30.15; cf. Toynbee 1965: 2.171–173 for a catalogue of Roman mass enslavements).

Rome made an alliance with the Achaean Confederation in its second war against Philip. Over the ensuing decades, a recurrent problem for the senators was a series of

Greek embassies wrangling over the issue of the incorporation of Sparta into the Achaean League: federal leaders were pressing for incorporation, while Sparta stubbornly resisted. This problem continued to smolder until well beyond the time of the so-called Third Macedonian War, which the Republic fought against Philip's son, King Perseus. After Perseus' defeat in 168 in the battle at Pydna, the Romans rounded up and incarcerated in Italy some 1,000 Greek statesmen whom they suspected of disloyalty. Even stances of political neutrality were grounds for arrest and expatriation. Many of these statesmen were Achaeans, the most famous of whom was the future historian Polybius (Champion 2004a: 15–18).

More than two decades later, in 146, the Achaeans acted independently of Rome in attempting to force Sparta into its confederation. They badly miscalculated at this time, thinking that the senators would look upon their unilateral action with indifference. The Republic dispatched an army, crushed the Achaeans quickly, and issued a warning against further recalcitrance by destroying the city of Corinth (see Gruen 1976). Both Aetolians and Achaeans had failed to understand properly that they were Rome's subjects and that Roman "freedom" was conditional (cf. the arrangements with the Campanians in 210 at Livy 26.34.7: "to be free on certain terms"). In the end, the two Greek federal states suffered the same fate as their Italian counterparts: extinction.

In the aftermath of the defeat of Perseus, other wayward client-states also had a price to pay. Both Rhodes and Pergamum had offered their services as third-party mediators in the interests of forging a peace settlement between the Republic and the kingdom of Macedonia. According to Roman social values, such a role would be unthinkable for a client in relation to his patron, but neither the Rhodians nor Eumenes II, king of Pergamum, seem to have understood that. For the insult, the island republic of Rhodes was crippled economically when the Romans made the island of Delos a duty-free port (Champion 2004b: 157–158); regarding Pergamum, the senators in a punitive frame of mind tried to destabilize the state by sowing seeds of dissension between the king, Eumenes II, and his brother, Attalus II (see Champion 2004a: 160–161 for discussion and sources).

Let us conclude this section with two poignant illustrations of Hellenistic monarchs being reduced to submissive servants to Roman power. Following the battle at Pydna, the Bithynian king Prusias II visited Rome in order to congratulate the Senate on Rome's victory. According to Polybius, Prusias had earlier abased himself as a freedman and suppliant before a Roman legation, and now he prostrated himself before the senators, hailing them as savior gods (*theoi sōtēres*). Polybius reports this behavior with censure and disgust; in his view it was a loathsome display of abject servility unbefitting for a king (Polyb. 30.18.1–7, with Erskine 1994). Also belonging to the aftermath of Pydna is the story of the Roman legate C. Popillius Laenas, the Seleucid king Antiochus IV Epiphanes, and the "Day of Eleusis." For generations Ptolemies and Seleucids had been involved in military struggles over the borders their kingdoms shared, and at this time Antiochus was engaged in an attempt to wrest territory from Ptolemaic control. Laenas met Antiochus at Eleusis on the outskirts of Alexandria with a senatorial decree ordering the king to desist from attacking the Ptolemaic realm. Laenas refused to show the conventional signs of friendship until after he had the king's response to the Roman mandate. When Antiochus asked for time to discuss the matter with his councilors, Laenas picked up a vine reed and drew a circle in the sand around him, demanding an answer before Antiochus should step out of it. Antiochus immediately submitted, and Polybius tells us that this dramatic event made it clear to all that they were to be from that point on the subjects and subordinates of the Romans (Polyb. 29.27.1–13, with Broughton 1951: 430; Habicht 1989: 344–346).

4 Conclusion

The ancient Greek political theorist Phaleas of Chalcedon apparently was an advocate of "arithmetical" political equality, according to which every citizen of a state would have equal political input in the commonwealth's functioning; indeed, he even proposed communistic property equalization in order to achieve intra-*polis* concord (Arist. *Pol.* 1266a31–67b21). And such notions found their way into the language of Greek international diplomacy, if not in actual Greek interstate relations (see Bolmarcich, Chapter 18). But ideas like these were anathema to Roman aristocratic values, which stressed a rigid hierarchy of status, reflected in socio-economic stratification in the most important popular assembly and even in seating at public entertainments. This was a social system of verticality in which nobles expected obedience, acquiescence, deference, respect, and at times even obsequiousness from their social inferiors. In light of such a value system, Cicero's remarkable statement that "equality is itself unjust" can make sense to us (*De rep.* 1.27.43, *ipsa aequabilitas est iniqua*, with Fantham 1973).

Patronage, the extra-constitutional social institution, as Badian called it, was one manifestation of these social values. It was as old as Rome itself (Cic. *De rep.* 2.9.16; Dionys. *Ant. Rom.* 2.9.2–3), and it helped to hold Roman society together, reifying the aristocrats' penchant for rigidly hierarchical social distinctions and status markers. Badian suggested that Roman social relations, and in particular the patron–client relationship, informed its foreign policy: subjected states were expected to behave as dutiful clients. While we cannot say that patronage in the strict sense was a template for foreign policy (Gruen 1984: 158–200), it is true that the underlying social assumptions of patronage—the crucial importance of hierarchical status distinctions, the demand for deference to authority and obedience from subordinates, and nearly constant performative reinforcements of rank—are evident in the Republic's behavior at the interstate level. Few scholars today would contest this point, and its elucidation is the enduring legacy of Ernst Badian's *Foreign Clientelae*. This chapter is presented in homage to that great work, and in employing its basic insight I hope to have shown how Roman social relations furnish a powerful lens through which to view questions of popular politics in the capital, Rome as a federal state, and the Republic's imperial behavior overseas.

NOTE

1 All dates are BCE.

REFERENCES

CAH = *The Cambridge Ancient History*. 2nd edn. Cambridge, 1989.
Badian, E. 1958. *Foreign Clientelae, 264–70* B.C. Oxford.
Badian, E. 1990. "The Consuls, 179–49 B.C." *Chiron* 20: 371–413.

Bederman, D.J. 2001. *International Law in Antiquity.* Cambridge.

Bispham, E. 2007. *From Asculum to Actium: The Municipalization of Italy from the Social War to Augustus.* Oxford.

Broughton, T.R.S. 1951. *The Magistrates of the Roman Republic*, vol. 1. New York.

Brunt, P.A. 1971. *Italian Manpower, 225 B.C.–A.D. 14.* Oxford.

Brunt, P.A. 1988. *The Fall of the Roman Republic and Related Essays.* Oxford.

Burton, P.A. 2011. *Friendship and Empire: Roman Diplomacy and Imperialism in the Middle Republic (353–146 BC).* Cambridge and New York.

Champion, C.B. 1997. "Review of *Contra arma verbis: Der Redner vor dem Volk in der später römischen Republik*, by F. Pina-Polo." *Bryn Mawr Classical Review* 97.2.8. Available at http://ccat.sas.upenn.edu/bmcr/. Accessed Apr. 2, 2014.

Champion, C.B. 2004a. *Cultural Politics in Polybius's Histories.* Berkeley.

Champion, C.B. ed. 2004b. *Roman Imperialism: Readings and Sources.* Oxford and Malden, MA.

Champion, C.B. 2007. "Empire By Invitation: Greek Political Strategies and Roman Imperial Interventions in the Second Century B.C.E." *TAPA* 137: 255–275.

Champion, C.B. 2009. "Imperial Ideologies, Citizenship Myths, and Legal Disputes in Classical Athens and Republican Rome." In R.K. Balot, ed., *A Companion to Greek and Roman Political Thought*. Oxford and Malden, MA, 85–99.

Cornell, T.J. 1995. *The Beginnings of Rome: Italy and Rome from the Bronze Age to the Punic Wars (c.1000–264 B.C.).* London and New York.

de Ste. Croix, G.E.M. 1981. *The Class Struggle in the Ancient Greek World: From the Archaic Age to the Arab Conquests.* Ithaca, NY.

Degrassi, A., ed. 1963. *Inscriptiones Latinae Liberae Rei Publicae*, vol. 2. Florence.

Dench, E. 1995. *From Barbarians to New Men: Greek, Roman and Modern Perceptions of Peoples of the Central Apennines.* Oxford.

Deniaux, E. 2006. "Patronage." In N. Rosenstein and R. Morstein-Marx, eds., *A Companion to the Roman Republic.* Oxford and Malden, MA, 401–420.

Doyle, M.W. 1986. *Empires.* Ithaca, NY.

Eckstein, A. 1995. "Glabrio and the Aetolians: A Note on *Deditio.*" *TAPA* 125: 271–89.

Eckstein, A. 2006. *Mediterranean Anarchy, Interstate War, and the Rise of Rome.* Berkeley.

Eckstein, A. 2008. *Rome Enters the Greek East: From Anarchy to Hierarchy in the Hellenistic Mediterranean, 230–170 B.C.* Oxford and Malden, MA.

Erskine, A. 1994. "The Romans as Common Benefactors." *Historia* 43: 70–87.

Fantham, E. 1973. "*Aequabilitas* in Cicero's Political Thought, and the Greek Tradition of Proportional Justice." *CQ* 23: 285–290.

Finley, M.I. 1983. *Politics in the Ancient World.* Cambridge, New York, and Melbourne.

Forsythe, G. 2005. *A Critical History of Early Rome.* Berkeley.

Gabba, E. 1976. *Republican Rome, the Army and the Allies.* Berkeley.

Gabba, E. 1994. "Rome and Italy: The Social War." In J.A. Crook, A. Lintott, and E. Rawson, eds., *Cambridge Ancient History*, vol. 92. Cambridge, 104–128.

Gargola, D.J. 1995. *Land, Laws, and Gods: Magistrates and Ceremony in the Regulation of Public Lands in Republican Rome.* Chapel Hill, NC and London.

Garnsey, P., T. Gallant, and D. Rathbone. 1984. "Thessaly and the Grain Supply of Rome during the Second Century B.C." *JRS* 74: 30–44.

Gelzer [1912] 1969. *The Roman Nobility.* Trans. R. Seager. Oxford.

Gruen, E.S. 1968. *Roman Politics and the Criminal Courts, 149–78 B.C.* Cambridge, MA.

Gruen, E.S. 1976. "The Origins of the Achaean War." *JHS* 96: 46–69.

Gruen, E.S. 1982. "Greek Πίστις and Roman *Fides.*" *Ath* 60: 50–68.

Gruen, E.S. 1984. *The Hellenistic World and the Coming of Rome.* Berkeley.

Gruen, E.S. 1990. *Studies in Greek Culture and Roman Policy.* Berkeley.

Habicht, Chr. 1989. "The Seleucids and Their Rivals." *CAH* 8: 324–387.
Hammer, D. 2009. "What Is Politics in the Ancient World?" In R.K. Balot, ed., *A Companion to Greek and Roman Political Thought*. Oxford and Malden, MA, 20–36.
Harris, W.V. 1979. *War and Imperialism in Republican Rome, 327–70 BC*. Oxford.
Hölkeskamp, K.-J. 2010. *Reconstructing the Roman Republic: An Ancient Political Culture Modern Research*. Princeton.
Hopkins, K. 1983. *Death and Renewal*. Sociological Studies in Roman History 2. Cambridge.
Jehne, M., ed. 1995. *Demokratie in Rom? Die Rolle des Volkes in der Politik der römischen Republik*. Historia Einzelschriften 96. Stuttgart.
Kallet-Marx, R. 1995. *Hegemony to Empire: The Development of the Roman* Imperium *in the East from 148 to 62 B.C.* Berkeley.
Lintott, A.W. 1990. "Electoral Bribery in the Roman Republic." *JRS* 80: 1–16.
Low, P. 2007. *Interstate Relations in Classical Greece: Morality and Power*. Cambridge.
MacMullen, R. 1974. *Roman Social Relations, 50 B.C.–A.D. 284*. New Haven and London.
MacMullen, R. 1980. "How Many Romans Voted?" *Ath* 58: 454–457.
MacMullen, R. 2000. *Romanization in the Time of Augustus*. New Haven and London.
McDonald, A.H. 1944. "Rome and the Italian Confederation (200–186 B.C.)." *JRS* 34: 11–33.
Millar, F. 1984. "The Political Character of the Classical Roman Republic, 200–151 B.C." *JRS* 74: 1–19.
Millar, F. 1986. "Politics, Persuasion and the People before the Social War (150–90 B.C.)." *JRS* 76: 1–11.
Millar, F. 1989. "Political Power in Mid-Republican Rome: Curia or Comitium?" *JRS* 79: 138–150.
Millar, F. 1998. *The Crowd in Rome in the Late Republic*. Ann Arbor.
Morstein-Marx, R.M. 1998. "Publicity, Popularity and Patronage in the *Commentariolum Petitionis*." *ClAnt* 17: 259–288.
Morstein-Marx, R.M. 2004. *Mass Oratory and Political Power in the Late Roman Republic*. Cambridge.
Mouritsen, H. 2001. *Plebs and Politics in the Late Roman Republic*. Cambridge.
Münzer, F. [1920] 1999. *Roman Aristocratic Parties and Families*. Trans. T. Ridley. Baltimore.
Nicolet, C. 1980. *The World of the Citizen in Republican Rome*. Trans. P.S. Falla. Berkeley.
North, J.A. 1990. "Democratic Politics in Republican Rome." *P&P* 126: 3–29.
Raaflaub, K.A. 1996. "Born to Be Wolves?" In R.W. Wallace and E.M. Harris, eds., *Transitions to Empire: Essays in Greco-Roman History, 360–146 B.C., in Honor of E. Badian*. Norman, OK, 272–324.
Rosenstein, N. 1990. *Imperatores Victi: Military Defeat and Aristocratic Competition in the Middle and Late Republic*. Berkeley.
Salmon, E.T. 1967. *Samnium and the Samnites*. Cambridge.
Salmon, E.T. 1970. *Roman Colonization Under the Republic*. Ithaca, NY.
Scheidel, W. 2008. "Roman Population Size: The Logic of the Debate." In L. de Ligt and S.J. Northwood, eds., *People, Land, and Politics: Demographic Developments and the Transformation of Roman Italy, 300 B.C.–A.D. 14*. Leiden and Boston, 17–70.
Sherwin-White, A.N. [1973] 2001. *The Roman Citizenship*. 2nd edn. Oxford.
Smith, C.J. 2006. *The Roman Clan: The* Gens *from Ancient Ideology to Modern Anthropology*. Cambridge.
Syme, R. 1939. *The Roman Revolution*. Oxford.
Syme, R. 1991. "Oligarchy at Rome: A Paradigm for Political Science." In A. Birley, ed., *Roman Papers*, vol. 6. Oxford, 323–337.
Tatum, W.J. 2009. "Democratic Rome?" In R.K. Balot, ed., *A Companion to Greek and Roman Political Thought*. Malden, MA and Oxford, 214–227.

Taylor, L. Ross. 1966. *Roman Voting Assemblies: From the Hannibalic War to the Dictatorship of Caesar*. Ann Arbor.

Toynbee, A.J. 1965. *Hannibal's Legacy: The Hannibalic War's Effects on Roman Life*, 2 vols. London, New York, and Toronto.

Wallace-Hadrill, A., ed. 1989. *Patronage in Ancient Society*. London and New York.

Waltz, K. 1979. *Theory of International Politics*. New York.

Yakobson, A. 1992. "*Petitio et Largitio*: Popular Participation in the Centuriate Assembly in the Late Republic." *JRS* 82: 32–52.

Yakobson, A. 1999. *Elections and Electioneering in Rome: A Study in the Political System of the Late Republic*. Stuttgart.

FURTHER READING

For an interesting discussion of the theoretical approaches modern scholars have taken to understand the exercise of political power in the ancient world, see Hammer 2009; and on politics in Greco-Roman antiquity generally, see Finley 1983. For the early Republic, Cornell 1995 and Forsythe 2005 are excellent studies, although their critical approaches to the primary sources differ markedly. The middle Republic is covered by Harris 1979 and Gruen 1984, again with widely different interpretations. For the late Republic, Syme 1939 is still unsurpassed; the essays in Brunt 1988 and Gabba 1976 are also essential. For the ad hoc, indirect nature of the Roman hegemony in Greek lands, which is complementary with the interpretation of Roman imperialism offered in this chapter, see the important work of Kallet-Marx 1995. On all matters of the Roman citizenship, Sherwin-White [1973] 2001 is of fundamental importance; see also Nicolet 1980. For the (Neo)-Realist school of international relations theory, see Waltz 1979, and Doyle 1986 for a summary treatment of this and other theories of imperialism. Eckstein 2006 and Eckstein 2008 use the systemic approach in interpreting the rise of Roman imperial power. On patronage, see the collected essays in Wallace-Hadrill 1989, and the recent discussion of Deniaux 2006. Badian 1958 is the classic work on the impact of Roman aristocratic social values on Roman foreign policy; MacMullen 1974 is of crucial importance for understanding Roman social hierarchies, though he concentrates on a later period than the main chronological focus of this chapter. Burton 2011 has now provided a counterweight to the approach taken in this chapter: adopting a tempered version of the Constructivist position of international relations theorists, he argues that since *amicitia* could exist in Roman society between friends who were unequal in power, wealth, and/or status, the same was true of states. Consequently the conventions and practices of interpersonal *amicitia* rather than patronage (as in Badian's *Foreign Clientelae*) can be used to analyze *amicitia* between Rome and weaker states.

PART X

Economic Life

CHAPTER 20

Production, Trade, and Consumption in Greek Democracy

David W. Tandy

1 Introduction

This chapter will articulate the outstanding characteristics of the economies of the Greek world in the archaic and classical periods. It will investigate the relationships between certain aspects of local economies and the corporate enactments generated by civic assemblies and law courts. Enactments of the assemblies of the Greek states could be salutary for the local economy and they could be problematic. Enactments shaped production as well as import/export patterns; assemblies set up standing and extraordinary regulatory offices that oversaw trade and collected import and sales taxes. Assemblies influenced wholesale grain prices and limited retail markup, sometimes even fixing the retail price, all with an eye to making consumption as affordable as possible for citizens and sometimes for all residents (though rarely with an eye on the economy more broadly). Verdicts delivered by democratic juries generated substantial fines to be paid by private citizens into state coffers, although it is difficult to argue that such fines were a significant percentage of annual revenue. (Verdicts that caused enormous transfers of wealth within communities would have had a small impact, if any at all, on productivity.) These actions, all good for the economy, had their costs. On the other hand, there were actions undertaken by assemblies that were unambiguous drags on the local economy, including the Athenian practice of paying citizens for both assembly attendance and jury service, unclearly wise expenditures of state resources. The majority of this inquiry will be focused necessarily on Athens, but there are other democracies and there are civic assemblies in moderate oligarchies whose public enactments affected economic realities in the *polis* and between the *polis* and the outside world.

We cannot do very much, except to exercise patience, about the paucity of hard numbers for ancient economic activity, but here are four: 130, 400, 60, 1,200. These are the total revenues, in talents, for the Athenian state for four different (but in that order) years in the fourth century BCE. We will return to them. For now, I share them to begin to make

A Companion to Greek Democracy and the Roman Republic, First Edition. Edited by Dean Hammer.

the case that any actions by the Athenian assembly to spend cash from the state's treasury must be understood within the annual stricture of revenue. That is, in any given year, seeing it coming or not, the Athenian citizens who authorized new expenses or reauthorized (even through inaction) existing ones were acting without understanding either specific limits on that spending or, as we will see, without understanding that planning might be a good idea, ever.

The study of the ancient Mediterranean economies has been dominated until the last decade by (1) the argument between formalists, who seek to explain the ancient economy in terms of the neoclassical notion of utility maximization under conditions of scarcity, and substantivists, for whom the economy is "[man's] interchange with his natural and social environment, in so far as this results in supplying him with the means of material want satisfaction" (Polanyi 1957: 243); (2) the argument between modernizers and primitivists; and (3) the argument between those who believe that these are a single argument and those who think them to be different. (Both substantivists and primitivists tend to speak of the economy being "embedded" within the broader array of social actions.) This chapter's proposed overview of the interaction between local economies and civic enactments by participatory communities does not promise to advance our understanding, for it is clear that some enactments were intended to be good for the local economy (and sometimes proved to be so), while others were not; it is also difficult to assess how intentionally economic a given enactment was.

The currently ascendant approach to the economies of the ancient Mediterranean is New Institutionalism, the analytical approach adopted in the recent *Cambridge Economic History of the Greco-Roman World* (Scheidel, Morris, and Saller 2007). This approach transcends these debates by focusing on the institutions (the social structures and forces) within which a society undertakes production, distribution, and consumption. These categories of economic activity can overlap, but will inform adequately the shape of this survey. Then a brief overview of the economic policies of Athens and the role of the assembly within them will precede examples of positive and negative actions of the assemblies of Athens and Eretria. A final section will return to Hugo Jones' question of sixty years ago (Jones 1952): Was the Athenian democracy parasitic on the Athenian empire? Jones focused on the obvious truth that the democracy met its many administrative costs by diverting funds collected from allies during the empires of the fifth and fourth centuries; it is clear as well that in fact the democracy, as proved by the latter part of the fourth century, was able to persist after empire was no more. In spite of the ambiguities of civic intentionality and because of our inevitable dependence on Athenian materials, I will reshape the question: Was the participatory community at Athens parasitic on the economy?

2 Production

Greek production may be divided into three areas: agriculture, manufacture, and extraction. It has long been understood that wealth in the Greek communities was fundamentally agricultural, that wealth resided in property and the production generated on it. When Solon in the early sixth century established his four classes (or added a new uppermost one to an existing trio), the determining factor for each status level was the number of measures of grain that the individual's property generated or was able to generate (on Solon's reforms, see Farenga, Chapter 6). In the fourth century, the wealthiest families at Athens, who were required to participate in the highest liturgical level, were identified by the value of their real property exceeding 4 talents (Davies 1971: xxiii–xxiv).

Cultivated lands throughout the Greek mainland and in the new communities flung far to the west and north were mostly under grains (wheat, barley, and oats), but much space was devoted also to pulses (beans, peas, lentils, vetches) and other vegetables, including roots. Fruit trees were cultivated in abundance, as were the vine and the olive, although the success of the lattermost was restricted by altitude and other geographical factors (Grove and Rackham 2001: 67; Foxhall 2007: 5–6). We can see the great variety in agricultural production as early as in Homer: Laertes' farm, while Homer understandably downplays the importance of grains, features pear, apple, and fig trees (*Od.* 24.340–341), while Alcinous' royal gardens feature the same trees plus pomegranates (7.114–116).

By the seventh century the Greek landscape was littered with enormous herds belonging to the fading monarchies and emerging aristocracies. This is clear from the roster of Odysseus' assets—Eumaeus tells us that Odysseus has 12 herds of cows, 12 flocks each of sheep and swine, and 23 flocks of goats (*Od.* 14.96–104), while Eumaeus himself keeps 960 swine (*Od.* 14.13–20)—and from the habitual behavior of Homeric heroes in their raids against the wealth of others—Nestor narrates with pride his successful raid into Elis, making off with 50 herds or flocks each of cattle, sheep, swine, and goats, as well as 150 mares, many with foals (*Il.* 11.677–681). The best bottomlands by 650 were devoted to grains, but many rich fields were under the hooves of animals large and small. By the classical period, enormous sacred properties held flocks for the provision of future sacrificial victims, under the management of local residents otherwise unaffiliated with the sanctuary (see Howe 2008; McInerney 2010); in 370, Jason of Pherae was able to mobilize a sacrifice of a thousand cattle on short notice for the Pythian Games (Xen. *Hell.* 6.4.29). It is uncertain whether the plains of Megara were particularly unfertile (Legon 1981: 22–24), but it is unambiguous that the Megarians covered them with sheep (see below).

Most ordinary free Greeks in the archaic period probably had a property (called an *oikos*) not dissimilar to Hesiod's in acreage (15–25) or hectareage (6–10) and population (10–12 persons). In the classical period farm sizes appear to have become smaller. (On Hesiod see Tandy and Neale 1996: 27–31; Tandy 1997: 211; land distribution varied widely from *polis* to *polis*, but Foxhall [1992] argues that in the classical period the size of the property of the vast majority of Athenians was very close to 13.75/5.5.) These smallholders would have oversown in the autumn and winter grain-growing seasons, the result of which would have been sufficient for the *oikos* in a lean year and would have produced a surplus in a good one. That surplus was probably too small to bring to the big markets in the local *polis*, but could have been exchanged locally or stored.

At Athens there were food markets at Piraeus and in the city. Large producers would have brought their surplus grains to sell there—Pericles brought his entire production for sale into the markets and then would purchase from the market foodstuffs as his *oikos* needed them (Plut. *Per.* 16.3.3–4). In the archaic period there had been border markets where produce could be brought (Dem. 23.37–40), no doubt in smaller amounts.

Most *ergasteria* ("workshops") were related to agriculture and animal husbandry (processing grown and husbanded materials: see the list in Davies 2007: 347 and n.74), but some not: pottery was produced and exported for at least one distant specific market (Osborne 1996), and the metic Cephalus' family owned a profitable shield factory (Lys. 12.19). Some *ergasteria* employed more than 100 persons and were economically powerful enough to lift their owners into the liturgical class (Stanley 1990: 13). In all, we can identify over 100 different crafts trades and estimate that a quarter to a third of the 40,000 Athenian citizens of the fifth and fourth centuries plied them (Migeotte 2009: 93).

Under the rubric of production we must register extraction of minerals, stone, and precious metals. Usable stone was available (though costly to transport, even over short distances) throughout the Baltic Greek peninsula, the Aegean, and Greek Anatolia; stone of lesser quality was available in Magna Graecia; valuable stone was available in a few locations, most famously Paros island. Athens enjoyed the income from the state-run and -leased mines in southernmost Attica at Laureion (and in fact one of our earliest intelligent economic planning documents is the portion of Xenophon's *Poroi* [§4] focused on this state-dominated industry). As coinage spread in the sixth century under Peisistratus, the Laureion silver was supplemented by that extracted in the north, mostly in Thrace. In addition, from the earliest period of colonization, iron was sought in the west. Later, at Thasos island and her *peraia* in the northern Aegean, gold and other precious metals were chased after.

Wealthy families invested also in non-agricultural productive ventures in manufacturing and extraction (Bissa 2009) and were involved in financial investments as well (Shipton 2000), many of them connected to long-range shipping (especially grains) and to the bottomry loans (loans with the ship as collateral) that began to be generated by the early fifth century at Athens and presumably elsewhere (Reed 2003: 40–41). Some scholars have observed that a certain amount of such business in Athens from the fifth century forward was driven by the need of the richest citizens to pay for their liturgies (Osborne 1990; Migeotte 2009: 141).

At Athens and in other *poleis*, much local commerce was in the hands of metics, Greeks from other places. This is true also of construction labor. In general free and slave labor was "intrinsically scarce" (Davies 2007: 352) throughout the Greek world; one may observe further that the population diminution in the course of the last years of the Peloponnesian War exacerbated the labor shortage and led to increases of slave labor and mercenarianism. The myth of the "standard Athenian wage of 1 drachma per day" has persisted to the present day, despite clear data and arguments to the contrary (Loomis 1998: 232–239), and there is ample evidence for variety in daily wages according to the job and for substantial sways up and down over the fifth and fourth centuries (Loomis 1998: 240–250). The vast sums of cash that came in from the Athenians' empire may be the best explanation for a possible 50 percent increase in wages between about 450 and 432; less forthcoming is a cogent explanation for the sharp increase in prices between 333/2 and 329/8, although labor costs had already risen before other prices, such as those of clothing and livestock (Loomis 1998: 246). (Loomis' collection of numbers is not perfectly organized [Osborne 2000], but the broad differences he is able to collect, especially in public-sector wages, show the absence of anything like a consistent economic picture over time.) There is no reason to think that there was not volatility of every sort in the course of any economic measuring period at any classical Greek *polis*. This was as true for wages as it was for state revenues (see below): the two in fact went hand in hand.

3 The Effect of Enactments on Production

The earliest enactments in our sources are the grants of productive land (τεμένεα) by the people to several heroes in the Homeric poems (e.g. *Il.* 6.191–195 [the Lycians to

Bellerophontes]; 20.184–186 [the Trojans to Aeneas]; 9.574–580 [the elders (*gerontes*) of the Aetolians to Meleager]; cf. 12.313ff., where Sarpedon and Glaucus enjoy their *temenos* and its production at the pleasure of the Lycians). Land in the early Iron Age was not certainly alienable, and the jury is still out on exactly what Solon was sorting through in the early sixth century at Athens; by the classical period, land was fully alienable everywhere in Greece where we have information, and juries, in at least Athens, apparently had the ability to transfer property from one citizen to another under judicial mechanisms such as *antidosis* (Gabrielson 1986, 1987; Christ 1990), although it is not certain to what extent there would be economic impact in such situations (except for the individual parties involved). More clearly of economic impact were fines that could be extracted from wealthy citizens through the process of *graphē paranomōn* (see further below; Rhodes, Chapter 8), since these fines were paid into state coffers and then spent out on behalf of the *dēmos*.

The earliest enactment in our historical sources is found within the economic reforms instituted by Solon and presumably approved by enactment of the *ekklēsia*. According to Plutarch (*Sol.* 24.1), the Athenians banned the export of all products except olives. This was undertaken, probably, as a strategy to keep a steady flow of grains into the local markets in Attica; Peisistratus in the next generation also manipulated production, again presumably with assembly ratification. In general, it may be observed that into the classical period the assembly was able to control and direct the disposition of surplus production (Bresson 2007: 103–122), with or without strong probouleumatic pressure.

But at other locations we may be able to discern greater corporate involvement in production. At Megara, there was clearly a government policy to support the woolens industry; this is how Megara thrived in the fourth century, when she had periods of democracy as well as moderate oligarchy (characterized by *sophrosyne*, "moderation," according to the contemporary Isocrates [8.119]), likely a reference to an equilibrium between the probouleumatic council and the assembly, whose enactments may have been as important to Megara's economic success as her two harbors. By the seventh century, it came to make sense to put the land under hooves instead of grain (Legon 1981: 89). Hence the cynic Diogenes' remark that at Megara it is "more advantageous to be a man's ram than a man's son" (Diog. Laert. 6.41). This collective policy led directly to a massive influx of wealth that was reflected in the local standards of living. "Although they farm land made of stone, they have built the greatest households in Greece" (Isoc. 8.117); "Megarians feast as if they will die tomorrow, but they build as if they will never die" (Diogenes *apud* Tert., *Apol.* 39.14). The assembly was in a position to enact regulatory policy and law that would massage production and export (see Legon 1981: 87–90, 280–281; 2004: 463–465; Tandy 2013).

To some extent, sacred laws that promoted the economic well-being of sacred precincts are examples of the assembly getting involved with the economy in its details; wars over these valuable sacred lands were declared by assemblies and subsequently fought (Howe 2008; McInerney 2010).

4 Distribution

Trade was not viewed favorably by most Greek elites. In Homer, nearly all trade is handled by unadmired non-Greeks; in the real world of Homer's audience, there is no scholarly agreement on who did the trading. By the fifth century, however, the evidence indicates that the majority of long-distance trade was undertaken by non-Greeks and by Greeks who were not local citizens, but this generally low esteem for traders did not prevent wealthy Athenians (and presumably wealthy citizens elsewhere) from investing in shiploads of grain and other commodities through bottomry loans and other instruments.

Nearly everything imaginable was carried between places by ships on the sea, from grains and specialty foods to timber, metals, and stone, from fine ceramics to human beings. That seaborne trade grew during the archaic into the classical period is suggested by increased discovery of shipwrecks (Horden and Purcell 2000: 371, table 5), but this may be an accident of archaeological recovery (Möller 2007: 362). As early as the seventh century, Hesiod considered seaborne trade one task (*ergon*) among many for the small-scale producer (Mele 1979; Tandy 1997: 75, 212–213). It may well be the case that an immeasurably large volume of trade was executed via *cabotage*, that is, via short-haul, smaller vessels. One excellent example of this is the early sixth-century wreck of a ship, at Pabuç Burnu on the coast of Caria, no larger than 10 tons, which carried unprocessed and processed foodstuffs that could be measured out to buyers (Greene et al. 2008; Leidwanger et al. 2012). There were also larger ships (perhaps purpose-built), such as the one that was wrecked in the middle of the seventh century at the coastal island of Kekova Adası off Lycia; it was carrying more than ninety Cypro-Levantine basket-handle amphoras as well as storage vessels from Samos and Corinth (Greene, Lawall, and Polzer 2008; Leidwanger, Özdaş, and Greene 2012). By the second half of the sixth century at latest, purpose-built merchant ships were carrying cargoes to and from nearly all points of the Mediterranean compass; some of these would on occasion carry grain.

There has developed a relatively new orthodoxy on when—not until after the Persian Wars—and to what extent—not drastically until later than that—Athens depended on outside suppliers for her grain (Garnsey 1988: 105–106: thus Morris 1994: 361 and Hornblower 2011: 31–32). Michael Whitby (1998: 121) is able to make an effective argument that there were years in the fourth century when the Athenians over-imported so much grain that Piraeus may have been the leading *exporter* of grain in the Aegean world. However, Alfonso Moreno (2007) has built a strong counter-argument to Garnsey's, based mostly on Garnsey's use of mathematics and assumptions about how much arable land was in Attica, how productive it was, how much people consumed, how many people there were, and so on. But Garnsey and Moreno, plus everyone else who has looked closely at the topic, agree that the assembly at Athens intervened extensively in the grain trade.

5 The Effect of Enactments on Distribution

We can start by observing that at the principal meeting of the Athenian assembly in each prytany (ten times per year) there were two required topics of discussion: the grain supply and border security (δεῖ ... περὶ σίτου καὶ περὶ φυλακῆς τῆς χώρας χρηματίζειν [*Ath.Pol.* 43.4]). The assembly also oversaw the election by lot or by vote of at least fifty (a number that grew to at least seventy-five in the fourth century) regulators of the grain trade alone (the following is drawn from the excellent, detailed synopsis by Moreno 2007: 334–336 [=appendix 4]):

- 10 *agoranomoi*, 5 each at Piraeus and the agora, elected by lot, kept order, controlled quality, prevented fraud, and collected the market tax from retailers.

- 10 *metronomoi*, 5 each at Piraeus and the agora, elected by lot, policed weights and measures.
- 10–35 grain guards (*sitophylakes*), 5 (later 15) at Piraeus, 5 (later 20) at the agora, elected by lot, kept accurate records and enforced (i) the prohibition of agricultural exports save olive oil; (ii) the prohibition of engaging in or underwriting any grain shipment not destined for Piraeus; (iii) the prohibition against hoarding; (iv) the prohibition against making profit more than one obol per *phormos* (3.3%, or if per wholesale drachma: 16.7%); (v) similar price and mark-up controls on millers and bakers; (vi) sale of loaves at prescribed weights; (vii) the levying of 2% tax on all grain entering or leaving Piraeus.
- 10 market overseers (*epimelētai emporiou*), at Piraeus, elected by lot, compelled traders (*emporoi*) to unload all grain at Piraeus and transfer 2/3 of it to the agora.
- 10 grain overseers (*epimelētai sitou*), at the agora, elected by assembly vote in 374/3, oversaw the sale, including the retail pricing, of the imported grain from the Cyclades islands. The law (RO 26; Stroud 1998) indicated how and when the grain was to be delivered to the agora and that the assembly was to determine the retail price people would pay for it. This is a good example of both the assembly's ability to set prices and its ability to provide citizens with affordable grain, but with the concomitant (negative) effect of potentially reducing the amount of cash the state might receive from the sale in support of Athens' war finances. (Stroud 1998: 75)

Even a rapid perusal of this list reveals the concerns the Athenians had both for provision of sufficient grain to the people of Athens and for the collecting of important taxes on grain (and other) imports (although the former seems the primary motivator). These officials oversaw the markets at Piraeus and in the city and served at the pleasure of the assembly, keeping tabs on wholesalers and retailers in both places, enforcing, for example, the limit (either 3.3 percent or 16.7 percent) on the amount per *phormos* (a measure otherwise unknown, but perhaps the same as a *medimnos*, a dry measure of 55 pounds) that retailers could charge above what they had paid in the wholesale market (this is not a fully understood arrangement: see Migeotte 1997; 2009: 148–149; Rosivach 2000: 49n.56; Bresson 2000: 183–210; 2007: 119–120). These officials may have had the power to act regarding prices without specific instructions from the assembly, but it is clear that the *dēmos* through this process directly influenced the cost of living of their community by fixing the retail price of this staple or by putting a ceiling on it, above all by empowering the officials to hold the retailers to the rules.

The assembly regularly generated downward pressure on wholesale prices by honoring traders who brought their ships laden with grains to Athens at a reduced price. Engen (2010: 140–213) has gathered the epigraphical evidence from the late fifth and fourth centuries that indicates that on many occasions the assembly voted to award honors, among them gold crowns, inscriptions, and statues, to traders who brought grains to Athens at the traditional wholesale price (5 drachmas per *medimnos*) instead of the current, "crisis" price (up to 16 drachmas and higher) (some brought grain in for free); the port officials would ensure that those purchasing at the retail stage would pay no more than the allowed amount. These gifts, usually from full-time, noncitizen traders, were made prior to the assembly votes for honors, but presumably on many occasions with the understanding that the gesture of generosity would lead to the assembly's vote of honor; posted inscriptions must have had a hortatory function as well (Luraghi 2010).

These honors in turn had a very specific positive impact on the economic well-being of the state, because (the prospects of) these very enactments brought downward pressure on the wholesale price of grain at Piraeus, especially at critical times; existing regulations enforced by market officials kept the retail price down commensurately. In one certain case (Engen 2010: 305) (and in all probability in other cases as well) there was a clear probouleumatic stage in the process, but in most cases this was not so. At what cost? A gold crown had a price tag of 1,000 drachmas, the outlay of which concerns Engen because it could represent a significant percentage of the state's revenue for the year (as much as 0.3 percent in a poor year: Engen 2010: 160).

The assembly enacted other decrees that manipulated grain prices favorably. In 333/2 the assembly decreed that traders from Kition on Cyprus would be allowed to purchase land and build a sanctuary to Aphrodite. Permission to noncitizens to purchase land was exceedingly rare, and the motive in this case appears to be strictly to curry the good will of Phoenician traders, just as the assembly at an unknown point in the past had done the same for Egyptians: "it is resolved by the *dēmos* to give to the traders of the Kitians the right to purchase a property on which they will build their sanctuary for Aphrodite, just as also the Egyptians have founded the sanctuary of Isis" (RO 91.38–45).

To the Athenian laws that forbade Athenians from issuing bottomry loans for grain cargoes that would be delivered to any port other than Piraeus and forbade any Athenian from transporting grain to any other port than Piraeus (regulated by the *sitophylakes* above), any violation of which offered the death penalty (Garnsey 1988: 139–140), we can compare this decree from the assembly at democratic (see Robinson 2011: 140–145) Teos in Ionia, enacted about 470 (ML 30A.6–12):

> ὅστις ἐς γῆν τὴν Τηίην κ-
> ωλύει σῖτον ἐσάγεσθαι
> ἢ τέχνηι ἢ μηχανῆι ἢ κατ-
> ὰ θάλασσαν ἢ κατ' ἤπειρο-
> ν ἢ ἐσαχθέντα ἀνωθεοίη,
> ἀπόλλυσθαι καὶ αὐτ-
> ὸν καὶ γένος τὸ κένο.
>
> Whoever interferes with grain being imported into Teian territory by any means at all, whether by sea or land, or exports (*or* pushes up the price of) what has been imported: may destruction visit both him and his family.

Similarly, although we cannot be sure to what extent the assembly initiated them, fifth-century civic enactments at Thasos empowered "fruit-reckoners" (*karpologoi*) to collect taxes and tariffs within the wine industry, protected local growers (*geōrgoi*) from unscrupulous traders (*emporoi*), restricted futures contracts, and forbade the movement by Thasian ships of non-Thasian wine within a broad patch of the northern Aegean stretching from Athos to Cape Pacheia south of Ainos (*SEG* 36 790–792 = Salviat 1986: 147–150, 152–153, 181–187; Stanley 1980).

6 Consumption

The ancient Greek diet comprised the Mediterranean triad of grains, grapes, and olives. It has been argued persuasively that up to 70 to 75 percent of a Greek person's caloric intake in the classical period was grains (Foxhall and Forbes 1982: 74; other calculations presented and discussed by Rosivach 2000: 32–33 and n.6); this helps to explain the fixation many states had on their grain production and/or importation. In general there was an increase in the standard of living, including ingestion of calories, from the beginning of the Iron Age (c.1100 BCE) into the classical period (Morris 2004).

There must have been large disparities of income in many *poleis*, and this was certainly true of Athens at the time of Solon, for if the bushel requirements for the economic classes in fact go back to Solon's restructuring, then most of the citizens at the time would have been placed in the lowest class of *thetes*; this means growing fewer than 200 *medimnoi* of grains and does not necessarily mean utter poverty, for 200 *medimnoi* would feed about thirty (Foxhall 1997: 130) or thirty-five persons (Rosivach 2002: 37–38). At the other end of our period, in 322 BCE, the Athenians passed a minimum wealth requirement, 2,000 drachmas, for retaining citizenship, which was met by only about 9,000 men (Diod. 18.18.4–5); this minimum amount would have been enough to buy about 3 hectares of land with a house on it (van Wees 2006: 357–358 with n.34). (More than 12,000 were forced out of the assembly.) Earlier in the century, Xenophon expresses concern about the reputation of Athens in the Hellenic world if she is unable to eliminate the poverty of her poorest citizens (*Poroi* 1).

Consumption patterns, especially among the wealthy, would have had a small demand effect on imports, such as specialty food products (eels and so on), and exotic spices and perfumes.

7 The Effect of Enactments on Consumption

It is difficult to say how much effect the actions of the assembly may have had on patterns of consumption. Sumptuary laws that were occasionally applied against excesses by wealthy citizens at Athens (from Solon [Plut. *Sol.* 21.5] to Demetrius [Cic. *De leg.* 2.66]) would have put a damper on specialty imports and thereby reduced the collection of the 2 percent import tax at Piraeus. As Davidson (1997) has pointed out, the specialty dietary imports were of ingestive interest only to the elite stratum of Athenian society, so assembly action might have reduced tax collection but would have increased the ability of the wealthy to afford the liturgical obligations placed on them.

When, near the end of the Peloponnesian War, grains became too expensive for many citizens, a daily dole of 2 obols (the *diobelia*) was instituted by action of the assembly. The *diobelia* advantaged only citizens, i.e. individual members of the assembly, while the regulations and price controls related to grain imports benefited *all* residents of Attica, and thus the assembly was undermining the advantage citizens had over noncitizens, which points to a disembeddedness of the economy, an attractive conclusion for substantivists (Rosivach 2000: 56). Disabled citizens were eligible for state support of 1 obol per day, increasing to 2 obols before 322 (Loomis 1998: 231). It would be mistaken to take the assembly's actions to pay assembly attenders and jurors as attempts to redistribute wealth, as the amounts involved, although large in the aggregate, would not have freed recipients from the poverty by which they were beset.

The assembly at Athens did not address disparities of income, although the debate over how to spend the windfall from Laureion in 383/2 (discussed below) was a reflection of the democratic commitment to the equality of citizens, whether the cash were to be distributed to all citizens equally or spent on triremes for the defense of all citizens.

8 Economic Policies and the Athenian Assembly

Labor and debt policies

Before the reforms of Solon, there had developed an intractable debt problem in the course of transition to private ownership of land. Residents of Attica appear to have accumulated debt collateralized by property and person. The reforms addressed this not fully understood problem by acting to forbid the use of human bodies as collateral.

Banks and private citizens were involved in the financing of many economic activities (Shipton 2000), perhaps most prominently long-distance trade and mineral extraction, but interest charged and other aspects of such loans were not regulated by any government body, including the assembly.

Because of the intrinsic labor shortage that I discussed briefly above, there was no recognizable labor market. It follows, then, that I do not believe that it is possible to speak of any ancient Greek state's "labor policy." The closest to this modern notion would be state pay for standing or campaigning armies and for laborers on state construction projects, although these are no more parts of a labor policy than the payments made to jurors and to assembly participants.

Fiscal policy

The Athenian assembly made fiscal policy at times whenever it responded to present circumstances. But until the Theoric Fund (public funds distributed to help cover the cost of admission to public festivals by poorer Athenian citizens) was properly born from the forehead of Eubulus shortly after 355 (Rhodes 1981: 514), it is difficult to identify, at any time, anything that might be called a "policy" that was directing the economy of the Athenians in any particular direction. This lack of policy is not surprising given the flimsiness of the grasp of the market found in Plato (Tandy 2003), although it can be said that Aristotle has an understanding of economic development and history (Meikle 1995) and Xenophon has an impressive if incomplete grasp of the possibilities of economic planning in the *Poroi*.

Monetary policy

Athens must not have been alone in pursuing monetary policies that appear intended to bring advantage to the local economy. Just as the spread of coinage in the sixth century facilitated the growth of extra-regional trade, so also efforts by the Athenian assembly to monopolize the monetary system must have brought benefits not only to Athens but also to all who brought goods to Piraeus. Shortly after 450, the Athenian assembly enacted a decree that required all members of the Delian League to use only Athenian coins, weights, and measures (ML 45). Although the beginning of the inscription is missing, it seems certain from a reference in §12 to a "previous decree" (*psēphisma*) that this is the work of the assembly. Uniform coinage would make it easier to handle the burgeoning, unprecedented volume of military and administrative payments that were flowing into Athens (Finley 1973: 168–169; Meiggs 1972: 167–172), while outsiders would be attracted because routinization of weights and measures meant a reduction in transaction costs (Martin 1985: 204; Lewis 1987). Add to this that more trade would come into Piraeus, which translates to increased employment and to taxes collected at higher levels and with greater ease. A law focused on the purity of silver coinage in use at Athens was passed in 375/4 (Stroud 1974; RO 25); this would have had similarly salutary effects on the revenue stream of the state. (Some [among them RO p. 116] believe that this and other laws that do not mention the "council and the people" must be the exclusive work of the *nomothetai*, while others [among them Stroud 1974: 163] hold that no mention of the people does not rule out a role for them in the process.)

9 Participatory Communities and Economic Decisions

The evidence with which we are forced to work can be difficult to sort through. Not only is the evidence capricious in its availability, but it is also the case, as I have mentioned already above, that it is often seemingly impossible to construct a clear motive for a given enactment. Unintended consequences must have been a regular outcome to enactments. I will present one example each of enactments that proved positive and negative.

A positive enactment

One very good example of assembly enactment is familiar to many readers. The vote to disburse the extraordinary income from a new seam at the Laureion silver mines in 483 for the building of warships instead of dividing up the enormous sum of 100 talents equally among all citizens was, by pure accident, a blessing for the Athenian economy and security (presumably years before those were the two regular topics of the main assemblies). Ordinarily, the income from the mines went into the Athenian treasury, although exceptional windfalls appear to have been divided equally among the citizens (Hdt. 7.144; Plut. *Them.* 4.1; we know the amount from *Ath. Pol.* 22.7). But on this occasion Themistocles convinced the assembly to approve, instead of the anticipated distribution, the diversion of the windfall to the building of ships for an expected war with Aegina. Although he was alone in making his proposal, it won the day, and this victory eventually led to his opponent Aristides' ostracism, probably in 482, as well as an Athenian navy better prepared for the Persian invasion of 480. Assembly action in support of a division to all citizens would have been entirely negative, for each citizen's share, according to Herodotus, would have been a mere 10 drachmas (more likely 15 drachmas in a population of 40,000). By directing the 100 talents to the task of shipbuilding, the assembly avoided the infusion of the 100 talents into the economy at large, which one has to assume would have put upward pressure on prices. However accidental this decision was, it was an economic blessing for the population of Athens. There must be many similar events in Greek political history when economic fortunes rose and fell in response to assembly decrees.

A negative enactment

A modest but good example of how a democratic assembly can decree itself into economic difficulties is to be found at Eretria. In 341, the Eretrians had thrown out the democrat-turned-tyrant Cleitarchus (installed with Philip's support) and made an alliance with Athens (Reber, Hansen, and Ducrey 2004: 654). When their most prominent festival, the Amarysia (referred to in the decree as the Artemisia), was to be celebrated in 340, the *dēmos*, acting probouleumatically, passed a decree that would make that year's edition especially spectacular and, apparently, especially inclusive (*IG* XII[9] 189 = Sokolowski 1969: no. 92 = RO 73). This is an example of a "sacred law", but it in fact reveals much more than how a festival was to be executed. It begins in typical fashion, indicating that this decree is the work of the council and the *dēmos*.

> [θ]εο[ί]
> 'Εξήκεστος Διοδώρου εἶπεν· ὅπωρ ἂν τὰ Ἀρ-
> τεμίρια ὡς κάλλιστα ἄγωμεν καὶ θύωριν ὡς π-
> λεῖστοι, ἔδοξεν τεῖ βουλεῖ τοῖ δήμοι·
> [[..]] τιθεῖν τὴμ πόλιν ἀγῶνα μουσικῆς ἀπὸ χιλίων
> δραχμῶν τεῖ Μεταξὺ καὶ τεῖ Φυλάκει καὶ παρέχει-
> ν ἄρνας τεῖ πρὸ τῶν 'Αρτεμιρίων πέντε ἡμὲρας, τ-
> ούτων δὲ δύο ἐγκρίτους εἶναι.

> Gods. Execestus son of Diodorus proposed: in order that we may celebrate the Artemisia as finely as possible and that as many people as possible may sacrifice, resolved by the council and the people. The city is to arrange a competition in music with a budget of 1,000 drachmas to the Moderator and Guardian and provide lambs there for five days before the Artemisia, two of them being choice animals. (RO 73.1–8, trans. Rhodes and Osborne)

We see that there is a clear democratic emphasis on the inclusion of as many citizens as possible (3–4); the very fact that the *dēmos* has made changes to this traditional festival is an assertion of the new political reality of the democracy at Eretria. Later there is a list of the prizes to be awarded:

> [τὰ δ]ὲ ἆθλα δίδοσθαι κατὰ τάδε· ῥαψωιδοῖ ἑκατὸν εἴ-
> κοσι, δευτέροι πεντήκοντα, τρίτοι εἴκοσι· αὐλωιδοῖ παιδὶ πε-
> ντήκοντα, δευτέροι τριήκοντα, τρίτοι εἴκοσι· ἀνδρὶ κιθαρισ-
> τεῖ ἑκατὸν δέκα, δευτέροι ἑβδομήκοντα, τρίτοι πεντή-
> κοντα πέντε· κιθαρωιδοῖ διηκόσιαι, δευτέροι ἑκατὸν
> πεντήκοντα, τρίτοι ἑκατόν. παρωιδοῖ πεντήκοντα, δευ-
> τέροι δέκα. (15–21)

> Prizes are to be given in the following way: to the rhapsode 120 [drachmas], to the second 50, to the third 20; to the boy singer to the pipes 50, to the second 30, to the third 20; to the adult lyre-player 110, to the second 70, to the third 55; to the singer accompanying himself on the lyre 200, to the second 150, to the third 100; to the singer of parodies 50, to the second 10.

A quick arithmetical check reveals that the prizes in the inscription add up to 1,035 drachmas—already over budget! In addition:

> σιτηρέσιον δὲ δίδοσθαι τοῖς ἀγωνισταῖς
> τοῖς παραγενομένοις δραχμὴν τῆς ἡμέρης ἑκάστοι ἀρ-
> ξαμένοις μὴ πλέον τρισὶν ἡμέραις πρὸ τοῦπροάγωνος, μέ-
> χρι οὗ ἂν ὁ ἀγὼν γένηται. (21–24)

> Maintenance is to be granted to the competitors who are present of a drachma a day for each of them, beginning not more than three days before the pre-competition event and continuing until the competition takes place.

The number of competitors is not indicated, perhaps not even known, so this is possibly an expense that will be burdensome. Finally,

> πωλεῖν δὲ ἐν τοῖ ἱεροῖ τὸμ βολόμενον ὅτι
> [ἂ]μ βόληται ἀτελέα μὴ τιθέντα τέλος μηδέν, μηδὲ πρ-
> [ή]ττεσθαι τοὺς ἱεροποιοὺς μηδὲν τοὺς πωλέοντ-
> ας. (32–35)

> Anyone who wants is to sell whatever he wants in the sanctuary, without tax and not paying any duty, and neither are the *hieropoioi* [temple overseers] to exact any tax from the sellers.

Although, as is often the case, this religious observance will be exempt from the collection of all taxes, one may be left to wonder where else in the process of the worship of Artemis would the assembly be rifling the treasury.

Was the participatory community at Athens parasitic on the economy?

It is intuitive to conclude that assemblies often acted in their own best interests, or at least without careful concern for the best interests of others. Hence it is appropriate to ask whether participatory communities in Greece were parasitic on the economies that they oversaw. The nature of the evidence requires us to begin and end with Athens. The example immediately above from Eretria, however, vividly (if largely trivially) suggests how an assembly can outspend its resources. Let us have a look at some of the expenses that the Athenian assembly had to meet each year just to keep the doors open. The Athenian assembly paid itself to meet. There is clear evidence of pay for assembly attendance also at Iasos on Rhodes after 330 BCE (RO 99), and Aristotle clearly states in his

Politics that pay for assemblers and jurors is typical for Greek democracies of his time, clearly not just of Athens (assembly: 1297a35–38, 1299b38–1300a4, 1317b30–38, 1320a17–22; jurors: 1294a37–40, 1298b18–19; both: 1293a1–10; see full discussion in de Ste. Croix 1975). De Ste. Croix draws our attention to the important fact that jury and assembly pay are found nearly only in literary sources, which goes a long way towards explaining why we do not know more about this arrangement in other democracies (de Ste. Croix 1975: 52). I present these examples of annual expenses, approved by the Athenian assembly, to indicate the impact of such civic withdrawals on the cash flow of the state in the 330s. (Pritchard [2014] has done much more detailed calculations for the following four categories, coming up with, respectively in the 330s, 29.5, 14.5, 45, and 26.7).

- There were about 350 magistrates in the fourth century, probably paid 1 drachma per day for the full 360 days of a year. (In fact, the number is uncertain—700 may be more like it, but it is not certain which magistrates were paid and which were not. (See Rhodes 1981a: 514; Hansen 1979 [on pay]; Hansen 1980 [on number].)
  COST: 21 talents
- The council of 500 were each paid 5 obols; the prytany members were paid an additional obol. The council met probably 300 times per year, for a starting cost of 21.25 talents. Not all members attended every meeting, so we can reduce this expense by about 30 percent.
  COST: 14+ talents
- The assembly attenders (or at least the first arrivals) were paid 3 obols by the time of the *Ekklēsiazousai* (c.392), at the motion of Agyrrhius, who was responsible also for the grain-tax law of 374/3; by the time of the *Ath. Pol.*, the attendance pay was 1 drachma for a meeting, 1.5 drachmas for the principal meetings. If the regular assembly met three times per prytany, that's 30 times a year; the principal meeting was 10 times a year. Rather than throw up our hands in frustration, let us assume an average attendance of 6,000, which was the required quorum for certain actions and seems to be the number that could fill the Pnyx. (In the last third of the fourth century the democratic polis of Iasos [on Rhodes], not a wealthy community, paid its assemblers 3 obols per monthly meeting [RO 99].)
  COST: 45 talents
- Finally, there were 6,000 jurors for courts that met about 200 days per year; pay was 3 obols per day, total cost 100 talents. By no means did all jurors find opportunities every day; the total should be cut by two-thirds or three-quarters. Juries could reassign property ownerships in disputes over loans or liturgies. Fines imposed by juries would have occasionally pleased a bureaucrat's heart, but surely the greatest impact the jury system had on the Athenian economy was the cost of paying jurors, not the fines generated by their decisions, which must have had very little effect on the performance of the economy.
  COST: 25–33 talents

To juror-pay may be compared payments voted by the assembly to pay for citizens' tickets to religious festivals; what these two programs have in common is that they are expenses from the treasury without any intended or unintended effect on the economy.

The festival money came from the Theoric Fund after 355; the most recent analysis of *theōrika* in the fifth century (but still no early Theoric Fund) is by Roselli (2009).

10 Conclusion

Let me conclude by taking up two issues. First, I do not add up the regulatory and judicial costs just above because there are too many unknowns, but by way of an answer, here is the place to return to the honors given to traders co-operative with Athenian interests, including the crowns about which Engen is worried (above). These honors, like magistrate pay, can be estimated and would have added several talents each year, but in the long term they would have been irrelevant. In the middle part of the fifth century, revenue was probably about 1,000 talents per year (Meiggs 1972: 258–259; Morris 2009: 167n.1) and probably fairly steady until the outbreak of the war in 432. But Engen is certainly right to be concerned about the fourth century, for by then the Athenians began to experience enormous fluctuations in annual revenues, ranging from a low of 60 talents (probably in 338 or 336) to a high of 1,200 twelve years later ([Plut.] *X orat.* 482f.), while we learn from Demosthenes (10.37–38) that earlier annual revenues varied from 130 (probably in 355) to 400 (probably in 346: on these dates see Engen 2010: 160), so there were definitely years in which there just was not enough cash in the treasury to pay for everything (including any new regulatory structures), and within that context from our perspective we can see how dangerous thoughtless voting could be, how perilous a political player like Agyrrhius could become. (Rhodes describes the low of 60 talents "hard to believe for any date" [Rhodes 2010: 368], seeing that the import tax at Piraeus immediately after the Peloponnesian War brought in 36 talents on its own [Andoc. 133]; Rhodes further wonders whether Plutarch's 60 should be emended to 600, adding that the reliability of Plutarch's numbers is further undermined by the magnitude of the high of 1,200 talents, attributed to Lycurgus by Plutarch, but by Duris [*FGH* 76 F 10 *apud* Athen. 12.542c] to Demetrius of Phaleron [Rhodes 2013: 222n.132]. Nevertheless, the numbers as we have them indicate a background noise of great and unpredictable variation in annual collections.)

Second: as noted above, genuinely frivolous or irresponsible proposals in assembly could be blocked in court by a *graphē paranomōn*, but it is clearly the case that this legal challenge was used primarily as a political tool to minimize the influence of rivals (Osborne 1985: 53). That said, a successful *graphē* could generate a large fine to the benefit of the state; a failed one could bring a fine from the originator of the suit. Perhaps significantly, the *graphē paranomōn* was introduced in about 415 as a replacement for ostracism. Enactments of ostracism at Athens and of petalism at Syracuse exiled citizens but did not confiscate property (Plut., *Arist.* 7.5), and thus (like an *antidosis* judgment) would have had no meaningful effect on either local production or distribution. But before the classical period, it is clear, as van Wees puts it, that "violent struggles among the élite were common and invariably involved groups of people going into exile or fighting their way back … therefore, power and property must have changed hands constantly as it was abandoned, seized, and recovered" (van Wees 2000: 66). Van Wees is generalizing from the Megara of Theognis, but this phenomenon is nowhere more clearly in play than in archaic Mytilene, where the exiled Alcaeus moans that he lives apart from his *polis* deprived of "the things my father and his father once owned" (130.20–24).

Such confiscations separated exiled individuals from overseeing cultivated properties and forced them to become marine competitors against their former *polis*—a doubly negative arrangement for the economic health of the *polis* (Tandy 2004; Tandy, forthcoming). Most states, like Athens, began to minimize the deleterious effects of the exiling of productive citizens by the beginning of the fifth century; they did so through enactments of the assembly, although it is manifest that these enactments did not contain anything resembling economic prescience or planning. The absence of planning over time reminds us that the skyrocketing of revenues at Athens in the 330s was coincident with the ceding of control of fiscal policy to central planners.

The Greek and Roman economies (see de Ligt, Chapter 21) start in similar places, namely, as small agrarian communities. And we see some similarity of attitudes toward trade and traders. In Greece, trade was recognized as essential but, as noted above, the best families did not themselves practice trade (except through investment), while at Rome trade was looked down on but admired if profits were converted into agricultural investment and if the investment in trade could be handled by middlemen, as de Ligt explains. But the developmental trajectory of these economies differed significantly, as did the political mechanisms for addressing different economic strains. The imperialisms of the Greek world took shape in very different ways from the *Imperium Romanum*. Spartan imperialism (like the co-operative *ethnē* that pooled member resources) was essentially defensive and integrated poorly with the outside world (as is clear from the Spartans' nearly exclusive use of iron bars for money at home), while Athenian imperialism suffers in comparison with Rome for at least three reasons: (1) Athenian imperialism was constructed and defined by the threat of a single outside power, Persia (and a single Greek power, Sparta); (2) the Athenian Empire was substantially smaller than its Roman counterpart; and (3) as important as Athens was as a center of trade, it never incorporated these economies but remained a *polis* protective of its distinct participatory identity.

ACKNOWLEDGMENTS

All the defects of this chapter are my own, despite the efforts of Sam Gartland, Dean Hammer, David Pritchard, Peter Rhodes, and Johanna Stiebert.

REFERENCES

Austin, M. and P. Vidal-Naquet. 1977. *Economic and Social History of Ancient Greece: An Introduction.* London.

Bissa, E. 2009. *Governmental Intervention in Foreign Trade in Archaic and Classical Greece.* Leiden.

Bresson, A. 2000. *La cité marchande.* Bordeaux.

Bresson, A. 2007. *L'économie de la Grèce des cités (fin VIe–Ier siècle a.C.). 1. Les structures et la production.* Paris.

Bresson, A. 2008. *L'économie de la Grèce des cités (fin VIe–Ier siècle a.C.). 2. Les espaces de l'échange.* Paris.

Christ, M. 1990. "Liturgy Avoidance and Antidosis in Classical Athens." *TAPA* 120: 147–169.

Davidson, J. 1997. *Courtesans and Fishcakes: The Consuming Passions of Classical Athens.* London.

Davies. J. 1971. *Athenian Propertied Families 600–300 B.C.* Oxford.

Davies. J. 2007. "Production." In Scheidel et al. 2007: 333–361.

Descat, R. 1998. "Public et privé dans l'économie de la cité grecque." *Ktema* 23: 229–241.

De Ste. Croix, G.E.M. 1975. "Political Pay Outside Athens." *CQ* 25: 48–52.

Engels, J. 2000. "Das athenische Getreidesteuer-Gesetz des Agyrrhios und angebliche 'sozialstaatliche' Ziele inden Maßnahmen zur Getreideversorgung spätklassischer und hellenistischer Poleis." *ZPE* 132: 97–124.

Engen, D. 2010. *Honor and Profit: Athenian Trade Policy and the Economy and Society of Greece, 415–307 B.C.E.* Ann Arbor.

Finley, M. 1973. *The Ancient Economy.* Berkeley; repr., with new introduction by I. Morris, 1999.

Foxhall, L. 1992. "The Control of the Attic Landscape." In Wells 1992: 155–160.

Foxhall, L. 1997. "A View from the Top: Evaluating the Solonian Property Classes." In L. Mitchell and P.J. Rhodes, eds. *The Development of the Polis in Archaic Greece.* London, 113–136.

Foxhall, L. 2007. *Olive Cultivation in Ancient Greece: Seeking the Ancient Economy.* Oxford.

Foxhall, L. and H. Forbes. 1982. "Σιτομετρεία: The Role of Grain as a Staple Food in Classical Antiquity." *Chiron* 12: 41–90.

Gabrielsen, V. 1986. "ΦΑΝΗΡΑ and ΑΦΑΝΗΣ ΟΥΣΙΑ in Classical Athens,." *C&M* 38: 7–38.

Gabrielsen, V. 1994. *Financing the Athenian Fleet: Public Taxation and Social Relations.* Baltimore.

Garnsey, P. 1985. "Grain for Athens." In P. Cartledge and F. Harvey, eds., *Crux: Essays Presented to G.E.M. de Ste. Croix on his 75th Birthday.* London, 62–75.

Garnsey, P. 1988. *Famine and Food Supply in the Graeco-Roman World: Responses to Risk and Crisis.* Cambridge.

Greene, E., M. Lawall, and M. Polzer. 2008. "Inconspicuous Consumption: The Sixth-Century B.C.E. Shipwreck at Pabuç Burnu, Turkey." *AJA* 112: 685–711.

Grove, A. and O. Rackham. 2001. *The Nature of Mediterranean Europe: An Ecological History.* New Haven.

Hansen, M.H. 1979. "*Misthos* for Magistrates in Classical Athens." *SO* 54: 5–22.

Hansen, M.H. 1980. "Seven Hundred *Archai* in Athens." *GRBS* 21: 151–173.

Hansen, M.H. and T. Nielsen, eds. 2004. *An Inventory of Archaic and Classical Poleis.* Oxford.

Horden, P. and N. Purcell. 2000. *The Corrupting Sea: A Study of Mediterranean History.* Cambridge.

Hornblower, S. 2011. *The Greek World 479–323 BC.* 4th edn. London.

Howe, T. 2008. *Pastoral Politics: Animals, Agriculture and Society in Ancient Greece.* Claremont, CA.

Isager, S. and J. Skydsgaard. 1992. *Ancient Greek Agriculture.* London.

Jones, A. 1952. "The Economic Basis of the Athenian Democracy." *P&P* 1: 13–31; repr. in *Athenian Democracy* (Oxford, 1957), 3–20.

Legon, R. 1981. *Megara: The Political History of a Greek City-State to 336 B.C.* Ithaca, NY.

Legon, R. 2004. "Megaris, Korinthia, Sikyonia." In Hansen and Nielsen 2004: 462–471.

Leidwanger, J., H. Özdaş, and E. Greene. 2012. "Sourcing the Cargos of Three Archaic Shipwrecks: Kekova Adası, Kepçe Burnu, and Caycağız Koyu." *Arkeometri Sonuçları Toplantısı* 27: 393–409.

Lewis, D. 1987. "The Athenian Coinage Decree." In I. Carradice, ed., *Coinage and Administration in the Athenian and Persian Empires.* Oxford, 53–63.

Loomis, W. 1998. *Wages, Welfare Costs, and Inflation in Classical Athens.* Ann Arbor.

Luraghi, N. 2010. "The *Demos* as Narrator: Public Honors and the Construction of Future and Past." In L. Foxhall, H.-J. Gehrke, and N. Luraghi, eds., *Intentional History: Spinning Time in Ancient Greece.* Stuttgart, 247–263.

Martin, T. 1985. *Sovereignty and Coinage in Ancient Greece.* Princeton.

McInerney, J. 2010. *The Cattle of the Sun.* Princeton.

Meiggs, R. 1972. *The Athenian Empire.* Oxford.

Meikle, S. 1995. *Aristotle's Economic Thought.* Oxford.

Mele, A. 1979. *Il commercio greco arcaico: Prexis ed emporie.* Naples.

Migeotte, L. 1997. "Le contrôle des prix dans les cités grecques." In J. Andreau, P. Briant, and R. Descat, eds., *Économie antique: Prix et formation des prix dans les économies antiques.* Saint-Bertrand-de-Comminges, 33–53.

Migeotte, L. 2009. *The Economy of the Greek Cities from the Archaic Period to the Early Roman Empire.* Trans. J. Lloyd. Berkeley.

Möller, A. 2007. "Distribution." In Scheidel et al. 2007: 362–384.

Moreno, A. 2007. *Feeding the Democracy.* Oxford.

Morley, N. 2007. *Trade in Classical Antiquity.* Cambridge.

Morris, I. 1994. "The Athenian Economy Twenty Years after *The Ancient Economy.*" *CPh* 89: 351–366.

Morris, I. 2004. "Economic Growth in Ancient Greece." *JITE* 160: 709–742.

Morris, I. 2010. *Why the West Rules—For Now: The Patterns of History, and What They Reveal about the Future.* New York.

Osborne, R. 1985. "Law in Action in Classical Athens." *JHS* 105: 40–58.

Osborne, R. 1990. "Pride and Prejudice, Sense and Subsistence: Exchange and Society in the Greek City." In J. Rich and A. Wallace-Hadrill, eds., *City and Country in the Ancient World.* London, 119–145.

Osborne, R. 1996. "Pots, Trade, and the Archaic Greek Economy." *Antiquity* 70: 31–44.

Osborne, R. 2000. Review of Loomis 1998. *CR* 50:185–187.

Polanyi, K. 1957. "The Economy as Instituted Process." In K. Polanyi, C. Arensberg, and H. Pierson, eds., *Trade and Market in the Early Empires.* Glencoe, IL, 243–270.

Pritchard, D. 2014. *Public Spending and Democracy in Classical Athens.* Austin.

Reber, K., M.-H. Hansen, and P. Ducrey. 2004. "Euboia." In Hansen and Nielsen 2004: 643–663.

Reed, C. 2003. *Maritime Traders in the Ancient Greek World.* Cambridge.

Rhodes, P.J. 1981. *A Commentary on the Aristotelian* Athenaion Politeia. Oxford; repr. with addenda 1993.

Rhodes, P.J. 2010. *A History of the Classical World, 478–323 BC.* 2nd edn. Oxford.

Rhodes, P.J. 2013. The Organization of Athenian Public Finance. *G&R* 60:185–202.

Robinson, E. 2011. *Democracy beyond Athens: Popular Government in the Greek Classical Age.* Cambridge.

Roselli, D. 2009. "*Theorika* in Fifth-Century Athens." *GRBS* 49: 5–30.

Rosivach, V. 2000. "Some Economic Aspects of the Fourth-Century Athenian Market in Grain." *Chiron* 30: 31–64.

Rosivach, V. 2002. "*Zeugitai* and Hoplites." *AHB* 16: 33–43.

Salviat, F. 1986. "Le vin du Thasos: Amphores, vin, et sources écrites." In J.-Y. Empereur and Y. Garlan, eds., *Recherches sur les amphores grecques.* Paris, 145–196.

Scheidel, W., I. Morris, and R. Saller, eds. 2007. *The Cambridge Economic History of the Greco-Roman World.* Cambridge.

Shipton, K. 2000. *Leasing and Lending: The Cash Economy in Fourth-Century BC Athens.* London.

Sokolowski, F. 1969. *Lois sacrées des cités grecques.* Paris.

Stanley, P. 1980. "Two Thasian Wine Laws: A Reexamination." *AW* 3: 88–93.

Stanley, P. 1990. "The Value of Ergasteria at Attica: A Reexamination." *MBAH* 9: 1–13.

Stroud, R. 1974. "An Athenian Law on Silver Coinage." *Hesperia* 43: 157–188.

Stroud, R. 1998. *The Athenian Grain-Tax Law of 374/3 B.C.* Princeton.

Tandy, D. 1997. *Warriors into Traders: The Power of the Market in Early Greece.* Berkeley.

Tandy, D. 2003. "Greece, Classical and Earlier." In Joel Mokyr, ed., *The Oxford Encyclopedia of Economic History.* Oxford, 2.467–472.

Tandy, D. 2004. "Trade and Commerce in Archilochos, Sappho, and Alkaios" In R. Rollinger and C. Ulf, eds., *Commerce and Monetary Systems in the Ancient World: Means of Transmission and Cultural Interaction*. Stuttgart, 183–194.

Tandy, D. 2013. "Skopas of Paros and the Fourth Century BC." In D. Katsonopoulou and A. Stewart, eds., *Skopas of Paros and his World*. Athens, 65–75.

Tandy, D. forthcoming. "On the Political Economy of Mytilene, 612/09–597/6." In A. Pierris, ed., *Symposium Philosophiae Antiquae Quintum Lesbium: Pittacus, Alcaeus, Sappho*. Patras.

Tandy, D. and W. Neale. 1996. *Hesiod's* Works and Days*: A Translation and Commentary for the Social Sciences*. Berkeley.

Van Wees, H. 2000. "Megara's Mafiosi: Timocracy and Violence in Theognis." In R. Brock and S. Hodkinson, eds., *Alternatives to Athens: Varieties of Political Organization and Community in Ancient Greece*. Oxford, 52–67.

Van Wees, H. 2006. "Mass and Élite in Solon's Athens: The Property Classes Revisited." In J. Blok and A. Lardinois, eds., *Solon of Athens: New Historical and Philological Approaches*. Leiden, 361–389.

Wells, B., ed. 1992. *Agriculture in Ancient Greece*. Stockholm.

Whitby, M. 1998. "The Grain Trade in Athens in the Fourth Century BC." In H. Parkins and C. Smith, eds., *Trade, Traders and the Ancient City*. London, 99–143.

FURTHER READING

The starting point for approaching the ancient Greek economy is Scheidel et al. 2007; previously Moses Finley (1973) had represented the orthodoxy of the late twentieth century. At the time of writing Bresson 2007 and 2008 were due soon to appear in English translation from Princeton University Press. The most straightforward introductions to agricultural production remain Isager and Skydsgaard 1992 and Wells 1992. On trade see Reed 2003 and Morley 2007; on the Athenian grain trade see anything by the topic's doyen Peter Garnsey and now Moreno 2007. For a sweeping collection of primary sources and intelligent discussion of the ancient economy see Austin and Vidal-Naquet 1977.

CHAPTER 21

Production, Trade, and Consumption in the Roman Republic

Luuk de Ligt

1 Introduction

Under the Republic, a period spanning almost 500 years, Rome developed from a small city-state struggling to defend its territory against Aequians and Volscians to a superpower dominating the entire Mediterranean world and parts of northwest Europe. This remarkable expansion went hand in hand with a succession of dramatic changes in agrarian and non-agrarian production, in levels of commercial activity, and in levels and patterns of consumption. Most of these changes were prompted or facilitated by the large-scale redistribution of economic resources resulting from military conquest.

However, while Roman imperialism transformed the lives first of the non-Roman peoples of Italy and then those of tens of millions of other people, the economic changes set in motion by imperialism also transformed Roman society itself. The aim of this chapter is to describe some of these transformations and to explore some of the institutional and non-institutional "enactments" by which the political elite of republican Rome responded to the countless new possibilities opened up by the conquests of the fourth to first centuries BCE. One of my questions will be: Under what circumstances were magistrates, senators, and other Romans of high social standing prepared to share at least some of the material benefits of imperial conquest, especially newly conquered tracts of agricultural land, with their fellow citizens? Another interesting theme is responses to the increase in the number and volume of commercial transactions that becomes visible from the late fourth century BCE. How was this development dealt with, politically, socially, and ideologically? Finally I will be looking at changes in patterns of consumption, especially in elite circles. As we will see, many elite Romans saw the unstoppable spread of "luxury," which seems to have accelerated in the 180s BCE, as deeply problematic. Why did many senators keep preaching simplicity while practicing extravagance? Was this a purely cultural concern, reflecting worries about the perceived loss of traditional Roman values?

A Companion to Greek Democracy and the Roman Republic, First Edition. Edited by Dean Hammer.

Or did senators and would-be senators have good reason to suspect that recent increases in expenditure on dinners and other forms of extravagant consumption were beginning to undermine social cohesion in and beyond elite circles?

2 Production

To judge by the contents of the Law of the Twelve Tables, of which a substantial number of fragments have been preserved, the economy of early republican Rome was overwhelmingly agricultural (Watson 1975: 157–165; Cornell 1995: 287). Since the same can be said of the economies of most other pre-modern societies, this inference may seem unspectacular. However, since the Twelve Tables contain no regulations concerning trade or manufacturing, it remains difficult to avoid the conclusion that the proportion of the population not primarily engaged in agricultural production was much lower in the fifth century BCE than it was to become in late republican and early imperial times.

Unfortunately, very little is known about the distribution of property rights and labor relations in the territory of early republican Rome. Late authors such as Varro and Pliny the Elder report that Romulus gave plots of land measuring 2 *iugera* (0.5 hectare) to each of his followers (Varro *RR* 1.10.2; Pliny *NH* 18). Since the chance that late republican or early imperial writers had access to reliable information concerning landholding patterns in regal Rome seems remote, there is every reason to reject such stories as completely fanciful. On the other hand, we do happen to know that 2-*iugera* allotments were given to colonists sent out to maritime colonies founded in the second half of the fourth century BCE. Since the sources relating to these foundations cannot easily be discredited, it has been inferred that the recipients of these tiny colonial plots must have had access to additional land. More specifically, it has been suggested that the colonists must have been given permission to "occupy" and cultivate plots of state-owned land in addition to their privately owned holdings (Livy 8.21 reports that 2-*iugera* allotments were given to colonists at Terracina in 329 BCE; access to additional land: e.g. Mason 1992; Pelgrom 2012: 86–89).

If the tradition of the Romulean 2-*iugera* allotments was inspired by patterns of landholding in regal Rome, we must surely conclude that the holders of these tiny allotments also had access to additional land. Since we have no further information on land tenure in Rome during the seventh and sixth centuries, any reconstruction of the specific arrangement or arrangements that made this possible must remain speculative. Some scholars have hypothesized that agricultural production in regal (and early republican) Rome took place in the context of an "infield-outfield" system in which peasants were allowed to occupy and cultivate some kind of "communal" or "gentilician" land in accordance with their possibilities and needs. Alternatively, it might be suggested that the legendary Romulean plots belong to the context of clientship, and that holders of 2-*iugera* allotments were expected to cultivate some the land owned or otherwise controlled by wealthier and more powerful neighbors, presumably in return for a rent (infield-outfield system: de Neeve 1984: 65n.13; *ager gentilicius*: Capogrossi Colognesi 1988, 1994; Franciosi 1995). Various scholars have suggested a connection between the legendary 2-*iugera* plots and the *heredium* of the Twelve Tables, which some later authors define as the "garden" (*hortus*) (Mommsen 1887: 3.23–24, building on Pliny *NH* 19.50; but see Gabba 1978 for the view that Pliny's claim goes back to a late republican antiquarian fantasy).

While this identification is conjectural, it is not entirely implausible. It must, however, be emphasized that the existence a system of land tenure in which *some* peasants (clients?) owned tiny plots of garden land by no means implies that only garden land could be privately owned in regal or early imperial Rome.

Whatever view of landholding patterns in early republican Rome we prefer to take, the existence of a substantial group of poor peasants is implied by the persistent tradition that rural indebtedness was a major social problem in fifth- and fourth-century Rome. From the Law of the Twelve Tables it appears that defaulting debtors could be sold across the Tiber (that is, to non-Romans) as slaves. Those who had incurred debts could avoid this fate by selling themselves as "debt-bondsmen" (*nexi*), meaning that they had to work off their debt by performing agricultural labor on other people's land. Judging by the literary tradition, this arrangement was widely perceived as harsh (Finley 1981 remains the best treatment of this topic; cf. also di Paolo 1996).

Perhaps understandably, the literary tradition has little to say about the less deprived sections of the rural population. Yet it seems certain that from the earliest times onwards the Roman citizen body included many non-elite landowners. One indication is the Roman system of recruitment in which all citizens owning a certain amount of property qualified for service in the legions. The Roman conquests of the fifth and fourth centuries BCE presuppose the existence of armies numbering several thousands of men. Although the critical threshold for legionary service is known to have changed in republican times, the conclusion that a very significant proportion of Roman citizens owned substantial plots of land cannot be avoided (army size and centuriate organization: Forsythe 2007; changes in threshold for legionary service: Rathbone 1993).

It also seems significant that the literary sources for the fourth century refer to subsistence farms considerable larger than 2 *iugera*. According to Livy (5.30), for instance, a few years after the capture of Veii (396 BCE) a large proportion of its former territory was distributed among Roman citizens (Livy 5.30.8). If he is to be believed, each Roman family received 7 *iugera* of land for each of its freeborn members. It may be noted that this scheme is far more generous than that which was implemented around 290 BCE after the conquest of Sabinum. Here, we are told, allotments measuring 7 *iugera* were given either to "plebeians" or to "legionaries," without any evidence of any families receiving multiple plots (Val. Max. 4.3.5; Colum. 1 *praef.* 14; on the social background of the beneficiaries of this scheme [mostly veterans] see Càssola 1988). Interestingly, references to farms comprising 7 *iugera* of arable land are also found in various legendary stories about Roman soldiers and generals who were called up for service during the wars of the early and middle Republic. It has been calculated that the crops harvested from 7 *iugera* (1.75 hectares) of arable land could have sustained a family of four, but only if the land was worked intensively (Roselaar 2010: 204–206).

While patterns of landholding in regal and early republican Rome remain shrouded in mystery, there are reliable indications that the Roman conquests of the fifth and early fourth centuries BCE fueled political conflicts over land. The reason for this was that newly conquered areas were incorporated as state-owned land (*ager publicus*). In theory this type of land may have been open to occupation by any Roman citizen. In practice, however, most of it seems to have fallen into the hands of rich landlords. This seems to be the background to later claims that all plebeians were "ejected" from *ager publicus* (Cassius Hemina fr. 17 P, discussed by Cornell 1995: 269). Regardless of whether we interpret such claims as referring to some formal regulation or simply to practical realities, there is no good reason to doubt the tradition that the plebeians of early republican Rome demanded that Roman public land should be distributed in small allotments that would become the private property of the recipients.

During the first 150 years of the Republic we hear about some twenty-five attempts to have state-owned land distributed under schemes of this type (Cornell 1995: 270). Judging by the literary tradition most of these attempts resulted in legislation ordering distributions being passed by the *concilium plebis.* However, since such laws could not take effect without the Senate's approval, very few of these distributions were implemented. Early exceptions include distributions of land in the former territories of Labici (418 BCE) and Veii (393 BCE), on the Volscian frontier (395 BCE), and in the Ager Pomptinus (383 BCE) (Pelgrom 2012: 37–38, 55).

Even after these programs of land distribution, much state-owned land remained in the hands of the rich and powerful. One clue is a passage in Livy that hints at the creation of large estates in the former territory of Veii (Livy 6.14.10). Another is the contents of the *lex Licinia de modo agrorum* of 367 BCE, which limited the amount of public land (or of land of any type) that a Roman citizen could lawfully possess to 500 *iugera* (125 hectares) (Cato *ORF*[4] fr. 167; Livy 6.35.4–5; Gell. 6.3.40; Varro *RR* 1.2.9; the best recent discussion is that of Rich 2008). In other words, political conflicts over land were initially defused by giving less well-off citizens a better opportunity to exercise their rights of occupation rather than by redistributing large amounts of public land in the form of privately owned allotments.

Between 340 and 240 BCE any lingering tensions arising from demands for land distribution were removed by further conquest. Following the defeat of the Latins and the incorporation of Campania (340–338 BCE) so-called "viritane" distributions were carried out in various parts of Latium and in the Ager Falernus. Under these schemes Roman settlers received plots of land in areas which continued to be administered directly from Rome rather than by the magistrates of a newly founded colony. The next couple of decades witnessed the implementation of similar programs of land distribution in other parts of Italy. Another important development was the foundation of a large number of Latin colonies. It has been calculated that between 334 and 263 BCE some 70,000 settlers were sent out to colonies of this type (Cornell 1995: 381). (Citizens of allied communities made up a large proportion of colonists. As Bradley 2006 points out, there are also some examples of indigenous populations being recycled as "colonists.") About half of these may have been Roman citizens. These schemes can be seen as so many enactments aimed at relieving social and political tensions in Roman society. It must, however, be emphasized that all of the land used for these schemes had been confiscated from defeated enemies. In other words, the successful scaling down of conflicts over land in mid-republican Rome was made possible by the large-scale expropriation of land belonging to non-Romans.

A very similar development can be discerned in the area of labor relations. As we have seen, debt bondage was an important source of dependent labor in early republican Rome. In 326 (or 313?) BCE, however, a law was passed declaring it forbidden for Roman citizens to become debt-bondsmen on a voluntary basis (that is to say, through self-sale). It has plausibly been suggested that this development would have been impossible without a steady supply of chattel slaves in the form of war captives (Finley 1980;

cf. Scheidel 2008: 116–119). In short, social tensions in mid-republican Rome were alleviated by increased opportunities to exploit outsiders (see also Stewart, Chapter 23, on this status as outsider).

During the third and early second centuries BCE few political struggles concerning land are recorded. The conflict ignited by Gaius Flaminius' proposal to use the *Ager Picenus et Gallicus* for viritane distributions (232 BCE) is a partial exception; but Flaminius won the day and his program of land distributions was carried out (Oebel 1993; Feig Vishnia 1996). Following the end of the Second Punic War more viritane distributions were carried out, and the period 194–177 BCE also saw a new wave of colonial foundations, especially in northern Italy (see Laffi 2007: 21–26; de Ligt 2012: 150–154).

It was only from the mid-second century BCE that conflicts over land began to resurface with new intensity, ultimately leading to the controversial land reforms of the Gracchi. The background to this new round of confrontation was quite complex. Earlier generations of scholars have identified the growth of agricultural slavery as the main problem. Of course there is an important element of truth in this theory. There are, however, good reasons to think that the number of slaves needed for the cultivation of cash crops for the market in Rome was considerably smaller than is often supposed. This has led some scholars to emphasize the geographical aspects of commercial agriculture based on chattel slavery. It has been suggested, for instance, that at least some of the social (and military) problems which the Gracchi sought to solve arose from the fact that, for purely economic reasons, the most attractive area for the setting up of slave-staffed estates was central-western Italy, which was precisely the area where the vast majority of rural citizens lived. It also seems likely that the Roman citizen body continued to expand during the most of the second century BCE, a development that could only intensify competition for land (competing reconstructions of background to Gracchan land reforms: de Ligt 2012: 157–182). In principle these tensions might have been alleviated by carrying out viritane distributions or colonial foundations outside central-western Italy, but, as the experiences of the Gracchan age were to reveal, it was virtually impossible to implement such schemes without raising fierce opposition from wealthy Roman landowners or allied communities. In the end the land committee set up under the *lex Sempronia agraria* of 133 BCE did manage to distribute some Italian land, mainly outside central-western Italy, but the program of land distribution set in motion by Tiberius Gracchus seems to have run out of steam after 129 BCE.

The enormous difficulties created by any attempt to use Italian land for distribution schemes is cast into relief by the ruthless policies of Sulla and the triumviri. While the former confiscated huge tracts of land to accommodate some 120,000 veterans, Antony and Octavian took the step of confiscating most of the agricultural land of the eighteen cities whose territories were known for their fertility (settlement of veterans by Sulla: Santangelo 2007: 147; territories of eighteen Italian cities promised to troops of triumviri: App. *B. civ.* 1.107).

Not surprisingly, such schemes carried enormous political costs. This explains why Octavian-Augustus, after eliminating all his rivals, decided to scale down veteran settlement in Italy. Henceforth most veterans would be settled in the provinces, where land could either be confiscated with relative ease or be snapped up at bargain prices.

Even from this deliberately superficial survey it emerges that Roman republican history offers many examples of political conflicts over land being fought between wealthy and less well-off citizens, but at least as many examples of less well-off citizens somehow gaining access to additional land with the help of members of the Roman elite. Part of the explanation for this seemingly contradictory picture is that peasants of citizen status formed the backbone of all republican armies. While this gave rural citizens considerable political leverage, it also explains why many members of the elite were happy to propose or to support colonial ventures or land distribution schemes, especially if such schemes were carried out at the expense of outsiders.

Ideologically, many elite Romans even seem to have relished stories about the legendary poverty of some military leaders of early and mid-republican times, who had allegedly been called away from their 7-*iugera* farms to command some of the Roman armies that had conquered Italy. In reality, very few wealthy Romans were inclined to follow the example of Cato the Elder, who took pride in the fact that he had done some farm work alongside his slaves, the majority view being that agricultural labor was "ungentlemanly toil" (Cic. *De fin.* 1.3). As Garnsey explained long ago, the Roman idealization of the peasant patriarch must be understood as an expression of the ideology of the ruling class of a militarist state (Garnsey 1976: 224).

Before rounding off my rapid survey of connections between economic and political life, I would like to add a few words about non-agrarian producers. There is hardly any need to point out that the interests of urban craftsmen found almost no political expression in republican Rome and that their ideological image was negative. Significantly, urban craftsmen were deemed to be unfit for legionary service. Only during the late 60s BCE and early 50s BCE do we find the craftsmen (and shopkeepers) of Rome making a significant contribution to political struggles. The best evidence refers to the social and political unrest of the years 58–52 BCE, when Publius Clodius recruited the craftsmen and shopkeepers living around the Forum Romanum for the gangs with which he terrorized the streets of Rome (Tatum 1999: 117–119; Lintott 1999: 77–83).

It has plausibly been conjectured that the fast expansion of the city of Rome, and especially the institution of permanent grain doles, had loosened traditional ties between rich patrons and clients involved in craft production and petty trade, a development which gave craftsmen and shopkeepers more political clout. Needless to say, elite authors such as Cicero made no attempt to conceal their contempt for these riotous "artisans and shopkeepers." About three decades later the emperor Augustus banned all private *collegia* that did not serve some officially recognized public purpose (Cic. *Flac.* 18: *opifices et tabernarios*; Augustan ban: de Ligt 2000).

3 Trade

In early republican Rome only a tiny part of production was traded. It is true that the city of Rome is likely to have had a substantial population as early as the sixth century BCE and that the existence of notable distinctions in wealth is suggested both by the literary tradition and by the archaeological record. The vast majority of the population, however, consisted of peasants who consumed most of what they produced and bought no more than a handful of items at weekly markets or annual fairs. Even if we make due allowance for a certain level of trade in luxuries or semi-luxuries (such as high-quality tableware) and the occasional importation of grain during food shortages, there can be no doubt that division of labor, and therefore commerce, stood at a much lower level in early and mid-republican times than in the final century of the Republic.

Of course these inferences are fully compatible with legendary stories which assume that as early as the seventh century BCE some goods were traded with neighboring peoples, for instance at the fair of Lucus Feroniae (Dionys. *Ant. Rom.* 3.23.1). There is also some evidence to suggest that some of these peoples enjoyed special rights when concluding commercial transactions with Romans. From various passages in Livy it appears that Latins concluding transactions with other Latins had the right of *commercium*, meaning (*inter alia*) that their sales and purchases were regarded as legally valid. From much later sources it may be gathered that this rule also applied to sales involving formal transfers of slaves, cattle, and perhaps land between Latins and Romans. Although firm evidence is lacking, it seems likely that this had been the case from early times (for a skeptical assessment of existing views on the early history of *commercium* see Coşkun 2009).

It seems reasonable to suppose that relationships of this type were rooted in a widely shared feeling that Latins and Romans belonged to some kind of community transcending local groupings. However, while such feelings are likely to have facilitated military co-operation, there is nothing to suggest that *commercium* prepared the way for political integration. Wars between Rome and the Latins were fought in 499 BCE and between 340 and 338 BCE, and when large numbers of Latins became Roman citizens in 338 BCE that was because this juridical status had been unilaterally imposed on them by Rome.

If we focus on levels of commercial development in central-western Italy, the late fourth century may be identified as marking an important watershed in levels of commercial agricultural production. Up to a point this take-off can be traced archaeologically, particularly by looking at shifts in the production of containers used to ship wine. During the fifth and fourth centuries the most important regions for the production of amphoras were Magna Graecia and Sicily. From the late fourth century, however, we witness the appearance of the so-called "Graeco-Italian" amphoras, most of which came from Vesuvian and northern Campania and from the coastal districts of Latium and Etruria (Morel 2007: 500–501). It may be inferred from this that the center of gravity of commercial wine-growing was beginning to shift from the Greek-speaking parts of Italy to a zone around Rome, almost certainly as a result of recent political developments and in response to population growth in the city of Rome.

Extensive archaeological investigations have revealed that considerable quantities of Graeco-Italian ware found their way to southern Gaul and the coastal districts of Spain and North Africa. This pattern of distribution resembles that of the black-glaze pottery produced by the "Atelier des Petites Estampilles," which was active in the late fourth and early third centuries BCE. Later types of pottery originating from central-western Italy, such as the Campanian A ware of the third and second centuries, were exported to the same areas but in much larger quantities.

Interestingly, the rise of commercial agriculture in Roman Italy appears to have had no discernible impact on existing attitudes towards trade, which were overwhelmingly negative. The main reason for this was that the marketing of agricultural surpluses could be conceptualized as a logical extension of "agriculture" and therefore as being entirely compatible with traditional elite values. This ideological strategy is reflected by the contents of the *lex Claudia de nave senatorum* of 218 BCE, which declared it forbidden for senators and their sons to own ships having a capacity of more than 300 amphoras. As Livy (21.63) comments, the idea behind this law was that it was all right for senators to own ships large enough to carry the produce of their estates but that it was dishonorable for them to dirty their hands by pursuing commercial profit (*quaestus*). We are also told that this law was carried against the wishes of the vast majority of the Senate. (On the contents and background of this law see e.g. Guarino 1982; Bringmann 2003. The evidence does not support the latter's view that the law was issued with the aim of barring senators from the transportation of troops and military supplies.) This might be taken to suggest that many senators found the provision of the *lex Claudia* too restrictive. There are, however, no indications of an attempt being made to question the underlying ideology by advocating a more positive conception of production for the market.

Late republican attitudes towards trade and traders are summed up in an often-quoted passage from Cicero's *De officiis* where we read that "large-scale trade is not to be greatly censured." In fact, "those involved in it even deserve the highest respect," but only if they withdraw from commerce and invest their profits into land (Cic. *De off.* 1.150–151). There is no reason to doubt that this view was shared by most of Cicero's fellow aristocrats. It is an entirely different matter whether negative attitudes towards trade dissuaded members of the Roman elite to finance trading ventures. Cato the Elder famously encouraged his debtors to form a *societas* operating fifty ships, with Cato taking a single share in the name of his freedman Quintio (Plut. *Cat. Mai.* 21). This set-up, which did not contravene the provisions of the *lex Claudia*, allowed Cato to reap large profits at minimal risk. In short, senators and other members of the Roman elite could feel free to reap substantial profits from commercial activities but only if they used middlemen to do the dirty work.

Alongside such middlemen we encounter many examples of Roman and Italian merchants without discernible ties with senators, *equites* or members of local elites. This type of merchant is well represented in the epigraphic record of Delos, where references to traders from central and southern Italy multiply after 167 BCE (Hatzfeld 1919). The inscriptions from Delos prove that social prejudice towards trade and traders did not stop Romans and Italians from becoming actively involved in profitable commercial activities. It also appears, however, that none of these traders belonged to the political elites of their hometowns. The evidence from Delos does not therefore in any way undermine the prevailing view that political power in Roman Italy continued to rest with aristocrats who defined themselves as a landowning elite, which was not supposed to dabble in any type of commerce other than the sale of crops grown on their rural estates.

Given the marginality of commerce in the ideology of the Roman upper class, one would not expect to find much evidence for Roman politicians or generals intervening in the interests of Roman or Italian merchants. Yet the surviving sources contain a couple of texts that seem to fit this description. An early example is a passage from Polybius relating to the origin of the First Illyrian War, which started in 229 BCE. We are told that after the Illyrians had long been in the habit of attacking ships sailing from Italy, the Senate decided to send an embassy to the Illyrian king Agron to complain about these depredations (Polyb. 2.8.1–3). When no satisfaction was given a Roman army was sent to Illyria. Another well-known example concerns the outbreak of the war against Iugurtha in 111 BCE. According to Sallust, when the town Cirta came under attack, the Italian businessmen (*negotiatores*) were confident that they would remain unharmed "because of the prestige of Rome." Unfortunately for them, Iugurtha decided to massacre not only all adult Numidian men but all traders carrying weapons as well. The Senate reacted by declaring war (Sal. *Iug.* 26.1–27.3; cf. Roselaar 2012: 149).

While these examples demonstrate that attacks on Roman or Italian merchants played a part in the outbreak of at least some wars, it does not follow that these wars were fought to secure markets or even to safeguard the commercial interests of merchants originating from Roman or allied communities. It seems more plausible that all military or diplomatic interventions undertaken on behalf of Roman or Italian merchants were prompted by the widely shared view that the political elite of Rome, especially the Senate, had to protect the lives and interests of all Roman citizens and of all citizens of allied communities, including merchants (Cf. Andreau 1994: 89). In other words, if Roman or Italian merchants wanted to prompt the central Roman government into action, they had to support their request by appealing to general political principles.

Interestingly, the only new "economic" group which gained considerable political clout in republican times was the *publicani*, a sub-group of the *equites*. The defining feature of the *publicani* was that they carried out various activities of "public" significance, such as road-building, supplying Roman armies with certain food items, the management of various types of public property, such as mines or lakes, and the collection of various indirect taxes, such as the pasture tax owed by those grazing more than a certain number of animals on state-owned land. In some older publications the *publicani* are characterized as a class of "businessmen" with interest differing from those of senators and *equites* holding most of their wealth in the form of land. Against this theory it has been pointed out that all *publicani* were major landowners (Brunt 1988a: 162–164; for good discussions of the juridical aspects of the *societates publicanorum* of late republican and early imperial times see Cimma 1981; Malmendier 2002). Any attempt to create an opposition between "entrepreneurial" and landowning *equites* must therefore be regarded as misleading.

It remains the case that opportunities to make money from contracts relating to the performance of public tasks increased during the final decades of the second century BCE and that the *publicani* became a powerful interest group in this period. The crucial turning point came in 123 BCE, when Gaius Gracchus issued two laws tailored to the political and material interests of the *equites*. The first of these laws gave the *equites* exclusive control over the *repetundae* courts, which dealt which cases of extortion by provincial governors; the other gave them the right to farm the direct and indirect taxes of the province of Asia, an area known for its wealth (judicial legislation: Brunt 1988b: 194–239; Mackay 1994; *lex de provincia Asia*: Merola 2001: 34–40). The tax-farming business could be combined with the extension of loans to defaulting communities, often at extortionate rates of interest. Meanwhile the publicans could lean on their friends in the *repetundae* courts to create trouble for any provincial governor trying to protect the tax-payers. A notorious case was the trial of Publius Rutilius Rufus, who tried to scale down levels of extortion when serving as *legatus proconsulis* in Asia in 94 BCE. After his return to Italy the jurors of the *repetundae* court found him guilty of corruption, after which he retired from Italy, first to Mytilene and then to the Asian city of Smyrna (Val. Max. 2.10.5 and 6.4.4). In 81 BCE a law of Sulla gave senators exclusive control over the *repetundae* courts, but eleven years later the *equites* regained two-thirds of the seats. Following this political success, the publicans remained a powerful group until 47 BCE, when the direct taxes of Asia ceased to be farmed out to them (for Caesar's reform see App. *B. civ.* 5.4; Dio 42.6; Plut. *Caes.* 48).

Taken in conjunction, the republican evidence suggests that the expansion of Roman and Italian commerce during the last three centuries BCE, rather than giving rise to a more positive assessment of trade and traders, prompted the political elite of Rome to reaffirm the ideological supremacy of landownership (see Jaeger, Chapter 5, on the importance of agrarian elements for Rome's founding identity). It is true that imperial expansion prompted some new "enactments" reflecting the material interests of the *publicani*, but as we have just seen, the main "business activities" undertaken by these people were tax collection and moneylending rather than trade.

4 Consumption

Despite the existence of legendary tales about destitute aristocrats owning no more than 7 *iugera* of arable land (see Jaeger, Chapter 5), there can be no doubt that profound distinctions in wealth existed in early republican Rome. Recent excavations, such as that undertaken at the Auditorium site, have confirmed the existence of large farmhouses at an early date, and if the tradition concerning the *lex Licinia* of 367 BCE can be trusted, landholdings measuring 500 *iugera* had been created some considerable time before the Roman conquest of Latium and Campania (for the suburban villa at the Auditorium site see Terrenato 2001). Of course the internal structure of the *comitia centuriata* of mid-republican times, with its five property classes (see Mouritsen, Chapter 9), also presupposes the existence of a society that was fairly steeply stratified in terms of wealth.

Changes in lifestyles and consumption patterns outside elite circles are badly documented, but there can be no doubt that the period 510–31 BCE witnessed some important developments that belong under this heading. At least some changes in patterns of consumption among wide sections of the population of Roman Italy reflect shifts in the relative importance of the various crops that could be grown on arable land. A well-known example is the progressive spread of the cultivation of various types of wheat at the expense of emmer (Latin *far*) and barley. Since wheat, especially soft wheat, was more suitable for bread-making than the traditional crops of archaic Rome, this evolution meant that less and less grain was consumed in the form of porridge (*puls*) (Spurr 1986 remains the best discussion of grain farming in Roman Italy). Even at this mundane level we must keep in mind the continued relevance of social distinctions. While the urban members of the Roman elite, and the ever-increasing population of the capital, clearly preferred high-quality bread made of wheat, many poorer citizens may have continued to consume large amounts of barley, which was about 50 percent cheaper (although it should be noted that Cato gave rations of wheat to his agricultural slaves: Cato *DA* 56).

Starting with the promulgation of the *lex Sempronia frumentaria* of 123 BCE, wheat began to be sold at a subsidized price to Roman citizens living in Rome. During the final decades of the Republic a far more generous scheme involving up to 320,000 recipients of free hand-outs came into existence. Caesar cut down the number of beneficiaries to 150,000. A couple of decades later, when their number had crept up again, Augustus introduced a *numerus clausus* of 200,000. But neither Caesar nor the first emperor dared to abolish the *frumentationes* (although Suetonius claims the latter contemplated this step), evidently because they regarded it as a political impossibility to disregard the "consumer interests" of the citizen population of the imperial capital. (For the historical evolution of the *frumentationes* see Garnsey 1988: 211–214 and 236–237; abolishment of grain doles contemplated by Augustus: Suet. *Aug.* 42.3.)

Various other clues suggest further changes in patterns and levels of consumption which never became politicized in the same way as wheat consumption in Rome. It seems a safe bet, for instance, that *per capita* levels of wine consumption increased as viticulture continued to expand between the sixth and first centuries BCE. There are also indications that the growth of urban populations in the last two centuries BCE stimulated the production of cheap wines (Purcell 1985). Another interesting topic is the historical evolution of meat consumption. Based on the chronological distribution of mammal bones excavated at rural sites across Italy it has been suggested that levels of meat consumption went up from about 300 BCE (King 1999; Jongman 2007: 190–192).

It remains exceedingly difficult to establish whether the changes just referred to imply a higher standard of living for the majority of the population of Roman Italy. It is true that we have good evidence for the existence of a fairly large group of moderately well-off country-dwelling citizens in mid-republican times (e.g. Rosenstein 2004: 163–164). The hundreds of thousands of veterans who benefited from the generous land distribution schemes of Sulla, Caesar, and the *triumviri* must also have belonged to this group (de Ligt 2012: 274–275). Furthermore it seems likely enough that the so-called urban *plebs media* of the early Empire started to develop during the final centuries of the Republic.

While the surviving evidence does not allow us to assess the relative importance of such middling groups, it is even more difficult to discern long-term trends in *per capita* levels of consumption in the entire citizen population. One possible way forward is to look at changes in average or mean body height between the early fifth and late first centuries BCE. Some years ago Jongman published an article that argued that the rise of Roman power, first in Italy and subsequently in the entire Mediterranean world and in northwest Europe, was accompanied by a spectacular increase in human stature as revealed by skeletal evidence (Kron 2005; Jongman 2007: 194). He inferred from this that the period 200 BCE–160 CE must have witnessed a very significant rise in *per capita* income and expenditure, in other words, very considerable economic growth. When larger amounts of bone evidence were examined, however, it appeared that these inferences do not apply to Italy. In fact, a recent study by Giannecchini and Moggi-Cecchi strongly suggests that Italian males of the Roman period were actually a bit *shorter* than those of the Iron Age (Giannecchini and Moggi-Cecchi 2008).

Any attempt to use changes in the average or mean body height of Italians as proxy evidence for increases or decreases in levels of consumption is complicated by the fact that the final decades of the Republic witnessed a fast expansion of cities in most parts of Italy. Since large cities were ideal environments for the spread of all kinds of infectious diseases that had a negative impact on the development of human bodies, we must reckon with the possibility that the Italian bone evidence might reflect a decrease in medical standards of living. Such a decrease might have taken place independently of any changes in material standards of living (Gowland and Garnsey 2010). In short, while we can be certain that the last two centuries BCE saw an increase in levels of expenditure and consumption well beyond elite circles, the evidence available at present is not sufficient to back up the theory that this period witnessed a general increase in levels of consumption benefiting the vast majority of the population of Roman Italy (in favor of rising (economic) standards of living: Scheidel 2007, but see Scheidel 2009 for a cautious reassessment of this issue).

While the issue of long-term changes in average living standards can only be studied on the basis of archaeological data sets, changes in consumption patterns among the political and social elite of republican Rome receive ample attention in the literary sources. As we have seen, there can be no doubt that substantial differences in wealth and income existed in regal and early republican Rome, and it seems reasonable to suppose that these differences were matched by distinctions in levels and patterns of consumption. Nonetheless, the admittedly fragmentary evidence suggests that the lifestyles of most members of the senatorial elite remained relatively simple until the late third or early second century BCE. In 275 BCE it was still possible for the censors to remove Publius Cornelius Rufus from the Senate because he had acquired silver vessels weighing 10 Roman pounds (3.23 kg) (Val. Max. 2.9.14; cf. Gell. 4.8.7.). A century later Cato the Elder was still admired for his frugal lifestyle but only because it was quickly becoming exceptional (Plut. *Cat. Mai.*, 4).

According to Livy, the triumphal parade of Gnaeus Manlius Vulso, held in 187 BCE to celebrate military successes against the Galatians, marked the beginning of the spread of luxury (*luxuria*). Having described the expensive furniture and tapestries that were carried through the streets of Rome on this occasion, he comments that "the origin of foreign luxury was introduced in Rome by the army from Asia" (Livy 39.6–7). It is probably no coincidence that later surveys of republican anti-luxury laws (*leges sumptuariae*), such as that compiled by the early fifth-century writer Macrobius, start with the *lex Orchia* of 182 BCE. We are told that Gaius Orchius, one of the tribunes of the *plebs*, was prompted by the Senate to propose a law that limited the number of guests that could be invited to dinner (*cena*). Twenty-one years later, a *senatus consultum* prescribed that the "leading statesmen" (*principes civitatis*) were to swear an oath that they would not spend more than 120 *asses* (forty times the daily wage of a Roman legionary) on banquets held at the time of the *ludi Megalenses*, and that only Italian wine would be served during these banquets (Macr. *Sat.* 3.17; cf. the extensive surveys of the Roman republican sumptuary laws by Sauerwein 1970 and Baltrusch 1989).

Later in the same year a *lex Fannia* laid down far stricter rules by limiting the number of guests that could be invited to dinner to three on ordinary days and five on market days, and by limiting expenditure on dinners to 100 *asses* per day. Various authors report that this law was evaded on a massive scale, leading to the introduction of a *lex Didia* (issued in 143 BCE), which extended its applicability to Roman citizens living outside Rome. Further laws, all regulating expenditure on dinners, were passed in 115, 102, 81, 70, 46, and 18 BCE.

The amount of legislation dealing with dinners stands in sharp contrast to the dearth of sumptuary legislation focusing on other types of extravagant expenditure. At first sight the *lex Oppia* of 215 BCE, which declared it forbidden for Roman women to "have" (meaning "to wear"?) more than half an ounce of gold jewelry or to wear colored clothing might seem to be an important exception, but the majority view is that this law was passed as an austerity measure to increase or express civic solidarity at a critical stage in the Second Punic War (Culham 1982). This would help to explain why, unlike any other piece of sumptuary legislation, this law was abolished in 195 BCE.

Livy's comments on the triumphal parade of 187 BCE belong to a moralizing discourse in which "foreign" luxury is held responsible for undermining traditional Roman *virtus* and as setting in motion a process of moral decline that would ultimately destroy the Republic (see Gruen 1992 for a wide-ranging discussion of cultural interaction with the Greek-speaking east as a catalyst for (re)formulations of Roman identity during the late third and second centuries BCE). At the same time, they hint at the existence of a causal connection between Roman imperialism and changes in lifestyles. Modern accounts use a completely different terminology to describe the complex transformations that took place in Roman-Italian society during the final centuries of the Republic. Nonetheless, most of them would accept that the successful campaigns to the Greek-speaking east had a dramatic impact on levels and patterns of elite income and expenditure.

While the timing of the sumptuary laws of the second century BCE poses few problems, modern historians have had a harder time finding a convincing explanation for the fact that these laws dealt quasi-exclusively with expenditure on food. One popular theory is that some of the new wealth generated by the military successes of the early second century was used for competitive expenditure on dinners and that the sumptuary laws of the second century BCE reflect a deeply felt concern about recent divergences in elite life styles and about a concomitant loss of social cohesion among senators and *equites* (Slob 1986: 182). It has, moreover, been pointed out that competitive expenditure on dinners must have put pressure on those members of the elite who did not want to spend large amounts of money on entertaining numerous guests at their dinner tables. The introduction of sumptuary laws might have been prompted by the wish to alleviate this kind of peer pressure (Daube 1969).

These considerations are certainly valuable. They do not, however, fully explain why the soaring costs of dinners were seen as more problematic than other kinds of competitive expenditure. In an article that addresses precisely this problem, Gabba suggests that the introduction of laws curbing expenditure on lavish dinners was seen as especially urgent because, unlike the acquisition of silver tableware or extravagant houses, this type of expenditure resulted in a permanent and irreversible diminution of private property. He concludes that the sumptuary laws of the last two centuries BCE should be seen as a form of aristocratic self-regulation aimed at ensuring the continuity of family fortunes and family power (Gabba 1981: 38–41).

A slightly different explanation is to be found in Catherine Edwards' *The Politics of Immorality in Ancient Rome*. Noting the centrality of foreign and expensive types of food in republican debates concerning "immoral" types of consumption, she observes that for Roman writers of the last two centuries BCE the delights of the dinner table seem to have epitomized the ephemeral nature of the pleasure that extravagant expenditure could buy (Edwards 1993: 186). While these observations contain an important element of truth, it is important not to lose sight of the social and political aspects of elite expenditure. At this point I would like to call attention to the fact that the republican sumptuary laws have close parallels in fourteenth-century Italy. One example is a Florentine law of 1330 prescribing that no more than forty guests were to be invited to wedding banquets and that no more than three courses were to be served to each of these guests. The same maximum numbers for guests and dishes are to be found in a Sienese law of 1343, but this law contained additional provisions concerning meals served after funerals: no more than thirty relatives of the deceased were to be invited to these meals and only one course was to be served (on these laws see Redon 1992: 111–112, 114–118). As the French historian Jacques Heers pointed out many years ago, the aim of such laws was to curb competition among powerful families who were in the habit of organizing large-scale dinners to extend their *clientela* networks (Heers 1977).

It does not seem far-fetched to suppose that Roman sumptuary laws such as the *lex Orchia* and the *lex Fannia* were prompted by similar considerations (de Ligt 2002, 2003; cf. also Dauster 2004; Rosivach 2006/7; Lonardi 2007). One argument in favor of such a reading is that networks of "friends" and "clients," however defined or conceptualized, are known to have played an important part in the social and political life of the Roman Republic. Secondly, the parallel evidence from Renaissance Italy provides us with a convincing explanation for the curious fact that the mid- and late republican sumptuary laws contained countless provisions concerning numbers of guests, types of food, and expenditure on dinners but hardly any regulations concerning other types of private expenditure. Finally, the series of sumptuary laws that started in 182 BCE runs parallel to a succession of laws dealing with political bribery (*ambitus*) (on these laws see Nadig 1997; Stolle 1999). It seems too much of a coincidence that a long series of *leges de ambitu* started in 180 BCE, only two years after the passing of the *lex Orchia*, and ended in 18 BCE, the year that also saw the introduction of the last sumptuary law, the *lex Iulia sumptuaria*.

In view of this striking parallelism it might be suggested that we are dealing with legislation trying to curb two types of behavior aimed at converting material wealth into political support, namely outright bribery of the electorate in the case of the *leges de ambitu* and attempts to multiply politically useful friendships in the case of the *leges sumptuariae*. Under the Principate many authors continued to express their concern about the corrupting effects of luxury, yet no new legislation was deemed necessary. The obvious explanation is that elite expenditure on extravagant dinners had ceased to be politically relevant.

5 Conclusion

The principal aim of this chapter has been to highlight the innumerable connections between Roman imperialism and a wide range of social and economic developments. While distinctions in wealth and disputes over rights of access to newly conquered land fueled political conflicts in early republican Rome, the ongoing conquests of the fourth and third centuries eventually made it possible to defuse internal tensions by abolishing *nexum* and using extensive tracts of newly conquered land for distribution. The price of these solutions was paid by outsiders who were deprived either of their farms or their freedom or both. Ideologically, the Roman elite continued to celebrate the superiority of farming over all other forms of economic activity, an attitude which could easily be combined with disdain for manual labor in the fields (see also Jaeger, Chapter 5).

When the volume of commerce increased, in part because agricultural production became increasingly market-orientated, attempts were made to reaffirm the traditional connection between landed wealth, social standing, and political power. Senators were prohibited from engaging in large-scale commerce. Large-scale commerce carried out by professional merchants could be seen as a respectable activity, but the acquisition of landed property remained the only route to high social standing and political power. In so far as diplomatic or military interventions were undertaken against those who had harmed Roman or Italian traders, this was invariably done not because the government of republican Rome felt a special responsibility for commercial entrepreneurs but because it was supposed to look after the interests of all Roman citizens and after those of its Italian allies, even if they were merchants.

Starting with the *lex Sempronia frumentaria* of 123 BCE, various Roman politicians initiated schemes that gave Roman citizens living in Rome access first to subsidized grain and later to free hand-outs. Part of the explanation must be that private hand-outs given by members of the Roman elite no longer sufficed to feed the growing population of Rome. At the same time the fact that Rome remained the epicenter of political life made it difficult to ignore the "consumer interests" of those of its inhabitants who happened to be of citizen status.

It is more difficult to establish whether the enormous increase in the amount of resources that began to flow to Italy after the first round of expeditions to Greece and Asia had a positive effect on the average standard of living of the majority of the Italian population. In recent years various scholars have asserted that this was indeed the case, but in view of the methodological problems posed by the interpretation of the archaeological evidence on which their claim rests it seems wiser to suspend judgment on this issue.

What can be said with confidence is that the conquests of the last two centuries BCE boosted elite income in a spectacular way. This prompted major cultural worries over the socially and politically disruptive effects of elite expenditure on dinners. These concerns found their way into a long series of sumptuary laws whose impact on actual behavior seems to have been negligible. An intellectually more sophisticated response is to be found in early imperial writers. In their view the spread of luxury had undermined traditional Roman values, thereby paving the way for the self-seeking politicians and generals who brought about the fall of the Roman Republic.

REFERENCES

Andreau, J. 1994. "La cité romaine dans ses rapports à l'échange et au monde de l'échange." In *Économie antique. Les échanges dans l'Antiquité: le rôle de l'état*. Saint-Bertrand-de-Comminges, 83–98.

Aubert, J.-J. 1994. *Business Managers in Ancient Rome: A Social and Economic Study of Institores 200 BC–AD 250*. Leiden.

Baltrusch, E. 1989. *Regimen morum: Die Reglementierung des Privatlebens der Senatoren und Ritter in der römischen Republik und frühen Kaiserzeit*. Munich.

Bradley, G. 2006. "Colonization and Identity in Republican Italy." In J.-P. Wilson and G. Bradley, eds., *Greek and Roman Colonization: Origins, Ideologies and Interactions*. Swansea, 161–187.

Bringmann, K. 2003. "Zur Überlieferung und zum Entstehungsgrund der 'lex Claudia de nave senatoris.'" *Klio* 85: 312–321.

Brunt, P. 1988a. "The Equites in the Late Republic." In *The Fall of the Roman Republic and Related Essays*. Oxford, 144–193.

Brunt, P. 1988b. "Judiciary Rights in the Republic." In *The Fall of the Roman Republic and Related Essays*. Oxford, 194–239.

Capogrossi Colognesi, L. 1988. "La città e la sua terra." In A. Momigliano and A. Schiavone, eds., *Storia di Roma I: Roma in Italia*. Turin, 263–289.

Capogrossi Colognesi, L. 1994. "*Ager publicus* e *ager gentilicius* nella riflessione storiografica moderna." In *Proprietà e signoria in Roma antica Rome*. Rome, 93–139.

Càssola, F. 1988. "Aspetti sociali e politici della colonizzazione." *DArch*, 3rd ser. 6(2): 5–17.

Champion, C.B., ed. 2004. *Roman Imperialism: Readings and Sources*. Oxford and Malden, MA.

Cimma, M.R. 1981. *Ricerche sulle società di publicani*. Milan.

Cornell, T. 1995. *The Beginnings of Rome: Italy and Rome from the Bronze Age to the Punic Wars (c.1000–264 BC)*. London.

Coşkun, A. 2009. *Bürgerrechtsentzug oder Fremdenausweisung? Studien zu den Rechten von Latinern und weiteren Fremden sowie zum Bürgerrechtswechsel in der Römischen Republik (5. bis frühes 1. Jh. v.Chr.)*. Stuttgart.

Culham, P. 1982. "The *Lex Oppia*." *Latomus* 41: 786–793.

Daube, D. 1969. "The Protection of the Non-Tipper." In *Roman Law: Linguistic, Social and Philosophical Aspects*. Edinburgh, 117–128.

Dauster, M. 2004. "Roman Republican Sumptuary Legislation." In *Studies in Latin Literature and Roman History 11*. Brussels, 65–93.

De Ligt, L. 1999. "Legal History and Economic History: The Case of the *Actiones Adiecticiae*." *Tijdschrift voor Rechtsgeschiedenis* 67: 205–226.

De Ligt, L. 2000. "Governmental Attitudes towards Markets and *Collegia*." In E. Lo Cascio, ed., *Mercati permanenti e mercati periodici nel mondo romano*. Bari, 237–252.

De Ligt, L. 2002. "Restraining the Rich, Protecting the Poor: Symbolic Aspects of Roman Legislation." In W. Jongman and M. Kleijwegt, eds., *After the Past: Essays in Honour of H.W. Pleket*. Leiden, 1–45.

De Ligt, L. 2003. "De Romeinse *leges sumptuariae* in vergelijkend perspectief." In J. Blok, J.-J. Flinterman, and L. de Ligt, eds., *Tesserae Romanae: Opstellen aangeboden aan Hans Teitler*. Utrecht, 9–22.

De Ligt, L. 2006. "The Economy: Agrarian Change during the Second Century." In N. Rosenstein and R. Morstein Marx, eds., *A Companion to the Roman Republic*. Oxford, 590–605.

De Ligt, L. 2012. *Peasants, Citizens and Soldiers: Studies in the Demographic History of Roman Italy 225 BC–AD 100*. Cambridge.

De Neeve, P.W. 1984. *Colonus: Private Farm-Tenancy in Roman Italy during the Republic and Early Empire*. Amsterdam.

Di Paolo, M. 1996. "Alle origini della *lex Poetelia de nexis*." *Index* 24: 275–288.

Edwards, C. 1993. *The Politics of Immorality in Ancient Rome*. Cambridge.

Fascione, L. 2009. "L'ambitus e la Pro Plancio." In B. Santalucia, ed., *La repressione criminale nella Roma repubblicana fra norma e persuasione*. Pavia, 357–382.

Feig Vishnia, R. 1996. *State, Society and Popular Leaders in Mid-Republican Rome, 241–167 BC*. London.

Finley, M.I. 1980. *Ancient Slavery and Modern Ideology*. London; revised by B. Shaw (Princeton, 1998).

Finley, M.I. 1981. "Debt-Bondage and the Problem of Slavery." In B.D. Shaw and R.P. Saller, eds., *Economy and Society in Ancient Greece*. London, 150–166.

Forsythe, G. 2007. "The Army and the Centuriate Organization in Early Rome." In P. Erdkamp, ed., *A Companion to the Roman Army*. Oxford, 24–41.

Franciosi, G. 1995. "*Gentes familiam habento*: Una riflessione sulla cd. proprietà gentilizia." In G. Franciosi, ed., *Ricerche sulla organizzazione gentilizia romana*. Naples, 35–49.

Gabba, E. 1978. "Per la tradizione dell'heredium romuleo." *Rendiconti dell'Istituto Lombardo* 112: 250–258.

Gabba, E. 1981. "Richezza e classe dirigente romana fra III e I sec. a.C."; repr. in *Del buon uso della richezza* (Milan, 1988), 27–44.

Garnsey, P. 1976. "Peasants in Ancient Roman Society." *Journal of Peasant Studies* 3: 221–235.

Garnsey, P. 1988. *Famine and Food Supply in the Graeco-Roman World: Responses to Risk and Crisis*. Cambridge.

Giannecchini, M. and J. Moggi-Cecchi. 2008. "Stature in Archaeological Samples from Central Italy: Methodological Issues and Diachronic Changes." *Journal of Physical Anthropology* 135: 284–292.

Gowland, R. and P. Garnsey. 2010. "Skeletal Evidence for Health, Nutritional Status and Malaria in Rome and the Roman Empire." In H.E. Eckard, ed., *Roman Diasporas: Archaeological Approaches to Mobility and Diversity in the Roman Empire*. Portsmouth, RI, 131–156.

Gruen, E. 1992. *Culture and Identity in Republican Rome*. London.

Guarino, A. 1982. "Quaestus omnis patribus indecorus." *Labeo* 28: 7–16.

Harris, W. 2007. "The Late Republic." In W. Scheidel, I. Morris, and R. Saller, eds., *The Cambridge Economic History of the Greco-Roman World*. Cambridge, 511–539.

Hatzfeld, J. 1919. *Les trafiquants italiens dans l'Orient hellénique*. Paris.

Heers, J. 1977. *Family Clans in the Middle Ages: A Study of Political and Social Structures in Urban Areas.* Amsterdam.

Hopkins, K. 1978. *Conquerors and Slaves.* Cambridge.

Jongman, W. 2007. "Gibbon Was Right: The Decline and Fall of the Roman Economy." In O. Hekster, G. de Kleijn, and D. Slootjes, eds., *Crises and the Roman Empire.* Leiden, 183–199.

King, A. 1999. "Diet in the Roman World: A Regional Inter-Site Comparison of the Mammal Bones." *JRA* 12: 168–202.

Kron, G. 2005. "Anthropometry, Physical Anthropology, and the Reconstruction of Ancient Health, Nutrition, and Living Standards." *Historia* 54: 68–83.

Laffi, U. 2007. "La colonizzazione romana." In *Colonie e municipi nello stato romano.* Rome, 15–35.

Lintott, A. 1999. *Violence in Republican Rome.* 2nd edn. Oxford.

Lonardi, A. 2007. "Alimentazione e banchetto: le leggi suntuarie di Silla e Cesare." In R. Bortolin and A. Pistellato, eds., *Alimentazione e banchetto: forme e valori della commensalità dalla preistoria alla tarda antichità.* Venice, 71–88.

Mackay, C. 1994. "The Judicial Legislation of Gaius Sempronius Gracchus." Diss. Harvard University.

Malmendier, U. 2002. *Societas publicanorum: Staatliche Wirtschaftsaktivitäten in den Händen privater Unternehmer.* Vienna.

Mason, G.G. 1992. "The Agrarian Role of *Coloniae Maritimae*: 338–241 B.C." *Historia* 41: 75–87.

Merola, G.D. 2001. *Autonomia locale, governo imperiale: fiscalità e amministrazione nelle province asiane.* Bari.

Mommsen, T. 1887. *Römisches Staatsrecht, III. Bürgerschaft und Senat.* Leipzig.

Morel, J.-P. 2007. "Early Rome and Italy." In W. Scheidel, I. Morris, and R. Saller, eds., *The Cambridge Economic History of the Greco-Roman World.* Cambridge, 487–510.

Nadig, P. 1997. *Ardet ambitus: Untersuchungen zum Phänomen der Wahlbestechungen in der römischen Republik.* Frankfurt am Main.

Oebel, L. 1993. *C. Flaminius und die Anfänge der römischen Kolonisation im "ager Gallicus."* Frankfurt am Main.

Patterson, H. 2006. "Colonization and Historiography: The Roman Republic." In J.-P. Wilson and G. Bradley, eds., *Greek and Roman Colonization: Origins, Ideology and Interactions.* Swansea.

Pelgrom, J. 2012. "Colonial Landscapes: Demography, Settlement Organization and Impact of Colonies Founded by Rome (4th–2nd centuries BC)." Diss. Leiden University.

Purcell, N. 1985. "Wine and Wealth in Ancient Italy." *JRS* 75: 1–19.

Rathbone, D. 1993. "The Census Qualifications of the *assidui* and the *prima classis.*" In H. Sancisi-Weerdenburg et al., eds., *De Agricultura. In Memoriam Pieter Willem de Neeve (1945–1990).* Amsterdam, 121–152.

Redon, O. 1992. "La réglementation des banquets par les lois somptuaires dans les villes d'Italie (XIIIe–XVe siècles)." In C. Lambert, ed., *Du manuscrit à la table: Essais sur la cuisine au Moyen Age et repertoire des manuscrits médiévaux contenant des recettes culinaires.* Montreal and Paris, 109–119.

Rich, J. 2008. "Lex Licinia, Lex Sempronia: B.G. Niebuhr and the Limitation of Landholding in the Roman Republic." In L. de Ligt and S. Northwood, eds., *People, Land and Politics: Demographic Developments and the Transformation of Roman Italy, 300 BC–AD 14.* Leiden, 519–572.

Roselaar, S.T. 2010. *Public Land in the Roman Republic: A Social and Economic History of Ager Publicus in Italy, 396–89 BC.* Oxford.

Roselaar, S. 2012. "Mediterranean Trade as a Mechanism of Integration between Romans and Italians." In S. Roselaar, ed., *Processes of Integration and Identity Formation in the Roman Republic.* Leiden, 141–158.

Rosenstein, N. 2004. *Rome at War: Farms, Families and Death in the Middle Republic.* Chapel Hill and London.

Rosivach, V.J. 2006/7. "The *lex Fannia sumptuaria* of 161 BC." *CJ* 102: 1–15.

Santangelo, F. 2007. *Sulla, the Elites and the Empire.* Leiden.

Sauerwein, I. 1970. *Die leges sumptuariae als römische Massnahme gegen den Sittenverfahl.* Hamburg.

Scheidel, W. 2007. "A Model of Real Income Growth in Roman Italy." *Historia* 56: 322–356.

Scheidel, W. 2008. "The Comparative Economics of Slavery in the Greco-Roman World." In E. Del Lago and C. Katsari, eds., *Slave Systems, Ancient and Modern.* Cambridge, 105–126.

Scheidel, W. 2009. "In Search of Roman Economic Growth." *JRA* 22: 46–70.

Slob, E. 1986. *Luxuria: Regelgeving en maatregelen van censoren ten tijde van de Romeinse Republiek.* Zutphen.

Spurr, M.S. 1986. *Arable Cultivation in Roman Italy, c.200 BC–c.AD 100.* London.

Stolle, R. 1999. *Ambitus et invidia: Römische Politiker im Spannungsfeld zwischen persönlichem Ehrgeiz und Forderungen der Standesloyalität.* Frankfurt am Main.

Tatum, W.J. 1999. *The Patrician Tribune: Publius Clodius Pulcher.* Chapel Hill, NC.

Tchernia, A. 2009. "L'exportation du vin: interpretations actuelles de l'exception gauloise." In J. Carlsen and E. Lo Cascio, eds., *Agricoltura e scambi nell'Italia tardo-repubblicana.* Bari, 91–111.

Terrenato, N. 2001. "The Auditorium Site and the Origins of the Roman Villa." *JRA* 14: 5–32.

Watson, A. 1975. *Rome of the Twelve Tables: Persons and Property.* Princeton.

FURTHER READING

There is no comprehensive account of social and economic developments in republican Rome. Morel (2007) covers the early and middle Republic but is overwhelmingly archaeological. Harris (2007) discusses late republican Italy but is weak on archaeology and on agriculture. Cornell (1995) provides a good discussion of the economic and social structures of early and mid-republican Rome but does not probe very deeply into various technical topics, such as debt bondage (*nexum*) and the rules governing control over *ager publicus.* For the latter topic the reader is referred to Roselaar (2010). Rosenstein (2004) is excellent on relationships between agriculture and warfare during the third and second centuries BCE, his account of these topics being superior to that of Hopkins (1978). On agrarian change during the second century BCE see also de Ligt (2006). On the complex interrelationships between Roman expansion and various social and economic developments see the essays in Champion (2004). Patterson (2006) reassesses the driving forces behind Roman colonization. Most of the recent literature on Roman commerce during the Republic focuses on legal developments or on the spread of various types of amphorae and other categories of pottery. See e.g. Aubert (1994), de Ligt (1999), Tchernia (2009). Most of the recent literature on living standards and the spread of "luxury" is given in the footnotes.

PART XI

Discourses of Inclusion and Exclusion

CHAPTER 22

Women and Slaves in Greek Democracy

Ryan K. Balot and Larissa M. Atkison

1 Introduction: Recovering Diverse "Outsiders"

Slaves, foreigners, and "metics" (resident aliens) were always excluded from the central activities of participatory citizenship in ancient Greece—that is, rendering judgment in legal cases and taking part in political decision-making. At least until the Hellenistic monarchies, the same held true for women, too; and even in those later and very different times, women's political power was based on royal status rather than a participatory ethic (on the legal status of women, see also Cohen, Chapter 10). It is important that the Greeks' exclusiveness in the political realm did not extend to the social, religious, or economic spheres of the *polis*: in all these areas, diverse "outsiders" could play central roles, as agricultural laborers and vendors in the marketplace, as wealthy bankers and high-ranking priestesses, and as celebrated courtesans, educators, and managers of household wealth (see also Cohen, Chapter 10). Certainly these "outsiders" always exercised informal power over citizens themselves, as mothers or sisters, as familial caretakers, and as friends and confidants of Greek citizens themselves. Such figures are most familiar, not so much from the historical record of daily life, as from the panhellenic poetry of the archaic period: think of the powerful and wise Penelope of Homer's *Odyssey* or the poet Sappho or Odysseus' loyal servant, Eumaeus the swineherd. At the same time, the case of Sparta, as often, proved to be unusual: many contemporaries, such as Aristotle, found fault with the high status of Sparta's women, while the city's state-owned slaves ("helots") differed from the ordinary chattel slaves of most other Greek *poleis*. Despite Spartan exceptionalism, however, it remains fair to say that, throughout archaic and classical Greece, men jealously guarded the privileges associated with their military and political roles, but, in both imaginative literature and in social life, they continually negotiated the statuses and roles of these outsiders, often communicating in the process a palpable sense of anxiety.

A Companion to Greek Democracy and the Roman Republic, First Edition. Edited by Dean Hammer.

Because of their exclusion from all forms of political power and familial authority, and because of their limited opportunities for education, these outsiders only rarely found an opportunity to represent themselves to the world as they desired. Hence, they surface in our sources infrequently, and in oblique ways dominated by the concerns of the male citizen elite. Nonetheless, scholars have begun to lay bare their particular contributions to civic practice and even, in certain cases, to recover their own self-understandings. For these purposes classical Athens provides our most extensive evidence, and it is there that scholars have been most successful at identifying the diverse character of those outside the participatory civic world. Edward Cohen, for example, has argued that household management and economic activity were mostly left to women and slaves, because traditional ideals of *andreia* excluded men from economic activity (Cohen 2003: 145; cf. Arendt 1998; Goff 2004: 25–76). Sara Forsdyke has reconstructed a cultural history of slaves to argue that women, slaves, and foreigners contributed to Greek social and political life through "a range of popular practices and discourses, including festival revelry, storytelling, and the spontaneous collective punishment of social offenders" (2012: 176). Barbara Goff, likewise, has recovered the history of women's ritual activity as it "constitutes women as its subjects"; Goff's work illustrates the ways in which ritual activity "conversely organizes female identity in order to subject it to the requirements of a male dominated society" (2004: 15; cf. Gould 1980; Just 1991). Together these scholars have shown that Athenian identities were constructed in opposition to both outsiders and "outsiders within," but in multiple ways—not only through rigid exclusions and binaries, but also through a more porous process of receptivity and incorporation of aspects of the other's identity.

Our aim is to build on this work and to show that representations of these outsiders both challenged and reinforced Greek participatory practices and identity formation. Again, the case of Athens—both unusual in certain respects and typical in others—will help to make clear how these processes worked at local sites of contestation and negotiation. How did Athenian representations of "others" contribute to an implicitly deliberative process in which normative conceptions of manliness and citizenship were held up for scrutiny, challenged, and refined? The Athenians advanced their deliberative work dialectically, through the self-critical and yet self-affirming mediums of tragedy, comedy, epitaphic oratory, and philosophy. This openness to dialectical self-criticism was a defining feature of the search for virtue, excellence, and self-understanding that characterized Athenian democracy (Balot 2009). To say this is not of course to idealize a political world founded on androcentric, slave-holding, and exclusionary orthodoxies. Yet, in Athenian reflections on the "other," we often find certain reasons to hope, insofar as these reflections provided new avenues of contestation, self-criticism, and self-knowledge (see also Cohen, Chapter 10).

We begin with Athenian tragedy, one of the most fertile sites for the interpretation of citizenship as a form of identity negotiated with and against such outsiders. Having illustrated tragedy's multiple engagements with the "other," we then explore the ideology of Athenian citizenship as embodied in Athenian epitaphic oratory—the surviving funeral orations. Even in this most explicitly "patriotic" of genres—speeches delivered to commemorate fallen soldiers—we observe civic identities being fabricated through altercations with and exclusions of non-citizens. Finally, against the backdrop of these representations, which were deeply entrenched within civic life, we investigate the novel challenges posed by Plato and Aristotle: who was to be marginal, after all, and why?

2 Athens' Tragic Theater: A Site for Critical Reflection on Citizenship

Performed in 472 BCE, eight years after the battle of Salamis, Aeschylus' *Persians* provides an unusually direct commentary on recent Athenian history (cf. Podlecki 1966; Harrison 2000). As Edith Hall has argued, the play provides a caricature of barbarian society and expresses strong disapproval of Persia's "hierarchialism, its immoderate luxuriousness, and its unrestrained emotionalism" (1989: 80). The Great King Xerxes laments like a Greek woman after rashly leading the Persian army to defeat (1040–1076); Persian society supports the ignorant and crass materialism of Queen Atossa, who concerns herself excessively with wealth and luxury (59–72, 237, 845–850) but knows nothing about the war in which her country is engaged (231–245); at Persia one also finds the historical revisionism and self-ignorance of the ghost of the dead King Darius (762–781); and, finally, the poet emphasizes the servile rejection of reason by the chorus—who, as a quasi-deliberative body enslaved to the Great King, stand in striking contrast to democratic participatory practices. In these dramatic representations, the play brings together the three forms of "outsiderism" most relevant to our inquiry: foreigners or "barbarians," women, and slaves. It highlights the contrast between the character of "barbarian" Persia and the democratic virtues of deliberation (Balot 2014). It blames the Persian defeat on effeminate and weak leadership, while depicting the Persian people itself as slavish. Aeschylus' tragic theater both affirmed a self-serving and patriotic narrative and taught the Athenians to comprehend more deeply the dignity, worth, and usefulness of their own political practices. In brief, even the robustly "ideological" *Persians* constituted the Theater of Dionysos as a theater of civic self-knowledge for the Athenians (see Balot 2014).

The chorus, in particular, reveals a great deal about Athenian attitudes toward both foreigners and slaves. Though self-identified as "trusted" counselors of the king (2, trans. Sommerstein), these men are servile and squeamish, lacking even a minimal understanding of political causation or power. While they demonstrate reasonable anxiety that Persia's aggressive military strategy is unsustainable (93–137), they attribute their fear not to the destructive logic of imperialism or to historical precedent (224), but to the possibility that Persia may encounter ruin due to the "the guileful deception of a god" (94, trans. Sommerstein). When asked by Queen Atossa for "good advice" (172, trans. Sommerstein), they suppress even these reasonable anxieties, affirming instead their desire simply to obey her command (173–174). When Atossa informs them of her premonitory dream foreshadowing Xerxes' defeat, they hide their anxiety and forecast, on the basis of their "intelligence" (224), that things will "turn out well for you in every way" (224–225, trans. Sommerstein). Their form of civic participation is limited to reinforcing traditional hierarchies and to reasserting, despite their own doubts, the conventional (if highly misleading) patriotic narratives that sustain those hierarchies.

Yet the members of the chorus also show that they possess the intellectual resources needed to break free from those mystifying narratives. When pressed by the queen for additional information, the chorus says openly that the Greeks are a formidable foe; they constitute both a sizeable and a proficient fighting force (236). The chorus recognizes the military importance of the Greeks' being both well armed and free. When asked by Atossa if this freedom will not make them easier to conquer, they point out that their freedom was no obstacle to destroying "the large and splendid army of Darius" (244, trans. Sommerstein). Despite the political pressures limiting their free speech and independent thought, the chorus apparently possesses all the factual and interpretative elements necessary to making prudent decisions; but the political environment prevents the old men from uniting these elements into a coherent and satisfying whole.

The chorus' anxieties are, of course, quickly confirmed, as a messenger arrives on the scene to announce the destruction of Xerxes' army and the defeat of the once wealthy and prosperous kingdom (249–255). They—and the audience—come to understand Xerxes' many critical failures of judgment. He trusted enemy intelligence and led his army into a strategically fatal position in the Hellespont (364–432) and on the island of Psyttaleia (456–771). Yet, while the messenger unequivocally highlights these failures (355–360) and Atossa focuses her blame on Xerxes (473–477; cf. 331–332), the chorus publicly blames the cruelty of the god (280–283, 515–516, 532–536). It is only when Atossa exits the stage that they reveal their authentic belief that "Xerxes handled everything unwisely" (552, trans. Sommerstein). Yet no sooner do they blame Xerxes than they retreat to a suspect image of Persian security under Darius (554–555). It is striking how quickly they forget that Darius too suffered a great loss to Greek forces (cf. Hdt. 6.112–117). Their fickleness and incoherence result directly from the culture's failure to provide a meaningful framework for honest deliberation and open civic participation.

Their self-deception is perpetuated by the ghost of dead King Darius who, predictably, provides an idealization of the past: he situates himself in a long line of glorious monarchs (759–781; cf. Hdt. 3.61–97), while offering little guidance to those struggling with the current affair (Balot 2014). He does not, for example, acknowledge a connection between his own military aggression and that of his son (765–786, 750–751). Atossa equally glorifies the reign of her god-like husband (709–714), while dismissing Xerxes' military expedition as a childish response to the teasing and shaming of short-sighted men (753–758). Perpetuated by the Persian leaders, and internalized by the people, these delusions also inflame the chorus' tendency to retreat from reality. They refer to the dead king as "godlike" (160, 651, 855–856), as the father "who never harmed us" (664, 671, 855–856, trans. Sommerstein), and as a leader who sacked many cities and ruled the Ionian Greeks with his "wisdom" (853–902). Just as they begin to digest the meaning of Xerxes' defeat (584–590), they fearfully reject the free speech that had seemingly been within reach (591–592). Happy and even unwitting slaves, they have lost the very desire for freedom.

As Aeschylus' dramatic treatment reveals, the Persians' despotism has corrupted the chorus' natural desire for freedom of thought and speech, instead "naturalizing"' a condition of slavery. This condition has become familiar and comfortable precisely because the chorus refuses to accept responsibility or to take on the burdens of independent thought, two elements that were central to the Athenian experience of participatory civic life. Hence, to an Athenian audience, this play served to confirm the suspicion that barbarian peoples were politically slavish and militarily effeminate, and that the two were closely interconnected. The problem was not, however, that these "barbarians" were born rationally deficient or weak. Rather, they had learned from their political culture that their servitude and weakness were "natural" and unchangeable elements of social and even religious order. This order was perpetuated by the weak and narcissistic Persian leadership—by the mystical reliance on Darius, by Darius' own self-aggrandizement, by Xerxes' rash military strategy and his effeminate sobbing, and by Atossa's uncomprehending association of wealth with security. In short, Aeschylus' *Persians* offers a comprehensive critique of Persia's entire political and social life—a critique centered on the concepts of gender, ethnicity, and enslavement (cf. Balot 2014; Harrison 2000). The play shows that imprudent and effeminate leadership led both to Persia's military failures and to a destructively servile *ethos* amongst the regime's most "trusted" advisors (2, 528).

By contrast, Euripides proved to be a more ambiguous, and therefore more deeply challenging, source for critical reflection on Athenian martial and masculine identity. The tragic theater's capacity to call into question and reify masculine norms—often at the same time—is best captured by Froma Zeitlin's influential concept of "playing the other." For Zeitlin dramatic portrayals of female characters presented a foil for the exploration of male identity; they "serve as anti-models as well as hidden models for the masculine self and concomitantly, their experience of suffering or their acts that lead them to disaster regularly occur before and precipitate those of men" (1995: 347). Building on Zeitlin's work, Helena Foley has interpreted tragic representations of women as reflective of shifting Athenian self-perceptions during the Peloponnesian War (Foley 2002). Laura McClure, on the other hand, reads women's subversive speech as a medium for exploring the ethical consequences of those citizens and orators who used rhetorical power to advance duplicitous and self-interested ends (1999: 264).

To take one especially poignant example of these themes, *Trojan Women* (of 415 BCE) invited its Athenian audience to confront the devastated figures, mostly women and children, of a fallen eastern dynasty. The play centers on Hecuba, the wife of Priam of Troy. In his presentation of this dethroned queen, the poet concentrates intently on "outsidership": Hecuba is equally foreign and female. She is also transformed from royalty to slavery—a transformation that inevitably raises questions about the "naturalness" of the Greeks' own slaves. In light of her otherness, it is striking that Hecuba nonetheless had already internalized the Solonian wisdom that no life should be considered blessed before death (509–510; cf. Hdt. 1.29–33; Arist. *NE* 1100a10–1101a22)—a foreboding reminder that may have given pause to the slave-holding and imperialistic Athenians themselves. Together with Hecuba, the audience was encouraged to confront the meaning of Troy's reversals through watching the suffering and death of her children. Cassandra, the notorious prophet, would be given to Agamemnon; whatever her own sufferings, though, her mantic truth-telling would prove victorious over the self-ignorant imperial male conqueror. Polyxena, the youngest daughter, was "slain at the tomb of Achilles as a gift to a lifeless corpse" (618–619, trans. Kovacs)—a seemingly vain and even meaningless "offering." Andromache, a model of domestic virtue (645–656), struggles to accept that she must betray Hector in the most gruesome possible way—by taking his slayer Neoptolemus as her husband. Although she had been Hector's war-won bride, she was inextricably attached to him through their son Astyanax, yet even that bond was destroyed when the Greek captors killed the child, to the horror of the Greek herald Talthybius (709–711, 786–789). Children have always been the most easily neglected outsiders in both ancient and modern worlds. Be that as it may, could an Athenian audience, in pitying the Trojan women, have failed to feel both indignation and contempt for the Greek perpetrators of these outrages (cf. Scodel 2012: xxiii)? If they were unsettled by Euripides' spectacle, then they were indeed empathetically closer to the foreign—female, enslaved, "barbarian"—than they might have imagined. No matter that their self-image depended on their status as Athenian male "insiders."

On the heels of this catalogue of suffering we meet an unruffled and still beautiful Helen, who skillfully, even if unconvincingly, deflects blame for her own wrongdoing onto Hecuba, who had "criminally" given birth to Paris (914–922). Through presenting a series of sophistical arguments, however unpersuasive, Helen manages to buy time before her execution (1042–1045) and to soften the resolve of her weak-willed husband (1047–1059). Helen's unflinching denial of responsibility and manipulation of appearances would have been all too familiar to the Athenian audience. As a woman and a foreigner, she represents a different sort of outsider whose behaviors they could nevertheless recognize as their own. In Helen's rhetoric they could discern the sophistic tendency to advance seemingly powerful yet deceptive arguments, the dark side of Athenian free speech (Goff 2009: 66). A disturbing thought: that, in this case at least, the "other" was not so different after all. By contrast, the chorus of *Trojan Women*, a surprising repository of good sense, begs the fallen queen to "destroy the persuasive force of her words," for "she speaks eloquently, although she is guilty, and that is a terrible thing" (966–968, trans. Kovacs). Yet while Hecuba offers a forceful condemnation of her step-daughter's guile and dishonesty, Menelaus cannot act on the better argument, and Helen will ultimately win (969–1032; cf. *Od.* 4.20). In light of their self-image as rationally self-governing men, the Athenians might begin to wonder whether sophistical rhetoric enfeebled them—that is, rendered them susceptible to the intrusion of the weak, the irrational, and the ungovernable into their own civic space. These uncomfortable questions would have been intensified by their recollection of the city's harsh and strategically unnecessary destruction of Melos (esp. Thuc. 5.17). The play invited Athenians to reflect on the logic of their own imperial ambitions and their own potential vulnerabilities. Were the sophisms and intrusions of "outsiders" ever far removed from the Athenians' own supposedly protected civic space?

3 Epitaphic Oratory: Commemoration, Celebration, Ideology

Delivered during the state-sponsored burial ceremony, the Athenian funeral orations served to contain unsettling questions, to resolve unnerving ambiguities, and to affirm the wisdom and strength of the democratic regime (see also Roisman, Chapter 16). Loraux (1986) has shown that state funerals supplanted private mourning and thereby placed under male control women's traditional roles in caring for and lamenting the dead. This transformation also signaled a new emphasis on the collective exceptionalism of the democratic city, as opposed to individual aristocratic greatness (Honig 2009). In light of these developments, how did the funeral orations serve to construct the identity of civic participants, and how was that self-construction related to the representation of particular outsiders?

In Lysias' funeral oration, we encounter democratic androcentrism in an appallingly unabashed form. Athenian civic ideology stressed that Athenians were born of the earth (they were *autochthones*), so that they possessed the same land as a "mother and a father-land" (2.18, trans. Herrman). In Lysias, this common birth was not a stable marker of identity; rather, capacities given at birth had to be enhanced and developed, with a view to their ultimate expression in common judgment (*gnōmē*) and the achievement of "many fine and amazing deeds" (20, trans. Herrman). The Athenians recognized that it was not only ties of birth, but also "freedom for all" that "provides the greatest unity" among the citizens (2.18, trans. Herrman). The Athenians parlayed their natal ties into a higher collective enterprise through establishing democratic law and free speech (2.18–20). Lysias implies that the common virtues of a shared fatherland, which were developed through long practice and sound judgment, came to supplant the attachment to the land as a common mother. Manliness and femininity were thereby mapped onto culture and nature respectively, a recurrent antithesis (Ortner 1984). Athenian autochthony illustrates the importance of the feminine as a point of origin and therefore as a foundation on which civic identity is built; yet what truly binds Athenians together and makes them politically and culturally distinctive are those outstanding feats of martial bravery and virtue that derive from manly Athenian deeds (2.19). For, above all, the orator celebrates the Athenians as distinctive in their commitment to virtue and just war, irrespective of the costs. He illustrates his point through offering stories of exceptional military capacity (2.4–6), burial of the war dead without partisanship (2.11–17), loyalty to foreign suppliants (2.7–10), and prudent leadership during the Persian Wars (2.20–43).

By this reckoning, Lysias implies, the casualties of war, including women and children, are a necessary (if lamentable) consequence of the Athenians' admirable civic ethos. Hence, while the public grieving performed by women was an ancestral custom and deserved respect, honorable death itself was the pinnacle of Athenian achievement, the ultimate human vocation (2.81). Even the safety of passage to the afterworld, traditionally conferred by women and ancient custom, was supplanted by the promise of immortal renown offered by the city. Civic honors, in other words, are not only superior to the honors granted by women through traditional ritual, but also diminish the significance of these rituals and their guardians. Lysias' speech exhorts his audience to understand these sacrifices experienced by and inflicted on the private sphere as less important than dedication to the goods cultivated by the city (cf. Thuc. 2.45).

The city's willingness to "build on" the feminine other, or to use women for its own purposes, is taken to its logical extreme by Lysias' more violent and disturbing representation of the Amazons. As Lysias tells it, the Amazons were the first to use iron (a traditionally masculine craft) and the first to attack enemies on horseback. They ruled many tribes and, when they learned of the Athenians, they were inspired by their "enormous reputation and great ambition" to launch a military campaign against the city (2.5, trans. Herrman). In Lysias' presentation, however, the Amazons had only to meet brave Athenian men before their "spirits were like their nature" (2.5, trans. Herrman): these outstanding female warriors reacted as women and recoiled from their male adversaries, yet (even though they were women) they were not spared or allowed to turn home. Rather, they were executed on Athenian land as a witness to Athenian virtue, which consisted, as we now see, not only of defending the city, but also of re-establishing proper relations between masculinity and war, and femininity and the home (2.6). The narrative allows Lysias to establish a simplistic and reassuring polarity between men and women, in which manliness is expressed in eliminating a female threat to—and perhaps also within—the city (Fantham et al. 1995: 128–135). Extraordinary violence underwrites ordinary political and domestic life. Men and women alike should see that the passivity of mothers and wives, along with their exclusion from public life, was part of a system in which their male counterparts embodied civic activity as a higher-order end. Yet even if this system had been practically imposed by violence, its workings were necessary and good, in that they constituted a fulfillment of human nature and an embodiment of natural order. Unlike the tragic poets, who emphasized culture and tragic contingency in the presentation of outsiders, Lysias found the ultimate differentia between Athenian men and Amazonian women to be natural.

By contrast, Demosthenes' funeral oration offers a different, less aggressive perspective on Athenian citizenship and participatory ideals. Delivered after the Athenians' defeat at Chaeronea (338 BCE), this oration struggles to keep Athenian civic ideals intact despite the Athenians' loss (see also Roisman, Chapter 16). This unusual rhetorical circumstance led Demosthenes to moderate Athenian androcentrism and to emphasize that "manly" courage could also be displayed in acts of self-sacrifice. This is why Demosthenes quickly glosses over the history of Athenian triumphs (60.6–12) on his way to praising the democratic principles that inspired these heroes to die nobly (60.27). Athenians are distinctive in encouraging freedom of speech and thus a desire for truth amongst the *dēmos*, which created a civically appropriate sense of shame. Shame of reproach (for speaking falsely or acting ignobly) was a central mechanism in motivating citizens to submit bravely "to the danger brought on by the enemy, and choose a noble death rather than a shameful life" (60.26, trans. Herrman). Shame was an internalized audit representative of the opinions and judgments of other living Athenians and heroic figures from the past (cf. Williams 1993). In Demosthenes' presentation, shame was cultivated by civic education—particularly by the community's self-chosen role models, who provided normative standards of behavior for all citizens. Among these role models, Demosthenes names the local heroes of each tribe, who encourage Athenian soldiers to be brave (60.27). Surprisingly, perhaps, Demosthenes offers several female examples (for a more detailed analysis, see Balot, forthcoming). The daughters of Pandion, for example, courageously took vengeance on the rape of Philomela by Procne's husband Tereus—a barbarian violator of the integrity of Athenian households and norms (Dem. 60.28–29). This model of justice in the service of self-respect provided inspiration for Athenians who could not tolerate any attacks on Greece. The Leontidae equally have as their internal guide the daughters of Leos, who sacrificed themselves in order to cure Athens of a plague (60.28–29). Finally, the Acamantidae must hold in their hearts the example set by their forefather Acamas, who sailed to Troy "to save his mother" (60.29, trans. Herrman). This final example not only establishes the importance of feminine role models but also reasserts the significance of attachments to and protection of women and the household (*oikos*) as worthy civic ends. Demosthenes shows that women too can be courageous, and in so doing he establishes the household and women as important partners in the formation of a collective sense of virtue and heroism. More than Lysias, Demosthenes brings to light the ambiguities in the Athenians' construction of gendered identities and helps to resolve, even if only provisionally, the competing claims represented by the feminine.

4 Philosophy's Provocations: Dialectical Reflections on Citizenship

Now that we have clarified Athenian participatory ideology, along with its internal ambiguities and tensions, we are well positioned to explore the challenges that arose from another quarter: fourth-century Athenian philosophy, particularly that of Plato and Aristotle. While these thinkers have often been charged with rejecting Athenian norms and foundations outright, we show that they engaged with Athenian practices dialectically, in ways that are especially illuminating for our diverse categories of outsiders (see also Morgan, Chapter 4, on the role of Plato in critically reflecting on myths of identity).

Consider Aristotle's discussion of slavery. Most scholars have read Aristotle's discussion as offering an alarmingly offensive justification for the enslavement of barbarian peoples, amongst whom, Aristotle says, "no naturally ruling element exists" (*Pol.* 1252b6–7, trans. Barker, rev. Stalley) and who "are more servile in character than Greeks ... and they therefore tolerate despotic rule without any complaint" (1285a19–22, trans. Barker, rev. Stalley). Garvey has offered an ideological interpretation of Aristotle's arguments: "[T]he function of the natural slave theory was to distract attention from the existence of these unnatural slaves by promoting a paradigmatic image of the 'real' slave, whom all could agree to be properly enslaved" (1996: 126; cf. Williams 2008: 114; Smith 1991:191). Other scholars, such as Kraut, Schofield, and Monoson, have tried to understand the case for natural slavery as consistent with Aristotle's larger philosophical and political aims (Kraut 2002; Monoson 2002; Schofield 2005). Instead of endorsing slavery as an essential institution of the *polis*, however, Aristotle offers his readers an example of the self-interrogation and critical questioning required of democratic citizens.

Aristotle first reports several popular views. Some propose that ruling over slaves is a species of knowledge within the genus of "ruling knowledge." Others argue that slavery is contrary to nature and therefore unjust, since it results from force alone. Aristotle wants to examine these perspectives in order to grasp their strengths and weaknesses and thereby to arrive at a more coherent outlook (1253b18–23).

In order to make progress on the question of "natural slavery," Aristotle observes that wherever there are natural wholes with a number of constituent parts, a ruling part and a ruled part always emerge (1254a20–31). The same hierarchical principle pertains to the relationships between human being and animal, between soul and body, and between man and woman (1254b2–16). Natural slaves, therefore, should in principle conform to the observed pattern. Yet do slaves differ from fully rational human beings to the same extent that the soul differs from the body and animals differ from humankind (1254b16–20; we address the relationship between man and woman shortly)? If this were true, then natural slave and beast would be paradoxically closer in kind than man and slave; to the contrary, however, Aristotle points out that while animals obey feelings, slaves apprehend rational instruction even though they lack the capacity to reason for themselves (1254b20–24). Nevertheless, Aristotle declares, a slave's proper function is similar to that of an animal, in that both naturally "provide bodily assistance in satisfying essential needs" (1254b25–26, trans. Barker, rev. Stalley). Aristotle has sharpened the questions surrounding the existence of natural slaves, but his analysis does not yield definitive answers.

Subsequently, the situation becomes even more complex, because the relationship between slave and free does not, in fact, reflect the hierarchical pattern observed in other natural partnerships. In particular, nature fails to provide a reliable visual standard for distinguishing between slaves and free men (1254b32–34; cf. Frank 2005; Balot 2006)—as it does, for example, in the distinction between animals and human beings or men and women. Could it be, then, that supposedly "natural" slave-owners must rely on human judgment and convention all over again?

Does the discussion of conventional slavery yield clearer results? Here again Aristotle explores several arguments. Many understand slavery as a just institution by virtue of the law that conquerors possess the goods and persons of those they conquer in war (1255a6–7). They view this law as having a rational basis, in that those who are victorious in warfare, and thus able to capture slaves, have a certain "excellence" (*aretē*), or otherwise they would not be so successful even in war (1255a12–16). To a limited extent, and in a certain sense, at least, Aristotle endorses the conventionalists' idea that "power [*to kratoun*] never goes without good qualities" (1255a15, trans. Barker, rev. Stalley); but neither Aristotle nor many conventionalists hold, with Plato's Thrasymachus, that justice implies simply the rule of the powerful (1255a18–19). The conundrum lies in the ambiguity of the Greek term *aretē*, which involves either traditional excellences such as strength and military prowess or "virtues" such as justice. Often the term seems to capture both ideas in an indistinct way. Clarifying the consequences of the positions he has surveyed and inquiring into the apparently high stakes involved in the dispute are Aristotle's goal in the discussion that immediately follows.

Aristotle allows the Thrasymachean thesis that justice consists in the rule of the stronger to disappear from view. By contrast, while he seems to accept in very general terms that those who excel in virtue ought to rule over their inferiors, he also raises numerous questions about the justice of slavery based on warfare. Certain wars are manifestly unjust and thus provide no foundation for natural slavery. More concretely, virtuous men do not deserve to be enslaved simply because they have been defeated in battle. Advocates of merely conventional slavery fall into hopeless contradiction because of the ethical arbitrariness of victory and defeat in battle. When they consider the opposition between Greek and barbarian, they come to agree that there are certain groups of people who are intrinsically virtuous, whether victors or vanquished, and who therefore deserve to be free, while others, such as barbarians, are slaves by virtue of their essence (1255a24–32). Hence, upon further consideration, the conventionalists can make sense of their position only through having recourse to a theory of natural slavery, such as the one Aristotle had already mooted. Aristotle concludes by pointing to a central failing of the conventionalist position: no theory of natural slavery yields a neat opposition between Greek and barbarian, because "nature ... is unable to bring it about" that virtue and vice are inherited within distinct cultures (1255b3–5, trans. Barker, rev. Stalley). Ethnicity, like physical appearance, is a weak marker of justice and goodness, because distinctions between ethnic groups also depend upon changeable conventions and fallible opinions.

It is not surprising that these passages have proved to be frequently misleading, for Aristotle's arguments against conventional slavery are at odds with his deprecating claims about barbarians elsewhere. At the beginning and end of the *Politics*, for example, he repeats the conventional view that the barbarian is slavish (1252b5–9; 1327b27–29). He also casts doubt on the naturalness of slavery when he recommends that all deserving slaves be awarded manumission in the presumably just regime described in Books 7–8 (1330a25–33). This idea does not cohere in any obvious way with Aristotle's conception of natural slavery. For how can a person who lacks practical reason, who is therefore a natural slave, and whose nature is apparently unchangeable (because natural), derive any benefit from freedom? Why would it be just to free such a person?

If we reflect carefully on Aristotle's dialectical mode of presentation, we will discover that, instead of offering a new, coherent vision of natural slavery, as he originally seemed to promise, Aristotle has led his readers into a state of perplexity. Far from affirming their pre-existing convictions, Aristotle invites his readers to consider whether the pursuit of virtue, particularly justice, is compatible with the possession of slaves. For slavery as practiced (for example) by the Athenians manifestly failed to conform to Aristotle's model of natural slavery, while nature in a broad sense failed to supply readily identifiable natural slaves. In a magisterial process of unsettling conventional beliefs, Aristotle laid bare existing opinions and then introduced a new, deeper set of questions about his contemporaries' ideals and practices, and their interrelations. Like the Athenian tragic poets, he offered his readers a provocation to critical self-questioning.

Plato's Socrates provided an equally controversial argument about women. Scholars have offered diverse interpretations of Socrates' discussion of women in Book 5 of the *Republic*: to certain readers the discussion appears comic (Bloom 1991); to others it is used instrumentally to advance Socrates' argument about philosopher kings (Annas 1976); to others it is "sacrificial," in the sense that female identity is absorbed or dissolved in the rationalism of the male *polis* (Saxonhouse 1976, 1985; Elshtain 1982); and to still others it is proto-feminist (Okin 1977; Vlastos 1994). Our question is how, if at all, Socrates' arguments would have challenged or provoked the Athenian participatory community to see gender relations in a new light.

Socrates' discussion of women ostensibly interrupts the dialogue's investigation of justice. Polemarchus and Adeimantus insist that Socrates elaborate on his earlier hint that women and children should be held in common (*Rep.* 449b–c; cf. 423e–424a). This suggestion, the interlocutors charge, had been passed off as though it were "something quite ordinary" (449c, trans. Bloom), when, in fact, it is startlingly bold. Their questions force Socrates to admit that comprehensive inquiry into justice cannot stop short of investigating conventions relating to both men and women. After all, since the participants in the conversation had thoroughly outlined the education and occupations befitting the new city's men, it made sense that they would also examine the role of women within this just regime (451c). The characters' surprise at Socrates' unconventional proposal might be paralleled by the shock of many readers who first learned of the necessity of thinking through the role of women—not to mention children—in their own regimes.

Be that as it may, Socrates' argument begins from an instrumental standpoint, established earlier in the dialogue (423e–424a), that women must become common members of the guardian class for the sake of procreating and rearing excellent children (450c). But he quickly extends this gambit beyond conventional recognition by arguing that if women are to live amongst the guardians, then they must be trained to perform as guardians; only equal training will lead to equal usefulness (452a). In taking up these questions, Socrates emphasizes the need to think freely about the issues themselves—which implies resisting the charms and comforts of traditional ideas. After all, just as the unfamiliar practices of others generally invite laughter, so too did many current Athenian practices once draw ridicule, even if they were later accepted as beneficial (452c–e). It is important to be aware, Socrates argues, that people often have poorly adjusted barometers for assessing what is laughable and praiseworthy, for it is common to everyone to "look seriously to any standard of beauty [he] sets up other than the good" (452c, trans. Bloom).

Is gender parity, therefore, held to be either conceivable or desirable? Socrates has led his interlocutors from the question of utility to that of the plausibility of gender equality. Like Aristotle, he begins innocuously, as though he were merely clarifying positions in order to advance debate for those who want to dispute the question further, whether in jest or seriously (453a). Yet Socrates does not hesitate to address the crucial issue at the right moment. "Can it be," he asks, "that a woman doesn't differ in her nature very much from a man?" (453c, trans. Bloom). Glaucon's predictably negative response invites Socrates to press the question more insistently. If women are truly different from men, he contends, then it does not make sense to assign women to the guardian class, for, according to their earlier understanding of justice, a just political order would locate each person in the role that suits his or her particular nature (453c). This point introduces a number of difficulties for Socrates' interlocutors. They see that the just mode of organization to which they had earlier agreed, in which classes were assigned on the basis of natural talent, must also involve a radical reinterpretation of the sexes, one that defies conventions presumed to be rational and therefore non-negotiable (454a–c). Could they be led, on the basis of the preceding arguments and their potentially explosive implications, to acknowledge explicitly that the differences between men and women are irrelevant to ruling or to studying philosophy? Just as it makes little difference whether a shoemaker is bald or hairy, so too should it make little difference whether an individual plays the male or female part in the reproductive process, if that person has the capacity to rule (454c–d). When it comes to assigning individuals to the appropriate class as a matter of justice, the only question that matters is that of aptitude for doing their work. This is a powerful argument—and therefore a challenging one.

Yet its radical power is obscured, perhaps, by other comments rooted in conventional views of the sexes. Socrates points out, for example, that in all tasks practiced by both genders, men excel women (455c). This leads the interlocutors to accept the still bold, but in their view more palatable, claim that "there is no practice of a city's governors which belongs to woman because she's woman, or to man because he's man; but the natures are scattered alike among both animals; and woman participates according to nature in all practices, and man in all, but in all of them woman is weaker than man" (455e, trans. Bloom). This reassuring claim may make Socrates' interlocutors more comfortable with the radicalism of his proposals, but in the meantime they have become increasingly open to the audacious suggestion that natural gender inequalities may be slight. They can, at least, confidently assert that insofar as women's nature resembles men's, women ought to have equal access to education and training (456b). Socrates underscores this shift by reminding the interlocutors that while they had previously thought that they were setting down laws that seemed impossible or like prayers, they were in fact identifying a law that is situated in nature (456b–c). For their investigations have revealed, in fact, that existing norms and laws, not gender equality, have been proven to be "against nature" (456c). Socrates' conventionally minded interlocutors are forced to agree that their theoretical investigation has not yielded merely a possible conception of the regime, but, in fact, what is best (456c–457a): "there is nothing better for a city than the coming to be in it of the best possible women and men" (456e, trans. Bloom).

Building on the Athenians' own traditions of self-criticism, the philosophers challenged and unsettled conventional opinions and political culture, however inconvenient or counterintuitive these interventions might have been—even, and perhaps particularly, for the philosophers themselves. We therefore agree with Vlastos (1994) that there is no necessary tension between Socrates' numerous negative presentations of feminine characteristics throughout the *Republic* (e.g. 387d–388a, 605d–e) and his revolutionary argument that women have a just claim to rule alongside men, because their natural capacities suit them to do so. The former are characterizations based on existing stereotypes, whereas Socrates' argument for female guardians attempts to interrogate these stereotypes in pursuit of the truth according to nature. While the question of the work's readership is contested, it is plausible to suppose that the *Republic* encouraged its Athenian readers to think for themselves about their own practices and beliefs (Yunis 2003). The challenges posed by Athenian philosophers reflect one especially potent outgrowth of a political culture that married robust ideology with intense moments of self-criticism and reflection. Socrates' attitudes toward convention thus reflect the Athenians' own practices of self-criticism and their interrogation of traditional perspectives. Both tragic poets and epitaphic orators illustrate the ways in which various "outsiders" can act as stimuli or vehicles of critical reflection on widely accepted ideologies and habits. It is a telling paradox that Aristotle, antiquity's greatest theorist of citizenship, was himself a metic and therefore an outsider to Athenian citizen culture. Like tragedy and epitaphic oratory, philosophy encouraged Athenians to explore these contradictions in the interest of clarifying potential injustices and promoting self-knowledge. As Plato's Socrates himself pointed out, democracy was the only regime open enough to permit the liberated philosophical thought of men (and even women?) such as himself (*Rep.* 561d).

5 Conclusion

Our discussion of Socratic political philosophy leads us to a surprising conclusion. From the perspective of the "manly" world of political participation and military service, the philosopher himself is an outsider. This is why, in Plato's *Republic*, Socrates explains that the philosopher will help to rule the ideal city; but he will not take part in the participatory politics of any other city (473d–e, 497b–c, 592a–b). In this sense, the philosopher is not only a marginalized critic, but also even the quintessential outsider—the outsider who considers his politically marginal status to be an essential feature of the highest human vocation.

In the Platonic *Gorgias* we see these themes illustrated with special power. The otherwise unknown Callicles characterizes Socrates as embodying many of the traits associated with women, slaves, and foreigners. In particular, Callicles accuses the philosopher of effeminacy and childishness (485b–c), precisely because he does not concern himself with men's competitive dealings in the *agora*, even though he is a fully mature citizen male (485d). The charge of immaturity—that philosophy is suitable for boys with lisps, whispering in a corner—blends easily with that of effeminacy, because Callicles implicitly views women as deficient men, as individuals who could have achieved a perfected masculine stature, but, to their discredit, did not. What should men be, then, in the view of an aspiring "manly" man such as Callicles? They should expand their desires, and, through "manly courage" (*andreia*) and intelligence, they should acquire the means necessary to fulfill those desires (491e–492a). Put differently, they should, like Callicles, aspire to become successful tyrants, or at least to act as the unchallenged leaders of tyrannical, imperialistic cities such as Athens. If Callicles is a happy tyrant, then Socrates is a wretched slave (485e–486c, 492a–c).

Plato draws the contrasts so sharply, and in just this way, in order to confront his readers with an unpleasant and little-noticed feature of Greek political androcentrism: namely, that it harbors within itself tyrannical impulses that are as destructive to the city as they are to its individual participatory citizens. This is why Socrates tries with increasing vigor to convince Callicles that conventional "manly" aspirations prove to be harmful to one's most precious possession—the soul—especially when young men take political ambitions to tyrannical extremes. To avoid inflicting this type of damage upon himself, then, Socrates would choose to suffer injustice (like a woman or slave) rather than to commit injustice (like a "manly" tyrant) (508b–509c). Socrates is cosmopolitan, even "philanthropic" (*Euthyphro* 3d–e; cf. Brown (2000) on Socrates' cosmopolitanism), not patriotic or specially committed to the good of any single, androcentric, and hierarchically organized regime. As the consummate outsider, Plato's Socrates reinvented the tradition of female, slavish, and foreign outsiders in order to criticize the self-destructiveness and injustice of the manly world within. Initiated within the life of the participatory Greek city, the outsiders' critique would eventually culminate in the Christians' cosmopolitan, effeminized, suffering image of the new hero, Christ, who suffered what was conventionally held to be a slave's death on the cross.

By presenting the philosophical life within the framework of these traditional dichotomies, Plato strikingly confirmed the point that it was outsiders and others—whether women, slaves, children, foreigners, the poor, or philosophers—who supplied a chief resource of criticism and imagination for Athens' participatory political community. It was the great merit of that community not only to permit outsiders to air criticisms publicly, but also, occasionally, to listen to those critical voices and to think through the problems they raised. Participatory discourse has a splendid potential, provided that it is underwritten by a spirit that is not simply "manly." One might go so far as to say, in fact, that the defining feature of the Greek, and above all democratic, participatory community was its willingness to question its own norms. Although the Athenians could be as patriotically self-absorbed and proud as any other Mediterranean community, they cherished freedom of speech and freedom of thought in a way that went far beyond the practices of other ancient cities, including Rome. Their profound reflections on diverse outsiders proved to be an integral feature of their self-questioning ethos.

REFERENCES

Annas, J. 1976. "Plato's Republic and Feminism." *Philosophy* 51: 307–321.

Arendt, H. 1998. *The Human Condition*. Chicago.

Arnson Svarlien, D., and R. Scodel. 2012. *Euripides: Andromache, Hecuba, Trojan Women*. Indianapolis.

Balot, R. 2006. *Greek Political Thought*. Oxford.

Balot, R. 2009. "The Virtue Politics of Democratic Athens." In Stephen Salkever, ed., *The Cambridge Companion to Ancient Greek Political Thought*. Cambridge, 271–300.

Balot, R. 2014. *Courage in the Democratic Polis: Ideology and Critique in Classical Athens*. New York.

Balot, R. forthcoming. "Transformations of "Manliness" in the Democratic Republic." In *Republicanism: Ancient and Modern*. Ancient Lessons for Modern Politics series. Toronto.

Barker, E., trans. 1972. *The Politics of Aristotle*. Oxford.

Bloom, A., trans. 1991. *The Republic of Plato*. 2nd edn. New York.

Brown, E. 2000. "Socrates the Cosmopolitan." *Stanford Agora: an Online Journal of Legal Studies* 1: 77–84.

Cohen, E. 2003. "The High Cost of *Andreia* at Athens." In R.M. Rosen and I. Sluiter, eds., *Andreia: Studies in Manliness and Courage in Classical Antiquity*. Leiden, 144–165.

Elshtain, J.B., ed. 1982. *The Family in Political Thought*. Amherst, MA.

Fantham, E., H.P. Foley, N.B. Kampen, S.B. Pomeroy, and H.A. Shapiro, eds. 1995. "Amazons: Women in Control." In *Women in the Classical World: Image and Text*. New York.

Foley, H.P. 2002. *Female Acts in Greek Tragedy*. Princeton.

Forsdyke, S. 2012. *Slaves Tell Tales: And Other Episodes in the Politics of Popular Culture in Ancient Greece*. Princeton.

Fowler, H.N., trans. 1999. *Plato. Euthyphro. Apology. Crito. Phaedo. Phaedrus*. Cambridge, MA.

Frank, J. 2005. *A Democracy of Distinction: Aristotle and the Work of Politics*. Chicago.

Garnsey, P. 1997. *Ideas of Slavery from Aristotle to Augustine*. Cambridge.

Goff, B. 2004. *Citizen Bacchae: Women's Ritual Practice in Ancient Greece*. Berkeley.

Goff, B. 2009. *Euripides: Trojan Women*. Duckworth Companions to Greek and Roman Tragedy. London.

Gould, J. 1980. "Law, Custom and Myth: Aspects of the Social Position of Women in Classical Athens." *JHS* 100: 38–59.

Grene, D., trans. 1988. *Herodotus: The History*. Chicago.

Hall, E. 1989. *Inventing the Barbarian: Greek Self-Definition through Tragedy*. New York.

Hall, E., R. Alston, and J. McConnell, eds. 2011. *Ancient Slavery and Abolition: From Hobbes to Hollywood*. New York.

Harrison, T. 2000. *The Emptiness of Asia: Aeschylus' Persians and the History of the Fifth Century*. Bristol.

Honig, B. 2009. "Antigone's Laments, Creon's Grief: Mourning, Membership, and the Politics of Exception." *Political Theory* 37(1): 5–43.

Irwin, T., trans. 1999. *Nicomachean Ethics*. 2nd edn. Indianapolis.

Just, R. 1991. *Women in Athenian Law and Life*. New York.

Kovacs, D., trans. 1999. *Euripides*, vol. 4: *Trojan Women. Iphigenia among the Taurians. Ion*. Cambridge.

Kraut, R. 2002. *Aristotle*. Oxford.

Lamb, W.R.M., trans. 1925. *Plato: Lysis. Symposium. Gorgias*. Cambridge.

Loraux, N. 1986. *The Invention of Athens: The Funeral Oration in the Classical City*. Trans. A. Sheridan. Cambridge.

McClure, L. 1999. *Spoken Like a Woman: Speech and Gender in Athenian Drama*. Princeton.

Okin, S.M. 1977. "Philosopher Queens and Private Wives: Plato on Women and the Family." *Philosophy & Public Affairs* 6(4): 345–369.

Ortner, Sherry B. 1974. "Is Female to Male as Nature is to Culture?" In M.Z. Rosaldo and L. Lamphere, eds., *Woman, Culture, and Society*. Stanford, 68–87.

Podlecki, A. 1966. *The Political Background of Aeschylean Tragedy*. 2nd edn. London.

Saxonhouse, A. 1976. "The Philosopher and the Female in the Political Thought of Plato." *Political Theory* 4(2): 195–212.

Saxonhouse, A. 1985. *Women in the History of Political Thought: Ancient Greece to Machiavelli*. Westport.

Schofield, M. 2005. "Ideology and Philosophy in Aristotle's Theory of Slavery." In R. Kraut and S. Skultety, eds., *Aristotle's Politics: Critical Essays*. Lanham, 91–119.

Smith, N. 1991. "Aristotle's Theory of Natural Slavery." In D. Keyt and F. Miller, Jr.,, eds., *A Companion to Aristotle's "Politics"*. Oxford, 142–155.

Sommerstein, A.H., trans. 2008. *Aeschylus: Persians. Seven Against Thebes. Suppliants. Prometheus Bound*. Cambridge, MA.

Strassler, R.B., ed. 1998. *The Landmark Thucydides: A Comprehensive Guide to the Peloponnesian War*. New York.

Vlastos, G. 1994. "Was Plato a Feminist?" In N. Tuana, ed., *Feminist Interpretations of Plato*. University Park.

Williams, B. 2008. *Shame and Necessity*. 2nd edn. Berkeley.

Yunis, H., ed. 2003. *Written Texts and the Rise of Literate Culture in Ancient Greece*. Cambridge.
Zeitlin, F.I. 1995. *Playing the Other: Gender and Society in Classical Greek Literature*. Chicago.

FURTHER READING

The best general discussion of the Greek construction of the "barbarian" remains that of Hall 1989. On women in classical antiquity, Fantham et al. 1995 is particularly useful because of the breadth of literary and material culture that it surveys; Just 1991 is a reliable guide to Athenian practices, especially within the framework of law. Loraux 1986 is deservedly considered the standard work on Athenian funerary oratory, helpfully linking ideas about gender to the orators' presentation of democracy. Garnsey 1997 covers the ancient sources on slavery in a succinct format. Readers will find it useful to argue with Schofield 2005 over Aristotle's theory of slavery. Plato's representation of women in the *Republic* is the subject of contentious debate; see the contrasting treatments of Bloom 1991 and Vlastos 1994.

CHAPTER 23

Women and Slaves in the Roman Republic

Roberta Stewart

The political revolution of fourth- to third-century BCE Rome included the definition of public offices of government, the reform of the legion as well as an expanded levy to create a more broadly based soldiery of Roman citizens, the social formation of the patricio-plebeian aristocracy as the ruling elite, the institutionalization of the tribunate of the plebs and the plebeian assembly as political, legislative institutions of the entire Roman community, and the development and institutionalization of chattel slavery (von Fritz 1950; Gabba 1975; Hopkins 1978; Hölkeskamp 1987, 1993). Within sixty-five years, from 338–273, Roman republican armies conquered peninsular Italy. The Romans developed categories or statuses to accommodate non-Romans within the highly stratified Roman system. Reports of levies describe non-Roman Italic peoples who served with the Roman army as *socii* and *Latini* (Brunt 1971: 544–548; Galsterer 1976: 18, 22). Roman religion recognized five categories of land, including conquered land, or *ager peregrinus* (on *sacra peregrina*, Festus in Lindsay 1913: 268), and prodigy reports indicate that prodigies occurring on the categories of conquered land in Italy were counted as affecting fundamentally the Roman state (Catalano 1978; Rawson 1991; Stewart 1998: 186–192). In other words, the Roman Senate and voting assemblies showed collective will to define mechanisms to accommodate non-Romans in a Roman system, militarily as *Latini* and *socii*, politically as allies with local autonomy, and legally and religiously as *peregrini* (Hölkeskamp 1987; Stewart 1998: 182–195; Williamson 2005: 131–238; see also Williamson, Chapter 11). Even the conquered peoples beyond Italy became non-Roman Romans within the Roman system as *peregrini* and as inhabitants of the *provinciae* of the Roman Empire beginning in 241.

Romans thus had developed categories to turn outsiders into insiders, *socii*, *peregrini*, *Latini*. They had also developed a new, different end of war that did not end in truce (*indutiae*), or enslavement, or massacre. It ended in a status of subordination as a non-Roman within the Roman system. The conquered foe was made an insider, a complex,

A Companion to Greek Democracy and the Roman Republic, First Edition. Edited by Dean Hammer.

twofold process of accommodation and assimilation that scholars study at the macro level (Cels-Saint-Hilaire 1985; Thomas 1996; Dench 2005) and, increasingly, at the micro level (e.g. Crawford 1996: 414–433; Stek 2009). The decision on statuses of non-Roman rested immediately with the conquering general in the field, who exercised enormous discretion in deciding who were restored as *peregrini* and who were enslaved (Dahlheim 1968, 1977). The Senate and senatorial commissions established terms of alliance. The conquered became an insider, although a non-Roman insider, in a relationship of subordination at the arbitrary discretion of the Roman commander and then of the Senate (see *CIL* I² 614, decree of the propraetor Aemilius Paullus in 189; *AE* 1984, 495, decree of L. Caesius C.f. in 104; Ebel 1991: 439–448; Rigsby 2005: 109–115, esp. 112–115).

Enslavement created a different category. Although the Twelve Tables identified a contrast of free citizen and debt slave, the *lex Poetelia* of 326/313 abolished debt slavery, and chattel slaves began to replace the dependent labor force as Roman armies conquered and enslaved Italic peoples and then those beyond peninsular Italy (Finley 1998; Hopkins 1978; Scheidel 2007; see also de Ligt, Chapter 21). At least by the third century, damage to the slave was compared to that to a herd animal, and the same statute (*lex Aquilia*) defined the legal remedy for both (Crook 1984, 1996). By contrast with the fate of the conquered non-Roman whose surrender resulted in restoration as a dependent insider, enslavement meant the sale of the conquered non-Roman as property. The Roman slave represented at once the ultimate outsider and yet the most intimate outsider: chattel denied the capacity to act as a human being in his or her own right, yet defined as representing, enacting, and so instantiating the will of the master in practical daily life and in business. Nevertheless, Roman manumission practice made the freed slave a citizen, a Roman practice well known and surprising enough to be mentioned in a letter of Philip V of Macedon who exhorted the Greeks to appreciate its political advantages (*IG* IX.517; *SIG*³ 543; *ILS* 8763). Slavery thus provided the mechanism to turn a non-Roman first into chattel and then into a citizen, a Roman naturalization process; and government policy in the early second century indicates that Latins had discovered enslavement and manumission as a "fast-track" path to naturalization as Roman citizens (Livy 41.9.9–12; Cels-Saint-Hilaire 1985; Coşkun 2009).

Understanding slavery and the slave as the furthest category of outsider and as the most intimate outsider requires investigation of the social interactions that created and defined the relationship of slavery: interactions of slaves with masters, with free persons outside of the slave's household, and with other slaves. The evidentiary base for studying slavery and the relationships of slavery in any slave society is skewed because of the extreme power differentials inherent in slavery itself (Scott 1990). Nevertheless, Cato's views on slave management and Plautus' public dramas illustrate the slave's role as the intimate outsider in the late third and early second century BCE, the earliest contemporary documentation of the Roman slave society after the political revolution that redefined the republican political and social structure. Cato's prescriptions on slave management, written for the self-consciously successful Roman elite, illustrate the idealized relationship of master and successful slave. He shows the economic role and social location of the slave: the slave's intimacy with the master, the complete loss of personhood at the basis of chattel slavery. But his prescriptions also imply the community of free poor and of slaves within which his successful slave lived, interacted, and functioned. Cato creates a parallel for evaluating Plautus, whose plays represent a piece of the larger public discourse in the general, heterogeneous Roman slave society (Richlin 2005: 21–30), a public discourse reflecting the process of enforced subordination and reinforcing the extrinsically imposed definition of the human being as chattel.

Plautus stages the interactions that are at the heart of slavery, the relationship of power enacted between master and slave and between slave and the larger community (Stewart 2012). Whether, as Fraenkel (1960) cogently argued, the slave trickster was a Plautine invention within the literary tradition of New Comedy and whether, as ancient commentators surmised, Plautus himself had experienced slavery, Plautus staged the slave as a regular character in Roman dramas performed at theatrical festivals at Rome, for a Roman audience. The extant corpus reveals Plautus as particularly aware of the problems of slavery for masters and for slaves (Stewart 2012): the master's strategies to subordinate the slave and the costs for the slave of various responses to enslavement (*Captivi*); the ubiquitous threat of violence to the slave, in both the household and the community (*Aulularia*, *Miles*, *Asinaria*); the problem of freedom for the freed slave in a society that did not have—and never developed—a view of freedom as a natural right (*Rudens*, *Menaechmi*); the problem of action from volition for the subordinated subject who figured out how to survive in slavery by maintaining a cloaked sense of self (*Pseudolus*). The Plautine corpus suggests how the master and the freeborn looked away from recognition of the slave as human "insider" and constructed the slave as an "outsider" lacking the personal character that defined the successful Roman (love of freedom; loyalty to family, or *pietas*; trustworthiness or *fides*; self-restraint). The plays also suggest the mechanisms whereby the slave survived in slavery. With *Persa* Plautus creates the illusion of a world peopled mainly by slaves and offers the Roman audience an imagined window onto the private, interpersonal relations of slaves with each other and with the free poor, i.e. the community imagined and regulated against by Cato. If the Roman republican society carefully distinguished "insiders" and "outsiders" politically, legally, and socially, Plautus imagines for the entertainment of his Roman audience—and so for us—the quotidian interactions of "insiders" and "outsiders" that now made and perpetuated the system of Roman republican slavery.

In chapter 5 of *De agri cultura*, Cato defines the jobs of the successful slave overseer. He requires an absolute identity of interest between the slave overseer and the master: the *vilicus* will not lend without the master's authorization, will heed only those whom the master orders him to heed, will keep the master apprised of all accounts (purchases, sales, loans), will not go out to dinner nor assume the role of patron of others. The prescriptions enforce the complete deracination of the successful slave who has no independent social, economic, or religious identity apart from the master. But the prescriptions imply the network of relationships within which the slave lived: social relationships of dependence with the master and his friends; economic relationships with neighbors with whom the *vilicus* engaged in reciprocal borrowing and with whom he might be invited to interact in the primary social institution of the banquet (Cato forbids the dinner plans); patronage over the local free labor force whom the *vilicus* would hire; personal relationships with the slaves whom the *vilicus* must maintain in good health, restrain from negligent work or crime, and discipline. In repeatedly enjoining that the *vilicus* must stand apart, Cato makes clear the interactions of slaves with each other and with the free community, and he suggests the potential relationships that might be formed by the successful slave because of his job, and because of the economic and social position of his master. Cato does not give a picture of these interactions, but he gives important evidence on the economic and social location of the successful slave, who functioned legally as the extension of the master, thus engaging as the master's proxy in business and interacting socially, because of his master's status and his job, with his master's friends, with free labor, and with locals of indeterminate status. According to Cato, the economic and social location of the slave reflected and embodied that of the master, and the master sought to regulate the slave's labor and the slave's expressions or actions for self, both social and economic. Cato's text shows that the slave did not inhabit a class, or status group, or caste, at least according to Roman thinking and an idealized Roman construction of mastery. The slave was thus an "outsider," qualitatively different from other human beings in his or her definition as "chattel"; yet the slave was an intimate "outsider" whose life practice reflected the volition and interests of the master. How did these interactions of slave with other slaves, with non-members (either free or slave) of the household actually look? Here Plautus can offer insight.

Within the Plautine corpus the *Persa* is conspicuous for staging a world of slaves who act and interact entirely without their masters. The plot is standard for Roman New Comedy: a forlorn lover needs money to purchase the freedom of his beloved from a pimp planning to sell her away; the lover asks funds from a trusted friend; the friend purloins the necessary funds (from his own master); the lover uses the funds from the friend to purchase his girlfriend, but he also beguiles the pimp into purchasing a freeborn young woman as a slave; the pimp is punished. Forlorn love, friendship, purchase of a slave—these are the actions of free men. But the lover and his friend are both slaves.

Persa and its deviations from dramatic convention have been studied as evidence for Plautine dramatic technique or for the Saturnalian, topsy-turvy quality of Latin New Comedy (Stärk 1991: 145–146; Lefevre 2001: 20–24). Although there is no extant Greek model for *Persa*, there is agreement that Plautus significantly altered the original in fundamental ways (Stärk 1991: 146–149; Lefevre 2001: 23–92). He conflated the conventional roles of forlorn lover and trickster slave in the character of Toxilus (Slater 1985: 37, 53–54; McCarthy 2000: 128, 130). He developed the character of the freeborn young woman Virgo (Sherberg 2001; Packman 1999), a startlingly rare role of a freeborn female (see Donat. ad Ter. *Adel.* 3.4.41, *aut nullam in scaena esse aut rarissimam vocem*, "an invisible or indeed most rare free female voice on stage"), whose sale into slavery is staged as a play within the play. He added a slave character Paegnium (Hughes 1984), who interacts with other slaves in distinctly Plautine verbal contests characterized by the verbal skills of punning, neologism, alliteration, rhyming, and metaphor (Wallochny 1992: esp. 59–97).

Yet *Persa* also tells a story about slavery. A male slave faces the prospect of his female slave partner being sold away and acts openly, in pursuit of his own self-defined interests, to collect the needed money in order to buy her into freedom. His slave friend, who works regularly as the business representative of his own master, tries to help him by diverting funds from money entrusted to him by his own master and faces whipping for the deed. The lover, his friend, and his female slave partner pursue affective relationships with each other, of friendship and of domestic partnership, even as they inhabit a slave world in which male and female slaves are seeking ways to secure their own freedom and show no natural alliance or conscious act of identification with each other. Slaves compete to dominate each other, illustrating the complete lack of community—or deracination—of the individual slave, as a lived experience, a personal decision, and a strategy for surviving in slavery. As contrast and foil to the slaves' experiences of slavery, Plautus stages the fictive sale of the freeborn Virgo, who offers commentary on the experience of deracination and the enduring consequences of slavery for a female. In *Persa* Plautus reveals keen awareness of the personal and structural problems militating against the creation of a slave community and of the slave family, i.e. the affective relations that offered a solution to the personal assault inherent in chattel slavery.

The opening of *Persa* confronted the Roman audience with the epistemological problem—probably a daily problem in the life of a slave society—of evaluating the doubleness of slaves as human chattel. The slave Toxilus delivers the opening six lines, presumably wearing the costume of a slave, but reciting the stock lament of the young, freeborn lover (Slater 1985: 38–39n.3; Stärk 1991: 144–145; McCarthy 2000: 130–131; Auhagen 2001: 97–98 and n.11). K. McCarthy (2000: esp. 122–123) has emphasized the jarring theatrical experience of competing dramatic expectations presented by Toxilus' representational role as a slave and the metatheatrical expectations created by his employing the language of the young, freeborn male lover. Toxilus' words insinuate him as "free" and "insider"; and his intentions betray him acting from his own volition and pursuing a personal, affective relation, that stands apart from his relationship to his master. The second slave monologue, an instance of Plautine doubling and mirroring, creates a similar destabilizing introductory image. In a second, syntactically and metrically parallel opening monologue (Fraenkel 1960: 218–219), the slave Sagaristio creates and frustrates the expectation of what Fraenkel (1960: 234–236, cf. Lefevre 2001: 69) has termed a catechism of good slave behavior (7–12). Sagaristio begins with the conventional language of the loyal slave (7–9), language that recurs in *Bacchides*, *Menaechmi*, *Mostellaria*, *Pseudolus*, and *Rudens*, in which a slave speaks to himself and to the audience about the skill set needed to succeed in slavery: prompt attention to assigned tasks, when the master is present or absent; healthy fear of the coercive authority of the master. Here, however, the monologue culminates with Sagaristio's assertion of his lack of enthusiasm and deliberate diffidence with regard to the master's persistent commands (7–10):

SAG: *qui ero suo seruire uolt bene seruos seruitutem,*
ne illum edepol multa in pectore suo conlocare oportet
quae ero placere censeat praesenti atque apsenti suo.
Ego neque lubenter seruio neque sati'sum ero ex sententia.

SAG: He who wishes to be a good slave in slavery for his master
that man need store many things in his breast
which he judges pleasing to his master when he is present and absent.
I neither willingly am a slave nor am I sufficient for my master, by design.

Sagaristio represents the successful slave whom the master trusts as a business representative (*hau quit tamen / quin mi imperet, quin me suis negotiis praefulciat*, 11–12). Both opening monologues thus exploit literary conventions in order to lay bare social presumptions about slaves and the slave system's definition of the slave as a non-subject, i.e. as an agent who acts only to fulfill the volition of the master (cf. Patterson 1982: 28). They also conjure up the illusion of the play as an authentic telescope onto the world of slave subjectivity. The theatrical conceit presumes a Roman awareness of a separate, slave world and an interest in seeing how slaves interact amongst themselves. Two slaves inform the audience that they hold parts of themselves separate from slavery and act—though in different ways—for their own self-interest.

The opening scene introduces Toxilus and Sagaristio as *amici*, "friends," a Roman category that in Roman (and ancient) thought defined a social relationship and measured the capacity to act as a human being in the fullest sense (Brunt 1988a: 351–381; Konstan 1995). The two slaves greet each other with reciprocal good wishes (16). Toxilus professes himself in love (24–25) and indicates that he seeks money in order to buy the freedom of his slave beloved, who is about to be sold away (33–34, *haec dies summa hodie est, mea amica sitne libera / an sempiternam seruitutem seruiat*, "today is the final day that will determine whether my girlfriend is free or is a slave in eternal slavery"). He asks Sagaristio to help him (33–37). Sagaristio questions where slaves experience love (*iam serui hic amant*, "do slaves now love here?" 25), perhaps to remind the audience that the play's action takes place away from Rome (*hic* indicating not at Rome), or to underscore the dramatic allusion of the play (*hic* indicating the stage). Sagaristio's words make explicit for the audience the divergence between Toxilus' status as slave and his intentions. Nevertheless Sagaristio identifies himself as an *amicus* of Toxilus and offers to help his slave-friend even before he knows what will be asked of him (19, *nimi' stulte amicis utere … imperare oportet*, cf. 33–34; Raccanelli 1998: 169–171; Lefevre 2001: 37). Furthermore, Sagaristio refuses to be bribed into helping Toxilus by the offer of food and high living (30a-b), promises which identify Toxilus as a trickster slave (Levine 1977: 108–110; Joyner 1986: 151) and which Sagaristio dismisses as dangerous (31, cf. *Pseud.* 946–949; Damon 1997: 49–50). His willingness to act selflessly for another slave, identified as his friend (cf. Lefevre 2001: 81–82), contrasts with his avowed, calculated reserve in working for his master's interests (as required and presumed by the slave society), even as he returns from penal servitude (21–22). Indeed in a subsequent monologue (259–271), he regales the audience with a description of his deliberate deception of his master, undeterred by the master's control of coercive violence, in order to help his friend (*amico prosperabo*, 263; *amico … largiar*, 265). In a regrettably broken line (the manuscripts have nothing beyond *ergo*, Lindsay added *volo* and adopted the additional words *et ego* appearing in T, the oldest recension we have), the slave nevertheless identifies himself as having the same desires as his friend (34b): *quid nunc vis ergo et ego <volo>* ("what now therefore you want, I too want"). So Sagaristio acts from a self-identified moral obligation to someone he identifies as his friend (21) and Toxilus claims that Sagaristio in helping him will earn his enduring friendship (35).

For his part, Toxilus acts to preserve a family unit, albeit a slave family unit, unrecognized by the slave society (Watson 1987: 77–81; Bradley 1987: 47–80), and he avows a perceived moral obligation that prompts an action running counter to his immediate self-interest, behavior that Plautine commentators have judged as illogical or poor dramaturgy (Lefevre 2001: 27). Yet Cato's proverbial suspicion of slave alliances and his regulations to commodify sexual relations among his slaves (slave relations were limited to those within the household, and male slaves paid for sex with female slaves within the household) suggests contemporary Roman awareness and perhaps anxiety about affective relations among slaves (Plut. *Cato Mai.* 21.2, 4; Astin 1978: 262–263). Moreover, relationships of male and female slave partners feature in *Casina* and in *Stichus*. In *Casina*, a master desires sex with a female slave raised in his household and seeks to assign her as consort to his male slave *vilicus* in order to facilitate his own liaison with her. Behind the stock conflict of philandering husband and shrewish wife that drives the plot and the play's moral exploration of the proper role of the male patriarch (Konstan 1983: 19–20, 51; Moore 1998: 158–180, esp. 166; McCarthy 2000: 77–121), two male slaves compete for the possibility of a long-term affective relationship with a female slave; the master's *vilicus* imagines torturing his rival in the country with hard work (*Cas.* 120–123), little food (126–129), and the experience of listening to the *vilicus* make love with the female slave over whom they are competing (132–140); and the rival male slave, given by his master the choice of freedom or a slave family, chooses family (290–294). Embedded in *Casina* as embellishment to the plot is the male slave's desire for a long-term affective relationship with a female slave partner. In *Stichus* two young wives dutifully await the homecoming of their spouses against the urgings of their father who insists that they divorce their absent husbands; the husbands return having achieved spectacular success in their business; the reconciled patriarch, his daughters, and their newly returned husbands celebrate their reunion offstage with a banquet; two male slaves celebrate onstage with a shared female slave partner, who is termed a *scortus* (730). The final banquet among the slaves, which doubles and mirrors the familial celebration of the freeborn, conflates Greek and Roman elements in order to create a typically Plautine inflation—and deflation—of the slave status: the slaves appropriate the language of Roman politics to describe their roles at banquet (696–704; Fraenkel 1960: 223–231), they identify as Roman and contrast the simplicity of their Roman tableware with Greek luxury (689–695; cf. Owens 2000: 401–402), and they dilate upon their affective relationships as shared (729–733) and commodified (750–751). In *Stichus* Plautus stages and denigrates slave relationships, as contrast and foil to the decorous relationships of the free (Owens 2000: 391–394). So Plautus' plays offer early evidence for slave relationships and the importance that the slaves themselves attached to their identification as family units, for example the use of the term *contubernalis* in later commemorative inscriptions (Treggiari 1981: 42–69). Contemporary slavery studies have emphasized the importance of the family as a solution to the problem of domination posed by slavery (Berlin 1998: 129–132, esp. 162–164). In a free person Toxilus' perceived obligation to family would have been heralded as *pietas*, as for example the self-sacrifice of the husband Ti. Sempronius Gracchus (consul 177, 163) for his wife (Pliny *NH* 7.122; Saller 1994: 108).

Both slaves at the opening of *Persa* thus act against their immediate self-interest to promote the identified good of another unrelated by blood, and Plautus' text gives early testimony to ethical thinking documented in the late Republic (Cic. *Att.* 12.37.3, cf. Arist. *NE* 8.2 1155b31; Konstan 1997: 1–23, esp. 13–14). In their actions and expressions, they reflect and posture according to the expected and honorable behavior of the free "insider."

The use of the substantive *amicus* elsewhere in Plautus elucidates the representation of slave relationships here in *Persa*. *Amicus* describes the relationship of free males with each other (see the appendix to this chapter, section a). The literary pedigree of the Plautine *amicus* as a character type may derive from the Greek New Comic tradition (Leo 1912: 127); but Plautus translates the idea with Roman conceptions, correlating the *amicus* with the *familiaris* (*Trin.* 89), *adfinis* (*Bacch.* 380), *cognatus* (*Miles* 1119, *Stich.* 580, *Trin.* 261–262 with 263–264, 702), and *sodalis* (*Bacch.* 475, *Cas.* 581, *Curc.* 332 with 330, *Merc.* 475, 951 with 947). He ascribes to the *amicus* a Roman set of expectations reflecting the alliance of interest among persons related or unrelated by blood (Hellegouarc'h 1972: 152–157, esp. 156–157). *Amicus* correlated with goodwill (*benevolens*, see *Asin.* 66, *Bacch.* 475, *Pseud.* 699, *Trin.* 1177) and with the late republican emphasis on intimacy (*cognatio* and *familaritas*, see Hellegouarc'h 1972: 64, 68) and concrete actions (*benevolens*, see Hellegouarc'h 1972: 150). The use of the word thus seems to reflect a real social category in Plautus, and Plautus' material correlates with the late republican evidence where we see *amicus/amicitia* describing a basic relationship that expressed the capacity for honor, of both participants, especially *fides* (*Bacch.* 541–542, *Merc.* 839, *Trin.* 1126, 1128; see *Thesaurus Linguae Latinae* s.v. "amicus," col. 1910, lines 41–66). The Plautine category does not include slaves, with two notable exceptions: a single occurrence in *Pseudolus* when the trickster slave Pseudolus grandiloquently identifies his audience as the people and all his acquaintance (127), and repeatedly in *Persa* where it is applied to the identity of interest of male slaves with each other on six occasions (14, 35, 255, 263, 265, cf. 293) and to the trickster's deceptive posture as protecting the interests of the person whom he is deceiving on three occasions (581, 595, 614, see below; cf. *Pseud.* 233).

Furthermore, the gendered use of *amicus/amica* in Plautus to describe the relationship of free and slave only describes the relationship of free males and slave women and only describes a sexual relationship, where the word contrasts with *uxor* and with *concubina* (see appendix, section b). Although both *amicus* and *amica* derive from the root *am* meaning "love" (Konstan 1997: 123–124), usage shows a limitation for women of the actions that would constitute "love," namely sexual relations, by contrast with the richly varied usage to describe the social and political capacities of men, thus reflecting a division of labor and a conceptual categorization of gender that Susan Moller Okin (1979: 10) traces throughout Western political philosophy. Finally, although the evidence for *amica* as a social category is literary and primarily poetic (*Thesaurus Linguae Latinae* s.v. "amicus," col. 1912, lines 65–68), both its appositives (*uxor* and *concubina*) are technical terms of the law and occur in inscriptions describing social relationships (Fabre 1981: 170–172). By exclusion, *amica* as a word seems also to reflect a real category of thinking about social relationships.

The use of *amicus/amica* in Plautus is thus conspicuous for what it excludes and what it recognizes: male slaves are excluded from social relationships not only with the free but with each other, and female slaves are only accorded a sexual identity in their relationships with masters (on the relationships, see Kolendo 1983). From the perspective of the master, usage suggests a conceptualization of the slave as incapable of social relationships (*amicus/amicitia*) founded in Roman terms on honor (*fides*). Moroever, even if the original identification of Sagaristio as an *amicus* represents an accidental anomaly or perhaps a relic of an original Greek play (so Raccanelli 1998: 169–171), the absence of the word elsewhere in Plautus to describe slave relationships and its repeated use in *Persa* are conspicuous. The slave community and slave friendship in *Persa* seem, then, intentional elements of the play, and indeed usage seems to mark a thematic contrast between the authentic alliance of slaves with each other and the posture of slaves with non-slaves.

As contrasts to the slaves' loyalty to each other, Plautus stages Sagaristio's reported dealings with his master and Toxilus' dealings with two free men, the parasite Saturio and the pimp. He also stages the slave dealings with each other, particularly Toxilus' interaction with two slaves, Paegnium and his slave girlfriend Lemniselenis, and Paegnium's interactions with the older female slave Sophoclidisca and then with the older male slave Sagaristio. The dramatic action emphasizes the enormous economic and social cost for free men who associate with a slave, but it also illustrates a complex web of relationships among the slaves themselves.

By contrast with the dinner invitation that is rejected by his fellow slave as dangerous, Toxilus secures the help of the freeborn parasite Saturio with the inducement of a meal. Behind the interaction of Toxilus and Saturio stands the literary and social reality of Roman patronage, a relationship of reciprocal obligation based on *fides* and functioning to guarantee for the client protection and preferment with respect to the larger community (Damon 1997: 37–79, esp. 48–57; Brunt 1988b: 382–442). Focusing on the character of the parasite, Damon (1997: 2, 8) has argued that the literary type allowed Romans to think about forms of social dependency and their dangers. The parasite also allowed Plautus to illustrate the difference between slaves and free men, for Toxilus shows himself unable to act as patron and uphold a relationship, ascribed to Romulus, wherein a patron served the state by taking care of a dependent (Wallace-Hadrill 1989). Saturio's first words on stage emphasize his self-conception as an honorable parasite within a long lineage of parasites (53–60), and Plautus cues his assumed superiority over the slave Toxilus by giving him the theatrical role of eavesdropper (Marshall 2006: 183). But the ensuing dramatic action reveals an inverse status hierarchy, for Toxilus exacts from the freeborn male an enormous price for the meal, namely his acquiescence in the sale of his daughter, and so her degradation and the consequent loss of his own honor (140–144; Damon 1997: 51 and n.33). Although the subsequent dialogue between Saturio and his daughter makes explicit the negative social judgment of his actions (344–348, 355–356, 383–384), and Plautus characterizes him as keenly—pimpishly-- self-interested to profit from his daughter (Marshall 2006: 184), with the interaction of Saturio and Toxilus, Plautus also stages a successful slave whose control of social resources results in the humiliation of his freeborn male dependent and the dependent's vulnerable, freeborn, virgin daughter. The dramatic action shows the slave incapable of enacting the role of the patron who provides the dependent with both scarce resources (Wallace-Hadrill 1989: 73) and protection (Drummond 1990: 104–105). Indeed Plautus constructs a plot in which Toxilus, in his desire to protect his slave girlfriend, demands the violation of the honor of a freeborn *virgo* (140–144). The male slave's threat to the chaste body of the freeborn woman is a trope appearing in the accounts of the first Sicilian slave rebellion (Diod. 34/35.2.11–12).

Similarly Toxilus deceives and humiliates the pimp Dordalus who is owed deference because he freed the slave girlfriend (Fabre 1981: 48). The pimp represents the universally loathed social outcast in New Comedy, and Plautus regularly exploits the theatrical expectations of animosity between pimp and trickster slaves in his plays (Segal 1968: 79–92). In *Persa*, however, Plautus complicates the enmity, because the pimp frees the trickster's own girlfriend and thus enjoys the status of patron. Indeed Toxilus deceives the pimp by playing upon his expectations of social obligation and reciprocity. In other words the pimp is deceived because he imagines—wrongly—that the slave possesses the expected sensibilities surrounding social relationships of patronage and friendship.

Having learned that his girlfriend is finally, legally freed and installed at his house, Toxilus avows himself the well-wisher of the pimp. He declares an identity of interest (489), claims the impulse to show reciprocity for the pimp's freeing of his girlfriend (492), an idea he repeats in encouraging Dordalus to buy Virgo (537–538), and professes candor (493), a virtue ascribed to friendship (Burton 2004: 214, 224–228). Although the trickster Toxilus never identifies himself as the *amicus* of the pimp, his assertions of goodwill and his actions are interpreted for the pimp—and for the audience—as the actions of friendship by the fellow slave Sagaristio, who asks Toxilus if he is the pimp's *amicus* (581), and then the pimp himself expounds on Toxilus' actions with gnomic statements on the role of the *amicus* when doing business (*quantum est adhibere hominem amicum, ubi quid geras*, 595) and on the mutual benefit of friends helping friends (*Tibi ibidem das, ubi tu tuom amicum adiuuas*, 614). With the sale concluded, Toxilus identifies the event as a favor (*beneficium*, 719) he has done for the pimp, who expresses his gratitude (*immo equidem gratiam tibi, Toxile, habeo*, 719–720; Woytek 1982: 393) and acknowledges the slave's labor (*te sensi sedulo mihi dare bonam operam*, 720–721). In other words, all characters represent and evaluate Toxilus' actions in recognizable Roman terms of the social institution of friendship and reciprocal obligation for favor (*gratia*). Moreover, Toxilus lures Dordalus to purchase Virgo by suggesting to the pimp that he can become his vision of himself within the social structure, as one who dispenses favor, or *gratia*, to an eager, attendant elite (567). Plautus thus stages the successful slave knowing, mimicking, and exploiting the social institutions of the free society and Roman social relations, even as he shows himself by his actions as disregarding those ideals and their obligations (cf. McCarthy 2000: 128–129). Toxilus whose opening lines suggested his theatrical role as "insider," as freeborn male lover, defines himself as "outsider" by his own actions. The successful slave's exclusion from free society stems from his actions, not from the arbitrary judgment of the slave society.

Persa stages a complex society among the slaves themselves. Toxilus seems to be the master of the slave Paegnium, perhaps reflecting the practice, recorded as early as Cato (Plut. *Cato Maior* 10.6; 21.7; Astin 1978: 263–264), whereby slaves, even though they could not technically own property, themselves bought (and traded) slaves (Buckland 1908: 239–249). Sophoclodisca is the *peculiare* of the slave woman Lemniselenis (201; Woytek 1982: 234–235), presumably her favorite slave, although again the slave woman could not technically purchase or own a slave. The male and female slaves enact among themselves a contest for domination that is the essential feature of slavery, thereby affirming the rightness of domination as a dynamic, and subordinating themselves within the system of slavery. They battle with each other in verbal contests that have been identified as Plautine creations (Wallochny 1992: esp. 59–97) and serve Plautine theatrical aesthetics of pacing (Marshall 2006: 181–184; Slater 1985: 42–43): the slave prostitute Lemniselenis with her old female slave Sophoclidisca (168–182), the younger male slave Paegnium with Toxilus (183–199), the old female slave Sophoclidisca (200–250) and the male slave Sagaristio (272–301; Hughes 1984: 50–54, Lefevre 2001: 70–76). The verbal play shows slaves adept at verbal skills which challenge the master's authority to define reality and become a vehicle of the slave's self-assertion with the master and with other slaves (Stewart 2012: 163–189; cf. Gates 1988: esp. 58, 66–67). Yet the verbal contests also reveal relationships and give repeated dramatic expression to essential elements of slave experience: the overwhelming physical assault that guaranteed the slave's obedience, the sexual exploitation of male and female slaves, the commodification of relationships of trust. The contests show how the slave's isolation from community, the deracination at the basis of chattel slavery, continued in slavery and was perpetuated by the slaves themselves.

Toxilus seeks to dominate Paegnium. Although we are never informed if Toxilus is truly Paegnium's master/purchaser, when he dispatches him to deliver a letter and a message for his girlfriend, he names and defines Paegnium—an example of Althusser's interpellation—with denigrating language that emphasizes the slave's corporal vulnerability and equates his low social worth with a low moral worth. Toxilus names Paegnium as a ***uerbereum caput*** or "whipping post" (184) and a *scelus* or "crime incarnate." The language of violence and denigration is ubiquitous in Roman comedy and variously interpreted, for example to reflect and mitigate the anxiety of Roman masters about their domination of their slaves (Parker 1989: 236; Hopkins 1993: 23). But the language reflects an enduring Roman reality and a way of thinking that defined the slave, fundamentally, as "less than human": masters disciplined slaves with corporal punishment, not with words, because, according to Roman thinking, slaves, by contrast with young freeborn males, lacked the personal capacity for correction by reason (Saller 1994: 133–160). Plautus here makes comedy with a slave applying the denigrating language—and thinking—of the slave society to another slave. When Paegnium quibbles on the exact meaning of his commands, Toxilus either promises or threatens him with something for his *peculium*, to ensure his compliance (*scelu' tu pueri es atque ob istanc rem ego aliqui te peculiabo*, 192). The verb *peculiabo* is a Plautine hapax, and Woytek (1982: 231) suggests a loaded meaning, in a positive sense offering Paegnium an addition to the personal property (*peculium*) at his discretion, or in a negative sense threatening him with sexual assault, a different *peculium* (cf. *Capt.* 965). Playing the master, Toxilus uses money or the threat of physical violence to force the male slave's compliance. The successful slave Toxilus, who works to free his slave girlfriend, thus parrots the objectifying and denigrating language and the thinking of the slave society: he has fully accepted domination and has no frame of reference apart from slavery. Paegnium responds by appropriating the master's words and using them against him, an example of double-voiced discourse studied by Henry Louis Gates (1988: 50). He proposes to obey precisely Toxilus' commands and so challenges Toxilus' ability to command, so for example at 190–191:

TOX: *sed ita uolo te currere, ut domi sis, quom ego te esse illi censeam.*
PA: *faciam.*
TOX: *quo ergo is nunc?*
PA: *domum: uti domi sim, quom illi censeas.*

TOX: Hurry so that you'll be at home when I told you to be there.
PA: Done.
TOX: Where are you going now?
PA: Home, so that I am there when you want me there.

Such verbal skill characterizes the interactions of master and slave throughout Plautine drama (e.g. *Poen.* 279–280, 292–297; Stewart 2012: 163–189), the folk tale of Aesop (Hopkins 1993: 3–27), and the trickster tales of the American South (Gates 1988). He makes explicit the arbitrary reality of the slave system—perhaps his role includes making explicit harsh realities (cf. lines 296–297 and below)—and he reminds Toxilus that the words and actions of the master with respect to a slave are guaranteed by no moral or institutional sanction (193–194):

Scio fide hercle erili ut soleat inpudicitia opprobrari
nec subigi queantur umquam, ut pro ea fide habeant iudicem

I know, by Hercules, that with respect to a master's good faith, shamelessness is wont to be censured, nor are they in any way able to be held accountable, so that they have a judge for that good faith.

Perhaps the humor here resides in the slaves' incapacity to make formal, binding agreements (Watson 1987: 90). But Plautus stages slaves who become masters and dominate their slaves, and he stages a slave who acknowledges and acquiesces in what he recognizes as an unassailable, emasculating power relation with another slave. The Roman audience witnessed slaves themselves battling with each other and thereby naturalizing and normalizing the arbitrary logic of domination (cf. *Pseud.* 905–951, esp. 926–933, 944–945).

Paegnium shows no deference or respect in his interactions with other slaves, either the female Sophoclidisca or the older male slave Sagaristio, and he parrots with them the denigrating language that Toxilus had applied to him. In Act 2, scene 2 (200–250), Paegnium and the old female Sophoclidisca meet as they deliver letters from their respective masters to each other (Slater 1985: 43; McCarthy 2000: 138–139). The slaves taunt each other: Sophoclidisca characterizes Paegnium as the most morally worthless person in her acquaintance (202, 209, 222) and calls him crime incarnate (217, cf. 220). Equally Paegnium identifies Sophoclidisca as criminal, morally inferior, the most morally inferior of beings, and purely bad (208, 220, 221, 238). Forms of *malus/peior/pessimus* occur throughout the passage with a wide range of meaning (e.g. "moral inferiority" at 220; "despicable" or "contemptible" at 238, with Woytek 1982: 248) and the instability of meaning forms the basis of verbal play (e.g. 209–210). Similarly, when Paegnium and Sagaristio meet, Sagaristio calls Paegnium "criminal," "poisoner," and "crime incarnate" (275, 278, 290). Paegnium replies by calling Sagaristio "cuckoo," "whipped," and "dead meat" (282, 279, 283). Wallochny (1992: 71–72) has argued that the Plautine verbal play is its own goal; but Plautus created scenes (Lefevre 2001: 72–73) that entertained a Roman audience with the image of slaves applying to each other the denigrating language that masters applied to them. For the slave society, the humor could arise from watching slaves who have so completely accepted the terms of domination and so combat each other.

Paegnium enacts with other slaves the negative reciprocity denied to him by the slave society. With the old woman Sophoclidisca, he claims that he chooses to be hateful (SOPH: *odiosu's*. PA: *lubet*, 236). When the male slave Sagaristio sees and addresses him, Paegnium refuses to acknowledge him (272–273):

SAG: *mane, etsi properas. Paegnium, ausculta.*
PA: *emere oportet, quem tibi oboedire uelis.*
SAG: *asta.*

SAG: Wait, even if you are in a hurry. Paegnium, listen.
PA: You need to buy the person whom you want to obey you.
SAG: Stop.

Paegnium knows that recognition reflects and enacts relationships of power, and acts accordingly (cf. *Cas.* 141). He insists on the logic of the slave system that commodified human relationships as relationships between purchasers and purchased: obedience is bought (273; cf. *Trin.* 1059, *Curc.* 223). He refuses to show respect for the older male slave (280). When Sagaristio threatens him with rope-whips (282), Paegnium threatens to smash his face (283), promising to retaliate and not to restrain the impulse to negative reciprocity (Scott 1990: 37–38). Obviously and simply, Paegnium, unlike Toxilus and

Sagaristio, does not pursue an identity of interest with other slaves. The deracination, or lack of community, at the basis of chattel slavery continues for him in slavery by his own volition. The dramatic action thus illustrates the complete lack of community—or deracination—of the individual slave, as a lived experience, a personal decision, and a strategy for surviving in slavery.

In their quest for freedom and the resources to procure freedom, the slaves display an essential amorality. In a monologue, a presumed private musing shared with the audience, Sagaristio reports that he has absconded with monies entrusted to him by his master in order to help Toxilus (255–262), and he faults his master for failing to account for his previously demonstrated independent will (*stultus, qui hoc mihi daret argentum, quoius ingenium nouerat*, 261). He dismisses his future punishment and represents his act as a military conquest as well as an attack on the privations of slavery and the system of slavery (263–267):

> *nunc et amico prosperabo et genio meo multa bona faciam,*
> *diu quo bene erit, die uno apsoluam: tuxtax tergo erit meo, non curo.*
> *nunc amico hominibus domitis mea ex crumina largiar.*
> *nam id demum lepidumst, triparcos homines, vetulos, avidos, ardos*
> *bene admordere, qui salinum servo obsignant cum sale.*

> Now I will help a friend and produce much good in my own interest,
> For as long as it will be well, on this one day I will acquit myself fully.
> There will be blows on my back. I don't care.
> Now, for my friend, from these my conquests, I will give largesse from my own purse.
> For this finally is pleasant, the thrice thrifty men, old, greedy, and hard,
> To bite them well, they who lock the salt cellar together with the salt to the disadvantage of the slave.

For the text at 265 (*hominibus domitis*, see Lindsay 1896: 333), there is no comparable use of "domitus" to describe human beings in Plautus, but the word elsewhere does describe conquered peoples in reports of military campaigns (Cic. *Prov. cons.* 5; Livy 21.5.3, 32.9.3, 38.28.5, *Per.* 100). Holt Parker (1998: 160–161) has observed a correlation between Roman moral clichés about hungry, bibulous, stealing slaves and the restricted quantities of food available to slaves. Here, however, Plautus conjures up the slave's justificatory logic, that his behavior responds to the circumstances of his slavery. Eugene Genovese (1974: 603–604) has observed the ubiquity across slave systems of the argument, which Plautus puts in the mouth of Sagaristio, whereby slaves justified their stealing from the master; and Levine (1977: 122–127) has traced the thinking in slave remembrances and trickster tales from the American South. Plautus thus stages here thinking characteristic across slave systems.

Similarly, the slaves of *Persa* represent their sexual attractiveness as a short-lived strategic asset that can bring freedom. They repeatedly deride each other about their sexual roles in slavery. Paegnium taunts the presumably older and unattractive (cf. 170) female slave Sophoclidisca as sexually aggressive and dominant (*subigitatrix*, 227, cf. 194; Woytek 1982: 244) and experienced (*peritae*, 233). The humor could arise from the conventional denigration of a woman as old, sexually insatiable, and loathsome, clichés evident in invective poetry a century later than Plautus (Richlin 1992a: 68, 109–116). But Plautus also stages a conversation that would never happen between a freeborn Roman female and a young male: male and female slaves talk about sex, are sexually aggressive, and the fortunes of their lives may depend upon sex. Similarly, in *Rudens*, the male slave Sceparnio speaks openly about sex to the female slave Ampelisca (416–418), looks at Ampelisca's body (420–423), and touches her (424–425). Again, Sagaristio taunts Paegnium as his master's repeated sex-mate (284: *video ego te: iam incubitatus es*, "I see through you. You are your master's boy toy"). Paegnium retorts that he at least, unlike Sagaristio, does not give sex for free (285). The taunt nods to Roman attitudes about penetration and compromised masculinity. But Paegnium identifies sex as a strategic transaction, useful to elicit *gratiae* or favor (228). The representation of the male slave is striking: unlike the romanticized images of delicate *pueri* in Latin literature and Hellenistic Greek epigram (Richlin 1992a: 34–44, esp. 38), Plautus stages the male slave conscious that sexual penetration was dishonorable (Williams 2010: 36–38) but could bring preferment (cf. *Cas.* 452–460) or freedom from the whip (cf. *Pseud.* 767–789). Paegnium avows that he allows the sex in order to become free (*Nam ego me confido liberum fore, tu te numquam speras*, "For I am confident that I will be free, you expect yourself never to be so," 286). So Plautus stages slaves who choose sexual behavior that was for a Roman stigmatizing, and they dismiss the stigma with a calculus of their freedom. For the master, the slave, once again, by his own actions implicates himself in a cycle of stigmatization that will lessen his freedom, his status as "insider." For the slave, sexual behavior is a survival strategy, and amoral. Plautus underscores the doubleness of the master's judgment of the sexualized slave and the slave's strategic decision-making with the fictive sale into slavery of freeborn Virgo.

The staged sale of Virgo, whose speaking role is probably a Plautine creation (Lowe 1989: 390–399; cf. Stärk 1991: 159–160), establishes a contrast to the behavior of the slaves, as Plautus conjures up the experience of sale into slavery and creates a commentary—uniquely given by a freeborn citizen woman—on the experience of deracination and the assault on corporal integrity inherent in chattel slavery (Stewart 2012: 37–47). The slave Toxilus had defined the parameters for a cogent fraudulent sale: a story of kidnap, a costume, and, most of all, the body of a freeborn woman which he knew would be most compelling as merchandise. He set up the credibility of the slave trader, by composing a letter—ostensibly from his absent master—that introduced the would be slave-trader and detailed the origins of the merchandise. The scene of freeborn Virgo's sale creates an extreme image of the loss of a woman's honor (383–384) that would have shocked the audience of Roman patriarchs (Marshall 2006: 189–190). Toxilus and Dordalus first silently watch Virgo, where the language emphasizes the appraisal of her physical form and the vulnerability of the female unprotected by family: Toxilus invites the lowlife pimp and the entire audience to join him in appraising her body (*taciti contemplemur formam*, 548; cf. 564). Virgo is subject to a penetrating and shaming gaze (Parker 1999: 163–168). The questioning of Virgo about her homeland parallels the requirements defined for slave sale by the edict of the curule aediles and would have grounded the dramatic action as a sensible, Roman experience for a Roman audience. Asked about her family and homeland (630–650), Virgo claims that her past, her homeland, and her personal identity were destroyed by enslavement. Nor does she truly have a present, for slavery does not allow her to judge her life experience. Plautus seems here to understand and reflect the deracination and complete loss of personal history caused by enslavement, as well as slavery's assault on personal judgment and emotion. Virgo's tears seal the sale, and the pimp attempting to console Virgo assures her that she will earn enough from her lovers in order to buy her freedom quickly (*ne sis plora; libera eris actutum, si crebro cades*, "Don't wail. You will be free directly, if you lie down for sex often," 656). Plautus thus stages the slave's experience in at once the most evocative, emotional terms for a Roman audience (the freeborn Virgo bereft of the protection of male family members) and the most deflecting manner (the would-be master is a lowlife pimp). Nevertheless the staging underscores slave experience as a radical isolation and a continuous assault on the integrity of the body with devastating consequences.

Plautus creates for *Persa* a final tableau that allows the play to end and the audience to go home, but the conclusion emphasizes rather than resolves the conflicting loyalties between the freed slave woman, her partner, and her former master. Toxilus celebrates his success in securing the freedom of his slave girlfriend, and the merrymaking fulfills the Saturnalian theme announced at the beginning of the play (29–30; Auhagen 2001: 103–106; Lefevre 2001: 23, 32) and once again allows the Roman audience to be voyeurs in the private lives of slaves (cf. the final scene of *Stichus* above). The slaves indulge their natural proclivities for sex and wine, enacting a cliché of intemperate slaves (Parker 1998). Toxilus and Lemniselenis embrace and recline together on the couch (763–766) and the slaves engage in a drinking party (771–776). But the dramatic action reveals the problem of a gendered slavery and a gendered freedom.

Toxilus announces that he celebrates the much-anticipated day, when he has obtained with divine help the right to embrace Lemniselenis as a free woman (*bene mihi, bene uobis, bene meae amicae, optatus hic mi dies datus hodiest / ab dis, quia te licet liberam med amplecti*, 773–774). The male slave thus proclaims Lemniselenis' role as the vehicle for his own self-assertion. Line 776 makes this claim explicitly: *bene ei qui invidet mi et ei qui hoc gaudet*. The line has been variously ascribed: Leo in his edition (1895–96) assigned the line to Toxilus; Woytek (1982: 411–412) suggests Sagaristio because Toxilus ought not to be speaking while his girlfriend drinks. The parallel for the line—a scene between lovers in *Mostellaria* (305–307)—suggests the sentiment belongs to a male lover. But even if the line is assigned to Lemniselenis, the sentiment only makes explicit the conclusion of the plot: Toxilus has claimed and secured his exclusive rights with respect to his slave consort. The contest over the body of the female slave in *Casina* (see above) corroborates the sensibilities implicit in Toxilus' action. The male slave has protected the body of the female slave, who thus serves as the vehicle for his self-assertion (and so for his victory over slavery).

Lemniselenis, who displays a noticeable silence throughout the play (Slater 1985: 43), finally speaks in Act 5, where her role is to have strong affective ties to Toxilus. In her first words she asks why she and Toxilus are apart (763). She literally defers to him for defining her desires (*omnia quae tu vis, ea cupio*, "Everything you want, I want those things too," 766). She avows that Toxilus is responsible for her being free (775) and thus endorses his self-assertion. Although Toxilus avers a reciprocity in their relationship (*mutua fiunt a me*, 766), he overwhelms Lemniselenis (cf. McCarthy 2000: 154–155; Auhagen 2001: 103). He declares her the *dictatrix* for the party (770), but he immediately undercuts her authority (and his proclamation), first by repeating her orders (771–772) and then by taking command of the toasting (773–776). The deference of the female freed-slave partner to her male slave partner replicates conventional conjugal roles: gender prevails over status in obliging deference.

The finale represents Lemniselenis' former master Dordalus and her slave partner Toxilus competing for the loyalty of the freedwoman. When Dordalus arrives, he first addresses Lemniselenis as his noble freedwoman (*bona liberta*, 797), thereby alluding to his former role and attempting to suggest the obligatory loyalty owed by a freed slave to a former master who now stood as patron (Lefevre 2001: 30n.132). When Lemniselenis addresses Dordalus as her *patronus* and invites him to go inside to dinner, he answers her and calls her *Ignavia mea*, ironically echoing her vocative, identifying her as the antithesis of the virtuous or *frugi* slave and again insinuating that she has failed in her moral obligations to him (849–851, cf. *Poen.* 845–846; Woytek 1982: 437–438). Similarly, when Toxilus exhorts Lemniselenis to obey him, he invokes the conventional logic of slavery to oblige her deference, that is, he claims that he gave money for her (*ego sum tibi patronus plane qui huic pro te argentum dedi*, "I am surely your patron who gave money to this guy for you," 842). Lemniselenis protests the mistreatment of her former master and patron, but Toxilus arrogates to himself the position of patron and accuses her of ingratitude (838–840):

TOX: *sed ita pars libertinorum est: nisi patroni qui advorsatust,*
nec sati'liber sibi videtur nec sati'frugi nec sat honestus,
ni id ecfecit, ni ei male dixit, ni grato ingratus repertust.

TOX: But such is the way of the freed, unless he shows opposition to his patron
he doesn't seem to himself to be free enough or successful enough or decent enough,
unless he does this, unless he speaks badly to his patron, unless he is revealed as ungrateful to one who deserves gratitude.

So Toxilus—once again—shows himself to understand the psychology of the slave system and able to exploit it successfully (McCarthy 2000: 157, cf. Woytek 1982: 434–435). The staging underscores the potentially autonomous action of the freed slave as the crux for the former master and for the slave society. The play ends when Lemniselenis follows her slave partner rather than her former master, and Toxilus redirects the ending by inviting the audience to applaud the punishment of the pimp, the appropriate social outcast (Stärk 1991: 149–154). The ending leaves unremarked the potential threat to the slave society of the freed female slave defining freedom in terms of affective relationship with another slave rather than her master/patron.

All of Plautus' plays share an essential conceit: the plays presumed to allow the Roman audience (and us) to watch slaves and to look within their behavior in order to see the elements of deferential roles, the logic of servile deference, and finally the existence of an independent servile identity that stood apart from slavery. Plautus shows slaves who deploy violence with each other and so normalize and naturalize the slave society's use of coercive violence. He stages slaves who deceive, steal, and prostitute themselves in order to gain freedom, thereby implicating themselves by their own actions in their social dishonor and exclusion. He presents slaves who gain resources and freedom but cannot act successfully in the human relationships of deferential honor that characterized Roman free society, thereby calling into question Roman policies of citizenship and inclusion. He seems, in other words, like Cato, to represent a piece of the multi-voiced Roman public discourse—by definition ideological—that formed and sustained the Roman slave society.

He appears, however, unlike Cato, to have recognized an alternative view. He also stages slaves who develop a matrix of affective relationships with each other, of friendship and of family. He shows slaves who justify their immoral behavior (deception, thieving, prostitution) as a response to the privations of slavery or as a strategy of survival. He presents slaves who understand and manipulate the psychology of the slave society, who know how to behave as slaves and how to make others resemble slaves. He seems, in other words, to have recognized slavery as a complex problem, a *relationship* of power between dominant masters, who justified their status with narratives of their own honor ("insiders"), and forcibly subordinated slaves, who experienced physical violence and the cognitive assault of being treated like chattels ("outsiders"). His own plays, the products of an artist's insight, do not take sides but reinscribe the contest in its complexity. Categories of "insider" and "outsider" emerge as narratives of power.

Both Greek and Roman discussions of excluded groups have shown how literary output was inflected by the ideological principles of the respective societies of democratic Athens and republican Rome. Literature, not simply the consciously formulated philosophical treatise but a wide range of literary texts and contexts, thus can be seen to function as a concomitant of government policy and social practice in creating and instantiating the discourses that created the citizen and the slave, which ideas (citizen, slave) are products of discourse. Balot and Atkison (Chapter 22) focus on literary representations of females and slaves in Athenian public drama, funeral oration, and philosophical treatises, as they reflect Athenian ideology, government policy and social practice, about what it meant to be a citizen through the construction of the other. Similarly, in this chapter I have considered the literary representations of slaves, male and female, in the public drama of Plautus to show how slavery and literary representations of slavery were constitutive of Roman citizen ideology (on women and law in Rome, see Williamson, Chapter 11). Alongside Roman government policies of inclusion and procedures of manumission granting citizenship, policies that presume a belief that subordinated peoples may be acculturated and enter into Roman social relationships, Plautus staged a drama, the *Persa*, that defined the slave by contrast with the citizen, in terms of capacity for honor and the social relationships, particularly patronage, founded upon it. Plautus stages a successful slave who cannot act with honor, treat others with honor, or live within the social relationships of honor. The slave's exclusion from Roman relationships becomes a product of his own actions, not the arbitrary thinking of the slave society. By contrast with Balot and Atkison, in the Roman context one does not adduce philosophical treatises because no Roman author wrote a philosophical treatise of slavery. Nevertheless the plays of Plautus reveal a sophisticated and complex Roman discourse of the problem of exclusion, enforced subordination, and integration.

Appendix. *Amicus/Amica* in Plautus

(a) Amicus

On *amicus* in Plautus, see *Amph.* 943, 1040; *Asin.* 246; *Aul.* 475; *Bacch.* 347, 377, 380, 386, 475, 477, 498, 539, 541, 547, 557, 619, 1156; *Capt.* 141, 180, 441, 645, 773; *Cas.* 241, 515, 581, 615; *Cist.* 114, 639–640; *Curc.* 332, 356, 685; *Epid.* 113, 119, 422, 425; *Men.* 700; *Merc.* 288, 385, 467, 475, 499, 534, 839, 887, 951; *Miles* 391,

660, 674, 724, 741, 1119; *Most.* 980, 1056, 1149; *Poen.* 349, 504, 508, 512, 573, 794, 852, 1090, 1213, 1339; *Pseud.* 127, 218, 228, 390, 699; *Rud.* 93; *Stich.* 128, 143, 503, 508, 509, 518, 520, 521, 522, 580; *Trin.* 23, 25, 48, 54, 75, 89, 91, 93, 94, 106, 180, 216, 263–264, 267–268, 326, 337, 347, 456, 620, 630, 651, 702, 716, 758, 759, 876, 895, 899, 909, 924, 926, 956, 1052, 1054, 1056, 1095, 1110, 1126, 1128, 1177; *Truc.* 172, 173, 216, 574, 880, 885; *Vid.* 68. Cf. *amica* describing the relationship of free females, see *Cas.* 203. *Amici* of the associates of a pimp, see *Pseud.* 878, 879, 880.

(b) Amica

On *amica* in Plautus, see *Amph.* 659 (contrasting with *uxor*); *Asin.* 83, 104, 183, 747, 812, 825, 852, 863, 879; *Bacch.* 61, 140, 145, 177, 194, 367, 390, 562, 574, 607, 717, 718, 755, 1115; *Cas.* 612; *Cist.* 1, 133, 227–228, 237, 406, 570; *Curc.* 593; *Epid.* 368, 457 (cf. 466, *concubina*), 481, 702, 704; *Men.* 173 (conjoined with *meretrix*), 300, 450, 561, 598, 652, 699, 741 (cf. 740, *uxor*); *Merc.* 181, 215, 341, 383, 479, 480, 545, 688, 753 (cf. 757, *concubina*), 794, 813, 863, 888, 925, 944, 966, 973, 974; *Miles* 105, 114, 122, 263, 274, 507; *Most.* 23, 310, 311, 538, 888, 974, 1139, 1160; *Poen.* 266, 393, 868, 1288, 1299, 1414; *Pseud.* 35, 174, 188, 231, 280, 341, 344, 347, 419, 435, 487, 673, 719, 722, 1277a; *Rud.* 351, 839; *Stich.* 572, 573; *Trin.* 651; *Truc.* 102, 167, 171, 239, 356, 497, 623, 893, 914, 917, 920. *Amica* describes the female slave partner of a male slave: *Stich.* 426, 431, 434, 437, 651 (correlate with *conserva*), 701, 711, 732, 735, 766. *Amicus* of male slave partners of a female slave: *Stich.* 679, 682, 766.

REFERENCES

CAH =, *The Cambridge Ancient History*. 2nd edn. Cambridge, 1989.

Astin, A.E. 1978. *Cato the Censor*. Oxford.

Auhagen, U. 2001. "Toxilus und Lemniselenis: ein paradoxes Liebespaar." In S. Faller, ed., *Studien zu Plautus' Persa*. Scripta Oralia 121. Tübingen, 95–111

Bastien, J.-L. 1998. "La clientèle, le triomphe et l'espace civique à Rome aux derniers siècles de la république." *Hypothèses* 1: 131–136.

Bellen, H. and H. Heinen, eds. 2003. *Bibliographie zur antiken Sklaverei*, 2 vols. Stuttgart.

Berlin, I. 1998. *Many Thousands Gone: The First Two Centuries of Slavery in North America*. Cambridge.

Bradley, K. 1987. *Slaves and Masters in the Roman Empire: A Study in Social Control*. Oxford.

Bradley, K. 1989. *Slavery and Rebellion in the Roman World, 140 B.C.–70 B.C.* Repr. edn. Bloomington and Indianapolis.

Bradley, K.m ed. 1991. *Discovering the Roman Family: Studies in Roman Social History*. New York.

Bradley, K. 1994. *Slavery and Society at Rome*. Cambridge and New York.

Brunt, P.A. 1971. *Italian Manpower, 225 B.C.–A.D. 14*. London.

Brunt, P.A. 1988a. "Amicitia." In *The Fall of the Roman Republic and Related Essays*. Oxford, 351–381.

Brunt, P.A. 1988b. "Clientela." In *The Fall of the Roman Republic and Related Essays*. Oxford, 382–442.

Buckland, W. 1908. *The Roman Law of Slavery: The Condition of the Slave in Private Law from Augustus to Justinian*. Cambridge; repr. New York, 1969.

Burton, P. 2004. "*Amicitia* in Plautus: A Study of Roman Friendship Processes." *AJP* 125: 209–243.

Catalano, P. 1978. "Aspetti spaziali del sistema giuridico-religioso romano. *Mundus, templum, urbs, ager, Latium, Italia.*" *ANRW* 2.16.1: 440–553.

Cels-Saint-Hilaire, J. 1985. "Les *libertini*: des mots et des choses." *Dialogues d'histoire ancienne* 11: 330–379.

Coşkun, A. 2009. *Bürgerrechtsentzug oder Fremdenausweisung? Studien zu den Rechten von Latinern und weiteren Fremden sowie zum Bürgerrechtswechsel in der Römischen Republik (5. bis frühes 1. Jh. v.Chr.)*. Stuttgart.

Crawford, M.H. 1996. "Italy and Rome from Sulla to Augustus." *CAH* 10: 414–433.

Crook, J.A. 1984. "*Lex Aquilia*." *Athenaeum* 62: 67–77.

Crook, J.A. 1996. "Lex Aquilia." In M. Crawford, ed., *Roman Statutes*, 2 vols. BICS suppl. 64. London, 723–726.

Dahlheim, W. 1968. *Struktur und Entwicklung des römischen Völkerrechts im dritten und zweiten Jahrhundert v. Chr.* Vestigia, Beiträge zur alten Geschichte 8. Munich.

Dahlheim, W. 1977. *Gewalt und Herrschaft: Das provinziale Herrschaftssystem der römischen Republik*. Berlin and New York.

Damon, C. 1997. *The Mask of the Parasite: A Pathology of Roman Patronage*. Ann Arbor.

Dench, E. 2005. *Romulus' Asylum. Roman Identities from the Age of Alexander to the Age of Hadrian*. Oxford.

Dixon, S. 1992. *The Roman Family*. Baltimore.

Dixon, S. 2001. *Reading Roman Women*. London.

Dixon, S. 2007. *Cornelia: Mother of the Gracchi*. London and New York.

Drummond, A. 1990. "Rome in the Fifth Century II: The Citizen Community." *CAH* 7(2): 172–242.

Ebel, C. 1991. "Dum Populus Senatusque Romanus Vellet." *Historia* 40: 439–448.

Edmondson, J. and A. Keith, eds. 2008. *Roman Dress and the Fabrics of Roman Culture*. Toronto.

Fabre, G. 1981. *Libertus: Recherches sur les rapports patron–affranchi à la fin de la République romaine*. Collection de l'École française de Rome 50. Rome.

Fantham, E. 2006. *Julia Augusti: The Emperor's Daughter*. London and New York.

Fentress, E. 2005. "On the Block: *Catastae, Chalcidica* and *Cryptae* in Early Imperial Italy," *JRA* 20: 220–234.

Finley, M.I. 1998. *Ancient Slavery and Modern Ideology*. Rev. B. Shaw. Princeton. (1st edn. 1980.)

Fitzgerald, W. 2000. *Slavery and the Roman Literary Imagination*. Cambridge.

Fraenkel, E. 1960. *Elementi Plautini in Plauto*. Trans. F. Munari. Florence.

Frier, B.W. and T. McGinn. 2004. *A Casebook on Roman Family Law*. Oxford.

Gabba, E. 1975. "Istituzioni militari e colonizzaxione in Roma medio-repubblicana (IV– III sec. a.C.)." *RFIC* 103: 144–154.

Galsterer, H. 1976. *Herrschaft und Verwaltung im republikanischen Italien: Die Beziehungen Roms zu den italischen Gemeinden vom Latinerfrieden 338 v. Chr. Bis zum Bundesgenossenkrieg 91 v. Chr.* Münchener Beiträge zur Papyrusforschung und antiken Rechtsgeschichte 68. Munich.

Gardner, J. 1986. *Women in Roman Law and Society*. Bloomington.

Garnsey, P. 1996. *Ideas of Slavery from Aristotle to Augustine*. Cambridge.

Gates, H.L., Jr., 1988. *The Signifying Monkey: A Theory of African-American Literary Criticism*. New York and Oxford.

Genovese, E. 1974. *Roll Jordan Roll: The World the Slaves Made*. New York.

George, M., ed. 2005. *The Roman Family in the Empire: Rome, Italy, and Beyond*. Oxford and New York.

George, M. 2013. *Roman Slavery and Roman Material Culture*. Phoenix Supplementary Volumes, 52. Toronto.

Grubbs, J. 2002. *Women and the Law in the Roman Empire: A Sourcebook on Marriage, Divorce, and Widowhood.* London and New York.

Hallett, J. and S. Murnaghan, eds. 1998. *Women and Slaves in Greco-Roman Culture: Differential Equations*. London and New York.

Harper, K. 2011. *Slavery in the Late Roman World,* A.D. *275–425.* Cambridge.

Hellegouarc'h J. 1972. *Le Vocabulaire latin des relations et des partis politiques sous la République*. 2nd edn. Paris.

Hölkeskamp, J. 1987. *Die Entstehung der Nobilität.* Stuttgart

Hölkeskamp, J. 1993. "Conquest, Competition and Consensus: Roman Expansions in Italy and the Rise of the Nobilitas." *Historia* 42: 12–39.

Hopkins, K. 1978. *Conquerors and Slaves.* Sociological Studies in Roman History 1. Cambridge.

Hopkins, K. 1993. "Novel Evidence for Roman Slavery." *P&P* 138: 3–27.

Hubbard, T. 2014. *A Companion to Greek and Roman Sexualities.* Chichester, West Sussex.

Hughes, D. 1984. "The Character of Paegnium in Plautus' Persa." *RhM* 127: 46–57.

Isaac, B. 2004. *The Invention of Racism in Classical Antiquity.* Princeton.

Joshel, S. 1992, *Work, Identity, and Legal Status at Rome. A Study of the Occupational Inscriptions.* Norman, OK.

Joyner, C. 1986. "The Trickster and the Fool: Folktales and Identity among Southern Plantation Slaves." *Plantation Society* 2: 150–156.

Kolendo, J. 1983. "L'esclavage et la vie sexuelle des hommes libres à Rome." *Index* 10: 288–297.

Koloski-Ostrow, A. and C. Lyons, eds. 1997. *Naked Truths: Women, Sexuality, and Gender in Classical Art and Archaeology.* London and New York.

Konstan, D. 1983. *Roman Comedy.* Ithaca.

Konstan, D. 1995. "Patrons and Friends." *CPh* 90: 328–342.

Konstan, D. 1997. *Friendship in the Classical World.* Cambridge.

Kraemer, R.S. 1992. *Her Share of the Blessings: Women's Religions among Pagans, Jews, and Christians in the Greco-Roman World.* Oxford and New York.

Kraemer, R.S. 2004. *Women's Religions in the Greco-Roman World: A Sourcebook.* Oxford and New York.

Kraemer, R.S. 2011. *Unreliable Witnesses: Religion, Gender, and History in the Greco-Roman Mediterranean.* Oxford and New York.

Kraemer, R.S. and M.R. D'Angelo, eds. 1999. *Women and Christian Origins*. Oxford and New York.

Lefevre, E. 2001. "Plautus' *Persa* zwischen Nea und Stegreifspiel." In S. Faller, ed., *Studien zu Plautus' Persa*. Scripta Oralia 121. Tübingen, 11–94.

LeGates, M. 2001. *In Their Time: A History of Feminism in Western Society.* New York.

Leigh, M. 2004. *Comedy and the Rise of Rome.* Oxford.

Leo, F. 1895–96. *Plauti Comoediae.* Berlin.

Leo, F. 1912. *Plautinische Forschungen: Zur Kritik und Geschichte der* Komödie. 2nd edn. Berlin.

Levine, L.W. 1977. *Black Culture and Black Consciousness: Afro-American Folk Thought from Slavery to Freedom.* Oxford and New York.

Lindsay, W. 1896. "Leo's Plautus." *CR* 10: 330–334; review of F. Leo, *Plauti Comediae*, 2 vols. (Berlin 1895, 1896).

Lindsay, W. 1913. *Sexti Pompei Festi De verborum significatu quae supersunt cum Pauli epitome.* Leipzig: Teubner.

Lowe, J.C.B. 1989. "The Virgo Callida of Plautus, Persa." *CQ* 39: 390–399

Marshall C.W. 2006. *The Stagecraft and Performance of Roman Comedy.* Cambridge.

McCarthy, K. 2000. *Slaves, Masters, and the Art of Authority in Plautine Comedy* Princeton.

McCoskey, D. 2004. "On Black Athena, Hippocratic Medicine, and Roman Imperial Edicts: Egyptians and the Problem of Race in Antiquity." In Rodney D. Coates, ed., *Race and Ethnicity—Across Time, Space and Discipline*. Leiden: Brill, 297–330.

McCoskey, D. 2012. *Race: Antiquity and Its Legacy*. Oxford and New York.
McKeown, N. 2007. *The Invention of Ancient Slavery*. London: Duckworth.
Miller, J., ed. 1999. *Slavery and Slaving in World History: A Bibliography, 1900–1991*. Armonk, NY.
Moore, T. 1998. *The Theater of Plautus: Playing to the Audience*. Austin.
Okin, S. Moller. 1979. *Women in Western Political Thought*. Princeton.
Olson, K. 2008. *Dress and the Roman Woman: Self-Presentation and Society*. New York.
Owens, W.M. 2000. "Plautus' Stichus and the Political Crisis of 200 B.C." *AJP* 121: 385–407.
Packman Z. 1999. "Feminine Role Designations in the Comedies of Plautus." *AJP* 120: 245–258.
Parker, H. 1989. "Crucially Funny or Tranio on the Couch: The *Servus Callidus* and Jokes about Torture." *TAPA* 119: 233–246
Parker, H. 1998. "Loyal Slaves and Loyal Wives. The Crisis of the Outsider-Within and Roman *Exemplum* Literature." In S. Joshel and S. Murnaghan, eds., *Women and Slaves in Greco-Roman Culture: Differential Equations*. London and New York, 152–173.
Parker, H. 1999. "The Observed of all Observers: Spectacle, Applause, and Cultura Poetics in the Roman Theater Audience." In B. Bergmann and C. Kondoleon, eds., *The Art of Ancient Spectacle*. New Haven, 163–179.
Patterson, O. 1982. *Slavery and Social Death: A Comparative Study*. Cambridge, MA.
Raccanelli, R. 1998. *L'Amicitia nelle Commedie di Plauto: un indagine antropologica*. Bari.
Rawson, B. 1986. *The Family in Ancient Rome: New Perspectives*. London.
Rawson, E. 1991. "The Prodigy Lists and the Use of the Annales Maximi." In *Roman Culture and Society*. Oxford.
Richlin, A. 1992a. *The Garden of Priapus: Sexuality and Aggression in Roman Humor*. Rev. edn. New York and Oxford.
Richlin, A., ed. 1992b. *Pornography and Representation in Greece and Rome*. New York and Oxford.
Richlin, A. 2005. *Rome and the Mysterious Orient: Three Plays by Plautus*. Berkeley.
Richlin, A. 2010. "What We Need to Know Right Now." *Journal of Women's History* 22: 268–281.
Richlin, A. 2011. "Writing Women into History." In A. Erskine, ed., *A Companion to Ancient History*. Oxford, 146–153.
Rigsby, K. 2005. "Agathopolis and Doloupolis." *Epigraphica Anatolica* 38: 109–115.
Saller, R. 1994. *Patriarchy, Property and Death in the Roman Family*. Cambridge.
Scheidel, W. 2007. "The Roman Slave Supply." *Princeton/Stanford Working Papers in Classics*.
Scott, J. 1990. *Domination and the Arts of Resistance: Hidden Transcripts*. New Haven.
Sebesta, J. and L. Bonfante, eds. 1994. *The World of Roman Costume*. Madison.
Segal, E. 1968. *Roman Laughter: The Comedy of Plautus*. Cambridge, MA.
Shaw, B. 2001. *Spartacus and the Slave Wars. A Brief History with Documents*. New York and Boston.
Sherberg, A.B. 2001. "Das Vater-Tochter-Verhältnis im plautinischen *Persa*." In S. Faller, ed., *Studien zu Plautus'* Persa. Scripta Oralia 121. Tübingen, 139–153.
Skinner, M., ed. 1986. *Rescuing Creusa: New Methodological Approaches to Women in Antiquity*. Special issue, *Helios* 13(2).
Slater, N. 1985. *Plautus in Performance: The Theatre of the Mind*. Princeton.
Stärk, E. 1991. "*Persa* oder *Ex oriente fraus*." In E. Lefèvre, E. Stärk, and G. Vogt-Spira, eds., *Plautus Barbatus: Sechs Kapitel zur Originalität des Plautus*. Scripta Oralia 25. Tübingen, 141–161.
Stek, T. 2009. *Cult Places and Cultural Change in Republican Italy: A Contextual Approach to Religious Aspects of Rural Society after the Roman Conquest*. Amsterdam Archaeological Series 14. Amsterdam.
Stewart, R. 1998. *Public Office in Early Rome: Ritual Procedure and Political Practice*. Ann Arbor.
Stewart, R. 2012. *Plautus and Roman Slavery*. Oxford.

Thomas, Y. 1996. "'Origine' et 'commune patrie': Étude de droit public romain (89 av. J.-C.–212 ap. J.-C.)." *CÉFR* 221. Rome.

Treggiari, S. 1981. "Contubernales in *CIL* 6." *Phoenix* 35: 42–69.

Treggiari, S. 1991. *Iusti Coniuges from the Time of Cicero to the Time of Ulpian*. Oxford and New York.

Treggiari, S. 2007. *Terentia, Tullia, and Publilia: The Woman of Cicero's Family*. London and New York.

Trouillot, M.-R. 1995. *Silencing the Past: Power and the Production of History*. Boston.

Von Fritz, K. 1950. "The Reorganization of the Roman Government in 366 B.C. and the So-Called Licinio-Sextian Laws." *Historia* 1: 3–44.

Wallace-Hadrill, A., ed. 1989. *Patronage in Ancient Society*. London and New York.

Wallochny, B. 1992. *Streitszenen in der griechischen und römischen Komödie*. Scripta Oralia 44. Tübingen.

Watson, A. 1987. *Roman Slave Law*. Baltimore and London.

Weaver, P.R.C. 1972. *Familia Caesaris: A Social Study of the Emperor's Freedmen and Slaves*. Cambridge.

Wiedemann, T. 1989. *Greek and Roman Slavery*. Repr. London.

Williams C. 2010. *Roman Homosexuality: Ideologies of Masculinity in Classical Antiquity*. 2nd rev. edn. Oxford.

Williamson, C. 2005. *The Laws of the Roman People: Public Law in the Expansion and Decline of the Roman Republic*. Ann Arbor.

Woytek, E. 1982. *T. Maccius Plautus Persa: Einleitung, Text und Kommentar*. Vienna.

Yavetz, Z. 1998. *Slaves and Slavery in Ancient Rome*. New Brunswick and London.

FURTHER READING

How the historian evaluates the extreme power relationship inherent in slavery (a process of enforced subordination; an extrinsically imposed definition of the human being as chattel), affects methodology and the type of history produced. For a comparative, methodological discussion, see Trouillot 1995. For those interested in the history of slavery, Finley 1980 (revised 1998) remains a necessary beginning. Finley identified the category of the "slave society" and argued for a comparative, historical approach. Shaw's Introduction to the revised edition orients Finley's work and responses to it within the broader context of the study of slavery. McKeown 2007 offers a broader survey of historiography. Patterson 1982 offers a comparative sociological study of the institution. Further considerations of the relationship between Roman political development, Roman militarism, and Roman slavery, see especially Hopkins 1978 and Scheidel 2011. Wiedemann 1989 provides a collection of sources, with judicious historical commentary. For the relationship of Roman master and slave, the works of Bradley 1987 and 1994 are foundational. For a general survey of ancient philosophical thinking about slavery (necessarily omitting the Roman republican era), see Garnsey 1996. For the slave and slavery as a theme within Latin literature, see the introductory survey of Fitzgerald 2000. For slave rebellions, see Yavetz 1998 and Shaw 2001. The foundational study of the slave wars remains Bradley 1989. For the slave's relationship to work, see Joshel 1992. On freedmen, see Treggiari 1969 and Weaver 1972. Uncovering the material reality of slaves, see George 2011 and Fentress 2005. For the late imperial history of slavery and the intersection between Christianity and slavery, see Glancy 2002 and Harper 2011. On the question of Roman racial, or racializing, thinking, see Isaac 2004 and McCoskey 2004; 2012. Excellent print bibliographies are in Bellen and Heinen 2003, indexed and with a full listing of works in English, French, German, Italian et al., arranged according to topic; Miller 1993; and http://www.oxfordbibliographies.com/view/document/obo-9780195389661/obo-9780195389661-0151.xml?rskey=lUYNWl&result=127&q= (accessed Apr. 3, 2014).

For those interested in the history of Roman women, Richlin 2009 offers a survey of the problem and the historiography, with recommended further reading. Dixon 2001 provides a useful survey of problems and methodologies. The recent spate of biographies of exceptional Roman women illustrates the opportunities and independence possible for Roman women, even as the series showcases the outstanding work of women historians: Dixon 2007; Fantham 2006; Levick 2007; Treggiari 2007. For those interested in locating ancient women's lives within the history of feminism and gender studies, see LeGates 2001.

The category of "gender," like the category of "slave," represents the product of a relationship of power that distorts relationships and records of relationships. For the methodological issues and very different analytical perspectives, see Skinner 1986; more discursively, a series of case studies, see Hallett and Murnaghan 1998. With a focus on ancient sexuality, see Hubbard 2014.

Amidst the explosion of new work in women's studies, I single out works that offer important methodological or analytical frameworks. Richlin 1992a showed how to understand words as weapons against women; see also Richlin 1992b. Kraemer 1994, 2012, and Kraemer and D'Angelo 1999; see too Kraemer 2004. Legal frameworks offer a way into understanding the quotidian frameworks within which women, including non-elite women, lived; with different approaches, see Frier and McGinn 2003; Grubbs 2002; for a survey, see Gardner 1986. On the social relationships (marriage, family) that framed women's lives, see Treggiari 1991. On the Roman family, see Dixon 1992. Good collections: Rawson 1987, Bradley 1991; George 2005. A good introduction to the use of material culture, the problems and the methodologies, see Koloski-Ostrow and Lyons 1997. Clothing reflected and constructed Roman status; on the adorned gendered body, see Sebesta and Bonfante 2001; Olson 2008; Edmondson and Keith 2008.

Online bibliographies, and images: http://www.stoa.org/diotima/biblio.shtml (accessed Apr. 3, 2014).

PART XII

Entertainment

CHAPTER 24

Tragedy and Comedy in Greek Participatory Communities

Keith Sidwell

Theater was already a well-established public art in the Greek world by the mid-fifth century: Aeschylus is said to have produced his plays in Sicily, comedy certainly flourished in Syracuse and appears also to have been important in Megara, while towards the end of the century the Athenian tragic playwrights Agathon and Euripides were involved with the production of tragedy in Macedon, for whose stage Euripides wrote a play entitled *Archelaos*, implicitly linking mythical antiquity with the current King Archelaos. But for nowhere outside Athens do we have sufficient data to attempt a comprehensive picture of the relationship of theater to its participatory community. This chapter, therefore, will concentrate on Athens and upon the two genres for which some political role can be argued, tragedy and comedy.

It seems at first sight that the place of the theater in political life in Athens simply must have been different from the way it was elsewhere (Rome included) because the context in which it occurred was determined and controlled by the *dēmos* rather than by private individuals (or groups) with political agendas. Hence, recent discussion about the politics of surviving theatrical texts has tended—in respect of tragedy especially—to use *dēmos* "values" as its template (e.g. Goldhill 1987, 2000; Rhodes 2003; Henderson 1990; Olson 2010). This chapter, by contrast, argues that, while the *dēmos* exercised various types of control over the theater, it operated in practice as a sort of private–public partnership, in which, because the production of plays was paid for by wealthy individuals as a form of tax and the playwrights were in competition with each other, there was ample room for the expression of private political agendas in the material presented before the public.

1 Social, Physical, and Legal Organization

In Athens, from an early point (around 501 BCE: *DFA*^{2}: 72), tragedy (probably with satyr plays) was drafted into the official calendar of the *polis* and formed (eventually the central)

A Companion to Greek Democracy and the Roman Republic, First Edition. Edited by Dean Hammer.

part of the celebration of two major festivals of Dionysus, the Lenaea (January: *DFA*^{2}: 25–42) and the Great or City Dionysia (March: *DFA*^{2}: 57–125). Comedy joined it in 486 BCE (*DFA*^{2}: 82: Suda s.v. *Chionides*). The plays presented were in competition with each other and their playwrights were chosen by the eponymous *archōn*, in a process of which we have no knowledge: the poet/producer (*didaskalos*) was said to have been "awarded a chorus" and the expenses of putting on the play(s) were paid by a *chorēgos*, in a form of higher taxation known as a liturgy (*DFA*^{2}: 86–90; Wilson 2000). There were prizes for the victorious dramatist and later (from 449 BCE: *DFA*^{2}: 93) for the main actor: these were allocated by a complex tribe-based system of voting which reflects in many ways the eager adherence to casuistic principles in the allotment of official roles by the Athenian democracy (*DFA*^{2}: 95–99). At the Dionysia, important official business of the *polis* was conducted in advance of the drama competitions (*DFA*^{2}: 58–59), and it has been argued that this effectively formed a quasi-political matrix for the audience's "reading" of the plays which followed (Goldhill 1987, 2000). No such "framing," however, existed for the competition at the Lenaea, or, as far as we know, for the competitions at the numerous *deme* theaters (at places like Thorikos, Aixone, and Piraeus).

The physical theater eventually used for the *polis* festivals developed from a space created temporarily in the *agora* (*DFA*^{2}: 28–29, 39–40) to the dedicated hillside site on the southeast slope of the Acropolis where the remains of what we call the "Theater of Dionysus" can still be seen (Pickard-Cambridge 1946; see also Hölscher, Chapter 26). Deme theaters also eventually had dedicated sites. Though the scale and proportions are necessarily different, since the *polis* festival theater had to accommodate some 5,000 spectators in the fifth century (Whitley 2001) and a much larger number in the fourth, the viewing places in the *polis* and demes had several features in common: an *orchēstra* ("dance-floor"), the focus of banked seating which encircled it on three sides, and a stage area.

Front seating in the Theater of Dionysus was reserved for magistrates (members of the *boulē*) and the priest of Dionysus (*DFA*^{2}: 268–270), but the make-up and seating position of the rest of the audience are matters of conjecture. It has sometimes been thought that seating was arranged by tribe (*phylē*), but this is uncertain (*DFA*^{2}: 270). If we could be sure of the date of the introduction of an attendance fee, on the one hand, and on the other of the *theōrikon*—a dole intended to help towards defraying the costs of attendance at festivals, including the purchase of theater tickets—we would perhaps be able to conjecture something of the social composition of the audience: but neither is certain (*DFA*^{2}: 265–268). There is evidence that boys attended (*DFA*^{2}: 263–264), but there is not enough to determine whether women were allowed admission (*DFA*^{2}: 264–265), or rather, since Plato tells us that in his day "educated women" did view tragedies (*Laws* 2, 658a–d; cf. *Laws* 7, 817c), at what stage and to what extent women were given access (i.e. were they, for example, able to watch *comedies*?).

The *polis* took the festivals seriously: it scrutinized the officials in charge (*DFA*^{2}: 68–70) and regulated various aspects of the competition. Regulation of content arises for tragedy in the instance cited by Herodotus of the fine levied and the ban imposed on his play *The Capture of Miletus*, on Phrynichus, for reminding the Athenians of "griefs close to home" (Hdt. 6.21.2). Since this was *post factum*, however, and Aeschylus' *Persians* and *Eumenides*, which arguably have political content, appear to have been produced without any untoward consequences for the playwright, this may well have been a "one-off" incident. There is evidence of a decree allowing Aeschylus' plays to be revived by anyone who wished (*DFA*²: 100). In the fourth century, it was probably *polis* legislation which allowed the introduction of "old dramas" into the festival (*DFA*²: 99), and certainly what decreed the tightly controlled treatment of the revivals of Aeschylus, Sophocles, and Euripides in the period of Lycurgus (*DFA*²: 100). In respect of comedy, the issue of *polis* control is contentious. Comic poets traditionally, but probably not legally, had the right to abuse individuals (Sommerstein 2004). The issue is clouded by the general acceptance by scholars of a serious legal challenge against Aristophanes by Cleon in 426 BCE. Unfortunately, since the basic evidence for this is within a comedy (*Acharnians* 376f.), it is entirely unclear whether or not such an action did take place or was invented for the purpose of humorous attack (Rosen 1988: 63–64), possibly within the confines of another comedy (Sidwell 2009: 78–79, 123). Nonetheless, most scholars do tend to accept the reality of at least one decree restricting comedy, that was passed in the archonship of Morychides (440 BCE) and was rescinded three years later (437 BCE), though its scope (*mē kōmōidein* "not to satirize") is difficult to pin down (scholion to Aristophanes *Acharnians* 67). Traces of other legislation, which also must underlie a version of the history of invective comedy of which we have only later, garbled, versions suggest, however, a continual battle between satirical comic poets and the *polis* over a considerable period of time (Sidwell 2009: 329–335; Sidwell, 2014). Measures enacted may have included: (1) restriction of naming in some form (*onomasti kōmōidein*); (2) restriction of visual satire; (3) restriction of targets to exclude citizens; (4) a total ban. Such a plethora of legal interference suggests, of course, that satirical comedy (what we usually call "Old Comedy") was seen as a serious political force, and for this reason scholars who wish to regard the genre as having no potential or actual political role or effect tend to argue this evidence away (e.g. Halliwell 1991).

2 Politics and Drama

Discussion of the political significance of Old Comedy almost always begins from the surviving plays themselves, on the assumption that they are relatively straightforward in what they can tell us (an exception is Heath 1987b). This confidence is induced by the existence in many Aristophanic plays of the common plot-theme of a "Great Idea" formulated to address, usually in a fantastic manner, some current political problem, and put into practice by the protagonist, normally interpreted (as in the cases, for example, of Dicaeopolis in Aristophanes' *Acharnians*, the Sausage-Seller in *Knights*, and Trygaeus in *Peace*) as a representative of the ordinary people, with whom the audience will identify (Sommerstein 1980: 11–13). However, interpretations based on close examination of the plots and their themes are even so not without difficulty. For example, understanding of the political lessons of *Acharnians* founders upon scholars' inability ultimately to provide a satisfactory account of the dissonance between Dicaeopolis' anti-democratic *modus operandi* and the actual workings of the *polis* (the *ekklēsia* will not listen to peace proposals and the "hero" makes a peace solely for himself and his family, mocks the *polis* representative of war, Lamachus, and is unwilling to share the benefits of his action with any consistency), or of the disjunction between the thrust of the plot (making peace with Sparta) and the authorial resistance (however comically expressed) to a settlement in the parabasis (655)—a section of the play where the chorus speaks directly to the audience about the poet's views (Sidwell 2009: 118–119).

If we begin from *external* evidence, however, and attempt to understand the nature of the genre as experienced by contemporaries, or from those who were in a position to have learned about the genre from such people, we find a different point of entry into the discussion. To the first category belong the account of comedy's satirical role in the pseudo-Xenophontic *Athenian Constitution* (2.18), Lysias' reference to attacks on Cinesias in comedy (fr. 53 Thalheim), Andocides' allusion to comic vilification of Hyperbolus and his father (fr. 5), Aeschines' mention of a comic attack on Timarchus (1.157) and Plato's utilization of Aristophanes' comic caricature of Socrates (*Ap.* 18c–d; 19c; *Phaedo* 70b–c). To these casual references we can add analysis of the attitudes towards Old Comedy of elite philosophers such as Plato (*Laws* 935d–936b), Isocrates (8.14), and Aristotle (*NE* 1128a23–25; *Rhet.* 1384b9–11; *Pol.* 1336a39f.). Aristotle's *Poetics*, composed certainly after satirical comedy became less of a force in Athens, provides scattered, but crucially important, evidence, of a *synkrisis* between his preferred mode of comedy and the unfavored satirical type (1451a36–38 and b5–15, 1449a32f., 1448b20–1449a5; Sidwell 2009: 320–326). And it is arguable that later writers relied on an account of the legislative history and eventual demise of Old Comedy produced by Aristotle, or someone else with attitudes and knowledge similar to his, to discuss (in a garbled fashion) the modes of attack used by the genre (Koster 1975, *Prolegomena*, *passim*; Sidwell 2014: 69–72). To these can be added significant, but rather general, pieces of information about individual poets: Aristophanes' civic crown and citation for support of the *dēmos* (*PCG* III^2, Testimonia on Aristophanes 1.35–39) and Eupolis' burial in the enemy city of Sicyon (Pausanias 2.7.3; Sidwell 2009: 38–44). Moving from the general to the specific, one may also adduce as quasi-external (because uttered in the poet's first-person voice) the evidence of the parabasis of the revised *Clouds* (518–561), a play never produced at a festival, but nonetheless addressed to an audience. This appears to have consisted of a group of patrons who had supported Aristophanes for at least ten years before this point, individuals with a political and intellectual agenda—against Cleon, against Socrates, for the Sophists, and for Hyperbolus, the radical democrat despised by Thucydides (Sidwell 2009: 3–30).

Paying close attention to the implications of the presentation (or intended presentation) of the revised *Clouds* before a *private* audience with a clearly focused political and intellectual agenda provides us with the neatest and simplest explanation of the way in which Old Comedy was political: comic poets were sponsored by special interest groups who supported specific political leaders—and despised others. Among other things, this meant that comic poets were locked also in a battle among themselves which reflected their political choices, and this explains the attention paid by Aristophanes in the revised *Clouds* parabasis (537–550) to lambasting the comic rubbish of his rivals, especially Eupolis (whom he probably hints at by a politically charged term, "to wear one's hair long" [545], something Aristophanes does *not* do, both because he is bald and because he is aligned with radical democrats, as opposed to the knights and/or laconophiles). However, it stands to reason that if the deployment of political attacks was to be at all effective, then Old Comedy cannot have operated in the way in which it was read by most later ancient scholars and as we traditionally read it, that is, with the chief iambic component being the jokes made against named individuals in the course of a plot which carries the main burden of the satire. Once again, the revised *Clouds* parabasis points us in the right direction: Aristophanes picks out the central *characters* of plays as the thematic focus of comedies (Cleon in *Knights*, Hyperbolus in Eupolis' *Marikas*—and, by implication,

Socrates in *Clouds*). This set of parameters, provided by Aristophanes himself, strongly suggests that satirical comedy ("Old Comedy") operated principally by ***caricaturing*** in the guise of its main characters real individuals, around whom it built a plot designed to ridicule the poet's sponsors' chosen targets (*contra* Heath 1987b: 43–54). Iambic naming of individuals thus takes place only within this wider structure and such jokes are focalized upon the character (or chorus) who speaks them: they are no guide, therefore, to the political thrust of the comedy itself (Sidwell 2009: 91–103).

That characters are not always given their real names (Paphlagon is the cover for Cleon in *Knights*, for instance) does not invalidate this reading of the evidence. A late source, Platonius, relying in my view upon a competent fourth-century writer, tells us that "In Old Comedy, they made the masks like the target of the satire, so that before the actors actually said anything the target was clear from the likeness of his face" (Koster 1975: *Prolegomena* 5, 1.57–59). The remarks of writers such as Plato and Isocrates, the scattered evidence of the scholia and the later *Prolegomena* on comedy also make it clear that satirical comedy was seen by some as a disruptive force and that attempts were made to restrict its ability to cause harm. In fact, the picture we can build up from analysis of the external contemporary references to Old Comedy confirms its perceived importance and potential dangers. This material tells us first and foremost that Old Comedy was designed to attack individuals who offended the ethos of democracy (Ps.-Xenophon *Ath. Pol.* 2.18) and that such attacks were used in public discourse by orators who assumed they meant there was no smoke without fire (e.g. Lysias fr. 53; Andocides fr. 5). Plato's portrait of Socrates' rejection of the caricature of Aristophanes as "having nothing to do with me" (*Ap.* 19c) was a philosopher's response, then, and both out of line with and indicative of the normal view. In this context, it is quite possible to believe that *rhētores* who felt that either they personally or—they might rather have argued—"the public interest" were threatened by such comic slurs might have wished to impose curbs, and that they might occasionally have been successful. There may have been, in fact, a comprehensive ban on satirical comedy between 440 and 437, the period of the Samian War and one, notably, where Cratinus was at the peak of his powers—and a severe critic of Pericles, whom he caricatured on stage as Zeus. Because of the ban on satirical comedy (which therefore obtained its own definitive generic descriptor as the *iambic form*), this very same period may well have given rise to the plot-based comedy peopled by type-characters (cooks, slaves, courtesans) which eventually became dominant in the fourth century (Arist. *Poet.* 1449b5–9; Sidwell 2009: 306–307; Sidwell 2014: 75–75), imported, so Aristotle tells us, from Sicily, and probably more specifically from Syracuse, where, no doubt under the tight political control of the tyrants, the comic poets, in particular Epicharmus, had developed the so-called "mythological burlesque," with comic plots focusing on Greek heroes such as Heracles and Odysseus. In fact, it seems highly likely that in the evidence for the banning of *onomasti kōmōidein* ("satirizing by name") preserved in the ancient scholia and *Prolegomena*, we may be seeing the outline of legislation which explains the fact that in our extant plays many of the central characters are not given their real names, even though the external evidence suggests they ought to be caricatures of real individuals. For the ancient scholars believed that *onomasti kōmōidein*, interpreted as "iambic naming," was *the* central feature of the genre (they wrote many books with titles like "Political Names in Eupolis": Sidwell 2009: 327), yet could not see any evidence at all for such a measure having been introduced. This means that they also could not have invented the phrase, which is likely, therefore, to derive from the terms of actual legislation. It could not, then, have meant "not naming individuals" *tout court*, but might very well have referred to the practice of not giving their real names to (certain classes of) individuals represented on stage in comedies.

Satirical comedy, then, was specific in its modes of attack and (therefore) subject to occasional regulation as time went on. The available evidence makes it difficult to be absolutely certain about the stages and pattern of this regulation, as has already been mentioned. As well as a possible total ban (440–437 BCE, a period where Cratinus' "mythological burlesque" *Dionysalexandros* might perhaps be dated) and a ban on giving the real names of some classes of individuals caricatured on stage, it seems likely that after the end of the Peloponnesian War, in the period of reconciliation, the opponents of satirical comedy were successful in achieving a ban on identification of these individuals (if they were Athenian citizens) by naming or by visual means (the famous "caricature-masks" which had apparently been normal for most of the fifth century). Later still, critics may have managed to have comic criticism (i.e. representation on stage) restricted to foreigners and slaves, and eventually to have the genre completely banned once again (Horace *Ars Poetica* 281–284) as had possibly happened between 440 and 437 (Sidwell 2009: 329–335).

If the reading of the revised *Clouds* parabasis allows the construction of a relatively simple model of how Old Comedy fits into the political life of Athens, our way into understanding how, if at all, tragedy operated politically is not nearly so straightforward, because its plots are mostly set in the heroic age. However, Aristophanes' continued on-stage caricature of Euripides over three decades (*Ach.* 425; *Thesm.* 411; *Frogs* 405) ought to mean, on the basis of the centrality of on-stage caricature to political interpretation articulated above, that he saw the tragic poet as a political opponent. Certainly, in *Frogs* he is figured as an opponent of democracy (952–953) and asked specific political questions, which he is unable to answer in such a way as to make him Dionysus' choice as Athens' savior (1427–1429, 1437–1438, 1440–1441, 1442–1443, 1446–1450). This is, of course, some way from demonstrating that Euripides did actually belong to a political group in the way that we can argue that Aristophanes did. Nonetheless, it does demonstrate that Aristophanes wished to represent Euripides as having to do with political process, and while this might simply be a joke resting on the fundamental absurdity of such a scenario, the way in which Aeschylus is treated points in a different direction.

Aeschylus in *Frogs* is also asked the same specific questions about political policy as Euripides, and his answers are formulated (at least in the version of the text accepted by most scholars) in such a way as to reflect realism about Alcibiades (1431–1432) and the current war policy of the *dēmos* (1463–1465)—in essentials, the same view as that of Pericles (according to Thucydides) at the war's outset (Sommerstein 1996a: 291). And Aeschylus is the tragic poet chosen to effect Athens'—political—salvation (1471). However, while Euripides might well have had a political posture—and that might have been generally known—Aeschylus had by this time been dead for some fifty years. The only way in which he could have been perceived as contributing to current political affairs will have been through the appropriation of his works by contemporaries. We are once more in contentious territory. We do have evidence of a decree that gave anyone who asked for a chorus to produce Aeschylus the right to be granted it (*Life of Aeschylus* 12). But modern scholarship is split in its view of whether we should take this seriously or not. On one side, there are those who explain as later scholiastic invention the evidence for fifth-century Aeschylean revivals (Hutchinson 1985; Biles 2006/7). On the other, there are scholars who take the phenomenon seriously (Newiger 1961: 427–430; Sommerstein 1996b: 31), though without connecting it in any thoroughgoing way with the political orientation of the final scene of *Frogs*. Certainty is impossible, though in my view the attention paid in *Frogs* in the contest to issues of *staging* (911f., 1028–1029) and the range of reference to Aeschylean material, in a period when the assumption that such a large audience could be reckoned *au fait* with a *written* text is questionable, point in the direction of a very strong tradition of such revivals, particularly during the war. The lack of correlation between the known dates of production of *Persians* (472) and *Seven Against Thebes* (467) and the order these are said to have been put on in *Frogs* (*Seven* before *Persians*: 1021–1026), the casual appropriation for parodic purposes of Aeschylean lines by several poets (Aristoph. *Knights* 836; Cratinus *Ploutoi* fr. 171.20–26; Eupolis *Marikas* fr. 207) and the scholiastic statement that "Aeschylus won not a few prizes after his death" (*Life of Aeschylus* 13) all suggest rather that revival of Aeschylus was something of an industry. It would not be unreasonable to conjecture, in fact, from the alignment of Aeschylus with Periclean policy in *Frogs* and from the well-established choregic relationship between the two (*IG* II^2 2318.9), that the decree had been designed by Pericles and with its provisions he aimed to continue using Aeschylus' name to support his own political agenda. Hence, Brockmann's suggestion that the expectation of an Aeschylus play by Dicaeopolis in *Acharnians*—disappointed by the command to Theognis to bring on his chorus (*Ach.* 9–11)—is to be explained by the notion that Theognis has asked for a chorus to produce an Aeschylus play (possibly *Persians*: compare *Ach.* 139 with *Persians* 496–497) is attractive (Brockmann 2003: 27–41). If the production had a political aim, however, it will not have been anything to do with Aeschylus himself, and the humor in *Acharnians* may rather have been understood as an interaction between (a) the identification by the audience of the real individual behind Dicaeopolis; (b) the audience's knowledge of his political allegiances; (c) the audience's recent viewing of Theognis' version of *Persians*(?); and (d) their knowledge of Theognis' political allegiances and recognition of the agenda the production was meant to serve.

In 387/6, the *polis* possibly issued a decree to allow revivals of the plays of other deceased tragedians, since in that year we have evidence from the *didaskaliai* that this was the first occasion when an "old tragedy" was "performed alongside" the new ones at the festival (*IG* II^2 2318; *DFA*^{2}: 105). Later on in the century, interpolation, especially in productions of Aeschylus, Sophocles, and Euripides, must have become an issue, since Lycurgus passed a decree establishing a fixed text of these playwrights with the requirement that actors not deviate from this in performance ([Plut.] *Vit. Orat.* 841f.). We have some confirmations of this phenomenon: Quintilian seems to have known that Aeschylean plays were revived in a changed form (10.1.66) and a gloss in Phrynichus refers to the word *epikattuein* ("to resole") specifically in relation to the adaptation of existing tragedies for revival performances; moreover, there have long been suspicions over the authenticity of whole plays (e.g. *Prometheus Bound*: Griffith 1977), and the status of portions of various texts (e.g. *Seven Against Thebes* 1005–1078: Hutchinson 1985: xliii and ad loc.); and we can see for ourselves that the account given of *Persians* by Dionysus at *Frogs* 1028–1029 is hard to match with the text *we* possess. Once more, however, we have very little information and scholars interpret what we have in more or less restrictive ways. However, if the evidence of *Frogs*, taken in conjunction with a firmly partisan political posture by Old Comic poets, suggests that tragedy too was regarded as having political force, then it is hard to believe that in either the fifth or fourth century the culture of revival was not firmly political too. Hence, we should be cautious about believing that Athenians will have had anything like our own attitude towards "authenticity" or "preservation" (the first evidence for this—if it is such—comes with Lycurgus' decree); rather, the fact that tragic plays were regarded as part of a political process should alert us to the possibility that interpolation—and even wholesale rewriting—may have been normal and have had an ideological basis.

3 Political Drama in Action

If the account given above of Old Comedy's political engagement is in any way accurate, we must acknowledge that our difficulties in reconstructing a full picture of the political networks it utilized will be immense: not knowing for certain who the on-stage targets are of any given play stands alongside the lack of any direct information (except for the inference from *Clouds* 551–559 of Aristophanes' adherence to Hyperbolus' group: Sidwell 2009: 24–26) about the *parti pris* of individual poets and the loss of all but a few fragments of the oeuvre of Aristophanes' rivals as the major impediments. Nonetheless, in the case of two plays, Aristophanes' *Knights* (Lenaea 424)—the most obviously political comedy we have—and Eupolis' *Marikas* (Lenaea 421), we do know one of the on-stage targets (Cleon for *Knights* and Hyperbolus for *Marikas*). Further, we are able to surmise that since Aristophanes supported Hyperbolus and reacted badly to his on-stage portrayal in *Marikas* (*Clouds* 553–556) this play was in some sense also an attack on him, especially because for once we do have a series of fragments from three different poets which reveal that there was a publicly debated issue about the relationship between *Knights* and *Marikas*. First of all Eupolis in *Baptai* fr. 89 *PCG* claims to have "co-written *Knights* with the bald fellow and given it to him as a gift," though Aristophanes in the revised *Clouds* parabasis says rather that *Knights*, promoted jointly by himself and his sponsors, was "turned inside out" by Eupolis in his *Marikas* (554; Sidwell 2009: 11), and Cratinus in the parabasis of *Pytine* (423 BCE) berates Aristophanes for "saying the things (i.e. words) of Eupolis" in *Knights* (fr. 213). Restrictive readings of this evidence, which either explain the relationship as a storm in a teacup based on the borrowing of one line (Sommerstein 1980: 51ff.) or as a sparring contest over originality (Storey 2003: 287), do not take into account the political dimension shown in the *Clouds* parabasis (Sidwell 2009: 3–44). Taking seriously some form of "collaboration" (Storey 2003: 281–288; cf. Kyriakidi 2007: 154–171) founders on the twin reefs of the general contempt in which co-authorship was held (Sidwell 1993: 373–375) and possible evidence for political antagonism between Aristophanes and Eupolis which *pre-dates Knights* (Sidwell 2009: 49, 80–82). Hence, although there is firm direct evidence from the fragments for the recycling of material from Eupolis to Aristophanes in *Knights* (Sidwell 1993: 381–384) and vice versa in *Marikas* (Storey 2003: 202–203), in the light of their political dissension, imitation is not a good explanation.

An alternative approach (Sidwell 2009: 48–56, 155–165) reads Cratinus' complaint in *Pytine* (fr. 213 *PCG*) as implying that, in *Knights*, Aristophanes had appropriated material from a pre-existing comedy by Eupolis. This play, possibly the *Noumeniai* ("Market-Day") produced at Lenaea 425 and lost already in antiquity, thus provided the overarching structure for *Knights* ("bad leader supplanted by worse leader") and at least two of its main characters (Paphlagon/Cleon and Dēmos). However, its main focus of attack was the "worse leader" who supplants Cleon. From several indications in Aristophanes (*Knights* 738–740, 1314–1315; *Peace* 680f.), and from a passage of Andocides (fr. 5), it seems possible that the idea of Hyperbolus as a lamp-maker/seller and as the leader of the *dēmos* derived from Eupolis' play, because in Andocides his profession is aligned with a completely fictional status for himself and his father (barbarian, slave), and leader (*prostates*) was a position he never held in reality. Thus Eupolis' focus of attack was clearly on the political favorite of Aristophanes and it is reasonable to suggest that in *Knights*, Aristophanes paid him back in kind by satirizing Eupolis' political sponsor (probably a knight) in the character of the Sausage-Seller. In *Marikas* (produced at Lenaea 421), Eupolis struck back, reusing his original scenario to attack Hyperbolus (the "bad leader") in the guise of a Persian (because of some recent change in Hyperbolus' policy towards Persia?) and perhaps to substitute for him as "worse leader" a politician with whom Aristophanes had only recently forged links—links which for some reason were deeply embarrassing. In each play, then, the pivotal figure will have been Dēmos and, given his satirical treatment and the evidence of [Xenophon] *Ath. Pol.* 2.18 that the *dēmos* did not allow itself to be satirized, he is likely to have represented a real individual somehow thought to have influential links with political figures and a status allowing him to claim that he represented the people. The suggestion (Sidwell 2009: 55–56, 75, 201) that he stands for a comic poet in each case (the same one in *Noumeniai* and *Knights*, but probably Aristophanes in *Marikas*) confirms the picture of close political association between comic poets and politicians which was inferred earlier from the *Clouds* parabasis.

Almost all identifications of fictitiously named characters as real individuals are, of course, problematic. Nevertheless, the underlying organizational structure revealed by the *Clouds* parabasis, in which a comic poet supports his own favorite by means of *attacking* his opponents by on-stage caricature and plots designed to ridicule them, is arguably visible in the *Noumeniai*(?)–*Knights*–*Marikas* series and resembles that of one type of sub-state-level politics in Athens we know about—the *hetaireia* (Ober 1989: 85). When we turn to the tragic texts, however, we are faced with even more serious difficulties, which even when approached by seeing how tragedy's political side is represented in Old Comedy, as interpreted in this chapter, are still difficult to overcome. We must first attempt to reconstruct the framework within which the humor operates, a hazardous occupation at 2,500 years' distance.

According to the template argued for above, the contest between Euripides and Aeschylus in *Frogs* will be enclosed within a satire of the individual represented as Dionysus. It seems likely that the choice of Aeschylus is supposed to be ironical for this individual, whose real-life allegiance, as well as that of his character in the play, will have been to Euripides. However, even if we could agree that this was the first step, making the identification is problematic and arguments towards it are necessarily convoluted, given that in any event these texts appear to have been constructed (perhaps because of legislative requirements, perhaps through fear of reprisal on the part of the poets) almost explicitly to *hide* these identifications (Sidwell 2009: 64–69, 328–335). Even in circumstances where we cannot be certain of the identification of Dionysus, however, we can see that the main joke of the satire is that Euripides agrees with the quasi-oligarchic message of the chorus (implicitly also reflecting the political agenda of the real individual behind Dionysus) and that Dionysus will be made to choose a poet whose stated policy choices agree with the current decisions of the *dēmos* (and before that of Pericles when the war began: Sommerstein 1996a: 291–292). Aeschylus himself, however, is not presented uncritically (Sidwell 2009: 291), and it may well be that the humorous point of the contest and its outcome is a joke being made about the political affiliation history of the individual behind Dionysus. Thus, the "advice" to the citizens given by Aristophanes in this play which led to a civic crown and a revival of the play (*after* the end of the war and the rule of the Thirty: Sidwell 2009: 41–44 *contra* Sommerstein 1996a: 21), may well have consisted not in anything said by Aeschylus, but rather in the implicit rejection of the recall of the oligarchs (which led after all to the regime of the Thirty), with whom the original of Dionysus must have been connected (Arnott, 1991; Sidwell 2009: 40–41, 285–288). When therefore Aeschylus is made to interpret *Seven* and *Persians* as inherently militaristic tragedies (1021–1028), designed to make the citizens noble by filling them full of the urge to fight and defeat their enemies, we are faced with an impenetrable wall of humorous possibilities: is he made to say this (1) because it is inherently absurd, or (2) because it reflects the way Athenians actually read the plays, but the individual satirized as Dionysus, being associated with the oligarchs, will actually have wished to make peace not war, or (3) because it expresses the *opposite* of the ideology Athenians would have seen behind those plays and Dionysus is being satirized by reacting in ways which undercut that supposition (Sidwell 2009: 295–297)? Currently, we do not have enough evidence to make a choice or even to know whether these are the only options.

Nonetheless, there does seem to be enough external evidence, through comedy, for a connection between tragedy and politics for it to be worthwhile investigating further. The socio-political structure within which tragedy will have been made to accommodate its political content will most likely resemble that of comedy. This will explain well the context of the final scene of *Frogs* and also the angle from which such potentially loaded material as the references to Argive alliance in *Eumenides* or the critical treatment of the assembly in *Orestes* was introduced into tragedy: utilizing well-established and easily understood contemporary filters of interpretation, the tragedian and his backers were bringing to the Athenians a view slanted in the direction of their own group's ideological take on contemporary issues. Nonetheless, since tragedy had to be "heroically vague" (Easterling 1997: 26), distancing itself in language and political context from the audience's present, those filters need to be reconstructed for modern readers who have no detailed knowledge of the political conditions under which specific plays were produced (and often do not know even the production dates—a fundamental point of departure), and have been conditioned by a long tradition of aesthetic criticism to believe in Athenian tragedy's universality (something which may exist notwithstanding an originally specific political agenda).

Let us begin with the way in which myth could be utilized in political argument. A passing comment in Thucydides (2.29) dismisses any relation between Teres, father of the Odrysian Thracian king Sitalkes, and the mythical Tereus. But it also shows that this connection was a live issue at Athens and was probably spoken about in public debate, in this case possibly as a deterrent to awarding Athenian citizenship to Sitalkes' son Sadocus. Other evidence of this type (e.g. Kallistratus' argument in Arcadia against their proposed alliance with Thebes and Argos on the basis of the mythical parricides who came from the one—Oedipus and Alcmaeon—and the matricide Orestes, from the other, Nepos, *Epaminondas* 6.1–2) strongly suggests that differently slanted versions of myth/history could be utilized in specific political discussions. What we could be seeing, then, in the variations tragedians incorporate in their plays is a response to the ideological requirements of the political group to which they belonged (as has been argued above the choice of on-stage targets operated for Old Comedy). Hence, though we cannot date accurately—or even be quite certain of the existence of—a revival of *Choephoroi* and *Eumenides* and we do not know for certain the date of Euripides' *Electra*, the two authors' plays are opposed to each other ideologically over the matter of Orestes' purity (Sidwell 1996a: 52) and this could certainly have represented the same sort of basis for argument about Athens' relations with Argos as we have seen is likely to be behind Thucydides' comment on Teres and Tereus and Kallistratus' arguments in Arcadia. This implies, of course, that Aeschylean plays were not just taken "off the peg"—they would be very unlikely to have fitted any given new ideological context very well—but might be heavily adapted, or even (as may have been the case with *Prometheus Bound*) written from scratch to an existing and recorded Aeschylean title. Indeed, the whole idea in *Frogs* that Aeschylus might be able to answer *current* political questions and save the city with his tragedy almost demands such a scenario as its background (cf. *Frogs* 868–869; Sidwell 2009: 295).

Tragedy may also have operated with other types of filter, however. If Euripides' *Trojan Women* was composed to sensitize Athenians to the consequences of their recent treatment of Melos, in which the men were executed and the women sold into slavery for their refusal to join the Athenians in war, then it may have done so as a sort of allegory, in which Troy stands for Melos. We do not have enough evidence to tell whether this was the case, though we can point to the use of the Trojan myth in Cratinus' *Dionysalexandros* to allegorize a current war (whether the Samian or the Peloponnesian is disputed: Storey 2006: 178–181; Bakola 2010: 213, 300–304). Nor can we entirely discount the notion that tragedy sometimes drew parallels between the mythical characters and contemporary Athenian political figures, as ancient scholiasts thought (Pelling 2000: 166) and some modern scholars have pressed further (e.g. Vickers 2008). Even if it is difficult to demonstrate the case effectively, this *modus operandi* was, I have argued, central to the way Old Comedy worked, and whether or not tragedy interacted with comedy, just as comedy did with tragedy, the audience would in any case not have had any problem understanding such a procedure given that the two genres shared a theatrical and festive space.

We must necessarily pay attention under the proposed political status of tragedy to the problem of "ideological interpolation" (Sidwell 1996b). It looks as though Aeschylus' name and the titles of his works were already in the fifth century being appropriated for various ideological purposes (not necessarily on all fours with each other, since "whoever wanted" would be granted a chorus to produce "Aeschylus": Sidwell 2009: 294–297). This process is likely to have continued into the fourth century (with the "actors," however, now responsible for the choice and production of the old plays) and this is one interpretation of what the Lycurgus decree about ensuring a fixed text for the fifth-century tragedians was about. In any case, other evidence for what have often been called "actors' interpolations" does show the phenomenon to have been rife (Page 1934; Hamilton 1974). It may be that the developing book culture of the later fifth century (Turner 1952) could have made wholesale rewriting less possible than it had been at the time of the Aeschylean revival decree. Hence the grafting on of material (in Phrynichus' gloss "resoling") may have been the only practicable way of altering existing plays to one's own purposes (though most modern attempts to disinter originals from their received form posit aesthetic rather than ideological motives: e.g. Kovacs 2003).

It is possible, for example, that such "resoling" is responsible for our inability to understand the ideological stance of Aeschylus in *Eumenides*: onto the version we possess, itself perhaps totally rewritten in the 420s with a purified Orestes to support an Argive alliance against those who would argue that Orestes' matricide polluted the city forever (Sidwell 1996a: 52), have been grafted passages which support the ideological role of the Areopagus outlined by Isocrates in the mid-fourth century, warn against *stasis* in a way which suits the atmosphere in Athens in the mid-340s and confirm a claim to land in Troy which relates one made by Athens in 360 and was linked with the current idea of Persian conquest (Sidwell 1996b: 191–201). The test for such ideological "resoling" will be in the first place the difficulty of aligning what looks like contemporary focusing with the known date of the first production and then the possibility of finding evidence for a revival where the ideological material makes a better fit.

4 Conclusion

Athenian theater in its major modes—satirical comedy and tragedy—was fundamentally political, and comedy especially so in a way which contrasts starkly with the apparently non-political "mythological burlesque" borrowed from Sicily by Athenian poets during the brief years of a ban on the satirical form (see also Fisher, Chapter 12, on the educational role of these performances). The *polis* exercised a measure of control over the phenomenon during the whole course of the fifth and fourth centuries, but the way politics was organized—around elite individuals and their supporting coteries, including dramatists—would have made it very difficult to outlaw the intrusion of ideological material and *parti pris*. Indeed, the evidence we have for *polis* interference strongly suggests an *aversion* from such censorship, with the possible exceptions of the decree against satirical comedy in 440–437 (and other measures to regulate satirical comedy's modes of attack) and the decree of Lycurgus controlling revivals of the fifth-century tragedians.

However, at our distance it is in most cases difficult to reconstruct, in the fine detail necessary to be convincing, the way in which the system operated. For Old Comedy this is mainly because many of the chief targets are not named, for tragedy because the modes of political interpretation may have been multiple and we have to reckon with wholesale forgery at one end of the spectrum and ideological interpolation at the other without having a firm substructure of dates of first production and revivals to guide our efforts.

The nature and state of the evidence does not allow the kind of analysis of the role theater played in the politics of the community that Shawn O'Bryhim gives for Rome in the parallel chapter in this section. On my account, the politics of the plays themselves were dictated by private agendas, within a system that was entirely controlled otherwise (in terms of buildings, occasion, choice of participants, and judging) by the *dēmos*. The aim of encoding in drama these divergent political *partis pris* was presumably, however, to influence the members of the audience in some way towards acceptance of one view of things rather than another. In tragedy, for example, while an account of Orestes' purification after his matricide might not directly make a political point, it would thereafter be available as a point of reference for public debates in which alliance with Argos was a live issue. In comedy, by contrast, the objective was surely to spread prejudice against specific individuals (not always politicians) by that most effective form of theatrical ridicule, caricature. Athenian orators certainly took advantage of these attacks to spread the prejudice they embodied (e.g. Lysias fr. 53) and comedy's prejudicial effect might also be inferred from the correspondence between Thucydides' description of Hyperbolus (8.73.3) as ***mokhtheron anthrōpon*** ("a vile fellow") and that of Aristophanes' *Knights* (1304) ***mokhtheron politēn*** ("a vile citizen"). True, it is often argued that the case of Cleon nullifies any argument about ***actual*** effect, since Cleon was elected general soon after Aristophanes won the prize with *Knights*. However, Aristophanes' own admission at *Clouds* 549 that the play had been an attack on Cleon guarantees the play's ***intent*** to affect people's view of him and, for all we know, Cleon's constituency may well have consisted of (country?) people who did not regularly attend the theater. But the classic case which shows that comic drama in its satirical form did have influence must surely be that of Socrates. Plato claimed (*Ap.* 18c–d, 19c) that Aristophanes' merciless on-stage caricature of Socrates in *Clouds* created an atmosphere of prejudice against him among Athenians (confirmed by the taunts of the Syracusan in Xen. *Symposium* 6.6f.). It is no wonder, then, that oligarchically minded Athenians (and others) disliked this form of attack (as many British politicians and public figures caricatured in the UK television show *Spitting Image* in the 1980s and 1990s also did): it bypassed argument in favor of the creation of powerful and in some cases unforgettable images—like that of Socrates in a basket, or possibly Hyperbolus as a lamp-maker—which could create real distaste, difficult then to undo or to counter effectively.

REFERENCES

DFA^2 = A. Pickard-Cambridge. 1988. *The Dramatic Festivals of Athens*. 2nd edn., rev. J. Gould and D.M. Lewis, reissued with a new supplement. Oxford.

PCG = R. Kassel and C. Austin, eds. 1983. *Poetae Comici Graeci*. Berlin.

Arnott, W.G. 1991. "A Lesson from the Frogs." *G&R^2* 38: 18–23.

Bakola, E. 2010. *Cratinus and the Art of Comedy*. Oxford.

Biles, Z. 2006/7. "Aeschylus' Afterlife: Reperformance by Decree in 5th c. Athens?" *ICS* 31–32: 206–242.

Brockmann, C. 2003. *Aristophanes und die Freiheit der Komödi: Untersuchungen zu Den frühen Stücken unter besonderer Berücksichtigung der Acharner*. Munich and Leipzig.

Carter, D. 2004. "Was Attic Tragedy Democratic?" *Polis* 21: 1–25.

De Ste. Croix, G.E.M. 1972. *The Origins of the Peloponnesian War*. London.

Easterling, P. 1997. "Constructing the Heroic." In C. Pelling, ed., *Greek Tragedy and the Historian*. Oxford, 21–37.

Goldhill, S. 1987. "The Great Dionysia and Civic Ideology." *JHS* 107: 58–76.

Goldhill, S. 1990. "The Great Dionysia and Civic Ideology." Rev. in J.J. Winkler and F.I. Zeitlin, eds., *Nothing To Do with Dionysos?* Princeton, 97–129.

Goldhill, S. 2000. "Civic ideology and the problem of difference: the politics of Aeschylean tragedy, once again." *JHS* 120: 34–56.

Griffin, J. 1998. "The Social Function of Attic Tragedy." *CQ* 48: 39–61.

Griffith, M. 1977. *The Authenticity of the Prometheus Bound*. Cambridge.

Halliwell, F.S. 1991. "Comic Satire and Freedom of Speech in Classical Athens." *JHS* 111: 48–70.

Hamilton, R. 1974. "Objective Evidence for Actors' Interpolations in Greek Tragedy." *GRBS* 15: 387–442.

Heath, M. 1987a. *The Poetics of Greek Tragedy*. London.

Heath, M. 1987b. *Political Comedy in Aristophanes*. Göttingen.

Henderson, J.J. 1990. "The Demos and Comic Competition." In J.J. Winkler and F.I. Zeitlin, eds., *Nothing to Do with Dionysos?* Princeton, 271–313.
Hutchinson, G.O. 1985. *Aeschylus: Seven Against Thebes.* Oxford.
Koster, W.J.W. 1975. *Scholia in Aristophanem, Pars I, Fasc. IA: Prolegomena de Comoedia.* Gröningen (= Koster, *Prolegomena*).
Kovacs, D., trans. 2003. "Towards a Reconstruction of *Iphigenia Aulidensis.*" *JHS* 123: 77–103.
Kyriakidi, N. 2007. *Aristophanes und Eupolis: Geschichte einer dichterischen Rivalität.* Berlin and New York.
Loscalzo, D. 2010. *Aristofane e la coscienza felice.* Alessandria.
Newiger, H.J. 1961. "Elektra in Aristophanes' Wolken." *Hermes* 89: 422–430.
Ober, J. 1989. *Mass and Elite in Democratic Athens: Rhetoric Ideology, and the Power of the People.* Princeton.
Olson, S.D. 2010. "Comedy, Politics and Society." In Gregory W. Dobrov, ed., *Brill's Companion to the Study of Greek Comedy.* Leiden, 35–69.
Page, D.L. 1934. *Actors' Interpolations in Greek Tragedy.* Oxford.
Pelling, C. 2000. *Literary Texts and the Greek Historian.* London.
Pickard-Cambridge, A.W. 1946. *The Theatre of Dionysus.* Oxford.
Rhodes, P.J. 2003. "Nothing To Do with Democracy: Athenian Drama and the *Polis.*" *JHS* 123: 104–19.
Rosen, R.M. 1988. *Old Comedy and the Iambographic Tradition.* Atlanta.
Sidwell, K. 1993. "Authorial Collaboration? Aristophanes' *Knights* and Eupolis." *GRBS* 34: 365–389.
Sidwell, K. 1996a. "Pollution and Purification in Aeschylus' *Eumenides.*" *CQ* n.s. 46: 44–57.
Sidwell, K. 1996b. "The Politics of Aeschylus' *Eumenides.*" *Classics Ireland* 3: 182–203.
Sidwell, K. 2009. *Aristophanes the Democrat: The Politics of Satirical Comedy during the Peloponnesian War.* Cambridge.
Sidwell, K. 2014. "Fourth Century Greek Comedy." In M. Revermann, ed., *The Cambridge Companion to Greek Comedy.* Cambridge, 60–78.
Silk, M. 2000. *Aristophanes and the Definition of Comedy.* Oxford.
Sommerstein, A. 1980. *Acharnians.* Warminster.
Sommerstein, A. 1989. *Aeschylus. Eumenides.* Cambridge.
Sommerstein, A. 1996a. *Frogs.* Warminster.
Sommerstein, A. 1996b. *Aeschylean Tragedy.* Bari.
Sommerstein, A. 2004. "Comedy and the Unspeakable." In D.L. Cairns and R.A. Knox, eds., *Law, Rhetoric, and Comedy in Classical Athens.* Swansea, 205–222.
Storey, I.C. 2003. *Eupolis: Poet of Old Comedy.* Oxford.
Storey, I.C. 2006. "On First Looking into Kratinus' *Dionysalexandros.*" In L. Kozak and J. Rich, eds., *Playing around Aristophanes: Essays in Celebration of the Completion of the Edition of the Comedies of Aristophanes by Alan Sommerstein.* Oxford, 105–125.
Turner, E.G. 1952. *Athenian Books in the Fifth and Fourth Centuries BC.* London.
Vickers, M. 2008. *Sophocles and Alcibiades: Athenian Politics in Ancient Greek Literature.* Stocksfield.
Whitley, J. 2001. *The Archaeology of Ancient Greece.* Cambridge.
Wilson, P. 2000. *The Athenian Institution of the Khoregia: The Chorus, the City and the Stage.* Cambridge.

FURTHER READING

The issues dealt with here are contentious and my view is different in both starting-point and conclusions from others. On politics in tragedy, Goldhill (1987, revised 1990 and 2000) has been highly influential, though not without his critics (e.g. Griffin 1998; Rhodes 2003; Carter 2004). On comedy, see De Ste. Croix 1972, appendix 29, 355–376, for an analysis of Aristophanes as a conservative critic (cf. Sommerstein *passim*), Heath 1987b for skepticism about comedy's political engagement (cf. Olson 2010), Henderson 1990, and Loscalzo 2010 for variations on comedy as providing service to the *dēmos*. Pelling 2000 provides a useful overview of politics in both tragedy and comedy.

CHAPTER 25

Tragedy and Comedy in the Roman Participatory Context

Shawn O'Bryhim

Nearly everything that a Roman aristocrat did in his public life was a spectacle geared toward maintaining or increasing his social standing. For members of the ruling class, the city was a stage where they all strove to be major players, seen and esteemed by others. The theater in particular provided the ruling class with an effective means to gain political power by influencing popular opinion.

1 Social, Physical, and Legal Organization

Throughout most of the Republic, plays were performed on temporary wooden stages with seating on bleachers or on the steps of a nearby temple. These structures were erected for a specific event and were disassembled immediately afterward. Even though it would have been less expensive in the long run to build a permanent structure to serve as a centralized venue for these performances (Tac. *Ann.* 14.21), there was no stone theater in Rome until the late Republic. It has been suggested that religion dictated this practice; temporary theaters had to be built next to the temple of the deity to whom a play was dedicated (Altheim 1936: 289–291; Hanson 1959: 9–25; Manuwald 2011: 60–61). But this custom may also have had a political motivation. According to Gruen (1992: 209–210), "the ritual of erecting and then dismantling temporary structures gave annual notice that the ruling class held decisive authority in the artistic sphere." Whatever the rationale, it seemed that this practice was coming to an end in 151 BCE, when the first stone theater in Rome was on the verge of completion.

In 154 BCE, the censors M. Valerius Messalla and C. Cassius Longinus let a contract for the erection of a stone theater that was paid for with funds allocated by the Senate. There is no indication that anyone objected when the building was first proposed or during the four years that it was under construction. But just as the theater was nearing

A Companion to Greek Democracy and the Roman Republic, First Edition. Edited by Dean Hammer.

completion in 151 BCE, P. Scipio Nasica Corculum persuaded the Senate to destroy it (Livy *Per.* 48; Val. Max. 2.4.2; Vell. Pat. 1.15.3; Oros. 4.21.4). He must have presented a powerful argument to halt such a large and costly undertaking, especially when it was on the verge of completion. According to Livy (*Per.* 48), Nasica told the Senate that a permanent theater would be "useless and harmful to public morals." It seems odd that he would have raised such an objection so late in the game. If utility and the preservation of Roman morals were his sole motivations for opposing its construction, it would have been better for him to voice these objections at the beginning of the project (Morgan 1990: 72–74). There must have been a compelling reason to destroy the theater in 151 BCE that did not exist when its construction was proposed three years earlier.

Nasica's opposition to a permanent theater is best understood in the context of the contemporary political situation. During the debate over the declaration of war on Carthage, he argued that Rome needed the fear of an external enemy to prevent the people from rejecting senatorial leadership and throwing the state into disorder (Diodorus Siculus 34/35.33.5; Plut. *Ca. Mai.* 27.1–2). It appears that Nasica made a similar argument about the dangers of a permanent theater in the same year, although the chronology of the source for this is confused. According to Appian (*B. civ.* 1.28), a certain L. Cassius (instead of C. Cassius) attempted to construct a permanent theater in 108 BCE. When it was nearly finished, the consul Caepio (instead of Scipio) persuaded the Senate to destroy it, either because he feared that the people would get used to Greek pleasures or because it might become a breeding ground for civil dissent. Given the many similarities to accounts of the destruction of the theater in 151 BCE, it is likely that Appian displaced a version of this story to 108 BCE (Taylor 1966: 30; Coleman 2000: 220; *contra* North 1992: 75–83). If so, then Nasica's arguments for allowing Carthage to survive and for the destruction of the stone theater both stem from his desire to avoid civil strife. Although the Senate rejected his argument that the preservation of a foreign threat would be salutary, it agreed that the construction of a permanent theater in Rome would be unwise. Therefore, both Carthage and the stone theater had to be destroyed.

In the same year, the Senate enacted a decree proposed by Nasica that forbade audiences to sit at theatrical performances that took place within one mile of Rome (Livy *Per.* 48; Oros. 4.21.4). Valerius Maximus (2.4) says that this decree was motivated by the belief that standing during performances was more appropriate to the virility of the Romans. Since they had been sitting at plays for more than a century, there must have been another reason for this ban on seating. A more likely explanation is that the Senate feared that the Romans would follow the example of the Greeks by using the theater for assemblies and impromptu gatherings of the people, which occasionally turned raucous and even violent (Stoops 1989: 84–87; MacMullen 1992: 171–173; Trebilco 1994: 348–350; Rumpf 1950: 40–50; *contra* Manuwald 2011: 59–60). Cicero (*Flac.* 16) describes how the Greeks were corrupted by "the unrestrained freedom and license of political meetings" that took place in theaters, and he remarks critically on the Greek practice of sitting in their assemblies. The danger of this occurring in Rome was mitigated by the fact that theaters were temporary. Therefore they could facilitate anti-government demonstrations only at festival times. However, a stone theater would provide a staging ground for protests throughout the year. By forbidding the construction of any type of theater beyond a simple stage, the Senate eliminated this possibility.

These restrictions on the theater may have been precipitated by the circumstances surrounding the war in Spain. In 151 BCE, the Senate ordered a levy to be conducted by lot to fill the ranks (App. *Spanish Wars* 49). Reports of the particularly difficult nature of this war made the Romans—especially the youth—reluctant to serve (Polyb. 35.4.1–14; Livy *Per.* 48; Oros. 4.21.1). Given the resistance to senatorial authority at this time, especially among men of military age, it would have been imprudent to provide a place for the people to assemble and express their opinion about the war in a fractious and potentially violent manner. Therefore the permanent theater was destroyed and the erection of temporary seating was forbidden.

While the desire to avoid political upheaval may have been the primary motive for the destruction of the stone theater in 151 BCE, it does not explain why the censors were willing to contravene tradition by building it in the first place. Nothing is known of the censor Messalla's part in this project, much less anything of his life beyond his political offices. He seems to have been little more than an unremarkable member of an important patrician family (Broughton 1951: 443 and 449; Suolahti 1963: 387–388). Since the censors could carry out building projects independent of each other, it is possible that the theater was Cassius' brainchild. Given his track record, it is not surprising that he would have made such a bold move against tradition. As consul in 161 BCE, he tried to become commander in the Macedonian war by arguing that the Senate should deprive his colleague of the opportunity to draw lots for the position. The Senate refused, and Cassius drew the lot for Gaul (Livy 42.31.1–32.5). Having failed to accomplish anything noteworthy in his own province, he embarked on an unauthorized campaign in Macedonia, the province of his colleague. When the Senate discovered that he had taken his army outside his province without permission, it ordered him to return without making war on anyone. Envoys to Rome then complained that Cassius had abused their people during his return from Macedonia. After the Senate signaled its willingness to put him on trial when he returned to Rome (Livy 43.5), he opted to serve as a military tribune in Macedonia and Illyria for the next three years (170–168 BCE), no doubt in an attempt to avoid prosecution. Cassius' quest for glory may have been what prompted him to undertake the construction of the first stone theater in Rome: even though his military exploits would profit him nothing, his name would be permanently associated with his theater. The Senate was apparently willing to go along with this in 154 BCE, but the political situation had changed three years later, when the impending war against Carthage and the opposition to conscription for the Spanish war brought an end to this grand monument to his ambition.

Instead of renewing the attempt to erect a permanent theater after the war, ambitious aristocrats turned their attention to building ever more elaborate temporary structures to enhance their career prospects. Valerius Maximus (2.4.6) lists a number of enhancements to the wooden theaters that aediles and praetors built during the first century BCE: a painted stage (99 BCE), a revolving theater (79 BCE), an awning for shade (69 BCE), and a stage lined with silver (66 BCE). M. Aemilius Scaurus built a spectacular wooden theater in 58 BCE, which Pliny (*NH* 36.114) calls "the greatest work of all those ever made by the hand of man." This theater reportedly held 80,000 spectators. Its stage consisted of three stories, the first decorated with marble, the second with glass, and the third with gilded wood. The interstices between its 360 columns held 3,000 bronze statues. Unable to compete with Scaurus financially, Gaius Curio aimed for an unforgettable special effect. For the funeral games of his father in 52 BCE, he built two theaters that pivoted to form an amphitheater. According to Pliny (*NH* 36.116–120), the motivation for Curio's unprecedented contraption was political: "through this he seeks influence in the meetings called by the tribunes." Given that Curio was elected tribune in the following year, it appears that his plan to use this theater to advance his political career was successful.

Other aristocrats produced lavish theatrical events to gain advantage over their political opponents. The more splendid the entertainment, the more likely the spectators would be to remember its sponsor at the polls (Plut. *Caes.* 5.8–9; Suet. *Iul.* 10.1; Shatzman 1975: 164–167; Manuwald 2011: 49–51). But memories fade, especially when they are supplanted by more spectacular memories. It is unlikely that the aediles and praetors who were responsible for mounting annual spectacles would have reaped perennial benefits from these performances (Hopkins 1983: 14–20; Beacham 1999: 30–31 and 36). Likewise, the provision of a richly appointed wooden theater would make an ephemeral impression on voters that would benefit the sponsor at the next election, but not beyond it (Shatzman 1975: 165; Jory 1986: 146; Holleran 2003: 51). While the Senate permitted such extravagances as part of the normal competition for public office, the construction of a permanent theater was another matter. The memory of a wooden theater, no matter how spectacular, would fade. A permanent theater, however, could influence voters for many years, especially if it displayed an inscription that reminded them of the donor's generosity (*L'Année épigraphique* 1957: 250; Edmondson 2002: 23). More importantly, it would render temporary theaters obsolete, thereby shutting down an important avenue for aristocrats to garner favor with voters (Holleran 2003: 52–53). The fact that there was no attempt to build a permanent theater for a century after Cassius' ill-fated endeavor suggests that aristocrats understood and accepted the importance of preserving this aspect of the annual competition for political office.

This situation changed in 55 BCE, when Pompey dedicated his stone theater in the Campus Martius, paid for out of the booty from his eastern campaigns. No doubt he hoped to profit politically from this extravagant gift to the Roman people. The construction of a stone theater might enable him to gain their favor, while depriving Caesar of popular support (Frézouls 1983: 203–204; Temelini 2006: 3). But this had to be done carefully, lest Pompey be condemned for flouting tradition (Tac. *Ann.* 14.20). Instead of calling the structure a theater, he built a temple of Venus above the seats and formally dedicated this complex (which also included a portico and a senate house) as a shrine of Venus Victrix (Gell. 10.1.7; Tert. *De spect.* 10.5; *contra* Phillips 2001: 211–220).

Thus, the prohibition on building stone theaters had two purposes. The first was to obviate the danger inherent in creating a permanent structure that could serve as a staging ground for sedition. The second was to prevent any aristocrat (and his descendants) from gaining a perennial advantage at the polls by giving the people a gift that would benefit them in perpetuity. This informal ban had no impact on the people, for whom theatrical entertainments continued as before, especially after the Senate's prohibition on seating ended. Rather, it served to regulate how the aristocracy would compete for office.

However, the Senate was not averse to making changes in the theater that negatively impacted the common man, so long as they bolstered the prestige of the aristocracy. In 194 BCE, the Senate modified the way that seats were allocated at theatrical events. Previously, there were no legal restrictions on seating (Livy 34.54). Everyone could sit wherever he pleased, at least in theory. In practice, the people voluntarily yielded the best seats to senators as a mark of respect (Val. Max. 4.5.1). This changed in 194 BCE, when Scipio Africanus proposed that the aediles reserve the seats in the orchestra for senators, thereby segregating them from the people (Ungern-Sternberg 1975: 157–163). While it was one thing to voluntarily surrender a seat to a senator, it was a different matter to be forced to do so. Scipio paid the price for his proposal with a loss of prestige among the people (Val. Max. 2.4.3), and he regretted suggesting this innovation during his consulship (Livy 34.54.8). In spite of the negative reaction to Scipio's reorganization of seating, the Senate segregated the theater to an even greater extent in 67 BCE. Prior to this, the knights sat with the people (Plut. *Cic.* 13.2), but now the law of L. Roscius Otho gave the knights fourteen rows of seats directly behind the senators (Cic. *Phil.* 2.44; Livy *Per.* 99; Vell. Pat. 2.32.3; Plut. *Cic.* 13.2; Pociña Pérez 1976: 435–442). The popular reaction was predictable. When Otho entered the theater in 63 BCE, the knights cheered, but the people booed (Val. Max. 2.4.3; Plut. *Cic.* 13.3). Their indignation reached such heights that the consul Cicero had to remove them from the theater to quell what was quickly becoming a riot (Pliny *NH* 7.117; Plut. *Cic.* 13.3–4). Popular discontent over this issue did not abate, and later attempts by emperors to enforce these restrictions were met with resistance (Barton 1993: 113–114).

The willingness of the aristocracy to create such unpopular rules testifies to the importance of this seating arrangement, which amounted to a visual demonstration of social status: senators sat in the front, knights behind them, and the lower class in the back (Moore 1996: 113–123). By noting his own place in the theater, anyone—male or female, free or slave—could determine his status relative to that of the other spectators. This system gave an appropriate amount of prestige to each social class, while reinforcing the social hierarchy by visually illustrating everyone's place in it. For the aristocrats, the opportunity to display their elevated social status vis-à-vis the rest of the people was well worth the resentment it engendered, for "the theater would be a visible reminder of the ascendancy of the *nobiles*" (Gruen 1992: 205).

This allocation of seats also provided a means to gauge popular sentiment toward political issues that were brought to the fore during theatrical productions (Nicolet 1980: 364–366; Bollinger 1969: 25–29; Coleman 2011: 347–349). With the audience separated according to class, aristocrats could easily identify the attitude of different segments of society based on the applause or hisses that emanated from each block of seats. Although this method of tracking public opinion may have been skewed at times because the system of ticket distribution allowed the sponsor of the event to populate the theater with his supporters (Holleran 2003: 49–50), the fact that aristocrats took note of these expressions of popular sentiment testifies to their perceived value (Cic. *Att.* 2.19, 14.3).

2 Politics and Drama

The extent to which Roman plays reflected or commented upon the political situation no doubt varied according to author, genre, and date. The prohibition against slandering living individuals on stage precluded authors from attacking politicians overtly (Cic. *De rep.* 4.10; Aug. *Civ. Dei* 2.12; Smith 1951: 169–172). Indeed, it was more prudent for them to avoid political themes altogether or, at most, to allude to contemporary situations only through very broad plot elements (Galinsky 1966: 203–235; Gruen 1996: 124–157; Moore 1998: 105–107; Manuwald 2011: 283–301). Otherwise, they might put their livelihood at risk by offending the very politicians who bought their plays (McCarthy 2000: 17–19).

This is not to say that some comedies did not reflect the concerns of Roman society. Plautine comedies are peopled with characters whose behavior was dictated by tradition. In some plays, these characters behave in an aberrant manner, which causes upheaval in their families. For example, the fathers who choose to behave like young lovers in *Mercator*, *Casina*, and *Asinaria* abandon their positions as heads of their families, thereby creating a power vacuum that allows less powerful characters to assume roles that are above their station: wives behave like husbands and slaves dominate their masters (see also Stewart, Chapter 23, on depictions of slaves in Plautus). This shift in behavioral paradigms brings comic society to the verge of collapse and threatens the traditional resolution of the plot. Therefore, these characters must be forced to return to their proper roles so that the play can end happily. Such comedies would have provided the audience with an object lesson on the dangers of abandoning traditional social roles: when those in positions of power abrogate their positions of leadership, the status quo is overturned and chaos ensues. Order is maintained by preserving the traditional social hierarchy, which is reflected in the division of seats in the theater.

Although it is unlikely that Roman plays openly mocked political figures, audiences eagerly searched for such animadversions in them (Nicolet 1980: 366–373; Coleman 2011: 345–347). Often an audience responded to a line that appeared to have some political relevance. Sometimes professional applauders, who were paid to foment demonstrations for or against political figures, tried to influence the audience's interpretation of a line (Cic. *Sest.* 115; Vanderbroeck 1987: 61–62 and 143–144). Actors would also manipulate lines so that they seemed to allude to controversial events and political figures (Gruen 1992: 184–185; Parker 1999: 171–172). When the actor Diphilus attacked Pompey in 59 BCE by emphasizing the lines "to our misery you are great" and "a time will come when you lament grievously that very strength of yours," the entire audience responded with resounding applause (Cic. *Att.* 2.19). After Cicero's return from exile had been announced during the *Ludi Apollinares* of 57 BCE, Aesopus roused support for him during a performance of Accius' *Brutus* by emphasizing significant lines, adding phrases from other plays, and incorporating a few lines of his own creation (Cic. *Sest.* 119–123). And during Afranius' *Pretender* (*Simulans*), the entire troupe of actors looked straight at Clodius and delivered a line that they intended to be critical of him (Cic. *Sest.* 118).

It would have been dangerous for actors to take such a bold step on their own initiative, especially in politically volatile situations. They were probably encouraged by aristocrats who wanted to gauge public opinion based on the audience's response to significant lines. Occasionally, they went so far as to select plays on a particular subject in order to manipulate the political views of the audience. Nicolet (1980: 370) suggests that the curule aediles of 57 BCE colluded with Pompey and the majority of the Senate to choose plays that would encourage Cicero's supporters to agitate for his return from exile. During Caesar's funeral in 44 BCE, selections from Pacuvius' *Arma Iudiciorum* and Atilius' *Electra* were sung to arouse pity and indignation over his death (Suet. *Iul.* 84). In the same year, Brutus planned to present Accius' *Brutus* at the *Ludi Apollinares* to muster support for his return to Rome (Cic. *Att.* 16.2 and 5; App. *B. civ.* 3.23–24; Sumi 2005: 143–148). In each of these cases, the plays that were selected for performance on politically significant occasions were written years before these events. Therefore it was not the playwrights themselves who were political. Rather, aristocrats politicized their plays.

3 Political Theater in Action

In addition to providing a venue for popular entertainment, the theater was a place where the Roman people could express their political views and, perhaps, influence politicians. Similarly, politicians used the theater to gauge the opinions of the crowd and to enhance their political prestige with voters. The latter was one of the main purposes of the *fabulae praetextae*, plays that dealt with significant events in early Roman history or with recent military victories. Often financed by generals who played an important role in the events depicted on stage, these plays could neutralize attacks from invidious politicians by portraying the generals as heroes to whom the gods had granted signal success in battle. Most were presented at the votive games that followed a military victory, but some were produced years later to coincide with the dedication of a temple that the general had vowed during an earlier war. In such cases, the play reminded the audience of the general's role as an intermediary with the gods for the benefit of the Roman people; he had promised the temple in exchange for victory and the gods had granted his petition. Flower (1995: 170–190) suggests that, in spite of the potential benefits to aristocrats and their families, *fabulae praetextae* were rarely presented because "they were too controversial and gave the patron direct control over audience reactions."

Public entertainments that were mounted for political purposes could produce a backlash from rivals. The contrasting games of L. Aemilius Paullus and Anicius Gallus are a case in point. After his defeat of the Macedonians at Pydna, Paullus celebrated victory games at Amphipolis in 167 BCE. He modeled these on the panhellenic festivals of Hellenistic monarchs, perhaps to signal Roman dominance over the Greeks through a format that was familiar to them (Edmondson 1999: 79). Paullus dispatched ambassadors to Greek cities throughout Greece and Asia Minor, inviting them to send representatives to lavish banquets, plays, athletic events, and musical competitions. Contestants were drawn from the best talent to be found in the eastern Mediterranean (Livy 45.32.9). Since he followed Greek custom during his victory festival, Edmondson (1999: 80) concludes that "Paullus wanted to show that even though he was a Roman, he understood exactly what was required in this key area of Greek culture." He was very successful in this, for the Greeks remarked on how observant he was of their customs, even in the nicest detail (Plut. *Aem.* 28.4–5).

In November 167 BCE, Paullus returned to Rome and celebrated a triumph over the Macedonians. Three months later, the Senate granted the propraetor Anicius Gallus a triumph over the Illyrians. Because Anicius offered the same types of entertainment at his triumph in Rome as Paullus had presented at his victory festival at Amphipolis, Edmondson (1999: 83) concluded that "he hoped to outdo Paullus' recent spectacles ... to enhance his cultural credentials and his political status at Rome." While there can be little doubt that Anicius wanted to increase his political status, he could not compete with Paullus on his own terms because Paullus had far greater financial resources at his disposal. Anicius had a much more sophisticated plan in mind.

Following Greek custom, Paullus had presented his entertainments in a theater at Amphipolis. Anicius' events, however, occurred on an enormous stage that he had erected in the Circus Maximus specifically for this occasion (Polyb. 32.22.1–12, paraphrased by Athenaeus 14.615b–d; Livy 45.43.1). Although the basic elements of their entertainments were the same, they could not have been more different in form. While Paullus showcased the talents of the best performers that the Greek world had to offer, Anicius seemed determined to humiliate them. According to Polybius, Anicius first brought out four of the best pipers from the Greek world and ordered them to play in unison to the accompaniment of a chorus. After they had played for a while, Anicius sent a lictor to tell the pipers that they were not doing a good job and that they should be more competitive. The pipers were confused until the lictor conveyed to them that they should turn against each other in battle. Thereupon, the chorus divided into two parts, which advanced against each other while the pipers improvised discordant tunes. When a chorus member adopted the stance of a boxer and moved aggressively against a piper, four boxers accompanied by horn players climbed onto the stage and joined the melee. Tragic actors followed, but Polybius refuses to say what they did because he thinks that his readers will not believe it.

Polybius' disgust at the humiliation of the best theatrical artists of Greece may have blinded him to Anicius' objective in offering an entertainment that appeared to be little more than a disorganized travesty. And by viewing this episode through Polybius' distorted lens, scholars may have erred in their interpretations of it. Some see it as a prime example of the inferior aesthetic sensibilities of the Romans, including Anicius (Gilula 1989: 106–107; MacMullen 1991: 425; Goldberg 1995: 38–39). Others believe that Anicius intended this performance to be a serious display of Greek virtuosity, but that he lost control of the spectacle to a mob of crass Romans (Garton 1972: 65; Edmondson 1999: 84). Neither is likely. Anicius' audience was not an unruly crowd of yokels that became bored with an unfamiliar form of entertainment. They could appreciate piping and dancing, which were regularly incorporated into the plays that were presented at Rome. Moreover, there is no evidence that Anicius lost control of the show to the audience. Polybius says that a lictor gave the order for the pipers to play against each other. Since lictors are not independent agents, but act at the behest of magistrates, Anicius must have ordered his lictor to relay his wishes to the pipers. Given the rather complex maneuvers that ensued (the splitting of the chorus and the mock battle), it is likely that the entire affair had been scripted and rehearsed ahead of time. Furthermore, a simple display of singing and dancing, followed by athletic contests and a tragedy, could easily have been accommodated on a typical Roman stage. But the great variety of simultaneous performances in Anicius' production required more space. The construction of a huge stage in the Circus Maximus strongly suggests that Anicius knew that this "melee" would occur and that he was aware of its logistical requirements (Edmondson 1999: 83; Franko 2013: 343–360). Clearly, he had planned all of this from beginning to end.

Gruen (1992: 217–219) argues that this farce contained a serious message. By compelling the best performers in the Greek world to behave in a disorganized, inept, and foolish manner, Anicius was able "to demonstrate that Hellas' frontline performers now worked at the behest of the Roman commander." However, it makes little sense for Anicius, who was celebrating a victory over Illyrians, to make such a statement about the Greeks. It is more likely that he was attempting to denigrate Paullus, whose victory over the Macedonians was casting a shadow over this celebration. In his comparison of their triumphal parades, Livy (45.43.1–4) says that Anicius' display was not contemptible when taken on its own merits, but that Paullus' was superior in every conceivable way, for he was of nobler birth, higher rank, had fought a more powerful enemy, and had returned to Rome laden with greater spoils. For Anicius to attempt to supplant Paullus' splendid triumph in the minds of the public would have been futile, since "the memory of the Macedonian triumph was still fixed not only in their minds, but almost before their eyes" (Livy 45.43.1; Diod. Sic. 31.8.9–13). Because Anicius could not diminish the magnificence of Paullus' triumph, he took aim at the victory games that Paullus had given at Amphipolis by presenting the same events, but in a farcical manner.

Anicius' parody of the games at Amphipolis was in large part for the benefit of Paullus' soldiers, who had recently returned to Rome in a foul mood. Paullus spent lavishly on his Greek games and paid the bill from the Macedonian royal treasury. This rankled his soldiers because he had not rewarded them as generously as they had expected out of the loot from the campaign. In fact, they were so angry with their commander that they attempted to block approval of his triumph, but the Senate berated them until they acquiesced (Livy 45.35.5–20). As punishment, they were given a lesser cash bounty than they would have received had they not opposed the triumph (Livy 45.40.4–5). In contrast, Anicius' soldiers marched happily in his triumph and sang many songs in his honor (Livy 45.48.8). With the support of his own troops already secured, Anicius may have intended to use his unusual theatrical event to gain the support of Paullus' disaffected soldiers by mocking their former commander.

Instead of holding this spectacle in a traditional theatrical space, Anicius moved it to the Circus Maximus. He probably chose this venue because it could accommodate a larger number of spectators than a theater and because the elimination of a stage building allowed the entire circus to be used as a theater in the round (Walbank 1979: 446). More importantly, there were no seating restrictions in the circus as there were in the theater. Paullus' soldiers could sit near the very senators who had granted him a triumph over their objections and had diminished their cash bounty. From there they could express their opinions freely and loudly.

By presenting the same types of acts as Paullus, Anicius was attempting to re-create his victory games at Amphipolis. But this time the setting was Rome and the entertainment was a parody intended to mock and belittle the great spectacle that had become the talk of the eastern Mediterranean. According to Livy, the Roman audience loved Anicius' offering and applauded enthusiastically after each new on-stage fiasco. It is not known whether this attack on Paullus helped him in his quest for higher office, but it certainly did not harm him in the long run. Anicius became consul in 160 BCE, the year of Paullus' death.

4 Conclusion

Roman aristocrats were well aware of the many ways that theater could be exploited for political gain. They accepted some of these as legitimate methods to acquire prestige and to attract votes, but sought to regulate others that were potentially disruptive to civic order and antithetical to the traditional means of accruing political power.

The Roman attitude toward theatrical venues is problematic. The Athenians had no aversion to the construction of permanent theaters, even though the opportunities for theatrical performances in Athens were few. In contrast, there was no permanent theater in Rome throughout most of the Republic, even though several festivals included a theatrical component. The Romans made do with temporary wooden structures that were disassembled after the conclusion of the event for which they were built. When the censor Cassius attempted to erect a stone theater in 151 BCE, the Senate had it torn down, partly out of fear that it could be used as a staging ground for civil dissent, as sometimes happened in Greek cities. A permanent theater also posed a threat to the traditional means of competing for political office. Candidates sought to impress the electorate by presenting the most impressive events possible, often in elaborate temporary theaters that they constructed specifically for this purpose. The erection of a permanent theater would eliminate the need for these temporary structures, thereby robbing candidates of one means to garner votes. Since theatrical events could be held in one centralized location that would display the name of the builder, he would receive sole credit for this gift to the Roman people, thereby diminishing the glory that would have accrued to other candidates if they had still been able to construct temporary theaters. As a result, there was no permanent theatrical venue in Rome until 55 BCE, when Pompey built the city's first stone theater, which he described as a monumental approach to his temple of Venus in order to avoid criticism for violating tradition.

The apportionment of seats was another way that Roman aristocrats sought to preserve their prestige and gain an advantage in elections. In democratic Athens, there seem to have been few restrictions on seating: elected magistrates and the priest of Dionysus sat in the front, while the other members of the audience were seated without regard to status. The Roman Senate, however, imposed restrictions on theater seating in order to solidify their social standing. They allocated seats in such a way that the theater provided a visual statement of each spectator's place in society: the Senate sat in front, the knights behind them, and the common people in the back. The theater, then, reflected the power structure of the Roman state. This arrangement also permitted aristocrats to gauge the attitude of the populace. By observing the reaction of each group to allusions to contemporary events in the plays, they could assess the popularity of certain policies and public figures. In essence, the theater was an informal polling place that allowed the ruling class to gauge the sentiments of a broad cross-section of the populace.

In both Athens and Rome, the attempt to manipulate public opinion through theatrical events sometimes gave rise to fierce competition. Athenian playwrights, perhaps with the backing of powerful individuals and interest groups, inserted political commentary into their works that either supported or ridiculed contemporary policies and the politicians who championed them. In Rome, few playwrights dared to include overtly political content. Some may have drawn implicit parallels between a myth and the current situation, but most seem to have limited themselves to supporting broad societal values, if anything. This stemmed in part from restrictions on slandering living individuals on stage, a prohibition that the Athenians also adopted at certain periods. But unlike the Athenian playwrights, Roman authors do not appear to have worked in support of specific politicians or groups. Writing a partisan play for a sitting magistrate could cause offense to his successors, who might have a very different political outlook. This could negatively affect the playwright's chances for selling future works. Generally it was the politicians themselves who politicized theatrical productions in Rome. Magistrates would sometimes select plays, often ones that were written years before, because they seemed to comment on current events. They might also encourage actors to emphasize significant lines for an audience that was attuned to political allusions. Sometimes the actors would even interpolate lines in order to make the play reflect a political point of view, the very type of "resoling" that Athenian playwrights carried out on the works of Aeschylus, for example. Thanks to the seating arrangement in the theater, politicians could gauge the reactions of different segments of the electorate to the policy that he was promoting with the play.

Some magistrates selected plays for performance with an eye toward magnifying themselves and belittling their opponents, while generals could present plays that recounted their recent victories in order to glorify themselves and defuse any criticism from their political enemies. The competition between Paullus and Anicius provides a particularly subtle example of this. After his victory over the Macedonians, Paullus presented spectacular entertainments in Greece. When he returned to Rome, he held a magnificent triumph despite the opposition of his soldiers, who were angry about their pay. Anicius, who celebrated his own triumph just three months later, saw an opportunity to increase his standing at Paullus' expense. Unable to compete with him in splendor, Anicius satirized his rival's Greek games in an attempt to belittle him and, no doubt, to deprive Paullus of votes.

Clearly, Roman aristocrats knew that theater could be an important tool for garnering the goodwill of the people, for gauging public opinion, and for competing with political opponents. With so much at stake, it is easy to understand why they expended so much energy on regulating theatrical venues, seating, and content.

REFERENCES

Altheim, F. 1936. *A History of Roman Religion*. Trans. H. Mattingly. London.

Barton, C. 1993. *The Sorrows of the Ancient Romans: The Gladiator and the Monster*. Princeton.

Beacham, R. 1999. *Spectacle Entertainments of Early Imperial Rome*. New Haven.

Bergmann, B. and C. Kondoleon, eds. 1999. *The Art of Ancient Spectacle*. New Haven.

Betts, J., J. Hooker, and J. Green, eds. 1986. *Studies in Honour of T.B.L. Webster*. Bristol.

Bollinger, T. 1969. *Theatralis Licentia: Die Publikumsdemonstrationem an den öffentlichen Spielen im Rom der früheren Kaiserzeit und ihre Bedeutung im politischen Leben*. Winterthur.

Boyle, A. 2006. *An Introduction to Roman Tragedy*. London.

Broughton. T.R.S. 1951. *The Magistrates of the Roman Republic*. New York.

Coleman, K. 2000. "Entertaining Rome." In Coulston and Dodge 2000: 210–258.

Coleman, K. 2011. "Public Entertainments." In Peachin 2011: 225–257.

Coulston, J. and H. Dodge, eds. 2000. *Ancient Rome: The Archaeology of the Eternal City*. Oxford.

Dodge, H. 2011. *Spectacle in the Roman World*. London.

Edmondson, J. 1999. "The Cultural Politics of Public Spectacle in Rome and the Greek East, 167–166." In Bergman and Kondoleon 1999: 77–89.

Edmondson, J. 2002. "Public Spectacles and Roman Social Relations." In Nogales Basarrate 2002.

Edwards, C. 1993. *The Politics of Immorality in Ancient Rome*. Cambridge.

Ehrhardt, N. and L.M. Günther, eds. 2002. *Widerstand—Anpassung—Integration: Die griechische Staatenwelt und Rom. Festschrift für Jürgen Deininger*. Stuttgart.

Flower, H. 1995. "*Fabulae Praetextae* in Context: When Were Plays on Contemporary Subjects Performed in Republican Rome?" *CQ* 45: 170–190.

Franko, G.F. 2013. "*Anicius vortit barbare*: The Scenic Games of L. Anicius Gallus and the Aesthetics of Greek and Roman Performance." In Harrison and Liapis 2013: 343–360.

Frézouls, E. 1983. "La construction du théâtre lapideum et son contexte politique." In *Théâtre et spectacles dans l'antiquité. Actes du Colloque de Strasbourg (novembre 1981)*. Travaux du Centre de Recherche sur le Proche-Orient et la Grèce antiques 7. Strasbourg and Leiden, 193–214.

Galinsky, K. 1966. "Scipionic Themes in Plautus' *Amphitruo*." *TAPA* 97: 203–235.

Garton, C. 1972. *Personal Aspects of the Roman Theater*. Toronto.

Gill, D. and C. Gempf, eds. 1994. *The Book of Acts in Its First Century Setting*. Grand Rapids.

Gilula, D. 1989. "Greek Drama in Rome: Some Aspects of Cultural Transposition." In Scolnicov and Holland 1989: 99–109.
Goldberg, S. 1995. *Epic in Republican Rome*. Oxford.
Gruen, E.S. 1992. *Culture and Identity in Republican Rome*. London.
Gruen, E.S. 1996. *Studies in Greek Culture and Roman Policy*. Berkeley and Los Angeles.
Günther, L.M. 2002. "Griechische Bühnenkunst bei den römischen Siegesspielen des L. Anicius (166 v. Chr.)—Klamauk oder Parodie?" In Ehrhardt and Günther 2002: 121–133.
Hanson, J. 1959. *Roman Theater-Temple*. Princeton.
Harrison, G. and V. Liapis, eds. 2013. *Performance in Greek and Roman Theatre*. Leiden.
Holleran, C. 2003. "The Development of Public Entertainment Venues in Rome and Italy." In Lomas and Cornell 2003: 46–60.
Hopkins, K. 1983. *Death and Renewal*. Cambridge.
Jones, T. 2009. "Pre-Augustan Seating in Italy and the West." In Wilmott 2009: 127–139.
Jory, E. 1986. "Continuity and Change in the Roman Theatre." In Betts, Hooker, and Green 1986: vol. 1, 143–152.
Kolendo, J. 1981. "La repartition des places aux spectacles et la stratification social dans l'Empire Romain." *Ktema* 6: 301–315.
Leigh, M. 2005. *Comedy and the Rise of Rome*. Oxford.
Lomas, K. and T. Cornell, eds. 2003. *"Bread and Circuses": Euergetism and Municipal Patronage in Roman Italy*. London.
McCarthy, K. 2000. *Slaves, Masters, and the Art of Authority in Plautine Comedy*. Princeton.
MacMullen, R. 1991. "Hellenizing the Romans (2nd Century B.C.)." *Historia* 40: 419–438.
MacMullen, R. 1992. *Enemies of the Roman Order*. London.
Manuwald, G. 2011. *Roman Republican Theatre*. Cambridge.
Moore, T. 1996. "Seats and Social Status in the Plautine Theater." *CJ* 90: 113–123.
Moore, T. 1998. *The Theater of Plautus: Playing to the Audience*. Austin.
Morgan, M.G. 1990. "The Perils of Schematism: Polybius, Antiochus Epiphanes and the 'Day of Eleusis'." *Historia* 39: 37–76.
Nicolet, C. 1980. *The World of the Citizen in Republican Rome*. London.
Nogales Basarrate, T., ed. 2002. *Ludi Romani: Espectáculos en Hispanis Romana*. Madrid.
North, J.A. 1992. "Deconstructing Stone Theaters." In *Apodosis: Essays in Honor of Dr W.W. Cruickshank*. London, 75–83.
Parker, H. 1999. "The Observed of all Observers: Spectacle, Applause, and Cultura Poetics in the Roman Theater Audience." In Bergmann and Kondoleon 1999: 163–179.
Peachin, M., ed. 2011. *The Oxford Handbook of Social Relations in the Roman World*. Oxford.
Phillips, D. 2001. "Tertullian on the Opening of Pompey's Theater in Rome." *Syllecta Classica* 12: 208–220.
Pociña Pérez, A. 1976. "Los espectadores, la lex Roscia Theatralis y la organización de la cavea en los teatros Romanos." *Zephyrus* 26–27: 435–442.
Rumpf, A. 1950. "Die Entstehung de römischen Theaters." *MDAI* 3: 40–50.
Scolnicov, H. and P. Holland, eds. 1989. *The Play Out of Context*. Cambridge.
Shatzman, I. 1975. *Senatorial Wealth and Roman Politics*. Brussels.
Smith, R. 1951. "The Law of Libel at Rome." *CQ* 1: 169–179.
Stoops, R. 1989. "Riot and Assembly: The Social Context of Acts 19:23–41." *JBL* 108: 73–91.
Sumi, G. 2005. *Ceremony and Power: Performing Politics in Rome between Republic and Empire*. Ann Arbor.
Suolahti, J. 1963. *The Roman Censors: A Study on Social Structure*. Helsinki.
Taylor, L.R. 1966. *Roman Voting Assemblies*. Ann Arbor.
Temelini, M. 2006. "Pompey's Politics and the Presentation of his Theatre-Temple Complex." *Studia Humaniora Tartuensia* 7.A.4: 1–14.

Trebilco, P. 1994. "Asia." In Gill and Gempf 1994: vol. 2, 291–362.
Ungern-Sternberg, J. 1975. "Die Einfhrung spezieller Sitze für die Senatoren bei den Spielen (194 v. Chr.)." *Chiron* 5: 157–163.
Vanderbroeck, P.J.J. 1987. *Popular Leadership and Collective Behavior in the Late Roman Republic (ca. 80–50 BC)*. Amsterdam.
Walbank, F. 1979. *A Historical Commentary on Polybius*. Oxford.
Wilmott, T., ed. 2009. *Roman Amphitheatres and Spectacula: A 21st-Century Perspective*. Oxford.
Wiseman, T.P. 1998. *Roman Drama and Roman History*. Exeter.

FURTHER READING

The bibliography for spectacle in the Republic is much more limited than for the Empire due to the relative paucity of sources for it. Coleman (2011: 335–357) provides the most recent overview. For Roman theater in general, Dodge (2011) provides a good introduction, while Manuwald (2011) concentrates on the Republic. Coleman (2000) reviews the available venues, and Holleran (2003) provides an overview of the politics associated with them. Jones (2009) discusses seating at events in general, while Moore (1996) deals specifically with the regulations for republican theaters. Nicolet (1980), Edwards (1993: 110–119), and Coleman (2011: 335–357) provide broad summaries of the politics of Roman theater. Boyle (2006) examines the political aspects of Roman tragedy, Leigh (2005) focuses on individual case studies for comedy, and Flower (1995) and Wiseman (1998) discuss the political uses of the *fabula praetexta*. Parker's (1999) chapter on audience reactions in the theater is excellent, as is Edmondson (1999) on Paullus and his imitators.

PART XIII

Visual Culture

CHAPTER 26

Art, Architecture, and Spaces in Greek Participatory Communities

Tonio Hölscher

1 Introduction: Democratic Visual Culture—or Visual Culture in Democracies?

When the Athenian statesman Cleisthenes introduced to Athens his political order of *isonomia*, which eventually led to the Greek form of *dēmokratia*, one of his major goals must have consisted in bringing the citizens together to form an interactive citizen-body. This strategy clearly implied a new concept of political spaces and of human behavior within them. Within the territory of Attica the local settlements of the *dēmoi* (demes) were made the basic units of the citizen-body; their citizens were brought together with those of *dēmoi* from other parts of the country in one of the ten *phylai* (tribes), thus creating a powerful network of political communication (see Rhodes, Chapter 8).

Within the city of Athens, the three great areas of public space, the *agora*, the great sanctuaries, and the common burial grounds, significantly changed their character, forming a clearly structured political center. On the one hand this new "image" of the urban spaces of Athens was caused by transformations of their physical appearance, on the other hand by changes in social practice, by the use the community made of them. For if democracy essentially means participation of the citizens in political affairs, and if such participation in Greek societies essentially meant concrete interaction of the members of the community ("présence civique": Christian Meier), then democracy can be expected to have exerted a deep impact on those societies' concepts of men's communicative actions, behavior, and visual appearance in space and time. This again may be expected to have had marked consequences for those cultural practices that were most intrinsically connected with visuality: the visual arts.

Yet we should be suspicious of clear-cut answers regarding a highly complex problem. The quest for the interrelation between democracy and visual culture can go in two different directions. On the one hand one may ask whether there was—in ancient Greece

A Companion to Greek Democracy and the Roman Republic, First Edition. Edited by Dean Hammer.

or elsewhere—a specifically democratic version of visual culture, differing from that of other, non- or less democratic societies. On the other hand one can aim to understand in which way a common repertoire of visual culture was adopted in specifically democratic contexts. Are we dealing with democratic culture and art—or with culture and art in democracies? (For some decidedly historical approaches to "classical" art: Osborne 1998; Hölscher 1998b; Tanner 2006; Stewart 2008).

"Visual culture" in this context is conceived as the entire spectrum (1) of the visual forms of social practice and behavior, (2) of the visual perceptions of the world, and (3) of the creations of visual "art." In ancient Greece, these three sectors were deeply interconnected. Greek culture can be defined as a "culture of immediate acting." All issues of political and social communities were carried out through immediate interaction of their members: political decisions were taken in face-to-face assemblies, war was fought in immediate encounters, man to man, athletic games were conducted in personal competition, and social communication, for example in the *symposion*, was realized in intimate situations of physical presence. All this entailed wide-ranging consequences for visual culture: face-to-face means eye-to-eye. Claims to public renown and position had to be negotiated in public situations where a charismatic public appearance (along with rhetorical skill) of individual persons was of paramount importance. Physical beauty was equated with a virtuous character, and both together were elevated to an exemplary model of (manly) "best-hood." Last but not least, this social *habitus* deeply stamped Greek art: human bodies, actions, and interactions constituted the primary themes in the world of images, which was an essential part of the social world.

From the origin of the Greek *polis*-state in early archaic times, "cities" were conceived as social spaces of a highly communicative character. The *agora* as the center of civic life, the urban and extra-urban sanctuaries, and the necropoleis outside of the city gates constituted distinct public areas where the citizens interacted with the members of their ideal tripartite *polis* community: with their co-citizens (*agora*), their gods (sanctuaries), and their ancestors (tombs) (Hölscher 1998a).

These spaces of public interaction were stages of visual performances; therein, works of art and handicraft played their role in public display as well as in private use. Images in ancient Greece (and Rome) were not works of "art" in the modern sense, destined for primarily aesthetic perception; they were elements and factors of the social world, conveying meaning to public and private spaces and actions. There they confronted the viewers with ideal models of physical and ethical valor. The visual world of human society and the images within this world merged in reciprocal interaction.

What was the impact of democracy or a more expansive participatory politics on this visual *kosmos*? Or conversely: how did democracy make use of these visual tools and strategies? Generally speaking, the fifth century was an age of emphatic political identity. The Greeks as a community fenced themselves off conceptually from the surrounding cultures of "barbarians," while individual city-states within Greece developed strong patriotic ideologies. Athenian democracy above all was a highly self-assertive enterprise. Through the reforms of Cleisthenes (507 BCE) and Ephialtes (461 BCE) policy became the most important aspect of civic life, increasingly dominating other cultural sectors such as religion, athletics, and theater, as well as the "private" sphere of the *oikos*. The new political order was not taken as a given fact but was under continual debate, and therefore in need of massive self-definition and self-assertion. No other *polis*-state brought its political identity so much to the fore as Athens did. In this process, public buildings and images, cults and rituals were of primary importance.

2 Urbanism: Shaping Societies

We begin with the space of the city itself. A significant role in urban planning was played by Hippodamos of Miletus, a city designer of high ambition. He is reported to have designed the newly founded harbor city of Athens, the Peiraieus (second quarter, fifth century) and Athens' daughter-city Thurioi in south Italy (444 BCE); controversial is his activity in the foundation of the city of Rhodos (409 BCE) (Castagnoli 1971; Gehrke 1989).

Hippodamos developed his concepts on the basis of orthogonal city planning which had its origin in archaic "colonial" cities, from the Black Sea to Sicily. In contrast to such forerunners, he seems to have introduced a clearer distinction between a small number of wide main streets (*plateiai*) and normal narrower streets (*stenōpoi*), delimiting shorter blocks of houses, as attested in Piraeus and in Rhodos, as well as in better-preserved fourth-century cities like Olynthos and Priene. Thereby the crisscross communication among the citizens was intensified, which corresponds to Cleisthenes' "bringing together" the citizens of Attica. Hippodamos' theoretical importance, however, seems to have been in his role as a political thinker, conceiving of an ideal society consisting of warriors, farmers, and craftsmen. His great achievement was a rational distribution (*diairesis*) of functional spaces. The territory surrounding the *polis* was to be divided into one-third for meeting the costs of the state's sacred institutions, one-third for paying the soldiers, and another third for "private" farming. Though specific information is lacking for the city space, some analogous principles may be assumed, such as sacred, political, and residential areas, each set into functional relation to the other. Most probably these concepts were never turned into reality, but they testify to the far-reaching ambition, characteristic of this period, to shape society through rational thinking.

On the other hand, the old cities that had grown for centuries from village settlements to urban centers never changed their irregular layout. Basic structures, such as the design of streets and the localization of sanctuaries, could not easily be changed; thus, innovations were restricted to single areas within the given structure. Athens was particularly efficient in reshaping its urban appearance. This was not a democratic feature as such since most of these measures are not specifically bound to democracy, but was a result of the specific political and economic dynamism Athens developed in its democratic phase. The driving force in this process was the "state," that is, the citizens' assembly which decided on public buildings. Until the middle of the fifth century, private persons like Cimon continued the archaic tradition of distinguishing themselves by financing public buildings; normally, however, their sponsorship was integrated, as an expected contribution (*leitourgia*), into the democratic state's budget and building programs. The power of urban development in democratic Athens is evinced in Thucydides' famous comparison with Sparta (1.10.2): once these cities were deserted, a future visitor would get the impression from their buildings that the latter was totally insignificant whereas the former would appear twice as powerful as in fact it was.

3 Political Spaces: Public Installations and Buildings

Athens

The new democratic order of Athens caused significant changes in the public spaces of the city. The configuration of civic spaces, with the *agora* and the Acropolis as ideal centers of the urban residential quarters, surrounded by the inland territory and the coastal zones, follows a clear structure. Although it seems doubtful, for chronological reasons, to ascribe this to a unique act of Cleisthenes, based on his exceptional capacity of geometric thinking (Levêque and Vidal-Naquet 1996), a sequence of substantial changes added up to an impressive system of democratic spaces.

The emergence of the *agora* of Athens and the impact of democracy in this process are issues of continuous scholarly debate. The prevailing view that an "old *agora*" (*archaia agora*), different from the later marketplace, was located in the northeast of the Acropolis was recently questioned with powerful arguments (see the discussion in Papadopoulos 2003; *contra*: Doronzio 2011). Most probably, the Athenian *agora* existed with its definite size in its definite place at least from the first half of the sixth century (Camp 1986: 35–60).

After Cleisthenes, political institutions became more and more predominant in the *agora*. Athenian democracy aimed to discuss and to decide on all matters of common interest by immediate interaction, face to face, which entailed an enormous increase of "civic presence." A large *bouleuterion* was built for the meetings of the 500 members of the council (*boulē*), as well as a circular building (*tholos*) for the council's fifty permanent representatives (*prytaneis*), where the official standard measures and weights of the state were also kept. For the increasing number of trials new law courts were installed all over the city; although they are difficult to identify, some of them are probably to be recognized in the northeastern part of the *agora*. These basic activities of the democratic state entailed the presence of hundreds, even thousands, of jurors, of relatives, friends, and supporters of the accused, and of all kinds of curious spectators. A group monument representing the ten eponymous heroes as exponents of the citizen-body served, with its high pedestal, as a board for public announcements for the people's assembly and for military service, addressing a wide public: a symptom of a growing city where the traditional face-to-face relations became more and more difficult. At the edges of the area various porticoes were erected as multi-functional spaces for business or personal encounters and for watching all kinds of events and rituals in the *agora*, protected from sun or rain: on the north side was the "painted portico" (*stoa poikilē*) containing a cycle of patriotic paintings; on the northwest side was the portico of Zeus Eleutherius (the Liberator) commemorating freedom from Persian domination; on the south side was a particularly long portico providing a series of rooms for offices and business banquets. Within the *agora* area a certain distribution of functions seems to have taken place: cults and jurisdiction were concentrated in the northwestern part, business on the south side, while market activities seem to have been expanded in the whole area and its periphery, especially towards the southwest and east (Rotroff 2009).

Through this development, the *agora* soon became so overcrowded with various mass events, like political assemblies, public trials, and religious festivals, that some of its functions had to be transferred to other places. First, dramatic competitions were installed in a new theater on the south slope of the Acropolis (where at the beginning of the event the tributes of the allies were publicly presented); then the people's assembly was moved to a theater-like meeting place on the Pnyx hill; finally, in the later fourth century, athletic contests moved to a new stadium in the southeast, outside the city walls. Political issues were so much at the center of democratic Athens that public spaces were more differentiated than in any other Greek city (Millett 1998).

In later periods, political installations were given great priority in times of a recovery of democracy (Knell 2000). Immediately after the catastrophic defeat in the Peloponnesian War (404 BCE) a new *bouleuterion* was built, the *tholos* of the *prytaneis* was restored, the state mint was installed in the *agora*, and above all the meeting place of the people's assembly on the Pnyx was totally rebuilt at great cost. Finally, during the revival of democratic power under the financial politician Lycurgus in the 330s a new monumental law court was begun on the *agora*, the Pnyx assembly site was greatly enlarged, and the theater of Dionysus was reshaped according to the actual exigencies of staging all kinds of performances and public events for large audiences. Still in this late period, such projects testify to the ongoing power of Athenian democratic institutions and practices (Hintzen-Bohlen 1997).

Other cities

Each city had its own spatial features. Metapontion in south Italy, with its well-investigated *agora*, containing a vast sixth-century circular meeting place, clearly shows that elaborate multifunctional installations for religious and political events could be conceived long before democracy. Similar facilities in Agrigento and Poseidonia, of fifth-century date, are difficult to relate to specific political systems (Mertens 2006: 315–323, 337–339). Mainland Argos, on the other hand, clearly demonstrates what democracy could achieve. Turned into a democratic state in 461 BCE, the city was quick to reshape its *agora*. New political needs were fulfilled by a large, columned hall for the city's council, built immediately after the democratic reform; by a large building including a court, perhaps serving for the youths' athletic training; and by a new rectangular theater for the people's assembly, some 200 meters away on the slope of the Acropolis hill. Through these buildings, the urban center was newly conceived as a constellation of differentiated spaces for all ages, for both sexes, and for the whole body of citizens as well as for the elite of the council (Marchetti and Kolokotsas 1995; Piérard and Touchais 1996: 40–54).

Yet public architecture did not so much depend on democratic constitution as on democratic self-consciousness, paired with economic power. Thasos, for example, as long as it was under Athenian dominion until the end of the Peloponnesian War, obviously made no great effort to adorn its *agora* or to erect buildings for its democratic institutions. Only in the fourth century BCE did the city give its public center a representative appearance: first with a temple of Zeus Agoraios Thasios and an altar with a statue of the famous athletic victor Theagenes, later by a two-winged stoa, perhaps the seat of the highest magistrates (*archontes*), a multifunctional building for the magistracies of public order, a *bouleuterion* for the council(?), and great porticoes delimiting the area. This sequence seems to mirror public priorities: first cults of patriotic identity, then administrative offices and installations for general comfort. The increasing impact of private donations that is characteristic of this period can be seen in the two-winged stoa at the *agora* as well as in a large hall for public meetings and banquets (Thersilocheion) further east, both with monumental inscriptions naming their rich sponsors (Grandjean and Salviat 2000).

For newly founded cities of the fourth century, the general plan, with public spaces for religious and political functions, was fixed from the beginning but only later filled out. Megalopolis, the new capital of Arcadia founded in 369 BCE after the defeat of Sparta, was designed with an impressive civic center, along a north–south axis: the center of the city was constituted by an *agora* including a spectrum of significant sanctuaries, as well as localities for the civic council (*bouleuterion*) and the magistrates (*archeia*), and framed by wide porticoes; further south, beyond the river Helisson, there followed installations for mass events: a large covered pillared hall (*Thersileion*) for the meetings of the Arcadian League, impressively towered over by a theater, the greatest in Greece, used for the citizens' assemblies (Lauter-Bufe and Lauter 2011). Likewise Messene, which at the same time was re-founded after the liberation from Sparta, got a vast *agora* with an adjacent theater, a temple of the city-goddess Messene, and further sanctuaries, followed by a sanctuary of Asclepius, and a kind of *stadion*, all aligned on the same axis (Müth 2007; Themelis 2010). Particularly revealing is the new foundation of Priene, around the middle of the fourth century BCE, where political installations were primarily laid out as functional spaces and only later shaped into representative state architecture (Rumscheid 1998; von Kienlin 2004).

4 Political Spaces: Imagery

Political monuments

The most conspicuous visual media of political self-assertion were monuments in the political space of the *agora*. Immediately after the institution of the new political order by Cleisthenes, the Athenians erected two monuments that embraced the whole spectrum of their political identity: On the Acropolis they celebrated the first victory of the newly conceived citizen army, against Chalcis and the Boeotians in 506 BCE, with what seems to have been the first Athenian state dedication to their city-goddess: a bronze four-horse chariot and the fetters of captured enemies (Raubitschek 1949: n.168). At the same time they honored the "tyrannicides" Aristogeiton and Harmodius with statues in the Athenian *agora* for their daring attempt on the lives of the tyrants Hippias and Hipparchus (514 BCE). This monument was in various respects a groundbreaking innovation. Whereas hitherto all monumental art had religious functions, as cult images in temples, votive offerings in sanctuaries, sepulchral images on tombs, these statues served exclusively political aims: commemoration of a great political achievement, in the political center of the city. In this sense they were not only a glorifying work of art but a political manifestation: first, they had to be decided on and pushed through, no doubt after controversial debates, by the citizens' assembly; afterwards, they served as compelling examples of civic bravery for all citizens that assembled in the *agora*: ideally, each Athenian citizen was to become a potential tyrant-slayer (Brunnsaker 1955; Taylor 1981; F. Hölscher 2010). Together, these monuments represented the political identity of Athens in its two main aspects: exterior military strength and interior civic freedom.

Portrait statues

The tyrannicides, heroes credited with having slain tyrants to make way for a more participatory community, were the first images of (nearly) contemporary individuals with a primarily political significance. In the archaic period images of individual persons were erected on tombs; sometimes also votive statues in sanctuaries could be given individual names through inscriptions. Aristogeiton and Harmodius, however, were celebrated by the political community in the political center as the founding heroes of the new political order. Such public honor, though, created problems in the context of democratic egalitarianism: How much should leading persons be elevated through lasting monuments over the collective community? The tyrannicides, having been put to death, were out of political competition and therefore beyond public debate. But afterwards, as long as a strong collective spirit prevailed in Athens, no living politician was distinguished by the Athenian people through a public image on the *agora*. The Marathon painting, being a private commission, was a different matter; yet even in this case controversies are reported to have arisen in the people's assembly whether Miltiades or, rather, the citizens' army merited the glory of defeating the Persians. Significantly, the portrait of Pericles on the Acropolis, set up through a private initiative probably after his death, shows him without any individual features, as a typical representative of the Athenian citizen-body.

Only in the fourth century, when a majority among the citizens was increasingly ready to acknowledge an exceptional position of renowned politicians, did the erection of public honorary images become a common feature of Athenian policy. Because of the great prestige that was conferred through an honorary statue, hot political debates revolved around questions such as: What deeds or virtues justified the erection of a public image? Should this be during the honorees' lifetime or after their death? Where should such monuments be erected? And even, who was to pay, the state or the honoree? From such continual discussions there developed a more or less well-defined practice of locating public images that was to become a basic feature of civic life in Hellenistic times (Tanner 2006; Ma 2013).

The public center of Greek cities was not just a space for setting up images of persons of public renown, but these statues in the course of time added up to a political physiognomy of the city. In Athens, other portrait statues were erected in other appropriate places: athletes on the Acropolis, philosophers in the places of their activity, in particular of their "schools," poets like the great tragedians Aeschylus, Sophocles and Euripides in the theater, as representatives of the city's cultural topography (Zanker 1995).

5 Sacred Spaces: Sanctuaries

Greek sanctuaries were not only places of personal religious piety: religion permeated the whole sphere of social life. Sanctuaries therefore played a paramount political role in Greek *polis* societies.

Athens

The Athenian Acropolis, which had been formed through the archaic period by the aristocratic elite and the tyrants as a splendid city sanctuary, was totally reshaped under the democracy into a space of patriotic pride (Hurwit 2004). The total destruction was used for a completely new concept. In a first phase, the ruins were left visible and even, by inserting the column drums into the rebuilt north wall of the Acropolis, transformed into memorials of the Persian sacrilege. Later, in 449 BCE, the radical democrat Pericles launched a highly patriotic building program that was financed, with much critique by his interior opponents as well as by Athens' allies, from the tributes of the Delian League (Hurwit 2004). The Parthenon, often wrongly described by scholars as a non-religious treasury house, conveyed to the cult of the city-goddess an overwhelming "imperial" impact through its incomparably rich sculptural decoration and its radiant colossal cult-statue (see below). The entrance building (*Propylaia*) to the precinct was shaped like a theater stage with side wings where ritual processions could enter and exit with great visual effect. Beside the entrance, a most elegant Ionian temple of Athena Nike (the Victorious) towered over the steep bastion like a triumphant victory crown. Last but not least the ancient cult of Athena Polias was united with many other cults of local gods and heroes, bound to venerable places, in a multiplex temple building, the Erechtheion. The Athenian Acropolis thereby became by far the most magnificent cult center of any Greek *polis*, exhausting the financial means of their allies and absorbing the best workers from all over Greece. When at the Panathenaic festival the delegations of the League were forced to participate in the public ritual, they became eyewitnesses to democratic Athens' political superiority that, paradoxically, was felt by many to be a kind of tyranny.

Within the city, the gigantic project of the tyrants to erect a monumental temple to Zeus Olympius was spectacularly abandoned and demonstratively left at an early stage of its development. Instead, new cult places were founded that marked the political claims of the community, notably celebrating the glory of the Persian Wars, as well as of individual politicians. On his own initiative, Themistocles, the ambitious general of the battle of Salamis, founded a private sanctuary of Artemis with the ambitious surname Aristoboule ("Giver of the Best Advice," i.e. regarding the strategy in the battle), thereby celebrating himself as the goddess's favorite—which caused considerable criticism among his fellow-citizens (see Travlos 1971, under the specific entries). Much more successful was his rival Cimon when in 476/5 BCE he transferred the bones of Theseus, who was reported to have helped the Athenians at Marathon, from his alleged tomb at Scyros to Athens, (re-?)founding this *polis* hero's sanctuary as a major precinct of young men's rituals. The Theseion was decorated with two large mythological panel paintings, representing the city hero Theseus as a prototype of two major ideological claims of present policy: his help to his friend Peirithoos in the fight against the centaurs, as an exemplary demonstration of Athens' aim to support allied cities in situations of danger, and the battle against the Amazons, as a testimony to her capacity of defending herself against aggression by foreign enemies. The affinity of these paintings to those of the Stoa Poikile testifies to close interconnections between sacred and profane public architecture (Castriota 1992: 33–63).

The second half of the fifth century saw a particularly powerful upswing of Athenian ideological claim to autochthony, i.e. to have lived forever in the Attic lands, and of local cults emphasizing Attic identity. Just as the Acropolis was embellished by the Erechtheion, so the *agora* was distinguished by the new temple of Hephaistus, father of the mythical Athenian king Erechtheus, towering on the Colonus hill over the civic center (Barringer 2008: 109–143). Complementary to this, the structure and sphere of the families (*oikoi*) were strengthened in the second half of the fifth century through an increased emphasis on cults and images of Aphrodite. Laws defining Athenian citizenship on the basis of marriage between genuine Athenians seem to have affected the cult of Aphrodite in the demes, in Athens as well as through Attica. Various sanctuaries were installed or re-equipped with new images of the goddess: one on the north slope of the Acropolis, another one, with a cult statue by Pheidias, northwest of the *agora*. Outside of the city, the old precinct of Aphrodite Ourania was distinguished through a new cult statue, graciously leaning on a pillar, created by the sculptor Alcamenes; replicas of this image were placed in parallel sanctuaries such as at Daphne (Weber 2006).

As in the realm of policy, the recovery after the catastrophe of the Peloponnesian War caused a revival of religious installations. While the Acropolis was defined as a monument to Athens' classical glory, a vast court building, the Pompeion, was erected near the main entrance gate of the city where the great procession of the Panathenaic festival was set up. Later, towards the end of the fourth century, the *agora* was equipped with two highly significant temples: for Apollon Patroos, the father god of the Ionian tribe within which Athens claimed the role of a leader; and for Zeus Phratrios and Athena Phratria, gods of the family groups (phratries). Both cults emphasized the archaic social roots of the Athenian citizen-body. Thus, in the final phase of classical democracy old and new structures were integrated in a concept of political and religious restoration (Hintzen-Bohlen 1997).

At the same time, the emergence of prominent benefactors within the democratic society became particularly evident in the elaborate tripod monuments erected by sponsors of victorious choruses in dithyramb competitions: conspicuously lined up along the Tripod Street on the east slope of the Acropolis, they gave prominence to an elite of wealth within the democratic society (Goette 2007).

Democratic Athens was also prominent in marking its claim on its unusually extended territory through conspicuous sanctuaries. From ca. 450 BCE the Acropolis project was supplemented by an ambitious program of temple building, mostly at the borders of Attica: splendid new temples were erected at Cape Sounion for Athena and Poseidon; at Brauron for Artemis; at Rhamnous for Nemesis; and at Eleusis for Demeter; while inland, probably at Pallene, a temple for Athena (and Ares?) was built (which under Augustus was transferred to the city *agora*). Through participation in great state rituals, processions, and sacrifices, the population of Athens, male as well as female, adults as well as children, could mark and experience their dominion over their territory (Parker 1996: 154).

Temples and cult places added up to a new concept of religious topography, conceived and reshaped in the spirit of a democratic society. As in the *agora*, the decisive feature of this sacred topography is that it is not only a static "image" but a semantic space to be used by the population, especially on the gods' or goddesses' public festivals: through processions and other rituals, animal sacrifices and subsequent banquets, by moving, viewing, and feasting, large parts of the Athenian citizen-body made a concrete experience of their city and territory.

Other cities

At Argos, too, the change to a democratic order around 460 BCE caused a new articulation not only of political spaces but also of religious topography, within as well as outside the city. Particularly impressive is the building activity in the famous extra-urban sanctuary of

Hera which represented the recently established power of democratic Argos within the territory of the Argolid: a new terrace providing an impressive, tribune-like flight of steps for spectators to watch processions as they arrived and the subsequent competitions, was destined to support a new temple; the cult-image image of the goddess, created by the great sculptor Polycleitus with gold and ivory, was to equal Phidias' Athena Parthenos in Athens. In both cities, democratic power expressed itself in similar forms (Piérard and Touchais 1996).

Among the newly founded late classical cities, Megalopolis as well as Messene had its political cults concentrated on and around the *agora* (see above). A significant feature of religious topography in these communities of groups of different provenance was the installation of new personified city-goddesses, Megalopolis and Messene, who addressed the whole people without privileging only one part (Lauter-Bufe and Lauter 2011; Müth 2007). At the same time Priene, which was transferred from its old to a new site, seems to have preserved its traditional separation of its religious and political areas: the central sanctuary of Athena Polias with the temple of the famous architect Pytheos was, together with the city wall, the first and most ambitious public project. Financial contribution by Alexander the Great confirms that at that time sacred buildings had the first priority for a city's identity. As in Athens, a festival called Panathenaea was celebrated. Beside this city cult a sanctuary of Demeter at the margin of the housing area was part of the original plan, offering a specific space to the female part of the population. Other cults were integrated in functional buildings, such as the Prytaneion (Hestia) and the theater (Dionysos) (Rumscheid 1998).

6 Sacred Spaces: Imagery

Temple decoration and cult images

Ever since archaic times the main temples of Greek *poleis* and their lavish treasuries in panhellenic sanctuaries had been distinguished by precious sculpted decoration, such as metopes, friezes, pediments, and acroteria. The themes of these figurative compositions, mostly mythological, celebrated exemplary feats of Greek heroes, without specific reference to the respective *polis*. Yet in the early fifth century the aristocratic city of Aegina chose for the pediments of its splendid extra-urban temple of Aphaia scenes of the first and second Trojan Wars in which Aeginetan heroes played a predominant role. At the same time, an analogous patriotic spirit is visible in the Athenian treasury at Delphi, later also in the temple of Hephaistus overlooking the Athenian *agora*, where the Athenian hero Theseus appears on public buildings, equal to the panhellenic hero Heracles. Thus, aristocratic and democratic states alike began to make use of indigenous heroes for their political self-assertion.

Most emphatically architectonic sculpture was used to arouse patriotic feelings in the Parthenon (Hurwit 2004: 106–154). Its themes develop a significant triad of ideological topics: in the pediments, the birth of the city-goddess Athena and the struggle between Athena and Poseidon for power over Attica signify divine protection; on the metopes, the fights of the gods against the giants, the Lapiths against the centaurs, the Athenians against the Amazons, and (although less directly) the Greeks against Troy are models of heroic prowess against the uproar of forces of *hybris* and godlessness, by implication referring to the recent victories of the Greeks, in particular the Athenians, over the Persians; while on the frieze the community of Athenians appears—despite all divergent interpretations—in a solemn religious procession, offering the new cloth (*peplos*) to the city-goddess at the festival of the Panathenaea. Divine favor, heroic virtue, and human piety add up to a comprehensive vision of a state claiming leadership all over Greece.

What the frieze presents is not the political structure of the Athenian state but the religious order of its community. Most surprisingly, however, in this order of the democratic citizen-body, great emphasis is given to the display of aristocratic traditions: four-horse chariots with warriors performing the ritual exercise of *apobatai* followed by a splendid cavalcade of young horsemen. Significantly, democratic Athens never developed a specific ideology of the people (*dēmos*) but ideally aimed at elevating the whole people to the rank of an aristocracy (Hurwit 2004: 133–146, 224–236).

The cult images in the temples of democratic cities were in principle stamped by the general development of the notion of gods during this period. Exceptionally, the Athena Parthenos in the Parthenon, with its colossal height of some 10 meters and its glittering surface of gold, ivory, and other precious materials, was meant to be an overwhelming demonstration of Athens' political power. Its sculptural adornment not only comprised the great myths of warlike valor, gigantomachy, and amazonomachy on the shield, and centauromachy on the edge of the sandals, but also the birth of Pandora, probably meant as a promise of gifts by the gods to humankind (Hurwit 2004: 146–154).

Votive offerings

Dedications to the gods have two sides: on the one hand they are an act of conveying gratitude and honor to the divine addressee, on the other they are a display of the dedicant's piety, and often also of his social rank and political power. Thus, monumental votive offerings could also become manifestations of a state's political order or a statesman's political ambition.

State dedications. Democratic Athens seems to have introduced a new device of state dedications to its city-goddess Athena. In archaic times, cities erected temple buildings with cult statues to their gods, whereas votive offerings, often in the form of sculpted images, were dedicated by individuals. Contrary to this, the chariot monument celebrating Athens' victory against Chalcis and Eretria in 506 BCE seems to have been the first dedication of the Athenian citizen-body. Later, towards the middle of the fifth century, the Athenians crowned the Acropolis with a colossal bronze statue, almost 10 meters high, of Athena Promachos ("Fighting for her City"), which was declared to have been built from the spoils of Marathon. Thus, the memory of the Persian defeat was towering over the sanctuary and the whole city (Hurwit 2004: 79–84). Pericles' rebuilding program of the Acropolis, starting in 449 BCE, was accompanied by statue dedications that, together with the older monuments of military victory, formed an impressive "entrance court" to the city sanctuary of democratic Athens. Thereby, the Acropolis became an almost oppressively overwhelming stage of state ceremonies, at the Panathenaic festival and on other occasions, in face of the Athenian allies and of all other Greek states.

Almost overpowering was the Athenian presence on the panhellenic stage of the sanctuary of Apollo at Delphi: a (statuary?) monument of unknown content beside the Athenian treasury house, erected immediately after Marathon; a large portico sheltering Athenian spoils from the expulsion of the Persians after their retreat from Greece; a monument of Athena on a palm tree after a great defeat of the Persians at the Eurymedon river (southern coast of Asia Minor) in the 460s; and a vast group of gods and Athenian heroes, surrounding Miltiades the general of Marathon, at the entrance to the sanctuary, dedicated around 460 BCE (Bommelaer 1991: 110–111).

Self-assertive monuments in panhellenic sanctuaries were not a specific feature of Athenian democracy: other states shared the same practice, which resulted in a competitive war of monuments, waged on the venues of great local and panhellenic sanctuaries (Hölscher 2010). In the early fifth century BCE, this competition began as a multi-voiced interplay between cities of various parts of the Greek world and of various political constitutions. Later, however, Athens became more and more the prominent player in this competitive concert of monumental dedications, occupying the most conspicuous places of the Greek world with its monuments, stressing her identity by her gods, mythical heroes and present-time politicians, and giving them an enduring presence through images in lasting material, bronze and marble.

Allies of Athens joined this practice: Argos, after reporting a common victory over Sparta together with Athens, soon after 460 BCE marked its change to democracy with a double monument of its own heroes, the "Seven against Thebes," one erected at Delphi (beside the Athenian Marathon monument), the other in its own local *agora*; Messenians from Naupactus dedicated a huge pillar monument, supporting Nike goddess of victory, in the sanctuary of Zeus at Olympia, again after defeating Sparta, together with Athens, in 425 BCE.

In other cases, Athenian predominance appears even more oppressive. When Samos was subdued after its revolt against Athens in 440 BCE, an over-life-size group depicting Heracles being introduced to Zeus by Athena seems to have been dedicated by the new pro-Athenian leaders, who thereby made Athens' city-goddess offensively present in the Samian sanctuary. Shortly afterwards, the neighboring city of Ephesus erected in its sanctuary of Artemis statues of wounded Amazons seeking asylum, created by Polycleitos of Argos, Pheidias of Athens, and Cresilas from Crete; thus, at the time when Athens marked its claim to the dominant position among Greek cities by the excessively ambitious building program of its Acropolis sanctuary, involving artists and artisans from all parts of Greece (see above), Ephesus emphasized the great mythical tradition of its own city cult with a monument commissioned from the most famous sculptors of the time (Hölscher 2000). Ultimately, however, the (pro-)Athenian memorials in Delphi and Olympia were overdone by even greater Spartan monuments after the final defeat at the end of the Peloponnesian War (404 BCE). Votive monuments were efficient weapons, used by various states in the political struggle for power.

Private dedications. In archaic times upper-class citizens used to emphasize their social rank by dedicating large-scale votive statues to the main city-gods. In the fifth century such private dedications seem to become rarer but even more politically ambitious. In Athens around 450 BCE, the conflict between "aristocrats" and "democrats" led to a competitive practice of erecting ambitious monuments: "aristocrats" like Callias, son of Didymus, or Pronapes presented themselves as athletic victors, while Pericles erected a group representing his father Xanthippos, a successful general in the Persian Wars, together with the poet Anacreon, anticipating his own concept of combining military strength and cultural power; after his death, Pericles himself was honored with a portrait statue at the entrance of the Acropolis, reminding visitors of the man who had initiated this program. While on the *agora* honorary statues were dependent on the community's decision, private votive statues on the Acropolis had to keep a balance between personal ambitions and critical reactions of the public (Raubitschek 1949).

Athletes' images

Already in archaic times, athletic victors in the panhellenic games began erecting votive statues of themselves in the sanctuaries of the gods in gratitude for their success. Although they mostly came from the upper classes, athleticism was in principle an egalitarian institution within the social elite since every participant could win social renown and political power by winning an athletic contest. Within the sanctuaries certain rules developed regarding the right to and practice of setting up an image. In the political context of democratic Athens, however, athletic valor was not among the highest-ranking distinctions. It is all the more revealing that in the critical phase around 450 BCE, when Pericles was about to assert his predominant position, some exponents of aristocratic circles like Callias and Pronapes expressed their opposing claims by highly ambitious monuments celebrating their athletic successes on the Athenian Acropolis. Later, Alcibiades marked the peak of his political career by celebrating his glorious victories in the four-horse chariot race at Olympia, Delphi, and Nemea through highly provocative paintings, arousing fury among the older and enthusiasm among the younger generation. Thus, in the context of Athenian policy the widespread traditional practice of athletic images was adopted as a strategy of aristocratic opposition, and to some degree as a compensation for the restricted honor of a public portrait statue (Rausa 1994).

7 Mythological and Historical Topography

Greek cities were stamped by traces of their mythical origins, which were held to be their "real" prehistory, and their subsequent historical past. Such traces were powerful symbols of political identity. The locations of mythical events were rarely remembered from primeval times but were mostly invented and attributed in later epochs. Dating such traditions is often difficult; some of them must go back to archaic times. Yet fifth-century Athens seems to have been particularly active in creating and emphasizing its mythical past. A conspicuous example is the Erechtheion on the Acropolis which includes traces of the combat between Athena and Poseidon over the possession of Attica in the north porch, and the Maiden porch over the tomb of King Cecrops. Aeschylus locates the camp of the Amazons, assaulting the Acropolis, on the Areopagus hill, and in the fourth century a whole topography of the glorious battle of the mythical Athenians under Theseus against the Amazons was "reconstructed" within the urban space of Athens.

At the same time, the topography of the Persian Wars was commemorated with particular emphasis: within the city was the area of the Persian camp, the place of assault on the Acropolis, while in the countryside of Attica there was the battlefield of Marathon, the place where Xerxes had observed the battle of Salamis, the shore where the Persian corpses were stranded, and so forth. Athens and Attica were transformed into a landscape of memories of their mythical and historical past (Hölscher 1998a).

8 Necropoleis

A particular aspect of classical Greek society appears in the space of cemeteries. Sepulchral art was a public manifestation of family structures and as such was in manifold ways linked to the sphere of politics. Democracy particularly affected burial customs. In Athens, the series of splendid aristocratic grave monuments of archaic times comes to an end around and after 500 BCE as a result either of a law, or of general social pressure, in an egalitarian spirit, against aristocratic expenditure (Morris 1992/3).

When after 440 BCE ambitious grave monuments re-emerge in Athens, they become the most significant form of social self-representation until the late fourth century, when Demetrius of Phaleron enacted a law that brought them to an abrupt end (Bergemann 1997). Typically, grave terraces, crowned by relief stelai and other figurative signs, contain burials of small or middle-sized families, mostly over two to four generations; no clans, no long genealogies. The stelai, accompanied by inscribed epigraphs, strongly emphasize the values of the family. The deceased, with their relatives and servants, appear in various combinations, in highly homogeneous civic attire and attitudes. The social focus is on the *oikos* as the nucleus of the *polis*. Its members, living and dead, are united in lifelike constellations; nevertheless, death is always present, either in explicit emotional gestures or through implicit knowledge of the stele's function. The threat to the survival of the *oikos* is conceived not only as a personal but also as a social concern.

Inscriptions show that the social range of this sort of self-assertion was wide, from the richest families to the middle classes, to foreign inhabitants (*metoikoi*) and even a few slaves. Yet, although the size and quality of the monuments indicate financial expenditure, they do not represent a clear social hierarchy. Obviously, the society's civic coherence and common values were regarded as more important than social distinction—at least in the realm of public sepulchral representation.

Perhaps the most powerful factor—product and producer—of the political identity of democratic Athens was the introduction, around 500 BCE, of the state burial for all victims of war (Loraux 1986; Arrington 2010). The democratic order required military service from all citizens; therefore, at the same time that sumptuous private burials became controversial the state provided collective compensation for the families that had lost one of their members in the service of the community. The site of the state burials, outside the Dipylon gate, was not a closed cemetery but an area where these graves were mixed with private tombs and other installations; nevertheless they were close enough to each other to be subsumed under the unifying term *dēmosion sēma*. They were supplied with lists of the victims, enumerated in columns of the ten *phylai*, and often adorned with reliefs representing scenes of fighting. The funerary celebrations, in the presence of the whole citizen-body, were highly charged with patriotic ideology and collective emotions. Public orations evoked the glory of the forefathers from the mythical origins of the city to the recent past, setting the achievements of the fallen co-citizens in this tradition. Emphasis is laid on struggle and death, emphasizing the value of self-sacrifice for the city. For future times these public graves added up to a conceptual facade of the city, outside of its main entrance gate.

The necropoleis of democratic Athens and its territory were the most extended burial areas with the most artistically accomplished grave monuments to be found in Greece. Since they were not fenced off cemeteries they were a part of ordinary life: the relatives of the deceased used to visit the tombs for regular cult and care activities, while travelers approaching the city could get a visual idea of the power of family traditions within this *polis*. Last but not least the state graves were one of the main places where, almost every year, the whole community of citizens came together for the public burial ceremonies, affirming and strengthening their political identity.

9 The Private Sphere

Houses

Private housing (see in general Nevett 1999) had developed during the archaic period in relatively small one-family units; in the old irregular cities this size was determined by social tradition, while in the newly founded "colony" cities it was in addition determined by the equal size of plots within the fixed grid system of orthogonal streets. As a general rule this was continued through the fifth century BCE, not least in the shorter housing blocks of the "Hippodamian" cities of Peiraeus, Thurioi, Olynthus, and Priene. However, the idea that Hippodamos also designed a "model house," to be adopted in an identical form in democratic states (Hoepfner and Schwandner 1994), seems to be a modernistic concept of egalitarian utopia: houses in classical cities are to some degree similar but never identical. Their similarity results on the one hand from the equal size of the plots, and on the other from a certain homogeneity in the functions that had to be fulfilled by specific types of rooms and spaces: a courtyard and a covered portico for outdoors activities in different climates, a main living room comprising a hearth and sometimes a bath tub, a secondary room, perhaps for women, and above all a dining room for the men's banquets (*andrōn*). If such rooms of a reasonable size were to be installed in a reasonable way—with the courtyard immediately after the entrance, the living rooms with the portico in the back part, the *andrōn* somewhat separated from the women's room—a certain similarity must have resulted without compelling prescripts. On the other hand, the well-explored houses at Olynthus demonstrate that considerable diversity could be reached through individual solutions, even within the frame of a rigorous frame of equal lots. Greek equality meant that everybody had an equal chance to become unequal.

From the late fifth century onward, social differences became more and more marked (Walter-Karydi 1998). Rich families no longer felt bound by the severe rules of an egalitarian lifestyle and invested more and more in their private housing. In Athens, Alcibiades was a protagonist of this tendency while in other places sumptuous residences become more and more frequent during the fourth century. At Eretria, the Maison aux Mosaiques is divided into two areas of different social accessibility, one representative part around a peristyle court, with three banqueting rooms for groups of varying size (with three, five, and nine couches), another part with private rooms and a less impressive court. Lavish mosaic floors, probably wall paintings, and costly furniture added to some degree of luxury. Demosthenes (*Olynth.* 25) reproached his wealthy co-citizens for spending their wealth more and more on private residences rather than public building. Although the often complained of decline of the public realm in late classical times is rather a modern myth than an ancient reality, a certain upswing of the private in comparison with the public sphere is undeniable.

Vase painting

Tens of thousands of painted vases are definitely the most significant testimony to social imagery and collective mentality of archaic and classical Greece. Though in great part exported to places outside of Athens, their themes mostly correspond to what Athenian producers supposed to be the common interests of their local and foreign customers. Destined for use in highly communicative social situations, such as the *symposion*, weddings, and burials, vases attest to a wide range of collective "visual discourses" (Neer 2002).

Representations from social life convey highly stylized concepts of normative civic behavior and its changes from one generation to the other. Significantly, the first decades after Cleisthenes are strongly stamped by a continuation of the archaic aristocratic repertoire, in particular the joys of symposia, the beauty of athletics, and the pleasure of hetero- and homoerotic relationships. Only after the Persian Wars do the scenes of aristocratic splendor become fewer and less extrovert, and themes of reflection on social roles and norms become predominant. Fights between Greeks and Persians are depicted according to antithetical concepts of normative Hellenicity and "barbarian" otherness. Moreover, the sphere of the *oikos* is more and more brought to the fore. Greek warriors are shown departing from their relatives, emphasizing the social importance of the family and the risks of the increasingly expanding warfare. From the middle of the fifth century, the world of women, in a relaxed atmosphere of conversation and music, comes more and more to the fore. Ultimately, in the last decades of the fifth, as well as during the fourth, century, the private sphere of love and pleasure becomes the dominant theme on Attic vases.

The experience of the human world is in multiple forms reflected in the sphere of myths and the gods. At the very beginning of the Cleisthenic era the Athenian hero Theseus was emphatically changed into a protagonist of the democratic state. Probably on the basis of an epic poem, Theseus was equipped with a biography of heroic deeds that elevated him, as a *polis* hero, to the level of the panhellenic hero Heracles (von den Hoff 2010). The Persian Wars then conveyed new actuality to the old myths of the fights of the gods against the giants, the Lapiths against the centaurs, and the Athenians against the Amazons. These mythical adversaries incorporated various aspects of conceptual otherness that were felt to be in opposition to, and menacing, the Greek order of life. On the other hand, the Greek gods and heroes were elevated to ideal representatives of male prowess and dignity. Particularly efficient was the self-assertion of Athenian identity which increasingly was emphasized through myths and heroes of Attic origin. The kings Codrus and Erechtheus, sprung from Attic soil, represented the exclusive Athenian ideology of "autochthony," of having lived in Attica from time immemorial (Shapiro 1998).

The powerful upswing of the individual sphere in the last decades of the fifth and throughout the fourth centuries BCE has its mythical counterpart in a wave of themes around the gods Aphrodite and Dionysus. Again, the female sphere comes to the fore. Aphrodite is often set in an idyllic garden landscape, surrounded by personifications of social and psychological ideals, such as Eudaimonia and Eutychia (Happiness), Himeros and Pothos (Longing), Eukleia (Good Renown) and Eukosmia (Good Order). At the same time the sphere of male desires is embodied by young satyrs enjoying the pleasures of Dionysus. The hard and long Peloponnesian War may have intensified these tendencies, yet the general shift from the social norms of the community to the ideals of individual bliss started before and was to endure for centuries after this event. It was a change of paramount importance in Greek history (Shapiro 1993; Borg 2002).

10 Art Forms, Political Ideals, and Social Values

A general phenomenon to which architecture and art contribute in democratic cities and societies is the politicization of public life. Buildings for political functions not only give space to the activities of political institutions but also, together with political monuments, convey to these spaces a new meaning. In Athens, the *agora* becomes a primarily political center, the Acropolis becomes a venue of political identity, the state "cemetery" becomes an area of patriotic emotions. In these spaces, the citizens constitute themselves in a new way as a political community: in the *agora* in interaction with each other, on the Acropolis with the city-goddess, in the burial areas with their ancestors.

For this purpose, "history" was of paramount importance. The discovery of "history" in the fifth century BCE was not a discovery of the past but of the present. For centuries the Greeks had lived with the great pre-history of their mythical origins, as a foundation of their political, social, and cultural order of life. Through honorary statues for the Athenian tyrannicides and others, political votive offerings and "historical" monuments celebrating the victories over the Persians, tragedies like Phrynichos' *Conquest of Miletus* and Aeschylus' *Persians*, public orations at state burials, and ultimately the *History of the Persian Wars* by Herodotus, the present time and its immediate pre-history were explicitly elevated to public significance, equal to the myths of the heroes of former times.

The politicization of public life was based on new and powerful concepts of identity: one's own state versus other states, Greeks versus barbarians, in particular those of the east. A strong political antithesis was created between Hellenicity and Asianity which served to define, fence off, and strengthen all that was considered to belong to the ideal identity of Greece in opposition to the culture of the Asiatic enemy (for various approaches see Castriota 1992; Miller 1997; Miller and Hölscher 2013). Stock elements in this self-image were a basic equality between citizens of a *polis*, ethical self-control, and modesty of lifestyle. In particular, the portrait of Pericles, the most powerful statesman of classical Athens, keeps within this normative frame. Only in late classical times, beginning with the late fifth century, dominant individuals and social distinction through wealth, together with a lavish lifestyle of an "oriental" type, are acknowledged within democratic societies.

At the basis of all this lies a new collective self-confidence of human beings. As the poet-philosopher Xenophanes put it (fr. 16): "Not from the beginning did the gods reveal all things to mortals, but men by searching found the better in the course of time." In this sense, Cleisthenes did not so much modify the old political norms as create a totally new order in which all members of the community had to take decisions on all essential issues of the state and even of the political order as such. It was a widespread optimism of being able to shape the human world and social life—with the gods' favor, but through men's own efforts.

The medic-philosopher Alcmaeon of Croton (fr. 4) developed a concept of health that primarily regards the human body but has implications for the political order of the state: health is the balance of powers, wet and dry, cold and hot, bitter and sweet, whereas illness is the predominance of one of these elements. In this context, "balance" and "predominance" are defined by political notions: *isonomia*, the key term of Cleisthenes' political order, and *monarchia*, as its negative counter-concept. As a medic, Alcmaeon must have considered health—and by implication political *isonomia*—to be feasible through theoretical insight, competent knowledge, and skillful practice. In the same sense, the sculptor Polycleitos of Argos conceived one generation later a canon of the human body that was radically based on the balance of antithetical forces. In his view, art was able to create a perfect human body, as Hippodamus of Miletus conceived his ideal state and the order of the city as a balance and reciprocal interaction between warriors, farmers, and craftsmen. Thus there were marked analogies between works of art and concepts of the state and society: analogies that in part resulted implicitly from general forms of thinking in terms of opposition and balance, and that in part were explicitly conceptualized.

11 Conclusion

The quest for the role of art in historical contexts should not lead to one-directional answers regarding the interrelation between art and the "historical" world of policy and society: while art to some degree results from historical circumstances because it has its place therein, art also affects and changes the world it is destined for.

Recent approaches have aimed to establish close connections between Athenian democracy and the general style of "classical" art (Tanner 2006; Neer 2010). Such attempts are most fruitful and challenging in integrating the forms of style within a specific political order. On the other hand, however, there remains the fact that this style, wherever it originated, immediately spread through the entire Greek world and was adopted in democratic as well as aristocratic and monarchic states. Therefore, one must consider also other social and cultural factors relevant to this change in the arts.

There is no "democratic architecture and art," but there is massive use of architecture and art by and for democracy. The Athenian democracy was imperialistic and voracious in many respects, not least in the field of art: within the realm of the Delian League, the allies were so heavily burdened with tributes that the number of public and private art commissions fell drastically, while Athens with its gigantic project of adorning its cityscape absorbed almost all capable artists from all parts of Greece. Yet from this it does not follow that this was essentially "democratic art": indeed, some specific phenomena, such as public portrait statues and the state cemetery, were developed in democratic Athens; moreover, the conflict between the claims of leading politicians to power and the constraints of the egalitarian community appears particularly sharp in Athenian public monuments. But most types and phenomena of public architecture and art were not restricted to this specific political order. What remains is that *democratic* Athens was the driving force in all tendencies towards the politicization of social life, the elevation of the present time to the rank of myth, the construction of patriotic and Hellenic identity, and the ideological promotion (and factual abandonment!) of typically "Greek" social and cultural values.

What is most important in this development is the enormous intensification of public life that occurred in the civic spaces of democratic Athens. People's assemblies, with a quorum of 6,000, meeting up to forty times a year, regular sessions of the council of 500 members, law courts with thousands of jurors every day, countless religious festivals celebrated in sanctuaries all over the city and beyond, athletic games and theater performances, public and private burials with great numbers of participants: all this added up to an unprecedented "civic presence" and encounters of inhabitants not only of the capital but also of the countryside. In this situation, public monuments, exalting the great feats of patriotic myth and history, prompted vivid discourses on matters of policy and patriotic identity. It was the combination of highly ambitious political and religious architecture with an intense concentration of civic energies in the realm of policy that made democratic Athens by far the most dynamic power in classical Greece.

In this respect classical Athens opened the way for a multiform practice of visual culture, installing communitarian spaces and erecting public monuments, in later states of democratic or republican constitution. The Roman Republic, not from its beginning but in its expansive phase from a *polis* state to a great territorial power in the fourth and third centuries BCE, adopted great part of these elements: transforming the Forum into a space of political agency, creating a religious topography of temples for divinities of political ideology and identity, and installing a practice of reciprocal claims and acknowledgment between the institutions of the community and its leading individuals in the visual forms of public monuments and rituals. This must also have affected public life, but in contrast to Athens the emphasis in these changes was laid on increasing public dignity and political magnificence, adequate to Rome's increasing ambition to rise among the great powers of the Mediterranean; accordingly, the Forum was reserved for political and elevated economic activities, while state cults were installed and performed for gods and goddesses of political concepts like Salus and Victoria, Virtus, Honos, and Pietas. Thus, in Rome the politicization of public spaces and monuments was developed into a powerful instrument of political contest, but the beginnings of this concept are to be traced back to Athens and other participatory communities in fifth-century Greece.

REFERENCES

Arrington, N. 2010. "Topographic Semantics: The Location of the Athenian Public Cemetery and its Significance for the Nascent Democracy." *Hesperia* 79: 499–539.

Barringer, J.M. 2008. *Art, Myth, and Ritual in Classical Greece*. Cambridge.

Bergemann, J. 1997. *Demos und Thanatos. Untersuchungen zum Wertsystem der Polis im Spiegel der attischen Grabreliefs des 4. Jahrhunderts v.Chr.* Munich.

Boedeker, D. and K. Raaflaub, eds. 1998. *Democracy, Empire, and the Arts in Fifth-Century Athens*. Cambridge, MA.

Boersma, J.S. 1970. *Athenian Building Policy from 561/60 to 405/4 B.C.* Groningen.

Bommelaer, J.-F. 1991. *Guide de Delphes: le site*. Paris.

Borg, B.E. 2002. *Der Logos des Mythos. Allegorien und Personifikationen in der frühen griechischen Kunst*. Munich.

Brunnsaker, St. 1955. *The Tyrant-Slayers of Kritios and Nesiotes*. Lund.

Camp, J.M. 1986. *The Athenian Agora*. London.

Castagnoli, F. 1971. *Orthogonal Town-Planning in Classical Antiquity*. Cambridge, MA.

Castriota, D. 1992. *Myth, Ethos, and Actuality: Official Art in 5th Century B.C. Athens*. Madison.

Doronzio, A. 2011. "L'*Archaia Agora* di Apollodoro e Melanzio." *Quaderni Ticinesi. Numismatica e antichità classiche* 40: 15–84.

Gehrke, H.-J. 1989. "Bemerkungen zu Hippodamos von Milet." In Schuller, Hoepfner, and Schwandner 1989: 58–63.

Goette, H.-R. 2007. "Choregic Monuments and the Athenian Democracy." In P. Wilson, ed., *Greek Theatre and Festivals: Documentary Studies*. Oxford, 122–149.

Grandjean, Y. and Salviat, F. 2000. *Guide de Thasos*. 2nd edn. Paris.

Gruen, E.S., ed. 2011. *Cultural Identity in the Ancient Mediterranean*. Los Angeles.

Hintzen-Bohlen, B. 1997. *Die Kulturpolitik des Euboulos und des Lykurg*. Berlin.

Hoepfner, W. and E.-L. Schwandner. 1994. *Haus und Stadt im klassischen Griechenland: Wohnen in der antiken Stadt* I. Munich.

Hölscher, F. 2010. "*Die Tyrannenmörder—Ein Denkmal der Demokratie*." In E. Stein-Hölkeskamp and K.-J. Hölkeskamp, eds., *Die griechische Welt. Erinnerungsorte der Antike*. München, 244–258.

Hölscher, T. 1974. "Die Nike der Messenier und Naupaktier in Olympia: Kunst und Geschichte im späten 5.Jahrhundert v.Chr." *JDI* 89: 70–111.

Hölscher, T. 1998a. *Öffentliche Räume in frühen griechischen Städten*. 2nd edn. Heidelberg.

Hölscher, T. 1998b. "Images and Political Identity: The Case of Athens." In Boedeker and Raaflaub 1998: 153–183.

Hölscher, T. 2000. "Die Amazonen von Ephesos: Ein Monument der Selbstbehauptung." In *Agathos Daimon: Mythes et cultes*. *BCEH* suppl. 38: 205–217.

Hölscher, T. and M. Miller. forthcoming. "Wealth, Luxury and Identity: East and West." In T. Hölscher, B. Parmann, K. Trampedach, and N. Zenzen, eds., *The Antithesis East–West before and after Alexander the Great*. Frankfurt.

Hurwit, J.M. 1999. *The Athenian Acropolis*. Cambridge.

Hurwit, J.M. 2004. *The Acropolis in the Age of Pericles*. Cambridge.

Knell, H. 2000. *Athen im 4. Jahrhundert*. Darmstadt.

Lauter-Bufe, H. and H. Lauter. 2011. *Die politischen Bauten von Megalopolis*. Darmstadt.

Levêque, P. and P. Vidal-Naquet. 1996. *Cleisthenes the Athenian*. Atlantic Highlands.

Loraux, N. 1986. *The Invention of Athens: The Funeral Oration in the Classical City*. Trans. A. Sheridan. Cambridge.

Ma, J. 2013. *Statues and Cities. Honorific Portraits and Civic Identity in the Hellenistic World*. Oxford.

Marchetti, P. and K. Kolokotsas. 1995. *Le nymphée de l'agora d'Argos*. Études Péloponnésiennes 11. Paris.

Mertens, D. 2006, *Städte und Bauten der Westgriechen*. Munich.

Miller, M. 1997. *Athens and Persia in the 5th Century* B.C. Cambridge.

Miller, M. and Hölscher, T. 2013. "Wealth and Social Identity: East and West: Between Cultural Anthropology and Political Ideology." In N. Zenzen, T. Hölscher und K. Trampedach, eds., *Aneignung und Abgrenzung. Wechselnde Perspektiven auf die Antithese von, Ost' und, West' in der griechischen Antike*. Heidelberg.

Millett, P. 1998. "Encounters in the Agora." In P. Cartledge, P. Millett, and S. von Reden, eds., *Kosmos: Essays in Order, Conflict and Community in Classical Athens*. Cambridge, 203–228.

Morris, I. 1992/3. "Law, Culture, and Funerary Art in Athens." *Hephaistos* 11–12: 35–50.

Müth, S. 2007. *Eigene Wege: Topographie und Stadtplan von Messene in spätklassisch-hellenistischer Zeit*. Rahden and Westfalen.

Neer, R. 2002. *Style and Politics in Athenian Vase-Painting*. Cambridge.

Neer, R. 2010.*The Emergence of the Classical Style in Greek Sculpture*. Chicago.

Nevett, L. 1999. *House and Society in the Ancient Greek World*. Cambridge.

Osborne, R. 1998. *Archaic and Classical Greek Art*. Oxford.

Papadopoulos, J. 2003. *Ceramicus Redivivus*. *Hesperia* suppl. 31. Athens.

Parker, R. 1996. *Athenian Religion*. Oxford.

Piérart, M. and G. Touchais. 1996. *Argos : Une ville grecque de 6000 ans*. Paris.

Pollitt, J.J. 1972. *Art and Experience in Classical Greece*. Cambridge.

Raubitschek, A.E. 1949. *Dedications from the Athenian Acropolis*. Cambridge, MA.

Rausa, F. 1994. *L'immagine del vincitore*. Rome.
Rotroff, S. 2009. "Commerce and Crafts around the Athenian Agora." In J.M. Camp and C.A. Mauzy, eds., *The Athenian Agora: New Perspectives on an Ancient Site*. Mainz, 39–46.
Rumscheid, F. 1998. *Priene: Guide to the "Pompeii of Asia Minor."* Istanbul.
Schuller, W., W. Hoepfner, and E.-L. Schwandner. 1989. *Demokratie und Architektur*. Munich.
Shapiro, H.A. 1993. *Personifications in Greek Art, 600–400 B.C.* Zurich.
Shapiro, H.A. 1998. "Autochthony and the Visual Arts in Fifth Century Athens." In Boedeker and Raaflaub 1998: 127–151.
Stewart, A. 1990. *Greek Sculpture: An Exploration*. New Haven.
Stewart, A. 2008. *Classical Greece and the Birth of Western Art*. Cambridge.
Tanner, J. 2006. *The Invention of Art History in Ancient Greece*. Cambridge.
Taylor, M.W. 1981. *Tyrant Slayers: The Heroic Image in 5th Century B.C. Athens*. New York.
Themelis, P. 2010. *Archaia Messene*. Athenai.
Thompson, H.A. and R.E. Wycherley. 1972. *The Agora of Athens*. The Athenian Agora 14. Princeton.
Travlos, J. 1971. *Pictorial Dictionary of Ancient Athens*. London.
Von den Hoff, R. 2010. "Theseus—Stadtgründer und Kulturheros." In E. Stein-Hölkeskamp and K.-J. Hölkeskamp, eds., *Die griechische Welt: Erinnerungsorte der Antike*. Munich, 300–316.
Von Kienlin, A. 2004. "Das Stadtzentrum von Priene als Monument bürgerlicher Selbstdarstellung." In E.-L. Schwandner and K. Rheidt, eds., *Macht der Architektur—Architektur der Macht*. Mainz, 114–120.
Walter-Karydi, E. 1998. *The Greek House: The Rise of Noble Houses in Late Classical Times*. Athens.
Weber, M. 2006. "Die Kultbilder der Aphrodite Urania in der 2. Hälfte des 5. Jh. V.Chr. und das Bürgerrechtsgesetz von 450/51 v. Chr." *MDAIAthen* 121: 165–221.
Zanker, P. 1995. *Die Maske des Sokrates*. Munich.

FURTHER READING

For a wider understanding of the issues dealt with in this chapter, international bibliography, including also French, German and Italian, has to be consulted. Among works in English a recent powerful account on classical Greece and the birth of Western art is Stewart 2008. Still worth reading is Pollitt 1972. In addition see the collection of essays in Boedeker and Raaflaub 1998 on a wide range of cultural topics in classical Athens. For good surveys of the political spaces of Athens see Thompson and Wycherley 1972 and, shorter, Camp 1986, on the *agora*, and Hurwit 1999, on the Acropolis. For new approaches on art and democracy see Neer 2002, 2010 and Tanner 2006. Important approaches of the French school of historical sociology, available in English translation, are Levêque and Vidal-Naquet 1996 on urbanism, and Loraux 1986 on ideologies of identity.

CHAPTER 27

Art, Architecture, and Space in the Roman Participatory Context

Ellen Perry

1 Introduction

One impediment to a comprehensive treatment of art and architecture that reflects the government of the Roman Republic is that the institution underwent considerable changes in its five centuries of existence. The Republic as it began to form at the end of the sixth century BCE bore little practical resemblance to the polity of two centuries later; and the Republic that developed into an international power in the late third and early second centuries BCE was not the same as the system that collapsed a century later, a victim of its own internal stresses (Flower 2010). In scholarship, the very words "Rome" and "Roman" necessarily shift in meaning. At first Rome is a city; in the end, it is an empire. However, the preponderance of evidence, material and textual, for the art and architecture of the Republic comes from the third century BCE or later, and so firm statements about the relationship between the art or architecture and the republican government are more frequent for these centuries. Much of what we can say concerning earlier periods is based on exiguous, retrospective, or highly contested evidence but this does not negate its value. Stories told in later centuries about the exemplary achievements of earlier times at the very least allow us to understand better the ideologies of those who did the storytelling.

A significant feature of Roman political life was the degree to which formal, constitutional power was acquired and reinforced through seemingly informal mechanisms (see Arena, Chapter 13). For example, among influential families, arranged marriage was used to create political alliances; and the institution of patronage, an extra-constitutional relationship between men of higher and lower status, had an undeniable impact on electoral politics. Because authority was created and maintained in so many ways, both formal and informal, the visual culture of power was ubiquitous. Political power in the Republic, therefore, shaped and was shaped by visual culture in a great variety of ways. The layout of

A Companion to Greek Democracy and the Roman Republic, First Edition. Edited by Dean Hammer.

a powerful man's house reflected and reinforced the rituals of patronage; and, in the late Republic, conspicuous consumption (*luxuria*) was employed by some men and reviled by others as a means for acquiring power. In addition, status was constantly assessed and re-assessed through various widely understood visual codes: What you wore, where you spent your time, where you sat at the theater or reclined at a dinner party, and even how you walked all signaled who you were and how others should react to you (Gleason 1994; Corbeill 2004; O'Sullivan 2011). These were just a few of the many important manifestations of visual culture as it related to the Republic.

2 Political Spaces: The Roman Forum and Roman Fora

If a *res publica*, literally the "public matter", is "government with the participation of the governed" (Flower 2010: 11), then that government required appropriate spaces and structures for the conduct of business. During the Republic, the Forum of Rome—and, for that matter the forum of any Roman city—was its social and political center, and contained government and commercial buildings, commemorative monuments and, at least at the outset, open space for large gatherings of citizens. The Roman Forum (Figure 27.1) was the location of a number of buildings and spaces essential to civic affairs. Most important among these was the Senate building or Curia and the Comitium, an open-air assembly space in front of the Senate building.

Sometime probably in the second half of the seventh century BCE, the flood-prone valley between the Capitoline and Palatine hills was drained and filled in, apparently as part of a deliberate reclamation project (Ammerman 1990). This project, though it pre-dated the establishment of the Roman Republic itself, was a necessary prerequisite for the area becoming the political and social center of Rome. During the Republic, the assembled citizens, the Senate, and the magistrates all conducted much of their business in or near the Roman Forum. The oldest place of assembly, the Comitium, was an open area where the *populus* gathered in a variety of ways to pass legislation and to listen to speeches made by the magistrates. Eight phases of the Comitium have been identified (Coarelli 1983: 120–127 after Gjerstad 1941). Two of these actually pre-date the Republic, but the third seems to be associated with its earliest days. Its first republican phase can be associated with the earliest speaker's platform or rostra, from which magistrates and orators addressed the crowd. Much later, this platform—or a similar one nearby—came to be known as the Rostra, or "beaks." The Romans had captured a number of ships from the Volsci, Latin allies, in 338 BCE at Antium (Anzio), in a decisive naval battle that took place towards the end of the Latin War. A motion was passed to burn the ships, but their metal "beaks" (prows) were salvaged and suspended from the speaker's platform (Livy 8.14; Pliny *NH* 34.20).

Because it was sometimes used for assemblies, the Comitium was inaugurated as a *templum*, a plot of sky and corresponding ground set apart from the surrounding area and sanctified by special rituals. Significant public business could not proceed in Rome before a magistrate took the auspices, and to do so a *templum* was required. The Comitium continued to be used regularly as a venue for public assemblies down to the second century BCE, when some officials, plebeian tribunes, began to speak from the back of the Rostra, with their backs to the Comitium proper and to the Curia. From the second century on, some assemblies met in front of the Temple of Castor, which may have formed a separate,

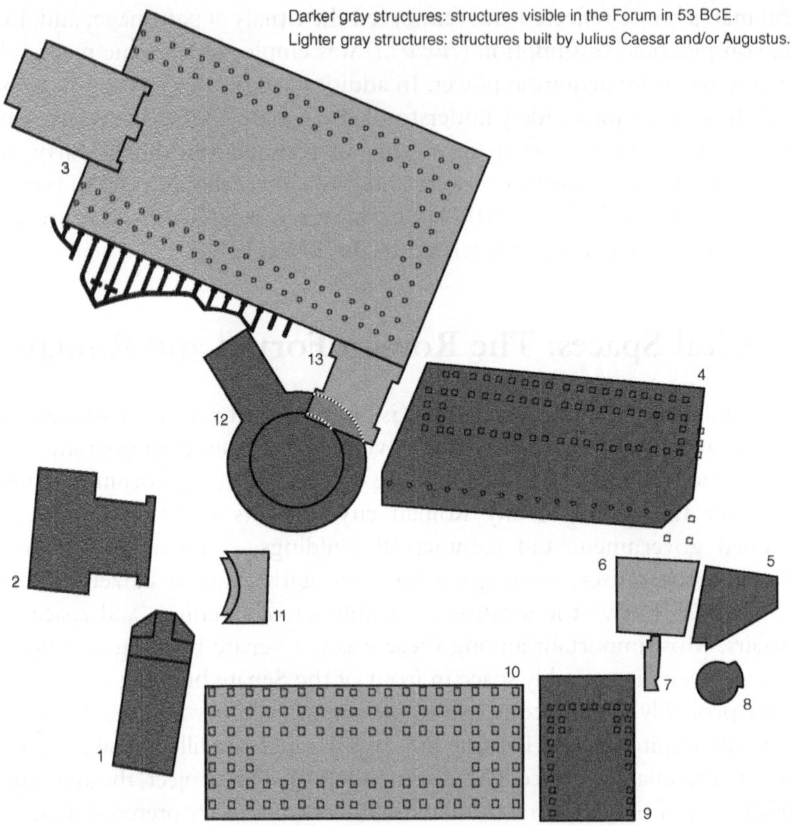

Figure 27.1 Schematic plan of major buildings in the Roman Forum during the late Republic and early Empire. (1) Temple of Saturn; (2) Temple of Concord; (3) Temple of Venus Victrix and Forum of Julius Caesar; (4) Basilica Aemilia; (5) Regia; (6) Temple of the Divine Julius Caesar; (7) Arch of Augustus; (8) Temple of Vesta; (9) Temple of Castor and Pollux; (10) Basilica Julia; (11) Imperial Rostra (12) Curia Hostilia and Comitium; (13) Curia Julia. Drawing by Barbara Geremia.

popular pole of political activity in the Forum, a deliberate contrast to the aristocratic area formed by Curia and Comitium (Sumi 2009). In 117 BCE a platform was attached to that temple for use by speakers. As early as the time of Julius Caesar in the first century BCE the Comitium was paved over with the paving that is visible today.

Like the Comitium, and for similar reasons, the adjacent Curia was inaugurated as a *templum*. For much of the Republic, this building, known as the Curia Hostilia, stood on axis with the Comitium, which, at least in its later phases, did double duty as a sort of staircase to the front entrance of the building. The building was expanded by Sulla but then, in 52 BCE, burned down in mob violence that followed the murder of Publius Clodius Pulcher. Julius Caesar in 44 BCE undertook to build a *curia* on a slightly different axis. The building no longer needed to follow the axis of the Comitium, and so instead aligned with Caesar's new Forum.

The Senate was by no means required to meet in the Curia Hostilia. It could meet in any space that had been consecrated as a *templum*. We therefore read of Senate meetings that took place in a number of other spaces around the city. Perhaps the most widely known example of this was the meeting that took place on the Ides of March, 44 BCE, when Julius Caesar was assassinated at the foot of a statue of his rival, Pompey, in the Curia Pompeia, a component of the latter's famous theater complex. The Senate might also meet in spaces that had thematic resonance with the chief order of business to be discussed on a particular day. Thus, on the Nones of December 63, when the Senate debated the punishment of those involved in the Catilinarian conspiracy, they met in the Temple of Concord, a building that was only a few feet away from the Curia Hostilia (Cic. *Cat.* 4.3), but that had been built after, and in consequence of, the murder of C. Gracchus (Plut. *C. Gracch.* 17; App. *B. civ.* 1.3.26). Both the deity housed here and the circumstances of the temple's construction suggested that the space was to be associated with the maintenance and restoration civic harmony. In addition to thematically appropriate locations, the Senate might meet in a *templum* that allowed for greater crowds—or greater crowd control. The largest attendance we know of for a meeting of the Senate, 417 members, took place at the Capitoline Temple in 57 BCE, when the subject under consideration was the recall of Cicero from exile (Cic. *Red. sen.* 26; Taylor and Scott 1969: 532). The open area in front of the temple will have provided enough space for this enormous meeting; while its location at the top of the hill might have made it possible to restrict the access that others sought.

3 Sacred Topography: The Capitoline Temple and Other Temples of Rome during the Republic

The fact that the Comitium, the Curia Hostilia and any of the many spaces where the Senate met were consecrated as *templa* reminds us that any distinction between sacred and secular is really an imposition of modern thinking on the Roman landscape. Thus a number of actual temples, in our sense of the word, were also essential to the functioning of government and to the creation and maintenance of Roman identity. Of these, the Temple of Jupiter Optimus Maximus on the Capitoline Hill, and the Temple of Saturn at its base, formed a dyad from the earliest days of the Republic.

The Capitoline Temple (Figure 27.2), although begun by the last kings of Rome, was, according to Roman tradition, completed and dedicated in 509, the first year of the Roman Republic. The archaeological remains of this structure are scanty, consisting of a part of the podium, some wall blocks, and a few other architectural elements. Nevertheless, the evidence is very good that it had three cellas to house the divine protectors of the city—Jupiter Optimus Maximus, Juno Regina, and Minerva—and that it overlooked the Roman Forum from the summit of the Capitoline Hill. Over time, the Capitoline Temple came to be incorporated as thoroughly into the civic life of republican Rome as the Parthenon was into the civic life of Athens. It became, for example, the location where all treaties between Rome and foreign powers were posted, and was the preferred place for foreign cities and rulers to offer gifts to the Roman gods. It was the place where Roman triumphs—parades that celebrated military victory—culminated in a sacrifice to Jupiter; and it was one of the locations visited by young men who were assuming the *toga virilis* (toga of manhood) in preparation for their enrollment among the voting citizenry and in the army. It was where the oracular Sibylline Books were stored under heavy guard, and consulted for divine guidance in times of civic crisis. And it was the site of the altar

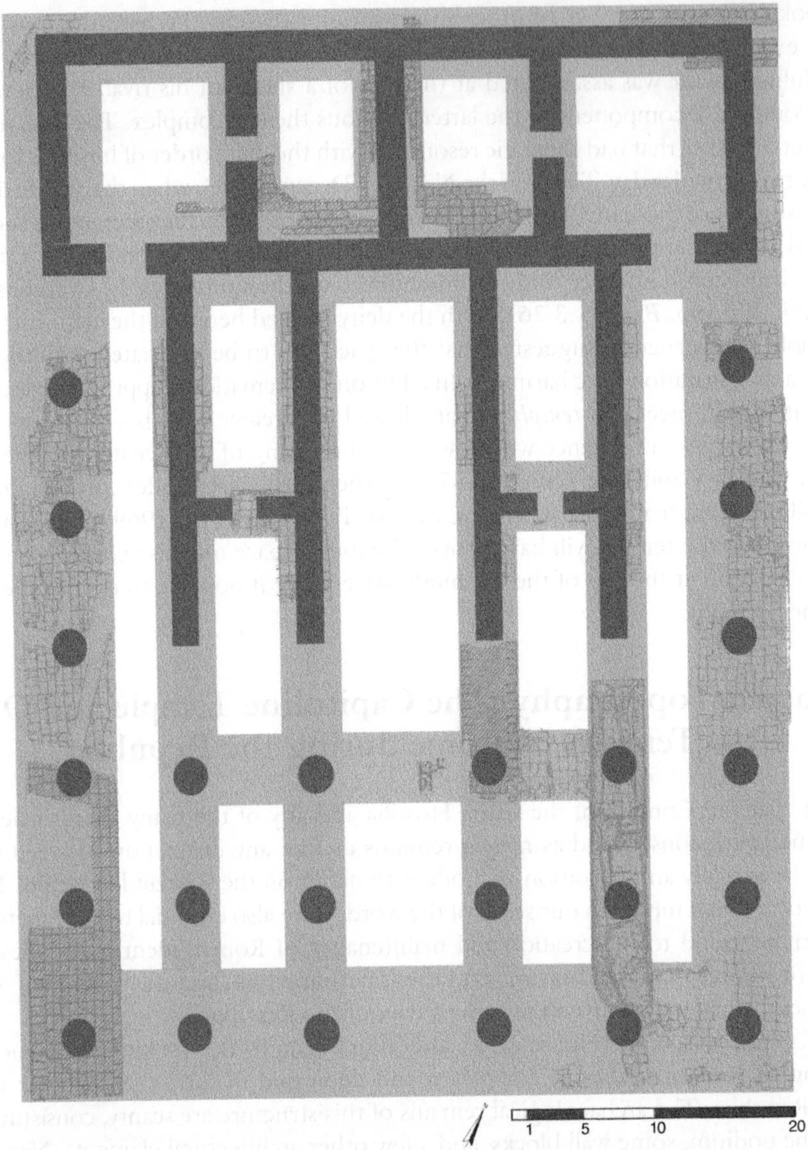

Figure 27.2 The Archaic Temple of Jupiter Optimus Maximus in Rome: plan of superstructure and foundations. Courtesy of John N. Hopkins (after A. Mura Sommella).

where, annually, Roman consuls took their oaths of office and sacrificed to the gods, as well as where the Roman Senate held its first meeting of each new year.

Tradition had it that, like the Capitoline Temple, the Temple of Saturn was also dedicated in the early days of the Republic. This structure was situated at the base of the Capitoline Hill and at the edge of the Forum, and so seems to have formed a pair, visually and perhaps conceptually, with the Capitoline Temple at the crest of the hill. Accounts of this temple's dedication date vary, but our sources generally place it sometime in the 490s BCE. The Temple of Saturn came early on to house the state *aerarium*, or treasury, and so served as headquarters for the quaestors, the city's chief financial magistrates. Like most Italic temples, the earliest Temple of Saturn must have had a high podium, accessible by steps from the front only; however, the podium that we see today appears to date from a reconstruction by L. Munatius Plancus in the second half of the first century BCE, and is made of concrete with a travertine facing. Neither of these materials was in use in the fifth century BCE, so the original podium must have been quite different, probably consisting of blocks of cappellaccio tufa. The *aerarium* may have been located in the podium of the structure, or it may have been a room accessible only from the temple's interior. (The current superstructure of the building, including the granite columns, is from a reconstruction of the fourth century CE.) The gable of the temple was decorated with sculptures of mythical sea creatures, and in the temple's cella was a cult statue of Saturn which seems to have been made of ivory, because it was filled with oil, a substance that was believed to prevent the ivory from drying out and cracking (Pliny *NH* 15.32).

A number of other important temples were attributed by later Romans to the first decades of the Republic: these included temples of Mercury (497 or 495 BCE), Ceres (493 BCE), Fortuna (486 BCE), and Castor and Pollux (484 BCE). Many of these structures were, like the Temple of Jupiter Optimus Maximus, actually dedicated to more than one god. Take, for example, the Temple of Mercury, whose cult was particularly attractive to merchants. To the best of our knowledge, the temple built in the 490s is the only temple to this god in Rome and it was also dedicated to his mother, Maia.

Our sources tell us that the Temple of Mercury was on the slope of the Aventine Hill overlooking the Circus Maximus. The Temple of Ceres was also located on the Aventine near the straight end of the Circus Maximus, and was actually dedicated to three agricultural gods, Ceres, Liber, and Libera. This is another structure whose remains have not been located, but Vitruvius tells us that it had terracotta statues on the roof, and we may presume that if there were three divinities, there were also three cellas. So the temple plan must have looked like that of Jupiter Optimus Maximus though on a smaller scale. This is a temple that was strongly associated with plebeian interests: in 449 BCE, the *plebs* seceded from the city, established a parallel government, and withdrew to the Aventine Hill, which at the time was outside the *pomerium*, the city's religious boundary, and therefore not technically in Rome. The Temple of Ceres became the headquarters for the magistrates known as the plebeian aediles, as well as the place where their archives were stored. Related items were also stored here: for example, fines collected from people who assaulted plebeian magistrates, and copies of senatorial decrees (so that plebeians could be kept informed). Finally, the Temple of Ceres was a place where, at various different periods of Roman history, food was distributed to the poor. This makes sense not only symbolically, since Ceres was an agricultural goddess, but because of its location right above the Forum Boarium, which in this period functioned as a port for the city of Rome.

4 Mythological Topography

Particular spots in the city of Rome had legendary associations. Just as the Capitoline Hill was a space dedicated by and large to Jupiter (and, to a lesser extent, Juno) and saw the construction, over time, of several temples to different aspects of the god, the Forum Boarium was the site of various monuments to Hercules. One of the oldest altars in Rome, known as Ara Maxima Herculis Invicti, The Most Important Altar of Hercules the Unconquered, stood somewhere in this area, possibly under the present church of S. Maria in Cosmedin. The legend was that, long before the foundation of Rome, Hercules rested here with the cattle of Geryon. While he was asleep, the monster Cacus stole some of these cattle, and Hercules killed him. Evander, the legendary founder of a Greek settlement in the area, recognized Hercules as a hero and either he or Hercules made the first sacrifices on the Ara Maxima (Livy 1.7 and Dionys. 1.39. Variants may be found in *Aeneid* 8.185–275; Ovid *Fasti* 1.543–586 and 5.643–652; Prop. 4.9; Macr. *Sat.* 1.12.28). Italian women were traditionally excluded from sacrifices at the Ara Maxima. This was supposedly because, when Hercules arrived in Italy thirsty, a woman celebrating the festival of the Bona Dea would not give him a drink, asserting that men could not partake of what was consecrated to the goddess.

The Romans believed that the Ara Maxima was older than the city itself. Its cult, however, was transferred from private hands to the state during the censorship of Appius Claudius Caecus in 312 BCE. Nearby were constructed at least two republican temples to Hercules, along with several smaller altars and shrines. Macrobius (3.6.10) distinguishes two temples dedicated specifically to Hercules Victor as the Temple of Hercules Victor "ad Portam Trigeminam"—a gate in the old republican city wall—and the Temple of Hercules Victor "in Foro Boario." The well-preserved round temple visible today in the Forum Boarium (Figure 27.3, sometimes still incorrectly identified as the Temple of Vesta) is likely one of these two temples. It was constructed towards the end of the second century BCE or the beginning of the first century BCE. It was built almost entirely of

Figure 27.3 Round temple in the Forum Boarium. Courtesy of Mark Landon.

marble—Pentelic originally, though later restorations were in Luna marble. (The superstructure of the temple has been destroyed.) This material, marble from the quarries of Mount Pentelikon outside Athens, reflects the expansion of Roman power in the Mediterranean during the second century.

Macrobius' second temple to Hercules might be associated with the remains of another round temple that once stood next to the church of S. Maria in Cosmedin, but was dismantled on the orders of Pope Sixtus IV. We can get some idea of its appearance from written descriptions and from a reconstruction drawing made a few decades later, in the early sixteenth century. It was larger than the extant round temple, perhaps 20 meters in diameter, with eighteen Tuscan columns. Nearby was found a gilded bronze statue of Hercules that is now displayed in the Capitoline Museums.

5 Roman Architectural Replication: Colonies, *Comitia* and *Capitolia*

Rome began the process of building an empire long before *the* Empire. Its power expanded first to and throughout the Italian peninsula and Sicily, and then around the shores of the Mediterranean. It would not reach its greatest geographic extent until well after the end of the Republic, but the custom of reproducing key architectural features of the mother city in the settlements under its rule was formulated earlier, during the expansion of the Republic.

In 273 BCE, Rome founded the coastal colony of Cosa in territory that was likely taken from the Etruscan city of Vulci seven years earlier. In Cosa's forum, the colonists constructed a *comitium*, and later a *curia*, that reproduced, conceptually though not literally, the complex in the Forum of Rome itself (Brown 1980: 23–27). Cosa's *curia*, a building with a rectangular footprint, stood on axis at the rear of the *comitium* (Figure 27.4), so the basic relationship of the two buildings in the colony was analogous to what could be found in the mother city, and was an architectural embodiment of Aulus Gellius' remark that Roman colonies seemed like little images and copies of Rome itself (Gell. 16.13: *quasi effigies parvae simulacraque esse quaedam videntur*; Gellius was referring, however, to the laws and institutions of such colonies). Like Rome, such cities were ruled by two chief magistrates and a senate, the so-called *decuriones*, so architectural replication might be understood as the outward manifestation of the replication of government traditions.

Still, the form of Cosa's *comitium* had as much in common with those of other early colonies like Alba Fucens (founded 303 BCE), Aquileia, Fregellae, and Paestum as it did with its predecessor in Rome. It was an open-air, square structure that enclosed a circular arrangement of steps—an arrangement that, in the Roman Forum, was only first approximated in the third century BCE and that spatial pressures may have made impossible to realize fully (Carafa 1998). And so, while the arrangement in Cosa did allude to the arrangement in the metropolis, it seems to have depended equally on the syntax of Roman colonial construction and to have helped establish that syntax for later foundations. Fregellae's *comitium* was also part of a *comitium–curia* complex on that town's Forum; and at Alba Fucens the *comitium* was located at the north end of the forum, though the condition of the remains has made it impossible to determine whether a *curia* was situated on axis with it.

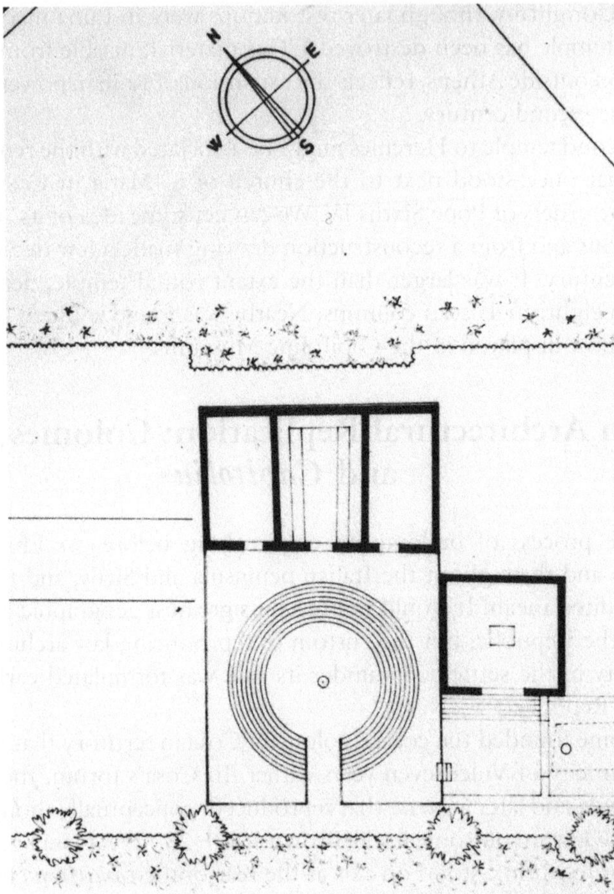

Figure 27.4 Plan of the *comitium* and *curia* at Cosa. Courtesy of the American Academy in Rome, Photographic Archive. Detail of AAR.Cosa I.AP.024.

Other cities demonstrated their connections to Rome, and to one another, through the construction of *capitolia*, temples located at prominent sites—generally either in the forum or on a hill—and dedicated to the Capitoline triad of Jupiter Optimus Maximus, Juno Regina, and Minerva. The best attested of these is the *capitolium* of Pompeii at the north end of that city's forum (Barton 1982). Identification of the Pompeiian temple is assured by the remains of a statue of Jupiter and by an inscribed dedication to Jupiter Optimus Maximus (*CIL* X.796). The extant hexastyle temple was apparently constructed after the foundation of the Roman colony at Pompeii in 80 BCE, on the site of an earlier, Samnite structure.

While one purpose of constructing these familiar monuments, the *comitium–curia* complex and the *capitolia*, was surely to assert Rome's dominance in local contexts, such an explanation is partial at best. Evidence from the countryside surrounding Cosa, for example, suggests that the Etruscan population that had been living in the area before 273 BCE must have been killed or forced to move. If so, the allusion to architectural forms would have had less to do with Romanizing the local population than with providing familiar forms and surroundings for the new colonists (Fentress 2000: 12–13). Their familiarity would have been both with the city of Rome and with the developing formula for how to construct a Roman colony.

6 Domestic Spaces: *Salutatio* and the Roman House

A great deal of exciting scholarship has recently been devoted to the archaeological assemblages from various houses at Pompeii. This work, however, necessarily provides us with a glimpse of the situation at the time of that city's destruction in 79 CE. To establish even the most rudimentary sense of an association between domestic spaces and the political circumstances of the Republic we must continue to resort to textual sources. Modern scholars have correlated the designs of wealthy republican houses with activities that helped its inhabitants to consolidate and maintain political power. In particular, the house plan that has come to be called the atrium house has often been associated with a morning ritual known as the *salutatio*, which was essential to the development and maintenance of a wealthy family's power base.

The authority of the Roman elite was articulated and constructed as much by the advice of elders as by the explicit powers that devolved on elected officials. Indeed, one of the key functions of the Senate was to offer its *sententiae*, its opinions or advice. The Roman patronage system also reflected the importance of advisors, though in a domestic setting, and the *salutatio* was the paradigmatic ritual of that system. So, while it was not an explicit feature of the Roman constitution, the patronage system was inextricably intertwined with the workings of government. It was, for example, essential for an ambitious family to participate in the patronage system so that its members could acquire and maintain the influence and clientele necessary to be elected to public office (see Arena, Chapter 13).

A schematic description of the morning *salutatio* might read as follows: in the early morning (Cic. *Fam.* 9.20.3; Mar. 4.8), the doors of the house were opened and dependents known as clients (*clientes*) were able to enter the front hall and wait their turn to speak with their patron (*patronus*). Perhaps they waited at a location towards the front of the house known as a *vestibulum*, or perhaps they waited on benches outside, but Vitruvius (6.1) makes it clear that they were permitted by right (*suo iure*) to enter the front hall or *cavaedium* and the peristyles (Allison 2004: 163; Leach 1993: 24–26). By the late Republic, some patrons may have established a sort of hierarchy of clients, with the more important ones sitting closer to the front door and entering before the others; however, this practice was frowned upon much later by Seneca the Younger so it may not have become common (Sen. *De ben.* 6.34).

Modern scholars most often identify the reception room for the *salutatio* as the *tablinum*, and locate this room opposite the entrance. It was often raised above the front hall like a compact proscenium stage (Dwyer 1994: 27). There was a direct visual axis from the front door to this room, though the path of the client was disrupted by an *impluvium*, a rectangular pool, which caught rainwater that came in through an opening in the ceiling known as a *compluvium*. Much of this architectural terminology can be found in Vitruvius (6.3), who also connects the rooms with the patronage system (6.5) when he asserts that people of a more common lot have no need for *atria* and *tablina* because they go around to others instead of being visited themselves (*quod in aliis officia praestant ambiundo neque ab aliis ambiuntur*). Though the most famous surviving examples of atrium houses are those in the Vesuvian cities of Pompeii and Herculaneum, such houses have been discovered at a number of Italian sites. The type dates back at least to the archaic period, since examples from this period have been found both in Etruria and in Rome itself (Donati 1994; Nielsen 1997; Carandini 1990).

Various sorts of business might be conducted during the morning *salutatio*. Dionysius of Halicarnassus, writing many centuries later, describes the legendary beginnings of the patron–client relationship under Romulus and lists some of the functions that Romulus is supposed to have assigned to the patron (Dionys. 2.10). These included providing legal advice and representation as well as help with finances, including contracts. Clients in their turn were not to bear witness against their patrons or to vote against them.

The decoration and furniture of the atrium reminded the visitor that the authority wielded by the patron was the authority of his entire family, which included its ancestors. Painted family trees were displayed in this space, and wax masks, known as *imagines*, of ancestors who had reached high public office were stored in individual wooden shrines. Pliny the Elder, writing in the first century CE, explicitly assigns these practices to the Roman *maiores*, elders, and contrasts them with the more lavish decorations of his day. He describes in detail how the wax masks were taken out for funerals and worn by actors who were similar in physical stature to the deceased (Polyb. 6.53; Pliny *NH* 35.6).

The location of a prominent politician's house could both advance and symbolize his status. By the late Republic, the Palatine Hill in Rome was without doubt the most desirable part of town and members of the aristocracy competed to see who could build the biggest, most lavishly decorated houses. Luxury became a tool for the consolidation of power, and competition meant that the stakes were constantly raised. Cicero purchased a house on the Palatine for 3.5 million sesterces. Interestingly, he made the purchase in 62 BCE, the year *after* he served as consul. This was apparently in keeping with his beliefs about when and why it was appropriate to own a house that broadcast one's status. Like Vitruvius after him, he argued that only important men with clients should own spacious houses (Cic. *De off.* 1.138–140). This is how he reconciled the contemporary moral condemnation of *luxuria* with the actual deployment of *luxuria* among his upper-class peers (Wallace-Hadrill 1994: 4–8): one was not supposed to buy a large house with an atrium and *tablinum* until one had the clients to justify it. A large house that was empty in the morning was a disgrace to its owner. So Cicero's moral objection was to obtaining a big house as a tool for becoming important politically, rather than as a reflection of the fact that one had *already* become important politically.

Although Cicero purchased his house in the fashionable part of town, he did not take steps to expand it. Indeed, he may have given his brother, Quintus, a slice of his land on the Palatine (Cerutti 1997: 418). He owned lavish villas in the countryside and so clearly had the wherewithal to expand his house in the city, so this must have been a conscious choice on his part. We might think of this as a deliberate political statement: his enemy, P. Clodius Pulcher, had expanded his own house by acquiring the property of a neighbor—Cicero claimed by poisoning him (*Dom.* 115). Then, when Cicero went into exile in 58 BCE, Clodius seized his house, burned it, and, famously, had the property converted into a shrine to the goddess Liberty. Cicero fought a successful legal battle to have his property restored to him on his return to the city the following year. By living on a relatively modest plot of land, Cicero may have wanted to demonstrate the stark contrast between his behavior and his rival's.

7 Art Forms and Social Values: Political Monuments

The Romans had a fondness for artistic depictions of the actual, historical events that brought glory and status; however, they were not sticklers for showing those events precisely as eyewitness viewers saw them. In particular, they often mixed elements of myth and the divine into their historical depictions. One of the earliest Roman historical reliefs still extant depicts the Battle of Pydna, which was fought by the Romans against Perseus of Macedon in 168 BCE. This relief decorated a tall statue pedestal at Delphi now known as the Monument of Aemilius Paullus. The monument was originally commissioned to honor Perseus, but instead ended up commemorating his defeat at the hands of the Roman general, L. Aemilius Paullus (Plut. *Aem.* 28; Polyb. 30.10.2; Livy 45.27). Details of the relief decoration identify the Battle of Pydna, including the depiction of a riderless horse that, legendarily, triggered the battle when it broke loose. Such details can create the illusion of realism, but it is only an illusion. The relief was placed at the top of a tall statue pedestal and was viewed from far below. Under such circumstances, a diligent reproduction of the melee of battle would have been difficult to read. Instead, the sculptors carved discrete, battling groups on a blank background with no landscape elements and without much spatial recession. All of these characteristics make for a nice, neat battle scene that is relatively easy to interpret from a distance.

Roman historical reliefs also sometimes honored government officials by depicting them practicing their duties. A set of reliefs discovered in 1637 and traditionally known as the Altar of Domitius Ahenobarbus is neither an altar nor convincingly associated with the Domitii. The reliefs once decorated a four-sided base, three sides of which depicted a mythological sea procession (*thiasos*). The fourth side (Figure 27.5), however, is unmistakably associated with the achievements of a Roman magistrate: it depicts a scene of the *lustrum* or sacrifice that marked the end of a completed census. It is, therefore, an early and well-preserved example of the sort of relief that late republican magistrates commissioned to commemorate their public deeds and benefactions. Other reliefs from the late republican period depict different magisterial achievements, like the subvention of the *ludi circenses* (competitions that took place in the Circus Maximus) and the *nuncupatio* (sacrifice made by a general departing for a military campaign); but the relative age and condition of the census relief makes it the prime example of a late republican historical relief that can be associated with the workings of government.

From left to right, we see two seated census officials interacting with two standing citizens. The official on the far left appears to be recording information. To the right of this group, two soldiers stand, formally dividing the actual census from the ceremony

Figure 27.5 The so-called Altar of Domitius Ahenobarbus. © RMN-Grand Palais / Art Resource, NY.

that ended the census, the *suovetaurilia* (sacrifice of a pig, sheep, and bull); another three soldiers are grouped at the far right of the scene. Together, these figures remind us that one of the several purposes of the census was to enlist young men in the army. In the center of the composition is an altar, to the left of which stands the god Mars, the recipient of the sacrifice. Mars is depicted on a larger scale than the other figures in the relief, though the veiled sacrificant who stands to the right of the altar—and who presumably represents the censor honored by the relief—is nearly as large and echoes the god's posture. Subsidiary figures in smaller scale who assist in the sacrifice include two musicians; three assistants behind and near the altar; and, to the far right of the composition, *victimarii* whose function is to lead the three animals to the altar in order of descending size (Holliday 2002: 164 citing Varro *Ling.* 6.93).

The aristocratic competition of the late Republic can be traced in public architecture as well as private. When Pompey the Great dedicated his enormous theater in 55 BCE, he was providing Rome with its first permanent theater, but he was also commemorating his own military victories (see O'Bryhim, Chapter 25). The theater and its adjoining portico were built from spoils of war, and the decorative program included sculptures that represented the fourteen nations he had conquered. The whole elaborate and architecturally innovative complex was dedicated to Venus Victrix, whose shrine was located axially at the top of the seating area. Only a year later Pompey's rival, Julius Caesar, was acquiring land that was ultimately used for the construction of the Forum Iulium, land that came to be dominated by a temple to Venus Genetrix, Venus the Ancestor. While the chronology is somewhat knotty—Caesar did not actually vow the temple to Venus until the battle of Pharsalus in 48 BCE—the Forum Iulium was in some sense a competitor to the Theater of Pompey (Ulrich 1993). Caesar took advantage of Pompey's defeat at Pharsalus to symbolically "steal" Venus from his rival. The Theater of Marcellus, which was planned by Caesar and completed under Augustus, offered another rival to Pompey's theater. Historical chance amplified this architectural competition: In 44 BCE, Caesar was assassinated at the foot of Pompey's statue in the Curia Pompeia, which was part of Pompey's theater complex. In response, a mob set fire to the Curia Pompeia (App. *B. civ.* 2.147).

8 Art Forms and Social Values: Funerals and Tombs as a Method of Fashioning Personal and Family Identity

Art historians have come to consider spectacle as an important manifestation of Roman visual culture (Bergmann and Kondoleon 1999; Dodge 2011). While it would be disproportionate to assign too much space to this topic in an introductory overview of the arts as they relate to republican government, a single example, the republican aristocratic funeral, will suffice to demonstrate the importance of spectacle in Roman political life. When a prominent man died, the wax masks of his illustrious ancestors were taken from the atrium of his home and placed on men who resembled the ancestors in stature. Polybius (6.53–54) also informs us that these actors or family members then also took up their ancestors' insignia of office—the highest public office each one achieved—and joined a procession to the Forum where a son or other living descendant made a speech in praise of the deceased and of his ancestors' achievements. Polybius supposed that this ceremony spurred the young men of great families to desire greatness of their own: the message was that, if they achieved high public office and did notable deeds, they would also live on eternally in the memory of their descendants.

After his death in 183 BCE, the descendants of Scipio Africanus, the legendary hero of the Second Punic War, were granted the right to keep his wax mask in the Capitoline Temple. Appian, writing in the second century CE, says that it was still the case in his day that the image of Scipio was carried from the Capitolium in his family's funeral processions. (This mask was almost certainly not the original, since the temple had burned down three times between Scipio's death and Appian's floruit.) The placement of Scipio's mask in the temple was, perhaps, in memory of his legendary visits to the Capitoline Temple to confer with Jupiter; but it may, in addition, have provided his descendants with an opportunity: the family lived very near the Forum, so funeral processions that did not include this detour must have been quite short. The display of Scipio's wax mask in the Capitoline Temple may have allowed the family to extend the duration of the procession, and so to advertise the illustrious men who had contributed to the fame of the family (Flower 1996).

By the late Republic, some wealthy Romans seem to have been building their tombs, like their houses, as acts of conspicuous consumption that aggrandized the achievements and family connections of the individual. Of course, the range of *luxuria* represented by the tombs of the wealthy was as great as the range of *luxuria* in their houses. Other prominent Romans were, during these decades, buried in tombs that were conspicuous only for their modesty: an example is the tomb of the consul Aulus Hirtius, who died in office during the siege of Mutina in 43 BCE, and was buried at state expense in an unassuming rectangular structure in the Campus Martius. Nevertheless, the handful of well-known, lavish tombs that have been preserved just outside the city must stand in for other examples that are no longer extant. These, in fact, span the period from the late Republic to the earliest Empire, when some degree of competition was still permissible.

One of the most famous examples belongs, extraordinarily, to a woman. This is the Tomb of Caecilia Metella (Figure 27.6) on the Via Appia, the road that led south out

Figure 27.6 The Tomb of Caecilia Metella. Courtesy of Mark Landon.

of the city. Caecilia is identified by an inscription on the tomb (*CIL* VI.1274) as the daughter of Q. Caecilius Metellus Creticus, consul of 69 BCE and the wife of a certain Crassus, that is, of somebody in the family of M. Licinius Crassus, the triumvir. The sculptural decoration on this tomb included a depiction of a captive barbarian at the foot of a trophy and so, although there is no evidence that the structure served as the burial place for anyone other than Caecilia Metella, it nevertheless seems to have served as an advertisement for the achievements of her family.

9 Art Forms and Social Values: Portraits

The Senate and People of Rome commissioned portraits to honor distinguished citizens, as did the inhabitants of other cities within the Roman sphere of influence. The portraits of those who were particularly marked for honor were displayed in prominent locations. Such dedications served simultaneously to express gratitude for past favors (*beneficia*) and to inspire loyalty in the recipients and in other ambitious members of the elite (Tanner 2000: 19–30).

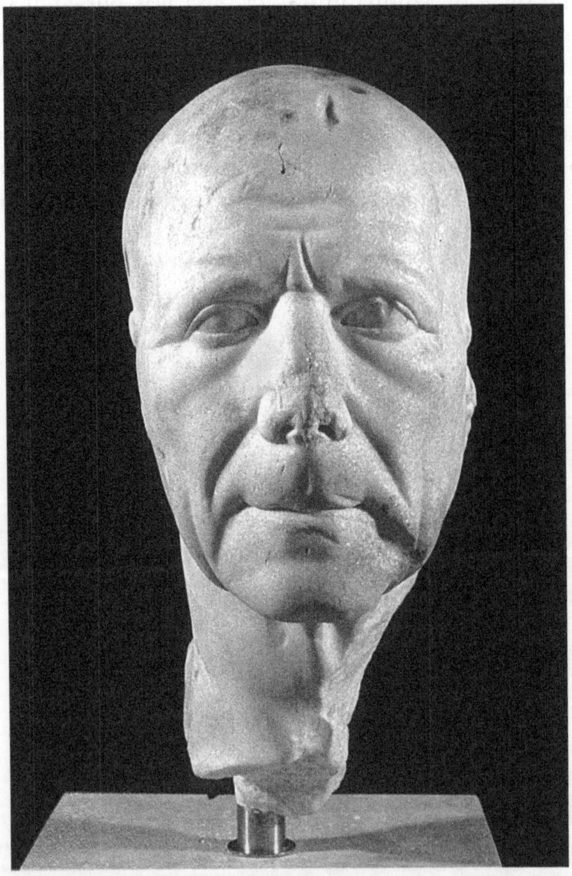

Figure 27.7 Veristic portrait: a priest of Isis, first century BCE, Palazzo Massimo Inv. 1184. Courtesy of the Soprintendenza Speciale per i Beni Archeologici di Roma.

Many of the extant portraits from the late Republic employ a style that modern scholars have come to call "veristic" (Figure 27.7), a term that means something close to, but is not identical with, "realistic." Verism involves not just the faithful reproduction of appearances, but the deliberate choice by the artist or customer of a particular visual syntax that emphasizes the seriousness and age of the sitter. Portraits in this style depict sitters who are almost without exception elderly men, with the many physical idiosyncrasies of aging—wrinkles, sunken cheeks, moles, and bald patches. Many of the examples we possess date to the first century BCE, though the type originated earlier. Because the first century was a period of civil war, and because most of the likenesses were of aged, unsmiling men, the type is often understood to reflect the instability of the times, and to convey the message that the sitters are wise and hardened survivors, and therefore ideal leaders in a time of crisis (Nodelman 1975). More recently, veristic portraiture has been associated with the values of the patron–client relationship described above. According to this reading, the sitter is depicted as, and encouraged to be, an ideal patron, an authoritarian father figure who is characterized by *gravitas* and *severitas*, both characteristics of old age (Tanner 2000). That Roman portraiture could be more than just a faithful rendition of appearance is also demonstrated by the likenesses of the emperor Augustus (27 BCE–14 CE), who overturned previous trends, and chose youthful, confident types that reflected the new prosperity of Rome under his rule.

10 Conclusion

Greek participatory communities and republican Rome shared certain basic, politically oriented elements of visual culture. Public spaces devoted to political activities developed in both sets of communities—the *agora* in different Greek *poleis*; the Forum in Rome. In each case, too, that central public space was dominated by a hilltop sanctuary whose chief deity served both as a protector of the city and as a symbol of domination over a *de facto* empire.

However, the concept of *isonomia* was a foreign one for the Romans. Participation in the affairs of state never meant equality, and much of Roman visual culture reflects this. A wide range of Roman art, architecture, and spectacle can be associated with the creation and maintenance of authority. In addition, the very informality of so much authority in the Roman Republic produced a visual culture that amplified differences in status rather than obscuring them. The rituals of the morning *salutatio*, for example, and the spaces in which it was conducted, served to amplify the authority of the patron and to remind clients of their dependent status. Similarly, particular temples and altars were of interest to distinct constituencies so that, for example, the Temple of Ceres was a focus of specifically plebeian activity; while women were ritually excluded from sacrifice at the Ara Maxima (Plut. *Quaest. Rom.* 60; Gell. *NA* 11.6.1–2), but were particularly associated with other religious locations like the Temple of Fortuna Muliebris (Dionys. 8.56).

Nevertheless, much of the art and architecture of the Republic served to unite Romans by creating a sense of common identity throughout the Roman sphere of influence. Unlike Greek city-states, the various towns and cities that came under Roman authority during the Republic did not maintain their own, distinct patriotic ideologies. The Capitoline Temple served as a constant reminder that Rome was the *caput mundi* because of its military victories, diplomatic successes, and effective government. As the power of Rome spread, the oft-replicated *curiae*, *comitia*, and *capitolia* promulgated a similar message. Thus the visual culture of the Republic reflected a sort of mosaic, a variety of individual constituencies that worked together to ensure the prosperity of Rome.

REFERENCES

Allison, P. 2004. *Pompeian Households: An Analysis of the Material Culture*. Cotsent Institute of Archaeology, Monograph 42. Los Angeles.

Ammerman, A.J. 1990. "On the Origins of the Forum Romanum." *AJA* 94(4): 627–645.

Barton, I.M. 1982. "Capitoline Temples in Italy and the Provinces (especially Africa)." *ANRW* II.12.1: 259–342.

Bergmann, B. and C. Kondoleon, eds. 1999. *The Art of Ancient Spectacle*. New Haven.

Brown, F.E. 1980. *Cosa: The Making of a Roman Town*. Jerome Lectures: Thirteenth Series. Ann Arbor.

Carafa, P. 1998. *Il Comizio di Roma dalle origini all'età di Augusto. Bolletino Comunale*, suppl. 5. Rome.

Carandini, A. 1990. "Palatino, pendici settentrionali : campagne di scavo 1985–1988." *Bolletino di Archeologia* 1–2: 159–165.

Cerutti, S.M. 1997. "The Location of the Houses of Cicero and Clodius and the Porticus Catuli on the Palatine Hill in Rome." *AJP* 118(3): 417–426.

Claridge, A. 2010. *Rome: An Oxford Archaeological Guide*. 2nd edn. Oxford.

Clarke, J.R. 1991. *The Houses of Roman Italy, 100 B.C.–A.D. 250*. Berkeley.

Coarelli, F. 1983. *Il foro romano I: Periodo arcaico*. Rome.

Coarelli, F. 2007. *Rome and Environs: An Archaeological Guide*. Berkeley.

Corbeill, A. 2004. *Nature Embodied: Gesture in Ancient Rome*. Princeton.

Dodge, H. 2011. *Spectacle in the Roman World*. London.

Donati, L. 1994. *La Casa dell'Impluvium: Architettura Etrusca a Rosselle*. Rome.

Dwyer, E. 1994. "The Pompeian Atrium House in Theory and Practice." In E.K. Gazda, ed., *Roman Art in the Private Sphere*. Ann Arbor.

Fentress, E. 2000. "Introduction: Frank Brown, Cosa, and the Idea of a Roman City." In Elizabeth Fentress, ed., *Romanization and the City: Creation, Transformations and Failures. Journal of Roman Archaeology* Supplementary Series 38, 11–24.

Fentress, J. and C. Wickham. 1992. *Social Memory*. Oxford.

Flower, H. 1996. *Ancestor Masks and Aristocratic Power in Roman Culture*. Oxford.

Flower, H. 2010. *Roman Republics*. Princeton.

Gjerstad, E. 1941. "Il comizio Romano dell'età repubblicana." *Opuscula Archaeologica* 2: 97–158.

Gleason, M. 1994. *Making Men*. Princeton.

Hanson, J. 1959. *Roman Theater-Temple*. Princeton.

Holliday, P.J. 2002. *The Origins of Roman Historical Commemoration in the Visual Arts*. Cambridge.

Hölscher, T. 1987. *Römische Bildsprache als semantisches System*. Heidelberg.

Leach, E.W. 1993. "The Entrance Room in the House of Iulius Polybius and the Nature of the Roman *Vestibulum*." In E. Moormann, ed., *Functional and Spatial Analysis of Wall Painting: Proceedings of the 5th International Congress of Ancient Wall Painting, Amsterdam 1992*. Leiden, 23–33.

Nash, E. 1968. *Pictorial Dictionary of Ancient Rome*. New York.

Nielsen, E. 1997. "An Atrium House of the 6th c. B.C. at Rosselle." *JRA* 10: 323–325.

Nodelman, S. 1975. "How to Read a Roman Portrait." *Art in America* 63: 26–33.

O'Sullivan, T.M. 2011. *Walking in Roman Culture*. Cambridge.

Platner, S.B. and T. Ashby. 1929. *A Topographical Dictionary of Ancient Rome*. London.

Richardson, L. 1992. *A New Topographical Dictionary of Ancient Rome*. Baltimore.
Steinby, E.M., ed. 1993–2000. *Lexicon Topographicum Urbis Romae*. 6 vols. Rome.
Sumi, G. 2009. "Monuments and Memory: The Aedes Castoris in the Formation of Augustan Ideology." *CQ* 59(1): 167–186.
Tanner, J. 2000. "Portraits, Power, and Patronage in the Late Roman Republic." *JRS* 90: 18–50.
Taylor, L.R. and R.T. Scott. 1969. "Seating Space in the Roman Senate and the Senatores Pedarii." *TAPA* 100: 529–582.
Torelli, M. 1992. *Typology and Structure of Roman Historical Reliefs*. Ann Arbor.
Ulrich, R. 1993. "Julius Caesar and the Creation of the Forum Iulium." *AJA* 97(1): 49–80.
Wallace-Hadrill, A. 1994. *Houses and Society in Pompeii and Herculaneum*. Princeton.
Zanda, E. 2011. *Fighting Hydra-Like Luxury: Sumptuary Regulation in the Roman Republic*. London.

FURTHER READING

The English-language reader is fortunate now to have two archaeological guides to Rome written by distinguished scholars, Claridge 2010 and Coarelli 2007, the latter a translation of chapters from three of Coarelli's Italian guidebooks. The imitative nature of Cosa's public architecture in relationship to Rome's is outlined in Brown 1980 and updated by Fentress 2000. A detailed treatment of the evidence for capitolia in the colonies can be found in Barton 1982. Readers who want more information on individual monuments in the city of Rome can consult three topographical dictionaries in English: Platner and Ashby 1929, Nash 1968, and Richardson 1992.

Dodge 2011 presents a very basic introduction to spectacle in Roman society, while Bergmann and Kondoleon 1999 offers scholarly articles about particular aspects of spectacle. Zanda 2011 is a recent study of *luxuria* in the Roman Republic, while the essential discussion of *luxuria* as it relates to the houses of the elite is Wallace-Hadrill 1994. A seminal work on the various theater-temple complexes that preceded Pompey's theater is Hanson 1959.

Essential resources for understanding Roman historical reliefs include Torelli 1992 and Holliday 2002. Our current understanding of how to interpret late republican portraits owes much to Nodelman 1975 and has been greatly enriched by Tanner 2000. A new phase in our understanding of how style creates meaning in Roman sculpture was ushered in by Hölscher 1987, a book that was translated into English in 2004 as *The Language of Images in Roman Art*.

Valuable foreign language resources include the most comprehensive topographical dictionary of all, Steinby 1993–2000. All of the works of Coarelli are worth consulting, but particularly his publications on the Roman Forum (1983) and the Forum Boarium (1988). P. Carafa (1998) has proposed an alternative interpretation of Rome's Comitium.

PART XIV

Conclusion

CHAPTER 28

Thinking Comparatively about Participatory Communities

Dean Hammer

Comparisons of political communities can be useful in identifying particular uniformities of practice with the goal of generating theories about politics (see White 2003: 836). But as David Konstan's introductory essay suggests, comparisons can also add complexity to our understanding by revealing the different trajectories, challenges, and responses of participatory communities. This volume has clearly been written in the spirit of the latter, not because there are no regularities to be observed, but because of an interest in expanding the conceptual resources we have for thinking about participatory communities. One clear take-away is that the caricature of Athens as a model of democratic reflectiveness is as unhelpful as that of Rome as an uncritical oligarchy. Viewed together, and in conjunction with other Greek *poleis*, we see how the concepts we associate with participatory communities emerge from practices that are deeply embedded in history and experience and linked to formal and informal relations and structures of power that sustain, limit, and at times undermine the participatory goals of these communities.

By saying that concepts are practices, I am suggesting that concepts cohere as a system of collectively learned meanings and dispositions. My interest is in locating these concepts in their political origins, in the experience of people acting together, rather than in a standard outside politics by which to give these ideas coherence and meaning. A number of theorists have sought to show how the concepts that communities employ are generated and given meaning through human enactments (see Geertz 1973; Douglas 1966, 1978, 1982; Arendt 1968: 157; 2005: 114–153; Turner 1974, 1988; Ricoeur 1986; Bourdieu 1977, 1990; Hodder 1985 in applications for archaeology; Hammer 2002, 2008). The implication is that the discourses by which political concepts are articulated contain layers of the past as practices, purposes, and symbols are formed through a history that is both learned and experienced. And through political discourse, new practices, purposes, and symbols are generated as participants encounter and communicate different experiences and opportunities. The concepts that emerge do not exhibit the logic of a system but the

A Companion to Greek Democracy and the Roman Republic, First Edition. Edited by Dean Hammer.

logic of practice (to borrow Bourdieu's phrase): the assimilation of different experiences into a composite image that guides people in turn in how they see and respond to other situations.

The purpose of this volume is neither to translate these concepts into modern terms (a translation fraught with difficulty) nor to confine these concepts to their respective pasts, but to provide perspective on how particular political concepts functioned as practices that sustained these participatory spaces. In this exploration these concepts emerge both as something unfamiliar—carrying with them different histories, experiences, and assumptions—and familiar—as we hear resonances of choices these communities had to face and identify the tensions they had to negotiate.

1 Liberty and Power

Greek and Roman political thought comes to us in pieces. Greece, almost exclusively Athens, emerges as an alternative to liberalism, whether as a reminder of the value of politics as the realm of human realization (Macintyre 1984; Nussbaum 1986; Arendt 1998), as lending perspective on our own democracy (Samons 2004; Saxonhouse 2006; Ober 2008), as a model of critical reflectiveness (Euben 1990), as a reminder of democratic ideals (Woodruff 2005), or as a reaction against the constitutional and bureaucratic order of the modern state (Wolin 1994). In these discussions, Rome looms unmentioned, more a reminder of a failure of political vision than anything to be studied (see Wolin 2004: 65; Hammer 2008: 13–37 on the neglect of Roman political thought).

The Romans have come to us most influentially by way of civic republican interpretations, notably those of what are often referred to as the neo-Romans. Concerned with the potential incivility of majoritarianism and populism—the very characteristics often valorized by those who look to Athens—the neo-Romans have found recourse in the institutional protections they associate with Roman liberty. The tradition is traced back to Cicero (Pettit 1997: 19), Sallust (Skinner 1998), and to some extent Livy (Skinner 1998), as well as to the later jurists. For the neo-Romans the tradition challenges the traditional dichotomy (articulated famously by Berlin) of communitarian, positive liberty (freedom to participate) and liberal, negative liberty (freedom from interference) (see Pettit 2002: 339; Skinner 1998: 113–116). Against this dichotomy the neo-Romans identify (and advocate) a third form of liberty, "republican" liberty (Pettit 1997: 19), born of a distrust of state power (both royal and, as Skinner looks to Sallust, oligarchic), characterized as non-domination.

The concepts that emerge from these discussions, particularly that of Greek freedom (*eleutheria*) and Roman liberty (*libertas*), seem to have little in common with each other. Brunt contends that a "negative sense of liberty was more congenial to the Roman mind than to the Greek," entailing a "mere absence of restraint in a great variety of contexts" (Brunt 1988: 313). Pitkin identifies a conceptual split between freedom, which is characterized by active participation, and liberty, which is a more passive protection from domination (1988). For Wirszubski, *libertas* appears as almost the surrender or displacement of power; it "is not so much the right to act on one's own initiative as the freedom to choose an 'auctor' whose 'auctoritas' is freely accepted" (Wirszubski 1950: 35). And Pettit similarly characterizes *libertas* as "antipower," claiming that to have liberty is to not be "susceptible" to the power of another (Pettit 1996: 577; also 1997: 298;

1993: 19). *Libertas*, as a surrender of or protection from power, is seen in dramatic contrast to the assertion of *kratos*, or power, of the people associated with Greek *eleutheria* (Ober 1997).

It is not that these conceptions of liberty are incorrect; they are incomplete, as even those seeing in Rome this more passive form of liberty recognize. Brunt notes that there are degrees of liberty (Brunt 1988: 297, 292). Pitkin acknowledges that "Rome developed two rival notions of *libertas*" (Pitkin 1988: 534). And Pettit recognizes that *libertas* does serve as a type of power, though he does not suggest what type (Pettit 1996: 589; also Brunt 1988: 312 and n.71). What these Greek and Roman concepts have in common, as I will develop below, is that they emerge as practices that transformed force, the dominance of individuals over others that is associated both with the household and tyranny, into power that is generative and sustaining of these participatory spaces (Arendt 1998: 148–149).

Sustaining the participatory space in Greece

The contours of Greek and Roman participatory politics acquire definition through a long historical and cultural process (see Raaflaub, Chapter 2 and Fronda, Chapter 3). Freedom (*eleutheria*) and liberty (*libertas*) both (and not just *libertas* as the neo-Romans often seem to assume) emerge in opposition to slavery, as a concept that is associated with citizenship in which individuals could both be protected and participate in deciding about the collective destiny of the community. For the Greeks freedom begins as an assertion against internal tyranny and then, during the Persian War, expands to be a claim about state sovereignty (see Raaflaub, Chapter 2 and Farenga, Chapter 6). For the Romans, liberty emerges as a reaction against the kings (and later oligarchic rule) that functioned more in the sphere of internal politics—whether as claims by the aristocracy or the populace—than as a reaction against foreign rule (see Schofield, Chapter 7; Raaflaub 2004: 254–266). In both cases freedom is associated with the legal status of a citizen that means that one is not a slave; that one is not subject to *dominium*, or, conversely, that one (whether individually or collectively) is a master of oneself (Greece: Thuc. 3.10; Raaflaub 2004: 53–55, 203–205, 261, 265; Farenga, Chapter 6; Balot and Atkison, Chapter 22; Rome: Pettit 1996: 576–577; 1997: 31–32, 36; Skinner 1998: 38–47; Brunt 1988: 283; Arena 2012: 14–16, 73–74; Schofield, Chapter 7; Stewart, Chapter 23).

While the different Greek city-states experimented with a range of participatory approaches (see Rhodes, Chapter 8), the fully democratic realization in Athens reaches a critical juncture with Solon who, as Farenga notes, combined law "with a concrete sense of agency that wielded *kratos*—and that empowered citizens to enact a concrete and complex agency as well" (Farenga, Chapter 6, and Wallace, Chapter 14; see also Hammer 2005). The *dēmos* was the whole state, a notion captured in Nicias' words to his troops that "you yourselves, wherever you settle down, are a city already" (Thuc. 7.77; also 2.37, 6.39: Athenagoras). Athenian democracy, in which all citizens were in some sense potential rulers (Raaflaub 2004: 211; Rhodes, Chapter 8), "was made possible by a set of uniquely Athenian circumstances" that included "the shared emergency and accomplishments of the Persian Wars, based on vital contributions by *all* Athenians, including the thetes; the continuation of the Persian Wars after 479, the foundation of the Delian League, and its transformation into an Athenian naval empire the rise of the fleet that increasingly and permanently assumed responsibility for the security, prosperity, and power of the polis; and the fact that thus the community came to rely on its lower-class citizens who mostly rowed the fleet" (Raaflaub 2004: 149).

In this release of energy, as Ober characterizes the emergence of democracy (1997: 70), in this expression of *kratos* as the "power of the demos to make things happen" (Ober 1997: 71), two concerns had to be addressed to maintain this space. The first is the instability of the power associated with this particular form of freedom because of the ease with which decisions could be changed. We can be rightfully suspicious of Cleon's oligarchic motivations in expressing his frustration with the *dēmos* changing its mind (Thuc. 3.37). But Cleon provides a window into the Athenian world, repeated by Plato in the *Gorgias*, of a people easily moved by oratory. Aristotle gives slightly better reasoning in arguing that there is danger in people getting used to revising the laws (Arist. *Pol.* 1269a12–18) since "law has no power to command obedience except that of habit" (*Pol.* 1269a20–21, trans. Everson). This instability is hardly surprising: in a political space in which decisions immediately followed debate, the people could be moved by fear or patriotic enthusiasm (or even good arguments) to change their minds (Thuc. 3.42–43). Moreover, in courts where precedent was not recorded, consistency in the application of the law could not be assured (see Cohen, Chapter 10, and Wallace, Chapter 14).

Yet these participatory realms were remarkably stable, owing in part to measures designed to secure precedent and give continuity to this space (Rhodes, Chapter 8). Persons could be prosecuted for proposing a law or decree that was later shown to be inappropriate "or in contradiction to an existing law" (*graphē paranomōn*: law contrary to existing law; Rhodes, Chapter 8; Boegehold 1996: 208). There were also entrenching clauses written into legislation that imposed sanctions against changes (Boegehold 1996: 208; also Lintott 1999: 63 for similar sanctions in Rome). And in 410/9 the Athenians appointed a commission to begin collecting and publishing all laws and later adopted a procedure for the review of old laws and the establishment of new laws by way of boards of lawmakers (*nomotheiai*), selected from the citizen-body (Ober 1989: 95–96). *Eleutheria* needed to be shaped by a relationship to memory and history to avoid that power from simply becoming inchoate.

If the first concern is the dissolution of the space through its instability, the second is the collapse of the space through the assertion of force by a powerful few. There are any number of pressures toward elite control: the sheer impossibility of every citizen being able to speak on a topic, the cost and logistics of participating, social and economic inequalities, an aggressive foreign policy that required military leadership, and crises (including the oligarchic coup and the loss of empire). Wallace identifies the paradox that at the height of Athenian democracy, strong leaders (*prostatai* and *dēmagōgoi*) had the most influence in the assembly (Wallace, Chapter 14).

Greece shared with Rome equality before the law (*isonomia*), which the Romans considered one of the pillars of the Republic. Unlike in Rome, though, where political inequality mirrored social inequality (Mouritsen, Chapter 9), in Athens social inequality was in dramatic contrast to political equality. All citizens experienced "reciprocal equality" through rotation in office (Farenga, Chapter 6), had freedom to speak (*isēgoria*), a right (and expectation) to serve on juries and office, and a right to speak openly and frankly (*parrhēsia*) (see Thuc. 2.37; Wallace, Chapter 14). There was a powerful *dēmos* ideology that reinforced the egalitarian dimension of this space, transmitted through education (Fisher, Chapter 12), rigorous training (in the case of Sparta), myths and visual artifacts (Hölscher, Chapter 26), public rhetoric (Roisman, Chapter 16; also Ober 1989: 304–311), ceremonies and rituals that created cohesion and attachment, and festivals (Fisher, Chapter 12). Some indication of the power of these traditions and norms is evidenced in Melos' refusal to surrender to Athens, citing their 700-year history of liberty (Thuc. 5.112).

There were important institutional provisions that protected this equality, shared in varying degrees with all the Greek city-states: selection of offices by lot with limited terms, a citizen-jury (in contrast to different census groups sitting on different types of juries in Rome), the ability to scrutinize magistrates before entering office (*dokimasia*), and the power to review conduct after leaving office (*euthynai*) (see Raaflaub, Chapter 2, and Rhodes, Chapter 8). Even *rhētores*, the politicians whom the *dēmos* looked to in order to speak and advance proposals in the assembly, never had a "sphere of influence, authority, or power for themselves that was independent of the continued goodwill of the people" (Ober 1989: 336; also Wallace, Chapter 14). In fact, a *rhētōr* could be indicted under *eisangelia*, a charge for anyone accused of trying to destroy the *dēmos*, which included sedition, conspiracies, betraying the military, or a *rhētōr* not saying what is in the best interest of the *dēmos* because of a bribe (Rhodes, Chapter 8, and Wallace, Chapter 14).

The actions by the oligarchic coup of 411 give us insight into what were seen as the sources of power that sustained this egalitarian space. It was precisely by way of arranged deception by the orators that the conspirators ushered in the coup (Thuc. 8.66). In a sharp departure from practice, only *rhētores* from the revolutionary party spoke and only said what had been approved by the party (Thuc. 8.66). New institutions were proposed (that actually bear similarity to what develops in the Roman Republic): property qualifications (Thuc. 8.65), a plebiscite, not unlike Sparta (or Rome), in which people had to either support or reject the proposal put before them (Thuc. 8.67), the elimination of salaries for office, and rule by a council, which would convene the select citizens when it chose (Thuc. 8.67). And what gave the coup strength speaks to the informal bond of trust that held together this participatory space. As Thucydides reports, by making "the general mass of people so mistrustful of each other," those joining the coup "made mutual suspicion an established thing in the popular assemblies" (Thuc. 8.66, trans. Warner). Trust takes a specific form: lacking differentiation of roles among its citizens or gradations of prescriptions by which to control its members (expulsion being its primary remedy), egalitarian communities depend on like-mindedness (*homonoia*), a sense that each individual is speaking on behalf of the group (see Wallace, Chapter 14, on the absence of parties or factions in Athenian politics), reinforced through myths of autochthonous origins and shared blood, serving as the premise for both equality and exclusivity (see Morgan, Chapter 4).

Sustaining the participatory space in Rome

Unlike in Greece, where elites never developed a sufficiently cohesive and exclusive basis of power, the Roman nobility developed solidarity in response to continual threats from neighbors, creating strong aristocratic clans that were able to retain predominance (Raaflaub 2004: 267; Raaflaub, Chapter 2; Fronda, Chapter 3; Wallace, Chapter 14; Hammer 2004). Rome provides a different constellation of power, one captured in Cicero's characterization of Roman politics: *potestas in populo, auctoritas in senatu*

(*De leg.* 3.12.28). *Potestas* (jurisdictional power) lies with the people but *auctoritas* (respect) with the Senate. Whereas Greek participatory communities rested in varying degrees upon practices and norms that structured the undifferentiated *kratos* of the *dēmos*, Roman politics was characterized by practices and norms that structured highly differentiated forms of power. The sheer range of Latin words for power—including *potestas*, *auctoritas*, *imperium*, *dominium*, and *vis*—gives us a sense of the difference (see Farenga, Chapter 6, and Schofield, Chapter 7; also Hammer 2014). Add to that the gradations of social and political roles and responsibilities and we see how differently power functioned (see Fronda, Chapter 3; Mouritsen, Chapter 9; Williamson, Chapter 11; Arena, Chapter 13; and Tatum, Chapter 15).

One often understands this differentiation of power by way of Polybius' characterization of Rome as a mixed constitution, in which democratic, aristocratic, and royal elements were reflected in the assemblies, the Senate, and the magistracies (see Millar 1998; Lintott 1999). But this takes us only so far, indicating to some extent how certain formal powers were distributed but not how power cohered (and ultimately fell apart) (see Hölkeskamp 2010 for a critique of Polybian approaches). More suggestive is Cicero's conception of this participatory space as a form of *societas*, a partnership of differential contributions (see Asmis 2004; Hammer 2014). *Societas* refers to a range of natural associations, including kinship ties (*De off.* 1.17.54), friendships (*De off.* 1.17.55–56), citizenship (*De off.* 1.17.53, 57), and the universal bond of common humanity (*De off.* 1.17.53, 3.6.28). But the term also has a more legal denotation, and one that arguably frames Cicero's understanding of political association: it refers to a type of partnership in which, as de Zulueta writes, individuals "contribute property or work or both to the prosecution of a common aim" (de Zulueta 1953: 2.179; see, for example, *Q. Rosc.* 8.24; *Quinct.* 3.11). In a partnership, as treated later by the jurist Gaius, profits and losses must continue to be shared, either equally or in proportion to an agreed upon recognition of differences in service or other contributions (Gaius *Inst.* 3.149–150). Social partnerships operate by a subjective notion of ongoing agreement (more than explicit objective conditions) (Daube 1938: 899). There are limits on the range of actions allowed in a partnership: one cannot be obligated to act contrary to morality (*boni mores*) (Gaius *Inst.* 3.157); one cannot have one's property taken against one's will (3.195); and one cannot reach an agreement to take someone else's property. But a distinctive aspect of partnerships, and of Cicero's conception of the *res publica*, is that the nature and extent of differential power are not fixed but are the subject of ongoing negotiation.

That negotiation of power is organized around the possession and disposal of property, including oneself and the *res publica* as a public thing (Schofield 1995; Hammer 2014). It is around this power that the Roman notion of *libertas* emerges. In one sense, *libertas* is a resisting power because it serves no master (*dominus*), acting as a jurisdictional limit to the *potestas* of a magistrate by restricting the ability to arbitrarily act against one's property or person (e.g. *De rep.* 1.32.48, 2.23.43; *Phil.* 3.4.8, 3.5.12; *De orat.* 3.1.4; *Clu.* 53.147; Schofield, Chapter 7: bond; Pettit 1996: 589, 602: "denied possibilities of arbitrary interference"; also Pettit 1993). Examples of specific laws in Rome include the requirement of a public trial in capital cases and restrictions on the legislating abilities of magistrates, but more fundamentally there must be equality before the law, the right of appeal for each of the partners, and opportunities to attain the highest political offices. Absent such equality, there can be no partnership because there is no jurisdiction over what is owned—neither oneself nor the *res publica* (*De rep.* 1.32.49, 3.32.44: without appeal, no protection of liberty; also *De off.* 2.12.41–42: no rights if no equality before law; *De orat.* 1.42.188: common law defined).

To conceive of *libertas* as "anti-power," as does Pettit, is to misunderstand how *libertas* is itself a form of power that rests on a more expansive notion of public ownership. When Cicero refers to the *res publica* as a *res populi*, he is saying that the *res publica* is itself a public thing in which the people have a share in determining how that thing will be used. One suggestive illustration of this assertion of public ownership occurs when the people apparently reclaim the Forum in the first half of the second century, reacting to it being filled by aristocratic portrait statues (Wiseman 2009: 49). To be free is to possess a commonwealth, which means, as Schofield notes, that the *populus* "has rights over its management and use" (Schofield 1995: 76; Schofield, Chapter 7; also Hammer 2014: 46–62).

Where the Greek participatory space emerges as an assertion of the *dēmos*, the Roman space is negotiated as a form of popular sovereignty (its decisions necessary to legitimate the outcomes of political processes) within the context of *auctoritas*, a concept for which there is no counterpart in Greek (Heinze 1925: 363–364; see discussion in Farenga, Chapter 6, and Schofield, Chapter 7; on the negotiation of ancestral traditions generally, see Arena, Chapter 13). *Auctoritas* is conventionally understood as influence that derives from respect for one's words and actions (*De rep.* 2.9.15, 2.12.23, 2.28.50; also *De off.* 2.9.33). "The word *auctoritas*," as Arendt writes, "derives from the verb *augere*, 'augment,' and what authority or those in authority constantly augment is the foundation" (1968: 121–122). Those endowed with authority were the elders, institutionalized in the Senate, "who had obtained it by descent and by transmission (tradition) from those who laid the foundations for all things to come, the ancestors, whom the Romans therefore called the *maiores*" (1968: 122). Arendt also relates *auctoritas* to the word *auctor*, the author who inspires the enterprise (in contrast to the actual builder). The authority of the Senate resides in augmentation, in the prestige associated with continuing the spirit of authorship.

We can understand the importance of *auctoritas* within the context of a partnership by way of a suggestion of Heinze, who argues that an *auctor* was originally used in legal terminology to refer to a person who, because of his position as seller of something, is responsible for ensuring the validity of the legal transaction or who, because of particular knowledge, is responsible for advice about the transaction. For Cicero, perhaps the most important aspect of a relationship, including political relationships, is "truth and fidelity to promises and agreements" (*De off.* 1.7.23). *Auctoritas*, for Cicero, answers to this concern, not by fixing something permanently in time, but by ensuring the bonds of trust and mutual accountability by which collective negotiations can occur. But it is a very different type of trust than one sees in Greek city-states, which were based on *homonoia*, or like-mindedness (see Morgan, Chapter 4, and Jaeger, Chapter 5). The *concordia* of the *res publica* was one of a common stake in which different (and progressively larger) groups with different interests see themselves as bound by negotiations that occur within a context of precedents, rules, and procedures, and connect to the future by ensuring that new promises are kept and protections assured.

If Athens' participatory space emphasized authorship and Sparta's rested on regimented discipline, then Rome's participatory space was premised on an overwhelming belief in tradition, a sense of duty to one's ancestors to follow, outdo, and augment their example (see Arena, Chapter 13; also Arendt 1968: 166). The breakdown of *auctoritas* threatens the power to stabilize, or, to recall Heinze, to ensure the validity of, negotiations of power. The alternative to *auctoritas* is either stalemate or violence as parties seek or block power so that negotiations do not have to occur. For Cicero, the loss of *auctoritas* is tied to the loss of politics as a public thing. The result for Cicero is that people are suppressed by violence (*Sest.* 58.105–108), the voice of the people replaced by hired crowds and mercenary gangs (*Phil.* 1.9.21–22), the Senate "abolished," the courts "closed" (*De off.* 3.1.2), the sentiment of affection replaced by fear (*De off.* 2.8.29), and constitutional forms replaced with dynasts who, in striving for *dignitas* at the expense of public *libertas*, could command their own army and popular support (Wirszubski 1950: 74–79). To recall the distinction that Cicero seems to set out between *auctoritas* and the *potestas* of the people, absent a partnership of power, and in particular the central role of *auctoritas* in giving context and continuity to those agreements, the public realm and the sovereignty of the people as the foundation of all laws, a principle uncontested in Roman republican politics, is unsustainable.

It is in this comparative context that *auctoritas* becomes revealing for its centrality to any discussion of participatory communities. *Auctoritas* points to the tension that all participatory communities must address of authoring within history. The authorship in Greek city-states occurred in the context of communities that defined themselves as both like-minded and exclusive, relations of power that as vigorously sustained the equality of the *dēmos* as excluded new groups from sharing in authorship (see Fisher, Chapter 12, on the fear that gripped Sparta after the helot revolt). The Roman state, in contrast, traced its origins to exiles and wanderers and its history to a continual refounding, authorship that could incorporate new groups into differential relations of power, but authorship that occurred within the authority of tradition and hierarchy (see Mouritsen, Chapter 9, and Williamson, Chapter 11). The Roman state could integrate new groups, but its space splintered as it obstructed authorship (notably of land reform), on the one hand, and ignored history (notably in the rise of military dynasts, whose assertion of *honores* and *dignitas* was no longer bound by ancestral precedent) on the other.

The sustaining power of these participatory spaces becomes particularly noteworthy in contemporary American politics, which has witnessed the breakdown of any notion of authoring within history. Efforts to suppress the urban vote, to reconfigure how votes get calculated for presidential elections (counting votes by district, akin to what the Romans did in their bloc voting), and to routinely block legislation by a minority of senators are revealing of the breakdown of authorship. But more significant is the dissolution of the very idea of trust, the invisible cultural bonds that are organized by history and experience by which negotiations can even occur. What the past helps us understand is how these tensions play out, how they must be continually negotiated within the particular historical, cultural, and institutional contexts of these communities, and what the costs are of this failure (or refusal) to do so.

2 Power and International Relations

The Greek and Roman cases alert us to another aspect of our modern conceptual vocabulary: an impoverished notion of power. Nowhere does this show up more dramatically than in the language of international relations, particularly as employed by the dominant strands of realism, neo-realism, and neo-conservatism. Although these approaches have different assumptions about human motivation (domination, security, ideology) and the goals of international relations (control, balance of power, spread of democracy), they share a conception of power as hegemonic; as an autonomous, zero-sum relationship of control, domination, and subordination in which any lessening of, for example, American power will both endanger the country and, for the neo-conservatives, the world (Morgenthau 1946: 192–196; 1950: 17–18; Morgenthau and Thompson 2001: 11; Waltz 1986: 111; Kagan, Schmitt, and Donnelly 2000: i–ii; Kristol and Kagan 1996; 2000: 5, 12–14; Kagan 2012b). One can hear these claims in Robert Kagan's recent words, which echo earlier calls for intervention: "The present world order—characterized by an unprecedented number of democratic nations; a greater global prosperity, even with the current crisis, than the world has ever known; and a long peace among great powers—reflects American principles and preferences, and was built and preserved by American power in all its political, economic, and military dimensions. If American power declines, this world order will decline with it" (Kagan 2012a). In this conception, power is something that one possesses—by way of resources, military strength, etc.—that one exercises over others. In fact, it is a reduction of power to force (see Arendt 1972; 1998: 200–204). And in that reduction, power is no longer seen as something that arises from individuals acting together; power appears as a form of control that is increased only by decreasing the ability of another to act.

These traditions variously define themselves within and against the ancient world, looking notably (and selectively) at Thucydides (Gilpin 1984: 291; Keohane 1986: 163–164; Bagby 1994; Kagan 2009), the Romans (in their imperial expansion) (Morgenthau 1950: 177, 403; Freedland 2002; Kaplan 2003; Madden 2008), and Augustine (in what some see as his rejection of ancient philosophic accounts of virtue to account for our fallen state) (Markus 1988: 83). Morgenthau, for example, sees in the destruction of Carthage "the methods of solving a technical political problem by the appropriate means without regard for any transcendent ethical considerations" (Morgenthau 1950: 177). And while scholars have questioned different aspects of the use of this ancient past—whether state cultures and institutions matter, for example—less attention is paid to how this past might challenge or expand our conception of power.

Equality and exclusivity in Greece

The Greek and Roman cases reveal the close, and perhaps unexpected, relationship between domestic ideologies and international politics. The *dēmos* ideology of Athens and Sparta created both equality and exclusivity: an association of freedom with absolute sovereignty that established a linkage of freedom with domination (Raaflaub 2004: 184, 261; also Arendt 1968: 164–165). The freedom of the Athenian citizen was, as Pericles even announces, the freedom of the master or the tyrant over the rest of the Greek world (Thuc. 2.63). Athens' (as well as Sparta's) association of freedom with absolute sovereignty underlies the Greek word for power, *kratos*, which was largely understood in terms of strength, might, and violence. Athenian power was exercised ruthlessly over other city-states, engendering sufficient hatred that, in Athens' mind, they either had to exert force or endanger themselves (Raaflaub 2004: 178; Thuc. 1.76.3, 6.82–83; see Bolmarcich, Chapter 18). The point here is not that Athens or Sparta happened to be imperial forces or happened to have a democracy (in whatever form) worth protecting. It is that their conceptions of freedom fueled a particular notion of domination.

There is a tragic sensibility in Thucydides: not one affirming the Athenians' belief in hegemonic power but one struggling with the inconsistency between a democratic conception of power as intangible, participatory, and generative (one articulated by Pericles) and an imperial conception of power as material, coercive, and ultimately destructive. In his discussion of the hegemonic position of the United States, Kagan seems to echo without a note of irony the proud words of (and about) Athens at the outset of the Peloponnesian War: that the United States' "naval power" is "predominant," that it can "defeat any competitor in a head-to-head battle," that it has the "richest economy," and that the "relative freedom" of the system allows it to better "adapt" by rewarding innovation (Kagan 2012a; Thuc. 1.70, 72–78). What the Athenians did not understand is that what gave them political strength—the intangible bonds, born of history and reinforced by culture, that united them as a people—also gave strength to others that could not be dissipated by force. As the Peloponnesian War progressed, a world interpreted through the lens of *kratos* became more precarious as massacres did nothing to prevent rebellion, neutral states joined with opposing forces, and Athens had to continually extend its force, since to allow power to exist somewhere was to threaten one's own freedom. The conception of power dramatically narrowed the range of options open to the Athenians. It is the logic, as Arendt notes, of tyranny: one is only strong when there is nothing left, when one rules a wasteland (Arendt 1998). The profoundly undemocratic aspects of the power that grew out of Athens' conception of freedom is missed when Euben calls for a "parallel polis with its Greek resonance" as a necessary condition "for the revival and extension of democratic politics" (2003: 139).

Hierarchy and integration in Rome

The Romans were not timid about empire either. For Cicero, the power of command (*imperium*) is not only natural (*De leg.* 3.1.3), but it is also the duty of the leaders to strive "by whatever means they can, in peace or in war, to advance the state in power, in territory, and in revenues" (*De off.* 2.24.85; also celebration of Pompey in *Cat.* 3.26; *De off.* 1.12.38: war pursued for glory; Gabba 1979: 120–122; Brunt 1978). And the Romans were always clear about one's primary attachments. Cicero articulates this Roman ideology: we are born for our country (*De off.* 1.7.22), our closest connection is citizenship (*De off.* 1.17.53, 57, 58; *De leg.* 2.2.5), we have a greater obligation to those closest to us (*De off.* 1.14.45, 1.17.54–55, 1.17.57), and we occupy a world that comprises both status (*De off.* 1.13.41) and ethnic differences (*Font.* 21; *Flac.* 24–26). So while the Romans do not offer us a particularly sanguine, or in Nussbaum's view, a logically coherent, vision of cosmopolitanism, they do offer us a cautionary one informed by the transformation of the Roman Republic into a global empire (Nussbaum 2000).

The Romans understood power in ways the Greeks never did, providing Rome with the ability to recognize in some form the sovereignty of other states and a range of ways of integrating new groups (Lintott 1993; Ando 2011: 64–80; see Champion, Chapter 19). Cicero asks how in a world of power differentials one constitutes relations between different peoples. And in contrast to a Greek conception of global relations as premised on might, in which justice extended no further than the borders of the *polis* and the possession of might served as the foundation of right, Cicero and the Romans reflect a more nuanced conception of both the different relations and the limits of global power (on the importance of Cicero's extension of justice in global relations, see Nederman 1993; Kinsbury and Straumann 2009).

One type of power is essentially a globalized version of the patron–client relationships that corresponded to aspects of Rome's domestic politics (see Champion, Chapter 19). These power relationships are personal, hierarchical, and reciprocal. The patron acts as a protectorate in the best interests of the clients (*De off.* 2.8.27), providing security, goods, or even access to Roman culture and entertainment. The client, in turn, returns the kindness (*De off.* 1.15.47–48; *Cat.* 4.22), both by recognizing the authority of the patron and by providing revenue and manpower. For Cicero, one must weigh the worthiness of the object of one's benevolence, taking into consideration the individual's moral character, attitude toward the benefactor, intimacy of relations to the benefactor, common social ties, and services to one's interests (*De off.* 1.14.45). A whole range of relationships of *beneficia* become possible, extending from alliances to grants of citizenship to groups or individuals in return for service (e.g. *Balb.* 2.6; see Steel 2001: 96–97, 108–112).

The distance, the personal relationships, and the small number of people actually in charge in these relationships made the temptations for corruption irresistible. Patron–client relations, which were always transactional, became vicious and exploitative when no longer bound by any limits, such as notions of duty or propriety (see *De off.* 2.8.7; *De Imperio Cn. Pompei* 5.13). It is in this context that Steel is correct in suggesting that Cicero "is operating, in the speeches, with a concept of empire which depends not on territory, but on the power wielded by individuals, and that this in turn means that the problems which arise in the running of empire can be presented as the result of personal failings rather than endemic to the structures of government: questions of morality rather than administration" (Steel 2001: 4; see *De off.* 2.8.28–29; *De Imperio Cn. Pompei* 13.36–39; 14.40–41).

A second type of arrangement, and one meant to mitigate the exploitative excesses that arise from power differentials, is a more legalistic one in which both parties have rights and duties that can be adjudicated. This approach, which has its origins in a Roman conception of the law of nations, is most extensively outlined in *On Duties* where Cicero writes that the rights of war must be observed (*De off.* 1.11.34): that the only reason for going to war "is that we may live in peace unharmed" (*De off.* 1.11.35), that war can only follow once an "official demand for satisfaction has been submitted" (*De off.* 1.11.36), that protection must be ensured to those who lay down their arms (*De off.* 1.11.35), and that any promises to foreign peoples must be kept (*De off.* 1.13.39). This approach is also the basis of the *leges de repetundis*, which were civil laws aimed at controlling the corruption and excesses of provincial administrators. These laws (and the extortion courts comprising juries of knights) themselves became the mechanism of corruption; a lucrative form of extortion in its own right as well as a forum for political vendettas.

A final approach involves wholesale incorporation through broad grants of citizenship, such as the near-doubling of the number of Roman citizens with the inclusion of the Italians after the Social War (see Champion, Chapter 19). Power is nominally equal, spanning vast geographic areas and ethnic groups. In its sheer breadth it begins to approximate in actuality the world citizenship that the Stoics imagine philosophically. Nussbaum, in frustration with Cicero's argument for claims that the Republic is different from "other more distant associations," questions the validity of his argument "since already Rome had complex civic and political ties with many parts of the world" (Nussbaum 2000: 204). I think that experience is precisely what haunts him: for Cicero the extension of citizenship, like the expansion of empire, made citizenship into an abstraction, altering the partnership of power that gave cohesion to the *res publica*. The problem of cohesion for Cicero is not that there are different groups with different histories and orientations. Rome's founding legend, after all, is premised on unity being forged from difference. The problem of cohesion is, instead, a problem of power.

For Cicero, not unlike Pericles, globalism comprises two images of power (Steel 2001: 168–170). The power of the *res publica* is political, exemplified in the public space of the Forum. It is a notion of power as a binding force that is built on, and organized by, affective relationships that are fostered by recognition: recognition of origins, of reciprocal obligations, of generosity, and of merit. The power of empire, however, is organized around *vis*, or might, exemplified in triumphal conquests by powerful military leaders (*Cat.* 4.22–23). The administration of empire required extended commands that concentrated power in the hands of military leaders (*De Imperio Cn. Pompei* 11.31–32; also Sal. *Iug.* 41.7–8; Hammer 2014: 153, 156–57). But even without conceiving of globalism in military terms, the vastness of global citizenship altered the affective basis of power. The extension of citizenship, as Rose notes, had revealed to Cicero the problem of "disaffected masses," whose loyalty could be purchased, whose quiescence could be enforced by fear, and whose supremacy in bestowing honors could be ignored (*De off.* 2.8.28; Rose 1995: 388).

In developing her own version of cosmopolitanism, Nussbaum ends up constructing a world essentially devoid of power relations; not just power as command, but the more challenging notion of an affective basis to power—of what holds a community together. Rejecting the sense of duty that derives from intimacy, Nussbaum suggests that families are just "arrangements" that, more than anything else, are useful in organizing care and resources (Nussbaum 2000: 203). For Cicero, though, the bonds of family derive from intimacy. The point for Cicero is that the more abstractly we understand our relations to each other, the less meaningful those relations become.

Sandel, in responding to the abstractness of global citizenship, suggests at one point, "The hope for self-government lies not in relocating sovereignty but in dispersing it. The most promising alternative to the sovereign state is not a one-world community based on the solidarity of humankind, but a multiplicity of communities and political bodies—some more, some less extensive than nations—among which sovereignty is diffused" (Sandel 1996: 345). The potential problem of dispersed autonomy, as Cicero's analysis suggests, is how it displaces, or replaces, one type of power with another. As the foundation of power shifts, from local affections to dispersed attachments, from the Forum to the provinces, from concrete citizenship to abstract fellowship, the risk is that the sustaining power of these participatory spaces can dissipate, as in Rome in which the *res publica* as a form of public ownership gave way to private loyalties and factions. But the Greek alternative of extending power while excluding those from participating, even if under the guise of a benevolent hegemony, is no better as it transforms *dēmos* power from participatory to tyrannical.

At the heart of this comparative approach is an understanding of how the internal and external conceptions of political relations, the two parts of this chapter, are related. In fact, by way of comparison with the Roman Republic, we can begin to answer Morris' question of why Athens, "the most modern Greek state with the biggest population, most advanced technology, most meritocratic administration, and deepest state capacity, failed to break through to become first a territorial Greek state and then a multiethnic empire" (Morris 2009: 167). In important ways, domestic political culture structures the range of viable conceptions of power (Thompson, Ellis, and Wildavsky 1990). The egalitarian Greek city-states, lacking sufficient mechanisms for establishing relationships with different groups, conceive of power internally and externally in diametrically opposite ways: as participatory and generative internally, and as exclusionary and repressive externally, functioning to protect the boundaries that define their identities. The hierarchical Roman Republic, with its variety of mechanisms for integration, simply had a broader range of practices by which power could be conceived. But the Roman participatory space collapsed when it could not resist the intrusion of force—the claim of sovereign power by military dynasts—that was brought home from the battlefield.

3 Humility, Confession, and Power

I want to end on what is perhaps an unexpected note, and that is with Augustine. When Augustine equates kingdoms with robbery, he is speaking with a comparative sensibility, looking at an ancient tradition, now at the end of its story, that continually grappled with the tragic dimensions and limits of power. Augustine's romp through Varro's categorization of the 288 different ways in which philosophers have attempted to understand what one means by, and how to attain, happiness points to a growing sense of the implausibility of attempts to systematize or perfect politics (*Civ. Dei* 19.1). Augustine does not replace ideals with cynicism, but grapples with the dimensions of power, violence, ambition, and authority that both sustained and destroyed the participatory aspects of these communities. In striking contrast to the images of virtue and non-domination that have filtered to us from the ancient past, a less appreciated aspect of their legacy is the unflinching glimpse they provide into the rawness of politics, whether of Thucydides' record of the decision by Athens to put the Melians to death, Livy's recounting of Rome's origins in rape and murder, Cicero's own role in suspending laws that perpetuated violence as a solution to politics, or how the competition for honor and glory turns a community against itself. Power, however defined, is necessary. But there is a tyrannical impulse that underlies a conception of power that is premised on, as Augustine writes, the will "want[ing] to be in its own power" (Aug. *De lib. arb.* 2.19.53.199), whether a desire to grab resources or a belief that peace will come when there is no longer anyone who can resist. It is this impulse to power that drives the extractive politics of distribution, the rise of military dynasts, and the relentless quest for empire.

For Augustine, the lesson of the past is a deceptively simply one, and one reminiscent of Socrates: "I don't know" (*nescio*) (see *De ord.* 2.6.19; also *Conf.* 1.6.7; Plato *Ap.* 23a–b, 29b). We are not creatures who know: we do not know the past, we do not know each other, we do not know other communities, we can only inadequately communicate ourselves, we are susceptible to both deceiving and being deceived, and we cannot achieve mastery precisely because we cannot know or control everything (see Hammer 2014: 403–7). It is knowledge that ends in confession, but a confession that is creative of power in two ways. First, confession relaxes the grip of habit by acknowledging that one's notion of what is good or what one should do may be premised on old habits of thought that one accepts as knowledge. It is this confession that underlies the role of frankness and openness in fostering *dēmos* power. Second, confession amounts to the recognition that participatory communities are relationships of people that require belief in the invisible. As the Greek and Roman cases both suggest, there must be trust, a faith in the invisible bonds of duty and in an orientation of love that underlies relations of authority and binds a people together. When Augustine asks, "If trust of this kind were to disappear from human affairs, who would not be aware of the confusion and appalling upheaval which would follow?" (*De fid. inv.* 2.4, trans. Campbell), he is reflecting on the lessons of this ancient past that we have explored in this volume.

I count Hans Morgenthau, one of the founders of what has become known as political realism, as among a handful of political scientists to reflect on both the ubiquity and ambiguities of power. I say this recognizing that I am reading Morgenthau against the grain. Not his critics but his supporters too frequently neglect his many essays (see collections in Morgenthau 1958, 1960, 1970, 2004), turning Morgenthau's confession about the limits of power into a celebration of the acquisition of power, his sense of fallenness from a moral order into an embrace of amoralism, his view of the mystery and darkness of the human heart into a rational science of calculation and prediction, his sensitivity to the plurality of human experiences and political forms into a reductionist account of interest, his humility into arrogance, his sense of a politics inextricably tied to culture into one abstracted from any affective context, and a view of politics as allowing the flourishing of different ends to one whose only aim is the containment of evil (exceptions include Lebow 2003, Frost 2003, and Brown 2007, though focusing primarily on tragedy as a mode of thought in international relations). We are moral beings who do not know how to be moral. "Thus, we are condemned by the nature of justice, and our own, to give and to receive too little or too much, or at least to be ignorant of whether we have received and given too little or too much. In the eyes of man, the accounts of justice never square. Yet we must try to square them" (Morgenthau 1970: 67). What a comparative study of the past reveals is this pull between politics in its ugliness and in its beauty, not as a choice of one or the other, but of their inseparability in forming and sustaining participatory communities.

REFERENCES

Ando, C. 2011. *Law, Language, and Empire in the Roman Tradition: Empire and After*. Philadelphia.

Arendt, H. 1968. *Between Past and Future: Eight Exercises in Political Thought*. New York.

Arendt, H. 1972. *Crises of the Republic*. New York.

Arendt, H. 1998. *The Human Condition*. Chicago.

Arendt, H. 2005. *The Promise of Politics*. Ed. J. Kohn. New York.

Arena, V. 2012. *Libertas and the Practice of Politics in the Late Roman Republic*. Cambridge.

Asmis, E. 2004. "The State as a Partnership: Cicero's Definition of *Res Publica* in His Work *On the State*." *History of Political Thought* 25: 569–599.

Bagby, L. 1994. "The Use and Abuse of Thucydides in International Relations." *International Organization* 48: 131–153.

Boegehold, A. 1996. "Resistance to Change in the Law at Athens." In J. Ober and C. Hedrick, eds., *Dēmokratia: A Conversation on Democracies, Ancient and Modern*. Princeton, 203–214.

Bourdieu, P. 1977. *Outline of a Theory of Practice*. Trans. R. Nice. Cambridge.

Bourdieu, P. 1990. *The Logic of Practice*. Trans. R. Nice. Stanford.
Brown, C. 2007. "Tragedy, 'Tragic Choices' and International Political Theory." *International Relations* 21: 5–13.
Brunt, P.A. 1978. "Laus imperii." In P.D.A. Garnsey and C.R. Whittaker, eds., *Imperialism in the Ancient World*. Cambridge, 159–191.
Brunt, P.A. 1988. *The Fall of the Roman Republic and Related Essays*. Oxford.
Daube, D. 1938. "*Societas* as Consensual Contract." *Cambridge Law Journal* 6: 381–403.
De Zulueta, F., ed. 1953. *The Institutes of Gaius*. Oxford.
Douglas, M. 1966. *Purity and Danger: An Analysis of Concepts of Pollution and Taboo*. London.
Douglas, M. 1978. *Cultural Bias*. Occasional Paper No. 34. London.
Douglas, M. 1982. *Natural Symbols: Exploration in Cosmology*. New York.
Eder, W. 2005. "The Political Significance of the Codification of Law in Archaic Societies: An Unconventional Hypothesis." In K. Raaflaub, ed., *Social Struggles in Archaic Rome: New Perspectives on the Conflict of the Orders*. Berkeley, 262–300.
Euben, J.P. 1990. *The Tragedy of Political Theory: The Road Not Taken*. Princeton.
Euben, J.P. 2003. *Platonic Noise*. Princeton.
Finley, M.I. 1983. *Politics in the Ancient World*. Cambridge.
Foucault, M. 1986. *The History of Sexuality*, vol. 3: *The Care of the Self*. New York.
Freedland, J. 2002. "Rome, AD … Rome, DC?" *The Guardian*. Sept. 17.
Frost, M. 2003. "Tragedy, Ethics and International Relations." *International Relations* 17: 477–495.
Gabba, E. 1979. "Per un'interpretazione politica del *De Officiis* di Cicerone." *Rendiconti dell'Accademia dei Lincei. Classe di Scienze morali, storiche, filologiche* 34: 117–141.
Geertz, C. 1973. *The Interpretation of Cultures*. New York.
Gilpin, R. 1984. "The Richness of the Tradition of Political Realism." *International Organizations* 38: 287–304.
Hammer, D. 2002. *The* Iliad *as Politics: The Performance of Political Thought*. Norman, OK.
Hammer, D. 2004. "Ideology, the Symposium, and Archaic Greek Politics." *AJP* 125: 479–512.
Hammer, D. 2005. "Plebiscitary Politics in Archaic Greece." *Historia* 54: 107–131.
Hammer, D. 2006. "Bourdieu, Ideology, and the Ancient World." *American Journal of Semiotics* 22: 87–108.
Hammer, D. 2008. *Roman Political Thought and the Modern Theoretical Imagination*. Norman, OK.
Hammer, D. 2009. "What is Politics in the Ancient World?" In R.K. Balot, ed., *A Companion to Greek and Roman Political Thought*. Oxford and Malden, MA, 20–36.
Hammer, D. 2014. *Roman Political Thought: From Cicero to Augustine*. Cambridge.
Heinze, R. 1925. "Auctoritas." *Hermes* 60: 348–366.
Hodder, I. 1985. "Postprocessual Anthropology." *Advances in Archaeological Method and Theory* 8: 1–26.
Hölkeskamp, K.-J. 2010. *Reconstructing the Roman Republic: An Ancient Political Culture and Modern Research*. Princeton.
Kagan, D. 1969. *The Outbreak of the Peloponnesian War*. Ithaca, NY.
Kagan, D. 2009. *Thucydides: The Reinvention of History*. New York.
Kagan, D., G. Schmitt, and T. Donnelly. 2000. *Rebuilding America's Defenses: Strategies, Forces and Resources For a New Century*. Report of The Project for the New American Century. Washington DC.
Kagan, R. 2012a. "Not Fade Away: The Myth of American Decline." *The New Republic*. Jan. 11. Available online at tnr.com.
Kagan, R. 2012b. *The World America Made*. New York.
Kaplan, R. 2003. "Supremacy by Stealth." *The Atlantic Monthly*. July/August.

Keohane, R., ed. 1996. *Neorealism and its Critics*. New York.
Kinsbury, B., and B. Straumann. 2009. "Reflections on the Roman Foundations and Current Interpretations of the International Political and Legal Thought of Grotius, Hobbes, and Pufendorf." In S. Besson and J. Tasioulas, eds., *The Philosophy of International Law*. New York, 33–51.
Kristol, W. and R. Kagan. 1996. "Toward a Neo-Reaganite Foreign Policy." *Foreign Affairs* 75 (July/ August): 18–32.
Kristol, W. and R. Kagan. 2000. "Introduction: National Interest and Global Responsibility." In R. Kagan and W. Kristol, eds., *Present Dangers*. San Francisco, 3–24.
Lebow, R. 2003. *The Tragic Vision of Politics: Ethics, Interests and Orders*. Cambridge.
Lintott, A. 1993. Imperium Romanum: *Politics and Administration*. London.
Lintott, A.W. 1999. *The Constitution of the Roman Republic*. Oxford.
Macintyre, A. 1984. *After Virtue*. 2nd edn. Notre Dame.
Madden, T. 2008. *Empires of Trust: How Rome Built—and American is Building—a New World*. New York.
Markus, R.A. 1988. Saeculum: *History and Society in the Theology of St. Augustine*. 2nd edn. Cambridge.
Millar, F. 1998. *The Crowd in Rome in the Late Republic*. Ann Arbor.
Morgenthau, H. 1946. *Scientific Man versus Power Politics*. Chicago.
Morgenthau, H. 1950. *Politics among Nations*. New York.
Morgenthau, H. 1958. *Dilemmas of Politics*. Chicago.
Morgenthau, H. 1960. *The Purpose of American Politics*. New York.
Morgenthau, H. 1970. *Truth and Power*. New York.
Morgenthau, H. 2004. *Political Theory and International Affairs: Hans J. Morgenthau on Aristotle's* The Politics. Ed. A. Lang, Jr., London.
Morgenthau, H. and K. Thompson. 2001. *Politics among Nations*. 6th edn. New Delhi.
Morris, I. 2009. "The Greater Athenian State." In I. Morris and W. Scheidel, eds., *The Dynamics of Ancient Empires*. Oxford, 99–177.
Nederman, C. 1993. "Humanism and Empire: Aeneas Sylvius Piccolomini, Cicero and the Imperial Ideal." *Historical Journal* 36: 499–515.
Nussbaum, M. 1986. *The Fragility of Goodness: Luck and Ethics in Greek Tragedy and Philosophy*. Cambridge.
Nussbaum, M. 2000. "Duties of Justice, Duties of Material Aid: Cicero's Problematic Legacy." *Journal of Political Philosophy* 2: 176–206.
Ober, J. 1989. *Mass and Elite in Democratic Athens*. Princeton.
Ober, J. 1997. "Revolution Matters: Democracy as Demotic Action (A Response to Kurt A. Raaflaub)." In I. Morris and K. Raaflaub, eds., *Democracy 2500? Questions and Challenges*. Dubuque, 67–85.
Ober, J. 2008. *Democracy and Knowledge: Innovation and Learning in Classical Athens*. Princeton.
Pettit, P. 1993. "Negative Liberty, Liberal and Republican." *European Journal of Philosophy* 1: 15–38.
Pettit, P. 1996. "Freedom as Antipower." *Ethics* 106: 576–604.
Pettit, P. 1997. *Republicanism: A Theory of Freedom and Government*. Oxford.
Pettit, P. 2002. "Keeping Republican Freedom Simple: On a Difference with Quentin Skinner." *Political Theory* 30: 339–356.
Pitkin, H. 1988. "Are Freedom and Liberty Twins?" *Political Theory* 16: 523–552.
Raaflaub, K. 2004. *The Discovery of Freedom in Ancient Greece*. 1st English edn. rev. and updated from the German. Trans. Renate Franciscono, revised by the author. Chicago.
Raaflaub, K., ed. 2007. *War and Peace in the Ancient World*. Oxford.
Raaflaub, K., J. Emlen, and A. Molho, eds. 1991. *Athens and Rome, Florence and Venice: City-States in Classical Antiquity and Medieval Italy*. Stuttgart.
Ricoeur, P. 1986. *Lectures on Ideology and Utopia*. Ed. G. Taylor. New York.

Rose, P. 1995. "Cicero and the Rhetoric of Imperialism: Putting the Politics Back into Political Rhetoric." *Rhetorica* 13: 359–399.

Samons, L. 2007. *What's Wrong with Democracy? From Athenian Practice to American Worship*. Berkeley.

Sandel, M. 1996. *Democracy's Disconnect: America in Search of a Public Philosophy*. Cambridge.

Saxonhouse, A. 2006. *Free Speech and Democracy in Ancient Athens*. Cambridge.

Scheidel, W., I. Morris, and R. Saller, eds. 2007. *The Cambridge Economic History of the Greco-Roman World*. Cambridge.

Schmidt, E.G., ed. 1996. *Griechenland und Rom. Vergleichende Untersuchungen zu Entwicklungstendenzen und -höhepunkten der antiken Geschichte, Kunst und Literatur*. Tblissi, Erlangen, and Jena.

Schofield, M. 1995. "Cicero's Definition of *Res Publica*." In J.G.F. Powell, ed., *Cicero the Philosopher: Twelve Essays*. Oxford, 63–83.

Shyrock, A. and D. Smail. 2011. *Deep History: The Architecture of Past and Present*. Berkeley.

Skinner, Q.R.D. 1998. *Liberty before Liberalism*. Cambridge.

Steel, C. 2001. *Cicero, Rhetoric, and Empire*. Oxford.

Thompson, M., R. Ellis, and A. Wildavsky. 1990. *Cultural Theory*. Boulder, CO.

Thucydides. 1972. *History of the Peloponnesian War*. Trans. R. Warner. New York.

Turner, V. 1974. *Dramas, Fields and Metaphors: Symbolic Action in Human Society*. Ithaca, NY.

Turner, V. 1988. *The Anthropology of Performance*. New York.

Waltz, K. 1986. "Anarchic Orders and Balances of Power." In R. Keohane, ed., *Neorealism and its Critics*. New York, 98–130.

White, S. 2003. "Return to Politics: Perestroika and Postparadigmatic Political Science." *Political Theory* 31: 835–851.

Wirszubski, C. 1950. Libertas *as a Political Idea at Rome during the Late Republic and Early Principate*. Cambridge.

Wiseman, T.P. 2009. *Remembering the Roman People: Essays on Late-Republican Politics and Literature*. Oxford.

Wolin, S. 1994. "Norm and Form: The Constitutionalizing of Democracy." In J.P. Euben, J. Wallach, and J. Ober, eds., *Athenian Political Thought and the Reconstruction of American Democracy*. Ithaca, NY, 29–58.

Wolin, S. 2004. *Politics and Vision*. Expanded edn. Princeton.

Woodruff, P. 2005. *First Democracy: The Challenge of an Ancient Idea*. Oxford.

FURTHER READING

My thanks to Sara Lupolt for her research assistance and Kerry Whiteside for his helpful comments.

There are very few comparative discussions of Greek and Roman participatory communities. A classic discussion of ancient politics is provided by Finley 1983. A review of methodologies for the study of the ancient world is provided by Hammer 2009. Eder 2005 provides a comparative discussion of the development of law codes. Raaflaub 2004 focuses on the Greek discovery of freedom but contains comparative discussions of Rome. There is also a helpful comparative discussion of freedom and sovereignty in Ando 2011. See also the edited collections by Raaflaub, Emlen, and Molho 1991 on city-states, Raaflaub 2007 on war and peace, and Schmidt 1996 on different aspects of Greek and Roman development. Scheidel, Morris, and Saller 2007 have provided comparative approach to ancient economies. Foucault 1986 looks at the Greek and Roman contexts for the care of the self. Arendt 1968 and 1998 draws on both Greek and Roman political ideas, placing them in a comparative context in thinking about politics. See also Shryock and Smail 2011 for an innovative frame for comparative study.

Index

Where appropriate, parallel entries and sub-entries have been provided for Greece and Rome.

A Companion to Greek Democracy and the Roman Republic, First Edition. Edited by Dean Hammer.

Printed and bound by [illegible]

Printed and bound by CPI Group (UK) Ltd, Croydon, CR0 4YY

15/09/2026

14962393-0006